Health Insurance Answer Book

Sixth Edition

This Sixth Edition of *Health Insurance Answer Book* replaces all previous editions and supplements.

Health Insurance Answer Book

Sixth Edition

John C. Garner

A PANEL PUBLICATION
ASPEN PUBLISHERS, INC.

This publication is designed to provide accurate and authoritative information in regard to the subject matter covered. It is sold with the understanding that the publisher is not engaged in rendering legal, accounting, or other professional services. If legal advice or other professional assistance is required, the services of a competent professional person should be sought.

—From a *Declaration of Principles* jointly adopted by a
Committee of the American Bar Association and a
Committee of Publishers and Associations.

Copyright © 2001 by PANEL PUBLISHERS
A Division of Aspen Publishers, Inc.
A Wolters Kluwer Company
www.panelpublishers.com

All rights reserved. No part of this book may be reproduced or transmitted in any form or by any means, electronic or mechanical, including photocopying, recording, or any information storage and retrieval system, without permission in writing from the publisher. Requests for permission to make copies of any part of this publication should be mailed to:

> Permissions
> Panel Publishers
> 1185 Avenue of the Americas
> New York, NY 10036

ISBN 0-7355-1469-0

Printed in the United States of America

2 3 4 5 6 7 8 9 0

About Panel Publishers

Panel Publishers—including the former Prentice Hall Law & Business, Little, Brown and Company's Professional Division, and Wiley Law Publications—is a leading publisher of authoritative and timely books, information services, and journals written by specialists to assist compensation and benefits managers, human resources managers, and other business professionals. Our mission is to provide practical, solution-based how-to information keyed to the latest legislative, judicial, and regulatory developments.

Other Panel products on related issues include:

Books and Manuals
- Managed Care Answer Book
- Employee Benefits Answer Book
- Employment Law Answer Book
- Flexible Benefits Answer Book
- State by State Guide to Human Resources Law
- COBRA Handbook
- Workers' Compensation Answer Book

Periodicals and Electronic Titles
- Panel Employee Benefits Library on CD-ROM
- Mandated Benefits: 2000 Compliance Guide
- Compensation & Benefits Management
- Medical Benefits
- Flexible Benefits
- On Managed Care
- COBRA Advisory

PANEL PUBLISHERS
A Division of Aspen Publishers, Inc.
Practical Solutions for Legal and Business Professionals
www.panelpublishers.com

SUBSCRIPTION NOTICE

This Panel product is updated periodically with supplements to reflect important changes in the subject matter. If you purchased this product directly from Panel Publishers, we have already recorded your subscription for this update service.

If, however, you purchased this product from a bookstore and wish to receive future updates and revised or related volumes billed separately with a 30-day examination review, please contact our Customer Service Department at 1-800-234-1660, or send your name, company name (if applicable), address, and the title of the product to:

**Panel Publishers
A Division of Aspen Publishers, Inc.
7201 McKinney Circle
Frederick, MD 21704**

*To my family and colleagues, whose support
made my work on this edition possible,
particularly Dilu de Silva
for her work on the manuscript.*

John C. Garner

About the Author

John C. Garner is President of Garner Consulting, a firm specializing in employee benefits consulting in Pasadena, California. Before founding Garner Consulting in 1987, Mr. Garner was a Principal in the Los Angeles office of Towers, Perrin where he worked for more than ten years. He previously managed claim offices for Lincoln National Life and for Prudential, where he also served as an underwriter.

Mr. Garner is President of the Los Angeles Chapter of the International Society of Certified Employee Benefit Specialists and is a Past President of the Los Angeles Life and Accident Claim Association and a past General Chairman and on the Board of Directors of the Western Claim Conference. He is also on the Board of Directors of the Employee Benefit Planning Association of Southern California. He is a Fellow of the International Society of Certified Employee Benefit Specialists and is listed in *Who's Who in the West* and *Who's Who in Managed Health Care*. Mr. Garner is chair of the advisory committee for the prenatal wellness program of the Southern California Chapter of the March of Dimes and is a member of the March of Dimes' Worksite Programs National Volunteer Advisory Committee.

Mr. Garner holds a Bachelor of Arts degree from Occidental College. He became a Chartered Life Underwriter in 1976, a Certified Professional Consultant to Management in 1991, a Certified Employee Benefits Specialist in 1993, and Certified in Flexible Compensation Instruction in 2000.

Introduction

This Sixth Edition of the *Health Insurance Answer Book* makes available the most current information about this rapidly evolving field. Specifically, it incorporates the latest information about the most recent regulations, including those governing flexible benefits and Form 5500s, as well as the model notice on the Women's Health and Cancer Rights Act.

Among key questions covered in the *Sixth Edition* are the following:

- Is there any guidance as to what the WHCRA notice should say?
- What does the city and county of San Francisco require regarding domestic partners?
- How many Medicare beneficiaries receive coverage through an HMO?
- How prevalent are employer-sponsored long-term care plans?
- What is a mental health carve-out?
- Are mid-year election changes permitted when a day care provider changes its rate?
- What is EFAST?

Also provided is some of the latest survey information about dramatic changes in the health insurance marketplace, such as the resurgence in healthcare inflation. As well, this edition cites recent case law to highlight hazards others have encountered. The author hopes that readers will find the *Health Insurance Answer Book, Sixth Edition*, with its expert guidance and practice-based solutions, to be a valuable and time-saving reference work.

How to Use This Book

The *Health Insurance Answer Book, Sixth Edition* is designed for professionals who need quick and authoritative answers to questions on the complicated administration of health insurance. This book uses simple, direct language and avoids technical jargon wherever possible. The following is a listing of some of this supplement's most useful features.

Question-and-Answer Format. The question-and-answer format, with its breadth of coverage and concise, plain-language explanations, effectively conveys the complex subject matter of health insurance, while providing quickly accessible, straightforward answers to common concerns.

List of Questions. A detailed list of questions follows the table of contents in the front of the book to help the reader locate areas of immediate interest. This list provides both the question number and the page on which the question appears. A series of subheadings helps to group and organize the questions by topic within each chapter.

Numbering System. The questions are numbered consecutively within each chapter. For example, Chapter 2 begins with 2:1, followed by 2:2, and so on.

Appendixes. For the reader's convenience, supplementary reference materials are contained within the appendixes at the end of the book.

Index. An index is provided as a further aid to locating specific information. All references in the index are to question numbers rather than page numbers.

Contents

List of Questions xxvii

Chapter 1
An Overview of Group Insurance 1-1

    Group Health Insurance 1-1

    The Uninsured 1-4

    Group Insurance 1-7

Chapter 2
The Health Insurance Marketplace 2-1

    Types of Insurance Professionals 2-1

    Choosing and Compensating Intermediaries 2-8

    Blue Cross/Blue Shield Plans 2-14

Chapter 3
Factors Influencing Insurance Plan Design 3-1

    Non-legal Factors Affecting Design 3-2

    Paying for Insurance 3-14

    Coverage 3-16

    Restrictions on Coverage 3-31

    Deductibles, Copayments, and Reimbursement 3-35

    Cost Containment 3-38

    Managed Competition 3-54

Chapter 4
State and Federal Laws 4-1

    Legal Factors Affecting Design 4-1

    State Law 4-11

    Federal Law 4-21

    Pregnancy Discrimination Act 4-29

    Family and Medical Leave Act 4-31

    Americans with Disabilities Act 4-36

Contents

    Health Insurance Portability and
    Accountability Act 4-44

    Taxation of Group Health Plans 4-63

    Reservists' Benefits 4-65

CHAPTER 5
Plan Rating and Funding 5-1

    Plan Funding 5-1

    Fully Insured Plans 5-2

    Alternatives to Fully Insured Plans 5-22

    Deferred Premium Arrangements 5-24

    Shared Funding Arrangements 5-26

    Retrospective Premium Arrangements . . . 5-28

    Reserve Reduction Agreements 5-30

    Minimum Premium Plans 5-32

CHAPTER 6
Plan Implementation and Administration 6-1

    Setting Up the Plan 6-2

    Reporting and Disclosure 6-6

Enrollment 6-12

Billing 6-16

Claims 6-18

Coverage, Renewal and Changes 6-25

Termination of Coverage 6-27

Computerized Administration 6-30

Chapter 7
Managing Health Insurance Costs 7-1

Factors Affecting Costs 7-1

Health Care Data 7-14

Utilization Review and Case Management . 7-24

Medical Savings Accounts 7-37

Coordination of Benefits 7-44

Additional Cost-Management Strategies . . 7-49

Billing Codes 7-57

Impact of AIDS on Insurance 7-58

Rationing Health Care 7-62

Contents

    The Employer's Role 7-65

Chapter 8
Managed Care Plans 8-1

    Introduction 8-1

    Health Maintenance Organizations 8-4

    Adverse Selection 8-16

    Legal Standards 8-18

    Evaluating HMOs 8-24

    Preferred Provider Organizations 8-29

    Managed Care Backlash 8-47

Chapter 9
Flexible Benefits 9-1

    Introduction 9-1

    Tax Advantages 9-3

    Cost Control 9-7

    Types of Plans 9-8

    Vacations 9-30

    Flexible Benefit Options 9-33

Implementation 9-37

CHAPTER 10
Medicare 10-1

    The Basics 10-1

    Medicare Order of Benefit Determination . 10-8

    Medicare Cost Containment 10-14

    Medigap 10-18

    Operation Data Match 10-20

    Medicare+Choice 10-23

CHAPTER 11
Nondiscrimination Rules 11-1

    Accident and Health Plans 11-1

    Group Term Life Plans 11-5

    Cafeteria Plans 11-8

    Dependent Care Assistance Plans 11-11

    Voluntary Employees' Beneficiary
    Associations 11-13

    Nondiscriminatory Classification 11-14

Contents

CHAPTER 12
Dental, Vision, and Other Benefits 12-1

    Dental Benefits 12-1

    Vision and Hearing Benefits 12-6

    Life Insurance Benefits 12-8

    Disability Benefits 12-10

    Disability Management 12-16

    Health Promotion and Wellness 12-20

CHAPTER 13
COBRA 13-1

    The Basics 13-1

    Covered Employers 13-8

    Covered Plans 13-13

    General Requirements 13-20

    Notification Requirements 13-23

    Premiums 13-30

    Election and Grace Periods 13-35

    Qualified Beneficiaries 13-39

Miscellaneous 13-43

CHAPTER 14
Form 5500 14-1

    Introduction 14-1

    Plan Years 14-3

    Administration 14-6

    Completing the Form 14-16

    Electronic Filing 14-17

CHAPTER 15
Retiree Health Benefits 15-1

    Determining Eligibility and Responsibility . . 15-1

    Determining and Allocating Costs 15-5

    Retiree Medical Liabilities 15-7

    Pre-Funding 15-15

    Medicare Solutions to Retiree Challenges . 15-24

    Regulatory Issues 15-32

CHAPTER 16
Pharmacy Benefit Management 16-1

Contents

The Basics	16-2
PBM Growth	16-5
Cost Control	16-7
Prescription Drug Management	16-19
Ensuring Quality	16-26
Prescription Drug Plans	16-29

CHAPTER 17
Self-Funding 17-1

Introduction	17-2
Reasons for Self-Funding	17-4
Decision to Self-Fund	17-10
Administration	17-13
The Marketplace	17-17
Effect of Self-Funding on Regulations	17-24
Stop-Loss Insurance	17-28
Voluntary Employees' Beneficiary Associations	17-37

Chapter 18
Third-Party Administration 18-1

    The Role of the TPA 18-1

    Performance Standards 18-6

    Legal Issues 18-8

    The TPA Market 18-12

Chapter 19
Quality Assurance 19-1

    Quality Measures 19-1

    Report Card Movement 19-13

    The Joint Commission and HEDIS 19-16

    Outcomes Measurement 19-17

Chapter 20
Home Health Care and Long-Term Care 20-1

    Home Health Care 20-1

    Home Health Care Fraud 20-12

    Long-Term Care 20-14

    Subacute Care 20-21

Contents

    Hospice Care 20-24

Chapter 21
Communication 21-1

    Developing Communication Strategies . . . 21-1

    Benefit Statements 21-5

    Periodic Benefit Reports 21-6

    Interactive Systems 21-7

    Online Services 21-9

    Communicating Employee Benefits 21-11

Chapter 22
Mental Health 22-1

    Mental Health Benefits 22-1

    Controlling Costs 22-9

    Substance Abuse 22-12

    Managed Mental Health 22-16

    Employee Assistance Programs 22-22

    Outcome Measurements 22-29

    Americans with Disabilities Act 22-30

Mental Health Parity Act 22-34

APPENDIX A
Health Information Resources A-1

    Government A-1

    Associations/Organizations A-4

    Accreditation Agencies/HMO Quality Review Organizations A-12

APPENDIX B
DOL Model COBRA Initial Notice B-1

APPENDIX C
DOL Model COBRA Initial Notice Incorporating Revisions C-1

APPENDIX D
Sample COBRA Notice Upon Occurrence of a Qualifying Event D-1

APPENDIX E
Model Certificate of Coverage E-1

APPENDIX F
Internet Resources F-1

Index I-1

List of Questions

Chapter 1 An Overview of Group Insurance

Group Health Insurance

Q 1:1	What are the various ways that individuals receive health insurance protection?	1-1
Q 1:2	What is the major difference between group and individual insurance?	1-2
Q 1:3	What are the advantages of group insurance over individual insurance?	1-2
Q 1:4	If all of an employer's employees are healthy, would the employer be just as well off with a series of individual policies as with one group policy?	1-3
Q 1:5	How prevalent is group insurance in the United States?	1-4

The Uninsured

Q 1:6	What portion of the population is uninsured?	1-4
Q 1:7	What are the characteristics of the uninsured?	1-5
Q 1:8	What is the impact of the uninsured on health insurance costs?	1-5
Q 1:9	Why are people employed by small companies less likely to have health insurance?	1-5
Q 1:10	Why aren't more people covered?	1-6
Q 1:11	What is underinsurance?	1-6

Group Insurance

Q 1:12	Why do most employers provide group insurance?	1-7
Q 1:13	What types of group protection do most employers provide?	1-7
Q 1:14	What is included in the term "group health insurance"?	1-8
Q 1:15	What are the characteristics of group health insurance?	1-8
Q 1:16	What caused the rapid growth of group health insurance?	1-8
Q 1:17	How important is group health insurance to employees?	1-9
Q 1:18	Is group insurance available only to single employers?	1-9
Q 1:19	What is a multiple employer trust?	1-10
Q 1:20	How can a labor union provide group insurance?	1-10
Q 1:21	What is an association plan?	1-10
Q 1:22	What is a MEWA?	1-11
Q 1:23	Are there any new requirements for MEWAs?	1-11
Q 1:24	What are state-sponsored coalitions?	1-11
Q 1:25	Have state-sponsored coalitions been successful?	1-11
Q 1:26	Do any local governments sponsor joint purchasing coalitions?	1-12
Q 1:27	What is joint purchasing?	1-12
Q 1:28	Is price the only focus of joint purchasing?	1-12
Q 1:29	What is an employer health care coalition?	1-12

Chapter 2 The Health Insurance Marketplace

Types of Insurance Professionals

Q 2:1	Can an employer work directly with an insurance company?	2-1
Q 2:2	What does the uncertainty in the insurance industry mean to employers?	2-2
Q 2:3	How can employers protect themselves against insurer failure?	2-2
Q 2:4	How can an employer obtain information from the principal rating companies?	2-3
Q 2:5	What are state insurance guaranty funds?	2-4
Q 2:6	What is a group health insurance underwriter?	2-5
Q 2:7	What is risk?	2-5
Q 2:8	What is a group sales representative?	2-6

List of Questions

Q 2:9	What is a client service representative?	2-6
Q 2:10	What is an intermediary?	2-6
Q 2:11	How do group sales representatives and intermediaries interact in the sale of a group health insurance plan?	2-6
Q 2:12	What services do intermediaries provide prior to the purchase of a group health insurance plan?	2-7
Q 2:13	What is an insurance broker?	2-7
Q 2:14	What is the difference between an agent and a broker?	2-7
Q 2:15	What is an employee benefit consultant?	2-8
Q 2:16	How does an employer determine whether to use an agent, broker, or consultant?	2-8

Choosing and Compensating Intermediaries

Q 2:17	How does an employer select a particular intermediary?	2-8
Q 2:18	Is the size of the intermediary important?	2-10
Q 2:19	Which brokerage firms are the largest?	2-10
Q 2:20	Which consulting firms are the largest?	2-10
Q 2:21	Can an employer use a personal or business advisor as its group insurance intermediary?	2-11
Q 2:22	How are intermediaries compensated?	2-11
Q 2:23	What are commission schedules?	2-11
Q 2:24	What is vesting of commissions?	2-12
Q 2:25	Are there laws that regulate the business practices of intermediaries?	2-12
Q 2:26	If an employer wants to self-fund the plan, which type of insurance professional would it need?	2-13
Q 2:27	Would an employer whose plan is fully insured use a TPA?	2-13
Q 2:28	How does an employer decide whether to use a TPA or an insurance company to administer its plan?	2-13
Q 2:29	If an employer has a TPA handle the administrative functions, would the employer's cost be decreased?	2-14
Q 2:30	How are TPAs compensated?	2-14

Blue Cross/Blue Shield Plans

Q 2:31	What is Blue Cross/Blue Shield?	2-14
Q 2:32	Are Blues plans similar to those offered by private insurance companies?	2-15
Q 2:33	Do most private insurers offer major medical supplements?	2-15

Health Insurance Answer Book

Q 2:34 How are the Blues different from private insurers? 2-16

Chapter 3 Factors Influencing Insurance Plan Design

Non-legal Factors Affecting Design

Q 3:1	Besides the legislative factors, what other issues must be addressed as part of the purchasing process?	3-2
Q 3:2	What are typical employer strategies?	3-2
Q 3:3	Who is an eligible employee?	3-4
Q 3:4	Who is an eligible dependent?	3-4
Q 3:5	Are employers providing benefits for domestic partners? .	3-5
Q 3:6	How have private employers responded to requests for domestic partner benefits?	3-6
Q 3:7	Why do employers offer domestic partner benefits?	3-8
Q 3:8	What criteria can employers use to determine the existence of a valid domestic partnership?	3-8
Q 3:9	What is the IRS position on benefits for domestic partners?	3-9
Q 3:10	What is the impact of the Defense of Marriage Act on domestic partner benefits?	3-10
Q 3:11	What type of public reaction can employers expect for recognizing domestic partnerships in their benefit plans?	3-10
Q 3:12	What does the city and county of San Francisco require regarding domestic partners?	3-12
Q 3:13	Do other cities have similar requirements?	3-12
Q 3:14	What is Vermonts Civil Union Law and does it affect benefit plans?	3-12
Q 3:15	What is a reciprocal beneficiary?	3-13
Q 3:16	What rights do reciprocal beneficiaries have?	3-13
Q 3:17	What has been the reaction of the business community in Hawaii to the reciprocal beneficiary law?	3-14
Q 3:18	Can a single group health insurance plan meet the benefit needs of an employer's diverse workforce?	3-14

Paying for Insurance

Q 3:19	How much can an employer expect to pay annually for group health insurance?	3-14
Q 3:20	Must employers pay the entire cost of group health insurance?	3-14

xxx

List of Questions

Q 3:21	What factors should an employer consider when deciding whether its group health insurance plan should be contributory or noncontributory?	3-15
Q 3:22	What legal constraints are imposed on the distribution of employer-employee costs for group health insurance?	3-16
Q 3:23	Can an employer self-fund a group health insurance plan?	3-16

Coverage

Q 3:24	What types of traditional group health insurance plans are available?	3-16
Q 3:25	What is a base-plus plan?	3-16
Q 3:26	What is a comprehensive plan?	3-17
Q 3:27	What types of services are generally covered by a group health insurance plan?	3-17
Q 3:28	Are alternative therapies covered?	3-18
Q 3:29	What are common types of alternative medicine?	3-20
Q 3:30	How popular is alternative health care?	3-21
Q 3:31	How much does alternative health care cost?	3-21
Q 3:32	What kinds of hospital charges are covered under a group health insurance plan?	3-22
Q 3:33	How is surgery covered under a health insurance plan?	3-22
Q 3:34	What is a reasonable and customary charge?	3-23
Q 3:35	What is a schedule of insurance?	3-24
Q 3:36	Why do some plans pay R&C charges and others schedule benefits?	3-24
Q 3:37	If the physicians' charges exceed the R&C amount or the schedule amount, is the employee responsible for paying the balance?	3-24
Q 3:38	How have hospital and surgical care changed recently?	3-25
Q 3:39	How are nonsurgical physicians' services covered?	3-25
Q 3:40	What alternatives to hospital care are common today?	3-25
Q 3:41	What kinds of hospital outpatient expenses are covered?	3-26
Q 3:42	Are all covered expenses reimbursed?	3-26
Q 3:43	Why would an employer want to limit reimbursement for covered expenses?	3-26
Q 3:44	How are covered expenses limited?	3-26
Q 3:45	What types of services are generally not covered by a group health insurance plan?	3-27
Q 3:46	Are experimental treatments covered?	3-28

Health Insurance Answer Book

Q 3:47	May treatments that are legitimately experimental be excluded from coverage?	3-28
Q 3:48	How do insurers decide whether to cover a treatment?	3-29
Q 3:49	What is an external review?	3-29
Q 3:50	What is the reason for an external review process?	3-30
Q 3:51	How common are external review programs?	3-30
Q 3:52	Does health insurance cover extended care facilities?	3-30

Restrictions on Coverage

Q 3:53	For what reasons do employers typically exclude employees from group health insurance coverage?	3-31
Q 3:54	Are there limitations on an employer's freedom to choose the employees it wants covered under a group health insurance plan?	3-31
Q 3:55	Why would an employer offer benefits to which some employees already have access?	3-32
Q 3:56	What are the drawbacks to duplicating benefits?	3-32
Q 3:57	Do employers provide group health insurance to part-time and temporary employees?	3-33
Q 3:58	Why don't more employers provide medical coverage to part-time employees?	3-34
Q 3:59	Can an employer provide enhanced health care coverage for key employees?	3-34
Q 3:60	Will an insurance carrier deny certain employees coverage under a group health insurance plan?	3-34
Q 3:61	Can an employer require different service waiting periods?	3-34

Deductibles, Copayments, and Reimbursement

Q 3:62	What is a deductible?	3-35
Q 3:63	What is a carryover deductible?	3-35
Q 3:64	For insured employees with dependent coverage, does the deductible for each person have to be satisfied before reimbursement begins?	3-36
Q 3:65	What is coinsurance?	3-36
Q 3:66	What are typical coinsurance percentages?	3-36
Q 3:67	What is a maximum out-of-pocket limit?	3-37
Q 3:68	Is the deductible included in determining an OOP maximum?	3-37

List of Questions

Q 3:69	Can medical expenses not covered by a health insurance plan be applied toward the deductible or OOP maximum?	3-38
Q 3:70	Do most policies include an overall limit to the amount reimbursable to one individual?	3-38

Cost Containment

Q 3:71	What specific factors should be considered relative to plan design philosophy?	3-38
Q 3:72	What factors should be considered relative to design theory?	3-39
Q 3:73	When might it be advisable to redesign the plan?	3-40
Q 3:74	Why might an employer consider excluding preexisting conditions?	3-41
Q 3:75	Why might it be advisable to carve out specific types of coverage?	3-41
Q 3:76	How can a plan increase cost sharing by employees? . . .	3-42
Q 3:77	Would increases in required employee contributions toward premium help control costs?	3-43
Q 3:78	Should employers that do not now require employee contributions for health care coverage introduce them? .	3-43
Q 3:79	What are average employee contributions for health coverage?	3-44
Q 3:80	What might an employer consider doing with regard to deductibles?	3-44
Q 3:81	What are typical deductibles?	3-44
Q 3:82	In what circumstances are deductibles waived?	3-45
Q 3:83	What are pay-based deductibles?	3-45
Q 3:84	What are the advantages of a pay-based deductible? . . .	3-45
Q 3:85	What are the disadvantages of a pay-based deductible? .	3-46
Q 3:86	What concerns should an employer have about per-condition deductibles?	3-47
Q 3:87	What is a front-end deductible?	3-47
Q 3:88	Do all comprehensive plans have front-end deductibles? .	3-48
Q 3:89	What is coinsurance forgiveness?	3-48
Q 3:90	What effect do increased deductibles and coinsurance have on utilization?	3-49
Q 3:91	How can health care plans be designed to encourage use of the most cost-effective care?	3-49

Q 3:92	Under what circumstances might an employer consider changing from reasonable and customary to a scheduled benefit structure?	3-49
Q 3:93	Does outpatient surgery coverage help control costs?	3-50
Q 3:94	What plan features prevent illness and injury, thereby reducing costs in the long run?	3-51
Q 3:95	Do any legal factors constrain employers from reducing health care benefits?	3-52
Q 3:96	Do these factors make it extraordinarily difficult for an employer to redesign its plan?	3-52
Q 3:97	What steps can employers take to reverse employee insulation from cost exposure?	3-53
Q 3:98	What can employers do to combat the problem of inappropriately designed plans?	3-53

Managed Competition

Q 3:99	What is managed competition?	3-54
Q 3:100	What elements are common to plans using the managed competition strategy?	3-54
Q 3:101	What should employers consider before incorporating managed competition into their health care benefits strategy?	3-55
Q 3:102	Why haven't all employers adopted managed competition in their health care benefits strategy?	3-56
Q 3:103	Are any employers using the principles of managed competition?	3-56
Q 3:104	Are employers who use managed competition incorporating quality improvement measures as well?	3-56
Q 3:105	What are the disadvantages of managed competition?	3-57
Q 3:106	Is there an advantage in groups of employers working together in a managed competition model?	3-57
Q 3:107	Does competition between HMOs reduce health care costs?	3-57

Chapter 4 State and Federal Laws

Legal Factors Affecting Design

Q 4:1	Are employers required by federal law to provide medical coverage to employees?	4-1

List of Questions

Q 4:2	What requirements do federal regulations directly impose?	4-2
Q 4:3	Are employers required by state law to provide medical coverage to employees?	4-5
Q 4:4	What medical coverage requirements do states impose?	4-5
Q 4:5	To help hold costs down, can an employer choose what specifically will be covered?	4-6
Q 4:6	When an employer self-funds to enhance flexibility in design, must it cover everything allowed by the IRS as a deduction?	4-6
Q 4:7	Is it necessary to cover things of which the employer disapproves, such as abortions or vasectomies?	4-7
Q 4:8	Can an employer require employees to purchase maternity (or family) coverage if they are single?	4-7
Q 4:9	Can an employer elect to make its plan secondary to Medicare after employees become eligible for Medicare?	4-7
Q 4:10	Can an employer assume that employees will choose the employer's plan as primary?	4-8
Q 4:11	Can an employer encourage its employees to select Medicare as primary?	4-8
Q 4:12	Can an employee who makes extensive use of the coverage be required to pay a greater premium or contribution?	4-9
Q 4:13	Must an employer cover spouses of employees?	4-9
Q 4:14	Are MEWAs governed by state or federal law?	4-9
Q 4:15	When state and federal laws change, what are an employer's obligations regarding a group health insurance plan?	4-10

State Law

Q 4:16	Are group health plans governed by federal or state law?	4-11
Q 4:17	Do both federal and state laws apply to self-funded group health plans?	4-11
Q 4:18	Has the Supreme Court affirmed this division between state insurance and federal law?	4-12
Q 4:19	What are the responsibilities of the state insurance department?	4-14
Q 4:20	What are the similarities among state laws governing group health insurance?	4-15
Q 4:21	What is a mandated benefit?	4-15
Q 4:22	Are self-funded plans exempt from state mandates?	4-16
Q 4:23	Why are some benefits mandated by state law?	4-16

Health Insurance Answer Book

Q 4:24	What are the most commonly mandated benefits?	4-16
Q 4:25	How extensive are state-mandated benefits?	4-17
Q 4:26	How much do mandates increase the cost of health insurance?	4-17
Q 4:27	What is a mandated offering?	4-18
Q 4:28	What are the state requirements for employee participation in a group insurance plan?	4-18
Q 4:29	What is the minimum number of employees allowed by state law to participate in a group health insurance plan?	4-18
Q 4:30	Is there a maximum number of employees that may be covered under a group health insurance plan?	4-18
Q 4:31	Are there state laws governing parental or family leave?	4-19
Q 4:32	What is the New York surcharge?	4-19
Q 4:33	What is the Massachusetts surcharge?	4-19
Q 4:34	Does the Massachusetts surcharge increase the coinsurance amount paid by the employee?	4-20
Q 4:35	What is a living wage ordinance?	4-20
Q 4:36	What can employers do to cope with mandated coverage?	4-20

Federal Law

Q 4:37	What federal laws affect group health insurance plans?	4-21
Q 4:38	What does the Newborns' and Mothers' Health Protection Act of 1996 require?	4-22
Q 4:39	Do all health plans have to provide minimum hospital stays in connection with childbirth?	4-22
Q 4:40	May group health plans, insurance companies, or HMOs impose deductibles or other cost-sharing provisions for hospital stays in connection with childbirth?	4-23
Q 4:41	Are there any regulations providing guidance on how to comply with NMHPA?	4-23
Q 4:42	Is there a notice requirement under NMHPA?	4-23
Q 4:43	May a group health plan require preauthorization of a maternity stay?	4-24
Q 4:44	How does ADEA affect group health insurance plans?	4-24
Q 4:45	Are employers required by federal law to cover retired employees under group health insurance plans?	4-25
Q 4:46	What requirements does ERISA impose on group health insurance plans?	4-25
Q 4:47	What does ERISA require regarding employee contributions?	4-26

List of Questions

Q 4:48	How were group health insurance plans affected by the HMO Act of 1973?	4-26
Q 4:49	What is the Women's Health and Cancer Rights Act?	4-27
Q 4:50	What are the notice requirements under WHCRA?	4-27
Q 4:51	Is there any guidance as to what the WHCRA notice should say?	4-27
Q 4:52	Does WHCRA apply to all group health plans?	4-28
Q 4:53	Does federal law prohibit employers from making any changes in coverage?	4-28

Pregnancy Discrimination Act

Q 4:54	What is the Pregnancy Discrimination Act?	4-29
Q 4:55	What does "the same" treatment for pregnancy-related medical conditions mean?	4-29
Q 4:56	What employers are subject to the PDA?	4-29
Q 4:57	Do the provisions of the Pregnancy Discrimination Act apply only to married employees?	4-30
Q 4:58	Does the Pregnancy Discrimination Act extend to benefits for spouses of employees?	4-30
Q 4:59	Does the PDA extend to other dependents?	4-30
Q 4:60	Must abortions be covered by employer health plans under the PDA?	4-30
Q 4:61	Are state laws preempted by the PDA?	4-31

Family and Medical Leave Act

Q 4:62	Are there federal laws governing family leave?	4-31
Q 4:63	Are there regulations regarding family leave?	4-32
Q 4:64	How does FMLA affect benefits?	4-32
Q 4:65	Does FMLA require any notices about benefits?	4-32
Q 4:66	What are the consequences for noncompliance with FMLA?	4-33
Q 4:67	What happens if an employee switches to a part-time schedule under FMLA?	4-33
Q 4:68	What if the plan changes while an employee is on FMLA leave?	4-34
Q 4:69	Can an employer pay an employee's premiums while the worker is on FMLA leave?	4-34
Q 4:70	What if a collective bargaining agreement requires more than FMLA?	4-34

Q 4:71	Does FMLA affect employee-pay-all benefits?	4-35
Q 4:72	What is the difference between maternity leave and parental or family leave?	4-35
Q 4:73	What features are typically found in employer family leave policies?	4-35

Americans with Disabilities Act

Q 4:74	What is the ADA?	4-36
Q 4:75	How does the ADA affect employers and their employees?	4-36
Q 4:76	What businesses are affected?	4-36
Q 4:77	What do employers need to do to comply with the ADA?	4-37
Q 4:78	What constitutes an undue business hardship?	4-37
Q 4:79	What is a disability?	4-38
Q 4:80	Are substance abusers considered disabled?	4-39
Q 4:81	Who is a qualified individual with a disability?	4-39
Q 4:82	What is an essential job function?	4-39
Q 4:83	What is reasonable accommodation?	4-40
Q 4:84	What effect has the ADA had on business?	4-40
Q 4:85	How does the ADA affect the hiring process?	4-42
Q 4:86	Are preemployment physicals permitted?	4-42
Q 4:87	How does the ADA affect health insurance benefits?	4-42
Q 4:88	Are health insurance plans that conform to state law exempt from the ADA?	4-43
Q 4:89	How does the ADA affect leave policies?	4-43
Q 4:90	Do the EEOC regulations offer detailed guidance for employers in specific employment situations?	4-43
Q 4:91	Where can employers obtain more information about the ADA?	4-44

Health Insurance Portability and Accountability Act

Q 4:92	When were the provisions of HIPAA effective?	4-44
Q 4:93	What does HIPAA require regarding preexisting condition exclusions?	4-44
Q 4:94	Does HIPAA apply to flexible spending accounts?	4-46
Q 4:95	Who is a late enrollee?	4-47
Q 4:96	What does HIPAA require regarding waiting periods?	4-47
Q 4:97	How can employees prove they had prior coverage?	4-47

List of Questions

Q 4:98	How can an employee who does not receive a certificate receive credit for prior coverage?	**4-47**
Q 4:99	Do plans that do not impose a preexisting condition exclusion have to provide certificates?	**4-48**
Q 4:100	Can plans contract with the insurer or HMO to provide the certificates for their employees?	**4-48**
Q 4:101	When must group health plans and issuers provide certificates?	**4-48**
Q 4:102	Is there a model certificate that group health plans and issuers can use?	**4-49**
Q 4:103	What if the plan or issuer does not know who the employees' dependents are?	**4-49**
Q 4:104	What is the minimum period of time that should be covered by the certificate?	**4-49**
Q 4:105	How does "crediting" for preexisting conditions work under HIPAA?	**4-49**
Q 4:106	Does COBRA count as creditable coverage?	**4-50**
Q 4:107	When employees change jobs, are they guaranteed the same benefits they had under their old plan?	**4-50**
Q 4:108	What are the HIPAA eligibility requirements?	**4-50**
Q 4:109	May an employer sponsor a group health plan that is available only to employees who pass a physical examination?	**4-51**
Q 4:110	Can employees lose health benefits if their health status changes?	**4-51**
Q 4:111	Does HIPAA require employers to offer health coverage or to provide specific benefits?	**4-51**
Q 4:112	What does HIPAA require regarding benefits and employee contributions?	**4-52**
Q 4:113	What does HIPAA require regarding special enrollment periods?	**4-52**
Q 4:114	What changes did HIPAA make to COBRA continuation requirements?	**4-53**
Q 4:115	What changes did HIPAA make to small employer health plans and individual health insurance policies?	**4-53**
Q 4:116	What is group-to-individual portability?	**4-54**
Q 4:117	Is it easy for people who exhaust COBRA to get individual policies?	**4-54**
Q 4:118	What does HIPAA require regarding renewal of policies?	**4-55**
Q 4:119	What does HIPAA require regarding reductions in benefits?	**4-55**
Q 4:120	Does HIPAA apply to small employers?	**4-56**

Health Insurance Answer Book

Q 4:121	Does HIPAA apply to self-funded group health plans? . . .	4-56
Q 4:122	What new kinds of information do group health plans have to give to participants and beneficiaries?	4-56
Q 4:123	What is the definition of a material reduction in covered services or benefits that is subject to the new 60-day notice requirement?	4-57
Q 4:124	Can employers use e-mail systems to communicate these new disclosures to employees and, if so, do employees have a right to get a paper copy of the information from their plan?	4-57
Q 4:125	What does HIPAA provide regarding electronic data interchange?	4-58
Q 4:126	What does HIPAA provide regarding long-term care insurance?	4-58
Q 4:127	What does HIPAA provide regarding accelerated death benefits?	4-59
Q 4:128	What does HIPAA provide regarding withdrawals from individual retirement arrangements for medical expenses?	4-60
Q 4:129	What requirements does HIPAA impose on multiple employer welfare arrangements and multiemployer plans?	4-60
Q 4:130	What requirements does HIPAA impose on insurers of small groups?	4-60
Q 4:131	What requirements does HIPAA impose on insurers of associations?	4-61
Q 4:132	Do the availability, renewability, and portability provisions of HIPAA apply to all types of health insurance?	4-61
Q 4:133	What disclosure requirements does HIPAA impose on insurers in the small employer market?	4-62
Q 4:134	Who enforces HIPAA?	4-62

Taxation of Group Health Plans

Q 4:135	What state tax laws apply to group health insurance plans?	4-63
Q 4:136	What is the federal tax status of group health insurance for employers?	4-63
Q 4:137	Are self-employed individuals treated as employers with respect to the deductibility of group insurance premiums?	4-64
Q 4:138	Are employer contributions treated as taxable income to employees?	4-64
Q 4:139	Do taxes apply if the employer reimburses an employee for the cost of an individual health insurance policy? . .	4-64

List of Questions

| Q 4:140 | Are the benefits from a group health insurance plan taxable to employees? | 4-64 |

Reservists' Benefits

Q 4:141	Must employers continue to offer health care benefits to employees and their dependents, even though they would be eligible for military benefits?	4-65
Q 4:142	What are the differences between USERRA and COBRA?	4-65
Q 4:143	Are reservists eligible for military benefits?	4-66
Q 4:144	Do most employers discontinue benefits for employees called to active duty?	4-66
Q 4:145	Do employers have any obligations for benefits provided by the Department of Defense or the Veterans Administration?	4-66
Q 4:146	Are dependents of military personnel eligible for medical care at military installations?	4-67
Q 4:147	What is TRICARE?	4-67
Q 4:148	Does an employer plan have any continuing responsibility to dependents covered by TRICARE?	4-68
Q 4:149	What rights do military personnel have when they return to civilian life?	4-68
Q 4:150	What requirements must a veteran meet to be eligible for reinstatement?	4-68
Q 4:151	To what benefits are reemployed veterans entitled?	4-69
Q 4:152	How does this rule (on reemployed veterans) apply to health benefits?	4-70
Q 4:153	How does the rule apply to sick leave?	4-70
Q 4:154	Do employers have to grant leave for training and reserve duty?	4-70
Q 4:155	How do state laws affect reservists' benefits?	4-71

Chapter 5   Plan Rating and Funding

Plan Funding

| Q 5:1 | What does plan funding mean? | 5-1 |

Fully Insured Plans

| Q 5:2 | What are the cost components of a health insurance plan? | 5-2 |

Health Insurance Answer Book

Q 5:3	What are expected claims?	5-2
Q 5:4	Why would claims be paid after the termination of the contract?	5-3
Q 5:5	How does an insurer know what claims to expect?	5-3
Q 5:6	What is a group health insurance actuary?	5-3
Q 5:7	How does an actuary estimate which individuals will incur claims?	5-4
Q 5:8	How can a plan find an actuary?	5-4
Q 5:9	How does plan design affect the expected claim calculation?	5-4
Q 5:10	How does the health plan's rate-guarantee period affect the rate?	5-5
Q 5:11	How does the insurer project the cost of the medical services expected to be provided?	5-6
Q 5:12	How is the expected cost of claims calculated for an employer with several locations?	5-7
Q 5:13	How is a margin for higher-than-anticipated claims developed?	5-7
Q 5:14	What is prospective rating?	5-7
Q 5:15	What is retrospective rating?	5-8
Q 5:16	How does a policyholder reimburse a deficit?	5-9
Q 5:17	What are reserves?	5-9
Q 5:18	How does an insurer determine what premium reserves are necessary?	5-9
Q 5:19	How are expenses projected?	5-10
Q 5:20	What percentage of the health insurance premium is generally an insurance company's profit?	5-10
Q 5:21	What is credibility?	5-11
Q 5:22	What is a manual rate?	5-11
Q 5:23	What is a pool?	5-12
Q 5:24	What is experience rating?	5-12
Q 5:25	What are paid claims?	5-12
Q 5:26	What are incurred claims?	5-12
Q 5:27	What is the difference between paid claims and incurred claims?	5-13
Q 5:28	Under what circumstances is it better to use incurred claims or paid claims?	5-13
Q 5:29	How is an experience rate combined with a manual rate to produce a final premium rate?	5-16

List of Questions

Q 5:30	Do all claims count toward an employer's claim experience, thus affecting the rate?		5-16
Q 5:31	What is a pool charge?		5-17
Q 5:32	What is retention?		5-17
Q 5:33	How does an employer determine whether a premium rate is reasonable?		5-18
Q 5:34	Are dependent rates developed separately from employee rates?		5-18
Q 5:35	What is a loss ratio?		5-19
Q 5:36	What is a tolerable loss ratio?		5-19
Q 5:37	Do TLRs vary from year to year and from employer to employer?		5-20
Q 5:38	What is lag?		5-21
Q 5:39	What is a lag study?		5-21

Alternatives to Fully Insured Plans

Q 5:40	Are there alternatives to fully insured (conventionally funded) plans?		5-22
Q 5:41	How do alternative funding methods differ from conventional funding methods?		5-22
Q 5:42	For whom might an alternative method of plan funding be appropriate?		5-23
Q 5:43	Does employer size affect the choice of alternatives?		5-23
Q 5:44	Do some employers elect to insure the entire risk of a health insurance plan?		5-24

Deferred Premium Arrangements

Q 5:45	What is a deferred premium arrangement?		5-24
Q 5:46	Why would an employer elect a deferred premium arrangement?		5-25
Q 5:47	Why don't all employers elect deferred premium arrangements?		5-25

Shared Funding Arrangements

Q 5:48	How does a shared funding arrangement differ from a conventionally funded plan?		5-26
Q 5:49	Why would an employer elect a shared funding plan?		5-26
Q 5:50	Why would an employer reject a shared funding plan as an alternative funding arrangement?		5-27

| Q 5:51 | Why don't all employers elect shared funding arrangements? | 5-27 |

Retrospective Premium Arrangements

Q 5:52	What is a retrospective premium arrangement?	5-28
Q 5:53	Why would an employer negotiate a retrospective premium arrangement?	5-28
Q 5:54	What is a deep cut retro?	5-28
Q 5:55	Why might an employer not negotiate a retrospective premium arrangement?	5-29
Q 5:56	To whom are retrospective premium arrangements available?	5-29

Reserve Reduction Agreements

Q 5:57	What is a reserve reduction agreement?	5-30
Q 5:58	Why would reserves decrease if an insurer eliminates its liability after contract termination?	5-30
Q 5:59	Why would an employer want to negotiate a reserve reduction?	5-30
Q 5:60	Why might an employer not change the conventional reserve arrangement?	5-31
Q 5:61	Do small employers typically implement reserve reduction agreements?	5-31

Minimum Premium Plans

Q 5:62	What is a minimum premium plan?	5-32
Q 5:63	At what level does the insurer become responsible for benefit funding under an MPP?	5-32
Q 5:64	If an individual incurs a shock claim (an unexpected claim of a high amount) under an MPP, does the full amount of that claim count toward the employer's trigger point?	5-34
Q 5:65	How are claims paid with employer funds under an MPP?	5-34
Q 5:66	Why would an employer benefit from establishing an MPP?	5-34
Q 5:67	Is there any reason why an employer would not elect an MPP?	5-35
Q 5:68	What employers typically elect MPPs?	5-36
Q 5:69	How are third-party administrative services used in an MPP?	5-36

List of Questions

Chapter 6 Plan Implementation and Administration

Setting Up the Plan

Q 6:1	After an employer selects a health insurance plan, how is the coverage put into effect?	6-2
Q 6:2	Is the coverage effective as soon as the insurer receives the application and enrollment material?	6-2
Q 6:3	When might an underwriter not approve an application for coverage?	6-3
Q 6:4	If an application is not approved by the underwriter, what happens?	6-3
Q 6:5	Why does the insurance company require detailed coverage information before issuing the policy?	6-3
Q 6:6	When an employer uses a TPA, what services does the administrator provide?	6-4
Q 6:7	Who provides the announcement materials necessary to inform employees about the plan?	6-4
Q 6:8	What is a certificate of insurance?	6-4
Q 6:9	What other materials are issued to employees?	6-5

Reporting and Disclosure

Q 6:10	Are there reports that an employer must file with the state or federal government?	6-6
Q 6:11	What new reporting rules were instituted under HIPAA?	6-7
Q 6:12	What is a qualified medical child support order?	6-7
Q 6:13	Can a QMCSO require a plan to offer a new benefit?	6-7
Q 6:14	Does OBRA '93 require plans to cover certain children?	6-8
Q 6:15	Does OBRA '93 require any notices?	6-8
Q 6:16	What is a summary plan description, and what information does it contain?	6-8
Q 6:17	Are there any changes pending regarding SPDs?	6-9
Q 6:18	What would the proposed regulations change?	6-9
Q 6:19	Do plan sponsors have to include information about HMOs in SPDs?	6-10
Q 6:20	Should an employer rely on the SPD to explain plan benefits to employees?	6-11
Q 6:21	Can an SPD be used for more than one purpose?	6-11
Q 6:22	What administrative material does the insurer initially provide to the employer?	6-11

Enrollment

Q 6:23	Why is enrollment in the plan encouraged?	6-12
Q 6:24	What information must individuals provide when enrolling in the plan?	6-12
Q 6:25	Can employers consider Medicaid eligibility when enrolling employees?	6-13
Q 6:26	Must individuals enroll in a noncontributory plan?	6-13
Q 6:27	Who enrolls the employees in the group health insurance plan?	6-13
Q 6:28	How long do employees have to complete their enrollment forms?	6-13
Q 6:29	Why would an employee who submits a late enrollment form not be allowed to participate as of the plan's effective date?	6-14
Q 6:30	Can an employee who declines coverage initially enroll at a later date?	6-14
Q 6:31	What is a special enrollment period?	6-15
Q 6:32	Is any kind of re-enrollment of employees in group health insurance plans necessary?	6-16

Billing

Q 6:33	How are employers billed for group health insurance premiums?	6-16
Q 6:34	Where can an employer get help in calculating premium payments?	6-17
Q 6:35	If an employer's premium payment is late, does coverage lapse?	6-17
Q 6:36	Does the insurer periodically audit employers that self-account?	6-18

Claims

Q 6:37	How does an individual submit a claim for payment? . . .	6-18
Q 6:38	Can employees submit claims after the effective date of the plan but before they receive their certificates of insurance?	6-19
Q 6:39	Do most individuals pay the health care provider for the service and receive reimbursement later from the plan? .	6-19
Q 6:40	What is assignment of benefits?	6-20
Q 6:41	Where can an employee get help in completing a claim form?	6-20

List of Questions

Q 6:42	How quickly are insureds reimbursed for their claim expenses?	6-20
Q 6:43	How rapidly should an employer or union expect claims to be processed?	6-20
Q 6:44	What changes would these DOL proposed regulations make to current benefit claim appeal procedures?	6-21
Q 6:45	Are there ways an employer can be assured of getting a good turnaround time for claim processing?	6-22
Q 6:46	Who receives the benefit check?	6-22
Q 6:47	What is an explanation of benefits?	6-22
Q 6:48	How does an employee appeal a claim determination?	6-23
Q 6:49	What is the plan administrator's obligation with regard to an appeal?	6-23
Q 6:50	What appeal processes are in place for workers and dependents?	6-24
Q 6:51	How can employers and health plans improve the appeal process to prevent failures and possible large damage awards?	6-25

Coverage, Renewal and Changes

Q 6:52	How does an employer renew its health insurance policy?	6-25
Q 6:53	When can an employer change its coverage?	6-26
Q 6:54	When the policy is renewed, are all employees automatically covered?	6-26
Q 6:55	If an employer believes that a renewal rate is too high, what options are available?	6-27
Q 6:56	What kinds of plan changes might an employer want to make during the plan year?	6-27

Termination of Coverage

Q 6:57	Can an employer terminate coverage in the middle of a plan year?	6-27
Q 6:58	If a contract specifies termination at year-end only, does an employer have any options?	6-28
Q 6:59	If an employer changes insurers, what protection do employees have against medical expenses?	6-28
Q 6:60	What protection does an employee who terminates employment have against medical expenses?	6-28
Q 6:61	What is a conversion privilege?	6-28
Q 6:62	How does COBRA affect the group conversion privilege?	6-29

| Q 6:63 | What are the conversion requirements for other group plans? | 6-29 |

Computerized Administration

Q 6:64	What role do computer systems play in managing health plans?	6-30
Q 6:65	What role would a computer system play in performing nondiscrimination testing?	6-30
Q 6:66	What sort of features should a COBRA administration system have?	6-31
Q 6:67	How would a computer help in administering flexible benefits plans?	6-32
Q 6:68	What types of computer communication programs are available?	6-33
Q 6:69	In buying or leasing an administrative computer system, what other features should a plan sponsor look for?	6-33
Q 6:70	Is it becoming practical to use the Internet/Intranet for employee benefit administration and communication?	6-34
Q 6:71	Are benefit professionals using the Internet/Intranet to communicate benefit information?	6-34
Q 6:72	What are the primary functions on the Internet/Intranet?	6-34
Q 6:73	What are the advantages of electronic communication?	6-35
Q 6:74	What are the different types of outsourcing?	6-35

Chapter 7 Managing Health Insurance Costs

Factors Affecting Costs

Q 7:1	What is the single most important factor affecting group health insurance in recent decades?	7-1
Q 7:2	Are health care costs coming under control?	7-2
Q 7:3	What are some of the factors that influenced the rise in medical costs?	7-3
Q 7:4	Which of the factors contributing to the rapid escalation of health care costs are to some extent under control?	7-4
Q 7:5	How does the proliferation of new and expensive medical technology contribute to rising medical costs?	7-5
Q 7:6	What effect do legal liability issues have on health care costs?	7-5
Q 7:7	What is cost shifting?	7-5

List of Questions

Q 7:8	How do higher claims affect health insurance costs? . . .	7-6
Q 7:9	How does overprovision of medical services contribute to the problem?	7-6
Q 7:10	Why do health care providers deliver unnecessary care? . .	7-6
Q 7:11	Why have consumers not purchased less care, as prices have increased?	7-7
Q 7:12	How does the inappropriate use of medical services exacerbate the problem?	7-7
Q 7:13	How does the oversupply of medical professionals and facilities contribute to the problem of rising medical costs?	7-8
Q 7:14	How does the practice of defensive medicine contribute to the health care cost spiral?	7-8
Q 7:15	How does the insulation of consumers from cost exposure for medical services contribute to rising medical costs? .	7-8
Q 7:16	How does consumer lack of medical understanding contribute to the cost problem?	7-9
Q 7:17	How does lack of communication contribute to the cost problem?	7-9
Q 7:18	What role do inappropriately designed plans play in the cost problem?	7-9
Q 7:19	How does mandated coverage contribute to the cost problem?	7-10
Q 7:20	Are employers to blame for high health care costs?	7-10
Q 7:21	How did employers create the high health care costs we know today?	7-10
Q 7:22	What are some specific, fundamental ways in which an employer's medical costs may be reduced?	7-12

Health Care Data

Q 7:23	Why have health data become an integral part of many employer cost-management programs?	7-14
Q 7:24	How can an employer know which programs to implement?	7-14
Q 7:25	Why are employer-specific data helpful?	7-15
Q 7:26	What elements are needed to analyze data effectively? . .	7-16
Q 7:27	What kinds of data are useful to better manage health care costs?	7-16
Q 7:28	What types of data are most useful for plan redesign purposes?	7-18

Q 7:29	If an employer wants to analyze claim data without assistance, what specific steps must be followed?	7-18
Q 7:30	How does an employer extract useful information from the data an insurance company or TPA can provide?	7-20
Q 7:31	What kinds of plan design features should employers implement, even without conclusive data on problems?	7-24

Utilization Review and Case Management

Q 7:32	What is utilization review?	7-24
Q 7:33	How does UR work?	7-24
Q 7:34	Do states regulate utilization review?	7-25
Q 7:35	With the growth of managed care, how is UR changing?	7-26
Q 7:36	What are treatment protocols?	7-26
Q 7:37	What kinds of utilization review are there?	7-27
Q 7:38	What is case management?	7-27
Q 7:39	How does case management work?	7-28
Q 7:40	With the growth of managed care, how is case management changing?	7-28
Q 7:41	Is hospital discharge planning different from individual case management?	7-29
Q 7:42	How does preadmission certification work?	7-29
Q 7:43	If hospital admissions are usually certified, why is UR necessary?	7-30
Q 7:44	What criteria are used to determine the length of a hospitalization?	7-31
Q 7:45	What happens during concurrent review?	7-31
Q 7:46	How does retrospective review help manage claim costs?	7-31
Q 7:47	Do the cost savings produced by UR justify the additional expense for the UR service?	7-32
Q 7:48	What is ambulatory care UR?	7-32
Q 7:49	How is ambulatory care UR different from inpatient UR?	7-32
Q 7:50	What techniques are used in ambulatory care review?	7-33
Q 7:51	How prevalent is ambulatory care UR?	7-33
Q 7:52	How much can ambulatory UR save?	7-33
Q 7:53	What is physician profiling?	7-33
Q 7:54	How much can physician profiling save?	7-34
Q 7:55	What is a second surgical opinion program?	7-34
Q 7:56	Which procedures should require second opinions?	7-35

List of Questions

Q 7:57	What is the difference between self-referral and referral by an SSO panel?	7-35
Q 7:58	How do mandatory SSO programs work?	7-36
Q 7:59	What is the current thinking regarding second surgical opinion programs?	7-36

Medical Savings Accounts

Q 7:60	What is a medical savings account?	7-37
Q 7:61	How do MSAs differ from flexible spending accounts?	7-37
Q 7:62	How would an MSA save money?	7-37
Q 7:63	Why do some people oppose MSAs?	7-38
Q 7:64	Who is eligible for a medical savings account?	7-38
Q 7:65	What is a small employer for MSA purposes?	7-38
Q 7:66	What happens if a small employer grows to have more than 50 employees?	7-38
Q 7:67	Which employees are eligible for MSAs?	7-39
Q 7:68	Can both employees and employers make contributions to an MSA?	7-39
Q 7:69	What other coverage is permitted for MSA participants?	7-39
Q 7:70	How much can be contributed to an MSA?	7-40
Q 7:71	What is a high-deductible plan?	7-40
Q 7:72	What is the deadline for MSA contributions?	7-40
Q 7:73	Are there nondiscrimination requirements that apply to employers with MSAs?	7-41
Q 7:74	What happens if an employer fails to comply with the comparability rule?	7-41
Q 7:75	Who has jurisdiction over high-deductible plans?	7-42
Q 7:76	What rules govern distributions from MSAs?	7-42
Q 7:77	What happens to an MSA when an employee dies?	7-42
Q 7:78	What are medical expenses for MSA purposes?	7-43
Q 7:79	What is the limit on the number of people with MSAs?	7-43
Q 7:80	Have MSAs been popular?	7-43
Q 7:81	Why haven't more people adopted MSAs?	7-43
Q 7:82	What happens at the end of the MSA pilot project?	7-44

Coordination of Benefits

| Q 7:83 | What is coordination of benefits? | 7-44 |
| Q 7:84 | How does COB help manage claim costs? | 7-44 |

Q 7:85	Which plan pays first when there is coverage under more than one plan?	7-45
Q 7:86	Are coordination of benefits rules controlled at the federal level by ERISA?	7-46
Q 7:87	Have all states adopted the rules exactly as written?	7-46
Q 7:88	What is maintenance of benefits?	7-46
Q 7:89	What are the forms of coordination available and what are the differences among them?	7-47
Q 7:90	May an employer elect to use any form of COB?	7-48
Q 7:91	What is the birthday rule?	7-48
Q 7:92	Have companies tried any other COB innovations?	7-48

Additional Cost-Management Strategies

Q 7:93	How does conventional insurance give an employer a predictable cash flow?	7-49
Q 7:94	How does conventional insurance give an employer protection against shock claims?	7-49
Q 7:95	If an employer determines that plan design features alone will not manage costs sufficiently, what other options are available?	7-50
Q 7:96	How does education contribute toward health care cost control?	7-50
Q 7:97	What is a hospital bill audit?	7-50
Q 7:98	How can negotiations with providers contribute toward cost management?	7-51
Q 7:99	What are centers of excellence?	7-51
Q 7:100	What types of procedures are usually referred to centers of excellence?	7-52
Q 7:101	How does using centers of excellence cut costs, and what are the resultant savings?	7-52
Q 7:102	Can employers be held liable for poor quality of care delivered as a result of health care cost control efforts?	7-52
Q 7:103	Are any cost control actions taken by an employer less risky than others?	7-53
Q 7:104	How do direct contracting arrangements between employers and health care providers work?	7-54
Q 7:105	What are coalitions?	7-54
Q 7:106	Who participates in health care coalitions?	7-55
Q 7:107	How can existing health care coalitions be located?	7-55
Q 7:108	What is value-based purchasing?	7-55

List of Questions

Q 7:109	Why might an employer consider requiring the use of an HMO?	7-56
Q 7:110	What are claim audits?	7-56
Q 7:111	What are performance guarantees?	7-56
Q 7:112	What are the most common performance standards and performance guarantees?	7-57

Billing Codes

Q 7:113	What are medical billing codes?	7-57
Q 7:114	Why do providers engage in code gaming?	7-58
Q 7:115	What kinds of code gaming are there?	7-58
Q 7:116	How can code gaming be detected?	7-58

Impact of AIDS on Insurance

Q 7:117	What is the impact of AIDS on health benefits?	7-58
Q 7:118	How much do AIDS claims actually cost?	7-59
Q 7:119	Why will the medical costs be so high?	7-59
Q 7:120	Are there restrictions on the information that may be requested to identify a person at risk for AIDS?	7-60
Q 7:121	Would all forms of care for AIDS patients be covered under an employer's health insurance program?	7-60
Q 7:122	What legal protections have been extended to persons with AIDS?	7-61
Q 7:123	Is testing for AIDS permissible?	7-61
Q 7:124	How does the Americans with Disabilities Act affect persons with AIDS?	7-61
Q 7:125	How should an employer respond to AIDS?	7-62

Rationing Health Care

Q 7:126	Is there objective evidence of the existence of illogical practice patterns?	7-62
Q 7:127	Is anyone considering rationing health care?	7-63
Q 7:128	What further developments have taken place concerning rationing?	7-63

The Employer's Role

Q 7:129	What are some actions individual employers can take to manage health care costs?	7-65

Health Insurance Answer Book

Q 7:130	Can an employer make cuts in its plan without hurting itself competitively?	7-65
Q 7:131	What steps can employers take to help reduce costs associated with new and expensive medical technology?	7-66
Q 7:132	What can employers do about the overprovision of medical services?	7-67
Q 7:133	How can employers combat the inappropriate use of medical services?	7-67
Q 7:134	How did employees' expectation of receiving benefits add to the problem of escalating costs for benefits?	7-68

Chapter 8 Managed Care Plans

Introduction

Q 8:1	How has the traditional reimbursement system in this country contributed to the escalating cost of health care?	8-1
Q 8:2	What is managed care?	8-2
Q 8:3	What caused the shift toward managed care in the health care marketplace?	8-2
Q 8:4	How are insurers and providers merging their services?	8-3
Q 8:5	How many people are enrolled in the largest managed care plans?	8-3

Health Maintenance Organizations

Q 8:6	What is an HMO?	8-4
Q 8:7	When were HMOs developed?	8-4
Q 8:8	Who develops and sponsors HMOs?	8-5
Q 8:9	How many people are enrolled in HMOs?	8-5
Q 8:10	What are the trends in HMO enrollment?	8-6
Q 8:11	Are there any reasons for the geographic differentials of HMO acceptance?	8-7
Q 8:12	Do physicians own HMOs?	8-7
Q 8:13	How are HMOs organized?	8-8
Q 8:14	What is the most popular type of HMO today?	8-8
Q 8:15	What is an IPA?	8-8
Q 8:16	How is a capitated payment structure different from a fee-for-service payment structure?	8-9
Q 8:17	What factors typically affect capitation payments?	8-9

liv

List of Questions

Q 8:18	Do employers pre-pay for health care services in traditional plans?	8-9
Q 8:19	Do employees pre-pay for health care through their payroll deductions for traditional plans?	8-10
Q 8:20	Does enrollment in an HMO entitle an individual to unlimited health care?	8-10
Q 8:21	What is a gatekeeper?	8-10
Q 8:22	Do HMOs require a deductible that patients pay before care is provided?	8-10
Q 8:23	What happens when an individual who is enrolled in an HMO needs to be hospitalized?	8-11
Q 8:24	Is an employee reimbursed for care received outside the HMO area?	8-11
Q 8:25	When can employees enroll in an HMO?	8-11
Q 8:26	How does an employee choose whether to enroll in an HMO or in the traditional health plan?	8-11
Q 8:27	What percentage of employees change plans every year, and why do they do so?	8-12
Q 8:28	Would an employee want to enroll in both a traditional plan and an HMO plan?	8-12
Q 8:29	Are HMOs more cost-effective for employees?	8-13
Q 8:30	How can an employer achieve 75 percent participation in its conventional plan if employees are allowed to enroll in HMOs?	8-13
Q 8:31	Why did enrollment in HMOs increase during the health care cost crisis?	8-13
Q 8:32	Why might employers experience lower costs with HMOs than with other health care plans?	8-14
Q 8:33	Do employers offer only HMOs?	8-14
Q 8:34	Do physicians treat HMO patients differently than fee-for-service patients?	8-14
Q 8:35	What is a self-funded HMO?	8-15
Q 8:36	When would converting to a self-funded HMO arrangement be advantageous?	8-15
Q 8:37	Are self-insured HMOs different from other HMOs?	8-16
Q 8:38	Can an employer self-fund with a federally qualified HMO?	8-16

Adverse Selection

Q 8:39	What is adverse selection?	8-16
Q 8:40	Does adverse selection occur in the HMO setting?	8-17

Q 8:41	Will the cost of an employer's conventional plan be affected by an HMO plan?	8-17
Q 8:42	Why might HMOs attract younger, healthier persons?	8-18
Q 8:43	Is the adverse selection obvious to employers?	8-18
Q 8:44	What can be done about adverse selection?	8-18

Legal Standards

Q 8:45	What is the Health Maintenance Organization Act?	8-18
Q 8:46	What standards must a federally qualified HMO meet?	8-19
Q 8:47	How prevalent are federally qualified HMOs?	8-20
Q 8:48	What is a community rating system?	8-20
Q 8:49	What was the dual choice mandate?	8-20
Q 8:50	Does the HMO Act specify how much an employer is required to pay for HMO coverage for its employees?	8-21
Q 8:51	What are the HMO financial nondiscrimination rules?	8-21
Q 8:52	Are HMOs subject to state regulations?	8-22
Q 8:53	What is ERISA preemption?	8-23
Q 8:54	Are state laws with respect to HMOs preempted by ERISA?	8-23

Evaluating HMOs

Q 8:55	How can a company compare costs of health plans?	8-24
Q 8:56	How does the quality of HMO care compare with that of conventionally insured medical care?	8-24
Q 8:57	How well do managed care plans score on quality of care measurements?	8-24
Q 8:58	Can changing managed care plans affect the quality of care?	8-25
Q 8:59	How do HMO participants rate HMO plans?	8-25
Q 8:60	Why do some HMOs have financial difficulty?	8-25
Q 8:61	How can a prospective HMO client get more information about the HMO?	8-26
Q 8:62	What are indicators of excellence?	8-28
Q 8:63	What is a triple option plan?	8-28
Q 8:64	What are the advantages and disadvantages of a triple option or multiple option plan?	8-29

Preferred Provider Organizations

Q 8:65	What is a PPO?	8-29

List of Questions

Q 8:66	How did the PPO concept develop?	8-30
Q 8:67	How does a PPO differ from an HMO?	8-30
Q 8:68	How is the PPO concept different from the Blues and Medicare contracts with providers?	8-31
Q 8:69	What is a preferred provider arrangement, and how is it different from a PPO?	8-31
Q 8:70	What is an exclusive provider organization?	8-32
Q 8:71	What is the difference between an EPO and a PPO?	8-32
Q 8:72	What services are offered by PPOs?	8-32
Q 8:73	Who sponsors PPOs?	8-33
Q 8:74	How prevalent are PPOs?	8-33
Q 8:75	What are the nationwide PPOs?	8-34
Q 8:76	What is involved in establishing a PPO?	8-34
Q 8:77	How are PPO providers selected?	8-35
Q 8:78	What else is necessary for ensuring cost-effective treatment in a PPO?	8-35
Q 8:79	What are the incentives for doctors and hospitals to be preferred providers?	8-36
Q 8:80	Must a PPO include UR controls?	8-36
Q 8:81	Are utilization controls important when using a PPO?	8-37
Q 8:82	Who does the utilization review?	8-37
Q 8:83	Are there federally qualified PPOs?	8-37
Q 8:84	Do state PPO standards or laws exist?	8-37
Q 8:85	What types of rate regulations apply to PPOs?	8-38
Q 8:86	What antitrust issues affect PPO development and negotiations?	8-38
Q 8:87	What incentives do employers have to include PPOs in their health plans?	8-38
Q 8:88	What kinds of employers can expect the largest discounts from a PPO health plan?	8-38
Q 8:89	Is an employer that elects a plan with a PPO sacrificing quality care for low cost?	8-39
Q 8:90	Can any employer include a PPO in its health care plan?	8-39
Q 8:91	How can an employer or trust evaluate a prospective PPO?	8-39
Q 8:92	How should a PPO be incorporated into an existing program?	8-40
Q 8:93	What types of discounts are available?	8-41
Q 8:94	When incorporating a PPO into a health plan, what employee education is necessary?	8-41

Q 8:95	What other kinds of health care delivery arrangements are available to employers?	8-42
Q 8:96	What are the advantages and disadvantages of a large network?	8-44
Q 8:97	What are hybrid HMO arrangements?	8-44
Q 8:98	What are the advantages and disadvantages of POS plans?	8-45
Q 8:99	What should employers look for when deciding to participate in a POS plan?	8-45
Q 8:100	Can an employer be held liable for negligent care provided by an HMO or PPO?	8-45
Q 8:101	How prevalent are point-of-service plans?	8-46

Managed Care Backlash

Q 8:102	How does the public feel about managed care?	8-47
Q 8:103	How do employers feel about managed care?	8-47
Q 8:104	How do health care providers feel about managed care?	8-48
Q 8:105	What form does the managed care backlash take?	8-48
Q 8:106	What are the essential elements in HMO complaint and appeal systems?	8-50
Q 8:107	Can managed care systems exclude physicians, hospitals, or other providers?	8-51
Q 8:108	How many states have passed any willing provider laws?	8-52
Q 8:109	Why is exclusion from networks such a controversial issue?	8-52
Q 8:110	How are doctors responding to these actions by managed care organizations?	8-53
Q 8:111	What is a gag rule?	8-54
Q 8:112	Are gag rules common?	8-54
Q 8:113	What is anti-managed care legislation?	8-54
Q 8:114	What are some examples of state managed care legislation?	8-55
Q 8:115	What are the categories of consumer protection laws?	8-55
Q 8:116	What is expanded liability legislation?	8-56
Q 8:117	What are external reviews?	8-56
Q 8:118	Do external reviews usually favor the patient?	8-57
Q 8:119	How is the managed care industry responding to the backlash?	8-57

List of Questions

Chapter 9 Flexible Benefits

Introduction

Q 9:1	What is a flexible benefits plan?	9-1
Q 9:2	How prevalent are flexible benefits plans today?	9-2
Q 9:3	How does the Code define a cafeteria plan?	9-2
Q 9:4	What are qualified benefits?	9-2
Q 9:5	Is a flexible benefits plan subject to the Employee Retirement Income Security Act of 1974?	9-3

Tax Advantages

Q 9:6	What are the tax advantages of a cafeteria plan?	9-3
Q 9:7	Can health benefits be provided to an employee on behalf of his or her domestic partner on a pre-tax basis through a cafeteria plan?	9-4
Q 9:8	Are employee contributions to a cafeteria plan subject to state income tax?	9-4
Q 9:9	How does the federal government view employee contributions under flexible benefits plans?	9-5
Q 9:10	When were flexible benefits plans first introduced?	9-5
Q 9:11	What is constructive receipt?	9-6
Q 9:12	Why were flexible benefits plans developed?	9-6

Cost Control

Q 9:13	How do flexible benefits help control costs?	9-7
Q 9:14	How successful have flexible benefits plans been in controlling costs?	9-8
Q 9:15	Are flexible benefits plans expected to increase in popularity?	9-8

Types of Plans

Q 9:16	Are there different types of flexible plans?	9-8
Q 9:17	What is a salary reduction premium conversion plan?	9-9
Q 9:18	What is a flexible spending or reimbursement account?	9-9
Q 9:19	What is a health care reimbursement account?	9-9
Q 9:20	Have there been any recent changes in what are considered eligible expenses for health care reimbursement accounts?	9-10

Q 9:21	Are there any exceptions to the rule regarding elective cosmetic surgery?	9-11
Q 9:22	What procedures are considered elective cosmetic surgery?	9-11
Q 9:23	What are some examples of medical expenses that are or are not eligible for reimbursement?	9-12
Q 9:24	What are the average participation rates and contributions for health care reimbursement accounts?	9-12
Q 9:25	What is a dependent care reimbursement account?	9-13
Q 9:26	When are dependent care services incurred?	9-13
Q 9:27	What are some examples of dependent care expenses that are or are not eligible for reimbursement?	9-13
Q 9:28	What are the average participation rates and contributions for dependent care reimbursement accounts?	9-14
Q 9:29	How are these reimbursement accounts structured?	9-14
Q 9:30	If an employee terminates employment, what happens to a reimbursement account?	9-15
Q 9:31	What happens if the benefits paid plus administrative costs are less than the total contributions plus interest earnings?	9-16
Q 9:32	What has been the experience under the uniform reimbursement approach?	9-16
Q 9:33	What steps can an employer take to reduce the risk that reimbursements will exceed contributions?	9-17
Q 9:34	Are there any new developments regarding plan changes?	9-17
Q 9:35	What kinds of changes may an employee make during the plan year?	9-21
Q 9:36	What changes in status permit participants in flexible spending arrangements to change their elections in mid-year?	9-23
Q 9:37	Are changes in the cost of medical care options grounds for changing elections in mid-year?	9-23
Q 9:38	If an employer introduces a new benefit mid-year, can participants increase salary reductions to elect coverage under the new benefit for the remainder of the year?	9-24
Q 9:39	Can a cafeteria plan permit a participant to make a mid-year election change if the participant's first election was a mistake?	9-24
Q 9:40	Are mid-year election changes permitted when a day care provider changes its rate?	9-24
Q 9:41	Is a mid-year election change permitted when a parent changes day care providers?	9-24

List of Questions

Q 9:42	Is a mid-year election to increase dependent care salary reductions permitted if the participant raises a nanny's salary?	9-25
Q 9:43	Can a participant who has elected cash in lieu of benefits make a mid-year election to opt into a benefit plan?	9-25
Q 9:44	Can medical coverage commence mid-year under a cafeteria plan to comply with a court order?	9-25
Q 9:45	Can coverage be effective before a participant makes a mid-year election?	9-25
Q 9:46	What is a modular plan?	9-25
Q 9:47	What is a core-plus plan?	9-26
Q 9:48	What is a working spouse plan?	9-26
Q 9:49	What is a full-menu or total flexible benefits plan?	9-27
Q 9:50	Are full-menu plans restricted to large employers?	9-27
Q 9:51	What are life cycle flex plans?	9-28
Q 9:52	What is a life cycle allowance?	9-29
Q 9:53	What types of benefits do cafeteria plans include?	9-30

Vacations

Q 9:54	How common is it to include vacation buying and selling in cafeteria plans?	9-30
Q 9:55	What are the tax consequences of letting employees transfer vacation days to other employees?	9-30
Q 9:56	What are some advantages of allowing employees to buy or sell vacation days?	9-31
Q 9:57	What are the disadvantages of allowing employees to buy or sell vacation days?	9-31
Q 9:58	What sorts of restrictions should be placed on vacation buying and selling options?	9-32

Flexible Benefit Options

Q 9:59	What medical insurance options are available under a cafeteria plan?	9-33
Q 9:60	Can a cafeteria plan reimburse employees for individual health insurance policies they purchase?	9-33
Q 9:61	Can a flexible plan include an HMO?	9-33
Q 9:62	Can a flexible plan include a PPO?	9-34
Q 9:63	Is all the insurance provided under a flexible plan provided by one insurer, or do insurers bid for pieces?	9-34
Q 9:64	What are the advantages of using one carrier?	9-34

Q 9:65	Does a cafeteria plan allow employees to select cash instead of benefits?	9-34
Q 9:66	Can a 401(k) plan be integrated into a cafeteria plan?	9-35
Q 9:67	What are the advantages and disadvantages of including a 401(k) plan in a flexible plan?	9-35
Q 9:68	Why would all employees not choose the plan options that offered the best coverage?	9-35
Q 9:69	What is the purpose of waivers in a flexible benefits plan?	9-36
Q 9:70	Why should there be controls on waivers?	9-36
Q 9:71	What sorts of policies have employers adopted regarding waivers?	9-37

Implementation

Q 9:72	How are flexible benefits plans funded?	9-37
Q 9:73	What factors should be considered when deciding between using pre- or post-tax contributions?	9-38
Q 9:74	Must flexible benefits plans be contributory?	9-38
Q 9:75	How does an employer determine its level of contribution to the flexible plan?	9-39
Q 9:76	How are employee contribution levels determined?	9-40
Q 9:77	How are employer and employee contributions made in a full flexible benefits plan?	9-40
Q 9:78	Can small employers self-fund flexible benefits plans?	9-40
Q 9:79	Is purchasing a flexible benefits plan similar to purchasing a traditional plan?	9-41
Q 9:80	How does adverse selection affect flexible benefits plans?	9-41
Q 9:81	What specific issues should an employer address in contemplating the purchase of a flexible benefits plan?	9-42
Q 9:82	How can an employer determine its employees' benefit needs?	9-43
Q 9:83	Are there any resources that would be useful in researching flexible benefit plans?	9-43
Q 9:84	How are flexible benefits plans implemented?	9-44
Q 9:85	How long does it take from the purchase of a flexible benefits plan until it can be implemented?	9-44
Q 9:86	What kinds of employee communications are advisable in advance of enrollment?	9-44
Q 9:87	How do employees enroll in a plan and select their benefits?	9-45

List of Questions

Q 9:88	Are "default" or "negative" elections permitted in a cafeteria plan?	9-46
Q 9:89	What is enrollment confirmation?	9-46
Q 9:90	How do the cost and pricing of a flexible benefits plan compare with those of a traditional employee benefit plan?	9-46
Q 9:91	How does renewal of a flexible benefits plan compare with traditional employee benefit plan renewal?	9-47
Q 9:92	What kinds of reports are necessary to ensure smooth implementation and administration of a flexible plan?	9-47
Q 9:93	How does an employer decide who will administer the flexible benefits plan?	9-48
Q 9:94	What type of billing arrangement is used: self-accounting or home office?	9-48
Q 9:95	What special rules apply to cafeteria plans under FMLA?	9-49
Q 9:96	If a company with a cafeteria plan is acquired by another company, what happens to the cafeteria plan?	9-50

Chapter 10 Medicare

The Basics

Q 10:1	What is Medicare?	10-1
Q 10:2	Who is eligible for Medicare coverage?	10-2
Q 10:3	How many people are covered by Medicare?	10-2
Q 10:4	What services are covered under Part A?	10-2
Q 10:5	What services are covered under Part B?	10-3
Q 10:6	What types of care are not covered by Medicare?	10-3
Q 10:7	Does Medicare cover transplants?	10-4
Q 10:8	What preventive services are covered?	10-4
Q 10:9	What is the Part A hospital deductible?	10-5
Q 10:10	What are the new indexed coinsurance requirements?	10-5
Q 10:11	Is there a maximum dollar out-of-pocket limit on the 20 percent coinsurance payable for Part B (physician) expenses?	10-5
Q 10:12	What are the Part B deductible and coinsurance amounts?	10-5
Q 10:13	What are the new Medicare premiums?	10-6
Q 10:14	What is the current Medicare payroll tax?	10-6

Q 10:15	How much does a typical Medicare beneficiary spend on health?	10-6
Q 10:16	When can someone enroll in Medicare?	10-7
Q 10:17	Are there any plans to extend Medicare to more people?	10-7
Q 10:18	Are there any proposals to add benefits to Medicare?	10-7
Q 10:19	What is balance billing?	10-7
Q 10:20	What are the federal Medicare balance billing limits?	10-8
Q 10:21	Are there any state balance billing requirements that affect employers?	10-8

Medicare Order of Benefit Determination

Q 10:22	How are Medicare benefits integrated with employer-provided benefits for older active employees?	10-8
Q 10:23	Can a group health plan be designed to exclude workers over age 65?	10-10
Q 10:24	Is Medicare primary for retirees with end-stage renal disease?	10-10
Q 10:25	Is there any guidance regarding Medicare secondary rules?	10-10
Q 10:26	How have the secondary payor rules been enforced?	10-11
Q 10:27	What are the rules for the disabled?	10-12
Q 10:28	Is there a penalty for failure to comply?	10-12
Q 10:29	How long must an employer plan provide primary benefits for individuals with end-stage renal disease?	10-12
Q 10:30	Who is considered disabled for Social Security purposes?	10-12
Q 10:31	What special rules apply to Medicare secondary requirements for disabled individuals?	10-13
Q 10:32	What other individuals are covered under the Medicare secondary rules?	10-14
Q 10:33	What is a large group health plan?	10-14

Medicare Cost Containment

Q 10:34	What steps has Medicare taken to limit costs?	10-14
Q 10:35	Why is Medicare cost containment important?	10-15
Q 10:36	What did Congress do about the impending bankruptcy of Medicare?	10-16
Q 10:37	How are payments determined on the basis of diagnosis?	10-16

List of Questions

Q 10:38	If the care delivered costs a hospital less than the DRG-allowed sum, does the hospital retain the difference?	10-16
Q 10:39	Is Medicare the only plan that uses the DRG reimbursement system?	10-17
Q 10:40	What is the RBRVS payment system?	10-17
Q 10:41	What is the difference between usual, customary, prevailing, and reasonable payments and RBRVS payments?	10-17
Q 10:42	What effect has RBRVS had on physicians' fees?	10-18
Q 10:43	How does Medicare reimburse ambulatory surgery centers?	10-18

Medigap

Q 10:44	What are the rules regarding Medigap policies?	10-18
Q 10:45	What do Medigap policies cover?	10-19

Operation Data Match

Q 10:46	What is Operation Data Match?	10-20
Q 10:47	What were the causes of Operation Data Match?	10-20
Q 10:48	What is an employer's responsibility in Operation Data Match?	10-21
Q 10:49	What is the process involved in Operation Data Match?	10-22
Q 10:50	What was the Medicare and Medicaid Data Bank?	10-22

Medicare+Choice

Q 10:51	What is Medicare+ Choice?	10-23
Q 10:52	Has Medicare+ Choice been successful?	10-23
Q 10:53	How are HMOs paid under Medicare?	10-23
Q 10:54	Are Medicare beneficiaries happy with HMO coverage?	10-24
Q 10:55	How many Medicare beneficiaries receive coverage through an HMO?	10-24

Chapter 11 Nondiscrimination Rules

Accident and Health Plans

Q 11:1	Is discrimination in health plans permitted?	11-1

Health Insurance Answer Book

Q 11:2	Which types of self-insured accident and health plans are not subject to discrimination testing?	11-2
Q 11:3	What is a highly compensated individual?	11-2
Q 11:4	What are the eligibility tests applicable to self-insured accident and health plans?	11-3
Q 11:5	What employees are excluded in applying the eligibility tests?	11-4
Q 11:6	What is the benefit test applicable to self-insured accident and health plans?	11-4
Q 11:7	What is the penalty for discrimination in a self-insured accident and health plan with respect to eligibility or benefits?	11-4
Q 11:8	How is the penalty determined?	11-5
Q 11:9	Are all self-insured accident and health plans aggregated for the purpose of applying eligibility and benefit tests?	11-5
Q 11:10	Are retiree plans subject to the same rules?	11-5

Group Term Life Plans

Q 11:11	What does Code Section 79 say?	11-5
Q 11:12	Who is a key employee under Code Section 416(i)?	11-6
Q 11:13	What nondiscrimination tests are applicable to group term life insurance?	11-6
Q 11:14	What are the eligibility tests applicable to group term life insurance plans?	11-6
Q 11:15	What employees may be excluded in performing these tests?	11-7
Q 11:16	What is the benefit test for group term life plans?	11-7
Q 11:17	Are all group term life insurance plans combined for testing purposes?	11-7
Q 11:18	What is the penalty for discrimination under group term life?	11-7
Q 11:19	Are group term life benefits for retired and former employees subject to nondiscrimination rules?	11-8

Cafeteria Plans

Q 11:20	What are the nondiscrimination rules for cafeteria plans?	11-8
Q 11:21	Who is a highly compensated individual for the purpose of cafeteria plan nondiscrimination rules?	11-8
Q 11:22	What is the eligibility test for cafeteria plans?	11-9

List of Questions

Q 11:23	Which employees may be excluded for purposes of this eligibility test?	11-9
Q 11:24	What are the benefit and the contribution tests for cafeteria plans?	11-10
Q 11:25	What is the concentration test?	11-10
Q 11:26	What is the health benefit test?	11-10
Q 11:27	What is the penalty for discrimination in cafeteria plans?	11-10
Q 11:28	Does a plan that is part of a cafeteria plan have to satisfy more than one set of discrimination rules?	11-11

Dependent Care Assistance Plans

Q 11:29	What are the nondiscrimination rules for dependent care assistance plans?	11-11
Q 11:30	What is the eligibility test for dependent care assistance plans?	11-11
Q 11:31	Who is a highly compensated employee with respect to dependent care assistance plans?	11-11
Q 11:32	What employees are excluded for purposes of nondiscrimination testing with respect to dependent care assistance plans?	11-12
Q 11:33	What is the benefit test for purposes of dependent care assistance plans?	11-12
Q 11:34	What is the concentration test for dependent care assistance plans?	11-12
Q 11:35	What is the average benefits test for dependent care assistance plans?	11-13
Q 11:36	What is the penalty for discrimination with respect to dependent care assistance plans?	11-13

Voluntary Employees' Beneficiary Associations

Q 11:37	What are the nondiscrimination requirements for VEBAs?	11-13
Q 11:38	Are there limits on compensation?	11-14
Q 11:39	What are the penalties for discrimination in a VEBA?	11-14

Nondiscriminatory Classification

Q 11:40	What is a nondiscriminatory classification of employees?	11-14
Q 11:41	How does the nondiscriminatory classification test work?	11-16

Health Insurance Answer Book

Chapter 12 Dental, Vision, and Other Benefits

Dental Benefits

Q 12:1	Do health insurance plans cover dental care?	12-1
Q 12:2	How common are dental benefits?	12-2
Q 12:3	How are dental benefits provided?	12-2
Q 12:4	What is direct reimbursement for dental care?	12-2
Q 12:5	What dental services are typically provided?	12-3
Q 12:6	Are all types of dental services covered by insurance?	12-3
Q 12:7	What cost-management features are built into dental plans?	12-3
Q 12:8	Is evidence of insurability required to become covered under a dental plan?	12-4
Q 12:9	Why is orthodontics often treated as a special coverage category?	12-4
Q 12:10	Are there special cost-control considerations for dental plans?	12-4
Q 12:11	What are dental plan incentives, and how do they work?	12-5
Q 12:12	What is precertification?	12-6
Q 12:13	Are some dental services excluded from coverage?	12-6

Vision and Hearing Benefits

Q 12:14	How is vision care covered?	12-6
Q 12:15	How prevalent is vision coverage?	12-7
Q 12:16	What are the different types of vision care delivery systems?	12-7
Q 12:17	How do indemnity vision plans work?	12-7
Q 12:18	How do managed vision plans work?	12-8
Q 12:19	How do discount vision plans work?	12-8
Q 12:20	Is coverage available for hearing evaluations and hearing aids?	12-8

Life Insurance Benefits

Q 12:21	Why would survivor benefits be included in a group health insurance program?	12-8
Q 12:22	What form do these death benefits take?	12-9
Q 12:23	How are these death benefits taxed?	12-9

List of Questions

Q 12:24	Does taxation differ depending on who pays for the coverage?	12-9
Q 12:25	Are employer contributions for group term life insurance subject to state income tax?	12-10

Disability Benefits

Q 12:26	How much of employers' payroll is used to pay disability benefits?	12-10
Q 12:27	How pervasive are disabilities in the United States?	12-11
Q 12:28	How do employees become disabled?	12-11
Q 12:29	What programs are available to compensate employees for disability?	12-11
Q 12:30	What is a short-term disability plan?	12-12
Q 12:31	Must employers provide short-term (nonoccupational) disability benefits?	12-12
Q 12:32	What is a long-term disability plan?	12-12
Q 12:33	How is disability defined?	12-13
Q 12:34	What are other important components of an LTD plan?	12-13
Q 12:35	How much do disabled workers receive from disability plans?	12-14
Q 12:36	How are employees taxed on disability benefits?	12-14
Q 12:37	Is an employee who leaves the service of his or her employer as a result of a total disability entitled to exclude certain payments from his or her qualified retirement plan from taxable income?	12-15

Disability Management

Q 12:38	How can employers achieve effective disability management?	12-16
Q 12:39	How does an employer, union, or insurer put a disability prevention program in place?	12-17
Q 12:40	What is an independent medical examination?	12-17
Q 12:41	How does rehabilitation fit into disability management?	12-17
Q 12:42	How does the rehabilitation benefit interact with pay?	12-18
Q 12:43	What portion of the disabled can actually be rehabilitated?	12-18
Q 12:44	Are some people better candidates than others for disability rehabilitation?	12-18
Q 12:45	What ingredients go into a rehabilitation program?	12-18
Q 12:46	Who staffs a rehabilitation team?	12-19

Q 12:47	What is a return-to-work program?	12-19
Q 12:48	What is an independent living program?	12-19
Q 12:49	What percentage of employers coordinate their overall approach to disability?	12-20

Health Promotion and Wellness

Q 12:50	What is health promotion?	12-20
Q 12:51	Which types of health promotion activities are most common?	12-20
Q 12:52	Why would an employer offer health promotion programs?	12-21
Q 12:53	Are there advantages to offering health promotion programs at the worksite?	12-22
Q 12:54	How does a company select a health promotion program?	12-22
Q 12:55	What is the life-style cost index?	12-23
Q 12:56	Why is interest in health promotion growing?	12-23
Q 12:57	Are employees satisfied with the information employers are providing?	12-23
Q 12:58	What is preventive care coverage?	12-23
Q 12:59	What kinds of benefits does preventive care coverage provide when it is part of a health care plan?	12-24
Q 12:60	How often are routine checkups usually covered under a preventive care plan?	12-24
Q 12:61	What is the current trend with regard to routine physicals?	12-24
Q 12:62	What has caused the move away from the traditional physical?	12-24
Q 12:63	Are there any specific guidelines available for health screening for particular risk factors?	12-25
Q 12:64	Are there guidelines on how frequently women should have mammograms?	12-25
Q 12:65	What tests are recommended in the preventive care program?	12-25
Q 12:66	Will providing preventive care coverage save money? . .	12-26
Q 12:67	What is a wellness program?	12-26
Q 12:68	What are some advantages and disadvantages of wellness programs?	12-26
Q 12:69	What types of wellness programs are there?	12-27
Q 12:70	What are typical components of wellness programs? . . .	12-28
Q 12:71	What are some characteristics of effective prenatal care programs?	12-29

List of Questions

Q 12:72	How can monetary penalties and rewards be used to enhance a wellness program?	12-29
Q 12:73	How prevalent are wellness programs?	12-30
Q 12:74	Do wellness plans work?	12-30
Q 12:75	How can the effectiveness of wellness plans be measured?	12-31
Q 12:76	In addition to behavioral modification and preventive programs, in what other ways can a company enhance health?	12-31
Q 12:77	Why would an employer want to include preventive care or wellness programs in a group insurance plan?	12-32
Q 12:78	Where can an employer obtain more information on wellness programs?	12-32
Q 12:79	Are wellness or health promotion programs usually insured?	12-32
Q 12:80	What is a health risk appraisal?	12-32
Q 12:81	How does the HRA fit in with health promotion?	12-33
Q 12:82	Would an employer use an HRA to determine the components of its group health insurance plan?	12-33
Q 12:83	Are HRA results used to set the price for health insurance coverage?	12-33
Q 12:84	Which works better as an incentive, participation or achievement?	12-34
Q 12:85	Which work better, positive or negative incentives?	12-35
Q 12:86	What are the arguments for positive incentives?	12-35
Q 12:87	When might the government take issue with the use of incentives?	12-35
Q 12:88	Do insurance companies provide financial incentives to companies to adopt preventive care programs?	12-36

Chapter 13 COBRA

The Basics

Q 13:1	What is COBRA?	13-1
Q 13:2	What are the highlights of the new COBRA regulations?	13-2
Q 13:3	When were the regulations effective?	13-3
Q 13:4	Where are the coverage continuation requirements found in federal law?	13-3
Q 13:5	What terminology is added to the employee benefits lexicon?	13-3

Health Insurance Answer Book

Covered Employers

Q 13:6	Which employers are covered under the COBRA requirements?	13-8
Q 13:7	Who is an employer for COBRA purposes?	13-9
Q 13:8	If an employer grows to more than 20 employees, when does COBRA apply?	13-9
Q 13:9	How are separate employers who are members of a controlled group of corporations treated with respect to the 20-employee threshold?	13-11
Q 13:10	Does the small-employer exemption apply to an employer in a multiple employer welfare arrangement?	13-11
Q 13:11	When a company is sold, does the buyer or seller have the responsibility to comply with COBRA?	13-11

Covered Plans

Q 13:12	What type of plan is covered under COBRA?	13-13
Q 13:13	What are the new rules regarding COBRA and flexible spending accounts?	13-14
Q 13:14	How is the term "group health plan" defined?	13-14
Q 13:15	What kinds of services are excluded from the term "group health plan"?	13-15
Q 13:16	Are any group health plans excluded from COBRA?	13-16
Q 13:17	When is a plan maintained by an employer?	13-16
Q 13:18	Are there special rules or exceptions for union plans?	13-18
Q 13:19	What are the requirements if there is more than one covered plan?	13-18
Q 13:20	Do the rules about core and noncore plans still apply?	13-18
Q 13:21	Can an employer make continuation of one plan dependent on another?	13-19
Q 13:22	Does COBRA apply to employees or plans in Puerto Rico?	13-20

General Requirements

Q 13:23	What are the general requirements of COBRA?	13-20
Q 13:24	How was the continuation of benefits under COBRA affected by OBRA '93?	13-21
Q 13:25	If benefits are changed or eliminated for active employees, what must an employer offer to COBRA continuees?	13-21
Q 13:26	If a qualified beneficiary in an HMO moves outside the HMO's service area, what must an employer offer?	13-21

List of Questions

Q 13:27	What disclosures must a plan make to health care providers inquiring about coverage for qualified beneficiaries?	13-22
Q 13:28	What is the relationship between COBRA and USERRA?	13-22
Q 13:29	If an employer withdraws from a multiemployer plan, what happens to that employer's COBRA continuees?	13-22
Q 13:30	When does COBRA apply for someone on FMLA leave?	13-23

Notification Requirements

Q 13:31	What are the COBRA notification requirements?	13-23
Q 13:32	Who is responsible for complying with the notification requirements?	13-24
Q 13:33	When must employees receive notice of their right to continue coverage?	13-24
Q 13:34	Does a group health plan need to notify a spouse of an employee of COBRA rights both initially and after a qualifying event?	13-25
Q 13:35	Who must receive notification?	13-26
Q 13:36	What must be included in the notification?	13-26
Q 13:37	Can the initial notice be placed in the summary plan description?	13-27
Q 13:38	Are there notice requirements that apply to employees, spouses, or dependents?	13-27
Q 13:39	What response must a plan administrator provide, once notified of a qualifying event?	13-28
Q 13:40	Must an employer send bills or payment reminders to continuees?	13-29
Q 13:41	If an employer chooses to administer COBRA, what should the employer look for in a COBRA administration software package?	13-29

Premiums

Q 13:42	How frequently may an employer change COBRA rates to a continuee?	13-30
Q 13:43	How is the COBRA premium (or the applicable premium) determined?	13-30
Q 13:44	How should a self-funded employer determine the COBRA rate?	13-32
Q 13:45	Has the IRS provided any guidance regarding applicable premiums?	13-34

Q 13:46	What should an employer do if the premium paid is less than the amount due?	13-34

Election and Grace Periods

Q 13:47	How do the time periods specified in COBRA work?	13-35
Q 13:48	What is the date of an election or a payment?	13-36
Q 13:49	What should an employer do if the monthly payment is postmarked one day after the grace period has expired?	13-36
Q 13:50	Must an employer provide coverage during these grace periods?	13-37
Q 13:51	Could this arrangement allow continuees to receive coverage without paying for it?	13-37
Q 13:52	How is the amount of the first payment due from a continuee determined?	13-38
Q 13:53	What should an employer do if a qualified beneficiary elects COBRA but does not specify whether the election is for family coverage?	13-38

Qualified Beneficiaries

Q 13:54	What class of individual may be a qualified beneficiary?	13-39
Q 13:55	Are there any persons who, although covered under the employer's plan, may not be qualified beneficiaries?	13-40
Q 13:56	If a qualified beneficiary gains a dependent, can that new dependent be covered as a qualified beneficiary?	13-41
Q 13:57	If a qualified beneficiary is eligible for the extension of COBRA as a result of a disability, can the other family members also extend COBRA?	13-43

Miscellaneous

Q 13:58	When does COBRA begin, at the qualifying event, or upon the loss of coverage?	13-43
Q 13:59	Can an employer minimize its financial exposure by reducing the medical plan benefits before a qualifying event occurs?	13-44
Q 13:60	What is gross misconduct?	13-45
Q 13:61	What are the penalties for failure to comply?	13-45
Q 13:62	May each qualified beneficiary make independent elections?	13-46
Q 13:63	May qualified beneficiaries change their minds about electing coverage?	13-47

List of Questions

Q 13:64	Can an employee pay the COBRA premium for a spouse or dependents?	**13-48**
Q 13:65	Can an employer require evidence of insurability from a qualified beneficiary?	**13-48**
Q 13:66	Can an employer create and offer a plan specially designed for COBRA continuation only?	**13-48**
Q 13:67	If an employer offers retirees coverage, does COBRA still have to be made available to retiring employees?	**13-49**
Q 13:68	What steps should an employer take if retiree coverage is offered as an alternative to COBRA?	**13-49**
Q 13:69	How are deductibles handled under COBRA continuation policies?	**13-50**
Q 13:70	How are pay-based deductibles computed?	**13-51**
Q 13:71	How are plan limits handled in a continuation policy? . . .	**13-51**
Q 13:72	Do flexible benefit plans create any unique or special considerations under COBRA?	**13-52**
Q 13:73	Do flexible spending accounts have any unique features in general?	**13-52**
Q 13:74	To offset the additional time and expense, can an employer receive extra compensation for administering a flexible spending account?	**13-53**
Q 13:75	If COBRA coverage is better and less costly than a conversion policy, should an employer advise all terminating employees to take COBRA?	**13-54**
Q 13:76	Under which circumstances may an employer terminate COBRA earlier than at the conclusion of the 18-, 29-, or 36-month periods?	**13-54**
Q 13:77	What is Medicare entitlement?	**13-55**
Q 13:78	If an employer makes an error that results in COBRA coverage being terminated prematurely, what steps should that employer take to rectify the situation?	**13-56**
Q 13:79	Is Medicaid or CHAMPUS/TRICARE considered another group plan?	**13-56**
Q 13:80	If Medicare entitlement does not cause an immediate loss of coverage, when is the 36-month "starting point" if employer coverage is subsequently lost for the spouse?	**13-56**
Q 13:81	If a COBRA continuee is covered simultaneously by a new employer's plan with a preexisting condition exclusion and the old employer's plan, which plan pays for which conditions?	**13-57**

Health Insurance Answer Book

Q 13:82	May an employee covered under another employer's plan switch COBRA coverage from family to single in order to maintain protection for a spouse with a preexisting condition?	13-57
Q 13:83	How does state legislation integrate with COBRA?	13-58
Q 13:84	Why were the continuation requirements stemming from an employee's disability included in the preceding list, when that is not a COBRA qualifying event?	13-64
Q 13:85	What has been the impact of COBRA on employers? . . .	13-65

Chapter 14 Form 5500

Introduction

Q 14:1	What is a Form 5500?	14-1
Q 14:2	Which welfare plans do not have to file a Form 5500? . . .	14-1
Q 14:3	What does filing forms in the 5500 series accomplish? . .	14-2
Q 14:4	Are these reports considered confidential or privileged in any way?	14-3
Q 14:5	When must 5500s be filed?	14-3

Plan Years

Q 14:6	When must 5500 forms be filed more frequently than annually?	14-3
Q 14:7	What is a plan year?	14-4
Q 14:8	What is a short plan year?	14-4
Q 14:9	Rather than operating a short plan year, may an employer operate a long plan year?	14-6

Administration

Q 14:10	Who is the plan sponsor?	14-6
Q 14:11	Who is the plan administrator?	14-6
Q 14:12	How are plan numbers assigned?	14-7
Q 14:13	How does an employer decide whether or not to combine plans?	14-8
Q 14:14	When is more than one Schedule A required?	14-9
Q 14:15	Could an employer combine all its plans into one filing? .	14-10
Q 14:16	What steps would an employer have to take to combine all its welfare plans into one filing?	14-10

List of Questions

Q 14:17	What attachments are included with a 5500 filing for plan years beginning in 1999 or later?	14-11
Q 14:18	Is a Schedule A required if an employer's assets include a GIC?	14-14
Q 14:19	What are some of the common errors made on Form 5500?	14-15

Completing the Form

Q 14:20	Why should some schedules not be completed?	14-16
Q 14:21	Can a private delivery service be used to file a Form 5500?	14-16
Q 14:22	Does a third party administrator have to hire its own auditor?	14-16
Q 14:23	Is a Schedule A needed for a stop-loss policy?	14-17
Q 14:24	How can a plan get an extension of time to file Form 5500?	14-17

Electronic Filing

Q 14:25	What is EFAST?	14-17
Q 14:26	Why was EFAST developed?	14-18
Q 14:27	What are the computer-scannable forms?	14-18
Q 14:28	Where can a copy of the software for the forms be obtained?	14-18
Q 14:29	Why use Form 5500 software for filing?	14-18
Q 14:30	How are the machine print forms filed?	14-19
Q 14:31	How is the hand print format different from the machine print format?	14-19
Q 14:32	How can one become an EFAST electronic filer or an EFAST transmitter (authorized transmitters of forms via modems)?	14-19
Q 14:33	Will EFAST perform edit checks on the Form 5500?	14-20
Q 14:34	What happens when a filing fails one or more edit checks?	14-20
Q 14:35	Should any payments owed be included with the filing? .	14-20
Q 14:36	What is the Delinquent Filer Voluntary Compliance program?	14-20

Health Insurance Answer Book

Chapter 15 Retiree Health Benefits

Determining Eligibility and Responsibility

Q 15:1	Why are retiree health benefits becoming a key area of focus for employers?	15-1
Q 15:2	How many employers provide health care benefits for their retirees?	15-2
Q 15:3	What are some factors an employer should consider before providing retiree coverage?	15-3
Q 15:4	How do companies determine who is eligible for retiree health benefits?	15-4
Q 15:5	How are these benefits generally structured?	15-4
Q 15:6	Does HIPAA apply to retiree medical plans?	15-5

Determining and Allocating Costs

Q 15:7	Are costs shared among companies and retirees?	15-5
Q 15:8	What is the annual cost of retiree health care versus health care for active employees?	15-6
Q 15:9	What is the cost difference between retirees younger than 65 and those older than 65?	15-6
Q 15:10	What are employers doing to reduce the cost of retiree health care?	15-6

Retiree Medical Liabilities

Q 15:11	What are FASB's rules governing accounting for retiree benefits?	15-7
Q 15:12	What do the rules require?	15-8
Q 15:13	What is a substantive plan?	15-8
Q 15:14	How does the employer determine the costs that must be reported?	15-8
Q 15:15	What additional disclosure requirements are there?	15-9
Q 15:16	Does FASB specify particular actuarial formulas?	15-9
Q 15:17	What were the effective dates of the FASB rules?	15-10
Q 15:18	Have employers found any ways to minimize the impact of FAS 106 without simpiy eliminating benefits for retirees?	15-10
Q 15:19	How have companies responded to FAS 106?	15-11
Q 15:20	Have there been any changes to FAS 106?	15-11
Q 15:21	Do these accounting rules apply to government entities?	15-12
Q 15:22	Does FAS 106 apply to multiemployer welfare plans?	15-12

List of Questions

Q 15:23	How should a company respond to FASBs accounting rules?	15-13
Q 15:24	How can a company limit its retiree health care benefit liability?	15-13
Q 15:25	What is a defined dollar approach?	15-15

Pre-Funding

Q 15:26	Do the FASB rules require companies to pre-fund retiree benefits?	15-15
Q 15:27	What options are available to an employer that wants to pre-fund for retiree health benefits?	15-16
Q 15:28	What are the rules governing VEBAs?	15-16
Q 15:29	How does the combination of a VEBA and stop-loss insurance work?	15-17
Q 15:30	How does COLI work to pre-fund retiree medical liabilities?	15-17
Q 15:31	How does TOLI differ from COLI?	15-18
Q 15:32	What is a 401(h) account?	15-18
Q 15:33	What are the terms for Section 401(h) transfers?	15-19
Q 15:34	What are the Department of Labor notice requirements for 401(h) transfers?	15-20
Q 15:35	Are there any other approaches to financing retiree health care?	15-20
Q 15:36	What types of defined contribution approaches are there?	15-21
Q 15:37	How may profit sharing plan accounts be used to provide health benefits?	15-21
Q 15:38	How can a company stock plan be used to provide retiree health care benefits?	15-22
Q 15:39	What is an HSOP?	15-22
Q 15:40	What is the position of the IRS on HSOPs?	15-23
Q 15:41	How can employee savings accounts be used to finance retiree health benefits?	15-23
Q 15:42	What are the advantages and disadvantages of the defined contribution approach?	15-24

Medicare Solutions to Retiree Challenges

Q 15:43	How can a retiree health plan be integrated with Medicare?	15-24
Q 15:44	What is a Medicare+ Choice HMO?	15-26
Q 15:45	How is the adjusted average per capita cost calculated? What effect does this have on employer premiums?	15-27

Q 15:46	How many employers are using Medicare+ Choice programs to manage retiree benefits?	15-28
Q 15:47	How do Medicare+ Choice HMOs reduce the cost of care?	15-29
Q 15:48	What are the disadvantages of Medicare+ Choice HMOs?	15-29
Q 15:49	What about prescription drug coverage?	15-30
Q 15:50	What criteria should be used in selecting a Medicare+ Choice HMO?	15-30
Q 15:51	How can employers persuade retirees to join Medicare+ Choice HMOs?	15-31
Q 15:52	Are there any special enrollment procedures for Medicare+ Choice plans?	15-31
Q 15:53	What if retirees want to switch back to traditional Medicare and the supplemental plan?	15-32

Regulatory Issues

Q 15:54	How are retiree health benefits regulated?	15-32
Q 15:55	Are there limitations on a company's ability to alter retiree benefits?	15-33

Chapter 16 Pharmacy Benefit Management

The Basics

Q 16:1	What is a prescription drug plan?	16-2
Q 16:2	What is a pharmacy benefit manager?	16-2
Q 16:3	What options do PBM prescription drug plans offer?	16-2
Q 16:4	What questions should a purchaser ask a PBM?	16-3
Q 16:5	What questions should a purchaser ask a PBM's current clients?	16-4
Q 16:6	Should the ownership of the PBM be a concern for employers?	16-4
Q 16:7	What educational programs for enrollees do PBMs offer?	16-5

PBM Growth

Q 16:8	Are many people enrolled in PBMs?	16-5
Q 16:9	Is nationwide service important for a PBM?	16-5
Q 16:10	Why are prescription benefits a growing concern for health insurance planners?	16-6

List of Questions

Q 16:11	Why are prescription drug costs increasing?	16-6
Q 16:12	How much are prescription drug costs increasing?	16-7
Q 16:13	How much do PBMs charge for their services?	16-7

Cost Control

Q 16:14	What factors influence the cost of the prescription benefit?	16-7
Q 16:15	What can employers and health plans do to control pharmacy costs?	16-8
Q 16:16	What is the role of utilization review in a managed prescription program?	16-8
Q 16:17	What is a formulary?	16-9
Q 16:18	What is the difference between an open and closed formulary?	16-9
Q 16:19	Where are open and closed formularies most commonly found?	16-10
Q 16:20	Are there any advantages to a closed formulary?	16-10
Q 16:21	Are there any disadvantages to a closed formulary?	16-10
Q 16:22	What role do generic drugs play in a prescription drug plan?	16-11
Q 16:23	What influence do PBMs have over formularies?	16-11
Q 16:24	Which drugs are typically excluded from formularies?	16-11
Q 16:25	How do PBMs get physicians to support a formulary?	16-12
Q 16:26	Are formularies usurping the role of physicians in prescribing medicine?	16-12
Q 16:27	Are there ways to manage costs even without a closed formulary?	16-13
Q 16:28	Why are formularies so controversial?	16-13
Q 16:29	How do new drugs affect formularies?	16-14
Q 16:30	Is Viagra covered?	16-14
Q 16:31	What are lifestyle drugs?	16-15
Q 16:32	What are therapeutic interchange protocols?	16-15
Q 16:33	What is the FDA's position on generic drugs?	16-16
Q 16:34	What is a MAC?	16-16
Q 16:35	What are disease state management programs?	16-16
Q 16:36	Can disease management offer real value to plan sponsors?	16-17
Q 16:37	Can proper drug usage reduce other costs?	16-18
Q 16:38	How are employers and health plans using disease management to cut prescription drug costs?	16-18

| Q 16:39 | How can a purchaser evaluate disease state management programs? | 16-18 |

Prescription Drug Management

Q 16:40	What role do prescriptions by mail play in the prescription drug plan?	16-19
Q 16:41	Why are mail service pharmacy programs underused?	16-20
Q 16:42	Have any studies been done on the effectiveness of mail service pharmacies?	16-20
Q 16:43	How does a health care purchaser know if an MSP is right for its insured population?	16-21
Q 16:44	Are prescriptions by mail safe?	16-21
Q 16:45	Is it common for a plan to have incentives to use a mail-order program?	16-22
Q 16:46	How is pharmacoeconomic research being used to cut prescription drug costs?	16-22
Q 16:47	What is a prescription drug card plan?	16-22
Q 16:48	What are the disclosure limitations in HMO pharmaceutical plans?	16-23
Q 16:49	How can employers protect themselves from HMO nondisclosure?	16-23
Q 16:50	What is the most important element to look for when considering a PBM?	16-23
Q 16:51	What kinds of reporting should a purchaser seek from a PBM?	16-24
Q 16:52	What is integrated claims information processing?	16-24
Q 16:53	How are PBMs compensated?	16-24
Q 16:54	What role does capitation play in pharmacy benefit management?	16-25

Ensuring Quality

Q 16:55	How do PBMs identify duplicate prescriptions?	16-26
Q 16:56	What error detection and reporting programs are available?	16-26
Q 16:57	How is electronic data interchange being used to review prescriptions?	16-27
Q 16:58	What is point of dispensing?	16-27
Q 16:59	Can PBM enrollees go anywhere to have their prescriptions filled?	16-27
Q 16:60	Can any size of company participate in a PBM?	16-28

List of Questions

Q 16:61	Besides lower costs, how can the quality of a PBM be measured?	16-28
Q 16:62	Are PBM satisfaction rates a valid way to measure the quality of services offered by a PBM?	16-28

Prescription Drug Plans

Q 16:63	What is the typical cost of prescription drug coverage?	16-29
Q 16:64	Are all prescription drugs covered under health care plans?	16-29
Q 16:65	Will some plans cover contraceptive prescription drugs?	16-29
Q 16:66	Why would an employer have a separate prescription drug plan?	16-30
Q 16:67	Why would an employer avoid a free-standing drug plan in favor of covering medication under a major medical or comprehensive health plan?	16-30
Q 16:68	Who offers drug plans?	16-30
Q 16:69	What are the largest PBMs?	16-30
Q 16:70	Is a flat copayment more common than coinsurance for prescription drugs?	16-31
Q 16:71	What are average prescription drug copays?	16-31
Q 16:72	What is a three-tier copay?	16-32

Chapter 17 Self-Funding

Introduction

Q 17:1	What is self-funding?	17-2
Q 17:2	How long has self-funding been in existence?	17-2
Q 17:3	What types of employers self-fund health insurance?	17-2
Q 17:4	What is a fully insured health plan?	17-3
Q 17:5	What law makes self-funding possible?	17-3
Q 17:6	What laws govern self-funded plans?	17-3
Q 17:7	Why do employers self-fund health insurance?	17-4

Reasons for Self-Funding

Q 17:8	Why do employers consider self-funding?	17-4
Q 17:9	What other reasons do employers have for self-funding?	17-4
Q 17:10	What should an employer consider in deciding to self-fund?	17-5

Q 17:11	What is a self-funded health plan?	17-5
Q 17:12	Does a distinction exist between self-funding and self-insurance?	17-6
Q 17:13	How does self-funding work?	17-6
Q 17:14	What are the advantages of self-funding?	17-7
Q 17:15	Have any challenges to these benefits been launched?	17-9
Q 17:16	What other advantages are available with self-funding?	17-9
Q 17:17	What are the benefits of self-funding to employees?	17-9
Q 17:18	What are the disadvantages of self-funding?	17-9

Decision to Self-Fund

Q 17:19	Is self-funding for all companies?	17-10
Q 17:20	Is self-funding primarily for large companies?	17-10
Q 17:21	What criteria should a small employer meet if considering self-funding?	17-11
Q 17:22	Can self-funding work for any small employer?	17-11
Q 17:23	Why would self-funding not work for a partnership?	17-11
Q 17:24	What should an employer that self-funds expect in the first year?	17-11
Q 17:25	What is stop-loss coverage?	17-12
Q 17:26	Does an employer that self-funds need to redesign its existing health plan?	17-13
Q 17:27	How does self-funding affect payroll deductions for health care?	17-13
Q 17:28	Does self-funding affect group term life insurance coverages?	17-13

Administration

Q 17:29	What organization takes the place of the insurer as administrator of the plan?	17-13
Q 17:30	Are there advantages in using a TPA versus an ASO arrangement?	17-14
Q 17:31	What services do TPAs and ASOs offer?	17-14
Q 17:32	How are self-funded plans classified?	17-15
Q 17:33	What are the existing approaches to financing employer medical expense plans?	17-16
Q 17:34	What are the distinguishing characteristics of a conventional, fully insured plan?	17-16

List of Questions

The Marketplace

Q 17:35	How have traditional insurers modified their conventional products to meet employer demand for self-funding?	17-17
Q 17:36	What are experience-rated plans?	17-17
Q 17:37	How do retrospective-rating agreements work?	17-18
Q 17:38	What is a minimum-premium product?	17-18
Q 17:39	What approaches are used for self-funding?	17-19
Q 17:40	Do any employers administer their own claims?	17-20
Q 17:41	Is a separate trust required when employers self-fund the medical expense benefits?	17-20
Q 17:42	What is the primary characteristic of a self-funded plan?	17-20
Q 17:43	Are covered employees affected by an employer's decision to self-fund?	17-20
Q 17:44	How does self-funding help an employer avoid cost shifting?	17-21
Q 17:45	How does self-funding help an employer get a reduction in risk financing costs?	17-21
Q 17:46	How does self-funding help an employer get more choices in claim administration?	17-22
Q 17:47	What effect does greater control over claim administration have?	17-22
Q 17:48	How does self-funding affect cash flow?	17-23
Q 17:49	What is a stop-loss intermediary?	17-24
Q 17:50	What is a producer-owned reinsurance company?	17-24

Effect of Self-Funding on Regulations

Q 17:51	What is the effect of self-funding on premium taxes?	17-24
Q 17:52	How does self-funding help employers with mandated benefit rules?	17-25
Q 17:53	Does self-funding play a role in health plan revisions?	17-26

Stop-Loss Insurance

Q 17:54	How does stop-loss coverage affect medical expense plans?	17-28
Q 17:55	How does specific stop-loss coverage work?	17-28
Q 17:56	What types of specific stop-loss plans are available?	17-29
Q 17:57	What does the term "incurred claim date" mean exactly?	17-30
Q 17:58	How does aggregate stop-loss work?	17-31

Health Insurance Answer Book

Q 17:59	Does stop-loss coverage affect the employer's responsibility to its workers?	17-31
Q 17:60	How do stop-loss contracts differ with respect to the reimbursement of claims?	17-32
Q 17:61	How do stop-loss contracts differ with respect to benefit period?	17-32
Q 17:62	How are claims incurred prior to the benefit period under the contract paid?	17-33
Q 17:63	Why are stop-loss provisions problematical?	17-33
Q 17:64	Can stop-loss policies be terminated mid-year?	17-33
Q 17:65	How has the regulatory environment affected employers' efforts to self-fund?	17-34
Q 17:66	What does the National Association of Insurance Commissioners say about self-funding?	17-34
Q 17:67	Do states regulate stop-loss insurers?	17-35
Q 17:68	Is there any alternative to stop-loss that provides similar protection?	17-35
Q 17:69	What is the difference between pooling and stop-loss insurance?	17-37

Voluntary Employees' Beneficiary Associations

Q 17:70	What is a voluntary employees' beneficiary association?	17-37
Q 17:71	What tax benefits do VEBAs confer?	17-38
Q 17:72	What other benefits can be provided through a VEBA?	17-38
Q 17:73	What benefits cannot be provided by a VEBA?	17-38
Q 17:74	What are the requirements for establishing a tax-exempt VEBA?	17-39
Q 17:75	How does a VEBA obtain tax-exempt status?	17-39
Q 17:76	May a VEBA be established to benefit only one person?	17-39
Q 17:77	May a VEBA benefit persons who are not employees?	17-40
Q 17:78	Who is an employee for VEBA purposes?	17-40
Q 17:79	What restrictions on VEBA membership are permissible?	17-40
Q 17:80	Who controls a VEBA?	17-41
Q 17:81	Is there a limit on deductible contributions to a VEBA?	17-41
Q 17:82	What are the restrictions on funding for post-retirement medical and life insurance benefits?	17-41
Q 17:83	What are the special rules regarding VEBA contributions for key employees?	17-42

List of Questions

| Q 17:84 | What is unrelated business income? | 17-42 |
| Q 17:85 | Are there special nondiscrimination rules for VEBAs? | 17-42 |

Chapter 18 Third-Party Administration

The Role of the TPA

Q 18:1	What is third-party administration?	18-1
Q 18:2	What is a third-party administrator?	18-2
Q 18:3	What is the role of TPAs?	18-2
Q 18:4	What is the history of using TPAs for employee benefit administration?	18-3
Q 18:5	What are multiple employer welfare arrangements?	18-4
Q 18:6	What are the regulatory differences between multiemployer plans and multiple-employer plans?	18-4
Q 18:7	When selecting a TPA, what characteristics should an employer seek?	18-4

Performance Standards

| Q 18:8 | What examples are available regarding performance standards or guarantees? | 18-6 |
| Q 18:9 | In lieu of performance standards or guarantees, do employers use bonuses and incentives for good service? | 18-8 |

Legal Issues

Q 18:10	What are the penalties for noncompliance with ERISA?	18-8
Q 18:11	Should employers expect legal opinions from TPAs?	18-8
Q 18:12	What laws govern TPAs?	18-9
Q 18:13	What is ERISA fiduciary responsibility?	18-9
Q 18:14	Why are ERISA's fiduciary requirements tougher than state insurance and normal business consumer protections?	18-10
Q 18:15	How does an ERISA fiduciary judge whether a deal is prudent?	18-10
Q 18:16	Who is subject to fiduciary duty?	18-11
Q 18:17	What are the risks for fiduciaries?	18-11

The TPA Market

| Q 18:18 | What do TPAs charge? | 18-12 |

Q 18:19	How many individuals are served by TPAs?	18-12
Q 18:20	Why has the market for TPAs grown?	18-13
Q 18:21	Have there been any discernible patterns of growth in the TPA business recently?	18-14
Q 18:22	What are the major markets for TPAs?	18-14
Q 18:23	What changes are underway in the TPA business?	18-15
Q 18:24	What is the future of the TPA business?	18-15
Q 18:25	What types of services do TPAs provide?	18-16
Q 18:26	What is a managed care TPA?	18-17
Q 18:27	What is the value of using a managed care TPA?	18-17
Q 18:28	How prevalent is the use of TPAs?	18-18

Chapter 19 Quality Assurance

Quality Measures

Q 19:1	What does quality mean in a health care context?	19-1
Q 19:2	What are quality measures?	19-2
Q 19:3	What is the NCQA?	19-3
Q 19:4	Why are quality measurements of health plans important to employers?	19-3
Q 19:5	How prevalent are quality measures?	19-4
Q 19:6	How do employers and health plans collect quality assurance data?	19-5
Q 19:7	Are any results available from Quality Compass?	19-6
Q 19:8	What can employers do to ensure that their health plans offer high quality services?	19-7
Q 19:9	Are any new systems available for employers to use in measuring and ensuring the quality of care offered through health plans?	19-9
Q 19:10	What is the American Medical Accreditation Program?	19-10
Q 19:11	What is URAC?	19-10
Q 19:12	Is quality important to employees when they choose a health plan?	19-11
Q 19:13	Are employers really concerned about quality?	19-12
Q 19:14	What is being done to help employees understand the quality issues?	19-12
Q 19:15	Are cost pressures affecting quality?	19-13

List of Questions

Report Card Movement

Q 19:16	Does the report card movement among managed care plans affect health care quality?	19-13
Q 19:17	What criticisms have been leveled against managed care report card efforts?	19-14
Q 19:18	Are customer satisfaction measures included on report cards?	19-14
Q 19:19	How common are patient satisfaction studies?	19-15
Q 19:20	Are there any national report card projects?	19-15
Q 19:21	How satisfied are people enrolled in managed care?	19-15
Q 19:22	What are some examples of report cards in use?	19-15

The Joint Commission and HEDIS

Q 19:23	What is the Joint Commission?	19-16
Q 19:24	What is HEDIS?	19-16
Q 19:25	Does the NCQA use HEDIS data as part of its accreditation process?	19-17
Q 19:26	Does HEDIS include financial measures?	19-17

Outcomes Measurement

Q 19:27	What is outcomes measurement?	19-17
Q 19:28	What type of system is need to measure outcomes?	19-18
Q 19:29	How can employers reduce the cost of obtaining outcomes data?	19-19
Q 19:30	What is a quality improvement organization?	19-19

Chapter 20 Home Health Care and Long-Term Care

Home Health Care

Q 20:1	What is home health care?	20-1
Q 20:2	What is the history of home health care?	20-2
Q 20:3	Is the market for home health care growing?	20-2
Q 20:4	Who provides home health care?	20-3
Q 20:5	Who uses home health care?	20-4
Q 20:6	What are the advantages of home health care?	20-4
Q 20:7	What kinds of services can be provided in the home?	20-5

Q 20:8	How are the frequency and the duration of services determined?	20-6
Q 20:9	How can employers foster the use of home health care?	20-6
Q 20:10	Who monitors home health care agencies?	20-7
Q 20:11	Does coverage for extended care facilities and home health care help an employer manage health care costs?	20-7
Q 20:12	How much can home health care save?	20-8
Q 20:13	Are there reasons an employer should not include home health care coverage as part of its medical plan?	20-8
Q 20:14	Is home health care coverage commonly found in medical plans?	20-8
Q 20:15	Which home care services are most employers providing?	20-9
Q 20:16	What is the procedure for installing home health care coverage?	20-9
Q 20:17	What kinds of information does accreditation provide?	20-9
Q 20:18	What information cannot be learned through accreditation?	20-10
Q 20:19	What is the best procedure to follow in dealing directly with the home care agency?	20-10

Home Health Care Fraud

Q 20:20	Why is home health care frequently cited as ripe for health care fraud?	20-12
Q 20:21	Who pays for home health care fraud?	20-13
Q 20:22	What is being done to stop home health care fraud?	20-13

Long-Term Care

Q 20:23	What is long-term care?	20-14
Q 20:24	What are the different levels of long-term care?	20-14
Q 20:25	What are the special issues connected with long-term care?	20-15
Q 20:26	What are the advantages of long-term care?	20-15
Q 20:27	How expensive is long-term care?	20-15
Q 20:28	What long-term care benefits does Medicare provide?	20-16
Q 20:29	What long-term care services are covered by Medicaid?	20-16
Q 20:30	How prevalent are employer-sponsored long-term care plans?	20-17
Q 20:31	Do employers contribute to the cost of long-term care policies?	20-17
Q 20:32	What does a typical long-term care benefit cover?	20-17

List of Questions

Q 20:33	Are benefits adjusted for inflation?	20-18
Q 20:34	What is the tax status of custodial care?	20-18
Q 20:35	Who provides long-term care insurance?	20-19
Q 20:36	How much does long-term care insurance cost?	20-19
Q 20:37	What considerations should be taken into account in evaluating long-term care insurance policies?	20-19
Q 20:38	Where can an employer obtain additional information on long-term care?	20-21

Subacute Care

Q 20:39	What is subacute care?	20-21
Q 20:40	What are the standards for assessing the quality of subacute care?	20-22
Q 20:41	Are there different levels of subacute care?	20-22
Q 20:42	What are some of the objections to using skilled nursing facilities to provide subacute care?	20-23
Q 20:43	How is subacute care paid for?	20-23

Hospice Care

Q 20:44	What is a hospice?	20-24
Q 20:45	Who pays for hospice care?	20-24
Q 20:46	Is hospice care effective at controlling costs?	20-25

Chapter 21 Communication

Developing Communication Strategies

Q 21:1	Why do employers focus on employee health care benefit communications?	21-1
Q 21:2	What makes a communication effort successful?	21-2
Q 21:3	How is a communication strategy developed?	21-2
Q 21:4	What should an employer consider when selecting communications media?	21-3
Q 21:5	What is an average budget for a communication campaign?	21-3
Q 21:6	When should employers communicate changes in benefit plans?	21-4

| Q 21:7 | Which is more effective for benefit communication, written or human resources? | 21-4 |
| Q 21:8 | What situations are appropriate for using event-based communications? | 21-5 |

Benefit Statements

| Q 21:9 | Why do employers issue benefit statements? | 21-5 |
| Q 21:10 | Do employees find benefit statements useful? | 21-6 |

Periodic Benefit Reports

Q 21:11	What is a periodic benefit report?	21-6
Q 21:12	How can periodic benefit reports communicate the value of benefits to employees?	21-6
Q 21:13	What types of information are typically included in a periodic benefit report?	21-7
Q 21:14	What risks are associated with using periodic benefit reports as an employee communication tool?	21-7

Interactive Systems

Q 21:15	What are the benefits of using interactive systems to communicate with employees?	21-7
Q 21:16	Why do some employees prefer interactive systems to access benefit information?	21-8
Q 21:17	What are the administrative advantages of using interactive systems?	21-8
Q 21:18	Are interactive systems expensive?	21-8

Online Services

Q 21:19	Are online systems being used to communicate benefit information?	21-9
Q 21:20	Can online technology be used for employee enrollment in benefit programs?	21-9
Q 21:21	What are the advantages for employers of using online services for enrollment activities?	21-10
Q 21:22	Are there any disadvantages to using online services for enrollment activities?	21-10

List of Questions

Communicating Employee Benefits

Q 21:23	What are some basic principles for successful employee benefit communication?	21-11
Q 21:24	What legal trends are developing in the area of employee communications?	21-11
Q 21:25	Under what circumstances may a plan administrator rely on electronic media to satisfy disclosure obligations under ERISA?	21-12
Q 21:26	What is important to include for enrollment communication campaigns?	21-13
Q 21:27	What information should be communicated to new employees?	21-14
Q 21:28	What information should be communicated to retiring employees?	21-14
Q 21:29	How should "bad news" be communicated?	21-15

Chapter 22 Mental Health

Mental Health Benefits

Q 22:1	Are mental illnesses usually covered by health plans?	22-1
Q 22:2	What are the concerns of employers in designing mental health benefit plans?	22-2
Q 22:3	Why have mental health benefits traditionally been structured differently from other health benefits?	22-2
Q 22:4	Do employers place limitations on mental health benefit coverage?	22-3
Q 22:5	Have changes in the clinical practices of mental health care changed the design of mental health benefits?	22-4
Q 22:6	What mental health benefits do health maintenance organizations typically offer?	22-4
Q 22:7	Is there any federal regulation of HMOs that provide mental health care?	22-5
Q 22:8	What benefit coverage should a behavioral health plan include?	22-5
Q 22:9	Are employers using lifetime maximum amounts for mental health benefits in their plan designs?	22-6
Q 22:10	What are some trends in mental health benefit plans?	22-6
Q 22:11	Is there disagreement about what constitutes mental health coverage?	22-7

Q 22:12	Why has attention focused on mental health care issues?	22-7
Q 22:13	What contributed to the increased utilization of mental health services?	22-8
Q 22:14	Can data from information systems help to coordinate medical care and behavioral care?	22-8
Q 22:15	What is the primary care physician's role in behavioral health care?	22-8

Controlling Costs

Q 22:16	How much do behavioral health benefit cost employers?	22-9
Q 22:17	How can mental health services be better managed?	22-9
Q 22:18	What strategies are employers using to control mental health care costs?	22-10
Q 22:19	What methods for reducing these costs are employers considering?	22-10
Q 22:20	Is there a downside to reducing benefits?	22-11
Q 22:21	How does case management of mental health services work?	22-11
Q 22:22	Is cost sharing an effective strategy?	22-12

Substance Abuse

Q 22:23	Is treatment for alcoholism and other types of substance abuse covered under typical health insurance plans?	22-12
Q 22:24	What benefits are typically offered for substance abuse treatment?	22-13
Q 22:25	How costly is substance abuse to companies and their employees?	22-13
Q 22:26	What are some strategies for employers to use when designing substance abuse benefit plans?	22-14
Q 22:27	Why should substance abuse or addiction treatments be restricted?	22-14
Q 22:28	Why have inpatient benefits for substance abuse treatment historically been more restrictive than for mental health treatment?	22-15
Q 22:29	Is substance abuse considered a treatable illness?	22-15

Managed Mental Health

Q 22:30	What is a pre-paid mental health plan?	22-16
Q 22:31	How is managed care affecting mental health and substance abuse benefit programs?	22-16

List of Questions

Q 22:32	In addition to cost savings, what else is driving the trend toward managed mental health benefits?	22-17
Q 22:33	What are the benefits of managed behavioral health care?	22-17
Q 22:34	What should employers consider when developing a managed care program for behavioral health benefits?	22-17
Q 22:35	What is a mental health carve-out?	22-18
Q 22:36	Why are carve-out plans appropriate for behavioral health care?	22-19
Q 22:37	Do carve-out plans limit access to behavioral health services?	22-20
Q 22:38	Do carve-outs cover services that traditional mental health and substance abuse plans do not?	22-20
Q 22:39	How do behavioral health carve-outs control costs?	22-21
Q 22:40	What are the advantages of carve-out plans for behavioral health care?	22-21
Q 22:41	What are the disadvantages of carve-out plans for behavioral health?	22-22

Employee Assistance Programs

Q 22:42	What is an employee assistance program?	22-22
Q 22:43	How prevalent are EAPs?	22-23
Q 22:44	Is EAP coverage cost-effective?	22-23
Q 22:45	How can EAPs be financed?	22-24
Q 22:46	Is an EAP an ERISA welfare plan?	22-24
Q 22:47	Do companies hire in-house counselors or use external resources?	22-24
Q 22:48	What components are needed for an effective EAP?	22-25
Q 22:49	What are the important elements of a well-designed EAP?	22-25
Q 22:50	Other than in-house or commercially, how else may EAP services be provided?	22-27
Q 22:51	What role do employee assistance plans play in cutting employers' behavioral health costs?	22-27
Q 22:52	What are the advantages of using an integrated EAP carve-out?	22-27
Q 22:53	Do employees appreciate EAPs?	22-28
Q 22:54	Is there evidence that EAPs are cost effective?	22-28

Outcome Measurements

Q 22:55	What performance indicators do employers use for behavioral health care programs?	22-29
Q 22:56	What other types of outcome measures are used in behavioral health care?	22-29

Americans with Disabilities Act

Q 22:57	Who does the Americans with Disabilities Act protect?	22-30
Q 22:58	Are any employees exempted from protection under the ADA?	22-30
Q 22:59	Does the ADA apply to employees with alcohol abuse problems?	22-31
Q 22:60	How is current drug abuse defined?	22-32
Q 22:61	What questions can an employer ask a job applicant regarding illegal drug use?	22-32
Q 22:62	Are there any regulations about employee confidentiality?	22-32
Q 22:63	What accommodations in the workplace might employees recovering from drug or alcohol abuse need?	22-33

Mental Health Parity Act

Q 22:64	What does the Mental Health Parity Act of 1996 require?	22-34
Q 22:65	Are there any regulations published regarding the Mental Health Parity Act?	22-34
Q 22:66	Does the Mental Health Parity Act require mental health coverage?	22-35
Q 22:67	Must benefits for mental health treatment be identical to the benefits for medical conditions?	22-35
Q 22:68	Are any employers exempt from the Mental Health Parity Act?	22-36
Q 22:69	How does a plan claim the 1 percent increased cost exemption under MHPA?	22-36
Q 22:70	Have many plans taken advantage of the 1 percent exemption?	22-36
Q 22:71	Can plans limit the number of inpatient days or outpatient visits for mental health treatment?	22-37
Q 22:72	Does the Mental Health Parity Act apply to substance abuse treatment?	22-37
Q 22:73	How much will the Mental Health Parity Act cost employers?	22-37

List of Questions

Q 22:74 How much would it cost to achieve treatment parity between mental health or substance abuse coverage and medical or surgical coverage? **22-37**

Chapter 1

An Overview of Group Insurance

Group insurance is a technique for providing a group of people with protection against financial loss resulting from death, disability, or the expenses associated with illness or injury. This chapter describes the different types of group insurance available and the various ways in which employers purchase it.

Group Health Insurance	1-1
The Uninsured	1-4
Group Insurance	1-7

Group Health Insurance

Q 1:1 What are the various ways that individuals receive health insurance protection?

Besides participating in group insurance plans, individuals may also be covered under federal and state government-sponsored programs such as Medicare and Medicaid, service-type plans such as Blue Cross/Blue Shield (the Blues), or so-called alternative health care systems such as health maintenance organizations (HMOs) and preferred provider organizations. Insurance may also be purchased privately on an individual basis, or through mass purchasing groups such as credit unions and professional or trade associations.

Q 1:2 What is the major difference between group and individual insurance?

The major difference between group and individual insurance involves evidence of insurability. To purchase individual insurance, a person must generally answer a health questionnaire and undergo a medical examination to provide evidence of insurability to the insurance company. An insurer may decline coverage on the basis of the applicant's personal habits, health, medical history, age, income, or any other factors that bear on risk acceptance. Or the insurer may issue a policy with limitations on coverage.

Under the provisions of the Health Insurance Portability and Accountability Act of 1996 (HIPAA) group health plans are issued without medical examination or other evidence of individual insurability. An insurer is willing to do so because it knows it can cover enough individuals to balance those in poor health against those in good health. The risk that an insurer will fail to achieve this balance is diminished as the size of the group increases, or as the insurer underwrites additional group policies and increases the total number of individuals covered. This is known as the "law of large numbers."

Q 1:3 What are the advantages of group insurance over individual insurance?

For an employer that intends to provide insurance protection to its employees, the group approach ensures that all employees, regardless of health, can be covered. Those with known health problems, who might otherwise be unable to obtain individual insurance, can be covered automatically upon employment without evidence of insurability. Although some limits may be imposed on new hires for certain conditions that predate their enrollment in the plan, most employees can receive coverage as soon as they are eligible.

Group insurance offers a lower cost per unit of protection than individual insurance does because of the economies of scale resulting from selling, installing, and servicing one plan covering many individuals. In addition, group plans are typically more flexible and tend to provide more liberal benefits than individual coverage.

Q 1:4 If all of an employer's employees are healthy, would the employer be just as well off with a series of individual policies as with one group policy?

No. One group policy is preferable for the following reasons:

1. Individual policies are subject to evidence of insurability. A prospective employee could have a current or preexisting medical problem that would make that person uninsurable. Evidence of insurability issues are avoided with group policies.

2. Individual policies are subject to individual re-rating. This could result in greatly divergent rates from one individual to another, with attendant recordkeeping and administrative difficulties.

3. Because an insurance company revises its policies periodically, at times under mandate of a state insurance commission, employees whose individual policies were issued at different times might receive different benefits.

4. The purchaser of a group policy has much greater bargaining power than that of an individual policy. As well, the purchaser of a group policy will be in a better position to modify the design, a task that would be impossible for the purchaser of even many individual policies. Naturally, the larger the covered group, the more latitude the purchaser will have.

An employee also gives up a great deal by not having a group policy. For example, individual policies generally provide more limited coverage than a similarly priced group policy. Even the best individual policies, which are quite expensive, cover far less than a well-designed group policy. That is because when an insurance company sells an individual policy, it measures its financial exposure against the projected cash flow that one policy will yield. It faces a risk that any given individual may present a large bill and then die or cancel coverage, ending further premium payments to the insurance company. In a group policy, although the cash flow coming from the premium will be reduced by the death of one member, it will not cease. The continuing cash flow allows the insurance company to recover losses stemming from any one large claim. Because a group plan is less likely to be canceled, the insurance company is presented with substantially lower risk by a group of individuals covered under a group policy than by those same individuals covered by an identical design, but by a series of individual policies. Lower risk translates into lower rates.

Q 1:5 How prevalent is group insurance in the United States?

By far, the most prevalent source of health insurance in the United States is employer-provided group coverage. According to a study by the Employee Benefit Research Institute (EBRI), 64.9 percent of the nonelderly (i.e., under age 65) population of the United States was covered by an employment-based health plan in 1998. Over 150 million people were covered by an employment-based plan.

The Uninsured

Q 1:6 What portion of the population is uninsured?

EBRI estimates there were 43.9 million uninsured people in 1998. This represents 18.4 percent of the nonelderly population. According to EBRI, the percentage of the population without insurance has been increasing. In 1987, 14.8 percent of the population was uninsured. EBRI attributes the increase in the uninsured between 1987 and 1993 to erosion of employment-based health benefits. EBRI explains the recent increase in the uninsured resulted from a decline in public sources of health insurance. The portion of Americans covered by employment-based health insurance increased from 63.5 percent in 1993 to 64.9 percent in 1998.

Although this and other similar estimates are generally recognized to be accurate, they have also been criticized as misleadingly low because they do not take into account people who are uninsured for only part of the year. When short-term lack of insurance and other factors are taken into consideration, the portion of uninsured Americans may be much higher.

EBRI estimates that 11.1 million children (15.4 percent of all children) in the United States were without health insurance in 1998.

Q 1:7 What are the characteristics of the uninsured?

The major determining characteristic of the uninsured seems to be source of employment: The self-employed and those employed by small companies are less likely to have health insurance than those employed by larger companies. For example, analysis by EBRI of the March 1999 current population study (CPS) by the Census Bureau showed that 12.7 percent of nonelderly workers employed by companies with 1,000 or more employees were uninsured. The same analysis showed that 33.9 percent of those employed by companies with fewer than 10 employees were uninsured and that 24.7 percent of the self-employed were uninsured.

Another important factor is type of employment. EBRI's analysis of the March 1999 CPS data indicates 33.8 percent of agriculture and construction workers were uninsured, compared to 7.8 percent of public sector employees.

Q 1:8 What is the impact of the uninsured on health insurance costs?

The uninsured still need and utilize medical services, but must either pay for them from their own pockets or not pay for them at all. If the services provided—by, for example, an emergency room or a nonprofit hospital—are not paid for by the individuals themselves, the costs will ultimately be shifted to other revenue sources and will be reflected in higher treatment costs for other payors.

A 1995 report by Lewin-VHI, Inc. concluded that about 16 percent of total employer health plan costs in California were attributed to some form of cost shift.

Q 1:9 Why are people employed by small companies less likely to have health insurance?

Health insurance generally costs more per person for small companies than for large companies. One reason is that there are certain fixed costs of setting up a group insurance policy. With a small group, those fixed costs are spread over fewer people. There also tends to be adverse selection in small groups. For example, a healthy business owner with two healthy employees may choose not to buy insurance.

But, if one or more of those three people gets sick, the owner may decide to buy health insurance.

According to a study by the Henry J. Kaiser Family Foundation, the average premium increase from 1996 to 1998 was 5.2 percent; however for groups of three to nine people, the average increase was 8 percent.

Q 1:10 Why aren't more people covered?

In a word: cost. A 1998 study by the UCLA School of Public Health found that payroll deductions required for family coverage with an HMO increased 90 percent from 1989 to 1996. This increase far outstripped the growth in wages, which was 23 percent during the same period. This increase came despite the fact that employers increased the percentage of premiums they paid from 60 percent in 1989 to 65 percent in 1996. A study by the GAO found that the average share of premiums paid by employees for single coverage more than doubled from 10 percent in 1988 to 22 percent in 1996.

The result of these increased costs (which averaged $1,778 in annual payroll deductions in 1996 for family coverage with an HMO) is that many employees cannot afford to pay for health insurance even when it is available.

A study by the Agency for Health Care Policy and Research found that six million employees turned down health insurance in 1996, an increase of more than 140 percent since 1987. More employees were offered health insurance coverage in 1996 than in 1987.

Q 1:11 What is underinsurance?

Underinsurance means a person has health insurance, but it has low maximum benefits or significant gaps. Consumers Union defines underinsurance as being at risk of spending more than 10 percent of income on health care bills in the event of catastrophic illness despite having health insurance. Consumers Union estimates 31 million Americans are underinsured.

Group Insurance

Q 1:12 Why do most employers provide group insurance?

Group insurance benefits have become a traditional and expected part of an employer's total compensation strategy. A comprehensive benefits package allows employers to attract and retain quality employees. In markets in which certain skills are in short supply, employers often vie for labor by offering more attractive employee benefit plans than the competition.

In addition, group insurance is a concrete way for employers to show concern for their employees' welfare. Group insurance is the only form of health coverage for many employees; without it, they would be susceptible to financial catastrophe from the expenses associated with illness or injury. By giving employees the peace of mind that comes from knowing that they and their families are protected against financial hardship, group insurance enhances employee morale; therefore, a formal benefits program is effective from both an employer and an employee standpoint.

Insurance protection purchased by an employer is also more valuable to employees than an equal amount of cash compensation. Because the premiums and, to a large extent, the benefits from group insurance, are not considered employee income, they are not taxable as such. (See the discussion of employer and employee taxation in Chapter 3.)

Perhaps most importantly, a group policy is cost-effective. For the same cash outlay, an employer buying a group insurance policy can purchase more coverage than could the same number of persons attempting to buy individual policies. Also, an insurance company will sell levels of coverage on a group basis that it would not even consider selling on an individual basis at any price.

Q 1:13 What types of group protection do most employers provide?

Although there are many variations of each, the four major types of insurance coverage provided by employers to their employees are life, accidental death and dismemberment (AD&D), disability, and health, including medical, dental and vision care. Some employers also provide additional coverage, including group legal, travel accident, and long-term care.

Q 1:14 What is included in the term "group health insurance"?

Group health insurance is sometimes used as a comprehensive term that includes medical, dental, vision, and prescription coverage, as well as disability and AD&D. In this text, group health insurance usually refers to medical and dental insurance. Comments in this text apply equally to insured and self-funded plans, unless otherwise noted.

Q 1:15 What are the characteristics of group health insurance?

Group health insurance provides full or partial reimbursement for various medical and dental expenses. Coverage almost always includes reimbursement for hospital and surgical expenses and for diagnostic x-rays, tests, and physicians' visits. The full extent of coverage depends on the master contract issued to the group. (For details on specific types of coverage, see Chapter 4.)

Q 1:16 What caused the rapid growth of group health insurance?

A number of factors contributed to the rapid growth of group health insurance. Among the more important factors are the following:

1. Industrialization and urbanization, which caused changes in the values of an increasingly affluent society, and lessened the family's responsibility for the health care of infirm family members; and
2. Wage controls during World War II, which caused employers to use rich employee benefits plans to attract employees during a period of short labor supply.

In addition, powerful labor unions demanded more and more benefits; favorable federal tax treatment made benefits a cost-effective way to increase employees' compensation. The rising demand for and cost of medical care made health insurance a necessity. Social legislation, together with refinements in the group insurance concept, led to more and different groups being covered and new benefits being added.

Q 1:17 How important is group health insurance to employees?

Medical benefits are very important to employees. Although health insurance was once thought of as a "fringe benefit," it is now a generally expected component of compensation, and one that is highly valued by employees.

A 1997 survey by Fidelity Benefits Center found that the three most important benefits to employees are medical insurance, a 401(k) plan, and dental insurance, in that order.

Employer-provided health insurance may be especially important to certain employees—for example, an employee whose spouse is self-employed or for some other reason does not receive medical benefits.

Also 67 percent of Americans surveyed by EBRI and the Gallup Organization, Inc. in 1994 said employee benefits were "very important" in their decision to accept or reject a job offer. Some 20 percent said it was "somewhat important," 4 percent said "not too important" and 7 percent said "not at all important." Twelve percent of respondents said they or a family member had passed up a job opportunity solely because of health benefits. In answering a related question, 17 percent of respondents said they had accepted, quit, or changed jobs because of benefits offered or not offered by an employer.

Q 1:18 Is group insurance available only to single employers?

No. Although the plan sponsor or policyholder is most often a single employer (corporation, partnership, or sole proprietorship), it can also be an entity such as a union or a professional association. In addition, a single group program may be issued to cover employees of a number of different employers. These vehicles are often used to insure individuals who are employed by companies too small to offer group coverage on their own.

Q 1:19 What is a multiple employer trust?

Under a multiple employer trust (MET), many small employers in the same or related industry participate in a group plan under a trust arrangement. The trust, rather than each participating employer, is the policyholder, and the master contract is issued to a trustee. Through mass purchasing, small employers can afford a level of insurance benefits that is normally available only to larger employers. METs are most common among employers with 10 or fewer employees, but some trusts also offer coverage to larger groups.

Q 1:20 How can a labor union provide group insurance?

A labor union can provide group insurance for its members under a policy issued to a trust jointly managed by union representatives and representatives of the employers employing the union members. The trust is the policyholder, just as the trust is the policyholder under a MET. A trust may purchase a group policy for a large number of members who are employed by the same company, or for union members working for different companies. Group insurance purchased through a trust is particularly advantageous in industries such as construction, where union members may work for many employers during a year.

Organized labor typically obtains insurance benefits for its members through collective bargaining with employers. As a result, union members are usually covered under group insurance plans sponsored by one or more than one employer. (See Chapter 18 for more information on multiemployer plans.)

Q 1:21 What is an association plan?

A professional or trade association can provide coverage for its members or member companies under a policy issued to the association. The association is the policyholder. Examples of association groups include various professional and retail associations and chamber of commerce groups.

When compared with employer group plans, the percentage of eligible association members who actually enroll in these plans is usually small because many association members have access to other insurance that may be less expensive or provide better coverage.

In all likelihood, an association plan would be considered a multiple employer welfare arrangement (MEWA).

Q 1:22 What is a MEWA?

A multiple employer welfare arrangement is an employee welfare benefit plan that provides medical benefits to the employees of two or more employers (including self-employed individuals.) A collectively bargained plan is not a MEWA.

Q 1:23 Are there any new requirements for MEWAs?

Yes. Starting in 2000, the administrator of a MEWA must file an annual report (Form M-1). New collectively bargained plans must file the report for three years.

Q 1:24 What are state-sponsored coalitions?

About 20 states have passed laws that promote health insurance purchasing coalitions (also called health insurance purchasing cooperatives). Some are alliances sponsored by the state. Other states have passed laws that encourage employers to form their own coalitions to purchase health insurance. Most of these laws are aimed at small employers, with the intent of making health insurance more available and affordable. Such coalitions also can provide group insurance expertise to employers.

Q 1:25 Have state-sponsored coalitions been successful?

Some certainly have been. Pacific Health Advantage, also known as PacAdvantage and formerly known as the Health Insurance Plan of California (HIPC), is often cited as a model for other states to follow. Since it was established by state legislation in 1993, it has enrolled 9,500 small businesses and covers more than 140,000 people. About 20 percent of those covered were previously uninsured. It offers almost 20 plans to businesses with 2 to 50 employees. For example, in a company with five employees, all five could choose a different health plan, but the employer would receive only one unified bill.

Q 1:26 Do any local governments sponsor joint purchasing coalitions?

Yes. In 1999, New York City launched a pilot program to help businesses with two to 50 employees offer health insurance. The effort is focused in some of the city's poorest neighborhoods. The Small Business Health Insurance Program includes a limited network of only three public hospitals.

Q 1:27 What is joint purchasing?

Several coalitions around the country are engaging in joint purchasing, in which member employers pool their purchasing power to negotiate better deals with hospitals, health insurers, HMOs, or other vendors. Some of these arrangements are very controlled, meaning employers agree not to negotiate separately. Others (called joint negotiations) are structured more loosely and allow employers to accept what is negotiated through the coalition or to contract separately.

Q 1:28 Is price the only focus of joint purchasing?

No. Price is, of course, a major concern, but an increasing number of coalitions are also attempting to measure and reward quality of care.

Q 1:29 What is an employer health care coalition?

An employer health care coalition is an association of health care plan sponsors (employers) that pool resources, share ideas, and gather information on insurers and health care providers. Coalitions may serve as go-betweens to obtain information or to assemble data to provide standard price lists and fee schedules and comparative statistics. They may also negotiate with providers on behalf of coalition members.

Chapter 2

The Health Insurance Marketplace

Because of limited resources and a lack of expertise, most employers use an insurance professional—an agent, broker, or consultant—to assist in the design, purchase, and administration of a group health insurance plan. This chapter introduces the various types of professional organizations and their services.

Types of Insurance Professionals	2-1
Choosing and Compensating Intermediaries	2-8
Blue Cross/Blue Shield Plans	2-14

Types of Insurance Professionals

Q 2:1 Can an employer work directly with an insurance company?

It is possible for an employer to deal directly with an insurer through a group sales representative to purchase group insurance; however, premium rates and underwriting practices vary considerably from one insurer to another. In addition, the coverage provided is rarely identical. Comparison shopping is often beyond the capability of all but the most sophisticated purchaser, typically the very large company that has internal employee benefit expertise. For this reason, many group insurance purchasers do not deal directly with insurance company underwriters or group insurance representatives, preferring instead to deal with an intermediary.

Most employers need a qualified professional to act as intermediary because they lack the resources and expertise to handle their group insurance needs. An intermediary can help them define their needs and objectives, design a plan to meet those criteria, select the proper purchasing and funding vehicles, obtain competitive quotes from insurers, and service the plan.

Q 2:2 What does the uncertainty in the insurance industry mean to employers?

While most of the attention has focused on life insurance policyholders, annuitants, and pension funds, the issue is relevant to health insurance policyholders as well. A failed health insurer can leave an employer's workers with unreimbursed medical expenses, as well as lack of coverage for future medical bills. The employer also faces the prospect of having to acquire insurance elsewhere, which is a time-consuming undertaking and can be especially difficult for the smaller employer with unfavorable claims experience.

Perhaps even worse, employees may seek redress or payment of medical bills directly by the employer. Depending on the degree of analysis the employer performed in choosing the insurer and the good judgment—or lack thereof—the employer exercised, the employer might not defeat employees' claims and the employees may obtain a settlement compelling the employer to pay the outstanding bills.

Q 2:3 How can employers protect themselves against insurer failure?

In addition to a prospective insurer's extent and types of coverage and the cost of its premiums, employers should pay attention to an insurer's financial health and claim-paying ability. A number of rating companies provide information on the creditworthiness of insurers. Ratings backgrounds provide information on the mix of assets in the insurer's portfolio. A company making its own financial assessments can obtain information directly from the insurer. Not all insurers are rated by all raters; a number of small companies may not be rated at all; and individual rater's systems may produce differing results.

A. M. Best is the most prominent of the ratings organizations, but some industry analysts have criticized its ratings as being too charitable. Best, in turn, criticized as disruptive Standard & Poor's (S&P) new rating process, called qualified solvency ratings. These ratings are based solely on information supplied to the National Association of Insurance Commissioners (NAIC) regarding total assets, statutory surplus, premiums, return on assets and revenue, portfolio profiles, and lapse rates. S&P continues to rate hundreds of other insurers using its traditional methodology, which examines more than just state filings.

Q 2:4 How can an employer obtain information from the principal rating companies?

The rating companies rank insurers as being superior or exceptional; excellent or very high; or good, high, or strong in their abilities to make claims payments. The ratings go lower, of course, but companies with lower ratings should be of little interest. The following is a list of rating companies, along with the highest ratings they assign to insurance companies:

1. A.M. Best Company, customer service and insurance company ID at 908-439-2200 extension 4742 (A++; A+; A; A-)

2. Moody's Investors Service, 212-553-0377 (Aaa; Aa1; Aa2; Aa3; A1; A2; A3)

3. Standard & Poor's, 212-438-7280 (AAA; AA+; AA; AA-; A+; A; A-)

4. Duff & Phelps Credit Rating Company, 312-368-3100 (AAA; AA+; AA; AA-; A+; A; A-)

5. Weiss Company, 800-289-9222 (A+; A; A-)

Information is free from all except Best and Weiss, which charge a nominal fee.

Q 2:5 What are state insurance guaranty funds?

Most, but not all, states have guaranty funds that are intended to support the financial promises of insurers that become insolvent. While most states have funds to cover property and casualty insurance policies such as homeowners and automobile insurance, funds for guaranteeing life and health insurance are not as common.

Unlike bank and savings and loan depositors, who are insured for up to $100,000 by the federal government, insurance policyholders are protected by a patchwork of regulations and guarantee funds that vary from state to state. The state funds are operated by guaranty associations, which are composed of members of the insurance industry. They are also thinly funded, drawing most of their assets from assessments against members made after an insurer becomes insolvent.

The funds are limited in several ways. First, there are usually separate arrangements for different types of insurance: life insurance and annuities, health insurance, and property and casualty insurance. Second, there are limits on the amounts that can be paid to policyholders. The limits depend upon the type of contract. There are different limits for different lines of insurance, and for individual versus group policies. Some states provide full coverage of obligations of insolvent insurers, while others have lower, albeit generous, caps.

Finally, there is the limitation imposed by the availability of funds to pay, generally restricted by caps expressed in terms of a percentage (usually 2 to 4 percent) of premiums paid to the insurers. This means that, even with higher percentage caps, small states with lower levels of overall insurance premium income have financing formulas that generate less money with which to pay policyholders. Larger states, naturally, tend to have higher volumes of premium payments, which results in better funding. (On the other hand, when there is an insolvency, larger states tend to have more policyholders to cover as well.)

Even if the specified level of protection is adequate, there is still a question of whether the reserves of state guaranty funds would be adequate should a major insurer fail.

One idea that has been discussed would take some of the authority to regulate insurance companies away from the states and give it to the federal government. This would mean changing the 1945 McCarran-Ferguson Act, which gave a limited exemption from federal antitrust laws to insurance companies and specified that insurers were to be regulated by the states.

Some states are seeking to tighten up investment standards for insurers; some already place limits on insurer holdings of medium- and low-grade investments. The NAIC has approved a model regulation that will limit junk bond holdings to 20 percent of an insurer's total assets.

Q 2:6 What is a group health insurance underwriter?

A group health insurance underwriter is a risk evaluator who analyzes each individual group to determine the financial risk it represents for the insurance company. To determine the acceptability of the risk a particular group represents, the underwriter examines the composition of the group as it relates to age, sex, prior claim experience, and the desired plan design.

Q 2:7 What is risk?

The risk an insurance company assumes when it agrees to cover a particular group is the possibility that claims will exceed the expected level. It is the chance of financial loss inherent in the group. Insurance companies use it to determine whether they will underwrite an insurance policy on a particular group.

A spread of risk is necessary not only because of the expected variations in a population's health but also because some policyholders—particularly very small groups—purchase group insurance to cover certain individuals with known health problems (see the discussions of adverse selection in Chapters 8 and 9). This is a more costly way to obtain coverage for those high-risk individuals, but often the only way possible, given the evidence-of-insurability requirement for individual policies.

Q 2:8 What is a group sales representative?

A group sales representative (also known as an account executive) is an employee of an insurance company who sells group insurance for that particular company and performs a variety of services directly for the policyholder in conjunction with the policyholder's intermediaries. The sales representative supplements the group insurance knowledge of the intermediary, especially with respect to the insurance company's products. Group sales representatives are often located in branch offices. They are compensated by the insurance carriers for whom they place business and service.

Q 2:9 What is a client service representative?

Some insurance companies have specialized personnel in their field offices who are trained to deal with intermediaries and clients in the ongoing administration of the health insurance plan. This enables the insurer to deal with clients' questions locally and to visit clients, if necessary. Such specialized personnel are often known as client service representatives or account managers.

Q 2:10 What is an intermediary?

An intermediary is a knowledgeable benefits professional who helps employers and other groups to develop, design, purchase, and service benefit plans. An intermediary may be a broker, an agent, an employee benefits consultant, or a third-party administrator (TPA).

Q 2:11 How do group sales representatives and intermediaries interact in the sale of a group health insurance plan?

Group sales representatives of different insurance carriers approach intermediaries to explain their insurance products. In turn, intermediaries request quotes for plans to meet the needs of their clients. They may work together to determine the most appropriate plans and to discuss the premiums required for those plans. The intermediary represents his or her clients' interests; the group sales representative represents his or her company's products and services.

Q 2:12 What services do intermediaries provide prior to the purchase of a group health insurance plan?

The services that intermediaries provide will depend, to a great extent, on (1) the employer's own employee benefit expertise and (2) the type of intermediary the employer chooses. For employers with little or no knowledge of health insurance, the intermediary can provide all of the following five services:

1. Designing the plan, including analyzing alternative programs from a cost standpoint;
2. Determining how the plan should be funded;
3. Providing necessary plan documents, including communications to employees;
4. Selecting an insurance carrier, HMO, or other health care provider; and
5. Servicing the plan, including claims analysis and preparation of annual reports.

Those employers that possess greater knowledge and resources will likely play a more active role in the decision-making process. The type of intermediary the employer selects will also determine the extent of services provided.

Q 2:13 What is an insurance broker?

An insurance broker is an employer's representative who provides counsel on insurance-related issues and assistance in dealing with insurance companies. Brokers may sell a variety of products and services, including business and group insurance, and market the products of many insurance companies.

Brokerage firms vary from the single broker operating independently to brokerage houses that employ thousands of professionals and operate offices nationally and internationally.

Q 2:14 What is the difference between an agent and a broker?

The basic difference between an agent and a broker is that, while the broker represents the employer, the agent is generally under contract with an insurance company to sell all of its products. That is, agents represent sellers (insurance companies) and brokers represent buyers (employers). Agents typically work with smaller single-employer groups.

If an agent's own company cannot meet the client's needs, the agent will deal with another insurance company, often through a broker; in this case, the distinction between an agent and a broker becomes blurred. In some states, brokers are licensed as agents, further confusing the terminology.

Q 2:15 What is an employee benefit consultant?

Employee benefit consultants specialize in the analysis and design of an employer's noncash compensation program. They should have in-depth knowledge of a particular client's company, having often been hired to analyze that company's benefit objectives in detail. Their expertise may be especially useful to larger employers that elect to self-fund their employee benefit plans partially or totally. Some consultants act as administrators in providing continuing service to their clients. Some employers believe a consultant offers a more objective viewpoint, because consultants are compensated directly by the employer, usually on a fee-for-service basis.

Q 2:16 How does an employer determine whether to use an agent, broker, or consultant?

Agents, brokers, and consultants provide many of the same services, and distinguishing among them is sometimes difficult. Generally, agents work with smaller companies that are less likely to require, or less able to afford, extensive analysis of their benefit strategies. Some brokers, especially those associated with large national brokerage houses, often provide some of the same services as consultants.

Choosing and Compensating Intermediaries

Q 2:17 How does an employer select a particular intermediary?

Most small employers select an intermediary just as they would hire any outside professional help. They consult friends, business associates, and authorities they respect. Based on this information, the employer can develop a list of potential candidates. It is generally advisable to speak with several candidates, because it is important that an employer trust the intermediary and feel comfortable doing business with that person. Many intermediaries, especially the larger ones, maintain client referral lists—lists of clients that have been satisfied with their services and have agreed to discuss their experience with prospective customers. Interviewing referred organizations similar in size and structure to one's own is a good way to determine whether the intermediary will meet one's needs.

Another thing to look for in selecting an agent, broker, or consultant is a professional designation. Some of the most pertinent designations are:

ALHC	Associate, Life and Health Claims
ASA	Associate of the Society of Actuaries
CBP	Certified Benefit Professional
CDMS	Certified Disability Management Specialist
CEBS	Certified Employee Benefit Specialist
CES	Certified Enrollment Specialist
CFC	Certified in Flexible Compensation
CFCI	Certified in Flexible Compensation Instruction
CLU	Chartered Life Underwriter
CPCM	Certified Professional Consultant to Management
CPDM	Certified Professional, Disability Management
FAHM	Fellow, Academy for Healthcare Management
FLHC	Fellow, Life and Health Claims
FLMI	Fellow of the Life Management Institute
FSA	Fellow of the Society of Actuaries
PAHM	Professional, Academy for Healthcare Management
REBC	Registered Employee Benefits Consultant
RHU	Registered Health Underwriter

Q 2:18 Is the size of the intermediary important?

Yes, but in different ways to different employers. Some employers only want to work with large firms, while others believe they receive more personalized service from smaller firms.

Q 2:19 Which brokerage firms are the largest?

According to the July 26, 1999 issue of *Business Insurance*, the 10 largest brokers in the United States, based on 1998 U.S. revenues, were:

1. Marsh & McLennan Cos. Inc.
2. Aon Corp.
3. Willis Corroon Group P.L.C.
4. Arthur J. Gallagher & Co.
5. USI Insurance Services Corp.
6. Acordia Inc.
7. Hilb, Rogal & Hamilton Co.
8. Norwest Insurance
9. Brown & Brown Inc.
10. Jardine Lloyd Thompson Group P.L.C.

These rankings include both property/casualty and life/health revenues.

Q 2:20 Which consulting firms are the largest?

Based on data from the December 13, 1999 issue of *Business Insurance*, the 10 largest employee benefit consultants in the United States are:

1. Hewitt Associates L.L.C.
2. Towers Perrin
3. William M. Mercer Cos. L.L.C.
4. PricewaterhouseCoopers, Global HR Solutions
5. Watson Wyatt Worldwide
6. Aon Consulting Worldwide

7. Buck Consultants Inc.
8. Deloitte & Touche/Human Capital Advisory Services
9. Ernst & Young L.L.P. – Human Resource Services
10. Arthur Andersen L.L.P. – Human Capital Services

These rankings include retirement plan consulting as well as welfare plan consulting and benefit communication consulting.

Q 2:21 Can an employer use a personal or business advisor as its group insurance intermediary?

Yes. The employer can use the broker or agent who handles the employer's business or personal insurance as an advisor, if the employer believes that this intermediary has the required degree of employee benefit expertise.

Q 2:22 How are intermediaries compensated?

Agents and brokers typically receive a percentage of premiums—commissions from the insurance companies with which they place business. Consultants generally charge either a fixed fee per project, a retainer, or an hourly rate to the employers for which they are providing services. In recent years, there has been a trend, especially among large brokerage houses, to negotiate a fee for services rendered. In addition, some individuals and firms will operate in either mode—commissions or fee for service.

Q 2:23 What are commission schedules?

Commission schedules are a type of monetary incentive that insurance companies use to encourage agents and brokers to do business with their companies. The two most common types of commission schedules are the high-low schedule and the level schedule. Both reward agents and brokers by providing a percentage of the premium for the insurance that is sold.

The high-low commission schedule encourages group brokers and agents to place new business with a particular carrier, by providing commissions that are a higher percentage of premiums in the first year of coverage and a lower percentage in renewal years.

The level commission schedule provides the same percentage of premium each year. This type of schedule encourages a group producer to keep business with a carrier, as there is no decrease in commissions after the first year. In theory, this commission schedule encourages the broker or agent to pay more attention to servicing existing clients rather than emphasizing sales of new business as the high-low schedule does.

The following table compares the two types of schedules:

Commission Schedules

Annual Premium	High-Low Schedule Year 1	High-Low Schedule Years 2–10	Level Schedule First 10 Years
First $1,000	25.0%	6.5%	7.5%
Next $8,000	20.0	3.0	5.0
Next $5,000	15.0	2.0	3.5
Next $10,000	10.0	2.0	3.2
Next $10,000	7.5	2.0	2.8
Next $25,000	5.0	1.5	2.0
Next $100,000	2.5	1.0	1.5

Q 2:24 What is vesting of commissions?

Vesting of commissions occurs when the insurer grants ownership of renewal commissions (commissions paid when coverage is renewed for another plan year) to the agent whether or not the agent continues to represent the policyholder. Although insurers differ in their vesting procedures, there is a general trend away from this concept, as it removes the agent's incentive to continue to provide services to the policyholder.

Q 2:25 Are there laws that regulate the business practices of intermediaries?

Laws determining agent and broker licensing requirements vary from state to state and may require consultants to be licensed as well. Insurance companies monitor the licensure status of intermediaries that place business with them. Most states allow agents and brokers to become licensed relatively easily if they are licensed in their state of residence.

Q 2:26 If an employer wants to self-fund the plan, which type of insurance professional would it need?

An employer interested in partially or fully self-insuring its group insurance plan often works with an employee benefit consultant or a third-party administrator; however, some brokers will have the expertise necessary to design and properly structure a self-funded plan. An insurance company may administer the plan even though it is not underwriting the entire risk.

Q 2:27 Would an employer whose plan is fully insured use a TPA?

An employer with a fully insured plan may employ a TPA to handle the administrative functions of the plan, including claim payment, with the approval of the insurance company; however, insurance companies provide most fully insured employers with administrative services.

Q 2:28 How does an employer decide whether to use a TPA or an insurance company to administer its plan?

Insurance carriers and TPAs provide valuable administrative services, which an employer would find difficult to provide internally. The choice between a TPA and an insurer should be based on service, ease of administration, and cost.

The employer should determine what services are most important. Some employers believe that local claim service is advantageous. The two traditional components of claim service are claim turnaround time and resolution of problems associated with claims. These services are not necessarily handled any more expediently with local service. Some employers may prefer a single source for all their insurance dealings.

In addition to accurate claims payment, an important service TPAs and insurance companies provide is giving the policyholder accurate information on benefits utilization. Examples of data reports should be requested from prospective administrators and compared. This is especially true for employers that have enough employees to be charged based on their own claim experience.

Q 2:29 If an employer has a TPA handle the administrative functions, would the employer's cost be decreased?

The expense portion of an employer's insurance premium would be decreased, because the insurance company's overhead costs are eliminated; however, the employer would be paying the TPA for the services. Depending on what those services are, their cost, and the efficiency of the TPA, the employer's overall cost could be higher or lower.

Q 2:30 How are TPAs compensated?

Most TPAs charge for their consulting services on either a fixed fee or an hourly basis. All sorts of arrangements are made for administrative services, but most TPAs charge for administrative services on a monthly or per-employee basis or as a fixed percentage of claims. Additional fees may be specified for installation, preparation of communication and enrollment materials, and other special services. The employer generally compensates the TPA directly; however, TPAs may also receive commissions from insurance products included in the program.

Blue Cross/Blue Shield Plans

Q 2:31 What is Blue Cross/Blue Shield?

Blue Cross/Blue Shield (the Blues) were similar to today's managed care plans, before the era of managed care, in that the Blues contract directly with physicians and hospitals to establish the level of charges the Blues will pay for services rendered to their subscribers. When an insured incurs a covered health care expense, the health care provider—a participating hospital or physician—bills the Blues directly. Payment is made to the provider based on the prearranged payment schedule, which is often accepted as payment in full.

This payment system between health care providers and the Blues network is an extension of the historically close relationship the Blues have maintained with the U.S. medical community over the years. This association dates back to the 1930s, when Blue Cross was established under the auspices of the American Hospital Association; Blue Shield was established by the American Medical Association in the 1940s. Blue Cross promised hospitals prompt payment and first-dollar reimbursement, thus guaranteeing that a patient's bill would be paid in full. In return, the hospitals gave Blue Cross a discount on hospital services for Blue Cross subscribers. The ability to obtain large discounts from hospitals has given the Blues a significant competitive edge over private insurers, and in some areas of the country, the Blues have gained a large share of the third-party reimbursement market.

At press time, there were 49 independent, locally operated Blue Cross/Blue Shield companies.

Q 2:32 Are Blues plans similar to those offered by private insurance companies?

Yes. Blues plans have traditionally been similar to private insurance company base-plus plans. The Blues usually offer both a base plan and a supplemental major medical plan, but some employers purchase only the base plan from the Blues. This is because the Blue Cross base plan in some areas is less expensive than private insurance; the Blue Cross hospital discounts can be significant. An employer may, however, elect a private insurer's major medical plan as a supplement because of its better price, coverage, or service.

The Blues have made the transition to managed care. Most people receiving coverage through the Blues are now covered by some type of managed care program—health maintenance organization (HMO), preferred provider organization (PPO), or point-of-service plan.

Q 2:33 Do most private insurers offer major medical supplements?

Generally, major medical plans offered by private insurance companies to supplement a Blue Cross base plan fall into two categories: supplemental major medical and wraparound major medical. The difference between the two is that the wraparound plan covers some basic expenses, such as surgery, and also covers major medical expenses, whereas the supplemental plan provides only major medical coverage. In the latter case, the surgical and doctor charges would usually be covered by Blue Shield, which may or may not be operating jointly with Blue Cross.

Employers that like the Blue Cross hospital coverage but want a different plan for all their surgical coverage often elect wraparound plans.

Q 2:34 How are the Blues different from private insurers?

The negotiated hospital discounts arranged through the Blues plans sometimes allow these insurers to offer lower rates to employers. Also, in most states the Blues are nonprofit organizations and, as such, pay no premium tax to the state. A few Blues plans are able to offer lower expense levels by not paying sales commissions, although the majority compensate brokers.

Other factors can work against these insurers. As quid pro quo for having exclusive rights to hospital discounting granted by the state, the Blues accepted state regulation of their rates and eligibility criteria for individual contracts. They have thus been prevented from denying coverage or raising rates on individual contracts as quickly as they wanted to (i.e., as quickly as private insurers). Group contracts then picked up the shortfall created by these costly individual contracts, causing frustration as many employers were presented with rate increases far outpacing their experience or actual trend.

Chapter 3

Factors Influencing Insurance Plan Design

This chapter covers generally the legal and environmental (internal) factors that affect the basic decisions concerning an employer's group health insurance plan. (Federal and state laws regulating the group health insurance market are primarily covered in Chapter 4.) This chapter also addresses managed competition. Several large employers have experienced considerable success through managed competition, and the expectation is that it will prove a positive strategy for medium-sized and small companies.

Non-legal Factors Affecting Design	3-2
Paying for Insurance	3-14
Coverage	3-16
Restrictions on Coverage	3-31
Deductibles, Copayments, and Reimbursement	3-35
Cost Containment	3-38
Managed Competition	3-54

Q 3:1   Health Insurance Answer Book

Non-legal Factors Affecting Design

Q 3:1 Besides the legislative factors, what other issues must be addressed as part of the purchasing process?

To some extent, general economic conditions will determine what type of plan an employer can select. For example, if the economy is depressed or the outlook for the employer's industry is poor, the employer may not be in a position to offer a generous benefit plan; however, the employer must simultaneously determine what role the group health insurance plan will play in its hiring strategy. Should the employer set up a "rich" plan in order to gain a recruiting advantage over competitors by providing employees and prospective employees with a more attractive benefit package, or will it settle for a less competitive plan?

Company demographics will also be a factor. If the majority of a company's employees are young and, therefore, would value certain types of benefits more than a predominantly older employee population would, the benefit plan can be structured to meet those needs. In addition, the employer will have to determine how its corporate culture should be manifested in the plan (for example, a traditionally employee-oriented company will want a benefit plan that reflects that orientation). Some employers may wish to consider that some employees may already have insurance from other sources.

Q 3:2 What are typical employer strategies?

Employer health insurance strategies generally fall into one of the four following categories:

1. Managed competition;
2. Total compensation;
3. Paternalistic; and
4. Flexible/market-driven.

Managed competition. Managed competition is a term that applies to a strategy that seeks to inject competition between health plans. Under the managed competition approach, employees are offered a choice of multiple health plans with financial incentives to select the lowest cost plan. Ideally, plans will compete for membership based on the perceived quality of the physicians in the network and customer service, in addition to cost. One of the goals of managed competition is to drive employees to the most cost-effective plan. One of the consequences of this is that the least cost-effective plan may become prohibitively expensive. Unless an employer is willing to let that happen, managed competition is not a good strategy.

Total compensation. Under a total compensation strategy, benefits are not viewed as separate from compensation. Base salaries, incentive pay, and employee benefits are evaluated and negotiated as a single package. A total compensation strategy works best with a flexible benefits plan that uses a credit formula.

Paternalistic. A paternalistic approach to health insurance is much less common today than in the past, but some employers still use this approach. At the extreme, some employers provide free family coverage for any benefit option. Other paternalistic employers require very modest employee contributions for each option.

Flexible/market-driven. The last strategy is what we have termed, "flexible/market-driven." This is the approach used by most employers. Rather than be tied to a dogmatic strategy, most employers prefer to retain flexibility in order to respond to employee needs and changes in the marketplace. The managed competition and total compensation strategies work well for employers that want to move employees out of preferred provider organizations and into health maintenance organizations (HMOs). For organizations that are interested in preserving preferred provider organizations (PPOs) as an affordable option, the paternalistic and flexible/market-driven strategies are more appropriate. At one time the conventional wisdom was that PPOs were only a transitional type of health plan that would disappear as more employers enrolled in HMOs. In recent years, employee choices during open enrollment have indicated that PPOs are becoming more popular, not less popular. The annual survey by Mercer/Foster Higgins shows that enrollment in PPOs has grown from 29 percent of employees in 1996 to 39 percent in 1999. During the same period, HMO enrollment has only grown from 31 percent to 32 percent.

Q 3:3   Who is an eligible employee?

An eligible employee is any employee who meets the definition in the plan for participation. Definitions of eligible employee vary widely from employer to employer, though they may be influenced by:

1. *Legal considerations.* For example, those employees who are not considered for purposes of nondiscrimination testing and those who are covered by a collective bargaining agreement may be excluded. Health Insurance Portability and Accountability Act of 1996 (HIPAA) prohibits using health-status related factors to determine eligibility.
2. *Company structure.* Eligible employee may be defined to exclude employees from different operating units, different geographical areas, or different employment categories (for example, salaried versus hourly). Self-funded medical plans must comply with nondiscrimination requirements, so excluding too many employees may jeopardize compliance (see Chapter 11).

Q 3:4   Who is an eligible dependent?

The definition of eligibility in the policy or document determines who is an eligible dependent under a group health plan (whether or not insured). It may include: former spouses of employees (if employees are responsible for the former spouse's medical expenses), privately placed pre-adoptive children and their birth mothers, domestic partners, resident parents, and resident children of an employee's minor child for whom the employee is financially or legally responsible. Unless an individual qualifies as a dependent under Section 152 of the Internal Revenue Code, the employee will be taxed on the fair market value of the employers contributions toward the cost of that dependents coverage.

Omnibus Safety and Health Act (OBRA '93) included a provision requiring group health plans to provide coverage for adopted children under age 18 that is equivalent to coverage provided to natural dependent children. Coverage must begin at the time the adopted child is placed with the plan participant (not the date of legal adoption). OBRA '93 also prohibits plans from imposing preexisting-condition limits or exclusions on adopted children. Note that only equivalent coverage is necessary: If the plan does not offer coverage of dependent children, it need not offer coverage to adopted children either.

Q 3:5 Are employers providing benefits for domestic partners?

Nearly 3,000 employers now offer domestic partner benefits. Municipalities and universities have led the way in providing domestic partner coverage, and a few private companies provide these benefits as well. According to a survey by the Society for Human Resource Management, about one in 10 U.S. companies offers domestic partner benefits.

Employers that provide this coverage have recognized that the traditional definition of family no longer applies to many lifestyles and relationships. The U.S. Census Bureau estimated that there were 5.6 million households in 1996 composed of unmarried couples, with almost one-third of these being same-sex couples. In response, many employers now recognize (for purposes of their benefits plan) a "domestic partner" (sometimes also called "significant other" or "cohabitant") to be the equivalent of a spouse in families not based on marriage. Domestic partners may be male-female or same sex, so the benefit includes both homosexual and heterosexual unmarried couples. Generally, these employers characterize a legitimate domestic partnership by the sharing of a residence, the sharing of finances, and the existence of a formal commitment to the relationship. For further discussion of how employers define domestic partnerships, see Q 3:8.

California has led the way in rethinking the definition of marriage and family. The State Joint Task Force on the Changing Family examined a number of issues, including those related to employee benefits. Los Angeles appointed a City Task Force on Family Diversity, and San Francisco instituted a domestic partners law that extended health insurance coverage to the domestic partners of city employees. Smaller cities like Berkeley, West Hollywood, and Santa Cruz provide some health benefits to the "significant others" of their employees. Other cities, such as New York City, Seattle, and Madison, Wisconsin, have laws or policies that recognize domestic partners as family for some purposes.

A recent state appeals court decision made Oregon the first state in which all government departments must offer insurance benefits to employees' same-sex partners. The case, *Tanner v. Oregon Health Sciences University*, may create a new employment-related cause of action that applies to all employers. Three lesbian employees filed suit in 1992 against OHSU when the university denied medical and dental benefits to their partners. The university argued it did not intend to discriminate by limiting coverage to married couples. The court ruled that because homosexuals may not marry, they do not have equal access to benefits. Some Oregon legislators have said they will introduce legislation to overturn the decision.

Q 3:6 How have private employers responded to requests for domestic partner benefits?

A survey by Hewitt Associates found that in 1997, 10 percent of employers offered benefits to the domestic partners of employees. While more and more private employers recognize domestic partnerships for benefit purposes, many are still reluctant to extend benefit coverage that far. That reluctance stems from the following seven concerns, some of which are probably unfounded:

1. Traditional views about what types of persons should constitute a family and thus would be owed financial obligations;

2. Concerns about the cost of expanding coverage to a new class of beneficiaries at a time when companies are already burdened by health care costs;

3. Lack of legal support in the form of recognition of these relationships (although a growing number of states and localities extend such recognition to one extent or another; Ohio, for example, recently extended its domestic violence statute to same-sex couples and California established a statewide registry of domestic partnerships that employers can use to determine eligibility);

4. Fear of burgeoning liabilities, especially those related to AIDS, associated with same-sex partners;

5. Reluctance by some insurance companies to expand coverage, even when employers are willing;
6. Concerns about community reaction (see Q 3:11); and
7. The problem of defining just how far the extended family extends.

The last issue may be the most troublesome. If the union is not legally sanctioned—with the attendant legal requirements and formalities that accompany not just the beginning but also the end of the union (i.e., marriage)—employers must determine for themselves what constitutes a legitimate union and what does not. Without some strict standards as guidance, companies could be vulnerable to situations in which individuals become a family simply to obtain benefits—domestic partnerships of convenience—with serious adverse-selection implications.

The early evidence from companies that have instituted the coverage suggests that fears of increased costs for domestic partners is unfounded. For example, Levi-Strauss & Co, the clothing maker, estimates that domestic partners cost them only 15 percent of what a traditional spouse costs in benefits. According to a survey by the Society for Human Resource Management, 85 percent of the organizations with domestic partner benefits said that health expenditures have not risen as a result of providing the benefits.

A closely watched lawsuit against AT&T extended the domestic partnership debate to the national level. The suit involved two women who lived together for 12 years following a ceremony before friends and family during which rings were exchanged. Although not recognized by the law, in the women's eyes and in the eyes of friends and relatives their relationship functioned as a marriage.

When one of the women died, the other applied to AT&T for the benefits she felt she was entitled to as a surviving spouse. AT&T refused to pay death benefits, which would have included a year's pay to her as an eligible spouse. AT&T's position was that its plans were designed to provide benefits for legal spouses only. As the law does not recognize same-sex marriages, no benefits were owed under its plans. The claimant contended that AT&T had an established corporate policy that prohibited discrimination on the basis of marital status or sexual orientation. In denying her spouse's benefits, she claimed, the company violated its own policies, and in so doing, violated ERISA as well. In 1993 a U.S. district court ruled in favor of AT&T.

Q 3:7 Why do employers offer domestic partner benefits?

According to the Employee Benefit Research Institute, employers offer domestic partner benefits for two reasons:

1. *Fairness.* Many employers believe that offering benefits to legally married partners of employees and not offering the same benefits to the partners of non-legally married partners of employees discriminates on the basis of sexual orientation and/or martial status. Many employers have a formal policy against discrimination on the basis of sexual orientation. The decision to offer domestic partner benefits communicates to employees that the employer is committed to its stated policy.

2. *Market competition and diversity.* A comprehensive benefits package that offers health and retirement coverage attracts employees. In today's tight labor market, designing a benefit package that appeals to a diverse work force enables an employer to maintain a recruitment edge and communicates that the employer values a diverse workforce. Employee morale and productivity has been found to improve in work environments where individuals believe the employer demonstrates that it values its employees.

Q 3:8 What criteria can employers use to determine the existence of a valid domestic partnership?

Included here are five of the criteria that are typically used to qualify domestic partnerships:

1. Standards similar to those used by many states for establishing common law marriages, including the couples' holding themselves out to the public as spouses and living (together) as a married couple for a specified number of years;

2. Legal or contractual obligations to provide mutual support, such as a formal contract to assume all of the financial obligations associated with marriage;

3. Mutual responsibility for children or other family members;
4. Other joint obligations, such as ownership of property; and
5. Registration or formal public notification of the existence of a domestic partnership (a number of municipalities and companies already require registration).

According to a report in *The New York Times*, the Montefiore Medical Center in the City of New York provides the same health care benefits to homosexual partners as to heterosexual spouses. The coverage is conditional upon the couple's providing proof of all of the following:

1. The two were living together (drivers' licenses showing same address).
2. The two were financially interdependent as evidenced by joint checking accounts.
3. Each of the two was the other's sole domestic partner, attested to by a sworn statement.

According to a survey by the Society for Human Resource Management, 42 percent of employers that provide domestic partner benefits require employees to show proof of common residency, 38 percent require a notarized affidavit of partnership status, and 26 percent do not require any certification.

Q 3:9 What is the IRS position on benefits for domestic partners?

Essentially, medical benefits provided to nondependents are taxed as income to the participant. The position of the IRS on the issue of cohabitant benefits was spelled out in a private letter ruling. [Ltr Rul 9034048] Nontaxable health coverage can only be provided to an employee's legal spouse or a dependent as defined under Code Section 152. To the extent that such coverage is financed by the employer, a beneficiary would be taxed on the fair market value of the coverage. Fair market value is based on what the employee's cost, at group rates, would have been to provide such coverage. The value of the coverage must be reported as income on the employee's W-2, and Federal Insurance Contribution Act (FICA) and Federal Unemployment Taxes Act (FUTA) taxes must be withheld.

The definition of "spouse" is a matter determined by the various state laws. In those states that recognize common law marriages, the IRS relies on state criteria for establishing such marriages. Even if the cohabiting adult does not meet any of the state standards for a spouse, the individual who meets all of the following criteria may still be deemed to be a dependent:

1. Receives at least half of his or her support from the taxpayer;
2. Is a member of the taxpayer's household; or
3. Lists the taxpayer's home as his or her primary residence.

In any case, when the relationship between the taxpayer and the cohabitant is in violation of local laws, the IRS will not recognize the person as either a spouse or a dependent.

If the requirements for establishing spousal or dependent status are not met, the IRS will deem any medical benefits provided on the individual's behalf to be taxable income. Even if a plan provides taxable coverage to domestic partners, the coverage and benefits provided to employees and other dependents would retain its non-taxable status.

Q 3:10 What is the impact of the Defense of Marriage Act on domestic partner benefits?

There is not much impact. The Defense of Marriage Act (P.L. 104-199) says the word "marriage" means only a legal union between one man and one woman and the word "spouse" refers only to a person of the opposite sex who is a husband or wife.

The Defense of Marriage Act basically affirms the IRS position on the taxability of domestic partner benefits.

Q 3:11 What type of public reaction can employers expect for recognizing domestic partnerships in their benefit plans?

While most employers have reported positive reactions to the extension of coverage, there have been cases of negative public response. Employers need to weigh the advantages of offering the benefits against the possibility of offending the values of the community within which they do business.

A prominent case involving Apple Computer Inc. recently brought this problem to light. Apple had decided to build a large new facility in Williamson County, Texas, based in part on the fact that the county commissioners had offered the company significant tax incentives; however, when the local press reported that Apple provided benefits to domestic partners, including same-sex partners, the commissioners balked and rescinded the original offer of tax abatements, stating that they did not want to subsidize benefits for homosexuals. The deal was eventually renegotiated on only nominally different terms (instead of outright tax abatements Apple received other financial incentives), but the brief controversy about Apple's policies suggests the worst possibilities of public reaction.

The Southern Baptist Church called for a boycott of Disney after it announced it was adding domestic partner benefits. The boycott had a negligible effect.

When Mayor Ed Rendell of Philadelphia ordered domestic partner benefits for his appointees, the city's Catholic cardinal sent an open letter to parishioners, asking them to organize protests.

In 1997, the Virginia Attorney General issued an opinion that domestic partner benefits offered by Arlington County violate state law. In 1997, the Georgia Supreme Court upheld an Atlanta ordinance providing health and other benefits to the domestic partners of city employees. The insurance commissioner attempted to block implementation, but in 1999 a court ruled the city could implement the benefits. In 1999, the Massachusetts Supreme Judicial Court ruled that state law prohibits the city of Boston from extending health insurance coverage to domestic partners.

There were protests by a group of Hasidic rabbis in 1998 when the New York City Council voted to treat unmarried couples, including gays and lesbians, in the same manner as married couples. The law is one of the broadest domestic partner laws in the nation, addressing not just benefits for city employees, but visitation rights in city-run facilities, tenancy succession rights, and disclosure of background information about domestic partners when seeking certain licenses, among other things. The rabbis protested outside City Hall, saying the mayor and other city officials would be cursed and wiped out because of their support for the legislation. The religious protestors read from the Bible about the destruction of Sodom and Gomorrah.

New York's Roman Catholic Cardinal John O'Connor also spoke out against the measure.

Q 3:12 What does the city and county of San Francisco require regarding domestic partners?

The San Francisco Administrative Code prohibits the city and county from entering into contracts with any contractor that discriminates in the provision of benefits between employees with domestic partners and employees with spouses. A U.S. District Court has ruled it is preempted by ERISA under certain circumstances. When dealing with most city contractors, the city acts as a "market participant" and the law does not violate ERISA's preemption provisions. When dealing with airlines at the city-owned airport, the city acts as a regulator and ERISA preempts the law.

Q 3:13 Do other cities have similar requirements?

On November 17, 1999, the Los Angeles City Council voted to prohibit city agencies from contracting with any business that "discriminates in the provision of bereavement leave, family medical leave, health benefits, membership discounts, moving expenses, pension and benefits between employees with domestic partners and employees with spouses." The ordinance applies to contracts over $5,000 and was effective January 1, 2000.

The Seattle City Council passed a similar ordinance on November 22, 1999. Seattles ordinance applies to contracts of $33,000 and was effective June 1, 2000.

Q 3:14 What is Vermonts Civil Union Law and does it affect benefit plans?

On April 26, 2000, Vermonts governor signed the nations most sweeping gay rights legislation. This groundbreaking law extends more than 300 benefits normally associated with marriage to gay and lesbian couples. These rights include inheritance rights, the authority to make medical decisions for an incapacitated partner, and the right to be treated as an economic unit for tax purposes. A civil union must be dissolved in a court proceeding similar to a divorce.

Because ERISA preempts state laws that relate to employee benefit plans, employers cannot be required to recognize civil unions as marriage for ERISA benefit purposes. Because Vermont created a "civil union" rather than allowing same-sex marriage, the new law does not challenge the Defense of Marriage Act (Q 3:10).

Q 3:15 What is a reciprocal beneficiary?

In 1997, the state of Hawaii created numerous rights for "reciprocal beneficiaries." To qualify as reciprocal beneficiaries, the people must be prohibited from marrying. In addition to two individuals of the same gender, this includes individuals who are related, such as a widowed mother and her unmarried son. In addition to being prohibited from marrying one another, both parties must be at least 18, unmarried, and not part of another reciprocal beneficiary relationship. Both parties must willingly file a notarized declaration of reciprocal beneficiary relationship with the state government.

Q 3:16 What rights do reciprocal beneficiaries have?

In addition to health benefits, Hawaiian law extends to reciprocal beneficiaries rights that are substantially equivalent to those extended to spouses, including:

1. Survivorship rights, including inheritance, workers' compensation, and state employee retirement beneficiary benefits;
1. Hospital visitation, auto insurance, mental health commitment approvals and notifications, and family and funeral leave;
2. Benefits and obligations relating to jointly held property;
3. Legal standing relating to wrongful death, victims rights, and domestic violence; and
4. Miscellaneous benefits, such as emergency use of government vehicles.

Q 3:17 What has been the reaction of the business community in Hawaii to the reciprocal beneficiary law?

A group of employers in Hawaii filed suit contending the bill is preempted by ERISA. A U.S. district court ruled in their favor, and the state did not appeal the decision.

Q 3:18 Can a single group health insurance plan meet the benefit needs of an employer's diverse workforce?

Most group health insurance plans are comprehensive enough to cover a wide range of medical expenses. They provide coverage to protect even those in the employer's workforce with the greatest need for health insurance. Many flexible benefit plans have been developed to address the needs of today's diverse workforce (see Chapter 9). Ironically, the comprehensive nature of today's group benefit plans has created two new problems: duplication of benefits and coverage levels not needed by many of today's workers. Because today's workforce contains a growing number of two-wage-earner families—with both earners entitled to health coverage from their own employers—the potential for duplication of benefits is great.

Paying for Insurance

Q 3:19 How much can an employer expect to pay annually for group health insurance?

According to the Mercer/Foster Higgins annual survey, total health benefit costs averaged $4,320 for active employees in 1999, compared with $4,037 in 1998.

Q 3:20 Must employers pay the entire cost of group health insurance?

No. Group health insurance plans can be noncontributory or contributory. Under a noncontributory plan, the employer pays the entire cost of the plan. Employees are automatically covered as soon as they become eligible for insurance coverage. Noncontributory plans have 100 percent participation; that is, if the employer pays the full cost, all eligible employees must participate unless they waive coverage in writing.

Under a contributory plan, the employee shares in the cost of the plan. Once employees are eligible to participate in a contributory group health plan, they usually have 30 days in which to enroll. An employee who does not elect coverage during the enrollment period may enroll at another time, but coverage can be subject to up to an 18-month exclusion for pre-existing conditions. Annual open enrollment periods are limited to specific times of the year, usually beginning January 1 and July 1. Special open enrollment periods apply if other coverage is lost or if the employee gets married or has a child.

Q 3:21 What factors should an employer consider when deciding whether its group health insurance plan should be contributory or noncontributory?

The decision depends primarily on how competitive the job marketplace is, what the competitors in the marketplace are doing, and the amount of money the employer can afford. Many employers want their employees to share in the cost of health coverage to make them aware of and responsive to its cost. Today, when more than half of all two-adult families are also two-paycheck families, contributions encourage employees to avoid duplicating coverage. The trend in health insurance is to place greater financial responsibility on the insureds for premiums and expenses, thereby helping to ensure that employees use their plans as efficiently as possible.

The Bureau of Labor Statistics reports that 31 percent of employees in small and medium firms had fully employer-paid health coverage in 1997, down from 49 percent in 1991, and only 20 percent received fully paid coverage for their families, down from 31 percent in 1991.

As more and more employers introduce contributions, those that retain noncontributory plans will pay more for insurance as a result of higher claims. Employees covered by contributory plans, whose spouses have noncontributory dependent coverage, will drop their employer plans and receive full benefits under their spouses' plans.

Q 3:22 What legal constraints are imposed on the distribution of employer-employee costs for group health insurance?

There are no legal requirements for employer-employee cost sharing with respect to medical and dental (and other health) insurance, although many states have provisions concerning employee contributions for life and disability insurance. An employer cannot discriminate financially against HMOs.

Q 3:23 Can an employer self-fund a group health insurance plan?

Yes. Companies with more than 200 employees often self-fund all or part of their group health insurance plans. The employer's objectives are to improve cash flow, save premium taxes, eliminate the insurer's risk charge, and benefit from better-than-expected claims experience (see Chapter 17).

Coverage

Q 3:24 What types of traditional group health insurance plans are available?

There are generally two types of traditional group health insurance plans available to smaller employers: a basic medical plus major medical plan, commonly referred to as a "base-plus" or "first-dollar" plan, and a comprehensive medical plan, called simply "comprehensive." Because it is believed to be more cost-effective, the trend in plan design is clearly toward the comprehensive plan. Traditional plans are being replaced in many areas by managed care plans.

Q 3:25 What is a base-plus plan?

A base-plus plan is a two-part health insurance plan. Basic medical coverage—for such expenses as hospitalization, surgery, physicians' visits, and diagnostic laboratory tests and x-rays—is provided under the first part. There may be limits on these expenses, such as a limited number of hospital days and a surgical schedule, but no deductible or coinsurance applies to the covered expenses. The employee is reimbursed starting with the first dollar of expenses.

The second, or major medical, part of the plan covers other health expenses. The coverage is broad, with fewer limits; however, a deductible is required before the employee is reimbursed for expenses. Coinsurance, usually 80 percent/20 percent, is applied until the maximum employee out-of-pocket expense is reached. Further covered expenses are reimbursed in full.

This two-part plan is the result of the historical development of health insurance. When first offered, group health insurance extended only to basic hospital and later surgical coverage. This was followed years later by broader coverage for more catastrophic illness. (Deductibles and coinsurance are discussed in Qs 3:62–3:70.)

Q 3:26 What is a comprehensive plan?

A comprehensive plan provides coverage for most medical services using one reimbursement formula. In a pure comprehensive plan, a deductible must be met before reimbursement for any covered expenses begins, and coinsurance applies to all covered expenses until the maximum employee out-of-pocket expense limit is reached. Additional covered expenses are then paid in full.

The pure comprehensive design has been modified in many ways to meet various market needs. For example, some employers have comprehensive plans with hospital expenses fully covered, with no deductible or coinsurance requirements. This form was first used by employers that wanted to move gradually away from base-plus plans.

Q 3:27 What types of services are generally covered by a group health insurance plan?

A covered expense is an eligible expense under a group health insurance plan. A covered expense is an expense incurred by a covered individual that will be reimbursed in whole or in part under the group health insurance plan.

Covered expenses vary by insurer and type of plan, but generally include the following:

Q 3:28 **Health Insurance Answer Book**

1. Professional services of doctors of medicine and osteopathy and other recognized medical practitioners;
2. Hospital charges for semiprivate room and board and other necessary services and supplies;
3. Surgical charges;
4. Services of registered nurses and, in some cases, licensed practical nurses;
5. Home health care;
6. Physiotherapy;
7. Anesthetics and their administration;
8. X-rays and other diagnostic laboratory procedures;
9. X-ray or radium treatment;
10. Oxygen and other gases and their administration;
11. Blood transfusions, including the cost of blood when charged;
12. Drugs and medicines requiring a prescription;
13. Specified ambulance services;
14. Rental of durable mechanical equipment required for therapeutic use;
15. Artificial limbs and other prosthetic appliances, except the replacement of such appliances;
16. Casts, splints, trusses, braces, and crutches; and
17. Rental of a wheelchair or hospital-type bed.

Q 3:28 Are alternative therapies covered?

Alternative therapies, such as herbal remedies, acupuncture, massage therapy, biofeedback, and music therapy, are usually not covered by health insurance. The American Medical Association's House of Delegates has approved a resolution encouraging doctors to educate themselves about alternative medicine.

The Insurance Commissioner in the state of Washington issued a controversial bulletin in December 1995 informing carriers they may not exclude categories of providers. A news release followed, explaining that insurers may not exclude acupuncturists, naturopaths, podiatrists, midwives, and others from coverage. Ten carriers sued,

Factors Influencing Insurance Plan Design   Q 3:28

contending the Insurance Commissioner's interpretation of a new law to take effect January 1, 1996 was incorrect. A federal judge ruled that the law is preempted by ERISA, but the Ninth U.S. Circuit Court of Appeals ruled that ERISA does not preempt the law and in February, 1999 the U.S. Supreme Court let that ruling stand. [Washington Physicians Service Association v. Gregoire.] In January 2000, the Washington Supreme Court upheld the law, removing what appears to be the final obstacle to full implementation.

Oxford Health Plans has begun offering employers in New York, New Jersey, and Connecticut the opportunity to buy coverage for a network of alternative medicine providers. Other HMOs are exploring doing so as well.

According to *Employee Benefit News*, the following complementary and alternative medicine therapies are frequently covered:

- Acupuncture
- Chiropractic
- Massage therapy
- Yoga

Also according to the same source, the following are rarely covered:

- Aromatherapy
- Color therapy
- Gems and magnets
- Reflexology

Employee Benefit News says the following therapies fall between the two extremes and are sometimes covered:

- Ayurveda
- Biofeedback
- Guided imagery
- Homeopathy
- Naturopathy
- Nutritional therapy
- Rolfing

- Traditional Chinese medicine
- Vitamins and herbs

According to a survey by Landmark Healthcare, 72 percent of HMOs offer at least one type of alternative care, with the most common being:

- Chiropractic (65 percent)
- Acupuncture (31 percent)
- Massage therapy (11 percent)
- Vitamin therapy (6 percent)
- Relaxation therapy (5 percent)

Q 3:29 What are common types of alternative medicine?

Some common types of alternative medicine include the following:

1. *Acupuncture.* This ancient form of healing uses thin needles inserted at specific points. The theory is that it adjusts the flow of energy through the body. It is often used to treat substance abusers.

2. *Aromatherapy.* Aromatherapy uses essential oils extracted from flowers, leaves, stalks and roots for therapeutic purposes.

3. *Ayurveda.* This ancient set of therapies uses herbs, relaxation techniques, massage, and posture exercises. It may be effective against cardiovascular problems.

4. *Biofeedback.* This mind-body therapy uses small electronic devices to teach patients how to control vital body functions like heart rate and blood pressure.

5. *Chiropractic.* This is the most common type of alternative medicine. It is largely focused on improving skeletal alignment to alleviate pain.

6. *Gems and magnets.* The theory behind this therapy is that gemstones and magnets carry vibrational rates that will change an aura's vibrational rate.

7. *Guided imagery.* Guided imagery has patients think about a certain outcome before an event (such as surgery) happens.

Factors Influencing Insurance Plan Design Q 3:31

8. *Homeopathy.* Homeopathy uses extremely diluted doses of toxic substances to fight disease.
9. *Massage therapy.* Massages and other hands-on therapies are used to improve circulation, release tension, and enhance overall health and energy.
10. *Naturopathy.* Naturopathy is intended to enhance a body's ability to heal itself. It includes acupuncture, counseling, herbal treatments, homeopathy, massage, nutritional treatments, physical therapies, and other approaches.
11. *Traditional Chinese medicine.* TCM focuses on trying to restore the balance of the body's energy, rather than on disease. TCM uses modalities such as acupuncture, herbal medicine, or exercises.
12. *Yoga.* Yoga uses breathing exercises, body postures, and meditation to manage stress, lower blood pressure, and enhance overall health.

Q 3:30 How popular is alternative health care?

An article in the March/April 1997 edition of *Archives of Family Medicine* reported that 50 percent of patients surveyed had used some form of alternative medicine.

According to the *Los Angeles Times*, there was 75 percent growth in herbal supplement sales from 1994 to 1997. A *Los Angeles Times* poll in 1998 found that 35 percent of Californians had tried high-dose vitamins, 32 percent had been to a chiropractor, 11 percent had tried homeopathy, and 8 percent had tried acupuncture. The statistics for California are about twice as high as the nationwide statistics.

Some alternative health care does not require any out-of-pocket expense, such as yoga, which can be practiced alone.

Q 3:31 How much does alternative health care cost?

Oxford Health Plans generally charges between 2 percent and 6 percent of the medical premium to add its rider for alternative health care coverage.

Q 3:32 What kinds of hospital charges are covered under a group health insurance plan?

Group health insurance plans typically cover a variety of inpatient and outpatient charges. Inpatient covered charges include room, board, and necessary services and supplies.

Room and board charges are covered on a per-day basis up to either a maximum dollar amount each day or the most common semiprivate room and board charges of the particular hospital. Private rooms are generally not covered. Base plans cover hospital stays up to a certain number of days, such as 120 or 365 days per calendar year. The major medical plan covers days exceeding the base plan limit. Comprehensive plans typically cover all hospital days at a percentage of the semiprivate room rate.

Hospital services and supplies include items such as drugs and use of the operating room. Some base plans allow maximum dollar amounts for these expenses, but most plans cover them in full when room and board charges are covered. Comprehensive plans cover the same services the base-plus major medical plans do but require a deductible and coinsurance. Of course, supplemental major medical also requires a deductible and coinsurance.

Intensive care is usually covered up to two or three times the room and board allowances for a semiprivate room under a base plan. Today, most plans cover intensive care at the reasonable and customary (R&C) charge for the service.

Managed care plans often negotiate per diem contracts with hospitals that pay a fixed daily amount for all services, including room and board. Percentage discounts that apply equally to all services are also common.

Q 3:33 How is surgery covered under a health insurance plan?

Surgical expense benefits are provided on a scheduled or non-scheduled basis. Scheduled plans specify an allowance for each kind of surgery, either in dollar terms or relative to other procedures listed. Nonscheduled plans cover surgical expenses on a reasonable and customary basis. Basic plans traditionally provided for surgery in conjunction with hospitalization. Today, base-plus plans cover surgery wherever performed, to discourage unnecessary hospitalization. The plan benefits include payment for the surgeon, assistant surgeon, and anesthesiologist. Charges associated with the surgery, such as for blood products, are also covered under the plan, although sometimes only up to a maximum amount, whereupon the major medical plan takes over.

Today most employers purchase a plan that does not treat surgical expenses differently from nonsurgical expenses. They purchase a wraparound major medical plan that covers surgery in addition to the standard major medical features. Comprehensive plans cover surgery after the insured satisfies a deductible. Coinsurance usually applies, but some plans encourage outpatient (as opposed to inpatient) surgery by waiving the coinsurance provision in an effort to manage medical care costs.

Managed care plans often negotiate fee schedules with physicians that specify the amount paid for each procedure, whether surgical or nonsurgical. Some plans use percentage discounts that apply to both surgical and nonsurgical services.

Q 3:34 What is a reasonable and customary charge?

An R&C charge, also called a usual, customary, and reasonable charge (UCR), or usual and prevailing (U&P), is the maximum amount that an insurer will consider eligible for reimbursement for a medical care expense covered under the group health insurance plan. These amounts are usually determined from a database that identifies the cost of each procedure or service in various regions of the country. For example, to determine the level at which to reimburse a surgeon's fee for a certain type of operation, an insurance company will examine the fees of all surgeons located within a certain geographic area. The R&C limit could be set so that some percentage, such as 90 percent of all surgeons' fees, would be covered. That is, if 1,000 surgeons' fees are reviewed, and 10 percent of the surgeons charge more than $5,000 and 90 percent charge $5,000 or less, the maximum covered charge would be $5,000 for that surgical procedure. That portion of the surgeon's charges over the R&C amount would not be considered a covered expense under the plan. R&C charges are adjusted periodically.

Q 3:35 What is a schedule of insurance?

A schedule of insurance sets forth a specific maximum amount an insurer will pay for each procedure, such as surgery or dental procedures. Schedules are sometimes denominated in units, rather than in dollars. These are called relative value schedules; a factor that reflects the level of charges in a geographic area multiplied by the number of units provided for each procedure determines the maximum amount the plan will pay.

Q 3:36 Why do some plans pay R&C charges and others schedule benefits?

These differences reflect, in part, the evolution of health insurance benefit coverage. The earliest plans used schedules paying limited and controlled amounts for the procedures covered. As plans were expanded, R&C fees replaced schedule amounts (usually for surgery) to meet the market demand for full payment for expenses incurred. As charges increased, reimbursement automatically increased.

Some employers would like to return to schedules, because without them their premiums increase significantly as physicians increase their R&C charges. This change would be difficult to implement. Employees would perceive it as a reduction in benefits, because of the more generous payment expectations today under the R&C system.

Managed care plans that have negotiated fee schedules have effectively returned to the old, scheduled approach, but have protected patients from balance billing.

Q 3:37 If the physicians' charges exceed the R&C amount or the schedule amount, is the employee responsible for paying the balance?

Yes. An insured is responsible for any charge that exceeds the R&C or schedule amount.

Most managed care plans protect patients from balance billing by network providers. Colorado and Hawaii have enacted legislation to require this protection.

Q 3:38 How have hospital and surgical care changed recently?

The number of hospital procedures has decreased considerably, and patients who do enter hospitals for care are released more quickly. In addition, procedures once considered unsafe on an outpatient basis are now performed that way routinely. These changes have resulted from improved technology, increased competition in the health care market among different kinds of providers and facilities, and the concern about rising health care costs.

Q 3:39 How are nonsurgical physicians' services covered?

Under a base-plus plan, the basic medical part often covers physicians' fees to hospital patients up to a specified maximum, and for a duration that normally coincides with the duration of the hospital benefits. Base plans usually also provide for limited home or alternative care facility physicians' visits directly related to recuperation after a hospital discharge. In addition, "office" visits are usually covered but are limited to a dollar amount per visit or per illness, or to a maximum number of visits per calendar year. Major medical plans pick up the coverage for physicians' visits where the base plan coverage leaves off.

Comprehensive plans cover physicians' services in the hospital, at alternative care facilities, at home, or in the office. Deductibles and coinsurance apply. Managed care plans also cover physicians services at any location, either in full, up to the negotiated fee, or subject to a copayment of a fixed dollar amount by the patient.

Not all physicians' services are covered by group health insurance plans. For example, physicians' services for dental treatments or examinations and for the prescription or fitting of eyeglasses or hearing aids are commonly excluded.

Q 3:40 What alternatives to hospital care are common today?

The most common alternative is the free-standing care center, also known as a "surgicenter" or "quick clinic." Some of these centers offer outpatient surgery under general anesthesia and some offer only routine, non-invasive care. Other alternatives are skilled nursing facilities. Patients discharged from acute care facilities find less expensive, more appropriate care at these extended care facilities during their convalescence.

Q 3:41 What kinds of hospital outpatient expenses are covered?

Three kinds of hospital outpatient care are covered: emergency treatment, surgery, and services rendered in the outpatient lab or x-ray department. Some comprehensive plans encourage the use of outpatient services (when appropriate) by covering them at a more generous level than hospitalization.

Q 3:42 Are all covered expenses reimbursed?

No. The fact that an expense is covered does not mean that the coverage is unlimited. Both base-plus and comprehensive plans have limits on the expenses for which they will reimburse. In addition, some form of deductible and coinsurance is often applicable.

Q 3:43 Why would an employer want to limit reimbursement for covered expenses?

An employer may want to impose a cap on some expenses in order to do the following:

1. Prevent abuse of a certain type of benefit;
2. Discourage community providers from raising their fees; and
3. Limit the total amount the plan will pay to any one person.

Q 3:44 How are covered expenses limited?

Covered expenses can be limited in an almost endless variety of ways. Among the more common are the following limitations, with examples for each:

1. *Time.* Coverage for mental health care provided for up to 30 days of treatment.
2. *Dollars.* The plan pays a maximum of $7,000 for a heart transplant, or up to $80 per office visit.

3. *Frequency.* The plan pays for 12 office visits per year, or for no more than two treatment programs for substance abuse per person.

4. *Combinations of these.* For the first 45 days of treatment, the plan pays 80 percent of up to $200 per visit for no more than 35 visits.

Coverage limitations may not, however, discriminate against protected classes of participants. For example, unreasonable coverage caps for AIDS-related diseases would likely be found to violate the ADA, because AIDS patients would qualify as disabled. The Mental Health Parity Act prohibits lifetime and annual dollar limits on mental health treatment.

Q 3:45 What types of services are generally not covered by a group health insurance plan?

Services that are generally not covered include those associated with procedures that are not medically necessary (for example, elective cosmetic surgery) and those that do not contribute materially to the treatment of an illness or injury, such as a hospital telephone or television. Also, in order to avoid duplicate payments, benefits that are available to an employee from another source, such as workers' compensation, are generally not covered.

Coverage that would create a substantial risk to the insurer are also excluded. For example, coverage for long-term nursing care has traditionally been excluded because of the unpredictability of the extent of the need for care and the resulting inability of insurers to price the coverage. In addition, care required as a result of war and care that would normally be provided without charge, such as care in certain state or federal hospitals, is not covered. Expenses for transportation are not covered, except for specified ambulance services.

Until recently, routine physicals and other preventive care procedures have not been covered, but some insurers now include a preventive care benefit.

Q 3:46 Are experimental treatments covered?

Health insurance plans have traditionally excluded experimental and untested medical treatments or procedures, but more and more plans are being forced to cover some of these treatments. The primary reason for this is the lack of accepted standards to determine adequately when a procedure or treatment is no longer experimental. This lack is exacerbated by vague or overly broad wording of exclusions in the plan contract or certificate. In a case in California, a jury awarded the estate of Nelene Fox more than $89 million in a judgment against Health Net (an HMO) stemming from its refusal to cover a bone marrow transplant for Ms. Fox's breast cancer. The HMO had refused coverage on the grounds that the treatment was experimental, but the jury concluded that the insurance contract did not adequately sustain the exclusion. [Fox v Health Net, Riverside Co Sup Ct, CA 1993] The parties later settled out of court for what was reportedly a much lower amount.

Q 3:47 May treatments that are legitimately experimental be excluded from coverage?

There is no easy answer. The major difficulty lies with the definition of the term "experimental" as it is used in the insurance contract's provision excluding such treatments from coverage. The provision is necessary to allow insurers to deny coverage for untested treatments that are valueless or may even be harmful; however, the distinction between what is and is not experimental is difficult to determine and—understandably, as the cases often involve terminally ill patients—usually controversial.

Insurers have tested various definitions of the term in the courts, with mixed results. Often, if the court finds any ambiguity in the term, it decides for the insured, as in the Fox case (see Q 3:46); however, the following language was found to be unambiguous by a court in Oregon that decided for the insurer in a case of denial of coverage for a bone marrow transplant, and is useful as a model of the type of definition often used:

> Experimental or Investigational Treatment: Services and supplies that are, in our judgment, experimental or investigational. These include, but are not limited to, any that are not recognized by medical practitioners as conforming to accepted medical

practice in the state of Oregon or any for which the required approval of a United States governmental agency such as the FDA, for other than experimental or investigational purposes, has not yet been granted at the time the services or supplies are provided. [West v Blue Cross & Blue Shield, US Dist Ct CV 91-581DA (D Or Oct 1, 1991)]

Q 3:48　How do insurers decide whether to cover a treatment?

Although many insurers and managed care organizations have broadened their coverage to include some treatments that have not been validated, they have usually done so on a case-by-case basis. In most cases, the decision as to whether a particular patient's treatment will be covered is made after consulting with a panel of outside medical experts hired by the insurer.

A report issued by the Government Accounting Office (GAO) found many insurers covering high dose chemotherapy with autologous bone marrow transplant as a treatment for breast cancer even though most experts say the benefits of the therapy are unproven. Twelve major insurers polled by the GAO said that they based their decision to cover the treatment chiefly on preliminary clinical research, but that nonmedical factors such as the fear of costly litigation and adverse public relations were also factors in the decision.

A California law requires HMOs and health insurers to establish a reasonable, external, independent review process by July 1, 1998 to examine coverage decisions regarding experimental or investigational therapies for people who meet certain specified criteria. The patient must have a terminal condition that has a high probability of causing death within two years. The patient's physician must certify the patient has a condition for which standard therapies have not been effective or are not medically appropriate. The physician must also certify that the recommended drug, device, procedure or other therapy is likely to be more beneficial, based on two scientific studies. This bill requires entities to be accredited by an organization under contract to the state.

Q 3:49　What is an external review?

Under an external review program, after a patient has exhausted a health plan's internal review process, the patient can take the matter to an independent third party for final resolution. Typically, the review is done by a specialist in the same field as the physician who suggested the treatment.

Q 3:50 What is the reason for an external review process?

Allowing independent appeals addresses widespread consumer concern that decisions are sometimes based on financial considerations, rather than what is truly best for the patient. External reviews should help to restore consumer trust in managed care plans.

Q 3:51 How common are external review programs?

According to the Bureau of National Affairs, 31 states, plus the District of Columbia, had enacted legislation requiring some form of external review. The Center for Health Dispute Resolution in Pittsford, N.Y. is the sole contractor for Medicare. Several leading health plans have also established such programs voluntarily.

Q 3:52 Does health insurance cover extended care facilities?

Extended care facilities offer one of three types of care: skilled nursing care, intermediate care, or custodial care. Most health plans cover skilled care facilities for a maximum number of days per calendar year per patient, or specify a dollar amount per day that will be covered. Some plans require that a patient must have been hospitalized within 7 to 14 days before entering a skilled nursing facility in order to be eligible for benefits. Health insurance plans do not cover custodial nursing care, and intermediate care may or may not be covered. Long-term care plans do cover custodial care.

Under base plans, stays in skilled nursing facilities are covered similarly to hospital expenses—a maximum benefit per day, to a maximum number of days in a calendar year. Major medical plans supplement this by providing additional days of care and by covering expenses associated with the care, all subject to deductible and coinsurance provisions until the maximum out-of-pocket (OOP) expense is reached. Comprehensive plans usually pay for a specific number of days of care, subject to deductible and coinsurance provisions until the OOP maximum is reached, whereupon the plan pays 100 percent of the R&C charges, as long as the care remains eligible, up to the limits of the policy. Most managed care plans will cover skilled nursing facilities only as an alternative to hospitalization and only if the patient cannot be treated at home.

Restrictions on Coverage

Q 3:53 For what reasons do employers typically exclude employees from group health insurance coverage?

There are a number of reasons that employers may exclude certain employees from coverage, for example:

1. Union employees who have coverage that was negotiated as part of a collective bargaining agreement would be excluded.
2. An employer may choose to cover employees working in different locations under different plans.
3. A subsidiary of an employer may be in a different industry, with different benefits needs; the subsidiary could be excluded and covered under a different plan.
4. An employer may want to give extra benefits to a special class of higher-paid employees and would therefore exclude all other employees from the extra coverage.
5. The expense of covering part-time and temporary employees may be too great for the employer to consider covering them.

Q 3:54 Are there limitations on an employer's freedom to choose the employees it wants covered under a group health insurance plan?

An employer may choose to cover only certain classes of employees under a group health insurance plan as long as applicable employment laws are not violated and the insurer approves the classification as one that precludes individual selection. Federal laws prohibit discrimination on the basis of age, gender, or race; therefore, these criteria cannot be used as the basis for exclusion from an employer's health plan. In addition, failure to include a significant percentage of employees, especially if those excluded represent a disproportionate share of lower-paid employees, may cause certain types of plans to be deemed discriminatory. This can result in tax penalties to certain highly compensated employees. (See Chapter 11 for a comprehensive discussion of nondiscrimination rules.) An employer must therefore weigh the cost of covering or making similar coverage available on a broad basis against the value of tax-free benefits for highly paid employees.

Under the terms of HIPAA, group health plans cannot establish any rules for eligibility or continued eligibility based on certain specified health-related factors and activities (see Chapter 4).

Q 3:55 Why would an employer offer benefits to which some employees already have access?

Health coverage has become an expected part of an employee's total compensation package, and if an employer hopes to attract and retain quality employees, medical coverage is among the first types of noncash compensation the employer should consider. A group plan allows all employees to participate without evidence of insurability. This is a valuable commodity to employees and their dependents who have health problems and are unable to purchase individual protection.

Although most employees have access to individual coverage, many do not elect it, usually because of the cost. Other employees may have "known" health conditions that either prevent them from obtaining individual coverage altogether or make the cost of that coverage so expensive that they cannot afford it. Employees who receive coverage from a spouse's plan are dependent on the continued employment of that spouse for health insurance. In addition, receiving dependent coverage through a spouse is generally more expensive for the employee's family than for that employee to be covered in a group plan where he or she works.

Q 3:56 What are the drawbacks to duplicating benefits?

That depends on the type of coordination of benefits provisions each plan has. At worst, the interaction between the plans might permit the employee to recoup 100 percent of medical expenses. While that might seem reasonable on the surface, current design theory holds that an employee must have some financial stake in the medical process in order to be motivated to use medical services with restraint.

Q 3:57 Do employers provide group health insurance to part-time and temporary employees?

Many employers do not cover part-time and temporary employees under their group health plans. Part-time employees are defined most often as those who work less than either 20 or 30 hours per week, depending on the industry. In general, employers believe that although these workers provide a valuable service, they do not justify the considerable expense associated with health benefits, particularly when they may be working for the company only a short time, or may already have coverage through another employer. A 1999 survey by Hewitt Associates reported that 78 percent of employers provide part-time employees with health coverage.

Some employers do cover part-time and temporary employees, although it is often difficult to find a carrier that will include these workers in a group health insurance plan. Changes in the tax law and in employment practices—such as job sharing among employees who choose to work part time while raising families—have led to more coverage being made available for part-time employees.

In 1998 the DOL sued Time Warner Inc., Time Inc., and its subsidiaries and plan administrators alleging that Time misclassified workers as temporary employees or independent contractors in order to deny them participation in benefits. The company has filed a motion to dismiss the suit.

According to the July 5, 1999 issue of *Business Insurance*, about half a dozen lawsuits have been filed against large employers by temporary employees. A suit against Microsoft involved stock options, but not health insurance. A suit against ARCO claimed medical and dental benefits as well as retirement benefits.

Q 3:58 Why don't more employers provide medical coverage to part-time employees?

The major reason is that medical benefit costs cannot be apportioned based on the hours worked. Employers pay employees for the time they work. Part-timers work fewer hours, so they receive fewer dollars in their paychecks. Once an employer grants an individual eligibility under its medical plan, he or she is entitled to whatever benefits the plan provides—a $10,000 surgical procedure for example. Faced with an all-or-nothing choice, most employers have opted for nothing.

Q 3:59 Can an employer provide enhanced health care coverage for key employees?

Under current tax law, different benefits can be provided to different classes of employees based on a condition of employment (for example, salaried versus hourly employees); however, discriminatory medical reimbursement plans (which typically cover any expense not reimbursed by the regular medical benefit plan for select employees) must be insured and exhibit risk shifting in order to avoid imputed income for selected employees covered under such a plan. [IRC § 105(h)]

Q 3:60 Will an insurance carrier deny certain employees coverage under a group health insurance plan?

Under the terms of HIPAA, group health plans cannot establish any rules for eligibility or continued eligibility based on certain specified health-related factors and activities (see Chapter 4).

Q 3:61 Can an employer require different service waiting periods?

Because employers use employee benefits to attract quality employees, it may make good business sense in some cases to cover all new hires under the group health insurance plan from the first day on the job. Some employers provide immediate health benefits only for certain job grades or levels, specifically indicating those individuals for whom the employer uses benefits as a recruiting tool. The other new hires are subject to a service waiting period—typically between one and three months for life and medical insurance and as much as one year for dental insurance—before their enrollment in the plan becomes effective.

A waiting period is advantageous to companies that suffer from significant turnover, because the administration involved in adding new employees to the plan and the risk associated with many short-term insurers is reduced considerably. Employees who are subject to a waiting period may purchase individual health policies to provide temporary insurance until they are eligible under the group health plan or, if they were previously covered by another employer's plan, elect to continue that plan under COBRA by paying the required cost. Rather than adjusting the waiting period, many employers reimburse select individuals for the cost of COBRA continuation under the prior employer's plan.

Deductibles, Copayments, and Reimbursement

Q 3:62 What is a deductible?

A deductible is a specific dollar amount that an individual must pay (or "satisfy") before reimbursement for expenses begins. The primary purpose of the deductible is to encourage employees to use health care services only when necessary, and to discourage submission of small claims to the insurance company because of the administrative expense involved. Deductibles typically range from $50 to $1,000. The higher the deductible, the lower the cost of the health insurance plan.

Q 3:63 What is a carryover deductible?

A carryover deductible allows covered expenses incurred in the last three months of the prior calendar year to be carried over to the new year and counted toward satisfying the new year's deductible. This provision is included to avoid the financial hardship of making an insured pay a deductible in the last quarter of one year and another in January of the next year. The trend is to eliminate the carryover provision and require each individual to pay an annual deductible, regardless of the timing of the claim, which is often within the control of the claimant.

Q 3:64 For insured employees with dependent coverage, does the deductible for each person have to be satisfied before reimbursement begins?

Each person covered under a group health insurance plan must meet a deductible before expenses will be covered; however, plans usually include some type of family deductible in order to limit a family's exposure for health care expenses.

The family deductible is usually some multiple of the individual deductible, generally two or three. For the family deductible to be satisfied, the combined expenses of covered family members are accumulated. Some plans require two or three family members to satisfy separate individual deductibles before the family deductible can be met.

Q 3:65 What is coinsurance?

Coinsurance is a feature found in most group health insurance plans. It sets forth the percentage of covered expenses that the employees and the health insurance plan will pay. Under a base-plus plan, no coinsurance is involved for basic medical coverage. For supplemental major medical and for comprehensive plans, a coinsurance provision applies. The most common coinsurance level is one in which the employee pays 20 percent of the expenses and the insurer pays 80 percent. This is called 80 percent coinsurance.

Q 3:66 What are typical coinsurance percentages?

Coinsurance percentages on both major medical and comprehensive plans are usually 20 percent for the employee, 80 percent for the employer. Some have changed to a 25 percent/75 percent split, or have decreased the employee's share when certain kinds of care are received. For example, a visit to an outpatient surgical center may be paid at 90 percent by the insurance company, while a hospital visit would be paid at 80 percent. Most plans limit the amount of coinsurance or out-of-pocket cost to an employee—typically $1,000 to $2,000 (20 percent of $5,000 and $10,000) per individual and twice that amount per family. According to a survey by Mercer/Foster Higgins in 1999, the average out-of-pocket limit for indemnity plans was $1,250, unchanged since 1995.

Q 3:67 What is a maximum out-of-pocket limit?

A maximum out-of-pocket limit is the maximum dollar amount the employee will have to pay for covered medical expenses during a specified period, generally per plan year. For instance, if a plan has an out-of-pocket limit of $1,000, the employee won't pay more than that amount for covered medical expenses. The out-of-pocket limit can be defined as (1) coinsurance amounts only, (2) coinsurance and deductibles, or (3) both, plus employee contributions.

In determining how the maximum will be accumulated, any one of those methods is not superior to the others; however, it is clearer and less complex to describe the "maximum" to employees as the maximum number of dollars an employee will pay. The maximum is usually expressed as two annual numbers, such as $3,000/$6,000. This means a single employee will face an annual maximum of $3,000, while a married employee, or a single employee with eligible dependents will face $6,000 per year. The family maximum is usually two or three times the single amount.

Some plans state the amount in terms of covered expenses. For example, a plan may pay 100 percent after covered expenses reach $10,000. This would yield the same benefit as an out-of-pocket limit of $2,000 for a plan with no deductible and 80 percent coinsurance. For a preferred provider organization or point-of-service plan, this approach yields a higher out-of-pocket limit for patients who do not use network providers.

Q 3:68 Is the deductible included in determining an OOP maximum?

Some group health insurance plans do not include the deductible in their OOP limits. In such situations, the insured employee would be responsible for paying the sum of the deductible and the OOP maximum. Other plans do include the deductible as part of the OOP maximum.

Q 3:69 Can medical expenses not covered by a health insurance plan be applied toward the deductible or OOP maximum?

No. Expenses incurred by the insured employee typically must be covered expenses under the health insurance plan to be applied toward the deductible or OOP maximum.

Q 3:70 Do most policies include an overall limit to the amount reimbursable to one individual?

Many policies have an overall lifetime limit. This is usually $1 million or $2 million. Some policies do not include an overall limit. Limits may be based on a calendar year or per illness or injury.

Some policies have a "reinstatement" provision that reinstates, or adds back, dollar amounts that have been counted toward the lifetime maximum limit each year, usually on January 1. Most plans automatically reinstate a small amount, such as $1,000. Higher reinstatement requests contingent on current health status used to be common, but are probably prohibited by HIPAA.

Cost Containment

Q 3:71 What specific factors should be considered relative to plan design philosophy?

First, an employer should answer the following questions:

1. How much should the plan pay, and how much should employees pay? This should be considered in terms of both contribution and in actual sharing of the cost for the medical services consumed by employees. Current design thinking is moving away from the concept of the plan paying all and moving

toward the idea that employees should be more financially responsible for their consumption of services.

2. Should the plan be there to help pay for common medical expenses, or should its role be only to prevent financial catastrophe?

3. What should be the plan's level of responsibility for dependents? Should the plan provide (or share the cost of) coverage for employees only? Should the plan pay all or any part of coverage for dependents? Benefits are compensation. These days, benefits can represent a sizable portion of compensation. If a plan subsidizes the cost of dependent coverage, an employer is, in essence, paying a married employee more than a comparable single employee.

4. Who are dependents? A spouse? Children? Adopted children? Generally these are automatic yeses. Foster children? Live-in mate? Significant other? Parents? Many employers balk at including some among that last group. Why? Employees can go just as broke paying for an ailing dependent parent, for example, as for a child. It is important to design a plan with deliberate thought and to consider what is mainstream and affordable as much as what is theoretically, politically, or socially correct.

5. Is it appropriate for an employer to restrict employees' choices to limit its own costs (and thereby perhaps being able to provide a higher or broader scope of coverage)?

6. Does the employer have the latitude to make design changes? Or is it constricted by union resistance, competitive pressure, or employee reaction? Might an employer gain understanding and agreement with any contemplated changes by explaining the reasons behind the changes?

Q 3:72 What factors should be considered relative to design theory?

The employer should take a careful look at its actual or proposed plan design to see if there are any built-in design fallacies or reverse incentives. In doing this, an employer should consult with its claim processor, which should be able to pinpoint any such problems in the plan.

Reverse incentives encourage employees to use a more expensive form of treatment because they get a higher level of reimbursement. This would include such features as the following:

1. 100 percent reimbursement for inpatient treatment, with a lower rate of reimbursement for outpatient treatment (commonly found in areas such as drug or alcohol treatment), or 100 percent coverage for use of a hospital emergency room, with a lower coverage for visits to a physician's office.

2. Higher rates of coverage for care given in an expensive setting. For example, some plans do not allow adequate (or any) coverage for hospice care, nursing home care for recovery, or home health care, but will provide continuing hospitalization coverage.

Does a plan provide financial protection, or does it actually encourage excessive use of the plan? Perhaps it only fails to encourage thoughtful or judicious use of the benefits available. If the employer's coinsurance rate is set too high, it will not encourage an employee to weigh the need for a medical service or supply. It can therefore be argued that 100 percent coverage for any medical service fails to encourage thoughtful use.

Comprehensive plan designs can address this matter. They require a front-end deductible, then require coinsurance until the 100 percent coverage level is reached. Only after an employee has paid an out-of-pocket maximum expenditure is 100 percent coverage attained. This is a very good design, provided the out-of-pocket maximum is well-placed. If it is placed too low, it will be easily reached. Once it is attained, further services (for that year) will cost the employee nothing. Other types of out-of-pocket limits are those that are specific to the condition or that are related to the employee's salary.

Q 3:73 When might it be advisable to redesign the plan?

An employer considering plan redesign should ask the following questions: Does the current plan support the employer's decisions regarding design philosophy? Is it sending mixed, counterproductive, or outdated messages to employees?

Factors Influencing Insurance Plan Design

If an employer is prepared to redesign all or parts of its plan, it should examine the plan's specific features and consider whether the redesign needs to be a wholesale revision or just a fine tuning. Some specific actions to consider include the following:

1. Exclude preexisting conditions.
2. Add or raise deductibles.
3. Carve out specific types of coverage, such as prescription drugs or mental health.
4. Change from "reasonable and customary" to a scheduled benefit structure.
5. Rethink covering working spouses.
6. Install managed care features.
7. Require use of HMOs.
8. Install wellness programs.

Q 3:74 Why might an employer consider excluding preexisting conditions?

Employers generally do not want to provide health care to employees who have sought employment specifically to obtain health care coverage; therefore, many employers exclude preexisting conditions for new hires and their dependents. Given the restrictions on preexisting conditions imposed by the Health Insurance Portability and Accountability Act of 1996, an employer can justify the use of this exclusion knowing that the only employees who will be excluded are those who did not have prior coverage for a significant period of time. As a result of HIPAA's rules, many employers have eliminated preexisting conditions exclusions. According to surveys by Charles D. Spencer & Associates, 29 percent of employers did not have a preexisting conditions exclusion before HIPAA, but that almost doubled to 47 percent after HIPAA.

Q 3:75 Why might it be advisable to carve out specific types of coverage?

Carving out a coverage means setting it apart from the body of the plan and treating it differently from the rest of the plan. For example, a plan might cover inpatient hospitalization at a 100 percent semiprivate room rate for 365 days, except for mental and nervous conditions, which are limited to 45 days of coverage. It is becoming increasingly popular to carve out mental and nervous conditions because plans have been subject to massive abuse by the provider community.

A still further carve-out is taking place within mental and nervous coverage to refine substance abuse treatments. With the support of the medical community and employee assistance programs, plans are now being structured to limit the number of courses of treatment for which the plan will pay. It has been found that leaving the number of treatments (for the same addiction) open-ended does not help the patient. A plan design worth considering is one that covers a course of treatment at 90 percent or 100 percent for the first time, 50 percent for the second time, and nothing thereafter.

Although it is frequently inadvisable to cover anything at 100 percent, treating an employee for addiction and getting him or her back to productive work is more important than getting a certain percentage of copayment.

There is usually a narrow window of opportunity during which the addicted person is amenable to receiving treatment. The chance to treat the person should not be lost because that person is worrying about coming up with the few hundred or thousand dollars necessary for a high copayment. It is, however, equally important for the person receiving treatment to know that this is a one-time event and that, without exception, the next treatment will involve a payment.

Q 3:76 How can a plan increase cost sharing by employees?

In this question, a cost-sharing increase does not refer to an increase in employee contributions to premium, although some employers have found this necessary in recent years. Here, cost sharing refers to increases in the individual's cost when he or she utilizes health care.

The simplest cost sharing is achieved through implementation of or increases in deductibles and coinsurance percentages. For example, base-plus plans may be changed to comprehensive plans to implement deductibles and coinsurance on all health care expenses. Employers can implement deductible amounts ranging from $100 to $1,000 (or even higher) per individual per calendar year. Special deductibles for certain kinds of care, or for care related to one illness or injury, may also be applied, and deductibles may be based on employee earnings. In a managed care plan, copayments for office visits or prescription drugs can be increased.

Q 3:77 Would increases in required employee contributions toward premium help control costs?

There is a school of thought that employees who are asked to contribute more to health care coverage will feel more entitled to care, and may be less likely to be concerned about the cost and the quantity of care they purchase; however, if an increase in employee contributions is suggested to employees as likely (if costs are not controlled soon), employees may be more responsive to benefit redesign as the alternative.

Some employers have not increased required employee contributions per se, but have offered employees choices in coverage by giving them a certain amount of benefit money to "spend" in order to purchase various insurance benefits. As a result of such plans, called cafeteria plans or flexible benefits plans, employees usually become more aware of the cost of care, because they themselves have made the decision about where to spend their benefit dollars and have elected medical coverage with increased deductibles and coinsurance. Further, some employers include a medical reimbursement account in their cafeteria plans, into which individuals place money through payroll deductions (on a pre-tax basis) to be used for medical care not covered by the health insurance plan. The money is perceived as their own money, and they usually spend it more wisely. It serves as a cushion that makes employees more comfortable with the idea of selecting a medical care plan with a higher deductible. (See Chapter 9 for a more detailed discussion of flexible benefits.)

Q 3:78 Should employers that do not now require employee contributions for health care coverage introduce them?

Yes. The majority of two-adult households are also two-wage-earner households, with nearly universal access to health coverage through employment. A husband and wife with both a contributory and a noncontributory health plan available to them will certainly opt for the plan that does not cost them to join; therefore, claims that would have been submitted to the other employer now become the full liability of the employer with the noncontributory plan. Such plans allow other employers to shift costs, and the only solution is to act defensively by structuring plans to balance or reverse the situation. Some employers "give" employees the money to make the contribution, because the intent is not to collect from employees, but to prevent selection.

Despite contributions, employees may choose to be covered by both available plans, resulting in overinsurance and, in all likelihood, overutilization as well. The level of contributions as well as reduced combined payments under the alternative coordination of benefits (COB) approach should act as disincentives to overinsurance.

Q 3:79 What are average employee contributions for health coverage?

According to a survey by Mercer/Foster Higgins in 1999, 74 percent of employers required contributions for individual coverage under an HMO and 88 percent for family coverage. The average monthly contribution was $38 for individual coverage and $147 for family coverage. For PPOs, the average monthly contribution for a PPO was $49 for individual coverage and $165 for family coverage.

Q 3:80 What might an employer consider doing with regard to deductibles?

It is hard to find an indemnity plan any more that does not contain a deductible. Deductibles may be added to practically any subset of medical coverage, from specific types of treatment to surgical fees. In fact, according to the 1999 Mercer/Foster Higgins survey, 89 percent of employees with indemnity coverage face annual deductibles.

Q 3:81 What are typical deductibles?

A 1999 survey by Mercer/Foster Higgins found median deductibles of $225 per individual and $500 per family.

Deductible rates had been rising steadily when health care costs were increasing sharply, and many employers increased deductible amounts or added separate deductibles for specific services, such as inpatient hospital confinements. For example, an employer that wants employees to stay out of the hospital whenever possible may require that a hospital-admission deductible be added to the plan. This may be in addition to the regular $200 deductible.

Q 3:82 In what circumstances are deductibles waived?

An employer that adds preventive care benefits to the plan may waive the regular annual deductible on that care to encourage employees to use it. The deductible may also be waived on outpatient services such as surgery and home health care to provide a financial incentive for their use. Conversely, an additional deductible may be required for unnecessary emergency room visits.

Q 3:83 What are pay-based deductibles?

Deductibles based on earnings may be achieved by use of a schedule or a formula percentage amount. For example, employees earning less than $20,000 a year may be subject to a $200 deductible; employees earning $20,000 to $40,000 a year, $300; and employees earning more than $40,000, $400. Or each employee may have his or her own deductible, figured as 1 percent or 1 percent of salary, to a maximum of $600. This adds complexity to the plan, may cause dissatisfaction among the more highly paid employees, and is difficult to obtain from commercial insurers. It does, however, provide an equitable way to control costs that takes into account an individual's ability to pay.

Q 3:84 What are the advantages of a pay-based deductible?

The intent of a deductible is to provide for cost sharing, as well as to discourage somewhat the unnecessary use of medical services. It is also intended to place some of the burden for necessary medical services on the user by preventing the plan from paying minor expenses unless the employee has first paid something. Continuing medical expenses are presumed to be creating a financial load on the employee with which he or she needs financial help.

Flat-dollar deductibles create an uneven burden, falling more heavily on lower-paid employees. If a deductible is tied to an employee's pay, every employee should receive an even-handed message that medical services are costly. Because more highly paid employees can shoulder a heavier financial load, it is fair and proper to require them to pay it.

Q 3:85 What are the disadvantages of a pay-based deductible?

It is possible to create some unfair situations. For example, consider a schedule of deductibles that looks like this:

Pay Range	Amount of Deductible
$0–$10,000	$100
$10,001–$20,000	$200
$20,001–$30,000	$300

At first glance, this seems reasonable and well thought-out; however, consider a situation in which two employees had each just received a $5,000 raise. The first employee went from $15,000 to $20,000, while the second went from $15,010 to $20,010. The first employee's deductible stays at $200, while the second employee's deductible goes to $300. Although it is certainly defensible from the employer's standpoint, and is a minor increase in cost compared to the raise, it may seem unfair to the employee who receives a raise and sees a significant percentage of that raise being offset by a higher deductible.

This type of problem can be avoided by making the deductible a fixed percentage of pay; however, there is the question of how pay should be computed. Assume the hourly rate is multiplied by 2,080 hours (to get an annual deductible amount). Should overtime be included? (It certainly affects the employee's ability to pay.) In the event that an employee receives an increase in midyear, should the deductible increase then also? Even with these and other questions resolved, the result will be varying deductibles unless the pay structure is unusually uniform. The administrative complexity of tracking different deductibles for each individual would be horrendous—and costly.

Pay-based deductibles require both additional communication and administration. Computer systems have made administration easier.

In addition, highly paid employees may infer that they are not worth as much to the company as lower-paid employees are. By giving them a benefit program that pays less, an employer would be going against the trend of giving better benefits as well as higher pay to those employees who are worth more to the company. Furthermore, the executives who must approve a pay-based deductible will themselves have to pay more, which is almost certainly a reason why pay-based deductibles are not more common.

Q 3:86 What concerns should an employer have about per-condition deductibles?

Per-condition deductibles are an old plan design feature that is rarely encountered today. There are a number of reasons why this approach is disappearing. Some of them are:

1. *Communication.* At a minimum, an employer will have to communicate so that employees understand their coverage.
2. *Administration.* The claim processor will have to establish a recordkeeping system capable of tracking and maintaining the data. If nothing else, this will add complexity with increased possibility of errors. It will certainly add cost because of the more complicated claim processing necessary. Many computerized claim payment systems cannot handle per-condition deductibles.

Furthermore, it is often difficult to separate expenses by condition. If a patient visits a doctor because of diabetes, high blood pressure, and chronic obstructive pulmonary disease and has satisfied the deductible for diabetes, but not the other conditions, it raises the question of whether the deductible should apply.

Q 3:87 What is a front-end deductible?

A front-end deductible is a deductible that must be satisfied before any covered health insurance expense will be reimbursed. It is also commonly called a first-dollar deductible and is included in a "purely" comprehensive health insurance plan.

Q 3:88 Do all comprehensive plans have front-end deductibles?

Some comprehensive plans do not require a front-end deductible for all covered health care expenses. Such plans most often have a full-pay hospital provision under which no deductible is required for reimbursement of hospital expenses; however, the employee would have to satisfy the deductible before being reimbursed for any other covered health care expenses.

This type of plan design can encourage unnecessary hospitalization because care as an inpatient is financially advantageous. This can, however, be controlled by also including a preauthorization review feature for all hospital confinements.

Q 3:89 What is coinsurance forgiveness?

Coinsurance forgiveness is the controversial practice of forgoing the patient's coinsurance payment by health care providers, accepting as payment only the insurer's portion of the costs of the medical services provided. Insurers and employers tend to view it as simple fraud (or at least breach of contract), but some physicians argue that it is an option for provider benevolence that should be left to their discretion. Except in cases where it is used in conjunction with fraudulent billing or certain advertising practices, forgiveness of coinsurance is not illegal in most states.

Coinsurance forgiveness can be used altruistically by providers that are willing to sacrifice some of their fees to provide services to needy patients whose coinsurance payments may represent a financial hardship, but it can also be used unethically as a marketing tool to attract patients, or even as a basis for health insurance fraud. In the worst cases of fraud, covered patients are provided some service for free (i.e., no coinsurance payment is collected by the provider), but their health insurers are later billed for tests and procedures far beyond what was actually provided. [Lachs, Sindelar, and Horwitz, "The Forgiveness of Coinsurance: Charity or Cheating?" 322 *New England J of Medicine* 22 (May 31, 1990)]

Whether it is motivated by altruism or greed, the effect of coinsurance forgiveness on health insurance is to disrupt the central purpose of the insured's copayment: to give the insured a stake in the cost of medical services, thereby acting as a disincentive to frivolous or unnecessarily expensive treatment. The *New England Journal of Medicine* article cited called coinsurance forgiveness a "common" practice, with 23 percent of surveyed patients in fee-for-service plans reporting having had their coinsurance waived by a provider at least once in three years.

Q 3:90 What effect do increased deductibles and coinsurance have on utilization?

A now famous study by the Rand Corporation demonstrated that although increased cost sharing decreased both inpatient and outpatient utilization, it did not prevent anyone, except the very poor, from seeking necessary care. And, except for the very poor, it had no impact on health.

Q 3:91 How can health care plans be designed to encourage use of the most cost-effective care?

Traditionally, coinsurance provisions have been the only incentive for individuals to seek less expensive care; however, their effectiveness is limited. Many individuals equate expensive care with quality care, and more care with better care. Physicians have encouraged superior care because there was no incentive for them to recommend otherwise, for patients with insurance. As costs have increased, more effective cost-management features have been developed, including coordination of benefits, outpatient surgery coverage, pre-admission testing, second surgical opinion programs, extended care facility coverage, home health care, hospital bill audits, and hospice care.

Q 3:92 Under what circumstances might an employer consider changing from reasonable and customary to a scheduled benefit structure?

A reasonable and customary (R&C) benefit structure is often limited to surgical procedures. Unfortunately, patients tend not to shop for surgeons—particularly not on price. In fact, patients often seek out expensive surgeons on the theory that the most expensive surgeon is likely to be the most expert practitioner. Also, R&C schedules allow the doctor to receive virtually instant feedback on the position of his or her fees in the marketplace. If the doctor's bill is too high, the insurance company will reduce its payment to the maximum of its allowable range and pay it. The doctor is thereby informed what the maximum for that procedure is. If a doctor leaves his or her fee at that level, that doctor contributes to raising the average. Thus R&C schedules have built-in inflation to which a plan automatically adjusts.

By changing to a fixed, scheduled amount, the employer decides when to adjust for inflation. Fixed schedules have never regained their early popularity, probably because too many physicians charged employees high surgical fees, which the employees had to pay because the plan had limited its payment. Employees with large medical payments are certain to complain to their employer about it. Employers who are not prepared to listen to complaints or to stand by the decision to shift the costs to employees may find fixed schedules to be better suited to such services as office visits, where employees are more likely to "price shop" for services.

Q 3:93 Does outpatient surgery coverage help control costs?

Outpatient surgery coverage helps reduce hospital admissions for procedures that can be performed safely in the outpatient department, in a free-standing surgicenter, or even in a doctor's office. These alternatives usually cost less. To encourage the use of such alternatives, some plans provide better payments for outpatient surgery than they do for inpatient care. For example, the plan may waive the deductible for a surgicenter procedure or pay the bill at 100 percent instead of 80 percent.

As more and more plans implement hospital preauthorization programs, differentials in benefit levels for inpatient and outpatient surgery become unnecessary, because utilization management, not benefits incentives, determines the most cost-efficient setting for care.

Factors Influencing Insurance Plan Design   Q 3:94

When a utilization review program is in place that directs employees to use outpatient facilities when appropriate, it is not cost-effective to reimburse such expenses at a higher coinsurance level, because it is not optional. The plan will not pay for unnecessary inpatient care, but pays regular plan benefits for appropriate alternatives; therefore, previous plan design must be considered when adding UR.

Many hospitals have now increased their charges for outpatient surgery to such an extent that outpatient procedures can be more expensive than inpatient confinement; therefore, many employers have eliminated incentives for outpatient surgery.

Q 3:94 What plan features prevent illness and injury, thereby reducing costs in the long run?

Preventive care programs that pay for routine physical examinations and screening tests can help detect symptoms of illness early and prevent its progression. Individuals who take advantage of covered physicals and tests may learn to take better care of themselves, as their physicians educate them on proper wellness care or preventive care strategies.

Other wellness programs, such as lower back care and nutrition workshops, can prevent injury and illness or improve an already existing condition. Programs for weight control, substance abuse, and smoking cessation can significantly affect employee health and the eventual cost of the employer's health care plan. Wellness features such as fitness courses (on-site or at a local facility) or health club memberships are gaining popularity.

Many employers provide their employees with periodic health risk appraisals (HRAs) to help increase awareness and, over the long term, change employees' health-related behaviors in the hope that healthier employees (and their dependents) will result in higher morale and lower claim costs. (HRAs are explained more fully in Chapter 12.)

Employers subsidize, in whole or in part, the cost of such programs either directly (cash payment) or indirectly by waiving deductibles or reducing premium contributions. The net cost of providing a wellness program is generally minimal. The view is that gains from increased productivity, reduced absenteeism, and reduced utilization of medical care will, in the long run, offset the cost if not exceed it. Although many employers make this claim, there is little hard data to support it. Nevertheless, such programs are an essential component of a long-term cost-management program.

Q 3:95 Do any legal factors constrain employers from reducing health care benefits?

Factors that restrict employers in redesigning health plans include, but are not limited to, collective bargaining agreements, state and federal laws and regulations, written agreements and verbal promises, booklets and employee benefit communication materials, and insurance carrier underwriting.

OBRA '93 prohibits group health plans from reducing or eliminating pediatric vaccines coverage.

Q 3:96 Do these factors make it extraordinarily difficult for an employer to redesign its plan?

No, but the redesign must be effected with thought and care. One often-overlooked tactic is simply to distinguish between current and future employees. For example, an employer might announce a plan change with an effective date in the future and state that the change applies to all employees hired (or retired) after that date, but not to employees hired before that date. Thus, the existing workforce is protected, and new employees are not subjected to a change in benefits.

There is, however, some downside to this tactic. First, there may be some discontent when one employee knows that he or she is receiving less "compensation" than a coworker. This potential can be ameliorated by openly and clearly explaining to prospective employees what the situation is and where they fit into the medical plan. Another difficulty with the concept is the increased recordkeeping and administrative tasks needed to track the two groups of employees.

Q 3:97 What steps can employers take to reverse employee insulation from cost exposure?

Consumers must be made aware that their reliance on employers or insurance companies to pick up the tab has greatly contributed to the problem of escalating medical plan costs. Further, consumers must either accept responsibility for making cost-appropriate decisions or accept the consequence of their failure to exercise appropriate judgment, which is to pay the bill out of their own pocket. Making cost-appropriate decisions presumes adequate knowledge on which to base those decisions. If employees do not acquire that knowledge, they must accept someone else's judgment (e.g., be told to enroll in an HMO of the employer's choosing). Failing either to make an appropriate purchase decision or to accept another's decision, they must pay higher prices in return for the freedom to choose their own providers.

Clearly, education is central to this process. It may not be fair to require employers to pick up the cost of educating their employees on issues of this magnitude, but employers do seem to be in the best position to do it. Other steps an employer can take are:

1. Establish a flexible benefits plan that allows employees to select among levels of medical coverage that realistically balance the premium an employee pays against the actual cost of the plan chosen.
2. Offer one or more high quality HMOs, either with or without an indemnity plan.

Q 3:98 What can employers do to combat the problem of inappropriately designed plans?

Employers should decide whether their plan encourages the purchase of medical services in an inappropriate or inefficient setting. Employers should seek assistance from their claim processor or insurance company, which can best see these patterns, if they exist. They can also assist with devising a more appropriate reimbursement structure.

Managed Competition

Q 3:99 What is managed competition?

The term "managed competition" was introduced to the general public and media during the legendary 1994 congressional health care reform debate, although its theory and strategy have been used in the health care marketplace since the late 1980s. Managed competition was conceived by Alan Enthoven, a management professor at Stanford University. He proposed that the health care marketplace would be able to control prices and improve quality if competition among health plans was increased and employees were responsible for paying at least a portion of their health care expenses.

The prototypical managed competition design can include HMOs, (PPOs), point-of-service (POS) plans, and even fee-for-service benefit plans. Under managed competition, all plans have standardized benefits but vary in premium price and special features. For example, some plans may offer health education programs or free membership in a health club. The employer encourages the employee to select the lowest cost plan by making that plan the most economically attractive. Employees have freedom of choice when selecting a health care plan, but pay more if they elect a high-priced plan.

Q 3:100 What elements are common to plans using the managed competition strategy?

The following two key features of plans incorporate managed competition into their benefits strategy:

1. Employees who elect coverage under indemnity and higher-cost managed care plans such as PPOs and POS plans pay more for their health care benefits.

2. Standardized benefits are offered among all competing HMOs. For example, if one HMO covers preventative health care such as immunizations and prenatal care, all HMOs contracted by the employer will offer the same coverage for those services. In addition, employers who strictly conform to the managed competition model limit their health care premium contributions to the full price of the lowest cost HMO contracted.

Employees who select more expensive options, typically POS or fee-for-service, must contribute more, either by paying higher premiums or receiving reduced benefits.

Q 3:101 What should employers consider before incorporating managed competition into their health care benefits strategy?

Before integrating managed competition into a health care benefits program, the employer should consider a number of questions:

1. *How is the employer's current health care benefit package structured?* Any change in the benefit that appears to take away benefit options or limit choices must be introduced carefully. Employee education and adequate time to become familiar with a new system are key in integrating any new benefit structure. This is particularly true for employees who have had a fee-for-service plan with low co-pays in the past.

2. *What benefits does the current health plan offer, and will the benefits be available under new plans?* Standardizing benefits among all HMO choices available to employees is an integral part of managed competition. Elements such as preventive care, the number of allowable physician visits, copays, and deductibles should be consistent over all plans offered.

3. *Which health plans does the employer currently work with?* Before changing carriers, an employer should determine if the current carrier offers, or can accommodate, plans that incorporate managed competition principles. Even traditional health insurance companies will often redesign their benefit offerings to suit the employer's needs. The value of utilization data and the current health plans' knowledge of the employer's operations and employees should be considered before making a decision to change plans.

4. *What are the employer philosophy and the competitive marketplace?* One potential consequence of managed competition is that the plan with the most freedom of choice may become prohibitively expensive. (See the discussions of adverse selection in Chapters 8 and 9.) If this is an unacceptable consequence, either because of the employers benefit philosophy or

competitive pressures, managed competition may not be a good fit.

Q 3:102 Why haven't all employers adopted managed competition in their health care benefits strategy?

Several factors deter employers from implementing managed competition as part of their benefits strategy. Confusion and misconceptions over managed care cause some companies to believe that HMOs offer not only lower-cost health care but also lower quality and fewer choices. The potential for employee dissatisfaction with plan changes and the cost and perceived difficulty of administration for multiple health care plans outweigh the potential benefits of managed competition for some employers. As mentioned, managed competition may not be a good fit, depending on the employers philosophy or the competitive marketplace.

Q 3:103 Are any employers using the principles of managed competition?

Several companies have gone beyond the experimental stage with managed competition. The two largest health plans in the country, the Federal Employees Health Benefit Plan and CalPERS (covering government employees in California), use variations on managed competition.

According to the 1997 Robert Wood Johnson Foundation Employer Health Insurance Survey, only about 27 percent of employees in firms offering a choice of plan face financial incentives to shop for the lower-priced plans, because most employers subsidize the difference in the price of plans by contributing more for the higher-priced plans.

Q 3:104 Are employers who use managed competition incorporating quality improvement measures as well?

The majority of companies using managed competition believe that quality outcomes—and the necessary data to track outcomes—are vital to the success of their programs.

General Motors ranks HMOs on a 100-point scale, with 50 points for quality and 50 points for cost. Based on the scale, HMOs are divided into six categories, with "benchmark" the highest rating. In 2000, employees enrolling in a benchmark plan only pay $35 per month for family coverage. Plans with the lowest ranking cost $190 per month for family coverage.

Q 3:105 What are the disadvantages of managed competition?

Critics of managed competition believe that health plans, specifically HMOs, will select only healthy enrollees and individuals who infrequently use the health care system. Others speculate about the possibility that a few large HMOs would dominate the health care marketplace. They fear that HMOs would wield enough power to dictate to employers, causing a "seller's" market governed by the health plan's rules. Of greater concern is that such a scenario could lead to lower quality care and inferior health outcomes. Another criticism is that managed competition would lead to the development of a two-tiered health care delivery system: one for healthy, high-income individuals who could select high quality plans regardless of cost; and one for lower-income individuals with more serious health problems who, unable to afford extra premiums, would be relegated to lower-cost plans offering potentially inferior quality.

Q 3:106 Is there an advantage in groups of employers working together in a managed competition model?

The larger the base of enrollees, the more negotiating power the health plan sponsor will have. This gives large employers an advantage; however, small businesses can form health care coalitions, joining together to increase the total size of the enrollee population. To the degree that employer groups can agree on specific aspects of a health plan and negotiate the lowest possible price for the benefit, their teamwork may have a great impact on overall health care costs nationwide.

Q 3:107 Does competition between HMOs reduce health care costs?

Yes. According to a study published in the July/August 1996 issue of *Medical Practice Management*, employer groups saw a slowdown in the growth rate of health premiums where there is a high market penetration by HMOs. On average, a 10 percent increase in HMO market penetration led to a 6.6 percent decrease in the rate of growth in health insurance premiums.

Chapter 4

State and Federal Laws

A variety of state and federal laws regulate the group health insurance market. This chapter covers most of these laws, except for Section 125 of the Internal Revenue Code, (addressed in Chapter 9), Medicare (covered in Chapter 10), nondiscrimination rules (discussed in Chapter 11), COBRA (covered by Chapter 13) and Form 5500s (addressed in Chapter 14).

Legal Factors Affecting Design	4-1
State Law	4-11
Federal Law	4-21
Pregnancy Discrimination Act	4-29
Family and Medical Leave Act	4-31
Americans with Disabilities Act	4-36
Health Insurance Portability and Accountability Act	4-44
Taxation of Group Health Plans	4-63
Reservists' Benefits	4-65

Legal Factors Affecting Design

Q 4:1 Are employers required by federal law to provide medical coverage to employees?

No.

Q 4:2 What requirements do federal regulations directly impose?

There are several major federal laws that directly regulate health plans once they are established. These include the Employee Retirement Income Security Act of 1974 (ERISA); the Health Insurance Portability and Accountability Act of 1996 (HIPAA); the Mental Health Parity Act of 1996; the Newborns' and Mothers' Health Protection Act of 1996 (NMHPA); Consolidated Omnibus Budget Reconciliation Act of 1985 (COBRA); the Pregnancy Discrimination Act (PDA); the Age Discrimination in Employment Act (ADEA); Omnibus Budget Reconciliation Act of 1993 (OBRA '93); the Women's Health and Cancer Rights Act (WHCRA); and Family and Medical Leave Act (FMLA). The PDA is an amendment to Title VII of the Civil Rights Act of 1964. There is also the HMO Act of 1973, which does not directly regulate plan design or operation, but affects employer contributions. A few of these laws have been amended repeatedly.

A brief statement of the requirements of these laws is set forth below. As appropriate, a more comprehensive treatment of the requirements of each law is dealt with in this or other chapters. Also omitted at this point is any discussion of IRS regulation as it pertains to health plans. IRS regulations are dealt with in the specific areas in which they have relevance, notably in flex plans and spending accounts in which Internal Revenue Code Section 125 has sway.

ERISA, as its name implies, was written mostly to protect pensions, not medical insurance plans; however, in defining a "plan," the law specifically includes "welfare plans" within its scope. The six general requirements of the law follow:

1. Plans must be established pursuant to a written document.
2. Plans must be administered according to the document, as it is written.
3. The document must be written in such a way as to be understandable by the "average" employee, and copies of a summary plan description (SPD) must be given to each participant.
4. The document must describe the benefits provided by the plan, and must specifically indicate conditions that will cause forfeiture or denial of benefits.
5. The document must indicate who administers the plan and who pays the benefits (how the plan is funded).

6. Annual financial reports must be provided to the government, with shortened versions (summary annual reports, or SARs) being provided to participants.

COBRA was a comprehensive piece of legislation covering a wide variety of topics, only a small portion of which applies to medical insurance. Notwithstanding, that small piece is of major consequence and has captured exclusive use of the acronym. Whenever reference is made to the COBRA legislation or its requirements, the reference is to the obligation levied on employers to allow employees or their covered dependents to have continuing coverage in the employer's medical plan beyond the date their coverage would otherwise have terminated, providing the insured person pays the full cost of coverage.

The PDA requires employers to treat disabilities or medical conditions resulting from pregnancy or childbirth in the same manner as any other disability or medical condition. This means that plans cannot contain limitations, restrictions, or caps that apply specifically to pregnancy or childbirth and not to any other condition. The law applies to all plans sponsored by an employer, including the following:

- Health insurance
- Disability or salary continuation plans
- Sick leave
- Employment policies, including seniority, leave extensions, and reinstatement

The ADEA prohibits discrimination in employment against individuals aged 40 and older. There is no upper age cap on the protection provided by this law. The law's primary intent was to prohibit mandatory retirement (with limited exceptions). Certain provisions of the law relate to health insurance. Employers with 20 or more employees must provide the same medical coverage to older employees as to younger employees. This requirement includes retaining the employer's plan as primary even if the employee is entitled to benefits under Medicare. Also specifically prohibited is the use of cost-justified reductions of health insurance coverage, despite the fact that such reductions are permitted for life and disability insurance.

The HMO Act mandated the "dual choice option." This provision has sunset. Any employer that chooses to offer a health maintenance organization (HMO) must comply with financial nondiscrimination rules (see Chapter 8).

Like COBRA, OBRA '93 is a comprehensive piece of legislation that includes significant provisions (though far fewer than COBRA) concerning employer health benefit plans. Its major effect is requiring coverage of children covered by qualified medical child support orders.

The FMLA requires most employers to permit employees to take as much as 12 weeks of unpaid leave annually in situations determined by Congress to be crucial to the well-being of the workers' family. Specifically, employees must be allowed to take FMLA leave upon the birth of a child; upon adopting a child or receiving a child for foster care; when the employee must care for a child, spouse, or parent who has a serious health condition; or when the employee is unable to perform his or her duties because of a serious health condition. Employees must be allowed to continue health insurance during FMLA leave.

HIPAA included the most sweeping changes to employer-provided health benefits since the COBRA group health continuation requirements were enacted in 1986. Among other things, the act does the following:

1. Restricts preexisting conditions exclusions.
2. Prohibits plans from dropping or denying coverage for employees with medical conditions.
3. Makes reforms to small employer plans and individual plans.
4. Creates medical savings accounts (MSAs) for small employers, for a test period.
5. Allows employers to provide long-term care insurance tax-free (but not through a cafeteria plan).
6. Allows chronically ill and terminally ill individuals to receive tax-free accelerated death benefits.
7. Amends the COBRA continuation requirements.
8. Includes anti-fraud provisions.

9. Disallows the interest deduction on corporate-owned life insurance.

The Mental Health Parity Act of 1996 prohibits employers with 50 or more employees from imposing annual or lifetime dollar limits on mental health treatment (but not substance abuse treatment). The Mental Health Parity Act is discussed in Chapter 22.

The Newborns and Mothers Health Protection Act of 1996 requires health plans to cover stays of at least 48 hours for normal delivery and 96 hours for cesarean section.

Under the Women's Health and Cancer Rights Act, group health plans offering mastectomy coverage must also provide coverage for reconstructive surgery.

Q 4:3 Are employers required by state law to provide medical coverage to employees?

There is only one state with legislation requiring employers to provide medical coverage for their employees. Hawaii is the only state with an active employer mandate, requiring that basic medical and hospitalization coverage be provided to employees working more than 20 hours per week.

Massachusetts was to begin a program to require employers with six or more employees to pay a tax or offer health insurance in 1992, but implementation of the plan was postponed repeatedly before the law was repealed. Oregon's plan to require large and medium-sized employers to provide coverage for employees could not be implemented because Congress did not grant a necessary ERISA waiver. The state of Washington created a plan that included both employer and individual mandates, but has repealed it. Minnesota also repealed a law calling for universal coverage.

Q 4:4 What medical coverage requirements do states impose?

Typically, when a state imposes a requirement it falls into one of three categories:

1. Mandating that a service, type of provider, or category of treatment be included as covered in a health plan;

2. Requiring actions by employers or insurers that they would not otherwise have taken, such as continuation of coverage under the plan beyond the point it would have normally ceased (i.e., at termination of employment); or
3. Categorizing the plan as a source of revenue and imposing surcharges or taxes.

Q 4:5 To help hold costs down, can an employer choose what specifically will be covered?

This answer varies, largely based on how the plan is funded. If the plan is conventionally insured, any one employer will have little or no latitude in choosing specific types of services or procedures that will be covered. An employer would not, for example, be able to obtain a contract that did not cover heart disease or cancer. The reason is that insurance companies must register their contracts with the state insurance commissioner of each state in which they do business. State insurance commissioners are interested in having broad spectrum coverage and would be unlikely to allow contracts with these types of exclusions. Further, most states have enacted legislation requiring that specific benefits or coverage be included in products being offered in their states. Such legislation broadens, rather than narrows, the scope of coverage.

If the plan is self-funded, it is immunized from this type of state regulation. ERISA provides a broad exemption to covered benefit plans by removing regulation from the state level and placing it in the federal level. Until the passage of the Newborns' and Mothers' Health Protection Act of 1996, federal-level regulation did not include mandating benefits. Thus, a self-funded employer can become somewhat more creative than a traditionally insured employer in structuring a plan to cover or not cover various items.

Q 4:6 When an employer self-funds to enhance flexibility in design, must it cover everything allowed by the IRS as a deduction?

No. Most medical plans confine their scope of coverage to curing an illness or treating an injury. Some plans are expanding their scope of coverage to include prevention and certain "wellness" programs. In contrast, the IRS will allow as a medical deduction many expenses that are not directly related to treating or curing a medical condition. For example, allowable deductions have been known to include air conditioners, air purifiers, and even swimming pools. Few medical plans would be prepared to accept these or other such items as covered expenses.

Q 4:7 Is it necessary to cover things of which the employer disapproves, such as abortions or vasectomies?

While in theory it is possible to exclude or limit specific types of coverage, in practice, an employer trying to do so would be on the defensive at best.

Regarding abortion: Federal law does not require coverage for voluntary abortions, nor does it prevent such an exclusion.

Q 4:8 Can an employer require employees to purchase maternity (or family) coverage if they are single?

No, but an employer could deny coverage for the child of an employee who had single coverage. Medical benefits, which include maternity benefits, are provided to the employed individual. On the basis of that relationship, an employer cannot require women to purchase additional coverage for something that would apply only to them (i.e., maternity-related benefits); however, an employer has no obligation to cover the child of an employee who does not have dependent coverage. In fact, plans can exclude maternity coverage for children even if the employee has family coverage because it is not discriminatory to exclude coverage for children of both male and female employees. Some states have laws that require coverage for complications of pregnancy.

Q 4:9 Can an employer elect to make its plan secondary to Medicare after employees become eligible for Medicare?

No. Federal law requires that employers provide coverage to older workers and their spouses on the same basis as younger workers. In that context, the employer's plan must remain primary to Medicare unless the employee elects otherwise. When employees or their spouses become eligible for Medicare, they must be offered the option of selecting which coverage will be primary—the employer's plan or Medicare. If the selection is for coverage under the employer plan, coverage under Medicare may be established as secondary; however, if the choice is for Medicare as primary, the employee must waive coverage under the employer plan. The employee may make independent decisions for himself or herself and his or her spouse.

Furthermore, under OBRA '93, group health plans are not allowed to take into account Medicaid eligibility when enrolling participants or paying benefits.

Regulations issued August 31, 1995 impose a $5,000 penalty for each violation of a new interpretation of this rule. The regulations say employers cannot offer Medicare beneficiaries financial incentives not to enroll in a group health plan.

Q 4:10 Can an employer assume that employees will choose the employer's plan as primary?

No. An employer must be diligent in its efforts to contact eligible employees to obtain their selection. The selection should be in writing, signed by the employee, and should clearly state which plan the employee is choosing as primary.

Q 4:11 Can an employer encourage its employees to select Medicare as primary?

No, an employer cannot provide any sort of encouragement or incentive to employees to cause them to make a decision in favor of Medicare as primary. Further, if the employee selects Medicare as primary, the employer cannot (1) provide secondary coverage, (2) provide supplemental coverage, or (3) pay for Part B on the employee's behalf.

Regulations issued August 31, 1995 impose a $5,000 penalty for each violation of a new interpretation of this rule. The regulations say employers cannot offer Medicare beneficiaries financial incentives not to enroll in a group health plan.

Q 4:12 Can an employee who makes extensive use of the coverage be required to pay a greater premium or contribution?

Under the terms of HIPAA, group health plans cannot base any benefits or premiums on any health-related factors, including claim experience.

Q 4:13 Must an employer cover spouses of employees?

No. Indeed, employers are even starting to move away from the old standard of providing spousal coverage at little or no cost to the employee. It is becoming common for employers to establish a fixed percentage of the premium they are prepared to pay for spouses. For example, a company might establish its share of the cost at 50 percent or 75 percent and require employees to pay the remainder. This is also true for family coverage.

Q 4:14 Are MEWAs governed by state or federal law?

As defined in ERISA Section 340A, a multiple employer welfare arrangement (MEWA) is an employee welfare benefit plan or other arrangement designed to provide benefits to employees of two or more employers. MEWAs are specifically referred to in ERISA Section 514 as generally being subject to state insurance laws governing required reserves and contributions needed to pay claims.

The language of ERISA has, however, caused confusion as to just what constitutes a MEWA and where the line between state and federal control lies. As a consequence, many self-funded MEWAs have gone unregulated and have been managed fraudulently, in some cases under the cover of bogus unions created for the sole purpose of selling insurance. By offering lower premiums, these self-funded MEWAs have attracted unsuspecting small businesses, which have been left with millions of dollars of unpaid claims when the MEWA folded. These cases are the subject of a series of ongoing lawsuits.

State insurance commissioners are working with the Department of Labor (DOL) to resolve the jurisdictional dispute. In an attempt to clarify the situation, the DOL has published a booklet explaining state and federal regulation of MEWAs: "MEWAs. Multiple Employer Welfare Arrangements Under the Employee Retiree Income Security Act: A Guide to Federal and State Regulation."

On August 1, 1995, the DOL proposed regulations on this subject. Effective in 2000, MEWAs must file an annual report (Form M-1) with the federal government.

Q 4:15 When state and federal laws change, what are an employer's obligations regarding a group health insurance plan?

Although it is the employer's responsibility to see that its plan complies with applicable laws, the complexity of these laws makes reliance on assistance from insurers or intermediaries essential. Insurers are required by law to write legally acceptable benefits plans and, therefore, take the responsibility for helping employers comply with the laws. Insurers generally take responsibility for informing employers about legislative developments. The insurer, with the intermediary, will explain exactly how the new law affects the employer and will outline how and when the employer's plan must change to comply with the new law.

Groups that self-fund must comply with laws that affect self-funded plans. Generally, the intermediary, third-party administrator, or insurance company, if it is administering the plan, will take responsibility for informing the employer about legislative developments.

Changes to laws that affect group health insurance plans usually fall into one of three categories: laws that (1) affect only policies issued after the effective date of the law, (2) not only affect newly issued policies but also require compliance at the next renewal date of an already existing policy, and (3) require compliance at any upcoming change to an existing policy, but at least at the next anniversary date of the policy. Some laws simply require that policyholders be offered the opportunity to purchase a new benefit. In that situation, the employer has the right to refuse to change the existing benefit plan.

Plans that are offered pursuant to a collective bargaining agreement will generally not be required to make legislated changes until the expiration of that agreement.

State Law

Q 4:16 Are group health plans governed by federal or state law?

Group health plans may be governed by both. As employee benefit plans, or welfare plans, they are governed by federal laws that contain provisions pertaining to such things as nondiscriminatory participation requirements, reporting and disclosure, continuation of coverage for former employees, and taxation.

If the benefits are provided under an insurance contract, the contractual provisions are governed by state, rather than federal, law. This was provided for by the McCarran-Ferguson Act, which, as of 1948, provided that federal law will regulate insurance only when state law does not. Each state has its own laws governing contracts, including those for insurance, and most states have laws specifically covering group life and health insurance.

States usually have an appointed official who oversees the operations of insurers in that state, commonly either a Superintendent or Commissioner of Insurance. In addition, the National Association of Insurance Commissioners (NAIC), a voluntary organization of state insurance officials with influence but no legislative authority, has developed standard model bills and procedures that are designed to provide some consistency from state to state. Although there has been general acceptance of model laws on a number of issues, leading to substantial uniformity, there are other issues on which the various states have chosen to pursue their own distinct policies.

Q 4:17 Do both federal and state laws apply to self-funded group health plans?

Most federal laws that govern group health insurance plans apply to all welfare plans and, therefore, to self-funded plans. State laws do not apply because ERISA preempts state laws governing self-funded plans; however, the matter is not quite that clear cut: Section 514 of ERISA states that ERISA will "supersede any and all State laws insofar as they may now or hereafter relate to any employee benefit plans," but that may not be "construed to exempt or relieve any person from any law of any state which regulates insurance, banking or securities." (The law goes on to say that neither an employee benefit plan nor a trust established under such a plan "shall be deemed to be an insurance company.")

Naturally, if federal law governs the plan and its provisions, but state law governs the insurance contracts and the benefits they provide, conflicts are bound to arise over where the jurisdictional line is actually drawn. Challenges to state authority over insured employee benefit plans have, however, generally been unsuccessful, as have state attempts to extend that authority to self-funded plans. This means that self-funded plans are safe from the threat of state mandates, and companies sponsoring welfare plans have their choice of two bodies of law. If they select a commercial insurer's product, they may choose to be governed by a combination of state insurance law and federal employee benefit law, or, should they decide to self-fund, they must comply only with federal law.

If an employer purchases stop-loss insurance, the insurance company providing stop-loss coverage must comply with state insurance laws; therefore, some indirect state regulation of nominally self-funded plans takes place.

Q 4:18 Has the Supreme Court affirmed this division between state insurance and federal law?

Yes. In *FMC Corp. v. Holliday,* involving a Pennsylvania law, the Supreme Court in a 7-1 decision ruled that self-funded plans fall under the jurisdiction of federal law and that state laws are preempted. [111 S Ct 403 (1990)] The case concerned the Pennsylvania Motor Vehicle Financial Responsibility Law, which prohibits subrogation or reimbursement from damage awards to a claimant in a tort proceeding. (Subrogation clauses in insurance policies allow the insurer to step into the shoes of an insured and press a claim against an injuring party as repayment for amounts the insurer paid as claims to the injured party.)

The FMC Corp. case stemmed from a 1987 incident in which Cynthia Holliday was injured in a car accident. Her father was employed by FMC Corporation, whose health care plan covered Cynthia as a dependent. The plan picked up $100,000 of her $178,000 medical bill. Subsequently, she was awarded a $49,875.50 judgment against the other driver. FMC claimed that it was entitled to this money under a subrogation provision of the plan, which required claimants to reimburse the plan from benefits received from other sources.

FMC argued that the Pennsylvania law prohibiting subrogation was preempted by ERISA. Both federal district and appeals courts sided with the state and with Cynthia's family in barring the subrogation, running counter to opinions on similar issues handed down by appellate courts in other jurisdictions. The Supreme Court, citing ERISA preemption, overruled the lower courts and found in FMC's favor.

The court's ruling reaffirmed a 1985 decision that barred states from regulating self-funded plans. The earlier challenge involved a Massachusetts law, which required group health insurance plans sponsored by private employers to provide mental health benefits of up to 60 days of inpatient treatment in a mental hospital and up to $500 of outpatient treatment a year. Metropolitan Life and Travelers balked, citing ERISA (as well as the National Labor Relations Act, which makes welfare benefits a mandatory subject of collective bargaining). [Metropolitan Life Ins Co v Massachusetts, 105 S Ct 2380 (1985)] The intent of Congress, the insurers argued, was to allow the marketplace to shape the design of such plans, and to allow Congress to establish whatever minimum standards were necessary on a uniform national basis, without the interference of each of the 50 states. The Supreme Court disagreed and upheld Massachusetts, but only for insured plans. It expressly did not extend the ruling to self-funded plans, or to those plans for which an insurer provides administrative services only.

Additional challenges to the strength of the ERISA preemption may meet with more success. Two recent examples further demonstrate how differently preemption is being interpreted:

1. Washington, D.C. attempted to modify its workers' compensation law to require that area employers provide disabled work-

ers with continuing medical plan participation, on the same basis as active employees received, for up to 52 weeks. Workers' compensation programs are within the states' purview and are specifically exempted from the requirements and regulation of ERISA. Notwithstanding, Justice Clarence Thomas, writing for the majority in an 8-1 vote, said that state laws may not "specifically refer" to any benefit plan protected by ERISA. Going still further, the court concluded that by linking the workers' compensation program to the federally regulated health program, the District had made its plan subject to the preemption. In a practical sense, this ruling will make it virtually impossible for a state to link any of its programs (i.e., workers' compensation, unemployment compensation, or disability benefits) to an ERISA-regulated plan. [Greater Washington Bd of Trade v District of Columbia, 948 F 2d 1317, 14 EBC 1791 (DC Cir 1991), *cert granted* 112 S Ct 1584 (1992)]

2. New York state imposed a surcharge on hospital fees. The surcharge was payable by any insured plan, self-funded plan, or HMO that paid for hospital fees on behalf of covered participants. The law varied the rate of the surcharge on the basis of the plan's funding. That is, a self-funded plan would pay a 9 percent surcharge, an HMO a 13 percent surcharge, and an insured plan a 24 percent surcharge. Plans insured by Blue Cross/Blue Shield were exempt from the surcharge. Suit was brought by Travelers Insurance Company, which prevailed in federal district court. The Supreme Court ruled that ERISA does not preempt this law because the surcharges do not "relate to" employee benefit plans within the meaning of ERISA's preemption. [New York State Conference of Blue Cross & Blue Shield Plans, et al v Travelers Insurance Company, et al, US Sup Ct No 93-1408]

Q 4:19 What are the responsibilities of the state insurance department?

The state insurance department is the administrative agency that supervises the insurance companies doing business in that state. The insurance department is assigned the task of making sure that carriers obey the insurance laws. Areas of responsibility include licensing companies and agents, issuing regulations, conducting examinations of companies, making legislative recommendations, monitoring fees and rates, handling customer complaints, adopting model bills, and performing any other duty that will ensure that state insurance laws are kept up-to-date and adequately enforced. Insurance contracts must be filed with and approved by the insurance commissioner before being offered for sale within that state.

Q 4:20 What are the similarities among state laws governing group health insurance?

Most states, having adopted NAIC model bills, have similar programs that govern each of the following: minimum participation, eligibility, certificates to insureds, payment of premiums, grace periods, claim processing, the appeals process, and the coordination of health insurance benefits among insurers' plans. Despite these somewhat standard provisions, laws governing specific required benefits vary considerably from state to state. These mandatory state programs generally fall into three categories: mandated benefits or coverage, mandated offerings of benefits, and right of direct payment. According to a study by the Blue Cross and Blue Shield Association, every state has at least one such requirement, and a number of states had more than 20.

Q 4:21 What is a mandated benefit?

A mandated benefit is a specific coverage that an insurer is required to include in its contract under state law. For example, most states require that coverage for substance-abuse treatment be provided. Other kinds of coverage that are mandated in some states include coverage for newborn children, mental and nervous disorders, and hospice care.

States may differ in the way they require the insurer to provide the mandated benefits. Some states require that benefits be provided on the same basis as for any other illness; others require that an insurer provide a minimum specified benefit (for example, an annual dollar amount or number of visits for each individual for claims relating to certain types of care).

Q 4:22 Are self-funded plans exempt from state mandates?

In general, state-mandated benefits are being viewed by the courts as an attempt to regulate plans. As such, these attempts are meeting with little success. ERISA does not, however, preempt states in their regulation of insurance. While at times the line between the business of insurance and employee benefit regulation is unclear and must be addressed by the courts, a Supreme Court ruling indicates that self-funded plans are exempt from state insurance mandates (see Q 4:18).

Q 4:23 Why are some benefits mandated by state law?

Some states mandate benefits because it is felt that a need is not being covered satisfactorily. Benefits that are mandated are usually intended to promote a widely recognized social goal, while limiting state expenditures for that type of care.

Q 4:24 What are the most commonly mandated benefits?

According to the National Underwriter, more than half of the 50 states have mandated some type of benefits for:

- Well baby care
- Psychological services
- Chiropractic services
- Extended protection for people with disabilities
- Conversion privilege
- Optometry
- Alcoholism treatment
- Dental care
- Continuation coverage
- Podiatry

According to a report by the Blue Cross and Blue Shield Association, the most popular new mandates in 1997 were:

- Emergency room services (20 states)
- Minimum hospital stay for mastectomy (14 states)
- Mental health parity (8 states)

Q 4:25 How extensive are state-mandated benefits?

States have passed more than 700 laws mandating various coverages. To state four generalizations:

1. Almost every state has a requirement for mandatory coverage of alcohol treatment; most also require substance abuse coverage.
2. Many states also mandate mental health coverage and list the types of providers that will be covered (e.g., social workers).
3. States regulate the coverage of employees' dependent children.
4. Many states mandate coverage of certain preventive or diagnostic services, such as mammography or Pap smears.

Q 4:26 How much do mandates increase the cost of health insurance?

Milliman & Robertson analyzed 12 common mandates and found that they could increase total costs by 15 to 30 percent. At the high end, that could amount to more than $1,000 per employee per year.

The detailed estimates are as follows:

Benefit	Estimated Additional Annual Cost
1. Minimum-stay maternity	Less than 1%
2. Speech therapy	Less than 1%
3. Drug abuse treatment	Less than 1%
4. Mammography screening	Less than 1%
5. Well child care	Less than 1%
6. Podiatry	Less than 1%
7. Papanicolaou (Pap) smears	Less than 1%
8. Vision exams	1% to 3%
9. Chiropractic treatment	1% to 3%
10. Alcoholism treatment	1% to 3%
11. Infertility treatment	3% to 5%
12. Mental health care	5% to 10%

Q 4:27 What is a mandated offering?

A mandated offering is coverage that must be made available to each policyholder. The coverage is extended to the employer as an additional price option; the employer is not required to purchase it. Unlike a mandated benefit, a mandated offering is not required to be part of every group insurance policy.

Q 4:28 What are the state requirements for employee participation in a group insurance plan?

State laws require that insurance companies set participation percentages to ensure against adverse selection, which could jeopardize the insurer's solvency. In most states, the participation requirement is 75 percent. This means that at least 75 percent of an employer's eligible employees must participate in a group health insurance plan.

Q 4:29 What is the minimum number of employees allowed by state law to participate in a group health insurance plan?

Most states require that an employer enroll a minimum number of employees (generally 10, but fewer in some states) for coverage in order to purchase and maintain a group health insurance plan. This minimum size requirement reduces the potential for adverse selection. Employers with fewer than 10 enrolled employees often participate in a group insurance trust, such as a multiple employer welfare arrangement.

Q 4:30 Is there a maximum number of employees that may be covered under a group health insurance plan?

There is no legal limit to the number of employees that may be covered under a group health insurance plan. Some plans cover tens of thousands of employees.

Q 4:31 Are there state laws governing parental or family leave?

Yes. Almost half of the states have enacted legislation that requires employers to permit natural or adoptive parents to take unpaid leave to care for a child. While the laws vary considerably from one jurisdiction to another, they generally provide that employers with a minimum number of employees (at least 25, although a number of states specify higher numbers such as 50 or 100) must allow employees (usually permanent employees, those who have been with the employer for a year or more) to take leave of from 6 weeks to 12 months within a specified period (12 to 24 months, usually commencing with the child's birth or adoption). The laws also govern matters such as notice of intent to return, reinstatement procedures, continuation of benefits, compensation, and penalties for failure to comply. A number of states have broader family leave laws. If state law is more generous to an employee than FMLA, the employer must comply with the state law.

Q 4:32 What is the New York surcharge?

Effective January 1, 1997, an 8.18 percent tax applies to all health care provided in the state of New York. Plans that do not file with the state of New York will have to pay an additional 24 percent surcharge. There are also professional education pool surcharges that vary by region, which can also be avoided by filing. The surcharge applies to services rendered in New York, even if people based elsewhere are only traveling through New York on vacation or business. The New York Health Care Reform Act of 2000 extended the surcharges through June 30, 2003.

Q 4:33 What is the Massachusetts surcharge?

From January 1, 1998 through September 30, 1999, a 5.06 percent surcharge applied to acute care hospital and ambulatory services provided in the state of Massachusetts. Effective October 1, 1999, the surcharge was reduced to 3 percent. The surcharge applies to any entity (including insurers, HMOs, TPAs, and self-administered plans) that pays hospital bills, whether it is based in Massachusetts or not. The surcharge applies to anyone receiving services in Massachusetts, regardless of the patient's state of residence or where the employer is based. Workers' compensation, Medicare, and Medicaid are exempt from the surcharge.

Q 4:34 Does the Massachusetts surcharge increase the coinsurance amount paid by the employee?

No. The surcharge is based on the payment to the facility. For example, if an insurer receives a $5,000 hospital bill, has a contract that calls for a payment of $2,500, and pays $2,000 (80 percent), the surcharge is 3 percent of $2,000. Therefore, the employee's coinsurance is not affected by the surcharge.

Q 4:35 What is a living wage ordinance?

Over 40 local governments have passed what is known as a living wage ordinance. These local laws mandate a wage higher than the minimum wage and typically mandate benefits, including health insurance. Most of these ordinances apply only to employers with city (or county) contracts or subsidies. The wages with benefits range from $6.25 an hour in Milwaukee to $10.44 in Detroit. San Jose mandates an hourly wage of $10.75 without benefits. Most are between $7 and $9 per hour. Other cities with living wages include Berkeley, Boston, Cambridge, Los Angeles, Miami, Oakland, Pasadena, Portland, San Antonio, San Francisco, and Tucson.

Q 4:36 What can employers do to cope with mandated coverage?

In the case of state government mandates, employers can become politically aware and active on these issues. Either individually, or as a member of a local business coalition, employers can make their opinions known to the appropriate legislators and work to prevent mandating—and perhaps even undo some existing mandates. For insurance company mandates, employers can meet with representatives from their insurance carrier to determine both whether that carrier has any such requirements and the medical or other justifications for them. The employer that disagrees with the requirement can ask to have it be removed from its contract. A third alternative is to self-fund. Self-funding provides broad-spectrum immunity against state mandates and practically perfect protection against insurance company mandates.

Federal Law

Q 4:37 What federal laws affect group health insurance plans?

Federal law has a pervasive influence on the design and operation of group health plans. The laws may be categorized in four ways:

1. Laws enacted primarily to protect employees from discrimination in employment. Although these laws may not specifically address group health insurance issues, they do contain relevant regulations. The most important of these laws are the Age Discrimination in Employment Act of 1967, as amended in 1968; Title VII of the Civil Rights Act of 1964, as amended; the Pregnancy Discrimination Act; and the Americans with Disabilities Act.

2. Laws addressing specific health insurance issues. The most important of these include the 1965 amendment to the Old Age, Survivors' and Disability Insurance Act (OASDI), which established Medicare, effective July 1966; the HMO Act of 1973, as amended in 1988, which governs the terms on which HMO coverage is offered to employees; COBRA, which requires that health care coverage continue to be made available to former employees and their dependents; the FMLA, which requires employers to continue health care coverage while an employee is on family or medical leave; the HIPAA, which limits pre-existing conditions exclusions; the NMHPA, which mandates minimum lengths of hospital stay for childbirth; and the Mental Health Parity Act of 1996, which prohibits certain types of maximums on mental health treatment.

3. Laws that set general standards for the operation of employee benefit plans. Most prominent of these is ERISA, which makes federal law preeminent regarding employee benefit plans, establishes standards for fiduciaries charged with administering these plans, and imposes standards for reporting and disclosure.

4. Laws governing the tax consequences of group health plans as they affect employers, employees, and the plans themselves. These rules, including standards that must be met to qualify for employer tax deductions and exclusion from employee income, are found in the Internal Revenue Code (Code), treasury regulations, IRS rulings, and periodic amendments to the law itself, such as the Tax Equity and Fiscal Responsibility Act of 1982 (TEFRA), the Deficit Reduction Act of 1984, and the Technical and Miscellaneous Revenue Act of 1988 (TAMRA).

The Supreme Court has also ruled that the federal Racketeer Influenced and Corrupt Organizations Act can apply to a health insurance plan. The case is *Humana Inc. et al. v. Mary Forsyth et al.* In this case, a group of Nevada residents sued Humana's Nevada plan alleging overcharging on copayments. Humana had agreed to pay 80 percent of charges after a deductible. Humana negotiated discounts with a hospital, but based the patient's 20 percent on the undiscounted amount.

Q 4:38 What does the Newborns' and Mothers' Health Protection Act of 1996 require?

President Clinton signed the NMHPA on September 26, 1996. It became effective for plan years beginning on or after January 1, 1998.

The legislation requires health plans to cover at least a 48-hour hospital stay for normal deliveries and at least 96 hours for cesarean sections. Plans cannot require precertification of maternity stays. Mothers can choose to leave the hospital sooner than 48 hours or 96 hours, but health plans cannot provide any incentives for them to leave early. Plans cannot impose any penalties on mothers who take advantage of the new minimum length of stay.

Q 4:39 Do all health plans have to provide minimum hospital stays in connection with childbirth?

No. NMHPAs requirements only apply to group health plans, insurance companies, and HMOs that choose to provide insurance coverage for a hospital stay in connection with childbirth. NMHPA does not require group health plans, insurance companies, or HMOs to provide coverage for hospital stays in connection with the birth of a child. If a plan covers only outpatient treatment in connection with childbirth, NMHPA does not apply.

Q 4:40 May group health plans, insurance companies, or HMOs impose deductibles or other cost-sharing provisions for hospital stays in connection with childbirth?

Yes. NMHPA does not prevent a group health plan, insurance company, or HMO from imposing deductibles, coinsurance, or other cost-sharing measures for health benefits relating to hospital stays in connection with childbirth as long as such cost-sharing measures are not greater than those imposed on any other types of hospital stays.

Q 4:41 Are there any regulations providing guidance on how to comply with NMHPA?

Yes, on October 27, 1998, the Departments of Labor, Treasury, and Health and Human Services issued interim regulations under the Newborns' and Mothers' Health Protection Act of 1996. Under NMHPA, plans cannot require precertification of maternity stays. The interim regulations clarify that plans can require patients to notify the plan in advance of an admission to reduce out-of-pocket costs. For example, if a plan generally covers 70 percent of the cost of a hospital stay, but will cover 80 percent if a patient calls and notifies the plan of the pregnancy, the notification requirement is permissable.

Q 4:42 Is there a notice requirement under NMHPA?

Yes. Plans can comply by including the following statement in their SPDs:

> Under federal law, group health plans and health insurance issuers offering group health insurance coverage generally may not restrict benefits for any hospital length of stay in connection with childbirth for the mother or newborn child to less than 48 hours following a vaginal delivery, or less than 96 hours following a delivery by cesarean section. However, the plan or issuer may pay for a shorter stay if the attending provider (e.g., your

physician, nurse midwife, or physician assistant), after consultation with the mother, discharges the mother or newborn earlier.

Also, under federal law, plans and issuers may not set the level of benefits or out-of-pocket costs so that any later portion of the 48-hour (or 96-hour) stay is treated in a manner less favorable to the mother or newborn than any earlier portion of the stay.

In addition, a plan or issuer may not, under federal law, require that a physician or other health care provider obtain authorization for prescribing a length of stay of up to 48 hours (or 96 hours); however, to use certain providers or facilities, or to reduce out-of-pocket costs, precertification may be required. For information on precertification, contact your plan administrator.

Q 4:43 May a group health plan require preauthorization of a maternity stay?

Plans, insurance companies, and HMOs generally can require employees to notify the plan of the pregnancy in advance of an admission if the patient wishes to use certain providers or facilities, or to reduce out-of-pocket costs.

Example 4-1. A group health plan generally covers 70 percent of the cost of a hospital stay in connection with childbirth; however, the plan will cover 80 percent of the cost of the stay if called and notified of the pregnancy in advance of admission and the plan designates the participating hospital the plan designates. In this example, the plan's notification requirement is permissible.

Q 4:44 How does ADEA affect group health insurance plans?

The Age Discrimination in Employment Act prohibits discrimination in employment against individuals aged 40 and older (until January 1, 1987, the maximum protected age was 70). Although the main intent of this law is to prohibit mandatory retirement (with certain exceptions), related provisions of the law apply to health insurance. ADEA, as amended in 1986, requires employers with 20 or more employees to offer all active employees and their spouses, regardless of age or eligibility for Medicare, the same coverage. ADEA does not permit cost-justified reductions for health insurance, although such reductions are permitted for life and disability insurance.

Q 4:45 Are employers required by federal law to cover retired employees under group health insurance plans?

No. Employment law generally applies to active employees. The decision to cover retirees is a human resource issue, rather than a legal requirement. The employer should examine its employee benefit objectives to decide whether to cover retirees. If a company is encouraging early retirement to manage expenses and avoid layoffs, it might be in the best interest of the company to provide health insurance coverage to retirees. Most retirees aged 65 and older have access to health insurance through Medicare, so coverage through an employer's plan would be supplemental. The cost of retiree coverage is high in spite of the share paid by Medicare.

A related issue is the right of employers to discontinue retiree health care once it has been made available. Attempts to do so have generally been challenged in court, with mixed results. (For more information, see the discussion of retiree health care in Chapter 23.)

Q 4:46 What requirements does ERISA impose on group health insurance plans?

ERISA was enacted primarily to effect pension equity, but it also protects the interests of welfare benefit plan participants and beneficiaries. Under ERISA, group health insurance plans must be established pursuant to a written instrument that describes the benefits provided under the plan, names the persons responsible for the operation of the plan, and spells out the arrangements for funding and amending the plan.

ERISA established a reporting procedure that requires that a summary plan description and an annual financial report be filed with the Department of Labor. Plan participants must be given copies of the SPD and the summary annual report. Simplified reporting requirements apply to plans with fewer than 100 participants because Congress considered the reporting requirements too burdensome for small employers (see Chapter 14).

ERISA also requires that fiduciaries be bonded. Bonding protects a plan against loss because of fraud or dishonesty. The bonding requirement does not apply to insured plans or totally unfunded plans.

Q 4:47 What does ERISA require regarding employee contributions?

The rule for transmitting participant contributions to a plan is that the contributions must be deposited to the plan within 90 days. DOL plan asset regulations require self-funded plan sponsors to deposit participant contributions into a trust, typically a 501(c)(9) trust. The rules generally require employers to transmit participant contributions to retirement plans within 15 days but welfare plans have up to 90 days.

If an employer can reasonably be expected to transmit contributions sooner, then the contributions must be transmitted sooner. Fully insured plans are exempt from the requirement.

Cafeteria plans are not currently subject to the 90-day limit. The preamble to the regulations clarifies that some after-tax contributions, such as COBRA premiums or retiree contributions, to a cafeteria plan will not affect the relief granted to cafeteria plans.

Q 4:48 How were group health insurance plans affected by the HMO Act of 1973?

The provision of the HMO Act that had the most significant effect on group health insurance plans was the "dual choice option." This provision required that employers with 25 or more employees in a health maintenance organization service area include HMO coverage as an alternative to the employer's regular health plan if requested by an HMO to do so. The law required that at least one group-practice and one individual-practice HMO be offered to employees if the employer received a request for inclusion by each type. HMOs were responsible for requesting inclusion by employers as alternative health plans, and were subject to certain federal requirements in order for employers to be required to recognize them.

This dual choice option (which expired in 1995 under a "sunset" provision included in HMO amendments passed in 1988) was established to encourage individuals to consider coverage under an HMO instead of under their employer's traditional plan. (HMOs are discussed in detail in Chapter 8.)

Now, employers that choose to offer an HMO must make contributions on behalf of their employees to an HMO sufficient to ensure that HMO enrollees are not discriminated against; that is, the contributions must be reasonable and assure a fair choice among competing health plans. This can mean equal dollars, equal percentage of premiums, equal contributions for demographic groups, or negotiated rates between employer and HMO.

Q 4:49 What is the Women's Health and Cancer Rights Act?

President Clinton signed the Women's Health and Cancer Rights Act of 1998 (WHCRA) into law on October 21, 1998. Under WHCRA, group health plans offering mastectomy coverage must also provide coverage for reconstructive surgery.

Q 4:50 What are the notice requirements under WHCRA?

A group health plan must furnish a written description of the benefits that WHCRA requires upon enrollment in the plan and annually thereafter. These notices must be delivered in accordance with the Department of Labor's disclosure regulations applicable to furnishing summary plan descriptions. For example, the notices may be provided by first class mail or any other means of delivery prescribed in the regulation. It is the view of the DOL that a separate notice must be furnished to a group health plan beneficiary where the last known address of the beneficiary is different than the last known address of the covered participant.

Q 4:51 Is there any guidance as to what the WHCRA notice should say?

On October 20, 1999, the Department of Labor and the Department of Health and Human Services issued questions and answers addressing the notice requirements of WHCRA. There are three notice requirements under WHCRA. The first notice should have been provided to all participants and beneficiaries by January 1, 1999. The second must be provided to participants upon enrollment. The third is an annual notice requirement.

The guidance indicates that the annual notice can be delivered anytime during a plan year. The annual notice must be sent by a method of delivery consistent with the regulations governing distribution of summary plan descriptions. The notice may be separate or may be included in other communications, such as open enrollment materials, a benefit newsletter, or a summary annual report.

To avoid duplication of notices a group health plan can contract with an insurance company or HMO to provide the notice. The same notice can be used as the enrollment notice and the annual notice. The guidance included the following model notice.

> Did you know that your plan, as required by the Women's Health and Cancer Rights Act of 1998, provides benefits for mastectomy-related services including reconstruction and surgery to achieve symmetry between the breasts, prostheses, and complications resulting from a mastectomy (including lymphedema)? Call your Plan Administrator [insert phone number] for more information.

Q 4:52   Does WHCRA apply to all group health plans?

All group health plans, and their insurance companies or HMOs, that provide coverage for medical and surgical benefits with respect to a mastectomy are subject to the requirements of WHCRA.

Q 4:53   Does federal law prohibit employers from making any changes in coverage?

Yes, in one instance. OBRA '93 effectively freezes the childhood vaccine coverage of every group health plan at the level it was on May 1, 1993. This provision specifically prohibits plans from reducing or eliminating coverage for pediatric vaccines that appear on a list compiled by the Health and Human Services Department's Advisory Committee on Immigration Practices.

Pregnancy Discrimination Act

Q 4:54 What is the Pregnancy Discrimination Act?

The PDA is an amendment to Title VII of the Civil Rights Act of 1964. It requires employers to regard disabilities or medical conditions associated with pregnancy and childbirth the same as other disabilities or medical conditions. That means that these conditions receive the same treatment as is afforded to similarly situated individuals who have not experienced pregnancy or childbirth. Similar treatment extends to the following:

- Disability benefits
- Health insurance benefits
- Short-term sick leave
- Employment policies including seniority, leave extensions, and reinstatement

Q 4:55 What does "the same" treatment for pregnancy-related medical conditions mean?

It means that, if employees are offered a choice among several different health care plans, pregnancy-related coverage must be available in all of them, and that there may be no distinction made in the applicability of such items as the following:

- Terms of reimbursement, including maximum reimbursable amount
- Deductibles, copayments, and out-of-pocket maximums
- Choice of physician and hospitals

Q 4:56 What employers are subject to the PDA?

Title VII of the Civil Rights Act applies to all private employers who employ 15 or more employees each working day for 20 or more weeks in the current or the preceding calendar year. Court decisions have interpreted coverage standards broadly, to include part-time employees, independent contractors, successor corporations, parent-subsidiary groups, and other groups of employers who are affiliated or under common control.

Q 4:57 Do the provisions of the Pregnancy Discrimination Act apply only to married employees?

No. Pregnancy-related disability benefits may not be restricted to married employees, unless all benefits are so restricted.

Q 4:58 Does the Pregnancy Discrimination Act extend to benefits for spouses of employees?

Yes. According to the Supreme Court, [Newport News Shipbuilding & Dry Dock v EEOC, 462 US 669 (1983)] if the employer provides health insurance coverage for spouses, benefits for pregnancy-related conditions of employees' spouses must be the same as those for non-pregnant spouses and the spouses of female employees.

Q 4:59 Does the PDA extend to other dependents?

Health insurance plans need not cover the pregnancy-related conditions of employees' daughters and other dependents, provided the pregnancy-related conditions of male and female employees' dependents are excluded on an equal basis. (Note: complications of pregnancy for dependent daughters are usually required to be treated as any other illness under many state laws.)

Q 4:60 Must abortions be covered by employer health plans under the PDA?

No, the act specifically states that employer plans are not required to provide for abortions, unless the mother's life would be endangered by carrying the fetus to term, or there are medical complications that have arisen from an abortion.

This does not prevent employers from choosing to provide abortion benefits, and most insurance carriers provide options regarding this coverage. Under the Equal Employment Opportunity Commission (EEOC) guidelines, those employers who choose to provide abortion benefits must do so in the same manner and at the same level as for benefits for other medical conditions.

Q 4:61 Are state laws preempted by the PDA?

Not necessarily. State laws that require more generous benefits than those required by the PDA have generally been upheld. Some state laws, such as those of California, extend the PDA mandates to employers who are not covered by Title VII. Many states have maternity provisions that require employers to provide benefits for "complicated maternities" on the same basis as for any other illness. These complications include caesarean delivery, therapeutic abortion, miscarriage, toxemia, and other defined conditions. Benefits for dependent children, in addition to employees and spouses, may be mandated as well.

Family and Medical Leave Act

Q 4:62 Are there federal laws governing family leave?

Yes. The Family and Medical Leave Act, originally vetoed by President Bush, was signed into law by President Clinton on February 5, 1993. It went into effect exactly six months later, on August 5, 1993.

The law requires employers with 50 or more employees to provide at least 12 weeks of unpaid leave to eligible employees for the birth and care of a newborn child, adoption of a child, or serious illness of the employee or the employee's spouse, child, or parent. In the case of the birth or adoption of a child, the 12 weeks must be taken within the 12 months following the birth or adoption.

An employee who meets the following three criteria is an eligible employee:

1. Employed by the employer for at least 12 months (not necessarily consecutively);
2. Worked a minimum of 1,250 hours during the last year; and

3. Works at a worksite that has 50 or more employees (or employs 50 or more people within 75 miles using surface transportation).

FMLA requires that the employee must be returned to the same or equivalent position on return from leave. The "equivalent position" provision is strict; it refers specifically to pay, benefits, privileges, and any other terms or conditions of employment (although it does allow a narrow exemption for key employees). The law also requires employers to maintain during the leave any health benefits normally provided to the employee while working.

Employees have responsibilities under FMLA as well. The law requires employees seeking leave to provide at least 30 days of notice when possible or, if not (as in a sudden medical situation), notice as early as is possible. Employers may also require employees to provide certification of the relevant medical condition and may obligate employees on leave to "check in" with the employer periodically in order to report status.

Q 4:63 Are there regulations regarding family leave?

Yes. The DOL published final regulations on January 6, 1995. They were effective April 6, 1995.

Q 4:64 How does FMLA affect benefits?

Under FMLA, covered employers must maintain any existing group health coverage during the leave and, when the worker returns, reinstate the employee to the same or an equivalent job with equivalent benefits. This includes family or dependent coverage, without any qualifying period, physical examinations, or exclusion of preexisting conditions.

Q 4:65 Does FMLA require any notices about benefits?

Employers must give advance written notice of the terms for paying premiums during FMLA leave. Employers cannot apply more stringent requirements to employees on FMLA leave than to those on other forms of leave. Employers also must give 15 days' notice that coverage will stop if the employee's premium is more than 30 days late. An employer with policies on other unpaid leave that permit ending the coverage retroactively (to the first date of the unpaid premium) may do so for FMLA leave if the 15-day notice was given. If no policy exists for other unpaid leave, coverage terminates at the end of the 30 days after payment was due, if the employer gave the 15-day notice. In addition, employers must post a notice about FMLA and give certain information to employees who document the need for FMLA. If an employer has an employee handbook, it must include FMLA policies.

Q 4:66 What are the consequences for noncompliance with FMLA?

An employer that violates FMLA by not maintaining group health benefits as required is liable for the employee's medical expenses that would have been covered. If a plan is insured, the employer becomes self-funded for this liability. There also are penalties if an employer fails to post the required notice.

Employees who believe their rights have been violated can file a complaint with the U.S. Department of Labor or file a private lawsuit. Employees who win lawsuits may be entitled to wages or benefits lost as a result of the employer's violation. If leave was denied, the employer may be required to pay any actual monetary loss sustained by the employee as a direct result of the violation, such as the cost of providing care. Amounts equal to the preceding sums also may be awarded as liquidated damages unless the court reduces the amount because the violation was in good faith and the employer had reasonable grounds for believing it complied with FMLA. When appropriate, the employee also may obtain employment reinstatement or promotion. Employees also may recover attorneys' fees, expert witness fees, and other costs.

Q 4:67 What happens if an employee switches to a part-time schedule under FMLA?

Full-time employees who switch to part time under FMLA must continue to receive the same (full) level of benefits they had before starting FMLA leave. The employee may not be required to pay more to maintain the same benefit level as before the part-time schedule, regardless of any employer policy applicable to part-time employees that would cause a different result. An employer can proportionately reduce the kinds of benefits based on the number of hours worked during the period, for example, vacation or sick leave. Life or disability insurance or other benefits determined by amount of earnings also may be reduced during the period.

Q 4:68 What if the plan changes while an employee is on FMLA leave?

Plan changes, such as premium increases or higher deductibles, that apply to active employees also apply to those on FMLA leave. The FMLA extends no greater right to benefits for eligible employees than they would receive if they worked continuously during the leave. An employee who would have lost benefits if continuously employed instead of taking FMLA leave is not entitled to retain the benefits simply because of the leave. This means employees who take FMLA leave before using all of their flexible spending account (FSA) for unreimbursed medical care will still forfeit unused amounts at year-end.

Q 4:69 Can an employer pay an employee's premiums while the worker is on FMLA leave?

Yes. An employer may elect to pay premiums continuously to avoid a coverage lapse in non-health benefits, such as life or disability insurance. If payments have been made, the employer is entitled to recover the employee's share of any premiums—even if employees argue that they did not want coverage during the leave.

Q 4:70 What if a collective bargaining agreement requires more than FMLA?

Nothing in FMLA diminishes an employer's obligations under a collective bargaining agreement or benefit plan to grant greater family or medical leave rights to employees than those under FMLA.

Q 4:71 Does FMLA affect employee-pay-all benefits?

Benefits paid by employees through voluntary deductions are excluded from the FMLA definition of a group health plan. Employers are not responsible for maintaining or restoring individual policies for employees who take FMLA leave.

Q 4:72 What is the difference between maternity leave and parental or family leave?

Maternity leave stems from the characterization of pregnancy as a "disability." Pregnancy disability laws, both federal and state, refer only to females and are in effect only as long as the attendant disability persists (or is legally presumed to persist). Family leave, on the other hand, is not conditioned upon the physical health of the employee.

Family leave under FMLA applies to both sexes.

The PDA protects those taking pregnancy leave. Additional time off, for males or females, to care for newborn children, newly adopted children, or children who are ill, is allowed by FMLA.

Q 4:73 What features are typically found in employer family leave policies?

In addition to what is required by the PDA and FMLA, many companies have policies regarding time off for expectant or new mothers, fathers, or other employees who need to look after a close relative. Following are six common features of such leave policies:

1. Paid maternity leave, combining prenatal and postnatal time off.
2. Unpaid leave for care of a newborn or newly adopted child for periods up to three years.
3. Continuation of some or all employee benefits during the period of absence.
4. Reinstatement provisions that guarantee reinstatement to the employee's original job if he or she returns to work within a specified period of time, usually not more than six months.

5. Reinstatement to a comparable job if return to work occurs after a stated period (for example, six months).
6. A best effort to place the employee in a job consistent with the employee's training, experience, and other qualifications if the period of leave exceeds a certain number of months.

Americans with Disabilities Act

Q 4:74 What is the ADA?

The ADA bars discrimination against persons with disabilities in transportation, public facilities, and employment.

The EEOC issued final regulations under the ADA on July 26, 1991. The EEOC has also released a technical assistance manual on ADA, and on June 8, 1993, approved interim enforcement guidelines on the application of ADA to disability-based distinctions in employer-provided health insurance.

Q 4:75 How does the ADA affect employers and their employees?

In addition to its prohibitions against discrimination in public accommodations, the ADA prohibits discrimination against disabled individuals in areas relating to hiring, firing, pay, promotion, training, and other terms and conditions of employment. The regulations embrace rates of and changes in pay and other forms of compensation; leaves of absence and sick leave; fringe benefits; all forms of training, including apprenticeships, training leaves of absence, and professional conferences and meetings; and employer-sponsored social and recreational programs.

Q 4:76 What businesses are affected?

Employers with 15 or more workers are required to comply with the law. Employers who can demonstrate that the required changes would cause an undue business hardship are exempt in certain circumstances.

Q 4:77 What do employers need to do to comply with the ADA?

Failing to make reasonable accommodation for an otherwise qualified individual with a disability, unless such accommodations would impose an "undue hardship" on the business, constitutes discrimination. It is difficult for employers to prove that necessary accommodations will actually cause undue hardship because the average cost of accommodation ranges from $100 to $380. In addition, tax credits are available for businesses with revenues of less than $1 million or fewer than 30 employees. Furthermore, failing to hire an otherwise qualified individual solely because the company would have to make a reasonable accommodation constitutes discrimination. Employers may not discriminate in this way, nor can they:

1. Select or administer preemployment tests in a way that reflects the impact of a disability rather than measuring relevant job skills or aptitudes;
2. Use qualifying standards or tests that screen out applicants with disabilities unless the standards are job-related and consistent with business necessity (i.e., driving ability for a driving job, physical requirements for pilots); or
3. Hire or promote individuals with disabilities who cannot perform the essential functions of the job with reasonable accommodation.

Q 4:78 What constitutes an undue business hardship?

The EEOC will look at the following four factors in reviewing an undue hardship claim by an employer:

1. The type and cost of the proposed accommodation;
2. The overall financial resources of the employer;
3. The type of business conducted at the location; and
4. The impact on the operation itself and the ability of the other workers to perform their jobs.

Q 4:79 What is a disability?

A person has a disability if he or she:

1. Has a mental or physical impairment that "substantially" limits one or more major life activities;
2. Has a record of such an impairment; or
3. Is perceived as having such an impairment.

Impairment can be any physiological or mental condition, including cosmetic disfigurement, even though compensated for or controlled by medication or a medical or prosthetic device. Major life activities include self-care, walking, seeing, hearing, speaking, breathing, sitting, standing, lifting, reaching, learning, working, or performing manual tasks. Whether the impairment substantially interferes with one or more of these activities will be determined by taking into consideration its severity, duration, and impact. A short-term or temporary impairment, such as a broken leg, would not be considered a protected impairment.

On June 22, 1999, the United States Supreme Court issued three decisions that narrow the definition of a disability under the Americans with Disabilities Act. The decisions overturn guidelines issued by the EEOC that said disability determinations must ignore mitigating measures, such as medication and prosthetic devices; therefore, someone who would be blind without eyeglasses, but whose vision is corrected by glasses, is not disabled under the ADA.

On May 24, 1999, the U.S. Supreme Court ruled that a person can pursue a claim under the ADA while simultaneously claiming disability benefits under Social Security. Social Security provides disability benefits to people who are unable to do their previous work and cannot engage in any other kind of substantial gainful work. The ADA only gives rights to employees if they can perform the essential functions of their jobs, with or without reasonable accommodation. Some lower courts had ruled that it was impossible to be disabled under Social Security while also being able to perform the essential functions of a job. The U.S. Supreme Court said employees should have the opportunity to proceed under both ADA and Social Security if they can explain the inconsistencies between their claims.

The Court noted there are differences in the definition of disability under ADA and Social Security. For example, Social Security determines disability without regard to accommodations; therefore, it is possible to qualify for Social Security disability benefits even though an accommodation would make it possible to perform a job.

Q 4:80 Are substance abusers considered disabled?

Individuals who are current users of illegal or controlled substances are not afforded ADA protection, although past substance abusers are.

Q 4:81 Who is a qualified individual with a disability?

The ADA defines a "qualified individual with a disability" as a person who has a mental or physical disability, but who is still qualified to perform the essential functions of a job. Employers may not discriminate against such individuals when they can perform these essential functions with or without reasonable accommodation.

Q 4:82 What is an essential job function?

While the determination as to what is an essential job function must ultimately be made on a case-by-case basis, job functions may be recognized as essential because they are: (1) so highly specialized that only a limited number of persons with special skills can fill the positions or (2) the principal reason that the job exists.

Employers may substantiate their decision as to what is essential and what is not through written job descriptions or through factors such as:

- The amount of time needed to perform the function
- The effect on the job of not performing the function
- Past experience of holders of the job
- The employer's own judgment

Q 4:83 What is reasonable accommodation?

Reasonable accommodation is any change in the work environment that permits a person with a disability to enjoy equal employment opportunities. Reasonable accommodation includes the following:

1. Converting existing facilities to make them accessible and usable by persons with disabilities;
2. Using part-time or otherwise modified work schedules;
3. Restructuring the job or reassigning the individual;
4. Acquiring or modifying equipment or devices used in the job; and
5. Restructuring training and support, including providing readers and interpreters.

Q 4:84 What effect has the ADA had on business?

Since its passage, the Americans with Disabilities Act of 1990 has reshaped employment, governmental services, telecommunications, public accommodations, and, perhaps most importantly, public attitudes, says Peter Blanck, a senior fellow with the Annenberg Washington Program in Communications Policy Studies of Northwestern University. A professor of law and psychology at the University of Iowa, and a commissioner on the American Bar Association Commission on Mental and Physical Disability Law, Blanck wrote an extensive report for the Annenberg Washington Program on the ADA accommodations made by Sears, Roebuck and Co. for its disabled workers. [Communicating the Americans with Disabilities Act Transcending Compliance: A Case Report on Sears, Roebuck and Co., The Annenberg Washington Program, Washington, DC, 1994] In his report, Blanck said:

> The ADA is the most comprehensive federal law to address discrimination against an estimated 49 million Americans with disabilities. Its implementation remains the subject of intense public policy debate, particularly in light of the larger and related debates on health care and welfare reform. . . . Sears, which employs an estimated 20,000 people with disabilities, provides a case study of a company with a long-standing commitment to its employees with disabilities.

> In the company's data on the cost of accommodating Sears associates with disabilities from 1978 to 1992, the most striking is the finding that almost all accommodation at Sears (97 percent) requires little or no cost. Such accommodation includes flexible scheduling, longer training periods, back-support belts, revised job descriptions, rest periods, enhanced lighting, adjusted work stations, and supported chairs or stools.
>
> Examples of higher accommodation costs include $1,275 for a work station for an employee with a visual impairment and $16,850 to accommodate an employee who is completely blind. Specific accommodation for the latter are a Braille display at $14,500, a voice synthesizer at $1,200, and software and hardware at $1,150.
>
> Other accommodation costs include $2,413 for work station additions (software at $2,200 and an audio-capture card at $213) for an associate with a physical disability, $500 for a railing in a rest room to accommodate wheelchair access for an employee, $400 for a light-controlled fire alarm system for an employee who is severely hearing-impaired, $80 for an electric stapler for an employee who suffers from Reynauds disease with resulting pain and lack of dexterity in her hands, and a no-cost schedule change to reduce stress for an employee who is subject to epileptic seizures.
>
> Sears also provided more expensive, state-of-the-art information technology accommodation that enabled groups of associates with and without disabilities to perform information-intensive jobs productively, cost effectively, and accurately. During 1993 the company spent $130,000 on information technology accommodation for 12 associates.

Blanck concludes his 47-page report by saying the ADA does not create onerous legal burdens, but rather a framework for dispute resolution and litigation avoidance.

Other observers agree. The Job Accommodation Network, in Morgantown, WV, an organization that assists employers in complying with the ADA, reports that employers generally have found that the changes needed to accommodate workers with disabilities are inexpensive. Network's staff members have surveyed more than 1,000 companies and found that half of the responding companies spent less than $200 on accommodation. The average amount spent on accommodation was $1,057, according to an article in *Business &*

Health [Medical Economics Publishing, Montvale, NJ] in July 1995. Many employers reported a return on their investment of $28 for every $1 spent on accommodation, Network officials said. Some 54 percent of the 1,000 companies surveyed said they had been able to hire or retain qualified workers, 29 percent eliminated the cost of retraining a new worker, 36 percent saved workers' compensation or other insurance costs, and 52 percent reported productivity increased.

Metropolitan Life Insurance Company has determined that 88 percent of employees with a disability can be accommodated under the ADA for less than $1,000 and 31 percent for less than $50.

Q 4:85 How does the ADA affect the hiring process?

An individual who is qualified may not be denied a position because of a disability. An employer may describe the essential functions of the job and inquire as to the applicant's ability to perform them, but may not inquire about the origins of an impairment or the prognosis for it. The ability to perform marginal, as opposed to essential, job functions may not be considered. Also, the application cannot contain a laundry list of impairments.

Q 4:86 Are preemployment physicals permitted?

Yes, but only after an offer is made, and only if such physicals are job-related and are required of all employees in the same job category, and if the results are confidential. Employment may, however, be contingent upon passing the physical.

Post-hire physicals for such illnesses as AIDS (or HIV infection) and cancer are prohibited unless the employer can demonstrate that they are job-related and a business necessity, or they are mandated by the government.

Q 4:87 How does the ADA affect health insurance benefits?

The regulations reemphasize the law's intent to ensure that employees with disabilities have equal access to the same health insurance coverage provided to other employees. That does not mean that certain plan provisions that have an especially adverse effect on employees with disabilities are necessarily prohibited. Preexisting condition clauses, for example, may be acceptable, provided they are not a subterfuge to evade the purposes of ADA. Limits on certain types of treatment or medications are also permissible (such as x-rays or experimental drugs), even if these would likely be more heavily used by people having certain categories of disabilities (e.g., blood transfusions for hemophiliacs), so long as the limitations apply across the board to all covered employees, and do not restrict access to other forms of treatment.

The impact of an individual's disability on health care costs, or the failure of the employer to cover expenses associated with an applicant's disability, may not be taken into account in making the hiring decision.

Q 4:88 Are health insurance plans that conform to state law exempt from the ADA?

Section 501 of the ADA provides a special exemption for employee benefit programs that permits insurers, HMOs, and sponsoring employers (for insured or self-funded plans) to classify, insure, and administer plans in ways that are in accord with accepted underwriting practices under the appropriate state insurance laws, provided the practice is not a subterfuge for avoiding the ADA.

Q 4:89 How does the ADA affect leave policies?

Leave policies that are applied evenhandedly to all employees are not per se discriminatory. Limits on sick leave will not violate the ADA even if such a policy would mean more of a hardship for disabled workers with disabilities, who might tend to use more sick time than other workers.

Q 4:90 Do the EEOC regulations offer detailed guidance for employers in specific employment situations?

No. The EEOC admits that while the regulations offer some guidance, many of the determinations as to what is discrimination and what is not will have to be made on a case-by-case basis. For employers familiar with the Rehabilitation Act of 1973 (which requires federal contractors to take affirmative action to employ and advance handicapped persons and to attempt reasonably to accommodate those persons), the ADA regulations may look familiar, as they are modeled on the Rehabilitation Act regulations.

Q 4:91 Where can employers obtain more information about the ADA?

The EEOC's *ADA Technical Assistance Manual* can be ordered from U.S. government bookstores.

Health Insurance Portability and Accountability Act

Q 4:92 When were the provisions of HIPAA effective?

Most of HIPAA's provisions were effective for plan years beginning on or after July 1, 1997. The requirement to provide certificates of coverage was effective June 1, 1997, regardless of the plan year. If later, HIPAA applies to collectively bargained plans on the first day of the plan year beginning after the expiration of a collective bargaining agreement in effect as of August 21, 1996, without regard to any extensions.

Q 4:93 What does HIPAA require regarding preexisting condition exclusions?

HIPAA provides that group health plans have to reduce any preexisting condition exclusion period by the length of time a person had prior coverage. Prior coverage does not count if there was a "significant break in coverage" (63 days or longer, not counting waiting periods). Creditable coverage includes the following:

- Group health plans
- Individual plans
- Medicare
- Medicaid

- Military-sponsored health care
- A program of the Indian Health Service
- A state risk pool
- The Federal Employees Health Benefits Plan
- A public plan (as defined by regulations)
- A plan of the Peace Corps

Creditable coverage does not include dental or vision coverage. It is not clear whether creditable coverage includes foreign coverage, either private or through a national health insurance program. Conservative employers and insurers will want to treat foreign coverage as creditable coverage until further guidance is available.

The act permits a group health plan to impose a preexisting condition exclusion if the exclusion relates to a condition (physical or mental) for which medical advice, diagnosis, care, or treatment was recommended or received within the six-month "look back" period ending on the "enrollment date." The exclusion cannot extend more than 12 months (18 months for late enrollees) after the enrollment date. The exclusion period is reduced by the period of prior coverage. The act defines enrollment date as the earlier of the date of enrollment or the first day of a waiting period (usually the date of hire). Genetic information is not considered a condition in the absence of a diagnosis of the condition. The legislative history makes it clear that states can require insured plans to be more generous, such as by shortening the 6- or 12-month periods.

Waiting periods must run concurrently with any preexisting condition exclusion. Preexisting condition exclusions cannot apply to newborn children or adopted children or children placed for adoption if they are covered within 30 days of birth, adoption, or placement. Preexisting condition exclusions cannot apply to pregnancies.

HMOs can impose preexisting condition exclusions only if they do not impose any waiting period. Any waiting period cannot exceed two months (three months for late enrollees).

A plan must inform employees if it has a preexisting condition exclusion. The plan must also notify employees of the right to show evidence of prior creditable coverage to reduce the preexisting condition period. If the plan does apply a preexisting condition exclusion, the plan must make a determination regarding each individuals creditable coverage. Within a reasonable time after the employee provides a certificate (or other information relating to creditable coverage) a plan is required to make a determination regarding the length of any preexisting condition exclusion period that applies to that individual and to notify the employee of the determination. The notice must also inform the employee of the basis of the determination, including the source and substance of any information on which the plan relied.

The plan may later modify its initial determination if it later determines that the employee did not have the creditable coverage claimed. The plan must notify the employee of its reconsideration and, until a final determination is made, the plan must act in accordance with its initial determination for purposes of approving medical services.

Q 4:94   Does HIPAA apply to flexible spending accounts?

ERISA Technical Release 97-01 clarifies the application of the HIPAA portability provisions to FSAs. The release clarifies that it is appropriate to treat benefits under certain health FSAs as exempt from HIPAA's portability provisions. If a health FSA is offered in conjunction with another group health plan and if the employer contributions do not exceed a specified amount, the benefits under the health FSA will not be subject to HIPAA. Accordingly, the coverage under the FSA will not be creditable coverage, and the FSA is not required to issue certificates for the coverage. The maximum benefit under the health FSA cannot exceed two times the employee's salary reduction election (or, if greater, the amount of the salary reduction election, plus $500).

Health FSAs funded solely by salary reduction will satisfy the exemption requirement as long as the employee is eligible for group medical coverage. Many health FSAs include an employer match; as long as the match does not exceed the salary reduction and group medical coverage is available, these plans will be excepted from HIPAA's requirements. Under credit-based cafeteria plans, if the employee can direct more than $500 to a health FSA, the FSA will be subject to HIPAA's requirements.

If a health FSA satisfies these requirements, it means that HIPAA's certification, portability, creditable coverage, and special enrollment requirements will not apply.

Q 4:95 Who is a late enrollee?

A late enrollee is an individual who enrolls in a plan other than on either (1) the earliest date on which coverage can become effective under the terms of the plan, or (2) a special enrollment date.

Q 4:96 What does HIPAA require regarding waiting periods?

HIPAA does not prohibit a plan from having a waiting period; however, a waiting period must run concurrently with any preexisting condition exclusion period.

Waiting periods do not count as either creditable coverage or a break in coverage. If an individual obtains an individual policy, the period between the date the individual files a substantially complete application for coverage and the first day of coverage is a waiting period.

Q 4:97 How can employees prove they had prior coverage?

Individuals can establish a creditable coverage period by presenting a certificate describing previous coverage, which can include limited or short-term coverage. HIPAA requires group health plans to provide a certificate of the periods of coverage under the plan, under COBRA continuation, and for waiting periods. This certificate must be provided when the individual ceases to be covered under the plan, after any COBRA continuation coverage ceases, and on the request of an individual within two years after coverage ceased. If possible, the certificate can be provided with the COBRA notice. Insured plans do not have to provide the certificate if the insurer provides it.

Q 4:98 How can an employee who does not receive a certificate receive credit for prior coverage?

The first step should be to contact the plan administrator of the former plan and request a copy. If the creditable coverage was insured or provided through an HMO, the employee can also contact the insurer or HMO for a certificate.

The employee who does not receive a certificate may demonstrate to the new plan that he or she had creditable coverage by producing documentation or other evidence of creditable coverage. Evidence includes pay stubs that reflect a deduction for health insurance, explanations of benefits, or verification by a doctor or other health care provider that the employee had prior health insurance. Accordingly, employees should keep these records in case they need them.

Q 4:99   Do plans that do not impose a preexisting condition exclusion have to provide certificates?

Yes.

Q 4:100   Can plans contract with the insurer or HMO to provide the certificates for their employees?

Yes. The law requires both the plan and the "issuer" (insurer or HMO) to provide a certificate. To avoid duplication of certificates, a plan may contract with the issuer to provide the certificate. Furthermore, if one entity (including a third-party administrator) provides a certificate to an individual, no other party is required to provide the certificate.

Q 4:101   When must group health plans and issuers provide certificates?

Plans and issuers (insurers and HMOs) must furnish the certificate automatically to individuals for whom the following event occurs, by the following deadline noted in parentheses:

1. Entitled to elect COBRA continuation coverage (by the deadline for a notice to be provided for a qualifying event under COBRA);
2. Losing coverage under a group health plan who is not entitled to elect COBRA continuation coverage (within a reasonable time after coverage ceases); and
3. COBRA coverage has ceased (within a reasonable time).

Plans and issuers must also provide employees with a certificate if the employee requests one, at the earliest time that a plan or issuer, acting in a reasonable and prompt fashion, can provide the certificate.

Q 4:102   Is there a model certificate that group health plans and issuers can use?

Yes. See Appendix E at the end of this book.

Q 4:103   What if the plan or issuer does not know who the employees' dependents are?

A plan or issuer must make reasonable efforts to collect the necessary information for dependents and include it on the certificate. An automatic certificate is not required until the plan or issuer knows (or, making reasonable efforts, should know) of the dependents' loss of coverage. This information can be collected annually, such as during an open enrollment.

Q 4:104   What is the minimum period of time that should be covered by the certificate?

It depends on whether the certificate is issued automatically or upon request:

1. For a certificate that is issued automatically, the certificate should reflect the most recent period of continuous coverage.
2. For a certificate that is issued upon request, the certificate should reflect each period of coverage ending within 24 months prior to the date of request.

At no time must the certificate reflect more than 18 months of creditable coverage that is not interrupted by a break in coverage of 63 days or more.

Q 4:105   How does "crediting" for preexisting conditions work under HIPAA?

Individuals receive credit for previous coverage that occurred without a break in coverage of 63 days or more. Any coverage occurring prior to a break in coverage of 63 days or more is not credited against an exclusion period.

> **Example 4-2.** An individual had coverage for two years, followed by a break in coverage for 70 days, and then resumed coverage for eight months. That individual would only receive credit against any preexisting condition exclusions for eight months of coverage; no credit would be given for the two years of coverage prior to the break of over 62 days.

Q 4:106 Does COBRA count as creditable coverage?

Yes. Under HIPAA any period of time an individual received COBRA continuation coverage is counted as creditable coverage as long as the coverage occurred without a break in coverage of 63 days or more.

> **Example 4-3.** If an individual was covered for five months by a previous health plan and then received seven months of COBRA continuation coverage, the individual would be entitled to receive credit for 12 months under a new group health plan.

Q 4:107 When employees change jobs, are they guaranteed the same benefits they had under their old plan?

No. When a person transfers from one plan to another, the benefits the person receives will be those provided under the new plan. Coverage under the new plan could be less or could be greater.

Q 4:108 What are the HIPAA eligibility requirements?

Group health plans cannot establish any rules for eligibility or continued eligibility based on any of the following health-related factors:

- Health status
- Medical condition (physical or mental)
- Claim experience
- Receipt of health care

- Medical history
- Genetic information
- Evidence of insurability (including conditions arising out of domestic violence)
- Disability

The legislative history makes it clear that the reference to evidence of insurability means people cannot be excluded because they participate in activities such as:

- Motorcycling
- Snowmobiling
- Riding all-terrain vehicles
- Horseback riding
- Skiing

While HIPAA's legislative history is clear that people engaging in these activities may not be excluded from coverage, HIPAA does not prohibit exclusions that would deny coverage for injuries related to these activities.

Q 4:109 May an employer sponsor a group health plan that is available only to employees who pass a physical examination?

No. A plan or issuer may not establish rules for eligibility that discriminate based on health status-related factors.

Q 4:110 Can employees lose health benefits if their health status changes?

No. Employees cannot be dropped from coverage just because they have an illness.

Q 4:111 Does HIPAA require employers to offer health coverage or to provide specific benefits?

No. The provision of health coverage by an employer is still voluntary. HIPAA does not require specific benefits nor does it prohibit a plan from restricting the amount or nature of benefits for similarly situated individuals.

Q 4:112 What does HIPAA require regarding benefits and employee contributions?

Group health plans cannot base any benefits or premiums on any health-related factors, but the legislative history makes it clear that plans can establish premium discounts or rebates or modify deductibles or copayments based on adherence to health promotion or disease prevention programs. The legislative history also makes it clear that entire groups can still be charged premiums based on their claim history. The act does preclude health plans from singling out individuals in a group for higher premiums or dropping their coverage.

Q 4:113 What does HIPAA require regarding special enrollment periods?

HIPAA requires special enrollment periods for people who lose other coverage, subject to the following conditions:

1. The employee or dependent had other coverage when declining an earlier opportunity to enroll in the plan.
2. The employee stated in writing that another source of coverage was the reason for declining enrollment. (This condition only applies if the plan required such a statement and provided the employee with notice of this requirement.)
3. The person has exhausted COBRA continuation or COBRA did not apply, but the loss of coverage resulted from what otherwise would have been a COBRA qualifying event.
4. The person requests enrollment within 30 days after the loss of other coverage.

Group health plans offering dependent coverage must allow at least 30 days in which to enroll new dependents following marriage, birth, adoption, or placement for adoption. If the employee is eligible, but not enrolled, the employee must also be allowed to enroll at the same time. Eligible spouses and other dependents must also be allowed to enroll within 30 days of birth or adoption. Coverage must be effective retroactive to the date of birth, adoption, or placement for adoption. After marriage, coverage must be effective no later than the first day of the month following the date the plan receives the enrollment request.

A special enrollee is not treated as a late enrollee; therefore, the maximum preexisting condition exclusion period that may be applied to a special enrollee is 12 months, and the 12 months are reduced by the special enrollee's creditable coverage.

A plan must provide the following description of special enrollment rights to anyone who declines coverage:

> If you are declining enrollment for yourself or your dependents (including your spouse) because of other health insurance coverage, you may in the future be able to enroll yourself or your dependents in this plan, provided that you request enrollment within 30 days after your other coverage ends. In addition, if you have a new dependent as a result of marriage, birth, adoption, or placement for adoption, you may be able to enroll yourself and your dependents, provided that you request enrollment within 30 days after the marriage, birth, adoption, or placement for adoption.

Q 4:114 What changes did HIPAA make to COBRA continuation requirements?

Under prior law, COBRA continuation coverage could be extended from 18 months to 29 months if a qualified beneficiary was disabled at the time of the qualifying event. HIPAA allows the extension if the disability exists at any time during the first 60 days of COBRA continuation. This extension of continuation coverage is also available to the spouse and dependent children of the disabled beneficiary.

HIPAA also modifies the definition of a qualified beneficiary to include a child born to or placed for adoption with the covered employee during the period of COBRA continuation.

Q 4:115 What changes did HIPAA make to small employer health plans and individual health insurance policies?

HIPAA includes provisions guaranteeing the availability of coverage to and through small employers. Small groups are those with 2 to 50 employees on a typical business day. New disclosure rules also apply to insurers of small employers. Medical savings accounts (MSAs) are available to self-employed individuals and employees of small employers covered under an employer-sponsored high-deductible plan. HIPAA allows federally qualified HMOs to offer high-deductible plans to people with MSAs. It requires guaranteed renewability of individual health insurance and guaranteed availability of individual health insurance to people with prior group coverage, and amends rules applicable to Medigap policies.

Q 4:116 What is group-to-individual portability?

HIPAA requires individual health plans to accept consumers who lose group coverage on a guarantee-issue basis, if certain criteria are met. Specifically, individuals must:

1. Have had prior medical coverage for 18 consecutive months, with the most recent coverage being a group plan.
2. Not have other coverage.
3. Not have lost the prior coverage as a result of fraud or nonpayment of premium.
4. Apply no later than 62 days after the loss of the last coverage.
5. Be ineligible for, or have exhausted, other coverage options, such as:
   a. COBRA
   b. State continuation requirements
   c. Medicare
   d. Medicaid
   e. Other group coverage.

Someone eligible for a conversion policy can still be eligible for group-to-individual portability.

Q 4:117 Is it easy for people who exhaust COBRA to get individual policies?

Not always. Some insurance companies still appear to be unaware of their responsibilities under HIPAA. Others are actively avoiding people entitled to coverage by setting sales commissions so low that agents have little incentive to sell the policies, by delaying processing of applications, or by charging high premiums. The General Accounting Office reports that some carriers have charged rates up to 600 percent of the standard premium. HIPAA does not restrict premiums, but it is possible that legislation will be introduced to stop price gouging. In July 1998, President Clinton signed an executive memorandum authorizing the office of Personnel Management to exclude health plans from the Federal Employees Health Benefits Program if they do not meet the letter and the spirit of the law.

Q 4:118 What does HIPAA require regarding renewal of policies?

HIPAA provides that health insurers (including HMOs) must renew coverage at the option of the plan sponsor, unless coverage is canceled as a result of the following:

- Nonpayment of premiums
- Fraud
- Violation of participation or contribution rules
- If the insurer leaves the geographic market (insurers leaving a market cannot return for at least five years)

Similar rules apply to Taft-Hartley plans and multiple employer welfare arrangements. Association plans can also terminate coverage if membership in the association ceases. Insurers that wish to stop offering a particular product to all employers must offer similar products and must give prior notice to each plan sponsor and participant. Insurers can modify products, but only if modifications are made on a uniform basis among all groups with that product.

Q 4:119 What does HIPAA require regarding reductions in benefits?

HIPAA provides that, if there is a material reduction in covered services or benefits, a summary of the changes must be furnished to participants within 60 days of its adoption.

Q 4:120 Does HIPAA apply to small employers?

The HIPAA health portability provisions apply to group health plans with two or more participants who are current employees.

Q 4:121 Does HIPAA apply to self-funded group health plans?

Yes.

Q 4:122 What new kinds of information do group health plans have to give to participants and beneficiaries?

HIPAA and other recent legislation made important changes in ERISA's disclosure requirements for group health plans. The Department of Labor issued interim disclosure rules in April 1997 to implement those changes. Under the new interim disclosure rules, group health plans must improve their summary plan descriptions and summaries of material modifications (SMMs) in four major ways to make sure they do the following:

1. Notify participants and beneficiaries of "material reductions in covered services or benefits" (for example, reductions in benefits and increases in deductibles and copayments) generally within 60 days of adoption. This compares to old requirements under which plan changes could be disclosed as late as 210 days after the end of the plan year in which a change was adopted.

2. Disclose to participants and beneficiaries information about the role of insurance issuers (e.g., insurance companies) with respect to their group health plan. In particular, the name and address of the issuer, whether and to what extent benefits under the plan are guaranteed under a contract or policy of insurance issued by the issuer, and the nature of any administrative services (e.g., payment of claims) provided by the issuer.

3. Tell participants and beneficiaries which Department of Labor office they can contact for assistance or information on their rights under ERISA and HIPAA.

4. Tell participants and beneficiaries that federal law generally prohibits the plan and health insurance issuers from limiting

hospital stays for childbirth to less than 48 hours for normal deliveries and 96 hours for cesarean sections.

Q 4:123 What is the definition of a material reduction in covered services or benefits that is subject to the new 60-day notice requirement?

Under the interim disclosure rules, a "material reduction in covered services or benefits" means any modification to a group health plan or change in the information required to be included in the summary plan description that, independently or in conjunction with other contemporaneous modifications or changes, would be considered by the average plan participant to be an important reduction in covered services or benefits under the group health plan.

The interim rules cite examples of reductions in covered services or benefits as generally including any plan modification or change that does the following:

1. Eliminates benefits payable under the plan.
2. Reduces benefits payable under the plan, including a reduction that occurs as a result of a change in formulas, methodologies, or schedules that serve as the basis for making benefit determinations.
3. Increases deductibles, copayments, or other amounts to be paid by a participant or beneficiary.
4. Reduces the service area covered by an health maintenance organization.
5. Establishes new conditions or requirements (e.g., preauthorization requirements) for obtaining services or benefits under the plan.

Q 4:124 Can employers use e-mail systems to communicate these new disclosures to employees and, if so, do employees have a right to get a paper copy of the information from their plan?

The interim disclosure rules provide a safe harbor for using electronic media (e.g., e-mail) to furnish group health plan SPDs, summaries of material reductions in covered services or benefits, and other SMMs (summaries of plan modifications and SPD changes). To use the safe harbor, among other requirements, employees must be able to access at their worksite documents furnished in electronic form. Participants also continue to have a right to receive the disclosures in paper form on request and free of charge.

Although the interim rule is not the exclusive means by which electronic media can be used to communicate plan information lawfully, the HIPAA safe harbor is limited to group health plans. The DOL has proposed extending the rule to other plans, including pension plans, and to other plan disclosures.

Q 4:125 What does HIPAA provide regarding electronic data interchange?

HIPAA includes administrative simplification standards designed to facilitate electronic data interchange. Regulations will be issued that will provide for a standard unique health identifier for each individual. HIPAA also includes penalties for wrongful disclosure of individually identifiable health information.

Q 4:126 What does HIPAA provide regarding long-term care insurance?

HIPAA clarifies the tax status of long-term care insurance. Long-term care insurance is now clearly treated as an accident and health insurance policy. This means employers can provide long-term care insurance to employees and the employees will not be taxed on either the value of the coverage or the benefits received. For policies that pay a flat per-diem benefit, rather than reimbursing actual expenses, benefits in excess of $175 per day are taxable ($190 in 2000; this amount is indexed by the medical component of the consumer price index.) Long-term care insurance cannot be provided through a cafeteria plan, nor can long-term care insurance premiums be reimbursed through a flexible spending account.

HIPAA defines long-term care insurance in such a way as to require policies to be guaranteed renewable. Furthermore, policies cannot provide cash surrender values. Refunds and dividends can only be used to decrease future premiums or increase future benefits, except for refunds on the death of the insured or the complete surrender or cancellation of the policy. HIPAA also limits deductible premiums to the following amounts, effective January 1, 1999:

Age	Annual Premium
40 or less	$ 210
Over 40, but not over 50	$ 400
Over 50, but not over 60	$ 800
Over 60, but not over 70	$2,120
Over 70	$2,660

These amounts are also indexed by the medical component of the consumer price index.

Even though long-term care insurance is treated as accident and health insurance, it is not subject to COBRA continuation requirements and cannot be part of a cafeteria plan.

HIPAA requires long-term care contracts to comply with a number of consumer protection provisions of the Long-Term Care Insurance Model Act and regulations of the National Association of Insurance Commissioners. HIPAA also includes disclosure requirements.

Q 4:127 What does HIPAA provide regarding accelerated death benefits?

HIPAA provides an exclusion from gross income for accelerated death benefits under life insurance contracts and amounts received for the sale or assignment of life insurance contracts to viatical settlement providers, if the insured is either terminally ill or chronically ill. The exclusion for the chronically ill applies to long-term care riders to life insurance contracts, provided the rider complies with the requirements for long-term care insurance policies. The exclusion does not apply to employers.

A terminally ill individual is defined as one who has been certified by a physician as having an illness or physical condition that reasonably can be expected to result in death within 24 months.

Q 4:128 What does HIPAA provide regarding withdrawals from individual retirement arrangements for medical expenses?

HIPAA allows penalty-free withdrawals from individual retirement arrangements (IRAs) for medical expenses. Withdrawals from IRAs to pay for medical expenses in excess of 7.5 percent of adjusted gross income can be made without the 10 percent tax. Additionally, penalty-free withdrawals can be made to pay for medical insurance without regard to the 7.5 percent floor if the individual has received unemployment compensation for at least 12 weeks in the current or preceding year. This rule ceases to apply once an individual has been reemployed for at least 60 days.

Q 4:129 What requirements does HIPAA impose on multiple employer welfare arrangements and multiemployer plans?

HIPAA provides that MEWAs and multiemployer plans cannot deny an employer continued access to coverage except for the following:

1. Nonpayment of contributions;
2. Fraud;
3. Noncompliance with plan provisions;
4. Plan ceases to offer any coverage in a geographic area; or
5. Failure to meet the terms of an applicable collective bargaining agreement, to renew a collective bargaining agreement or other agreement requiring or authorizing contributions to the plan, or to employ employees covered by such an agreement

Q 4:130 What requirements does HIPAA impose on insurers of small groups?

HIPAA requires insurers (including HMOs) that offer health insurance in the small group market (2 to 50 employees) to accept every small employer that applies and to accept every eligible employee who applies during the period in which the employee first becomes eligible. The insurer cannot impose restrictions based on health status of the employee or his or her dependents.

Q 4:131 What requirements does HIPAA impose on insurers of associations?

HIPAA requires renewal and continuation of coverage, but does not require guarantee issue to associations. Nondiscrimination rules apply to association plans, and no employee or dependent can be excluded from coverage on the basis of any health-related factor.

Q 4:132 Do the availability, renewability, and portability provisions of HIPAA apply to all types of health insurance?

No. HIPAA specifically excludes the following:

- Accident insurance
- Disability insurance
- Liability insurance
- Workers' compensation
- Automobile medical insurance
- Credit insurance
- On-site medical clinics
- Long-term care insurance
- Specified disease insurance (such as cancer insurance)
- Fixed indemnity insurance (such as plans that pay a certain amount for every day hospitalized)
- Medicare supplement insurance
- Coverage supplemental to military health care

"Limited scope" dental or vision benefits are not subject to HIPAA. But, this applies only if the benefits are provided under a separate contract, policy, or certificate of insurance or the benefits are otherwise not an integral part of the plan. Such benefits are deemed to be an integral part of the plan unless:

1. A person has the right to elect not to become covered for them; and

2. If the coverage is chosen, the person must pay an additional premium or contribution for it.

"Limited scope" benefits are defined as those that are sold under a separate policy or rider, and are limited in scope to a narrow range or type of benefits that are generally excluded from hospital/medical/surgical plans.

Q 4:133 What disclosure requirements does HIPAA impose on insurers in the small employer market?

HIPAA requires insurers offering any health insurance coverage to small employers to make a reasonable disclosure of the availability of information as part of solicitation and sales materials. At the small employer's request, the insurer must provide the provisions of the plan concerning the right of the insurer to change premium rates and the factors that could affect such changes, the provisions of the plan relating to renewability, any preexisting condition provisions, and the benefits and premiums under all health insurance coverage for which the employer is qualified. The information must be understandable by the average small employer and sufficient to inform small employers reasonably of their rights and obligations under the health insurance coverage.

Q 4:134 Who enforces HIPAA?

The Secretary of Labor enforces the health portability requirements on group health plans under ERISA, including self-funded arrangements. In addition, participants and beneficiaries can file suit to enforce their rights under ERISA, as amended by HIPAA. The Secretary of the Treasury enforces the health portability requirements on group health plans, including self-funded arrangements, through excise taxes under the Internal Revenue Code.

States have the primary enforcement responsibility for group and individual requirements imposed on health insurance issuers, including sanctions available under state law. If the states do not act in the areas of their responsibility, the Secretary of Health and Human Services may make a determination that the state has failed substantially to enforce the law, to assert federal authority to enforce, and to impose sanctions on insurers as specified in the statute, including civil monetary penalties. California, Missouri, and Rhode Island have failed to enact enabling legislation; therefore, the federal government is responsible for enforcing the group-to-individual portability provisions in those states. As of press time, Congress had yet to appropriate funds for enforcement.

Taxation of Group Health Plans

Q 4:135 What state tax laws apply to group health insurance plans?

All states tax the premiums that group insurance policyholders pay to insurers based on the residence of covered employees. These taxes range from 1 percent to 3.3 percent of premiums. The cost of the tax to insurance companies is passed along to the policyholder.

Q 4:136 What is the federal tax status of group health insurance for employers?

Under Code Section 162, an employer's contributions to a group health insurance plan are deductible as ordinary and necessary business expenses. There is no limit on the amount that can be deducted for current expenses, as long as the contributions qualify as additional reasonable compensation to the insured and the benefits are payable to the employees, not the employer.

An exception to the general rule on deductions concerns group insurance plans funded through voluntary employees' beneficiary associations (VEBAs), also known as Section 501(c)(9) trusts. VEBAs that establish a reserve fund for the payment of future benefits are subject to special deduction limits under Code Sections 419 and 419A. Failure to comply with all of the requirements of these sections can result in loss of deduction, unrelated business income tax on excess reserves [IRC § 512], and/or excise tax on "disqualified" (discriminatory) benefits (see Chapter 11). [IRC § 4976]

Q 4:137 Are self-employed individuals treated as employers with respect to the deductibility of group insurance premiums?

No. Self-employed individuals (those who own any part of an unincorporated business, partners in a partnership, and individuals who own 2 percent or more of an S corporation) are treated differently. Under the 1998 Appropriations Act, they may deduct 45 percent of their health insurance premiums from their taxable incomes in 1998, 60 percent in 1999 through 2001, 70 percent in 2002, and 100 percent in 2003 and thereafter.

The deduction is not allowed for any month in which the individual is eligible to participate in a subsidized health plan of a spouse or another employer.

Q 4:138 Are employer contributions treated as taxable income to employees?

No. Under Code Section 106, contributions by an employer to a health insurance plan are not considered part of an employee's taxable income.

The value of a discriminatory self-funded benefit (see Chapter 11) may be taxable to highly compensated employees under Section 105(h) nondiscrimination rules.

Q 4:139 Do taxes apply if the employer reimburses an employee for the cost of an individual health insurance policy?

If the employer requires proof that the premiums were paid by the employee, the reimbursement would be excludable from gross income under Code Section 106. The employer should have a written plan describing this practice.

Q 4:140 Are the benefits from a group health insurance plan taxable to employees?

No. Generally, payments of employee or dependent medical expenses by a group health plan are not includible in the employee's taxable income. [IRC § 105] There is an exception if a person does not qualify as a dependent under Code Section 152. This applies most frequently with domestic partners. Code Section 152 requires that the taxpayer provide over half of the support of the person claimed as a dependent. Code Section 151 provides an exemption from this requirement for children under age 19 and students under age 24.

In plain English, this can best be summarized in the wording of IRS Publication 17, *Your Federal Income Tax for Individuals* [1999]:

> Generally, you cannot take an exemption for a dependent if that person had gross income of $2,750 or more for the year. This test does not apply if the person is your child and is either under age 19, or a student under age 24.

Reservists' Benefits

Q 4:141 Must employers continue to offer health care benefits to employees and their dependents, even though they would be eligible for military benefits?

The Uniformed Services Employment and Reemployment Rights Act of 1994 (USERRA) gives employees the right to continue health care benefits. An individual on leave fewer than 31 days can only be required to pay the same amount as an active employee. Employees on longer leaves can continue coverage for 18 months from the date leave begins and can be required to pay 102 percent of the plan's cost.

Q 4:142 What are the differences between USERRA and COBRA?

The key differences between USERRA and COBRA are:

1. USERRA has no exception for small employers.
2. USERRA coverage cannot be extended beyond 18 months.
3. USERRA can be terminated the day after the employee fails to return to or reapply for employment within the time allowed (anywhere from 8 hours to 90 days depending on the length of active duty).

4. Whenever the uniformed service leave of absence is less than 31 days, the employee cannot be required to pay more than an active employee.
5. USERRA does not include any notice requirements.
6. USERRA does not permit termination when someone becomes entitled to Medicare or becomes covered by another group health plan.
7. USERRA does not include a grace period.

Where rights under USERRA and COBRA differ, the employee or dependent is entitled to the greater benefit.

Q 4:143 Are reservists eligible for military benefits?

Persons subject to involuntary call to active duty for more than 30 days are eligible for a range of military and dependent benefits, notably health care benefits, to replace those that would normally be supplied by an employer.

Q 4:144 Do most employers discontinue benefits for employees called to active duty?

A survey of 47 large private companies conducted by Hewitt Associates found that:

1. Twenty-nine continued to compensate the reservists in some manner.
2. Sixteen continued life insurance coverage.
3. Ten continued health care benefits.
4. Seven provided health care coverage for dependents for a limited period of time.

Q 4:145 Do employers have any obligations for benefits provided by the Department of Defense or the Veterans Administration?

Yes. Veterans Health Care amendments in COBRA permit the Department of Defense and the Veterans Administration (VA) to recover the cost of providing medical care to non-service-disabled veterans from employer-sponsored health plans. OBRA '90 extended this rule to include the cost of care for non-service-related illnesses and injuries provided to veterans with service-related disabilities. The VA determines what is a service-related disability and what is not; generally, that determination is final and not subject to review.

Q 4:146 Are dependents of military personnel eligible for medical care at military installations?

Dependents of active duty military personnel are eligible for inpatient and outpatient care at any military medical facility. Inpatient care at these facilities costs dependents $8.35 a day; outpatient care is free. When the dependent lives too far from a military medical facility, or when the necessary care is not provided by the military facility, treatment by a civilian provider may be partially covered by TRICARE.

Q 4:147 What is TRICARE?

TRICARE, formerly known as the Civilian Health and Medical Program of the Uniformed Services (CHAMPUS) covers some of the costs of medical care provided by civilian facilities to military dependents when a military medical facility is unavailable (provided that, for inpatient care, the dependent first receives a "statement of nonavailability"). Dependents include spouses and unmarried children (up to age 21; 23 if a full-time student) of active duty military personnel, as well as of reservists who are called up for more than 30 days.

Coverage offered under TRICARE for dependents requires no premium, but may not be as generous as benefits provided by the individual's employer. TRICARE offers eligible beneficiaries three choices for their health care:

1. TRICARE Prime – where Military Treatment Facilities (MTFs) are the principal source of health care.
2. TRICARE Extra – a preferred provider option; and
3. TRICARE Standard – a fee-for-service option (the old CHAMPUS program).

Q 4:148 Does an employer plan have any continuing responsibility to dependents covered by TRICARE?

Yes, TRICARE is always the secondary payer. This means that when dependents continue to be covered under an employer's plan, the plan will be charged for care even when it is provided at a military facility.

Q 4:149 What rights do military personnel have when they return to civilian life?

The Uniformed Services Employment and Reemployment Rights Act of 1994 states the following:

> [A] person who is a member of, applies to be a member of, performs or has performed, applies to perform, or has an obligation to perform service in a uniformed service shall not be denied initial employment, reemployment, retention in employment, promotion, or any benefit of employment by an employer on the basis of that membership, application for membership, performance of service, application for service, or obligation.

The definition of employer is sweeping and includes "any person, institution, organization, or other entity that pays salary or wages for work performed or that has control over employment opportunities."

Q 4:150 What requirements must a veteran meet to be eligible for reinstatement?

The veteran must meet the following three requirements:

1. The veteran must have received an honorable discharge from the armed forces.

2. He or she must make timely application, unless discharge was followed by a period of hospitalization not exceeding one year.

3. The veteran must be physically qualified to perform the functions of the job. If the veteran incurred a disability while on military duty that prevents him or her from performing the duties of the former job, the individual must be offered another

job with similar pay, seniority, and status, with requirements that are not beyond his or her abilities.

Q 4:151 To what benefits are reemployed veterans entitled?

Veterans who are entitled to reemployment are entitled to participate in the "same insurance and other benefits" offered to employees under the employer furlough and leave of absence policies in effect at the time the individual entered the armed forces.

The federal veterans' reemployment rights statutes have been interpreted by a number of Supreme Court cases, which look to the underlying nature and purpose of the benefit in question. A returning veteran may assert the right to those benefits that would have accrued "but for" an absence for military service. Where the benefit is found to be a "perquisite of seniority" that rewards length of service and is reasonably certain to have accrued during the period of absence, the rehired veteran is entitled to participate in the benefit as if he or she had been working for the company all along. [Alabama Power Co v Davis, 431 US 581 (1977)] On the other hand, where the benefit is designed to be a short-term reward for actual services rendered, or is subject to a significant contingency, the veteran will be eligible for such benefits only if other employees on leaves of similar duration are similarly entitled.

The rule just described was originally applied to defined benefit plans. The Sixth Circuit Court of Appeals rejected a lower court's line of reasoning that would have applied the rule to profit sharing plans as well. [Raypole v Chemi-Trol Chem Co, No. 84-3039 (6th Cir 1984), rev'g CIR No 79-137 (ND Ohio 1983)] The profit sharing plan in question was more properly characterized as a form of compensation, the appellate court reasoned, tied to the performance of actual work, with no added benefits for seniority and no guarantee of benefits after a period of service. Contributions to the plan were contingent on profits and at the discretion of the company's board of directors. Veterans are not guaranteed a continuation of compensation during military service. Rather, they enjoy protection against a loss of the kind of status that comes through the accumulation of years of service.

In *United States ex rel Reilly v. New England Teamsters & Trucking Industry Pension Fund* [737 F 2d 1274], the scope of the Veterans Reemployment Act was broadened further to apply to defined contribution plans and multiemployer plans. Holding that the pension benefit was a perquisite of seniority, the court ruled that Reilly was entitled to service credit for periods of reserve duty with the National Guard.

Q 4:152 How does this rule (on reemployed veterans) apply to health benefits?

A veteran should be eligible for coverage on the first day of his or her return to work, even though the governing collective bargaining agreement would require a delay until the first day of the following month. [Dufner v Penn Cent Trans Co, 374 F Supp 979 (1974)]

Note. Where a collective bargaining agreement benefit description conflicts with the intent of the reemployment law, the law prevails.

The veteran will be treated as if he or she had never left employment, so that there is no lapse of coverage or reimposition of waiting periods; however, an exclusion or waiting period may be imposed for coverage of any illness or injury determined by the Secretary of Veterans Affairs to have been incurred in, or aggravated during, the performance of uniformed service. Service-related conditions are treated at no charge by VA facilities.

Q 4:153 How does the rule apply to sick leave?

Sick leave benefits are earned on the basis of work and not on the passage of time, so courts interpreting the old law have determined that reemployed veterans were not entitled to sick leave, as this would put the veterans in a better position than other employees. [Li Pani v Bohack Corp, 546 F 2d 487 (1976)]

Q 4:154 Do employers have to grant leave for training and reserve duty?

Employers are required to accede to requests from reservists and National Guard members for leaves of absence for training or other military obligations. Employers are entitled to reasonable advance notice unless precluded by military necessity.

Q 4:155   How do state laws affect reservists' benefits?

As always, the rules vary from state to state. Some states require the continuation of employer-sponsored coverage for a limited time (for example, 30 days) following the reservists' call-up.

Chapter 5

Plan Rating and Funding

Plan rating and funding are important aspects of group health insurance. The approach used is the basis on which the cost of the plan to the employer is determined. This chapter covers plan rating and funding techniques, including conventional funding, shared funding plans, deferred premium, retrospective premium arrangements, reserve reduction arrangements, minimum premium, pooling, experience rating, and stop-loss insurance. Self-funding is addressed in Chapter 17.

Plan Funding	5-1
Fully Insured Plans	5-2
Alternatives to Fully Insured Plans	5-22
Deferred Premium Arrangements	5-24
Shared Funding Arrangements	5-26
Retrospective Premium Arrangement	5-28
Reserve Reduction Agreements	5-30
Minimum Premium Plans	5-32

Plan Funding

Q 5:1   What does plan funding mean?

Plan funding refers to the way claim liabilities and administrative costs will be financed. The fully insured insurance contract represents the most common method of financing claims: The policyholder pays a monthly premium to an insurance company that is responsible for administering and paying claims for covered expenses. For most small employers, this is the conventional and most appropriate approach to funding the costs of a health care plan.

Fully Insured Plans

Q 5:2   What are the cost components of a health insurance plan?

No matter what funding vehicle is used, the cost components of a plan are similar:

- Expected claims
- Margin for higher claims than expected
- Reserves for future claims
- Expenses
- The insurer's profit charge

Q 5:3   What are expected claims?

The insurer estimates the amount of claims that will be incurred during the policy year. The estimate includes claim payments that are expected to be made during that policy year as well as claim payments for expenses incurred during that year, but not reported until after the end of the year. Thus, expected claims are of the three following types:

1. Expected to be reported and paid in the policy year;
2. Incurred during the year but not paid in that year; and
3. For which the insurer is liable after the contract terminates, such as extensions for disabled individuals.

Although claims that will be paid after termination of the contract are also typically included in this "expected claims" projection, the claims for which an insurer is liable vary from contract to contract.

Q 5:4 Why would claims be paid after the termination of the contract?

The insurer usually guarantees certain benefits after the termination of an insurance contract.

Example 5-1. Consider a situation in which an expense was incurred in April, but the claim was not submitted to the insurer until May; the employer has terminated coverage with the insurer as of April 30. The insurer is typically liable for paying the claim, because the expense was incurred while the coverage was in force, even if the employer has signed a contract with a new insurance company.

In addition, under most policies, the insurer is liable for "extended benefits" for employees who are disabled when an insurance contract terminates. Policies vary, but these benefits often cover expenses for a year or more after termination.

Q 5:5 How does an insurer know what claims to expect?

Insurance actuaries base expected claim estimates on their past experience with large numbers of insureds, as well as on published statistical information regarding (1) the probability that individuals will incur medical expenses, (2) the plan design (what expenses are covered), and (3) the probable cost of those expenses. Deviations between "expected" and "actual" claims are common on a policy-by-policy basis. An insurer hopes to estimate expected claims accurately for its entire block of business, thus collecting enough premium to pay claims overall.

Q 5:6 What is a group health insurance actuary?

A group health insurance actuary is an accredited insurance mathematician who analyzes health care providers' costs associated with delivering health care and insurance companies' costs associated with insuring against the risk of incurring health care expenses. Traditionally, actuaries have focused on group morbidity and mortality and insurance administrative expenses to develop premium rate structures for health coverage.

Q 5:7 How does an actuary estimate which individuals will incur claims?

Group insurance actuaries do not estimate which individuals will incur claims, but instead use the law of large numbers to predict costs for a group. Actuarial data that reflect claim probabilities for groups of individuals, according to certain characteristics, are continuously compiled and updated. These data are available to actuaries through various insurance industry channels. The probability of incurring a medical expense is based primarily on age and sex, but some actuaries also consider the effects of income and occupation or industry.

For example, expected claims for an architectural firm where the average age is 35 and 80 percent of the employees are male would usually be lower than for a retail store where the average age is 45 and only 40 percent of the employees are male. This is because younger people are generally healthier, and women generally incur more claims than men, especially during their childbearing years.

Actuarial statistics show that the incidence of claims is often higher for employees who change jobs frequently; they use health care coverage when they have it, for fear that they may not have it at some point in the near future. And because better health is generally tied to higher socioeconomic status, all else being equal, insurers expect fewer claims but higher claim dollars from professionals as compared with other employees.

Q 5:8 How can a plan find an actuary?

For a fully insured plan, the insurance company provides the actuary. For a self-funded plan or a study of the feasibility of self-funding, administrators, reinsurance companies, and consulting actuaries can provide actuarial services.

Q 5:9 How does plan design affect the expected claim calculation?

Claims will be higher for a base-plus major medical plan (see Chapter 3) than for a comprehensive major medical plan. This is caused by a plan design that not only increases the actual dollar benefit for each hospital stay (typically 100 percent coverage rather than the 80 percent usually found in comprehensive designs), but also encourages use of the more expensive inpatient care. For example, if an employee is given a choice of receiving inpatient treatment at 100 percent and outpatient at 80 percent, there is a greater likelihood that the employee will elect 100 percent coverage.

The plan's deductible can be of equal importance in determining the magnitude of expected claims. The lower the deductible, the higher the claim expenses for the insurer.

The single most influential determinant of the cost of any plan is deciding which items or services to cover. With that determination made, the amount of the deductible and the coinsurance percentage are the next most significant factors determining cost, because of a simple truth: Small claims are a certainty, large claims are a possibility. If the plan design provides for payment to begin at low dollar amounts, employees will rightfully save and submit every receipt they can; however, if reimbursement begins at a higher threshold, it might not be worth the trouble to save receipts; the threshold might not be attained or other factors might result in claims not being submitted.

Another plan design factor that has significant influence on the expected claim calculation is utilization review. With utilization review included, hospital admissions and lengths of stay are expected to be lower than average. Hospitalization normally represents a large portion of the total claims; therefore, any savings there tend to be significant.

Q 5:10 How does the health plan's rate-guarantee period affect the rate?

Monthly premium rates are guaranteed to remain fixed for a specified period, such as one year. The longer the rate guarantee, the higher the rate. This is because it is difficult to project the cost of health care in the future and health care costs are expected to continue to rise at least as fast as the consumer price index.

When an employer's own claim experience is the basis for setting premium rates, the older those data, the more "trend" or projected cost increase is built in to the premium. Trend is typically calculated from the midpoint of the experience period to the midpoint of the rate guarantee period.

Q 5:11 How does the insurer project the cost of the medical services expected to be provided?

The two major components of claim cost projections are geographic location and medical care inflation trend.

Geography. As with other goods and services, health care costs more in certain areas of the country. For example, according to a 1999 survey by Mercer/Foster Higgins, the amount spent on medical insurance per employee averaged $4,671 per year in the Northeast, compared to only $3,716 in the South.

Medical care inflation trend. Historically, "trend" has been a component of every insurer's rate structure. It is a measure of the annual inflation rate of medical care goods and services and the effects of increased technology and utilization of services. In the mid-1990s trend fell sharply as the rate of increase in health care costs declined, but it has begun increasing again. According to a survey by The Segal Company in 1999, the trend component of a preferred provider organization (PPO) averaged 9.4 percent. That is, insurers estimated that prices would rise 9.4 percent during the year the contract was effective and therefore set their initial rates to cover the expected increases. For health maintenance organizations (HMOs), the survey found a trend of 6.8 percent. The trend for point-of-service plans was 7.8 percent and for non-network fee-for-service plans it was 12.0 percent.

In December 1999, *Business Insurance* magazine forecast that indemnity increases in 1999 would be 9 percent and above, PPO increases 8 percent to 20 percent, point-of-service increases would be 7 percent to 12 percent, and HMO premiums would increase 8 percent to 20 percent.

A survey by Towers Perrin predicted 8 percent increases in health care benefit costs in 2000, for PPOs, HMOs, and point-of-service plans and, 10 percent increases for indemnity plans.

Q 5:12 How is the expected cost of claims calculated for an employer with several locations?

The costs in each location are analyzed to develop claim projections. If there are large numbers of employees in more than one location, there may be separate rates for each location.

Q 5:13 How is a margin for higher-than-anticipated claims developed?

Insurance company actuaries project how much fluctuation is likely in their expected claim estimates, based on their experience with rate setting and the volatility of the medical care climate at the time a group rate is set. The margin that is added to the expected claim figure is based on the probable stability of the group, which varies with the size of the group and, for larger groups, is based on the past experience of the group. Margin is a potential cost for retrospectively rated groups and a guaranteed cost for prospectively rated groups. (Purists hold that margin is not applicable to prospectively rated groups, but the practice of most carriers today is to include a provision for margin in all but the smallest groups.)

Q 5:14 What is prospective rating?

Prospective rating is the process of estimating the claims or expenses a group will encounter in the coming year and dividing that expectation back into the number of persons covered in the group.

Example 5-2. If there are ten people in a plan and the expected claims for the year are $120, the prospective rate for persons in the group would be $1 per month ($1 × 10 × 12). Naturally, in an actual situation there would probably be a different rate based on the marital status of the members of the group. Further, the rate would be constructed to provide funding for greater-than-expected claims and to cover expenses. In this example, administrative concerns can be accounted for by modifying the expected claims to equal $100, with expenses, profit, margin, and other factors equaling $20. Still needed is $120, or $10 per month per person.

Prospectively rated plans (also known as conventionally rated or fully insured plans) do not share in any gain or loss resulting from their having paid more or less than required for the claims they generated. The premium paid by these plans goes into the carrier's overall "pool" (Q 5:23) The carrier accepts the risk that while it may not estimate accurately on any one plan, taken together, the accuracy level will be much higher over the larger pool.

This method of funding has obvious appeal for small groups, which generally are not prepared to take the financial risk of being self-funded, or even experience-rated (see Q 5:24). They find the greatest value in a rating structure that allows them to pay their premium and not be concerned about their day-to-day claim usage. Of course, they do have to worry about rate increases from year to year.

One variant of prospective rating introduces an element of experience rating into the process. This is commonly known as split funding and may involve the use of a rate stabilization reserve. In instances where this is done, the rate is still fully guaranteed to the purchaser. This variation preserves the benefits of budget stability, while introducing the possibility of savings if long-term claim patterns are lower than the rest of the pool. Other hybrids are available that, among other things, bring trade-offs of additional premium in return for the possibility of refunds. This is getting into retrospective rating and is no longer pure prospective rating.

Q 5:15 What is retrospective rating?

Retrospective rating means that the cost of a plan is established at the end of a policy year, rather than fixed in advance as under prospective rating. The policyholder pays an estimated premium throughout the year. Claims plus expenses are reconciled with the premium at year end, and a settlement or dividend calculation is produced. If the result is positive, the policyholder receives a dividend; if the result is negative, the policyholder must reimburse the carrier for the deficit. It is therefore only retrospectively, after the settlement process is complete, that the net cost for a plan year is known.

Q 5:16 How does a policyholder reimburse a deficit?

There are five basic approaches to reimburse a deficit, but policyholders may negotiate a settlement that combines attributes of more than one method:

1. Paying in a lump sum, single payment, or installment, with interest charged from the midpoint of the policy year;
2. Transferring a surplus developed from another line of coverage (some carriers insist on this);
3. Building deficit recoup into subsequent years' estimated premium by increasing the margin;
4. Placing the deficit into an agreement (between policyholder and insurance company) to pay upon contract termination, in exchange for lower or no interest payment on the deficit; and
5. Drawing down a special reserve, called a premium stabilization reserve, that was accumulated out of previous surplus not received as a dividend. (Note: The combination of all reserves, including incurred-but-not-reported reserves, cannot exceed the safe-harbor limits set by the Deficit Reduction Act of 1984 (DEFRA) unless actuarially certified.)

Q 5:17 What are reserves?

In broad terms, reserves are a measure of an insurance company's liability for future claims. Insurers establish a dollar amount for each group they insure that is an estimate of the amount of money they will need to fund claim payments, for which they may be liable after policy termination. This reserve estimate is added to the claim estimate developed for the claims incurred in the present plan year to get an "expected claims" projection for a group. The carrier, rather than the employer, is responsible for claim payments under insured plans, so reserves are legally required to prevent insolvency.

Q 5:18 How does an insurer determine what premium reserves are necessary?

Insurance company actuaries develop projections of future claim liability for their entire pool of insured groups. They base their projections on the past experience of similar groups, and they factor in the expected cost increases for medical care and expected changes in utilization.

For smaller employers, an average percentage of premiums is usually used to estimate the expected incurred claims and set the premium reserves.

The insurance company underwriting a new contract on a larger employer typically reviews the incurred but not reported, or "run-out," claims of prior years to get an idea of the reserves that should be established for future liability. As a result of claim run-outs, "lag studies" are generated for underwriters to analyze (see Q 5:39).

Q 5:19 How are expenses projected?

The expense components of premium include the following:

1. The insurer's initial underwriting work;
2. Issue of the contract and the plan materials, such as employee booklets;
3. Ongoing plan administration (for example, billing, the cost of paying claims, and underwriting work for plan changes and renewals);
4. Premium taxes;
5. Broker and/or agent commissions; and
6. Contribution to the insurance company's overhead.

For small employers, average expenses are used, but for large employers, expenses are often itemized. For example, a charge for each claim paid could be agreed to by the policyholder and the insurer at the beginning of the plan year.

Q 5:20 What percentage of the health insurance premium is generally an insurance company's profit?

Generalizations regarding insurer profits are difficult to make. One reason for this is that profit charges, like expense charges and methods of calculating expected claims, vary by insurer (many states place some kind of maximum on insurer profits). Part of the reason for the variation is the role that different accounting methodologies can play in profit reporting. Finally, the sharp rise in costs during the 1980s held down profits, while moderating costs in the 1990s led to increased profits.

Q 5:21 What is credibility?

Credibility refers to the belief in past claim experience as an indication of future claim experience. Each insurer interprets claim history differently, and each has a certain credibility formula that applies to groups that are large enough to be experience rated. The basis for the formula is the size of the employer in terms of both covered employees and plan design. Credibility increases with predictability, the more claims available for projection purposes, the higher the credibility.

For example, an employer with 100 covered employees and a wraparound major medical plan (with Blue Cross for hospitalization) would be less credible than the same group with a comprehensive major medical plan where all claims are included in the analysis; however, a group of 250 covered employees with a wraparound plan would be as credible as a 100-employee comprehensive plan.

The greater the frequency of claims, the higher the credibility as well. Dental claims are more predictable than medical claims, because of greater frequency and lower potential costs. Hospitalization—less frequent than nonhospital treatment—is also less predictable and often given less credibility for purposes of projecting claims.

Q 5:22 What is a manual rate?

A manual rate is the rate generally charged to groups with too few employees to create credible claim experience. It is a combination of the expected claim factor with margin for higher-than-anticipated claims, expenses, and profit. All four components are based on actuarial formulas that produce an approximation of expected "average" claims and expenses, given the size and demographics of the group based on the experience of the insurance carrier's entire pool of business. Manual rates are occasionally referred to as "pooled rates."

Q 5:23 What is a pool?

The term "pool" refers to a large number of small groups that are analyzed as a single large group. Claim projections for a group of policyholders can be more accurately estimated than for small policyholders individually—thus, the term "pooled rates" (see also Q 5:30).

Q 5:24 What is experience rating?

Experience rating is the process of setting rates based on a group's own claim experience.

Smaller plans will have less of their experience used as a component in creating their premium rate. Larger plans tend to move toward the ultimate experience rate, self-funding.

Q 5:25 What are paid claims?

Paid claims is a method of measuring the performance or usage of a medical or dental plan. It is perhaps the simplest method, although it might be considered misleading under certain circumstances. The paid claim figure is the sum dollar total of all claims paid under a plan during the measurement period (usually the policy year), without regard to when the service for which the payment is being made was performed. For example, suppose a person covered under the plan received some medical services in December 1999, but the request for payment did not reach the insurer until February 2000. Under the paid claims method, that amount would appear as a 2000 charge.

Q 5:26 What are incurred claims?

Incurred claims is another method of measuring the performance or usage of a medical or dental plan. Under the incurred claims method charges are assigned to the period of time during which the plan had a liability, ignoring whether the charges were paid or even known about during that time. In the previous example the charge would be assigned to the 1999 experience year under the incurred method.

Q 5:27 What is the difference between paid claims and incurred claims?

Paid claims are claims actually paid in a defined period. Incurred claims are a combination of claims that are actually paid, claims that have been incurred but have not yet been submitted for payment, and claims for which an insurer will be liable after termination of the contract. When an insurer develops a premium rate, incurred claims are used to set the rates, because the incurred claim estimate represents the insurer's liability.

Q 5:28 Under what circumstances is it better to use incurred claims or paid claims?

The answer depends greatly on what the employer is trying to measure or analyze. Paid claims will probably give a truer picture of cash flow if viewed on a month-to-month basis. This view of claims will be useful at renewal in determining the rate of trend to use for the upcoming year.

By assigning claim charges to the period in which they occurred, which is the purpose of incurred claim accounting, employers can more accurately measure the effect of plan changes or new limits. For example, if an employer changed the deductible on the plan from, say, $100 to $400 per person, an employer would be able to determine whether claims were being evenly incurred—whether or not paid evenly—during the course of a year.

One of the best methods of determining whether the plan is adequately reserved, under-reserved, or over-reserved is to analyze when claims are incurred versus when they are paid (commonly referred to as a "lag" report). In this instance, suppose an employer analyzing the claim lag finds that during the course of a plan year 30 percent of the claims paid during that year stem from prior time periods. Then, knowing the extent of the liability that would remain to be paid even in the event of the plan's termination, the employer has a valid basis for determining if the reserves are correctly set. Conventionally insured employers that do not know the amount the insurance company is holding in reserve can request this information from the insurance company or look at Schedule A, Form 5500, Part III, Line 8 d(2) and d(3). If an employer does both—looks and asks—the numbers should be identical. If not, the insurance company should provide a good explanation as to why there is a difference.

At renewal, the insurance company will want to use incurred claim figures because, theoretically, an incurred claim amount will represent the most current and accurate data available for projecting trend and predicting future claims. To aid in understanding why this is important, consider this:

Example 5-3. The plan paid only for one service, and one person each month received that service. In the first month the service cost $1, but was subject to inflation at the rate of 2 percent per month; therefore, in the second month, the cost was $1.02, then $1.04 in the third month, and so on. That would generate a schedule over one year as follows (amounts rounded off to two places):

Month	Cost
1	$1.00
2	1.02
3	1.04
4	1.06
5	1.08
6	1.10
7	1.13
8	1.15
9	1.17
10	1.20
11	1.22
12	1.24

Toward the end of the first year, around month 10, the insurance company would present data to the employer in the renewal discussions; however, the insurer would have data available only through, roughly, month 7, because of the normal process of claim lag. On a cash basis, plan costs could therefore have been $7.43 (the sum of months 1 through 7). That would average $1.06 per month and annualize out to $12.74 (($7.43/7) × 12), whereas the plan would have actually absorbed costs of $13.41 by the end of month 12. Further assume that the insurance company expected claims to occur at the one-per-month rate. Assuming the insurer suspected that claims were trending at about 20 percent, it would be reasonable for the insurer to take the average ($1.06/mo.) and use the suspected trend rate and a midpoint-to-midpoint calculation to "fill in" the remaining months of the year. The midpoint of the base period is March 15. The midpoint of the remaining months is October 15. The underwriter would therefore project seven months of trend.

	20	annual trend
÷	12	
	1.67	monthly trend
×	3.67	month of trend
	11.67	round to 12% trend
	1.06	base period experience
×	1.12	trend
	1.19	projected average for remaining months
×	5	remaining months
	5.95	projected total for remaining months
+	7.43	base period experience
	$13.38	projected total for year

This is very close to the $13.41 "real amount."

This example demonstrates the logic of adding incurred claims rather than simply using paid claims. Because it is a simplified example, the elaborate gyrations of projection seem unnecessary;

however, the real world is never so simple, and real data are seldom quite so revealing.

Q 5:29 How is an experience rate combined with a manual rate to produce a final premium rate?

For a case that is 50 percent credible, half of the experience rate and half of the manual rate would combine to form the final rate. Each carrier follows a different credibility formula based on size and available claim experience. For example, Blue Cross historically used low credibility and based most of the premium rate on company average, even for larger clients; therefore, groups with poor experience could obtain lower rates from Blue Cross than from commercial carriers that used higher credibility formulas.

Small groups, which ordinarily would not benefit from good claim experience with carriers whose formula is based on size, may obtain partial credibility from carriers that use a "life years" formula. For example, if a carrier would consider a "500 life year" group fully credible, an employer with 100 employees and three years of available experience data would be considered the same as a group of 300 employees (3 years multiplied by 100 employees) and be 60 percent credible (300 divided by 500); therefore, 60 percent of the premium rate would be a function of claims and 40 percent would be a function of company average or manual. The "life year" approach typically incorporates weighting in order to give more credibility to recent claims than to prior years' claims, given the expectation that the group is more like the group that incurred the most recent claims.

Q 5:30 Do all claims count toward an employer's claim experience, thus affecting the rate?

Arrangements are usually made for insurers to "pool" claims over a certain dollar limit so that large, infrequent claims do not adversely affect the employer's loss ratio. The employer pays a premium to the insurer for this protection, which keeps large claim amounts out of the experience analysis, so rates will not increase solely as a result of occasional unpredictable claims; however, employers with large claimants often find the carrier increasing the pooling level (less of the claim is forgiven) or increasing the charges for pooling protection. The higher the pooling point, the less risk to the insurer that such a claim will occur, and the lower the pool charge.

Many large employers (5,000 employees and up) forego individual claim pooling entirely because their own "pool" is large enough to absorb such claims. Smaller employers are wise to purchase protection, usually set at 5 percent to 25 percent of expected claims.

Q 5:31 What is a pool charge?

Some risks are excluded from an employer's experience, such as very large claims that are "pooled" rather than counted as part of the employer's claim experience for rate setting. The fee for this protection is called a pool charge.

Small group rates include a provision for the risk of large claims, which is not negotiable. Larger employers, on the other hand, may choose to pool claims at a certain dollar level, based on the risk the employer wants to assume. Claims included in an employer's experience analysis will cause premium rates to fluctuate. A large employer must decide whether it is a better financial decision to pay a larger pool charge to be protected against claims, or to pay a smaller pool charge but be less protected from the risk of large claims. The decision is based on the potential cost of a large claim versus the guaranteed cost of a fixed premium charge for shifting the risk.

Q 5:32 What is retention?

An insurance company's retention is the premium charged for expenses and profit. Retention is generally an average charge for small employers, based on how much administration is typically required, the risk assumption involved, and the insurance company's profit margin. It is expressed as a percentage of premium. For small groups, the term "retention" is not generally used to refer to expenses and profit, because the entire premium is retained by the carrier.

For larger employers or for policies that have alternative funding arrangements, the term "retention" is used and is usually a negotiated percentage of premium, ranging from 6 percent to 20 percent, based on the services and risk assumption the employer requires from the insurer and the size of the group (smaller groups have higher retention percentages because the fixed costs of administration are spread over a smaller base).

Q 5:33 How does an employer determine whether a premium rate is reasonable?

Employers have a hard time determining the reasonableness of rates because it is difficult to compare the various plan quotes by insurance companies when their coverage provisions vary so much.

For employers whose rates are manual, the intermediary typically offers "spreadsheet" quotes from several carriers. Rate comparisons can be made, but differences in benefits must be carefully reviewed. Rate alone is not a good basis for choosing a plan.

For employers whose rates are partially or fully experience rated, the intermediary obtains quotes from several insurers; however, because the quotes are based on more subjective information, which each insurer analyzes somewhat differently, there will be more rate negotiation than on smaller policies. One significant variation is in the amount of credibility the insurer assigns to a particular employer's past claim experience.

Q 5:34 Are dependent rates developed separately from employee rates?

No. Dependent rates are artificial and are based on company average relationships between employee and dependent loss ratios. Usually, spouses' actual ages are not required; their ages are assumed to average out to be the same as employees' ages. For the experience portion of a premium rate, the employer's loss ratio is reviewed as a whole, rather than by the employee and dependent; thus, even if only dependent claims were resulting in high loss ratios, employee rates as well as dependent rates would reflect these high losses. Although rates quoted to the employer are separate, all premiums—both employee and dependent—are combined, as are claims.

With the increase in employee contribution requirements, many carriers are adjusting the historical relationship between employee and dependent rates, increasing the employee rate, and decreasing the dependent rate in order to obtain sufficient premium if contributory dependent coverage is waived. Employers should obtain separate rates that are more nearly "self-supporting" for the purpose of determining employee contributions.

Q 5:35 What is a loss ratio?

An employer's loss ratio is an expression of claims compared with premium. A low ratio indicates "good" claim experience: The premium collected was more than required to fund the actual claims. A loss ratio greater than one (usually expressed as a percentage over one hundred) indicates that claims exceeded premium.

If a plan paid $1,000 in premium and had $1,000 in claims, its experience (loss ratio) would be 100 percent. Similarly, if the plan paid $1,000 and had $2,000 of claims, its loss ratio would be 200 percent. An experience rate, then, is a rate based on the plan's actual claims. It is the actual claims divided by the premium paid for the same period. For this purpose, an insurance company might use either "paid claims" (see Q 5:25) or "incurred claims" (see Q 5:26) when making the calculation. While use of one or the other might markedly change the result, the more important factor is not which claim figure is used, but rather that the same definition of claims be used consistently from year to year.

For the insurance company, the ideal experience would be in the 80 percent range on all cases. The remaining 20 percent is necessary to cover the expenses of administering the plan, risk charges, and profit.

Q 5:36 What is a tolerable loss ratio?

A tolerable loss ratio (TLR), or acceptable loss ratio (ALR), is the loss ratio the insurer can tolerate without losing money on the group. The insurer projects the claims expected for a certain group. Premium rates are set based on that projection of claims, plus the charges necessary to cover the insurer's expenses. A typical small employer's premium might be 82 percent for expected claim payments and 18 percent for expenses—underwriting, issue, administration, claim processing, commissions, overhead, and profit. The TLR in this case would be 82 percent of premium. A loss ratio of over 82 percent for this employer group indicates that the insurer did not accurately project claims.

The insurer has a TLR for its block of cases as a whole, as well as a target TLR for each policy. If the overall loss ratio exceeds the TLR, profits may be reduced or eliminated. If an insurance carrier has set rates properly and the loss ratio is exactly at the tolerable level, at renewal the rate will still be increased to anticipate "trend." (Trend is the rate at which medical costs are increasing. It includes inflation, utilization, and new technology costs.) Rates will be continued or decreased only if the carrier charged too much in the year prior to the renewal and the case is using some degree of experience rating. For cases that are fully pooled (that is, have no experience rating), even if the loss ratio is down at 20 or 25 percent for the prior year, there will be no rate reduction.

Q 5:37 Do TLRs vary from year to year and from employer to employer?

TLRs vary annually because expected claims and expenses vary from year to year. Expenses vary with the size of a group and with the plan design elected by the employer. Expected claims vary by group and plan design, and they also vary considerably from the first year of coverage to later years.

For the first year in which an insurance company underwrites an employee group, the claims actually paid are expected to be less than 80 percent of premium. Typically, first-year paid claims are estimated to be between 45 percent and 60 percent of premium. This is because claims that were incurred in the prior year under another insurance contract are usually paid by the prior insurer. Thus, the prior insurance company is liable for claims incurred but not reported, instead of the present insurer.

The premiums charged by the new insurance company may appear, at first glance, to be much too high, based on the expected paid claims for that first year the contract is in force; however, because the new insurer will be liable for all claims incurred during the period, even though they may not be reported and paid until later, it must collect premiums to fund the claims that will be paid at a later date. These premiums are known as "reserves" (see Q 5:17).

Q 5:38 What is lag?

Lag is the time between claim incurrence and claim payment. Lag varies by type of service and amount of claim. For example, hospital bills are usually submitted directly by the provider within a short period of time; however, routine medical expenses that do not represent a substantial out-of-pocket expense may be accumulated by the employee for weeks or months before being submitted, while large bills such as for surgery are likely to be submitted within a moderate period of time. The average lag, weighted for dollars, is determined and expressed as a number of months, a percentage of claims, or, in the first year, a percentage of premium. If the average lag is expected to be three months, a 25 percent (3 ÷ 12) reserve for incurred-but-not-reported claims is necessary. (The full reserve will be higher than the lag estimate, because the reserve must also cover claims for disability extensions after contract termination.)

Lag for basic hospital expenses is usually two and a half to three months, partly because of the need for large claims to be reviewed. Dental lag is similar. Major medical lag can, however, be five or six months. For comprehensive plans, the combination of hospital and nonhospital lag typically ranges between four and four and a half months, depending on the mix of claims and the deductible level.

Claims are generally submitted more promptly under managed care plans than under traditional indemnity plans because providers typically submit claims directly, without requiring employees to complete claim forms; therefore, lag times are shorter.

Q 5:39 What is a lag study?

A lag study is an analysis of the historical timing patterns of claim submissions. The results are used to estimate claims expected to be submitted after the end of the policy period. Lag studies are rarely done for employers with fewer than 2,000 employees, because of the high volume of claims necessary to make the studies believable projections; however, actuaries compile lag studies for their entire case block to establish reserve requirements for the expected total run-out liability on their entire block of business, and apply formula reserve requirements based on these studies.

Alternatives to Fully Insured Plans

Q 5:40 Are there alternatives to fully insured (conventionally funded) plans?

Alternative funding vehicles allow the employer to absorb some of the risk that the insurer assumes under a conventionally funded insurance plan. The alternatives can be characterized as those that increase cash flow, including the following:

- Deferred premium (extended grace period)
- Retrospective premium arrangements
- Reserve reduction agreements
- Minimum premium plans

and those that increase employer risk, including the following:

- Shared or split funding (high self-funded deductibles)
- Self-funding or administrative services only plans

Employers that elect alternative funding can be either partially self-funded or fully self-funded. See chapter 17 for more information on self-funding.

Q 5:41 How do alternative funding methods differ from conventional funding methods?

The fundamental differences between conventional and alternative funding methods are the split of risk between insurer and policyholder and the expenses associated with the alternative funding arrangement. The split of risk changes the insurer's liability for claims during the plan year as well as after contract termination. For example, the employer may elect to be responsible for "run-out" claims (claims submitted after plan termination). By assuming additional risk, the employer can reduce its premium to the insurer.

Expenses payable to the insurer vary, depending on the types of risks and services for which the insurer retains responsibility. For instance, premium taxes are reduced to the extent premium is reduced when the employer assumes more risk, as are risk charges.

Q 5:42 For whom might an alternative method of plan funding be appropriate?

The high cost of health care has resulted in increased interest in funding alternatives by many employers that want to do the following:

1. Improve their cash flow.
2. Reduce premium taxes and insurance company charges.
3. Eliminate or reduce services provided in conventionally insured plans.
4. Enjoy an exemption from state-mandated benefits.

An employer can achieve any of these objectives by assuming some of the risk the insurer traditionally assumes. Whether a particular employer should attempt to do this depends on the size of the employer, the past claim experience of the group, the current health status of the employees, the risk tolerance of the employer, and the willingness of an insurer to provide the employer with protection against whatever share of the risk the employer is unwilling to assume.

Q 5:43 Does employer size affect the choice of alternatives?

Most employers with fewer than 250 employees do not elect an alternative funding arrangement; however, employers with as few as 100 covered employees are sometimes candidates for nonconventional funding. Some insurers have special funding products for employers with as few as 50 employees.

Employers with fewer than 500 employees are unlikely to self-fund fully. Those that do almost always have stop-loss insurance as protection against large individual claims or substantial variations from the employer's expected claim level. This is because a small employer might be able to absorb a $10,000 claim on one person, but few small employers can absorb a $750,000 claim. Accordingly, an employer must analyze its financial condition and determine the dollar level at which the employer should place its stop-loss trigger.

Q 5:44 Do some employers elect to insure the entire risk of a health insurance plan?

Some very large employers may elect fully to self-fund. Depending on their risk capacity, even these employers may purchase some form of stop-loss insurance. When an employer elects fully to self-fund a plan but have an insurer administer it, a contract for administrative services only may be arranged. Self-funded plans typically retain the less expensive claim payment services of a third-party administrator (TPA).

Deferred Premium Arrangements

Q 5:45 What is a deferred premium arrangement?

A deferred premium arrangement is the simplest of all alternative funding arrangements. Conventionally funded plans allow the employer a 31-day grace period, during which premium for the current month is overdue but payable without allowing the policy to lapse. Insurers will defer premium receipt for certain employers by an additional 30 or 60 days, thus extending the grace period to 60 or 90 days. This enables the employer to retain funds for an extended period, thereby allowing investment income on those funds to accrue to the employer rather than to the insurer. It also permits the policy to remain intact without payment of premium.

Because 90 days worth of premium is typically equivalent to the reserves required by the insurer, this deferred premium arrangement effectively eliminates the cash reserve usually held by the insurer. If the policy terminates, then all of the deferred premium is typically due as of the date of termination.

Q 5:46 Why would an employer elect a deferred premium arrangement?

The employer's cash flow is improved because the employer is able to use the premium deferred in the business or elsewhere.

An employer must compare its use-of-money cost to the interest charged by the insurance carrier on what is effectively a loan. The following three factors must be taken into account:

1. Does the carrier charge interest, and, if so, at what rate?
2. When is the interest compounded? From the first day premium is due? From the thirty-first day?
3. What cost, if any, does the company incur from borrowing the same dollars through normal commercial channels?

The insurer's profits depend significantly on cash flow; therefore, there will be a charge to the company. If there is no direct interest charge, there may be an increase in retention (see Q 5:32).

Carrier interest charges are typically set annually and rarely float (although some carriers index and adjust the rates monthly); therefore, positive cash flow may be possible to achieve in periods of rising interest. When interest rates fall, however, the carrier's rate is likely to be much higher, and the arrangement should be terminated.

Q 5:47 Why don't all employers elect deferred premium arrangements?

Insurers do not provide deferred premium arrangements for most employers. This practice is essentially an extension of credit, and insurers are not inclined to underwrite that risk without protection, such as a letter of credit. In addition, the insurer charges a fee for its loss of income when premiums are deferred. The combination of the costs of determining and ensuring the employer's credit worth, plus the loss of investment income to the insurer, results in an increased expense for the insurer and may produce a small net saving for the employer. Under the final COBRA regulations, plans with deferred premium arrangements must allow COBRA continuees a comparable grace period.

Shared Funding Arrangements

Q 5:48 How does a shared funding arrangement differ from a conventionally funded plan?

Shared funding (also called high self-insured deductible (HSID) plans) allows the employer to self-fund all of an individual's covered expenses for health care up to a specific limit. The employer chooses the "employer deductible" level, such as $2,000, and pays covered expenses for anyone who incurs claims, up to that maximum. The insurance company typically provides eligibility review, claim processing, and assumption of the risk above $2,000 per individual.

Basically, shared funding is a minimum premium plan (MPP) for small employers. Most carriers will not offer MPPs to employers under a certain size because of underwriting or state filing limitations. Certain carriers specializing in small groups have adapted the concept for their clients.

Q 5:49 Why would an employer elect a shared funding plan?

Shared funding requires less premium to the insurer for both current and future claims. The employer retains funds that would usually be paid to the insurance company, thereby improving its cash-flow position. The employer must fund current claims up to the employer deductible level, but may be able to pay funds out less quickly than if the plan had been totally insured, depending on the timing of the claims. Also, if claims are less than would normally be expected, the employer will come out ahead. This is because the insurance company would have set premiums at a level to fund "expected claims"; thus, if the plan experiences lower-than-expected claims, the employer will spend less. Conversely, the timing and claim level may result in a greater cost, which is the risk inherent in these types of plans.

The employer may also save money because it will pay the insurer no premium tax on the self-funded part of the plan; therefore, even if the employer self-funds claims that are nearly equal to what the insurer would have expected, it will still save money by avoiding the premium tax.

Q 5:50 Why would an employer reject a shared funding plan as an alternative funding arrangement?

An employer with a shared funding arrangement could pay out more than for a conventionally funded plan in some years. Also, additional administration is involved and budgetability is virtually impossible for smaller groups.

The employer could pay more, in total, for the shared funding plan than for a conventionally insured plan if any of the following three situations exist:

1. Claims for which the employer is liable exceed expected levels. In this case fully insured premiums would have been a better investment, based on the fact that an insurer that accepts a fixed premium is not entitled to additional premium to fund higher than expected claims.
2. The employer assumes liability upon contract termination, and run-out claim liabilities for claims up to the employer deductible are excessive.
3. The employer uses a TPA to administer claims and perform other services the insurer usually performs, and the combination of the TPA's expenses plus the insurer's expenses is higher than the expenses would have been under a conventionally insured plan. This sometimes happens because of the split of services and extra coordination work done by the TPA and employer that traditionally is done by the insurer.

Q 5:51 Why don't all employers elect shared funding arrangements?

Only employers that have 50 or more covered employees and are willing to absorb a piece of the risk usually taken by the insurer are the logical candidates for shared funding arrangements. The employer must be able to absorb peaks of outgoing cash flow over months and years.

Employers with more than 500 covered employees typically elect other funding alternatives that have the potential for greater savings.

Retrospective Premium Arrangements

Q 5:52 What is a retrospective premium arrangement?

Under a retrospective (retro) premium agreement, the insurer agrees to collect less than the conventional premium from the employer. At the end of the year, the insurer has the right to collect additional premium from the employer if the actual loss ratio exceeds the loss ratio agreed to at the beginning of the retro agreement period. Typically, the initial premium reduction is equal to the margin built into the rate. The maximum additional premium payable is capped; it is agreed to at the beginning of the policy year and may raise the total premium to more than would have been paid in the absence of the retro agreement.

In effect, the insurer is agreeing to collect premiums at the expected claim level, collecting no premium for fluctuation. If claims exceed the expected level, some or all of the retro may be "called."

Q 5:53 Why would an employer negotiate a retrospective premium arrangement?

Retrospective premium arrangements were originally known as "advance dividends." The margin in excess of expected claims was presumed to be the dividend payable if claims were as anticipated. Rather than wait until the close of the policy year plus three months to perform the settlement calculation, the "dividend" is "paid" in advance and is available to the policyholder throughout the year.

The employer retains funds it ordinarily would remit to the insurer during the year, thus improving its cash-flow position. The employer assumes some additional risk if the retro agreement states that more than the conventional premium can be collected if claims exceed a set level, but this risk is limited because a maximum retro is agreed upon at the beginning of the policy year.

Q 5:54 What is a deep cut retro?

Typically, only the margin is placed in a retro; however, some carriers, especially Blue Cross, allow retrospective arrangements for as much as 20 percent of expected premium. This includes not only margin, but a portion of the reserves—the piece attributable to the increase in reserves that will accrue by the end of the policy year.

Deep-cut retros can be negotiated when the reserve change is expected to be negative (for example, when there is a reduction in covered persons, a plan change that reduces expected benefits, or significantly improved claim levels).

Q 5:55 Why might an employer not negotiate a retrospective premium arrangement?

An employer that implements a retro arrangement may find that the savings are minimal, because of the insurance company's increased retention charges. These include an interest charge for the loss of the use of money during the policy year and a charge for assuming the credit risk of the employer. The employer may be required to pay additional premium at policy year-end. If the retro agreement specifies that the collectible additional premium is capped, but at a level that makes the total potential premium higher than the conventional premium would have been, the employer can pay more than under a conventional plan. In order to guarantee payment of the retro, the insurer may require a letter of credit. This will result in a bank fee, usually 1 percent of the retro amount, which together with the carrier's interest charges might exceed a policyholder's cash flow.

Q 5:56 To whom are retrospective premium arrangements available?

Insurers are unwilling to provide retrospective premium plans to employers with fewer than 50 covered employees and, in fact, rarely allow retro plans for employers with fewer than 150 employees. Retrospective premium arrangements are most often arranged for employers with between 200 and 500 employees whose past experience requires rates that the employer and intermediary believe are too high. They may negotiate a lower premium rate with the insurer by agreeing to pay a retro, but only if claims do accumulate to the insurer's original projections. To ensure that the retro will be paid if it is called, insurers will confirm the creditworthiness of the employer requesting a retrospective arrangement.

Some insurers offer retrospective premium arrangements to small employers whose experience is habitually better than the manual pool. These employers, whose rates are based partially on experience and partially on manual rates, are becoming more willing to assume some of the risk the insurer has traditionally assumed. Rate increases may be necessary in general, because of increasing claim costs, but for small employers whose claim experience is better than average, a modified retro agreement may be available.

Reserve Reduction Agreements

Q 5:57 What is a reserve reduction agreement?

Reserve reduction agreements take two forms: (1) an upfront amendment to the insurance policy, which eliminates the insurer's liability after contract termination; and (2) an agreement between employer and insurer that the employer will retain the reserves traditionally paid to the insurer, but the insurer will be liable for benefits after termination and the employer must return the reserves to the insurer. Both arrangements result in decreased premiums payable to the insurer.

Q 5:58 Why would reserves decrease if an insurer eliminates its liability after contract termination?

Traditionally, the insurer is liable after contract termination for extended benefits for disabled employees and for claims incurred but unreported prior to termination. Some employers are willing to assume this liability, thereby eliminating the reserves held by the insurer.

Q 5:59 Why would an employer want to negotiate a reserve reduction?

Premiums decrease for employers that modify benefits payable on contract termination or hold the reserves traditionally held by the insurer. This is especially true in the first year, when the insurer typically establishes reserves with a percentage of the initial premium.

Q 5:60 Why might an employer not change the conventional reserve arrangement?

When an employer holds the reserves usually paid to the insurer, the insurance company still typically retains liability for certain claim payments after contract termination. The insurer must therefore have access to the funds, and the employer may be required to provide them at a most inconvenient time. The insurer also typically requires some form of arrangement to protect its credit risk, such as a letter of credit from a bank, for which there is a charge. This may be in addition to the maintenance of the minimum balance in an account where the reserves or a portion of the reserves will be held.

Some arrangements require the employer to invest the funds (the amount of the conventional reserve requirement) in certain accessible securities; the employer may not be allowed to use the captured reserves as working capital in the business, because of the risk of loss and the inaccessibility of funds. This arrangement is agreed to by employer and insurer, and although the funds are the employer's property, the insurer has the contractual right to withdraw money to fund obligations after contract termination.

The administration required for these arrangements can be cumbersome. Furthermore, an insurer may be unwilling to allow the employer to retain reserves, based on an assessment of the employer's credit worthiness and the practical effectiveness of letters of credit.

The reserve level must be adjusted annually and carried on the employer's books if a hold-harmless agreement has been executed. If the carrier retains liability, interest charges will be accumulated and charged in the carrier's retention.

Q 5:61 Do small employers typically implement reserve reduction agreements?

The release of reserves is rarely available to smaller employers. The additional administration involved requires that a significant reserve amount be involved in order for the employer to net savings. Generally, the smaller the employer, the lesser the benefit expertise. Administration of the banking arrangements requires a knowledgeable employer and intermediary.

Minimum Premium Plans

Q 5:62 What is a minimum premium plan?

Minimum premium plans are fully insured plans in which the employer agrees to fund expected claims; the insurance carrier funds claims in excess of the employer's aggregate claim liability and claims in excess of a specific high-amount claim per individual. It is, however, fully insured, because the insurance carrier is ultimately liable for all benefits due under the terms of the plan, including those incurred but not reported at termination.

Two kinds of MPP are available:

1. The insurer holds reserves similar to those required under a conventionally insured plan.
2. The employer is permitted to hold reserves to fund this liability.

The insurance carrier is responsible in both cases for benefit obligations after termination of the contract.

Q 5:63 At what level does the insurer become responsible for benefit funding under an MPP?

The employer and insurer establish a "trigger point" beyond which the insurer is liable. This liability can be set on a monthly cumulative basis or on an annual basis. The trigger is negotiated between each employer and insurer, based on expected claims. A trigger point of 105 percent of expected claims is one example.

Under a monthly cumulative arrangement, the employer is protected against fluctuation in claims from month to month. If cumulative claims exceed the monthly trigger point, the insurer pays claims from its own funds. In a subsequent month, if claims are below the trigger point, the insurer is usually allowed to recoup the

Plan Rating and Funding

Q 5:63

amount from the employer to cover the payments made in the month when claims exceeded the trigger point. For example:

Month	Employer Obligation	Claims	Employer Pays	Insurer Pays	Unexpended Employer Funds
1	$ 100	$ 60	$ 60	$ 0	$40
2	200	70	70	0	70
3	300	120	120	0	50
4	400	150	150	0	0
5	500	100	100	0	0
6	600	110	100	10	0
7	700	40	50	−10	50
8	800	100	100	0	50
9	900	130	130	0	20
10	1,000	50	50	0	70
11	1,100	180	170	10	0
12	1,200	140	100	40	0

Under an annual arrangement, the employer funds all claims until the annual trigger point is reached. For example:

Month	Employer Obligation	Claims	Employer Pays	Insurer Pays	Unexpended Employer Funds
1	$1,200	$ 60	$ 60	$ 0	$1,140
2	1,200	70	70	0	1,070
3	1,200	120	120	0	950
4	1,200	150	150	0	800
5	1,200	100	100	0	700
6	1,200	110	110	0	590
7	1,200	40	40	0	550
8	1,200	100	100	0	450
9	1,200	130	130	0	320
10	1,200	50	50	0	270
11	1,200	180	180	0	90
12	1,200	140	90	50	0

The insurer and employer are both obligated to fund the same amounts under both arrangements by the end of the year. The only difference is the timing of that funding.

Q 5:64 If an individual incurs a shock claim (an unexpected claim of a high amount) under an MPP, does the full amount of that claim count toward the employer's trigger point?

Whether or not the full amount will count toward the trigger point depends on whether an arrangement has been made to "stop the employer's losses" at a certain point per claimant per policy year (specific pooling or stop loss). Some employers elect to buy individual high-amount claim pooling and pay a pool charge as part of the "minimum premium."

Q 5:65 How are claims paid with employer funds under an MPP?

The employer establishes a bank account to which the insurer has access to pay claims. The account is funded as claims are submitted for payment. Three days to two weeks worth of expected claims, called an "imprest balance," are required, however, to be maintained in the account. Claim processing is typically performed by the insurer, although some employers use third-party administrators instead, who would have access to the funds just as the insurer would if it were the administrator.

Q 5:66 Why would an employer benefit from establishing an MPP?

The employer retains significant funds under an MPP, paying the insurer a "minimum premium," which consists of administrative expenses, reserves (unless the employer holds the reserves), and predetermined premium for stop loss to fund claims above the trigger point. In the first year, when the insurer establishes reserves, premium could be as much as 35 percent of the conventionally insured premium, but in later years, premium could be as little as 7 percent of the conventionally insured level, covering only administration, a change in reserves resulting from a change in claim levels, and premiums for claims above the trigger point.

Premium tax is usually not payable for the employer-funded portion of the plan; however, in California an insurance company's obligations to pay premium tax are not changed for MPPs. In this case, the employer pays premium tax to the insurer, which, in turn, remits it to the state insurance department. Usually, an agreement for this contingency is reached initially. Most insurers require a "hold-harmless" agreement that relieves the insurer of any obligation to pay taxes other states might assess in the future. (Hold-harmless agreements are also used when insurers need assurance that an employer will release reserves it has been holding in various funding arrangements.)

Employers that were previously fully retrospectively rated will have the same claim cost under conventional and MPP funding. Thus, the savings are usually realized not from positive claim experience but from decreased premium taxes and from investment income on reserves.

Q 5:67 Is there any reason why an employer would not elect an MPP?

Properly structured, MPP arrangements expose employers to no more of the risk than they assume under conventional, retrospectively rated plans; however, the administrative work required to establish and maintain the banking arrangements requires expertise and effort too burdensome for some employers.

The insurer's risk charges may be substantial for some employers whose creditworthiness is questionable, especially if a letter of credit is used, which is expensive to arrange.

If the carrier (or the state) does not permit the release of the reserves, MPP savings may be minimal. Without the interest gain on the reserves (approximately 20 percent of conventional premium), the premium tax savings (as low as 0.5 percent to 1 percent in most states; up to 2 percent or 2.5 percent in some states) may be offset to a large degree by banking expenses and additional internal administration.

MPP is not attractive in California, which taxes the employer-funded portion of the plan.

The same level of retention savings (but not premium tax savings) can be obtained in a conventionally insured plan with a 90-day premium deferral.

Q 5:68 What employers typically elect MPPs?

Employers with MPPs usually have at least 200 employees enrolled in the health plan. Insurers also require some protection against the credit risk an MPP represents; thus, if an employer cannot supply a letter of credit or excellent financial statements, an MPP may not be an option. MPPs are not available in every state.

Q 5:69 How are third-party administrative services used in an MPP?

An employer may elect to have administration, including claim processing, performed by a source other than the insurer, if the service the TPA can provide is better or less expensive. In this situation, the insurer only assumes risk; the TPA provides documentation to the insurer for claim payments for which the insurer is liable over the trigger point. The TPA must be approved by the insurer, and not all insurers are willing to engage in such arrangements.

Chapter 6

Plan Implementation and Administration

Proper administration of a health insurance plan is essential if both employer and employee are to receive maximum value. Plan administration begins before the effective date of the plan and continues throughout the plan year. This chapter examines plan administration and implementation and covers such topics as setting up the plan, employee enrollment, claim filing, billing procedures, the renewal process, terminating employees, and the use of computers in plan administration. COBRA administration, an important part of plan administration, is covered in Chapter 13 and discrimination testing is covered in Chapter 4.

Setting Up the Plan	6-2
Reporting and Disclosure	6-6
Enrollment	6-12
Billing	6-16
Claims	6-18
Coverage, Renewal, and Changes	6-25
Termination of Coverage	6-27
Computerized Administration	6-30

Setting Up the Plan

Q 6:1 After an employer selects a health insurance plan, how is the coverage put into effect?

After reviewing proposals and selecting the plan, the employer makes a written application and pays a binder that approximates the first month's premium to the selected insurer. A worksheet usually accompanies the application. It provides a precise explanation of all the information required for the smooth operation of the plan. This includes, but is not limited to, the legal name of the policyholder and the locations of employees who will be insured, classes of employees eligible for coverage, the effective date of the plan, details of the coverage requested, the amount of employee contributions and policyholder premium payment, the claim payment method, and the intermediary involved. The process is similar for self-funded plans. Most self-funded plans hire insurers or third-party administrators (TPAs) to pay claims; they also require applications that request similar information.

In addition, enrollment of employees must take place before the underwriter will approve coverage (accept the group as a risk) and issue final premium rates. Changes in enrollment from estimates on which the proposal was based can significantly affect the cost of the plan. Thus, the employees are told about the new coverage and required to enroll prior to final approval by the insurer.

Q 6:2 Is the coverage effective as soon as the insurer receives the application and enrollment material?

No. The enrollment forms accompany the application materials to the insurance company's home office, where the underwriter reviews the enrollment and the final coverage requested. This pre-issue work typically occurs during the month prior to the effective date of the coverage, although the extra preparation required for implementation of some plans, such as flexible benefit plans, must be done several months earlier. Only after the final review and approval by the insurer is the coverage effective.

Under the terms of the Health Insurance Portability and Accountability Act (HIPAA), insurers must accept every eligible employee who applies for medical coverage. Insurers also must accept every small employer (2 to 50 employees) that applies for medical insurance. An insurer can decline to insure a group with over 50 employees, but if it accepts the risk, it must accept all employees, regardless of health.

Q 6:3 When might an underwriter not approve an application for coverage?

There are two general reasons why an underwriter would not approve an application: The coverage details are substantially different from the plan the underwriter had originally agreed to, thus materially changing the risk, or the group's enrollment produces a substantially different final group than expected.

If the group has 50 or fewer employees, the insurer must accept the risk for medical insurance, but not necessarily for dental, vision, long-term care, disability, or life insurance.

Q 6:4 If an application is not approved by the underwriter, what happens?

Usually, the intermediary and group representative work together to make changes to the plan or the premium to make the group an acceptable risk for the underwriter.

Q 6:5 Why does the insurance company require detailed coverage information before issuing the policy?

It is important that the master contract reflect precisely the coverage desired, because claims are paid on the basis of the contract. Although the underwriter may have a detailed record of what coverage is desired and who is likely to participate based on the materials submitted for the initial quote, the final master contract must be developed from current information.

Another reason for requiring detailed coverage information is that some insurers allow policies with fewer than 100 participants to be "field underwritten." This means that the initial quote is developed by a field sales representative. As a result, the home office may have no prior knowledge of the employee group, and the application and enrollment forms may be the first information the underwriter receives.

Q 6:6 When an employer uses a TPA, what services does the administrator provide?

The TPA or a service bureau may take care of changes in enrollment, premium payment, claim determination, and reporting functions. When the TPA also acts as an intermediary, plan change and renewal administration would be included. Depending on how much of the plan is self-funded, the TPA will perform various services that the insurer performs for a conventionally insured plan. Typically, when an employer self-funds, one of the reasons is to unbundle administrative services and eliminate duplicate carrier administration, which adds unnecessarily to the cost of the program; therefore, even though TPAs offer most services available from insurance carriers, many self-funded employers perform as many tasks as possible in-house and buy any necessary adjuncts from one or more third parties.

Q 6:7 Who provides the announcement materials necessary to inform employees about the plan?

Typically, a concise letter from the employer to employees explains what benefits the new plan will provide, who is eligible to enroll, how much an employee's monthly contribution will be (if the plan is contributory), and when the coverage will become effective. An insurance company representative may provide form letters to the policyholder that can be customized to meet the employer's needs. When substantial changes are being made or the plan is complex, professionals may be retained to provide special communications.

Q 6:8 What is a certificate of insurance?

Once the plan becomes effective, a certificate of insurance is given to each employee. This may or may not be mandatory; certificates are not required in all states. The certificates provide employees with a summary of coverage, just as the master contract does for the employer. (The "cert" does not, however, constitute a contract between the employee and the insurer.)

Insurers typically provide covered employees with booklets that describe coverage in less technical language than in the master contract. These booklets are not filed with the state insurance department as certificates are usually required to be. Booklets explain coverage in readable language and are becoming increasingly common, in part because of state "readability" laws. It is also common for insurers to provide "booklet certs" that include both a technical coverage explanation and a lay person's explanation under one cover. Neither the booklet nor the certificate automatically satisfies the summary plan description (SPD) requirement of the Employee Retirement Income Security Act (ERISA). Special wording must be added to standard insurance company-provided material in order to meet ERISA requirements.

Q 6:9 What other materials are issued to employees?

Many plans include identification cards so that each employee has a wallet-sized card to refer to when questioned by a provider or when filing a claim. Some employers purchase hospital guarantee cards from their insurers as part of their plans instead of ID cards. The guarantee card typically ensures that a hospital will accept a patient even if the hospital cannot reach the insurance company to verify coverage. Cards usually guarantee coverage for 72 hours and are meant to serve as temporary coverage confirmation on weekends and holidays when a provider would not be able to contact the insurer. Cards may be provided to covered dependents as well as employees.

Other materials involve preferred provider organizations (PPOs). In order for an employee to visit a preferred provider, he or she must know who those providers are. The insurance company, third-party administrator, or PPO publishes a list of the preferred providers periodically, because additions and deletions are made during the year.

If the health care plan includes a prescription drug card plan, employees are issued cards as soon as possible after the effective date of the policy. The prescription drug administrator produces the cards and often ships them directly to the employer. The employer can specify that it wants cards for employees only or cards for covered dependents and employees. A guide to participating pharmacies that will accept the card is necessary with such plans. In some instances the ID card is combined with the prescription drug card.

Various other materials are distributed, especially when a new policy provision is being added. If new limitations are being placed on coverage or if expansions are being made to coverage, employers and insurers want to communicate the changes so that employees understand what benefits will be payable. For example, if utilization review (UR) is added to the health plan, employees will need to understand when they must contact the UR organization, where to call or write, and what the ramifications will be if they do not follow the UR procedures.

HIPAA added a new requirement that reductions in benefits be communicated within 60 days. A summary of material reduction (SMR) must be distributed to participants with 60 days of adoption.

Reporting and Disclosure

Q 6:10 Are there reports that an employer must file with the state or federal government?

Yes. Generally, employers and other plan sponsors must file annual reports. These reports, known as the Form 5500 series, are due within seven months after the close of the plan year, unless an extension has been requested. Plans must file a Form 5500 each year, but some plans with fewer than 100 participants qualify for an exemption from the filing requirement. Failure to comply with ERISA reporting requirements can result in fines of up to $1,000 a day for each day of noncompliance. For a complete discussion of Form 5500 filing, see Chapter 14.

Effective August 5, 1997, the Taxpayer Relief Act of 1997 eliminated the requirement to file summary plan descriptions and summaries of material modification with the Department of Labor (DOL).

Q 6:11 What new reporting rules were instituted under HIPAA?

One of the provisions of the Health Insurance Portability and Accountability Act of 1996 set into place rules requiring employers to report certain changes to employees.

HIPAA provides that if there is a material reduction in covered services or benefits, a summary of the changes must be furnished to participants within 60 days of its adoption. Alternatively, plan sponsors may provide a description of changes at regular intervals that do not exceed 90 days.

Q 6:12 What is a qualified medical child support order?

The Omnibus Budget Reconciliation Act of 1993 (OBRA '93) mandates that group health plans provide benefits according to qualified medical child support order (QMCSO) requirements. QMCSOs are judgments, decrees, or court orders that create or recognize a child's right to receive benefits under a group health plan. QMCSOs also must specify the following:

1. The name and last known address of the participant and each child covered by the order;
2. The type of coverage the plan will provide each child or how the coverage will be determined;
3. The period the order covers; and
4. Each plan to which the order applies.

OBRA '93 requires that each group health plan establish reasonable procedures to determine whether medical child support orders are qualified. It also requires group health plans to administer benefits under QMCSOs. Procedures for meeting these requirements must be in writing and must include notifying each person eligible for benefits under the plan as well as allowing the child to designate a representative to receive notices.

Q 6:13 Can a QMCSO require a plan to offer a new benefit?

No. QMCSOs cannot require a plan to "provide any type or form of benefit or any option, not otherwise provided under the plan."

Q 6:14 Does OBRA '93 require plans to cover certain children?

Under OBRA '93, states must pass legislation prohibiting insurers from denying a child enrollment under the parent's health coverage—even if the child is:

1. Born out of wedlock;
2. Not claimed as a dependent on the parent's federal income tax return; or
3. Not living with the parent or in the insurer's service area.

States also must enact laws requiring the insurer or employer to allow the parent to enroll any eligible child under the QMCSO, regardless of open enrollment period restrictions. The plan may not terminate the child's coverage unless the QMCSO is no longer in effect or the child has (or will have) comparable coverage by the termination date.

State law also must permit employers to withhold any payroll deduction needed to cover the child and require insurers to do the following:

1. Give custodial parents any information they need to obtain benefits;
2. Submit claims without the noncustodial parent's approval; and
3. Make payments directly to the custodial parent.

Q 6:15 Does OBRA '93 require any notices?

Yes. The plan administrator must notify the participant, the child, and the child's guardian or custodial parent of receiving a QMCSO and the plan's procedures for determining whether the order is qualified. OBRA '93 also mandates that plan administrators determine whether an order is qualified and notify the same people within a "reasonable" time.

Q 6:16 What is a summary plan description, and what information does it contain?

A summary plan description furnishes the DOL with specific information about the health plan. It includes the name and address of the policyholder; the type of benefit plan; the name, address, and telephone number of the plan administrator; the name and address of the person designated as agent for service of legal process; and the names and addresses of the plan trustees, if any. It also includes eligibility requirements, contribution requirements, claim processing procedures, benefit denial guidelines, and an explanation of the appeals process. Each plan participant must be provided with an SPD. Effective August 5, 1997, the Taxpayer Relief Act of 1997 eliminated the requirement to file SPDs with the Department of Labor.

HIPAA amended the SPD requirements. SPDs now also need to include the following information:

1. Whether an insurer is responsible for financing or administering the plan;
2. The insurer's name and address; and
3. The office of the Department of Labor where plan participants can obtain information regarding their rights.

Q 6:17 Are there any changes pending regarding SPDs?

Yes, on September 9, 1998, the DOL published in the *Federal Register* proposed regulations governing the content of SPDs. The proposed regulations would clarify benefit, medical provider, health maintenance organization (HMO), and other information that plans must disclose to plan participants and beneficiaries in, or as part of, the plan's SPD.

Q 6:18 What would the proposed regulations change?

The proposed SPD content regulation would provide that health plan SPDs must describe:

1. Any cost-sharing provisions, including premiums, deductibles, coinsurance, and copayment amounts for which the participant or beneficiary will be responsible;
2. Any annual or lifetime caps or other limits on benefits under the plan;

3. The extent to which preventive services are covered under the plan;
4. Whether, and under what circumstances, existing and new drugs are covered under the plan;
5. Whether, and under what circumstances, coverage is provided for medical tests, devices and procedures;
6. Provisions governing the use of network providers, the composition of the provider network and whether, and under what circumstances, coverage is provided for out-of-network services;
7. Any conditions or limits on the selection of primary care providers or providers of specialty medical care;
8. Any conditions or limits applicable to obtaining emergency medical care; and
9. Any provisions requiring preauthorizations or UR as a condition of obtaining a benefit or service under the plan.

The proposed regulations would also make clear that SPDs must describe, among other things, their procedures related to qualified medical child support orders, the plan sponsor's authority to terminate the plan or eliminate benefits under the plan, COBRA continuation rights, and must include updated information on ERISA rights.

The proposed regulations also would repeal the limited exemption with respect to SPDs of health plans providing benefits through qualified HMOs. The proposed regulations would result in health plans that provide benefits through a federally qualified HMO having to comply with the revised SPD disclosure rules being proposed for other health plans.

Q 6:19 Do plan sponsors have to include information about HMOs in SPDs?

If the HMO is not federally qualified, the SPD must include the same information for HMOs as for indemnity plans. For federally qualified plans, the SPD need only include information about HMO availability, and refer to sources of additional information and to HMO-prepared materials that are to be distributed in conjunction with the SPD. The DOL has proposed eliminating this exemption.

Q 6:20 Should an employer rely on the SPD to explain plan benefits to employees?

The SPD is a legal document with specified contents. It is helpful to supplement the SPD with some down-to-earth employee communication materials. Ongoing education of employees will lead to more effective use of the health care system, along with better quality of care and improved health cost management. It will also maximize the employee relations value of providing benefits.

Q 6:21 Can an SPD be used for more than one purpose?

Yes. As explained in Q 6:16, the SPD is a legal document that provides information required by law. These requirements are minimum requirements, and the SPD can contain even more information than that legally required. Many employers write their benefit communication booklet in straightforward terms, adding a few pages at the back that contain the data necessary to fulfill the SPD requirements.

Another approach is to use the benefit book/SPD as the plan document itself. This can be done most easily if the plan is self-funded; in that case it will not be necessary to overcome the objections of an insurance company that wants to use its own materials. A significant advantage of using the booklet/SPD as the plan document is that it prevents any differences between the booklet and the document that may cause a conflict in interpretation. ERISA requires a "summary" plan description, which implies that the SPD summarizes a separate document; therefore, some benefit practitioners believe a separate plan document is required.

Q 6:22 What administrative material does the insurer initially provide to the employer?

The employer is usually given a supply of enrollment forms, certificates, and booklets for additional enrollees; premium reporting forms; claim forms; the master contract; a final employee roster or listing; an administrative manual; and all forms required to administer changes (additions and deletions), including conversions and COBRA.

Enrollment

Q 6:23 Why is enrollment in the plan encouraged?

The employer is attempting to meet its employees' coverage needs by providing a health care plan. If employees are not educated about the plan and encouraged to enroll, the employer will not have achieved that objective. Further, because a larger insured group sometimes results in a better spread of risk, the rates may be better as enrollment increases. Administrative charges by the insurer also may reflect economies of scale in the rates.

Q 6:24 What information must individuals provide when enrolling in the plan?

Enrollment forms ask enrollees to provide some or all of the following information:

- Name
- Sex
- Age
- Social Security number
- Salary
- Occupation (rarely required for health care coverage)
- Election or rejection of coverage (if contributory)
- Marital status and election or rejection of dependent coverage (if contributory)
- Dependents to be covered (this information is now mandatory—HIPAA requires that dependents be named on certificates of coverage.)
- Selection of coverage if more than one is offered
- The employee's beneficiary for life insurance
- Authorization for payroll deductions (for contributory plans)

This information is more detailed and up-to-date than the census data provided to the insurer for the initial quote.

Q 6:25 Can employers consider Medicaid eligibility when enrolling employees?

No. OBRA '93 amends ERISA specifically to prohibit employers from taking Medicaid eligibility into account when enrolling participants or beneficiaries in a group health plan. [ERISA § 609(b)]

Q 6:26 Must individuals enroll in a noncontributory plan?

Yes. Although the employer knows that everyone will be covered, demographic information and a beneficiary designation (for life insurance coverage) is necessary for the insurer to develop a final premium rate and, for some plans, to establish the employee records needed to pay claims. Because HIPAA requires that dependents be named on certificates of coverage, employers must find out the names of covered dependents.

Q 6:27 Who enrolls the employees in the group health insurance plan?

The company's employee benefit administrator, with or without the assistance of the intermediary or insurance representative, enrolls employees. Small employers may not need help because of the limited number of employees. Employee meetings to explain the new plan and distribute the enrollment forms are conducted by the employee benefit administrator, but may include representatives of insurance companies and HMOs.

Q 6:28 How long do employees have to complete their enrollment forms?

Because the enrollment forms must be submitted to the insurance company before the effective date of the plan, employees are encouraged to return them as quickly as possible. An arbitrary time period to return the form, such as a week, is typically established by the employer. Employees who submit forms late may or may not be allowed to participate in the plan as of the effective date of the plan.

Q 6:29 Why would an employee who submits a late enrollment form not be allowed to participate as of the plan's effective date?

Insurance companies have established rules regarding late enrollment in order to ensure consistent, accurate premium and coverage records and to protect the plan against adverse selection. Whether the employee obtains coverage as of the plan's effective date depends on how late the form is submitted. If the insurer does not have the form before the effective date, the employee is typically added to the plan on the date the form is received, if it is received within 31 days of the effective date. An employee who does not enroll within 31 days of becoming eligible is assumed to have declined coverage. Insurers try to have employees return enrollment forms that note if they are actually declining coverage in order to protect themselves and to ensure that no employee is inadvertently excluded from enrollment in the plan.

Under HIPAA, group health plans offering dependent coverage must allow at least 30 days in which to enroll new dependents following marriage, birth, adoption, or placement for adoption. Cafeteria plan rules generally require elections prior to the effective date of coverage, but regulations allow plans to comply with HIPAA while allowing pre-tax contributions.

Q 6:30 Can an employee who declines coverage initially enroll at a later date?

For contributory plans, an employee who initially declines coverage, whether as of the initial effective date of the plan or as of his or her initial eligibility date (a new hire or an employee who becomes part of an eligible class after the initial plan effective date), was formerly required to supply evidence of insurability in order to enroll in the plan later. Otherwise an employee might elect health care coverage only after having been injured or becoming ill. This is known as adverse selection (or antiselection) and can significantly increase the cost of the medical plan beyond the anticipated levels. Some states prohibit preexisting condition exclusions in plans beyond a certain size or specify a limited benefit for preexisting conditions, such as $5,000 in the first 12 months of coverage.

HIPAA prohibits evidence of insurability requirements. Late enrollees may have to satisfy a waiting period before coverage becomes effective and may have preexisting conditions excluded for up to 18 months (including any waiting period), but they must be allowed to enroll, no matter how sick they are. HIPAA does not require plans to allow late enrollment, but if a plan allows late enrollment, evidence of insurability or any other health-status related factor cannot be used to determine eligibility, benefits, or contributions.

Q 6:31 What is a special enrollment period?

HIPAA requires special open enrollment periods for people who lose other coverage, subject to the following conditions:

1. The employee or dependent had other coverage when declining an earlier opportunity to enroll in the plan.
2. The employee stated in writing that another source of coverage was the reason for declining enrollment. (This condition only applies if the plan required such a statement and provided the employee with notice of this requirement.)
3. The person has exhausted COBRA continuation or COBRA did not apply, but the loss of coverage resulted from what otherwise would have been a COBRA qualifying event.
4. The person requests enrollment within 30 days after the loss of other coverage.

Group health plans offering dependent coverage must allow at least 30 days in which to enroll new dependents following marriage, birth, adoption, or placement for adoption. If the employee is eligible, but not enrolled, the employee must also be allowed to enroll at the same time. Eligible spouses must also be allowed to enroll within 30 days of birth or adoption of the couple's child. Although the law does not so state, it appears that the IRS is interpreting this requirement to allow enrolling other children as well. Coverage must be effective retroactive to the date of birth, adoption, or placement for adoption. After marriage, coverage must be effective no later than the first day of the month following the date the plan receives the enrollment request.

Q 6:32   Is any kind of re-enrollment of employees in group health insurance plans necessary?

Periodic re-enrollment is desirable—even necessary. The employer's list of eligible participants needs regular updating, or the employer may be paying benefits for ineligible people. Employees come and go; dependent status changes; employees marry, divorce, and have children. All of these changes require updating of eligibility lists. A regularly scheduled re-enrollment will minimize the chances of paying health benefits for someone who is ineligible or no longer eligible.

Other reasons for re-enrollment include:

1. Change of carrier
2. Change in benefits or cost to employees (required to re-authorize employee contributions)
3. Annual open enrollment elections

Even in noncontributory plans, periodic updates of employee and dependent information are advisable to assure continued eligibility and correct claims determination.

Billing

Q 6:33   How are employers billed for group health insurance premiums?

Today, there are two basic kinds of billing and eligibility arrangements between employers and insurers.

Large employers generally provide eligibility information on magnetic tape, computer disk, or via modem. The insurer then calculates the bill based on eligibility.

Smaller employers that elect home-office accounting (also known as roster or list billing) are required to submit individual changes in insured status to the insurer so that accurate bills can be generated from the insurance company's home office. For example, when a new employee is hired and completes an enrollment form, the form is submitted to the insurer, and the insurer establishes a file on that employee, thereby increasing the required monthly premium. A bill reflecting that will be produced for the coming period. The initial enrollment forms provide the insurer with the information required for computerized claim payment and billing.

An older arrangement, known as self-accounting, is still in use. With self-accounting, the employer only reports total numbers of employees covered. Typically, the employer uses the last premium, adds the number of new hires, deletes the number of terminations, and makes any changes in family status. This arrangement is generally used with policyholder certification of eligibility, as described in Q 6:37.

Q 6:34 Where can an employer get help in calculating premium payments?

A service representative of the insurance company located in one of the insurer's field offices can be contacted by phone.

Some insurers provide their policyholders with the name of their billing representative in the home office.

Q 6:35 If an employer's premium payment is late, does coverage lapse?

Generally, policyholders have 31 days from the premium due date to remit the premium; however, if the insurer does not receive the premium by that date, the coverage usually is not canceled immediately. Instead, the insurer attempts to collect the premium by sending late notices and then a formal cancellation notice, assuming, until proven otherwise, that the employer wants to maintain coverage. Insurance companies have different time requirements and procedures regarding late premium payment.

Usually the employer pays the late premium, and the policy remains in force. If the insurer has made it clear when the premium must be paid to avoid policy termination, and the employer still does not remit the premium, the policy will be terminated.

Reinstatement of a terminated policy is not automatic upon payment of the late premium; an insurer may offer revised premium rates as a condition of reinstatement or may want to ascertain whether large life or health claims have been incurred. The insurer may refuse to reinstate coverage.

Q 6:36 Does the insurer periodically audit employers that self-account?

Yes. Audits are done randomly or for employers that have requested help to solve a significant billing problem. The audits are performed in order to ensure that the employer is adhering to the administrative requirements of the plan, especially with respect to enrollment of employees and premium payment.

Proper enrollment of employees is crucial to claim payment. The administrator must understand when employees can be enrolled, when coverage becomes effective, and when premium payments must start in order to ensure coverage. Audits help the insurer understand what needs to be more clearly explained to administrators and identifies employers that may be having problems.

Claims

Q 6:37 How does an individual submit a claim for payment?

Certain information regarding the medical expense must be provided to the insurer or the TPA for review. This can be communicated on a claim form or electronically, depending on the provider's and insurer's or administrator's procedures. The majority of private insurers require that the insured obtain a claim form from the employer, have the provider complete information about the care provided, and then submit it for payment. This is known as a "direct claim" because the employer does not become involved in certifying eligibility; the claim goes directly from employee to insurer/administrator. Of course, the insurer/administrator must be continually updated regarding enrollment changes.

Some employers require that an insured request a form from the benefit administrator, who certifies eligibility by signing the form before it is provided to the employee. The insurer does not ascertain eligibility for these insurers, because the employer has already done so. Few employers today use the "policyholder cert" approach, although it is effective in limiting claims by ineligible individuals.

Some plans require no claim forms for employees. For example, an employee may present a card to the health care provider. The provider submits charges directly to the insurer/administrator for services rendered. Usually, the card shows what coverage the employee has, and the provider knows what fees and services are eligible. Sometimes services for which there is only partial coverage are provided. In that case, the insured is billed for the balance.

Electronic claim submission is becoming increasingly common. Most large hospitals and many physician groups have the capability to submit claims electronically. Most insurers, HMOs, and large TPAs have the capability to accept claims electronically. HIPAA requires that plans paying claims under Medicare and Medicaid accept claims electronically, either directly or through a clearinghouse. The effective date of this requirement depends on when regulations under HIPAA are issued by the Department of Health and Human Services.

Q 6:38 Can employees submit claims after the effective date of the plan but before they receive their certificates of insurance?

Yes. Claims for medical care received after the plan effective date (other than those resulting from a preexisting condition not covered by the plan) can be submitted and paid as soon as the underwriter approves the policy and the enrollment information is filed at the home office of the insurer.

Q 6:39 Do most individuals pay the health care provider for the service and receive reimbursement later from the plan?

Individuals either pay providers at the time of service and receive reimbursement later or "assign benefits" to the provider, thus avoiding payment at the time of service. (The practice of assigning benefits originated to assure payment for services rendered; some insureds requested reimbursement from the insurer but did not pay the provider with the money they received, thus creating cash-flow and bad-debt problems for the providers.)

Managed care plans, such as preferred provider organization plans, generally require their physicians and other health care professionals to bill the plan directly for the convenience of the insured. Most hospitals accept assignment, even if they are not part of the network. Other non-network providers may require payment by the insured at the time of service.

Q 6:40 What is assignment of benefits?

The insured authorizes the insurance company to pay any benefits directly to the provider of medical care, rather than to the insured.

Q 6:41 Where can an employee get help in completing a claim form?

The employer's benefit administrator can usually help employees, but many insurers can also provide assistance. A toll-free number is sometimes provided by the insurer for benefit questions.

Q 6:42 How quickly are insureds reimbursed for their claim expenses?

Claim turnaround time varies by insurer from several days to several months. The information an insurer requires in order to determine reimbursement is sometimes detailed and comes from various sources. Providers are sometimes asked to provide additional information when the claim form is completed improperly or the reasons for the procedures and charges are unclear. If benefits are to be coordinated with other insurance programs, information from other insurers must be requested in order to determine each insurer's payment.

Q 6:43 How rapidly should an employer or union expect claims to be processed?

Processing time can vary considerably, but a good rule of thumb is that about 90 percent of claims should be turned around within ten working days. Some claims will be delayed because of processing difficulties; some will require investigation or additional information from the provider; others will be incomplete. Nevertheless, about 98 percent of all claims should be processed within 30 calendar days.

For cash-flow purposes, slower turnaround can be desirable. This can be accommodated under self-funded arrangements, but generally not under insured programs.

Under ERISA, if a claimant submits a claim and does not receive a response within 90 days, the claimant can initiate appeal proceedings. Many states have laws specifying that no legal action can be taken to collect on claims before 60 or 90 days have passed without a response. Some states have passed laws or promulgated regulations defining what constitutes fair or unfair claim practices. These laws generally require payment within 30 or 45 days, unless investigation is needed, in which case a notice of delay is usually required.

On September 9, 1998, the DOL published in the *Federal Register* proposed regulations governing claim procedures. The proposed claim procedure regulation would modify the benefit claim and appeal process for all ERISA-covered employee pension and welfare benefit plans.

Q 6:44 What changes would these DOL proposed regulations make to current benefit claim appeal procedures?

The proposal would establish shorter time limits for making health benefit claim decisions:

1. For urgent care claims, as soon as possible, but not later than 72 hours for an initial decision and no later than 72 hours for appeals; and

2. For non-urgent health care claims, within a reasonable period of time, but no later than 15 days for the initial decision and no later than 30 days for appeals.

Other requirements under the proposed regulations include:

1. Plans would have to provide participants with more timely information about the plan's claim procedures and more information about the decision when a claim has been denied.

2. Appeals would have to be decided by a party who is neither the initial claim reviewer nor a subordinate of the initial claim reviewer. For decisions based on medical judgments, the reviewer of a denied health care claim must consult with a medical professional.
3. Claimants would have access to judicial review when plans fail to establish or to follow reasonable claims procedures that comply with the new regulations.
4. All ERISA-covered health plans, including plans that provide benefits through federally qualified HMOs, would have to comply with the new claims procedure rules.

Consumer advocates strongly support the regulations, while managed care plans and many employers oppose certain aspects as unworkable.

Q 6:45 Are there ways an employer can be assured of getting a good turnaround time for claim processing?

Insurance companies and TPAs are increasingly willing to offer processing guarantees as part of their contracts. The guarantees may specify such things as the turnaround time, financial accuracy, and processing accuracy.

Q 6:46 Who receives the benefit check?

The employee normally receives the payment. If reimbursement is for a service received by a dependent, the insured (the employee) still receives the payment unless it has been assigned. Some employers prefer to receive the checks from the insurer and distribute them to employees. If the employee has assigned benefits to a provider, the provider is paid directly. An explanation of benefits (EOB) accompanies the check.

Q 6:47 What is an explanation of benefits?

An explanation of benefits summarizes how a reimbursement was determined. It usually includes the services provided, the providers involved, the date of the care, and an explanation of what services were covered or not covered. If payment is made directly to a provider, a facsimile of the check is often provided to the insured, with an EOB. Claim systems have improved so much that some EOBs now provide year-to-date information regarding deductibles and maximums. Many administrators include the name of the person who processed the claim to improve customer service. Typically, the EOB material also explains how the claim appeal process works. ERISA requires this explanation whenever a claim is denied.

Q 6:48 How does an employee appeal a claim determination?

ERISA regulations establish and define the appeal process for both insurer and employee. Generally, by law, the claimant can be required to complete reasonable forms for the insurer. Claimants have at least 60 days to appeal claims, and the insurer or plan administrator must answer the appeal within 60 days unless special circumstances require an extension. If there are special circumstances, such as the need to hold a hearing, the decision must be made within 120 days after receipt of a request for review. If a claim is denied, the insured must be provided with a written explanation of the reasons for the denial and references to the policy provision on which the denial is based. This procedure is followed for initial claim denial as well as for an appeal denial.

Under the rules proposed by the Department of Labor in 1998, the length of time a claimant has to appeal a health or disability claim would be extended to 180 days. The decision on appeal would have to be made within 72 hours for urgent care claims, 30 days for other health plan claims, and 45 days for disability claims. It would remain 60 days for other claims.

Q 6:49 What is the plan administrator's obligation with regard to an appeal?

ERISA requires that the plan afford a reasonable opportunity for a full and fair review. A court decision illustrates what is and is not a full and fair review.

The U.S. District Court for the District of Connecticut ruled that the Xerox Corporation and the administrator of Xerox's benefit plans

(Patricia Nazemetz) did not provide a full and fair review of an employee's appeal. [Crocco v Xerox Corp, DC Conn, No. 5:91-CV-779] The court said Xerox conducted a "cursory and one-sided review" of the appeal. The court remanded the claim to Xerox for a fair hearing and reconsideration by the plan fiduciary. Ms. Nazemetz explained to the court that the only objective of her review was to determine whether American PsychManagement (which was dismissed as a defendant) had followed proper procedures. The court observed that "she made no independent effort to determine whether that decision was correct, she did not speak to (the employee) or her psychiatrist, she did not look at the medical record, and did not even consider seeking the advice of a third party."

The court went on to say "Logic, fairness and ERISA require that Nazemetz do more than check APM's procedures and the superficial rationality of its decision. . . . There can be no doubt that the steps taken by Nazemetz did not constitute a full and fair review of the case." The court pointed out that Nazemetz had assumed a fiduciary responsibility to act in the best interests of benefit plan participants, while APM did not have this responsibility.

The regulations proposed by the DOL in 1998 would require plan administrators to provide claimants with "all documents and records relevant to the claimant's claim for benefits, without regard to whether such records were considered or relied upon in making the adverse benefit determination."

Q 6:50 What appeal processes are in place for workers and dependents?

When a health plan does not meet expectations, any member or covered dependent can make an appeal. Whether the appeal is made because payment of a claim, authorization of treatment, or referral to a specialist has been denied, or simply because care seems unsatisfactory, the patient has 60 days (under ERISA) from the date of denial or decision to submit the appeal, listing the reasons why the request should be honored. (A proposal is pending to extend the limit to 180 days for health and disability claims.) If the appeal is denied, a patient who wants to pursue the appeal further may file the appeal with the appropriate regulatory body, such as the state Department of Insurance (DOI). If the patient is a senior on Medicare, the follow-up appeal should be filed with Health Care Financing Administration (HCFA), rather than the DOI.

Appeals are submitted to the health plan's appeals board, which typically comprises medical and administrative personnel. The board reviews the medical history and condition of the appeal applicant and the reasons listed for honoring the patient's request. A determination is made as to whether the original decision should be reversed, and the patient is notified of the board's finding. Some health plans allow the patient to make a statement in person to the board.

Q 6:51 How can employers and health plans improve the appeal process to prevent failures and possible large damage awards?

Appeal processes fail largely because of a lack of education. In many cases, plan participants have not been informed about how to best use their health care program, and when unexpected medical needs arise, they are not prepared to proceed according to plan guidelines. The most common appeals are made for reconsideration of decisions originally made according to plan provisions when the patient, although clearly in error, claims to have been unaware of standard operating procedures.

A concerted effort to develop good rapport among employers, employees, physicians, and health plans will have a positive effect. If the health plan effectively communicates that coverage decisions made are in the patient's best medical interest, rather than just to save health care dollars, participants will be far less likely to file a complaint with the Department of Insurance or to pursue a lawsuit. Patients will also take a more proactive role in their own treatment (e.g., preventive measures such as weight loss and smoking cessation) if the health plan provides them with education and support.

Coverage, Renewal and Changes

Q 6:52 How does an employer renew its health insurance policy?

The insurer assumes that the policyholder wants to renew its policy and maintain the same plan design unless it hears differently from the employer's intermediary. Thus, policy renewal can be as simple as the insurer re-rating the group to determine a premium rate for the coming policy period (typically a year) and sending the notice of the renewal rate to the policyholder or intermediary.

Small employers whose policies are manually rated have little or no opportunity to negotiate their premium. Unless they request a plan change, such as an increase in the deductible or the addition of a utilization review service, the coverage will remain in force as it has been, although the rate may change. If the insurer does not have an up-to-date employee census, the employer will be asked to submit one about three months before the policy anniversary date, so that a new policy rate may be calculated. A notice must be sent to the policyholder before the policy anniversary date, based on the contractual agreement regarding the timing required for premium changes.

For employers with more than 50 covered employees, the renewal process usually involves an analysis of the policy period's claims in order to develop the experience-rated portion of the rate. For more complicated policies, such as for collectively bargained groups and flexible benefits, the renewal process involves more negotiation on benefits and rates, and the process must start earlier.

Q 6:53   When can an employer change its coverage?

Plan changes can be made at any time, given the insurer's approval. The employer discusses its needs with the intermediary, and a request is made to the insurer for the change in premium that would result from a change in coverage.

The insurer can make plan changes for the employer at any time, but the most common point is coincident with renewal. Typically, the underwriter develops a renewal rate based on the in-force plan, and then calculates a different rate based on the proposed changes. Often, the request for a plan change follows an underwriter's premium rate change notice.

Q 6:54   When the policy is renewed, are all employees automatically covered?

Only employees who have previously enrolled are automatically covered. In the past, others, known as "late enrollees," had to submit evidence of insurability. The Health Insurance Portability and Accountability Act of 1996 prohibits group health plans from establishing eligibility rules based on health-related factors, such as evidence of insurability. Plans can impose waiting periods on late enrollees, but the length of the waiting period cannot be based on health status-related factors. Late enrollees can be subject to a preexisting condition exclusion of no more than 18 months reduced by the length of prior coverage. A late enrollee who previously declined coverage because he or she was covered under another plan may be eligible for a special open enrollment upon losing that other coverage.

Q 6:55 If an employer believes that a renewal rate is too high, what options are available?

The intermediary can attempt to negotiate a decrease in the renewal rate or get quotes from other carriers.

Q 6:56 What kinds of plan changes might an employer want to make during the plan year?

An employer might want to implement cost-management provisions in the middle of a plan year if concerned that the renewal rate will call for a large increase. Employers that are going through significant organizational changes or experiencing economic difficulties may choose to make changes immediately, rather than waiting for the renewal date. If employees are asked to choose a plan during an open enrollment period, changes are typically made only coincident with the effective date of the choice.

Termination of Coverage

Q 6:57 Can an employer terminate coverage in the middle of a plan year?

Yes, but the employer will be held responsible for all premiums due and unpaid up to the official termination date. The request for termination must be in writing and dated prior to the requested termination date. Some Blue Cross contracts permit termination only upon anniversary.

Q 6:58 If a contract specifies termination at year-end only, does an employer have any options?

Maybe. Regardless of what the contract says, the employer's carrier should, however, be consulted. Few carriers want to hold clients against their will. They will likely be willing to negotiate an earlier cancellation once they have received assurance that large claims will not remain when the employer leaves. Also, the contract should be checked for provisions dealing with nonpayment of premium. Nonpayment of premium may (and probably does) provide for automatic cancellation after premiums are delinquent for 60 or, at most, 90 days.

Q 6:59 If an employer changes insurers, what protection do employees have against medical expenses?

Normally, there is no gap in coverage for employees. If an employer terminates coverage with one insurer, the new insurer usually agrees to pick up the protection as of the minute the other coverage is terminated.

Q 6:60 What protection does an employee who terminates employment have against medical expenses?

Some states require continuation of coverage for a certain period. Otherwise, those who terminate employment, either involuntarily or voluntarily, become insured under a new employer's plan, elect a conversion policy from the previous employer's insurer, or elect to continue coverage under COBRA.

Q 6:61 What is a conversion privilege?

Individuals insured under a group plan (in most policies, after being insured for at least three months) can convert to an individual policy without evidence of insurability. Individuals eligible for similar group coverage under another plan offered by the same employer and those aged 65 or older are typically not allowed to convert. Coverage is available to the employee as well as to his or her dependents.

The individual often has several plans to choose from, but rarely do these options include a plan that provides benefits similar to those of the group plan. The actual plans available are those normally issued by an insurer in the state in which the terminated employee resides. Most states require specific benefit offerings and policy forms.

For an additional premium, self-funded employers may purchase the conversion privilege from either the life insurance carrier or the carrier that provides stop-loss insurance. Fully self-funded plans are not required to offer conversion, because they are not subject to state insurance laws.

Q 6:62 How does COBRA affect the group conversion privilege?

Many employees and their dependents are eligible for COBRA continuation coverage and elect this rather than a traditional conversion policy, which is probably more expensive and offers less coverage. The Health Insurance Portability and Accountability Act of 1996 makes individual health insurance policies available to people who lose group coverage. To be eligible a person must have at least 18 months of creditable coverage; therefore, people with more than three months, but less than 18 months of coverage, will still want conversion policies.

Q 6:63 What are the conversion requirements for other group plans?

Similar to group health plans and depending on the state of issue, life insurance plans are required to offer conversion options upon termination of coverage. Many long-term disability and accidental death plans offer conversion privileges as well.

Computerized Administration

Q 6:64 What role do computer systems play in managing health plans?

Even when significant portions of the administrative job are performed by insurers or TPAs, computers are still extremely useful in helping the employer perform mandatory or voluntary functions. These functions include:

- Gathering data
- Performing nondiscrimination tests
- Tracking flexible benefits credits
- Administering COBRA benefits
- Tracking costs and utilization
- Preparing management reports
- Preparing employee statements
- Providing interactive communication with employees

The ultimate responsibility for assembling most of the necessary data (the "input") for almost all of these administrative functions falls on the employer. This includes personal data on the employee and dependents, eligibility data, compensation, contributions, plan option choices, and claims filed.

Q 6:65 What role would a computer system play in performing nondiscrimination testing?

Actually performing the nondiscrimination tests (see Chapter 11) is difficult enough; getting ready to do so can be even more demanding. One of the most difficult aspects of nondiscrimination testing is "categorizing." Employees must be categorized and tracked according to their status. Categories include the following:

1. Highly compensated versus non-highly compensated, and key versus non-key employees;
2. Ineligible, eligible, and participating employees; and
3. Employees in separate lines of business.

Nor are these categories static. An employee who falls into one category one year may fall into another in another year, either because the definitions change (e.g., a cost-of-living adjustment in compensation criteria for highly compensated employees) or because the employee's circumstances change.

For employers with significant numbers of employees or plan options, the only way of keeping all this information current and accurate is by means of a system that accepts data from the personnel recordkeeping system and has been programmed to assign everyone to the proper slots.

Q 6:66 What sort of features should a COBRA administration system have?

At a minimum, a system for administering COBRA should be able to do the following:

1. Produce notices and form letters for qualified beneficiaries;
2. Calculate premium amounts and prepare billing notices;
3. Keep track of qualified beneficiaries and the payment records and status of each;
4. Keep track of all transactions, producing an auditable report; and
5. Generate a variety of management reports.

It should, of course, also reflect all the latest requirements and be easily modified to handle future changes or additions to the regulations.

Many COBRA administration software packages will produce payment coupons that can be provided to the continuee. The employer is not required to provide these to the continuee, nor can an employer demand that the continuee return the payment coupon along with the monthly payment. If this feature is of interest to an employer, the following are some additional points to consider while shopping for the software:

1. The coupons should not be produced for the entire period of continuation at the start of the continuation period. The first

batch of coupons should cover the period from the inception of the continuation period to the end of the first plan year. That is the most likely time a rate increase will take effect, and new coupons will need to be produced showing the new premium.

2. The program should allow for changing the premium rate at any time, and the printing of new coupons from that occurrence. This is necessary because rate increases could occur more frequently than annually. Under these circumstances, an employer would want to insert the most current rate, if only for future continuees.

3. Continuees might lose the coupons and request that they be provided with a replacement supply.

4. The software should be capable of producing coupons for all persons currently in continuation status. When a premium rate change that is to apply to all persons does occur, the employer would want to (a) input the new rates once, (b) then have the software produce coupons for all affected parties as one process, and (c) not require the employer to input the same rate over and over, for each individual.

Q 6:67 How would a computer help in administering flexible benefits plans?

The more options available in a flexible benefits plan—including the option to change one's mind from time to time—the more data that has to be managed. A computer flex system can do the following:

1. Determine and communicate to the employee and the company the costs of various options;

2. Calculate premiums due to insurers;

3. Monitor individual accounts, including contributions or credits, and charges against those accounts;

4. Prepare employee statements of account balances; and

5. Monitor the nondiscrimination requirements that apply to flex plans, for overall requirements and each underlying benefit.

Q 6:68 What types of computer communication programs are available?

There are several types of communication programs available:

1. *Statement and correspondence systems.* These can be used to provide customized employee benefit statements and letters that incorporate individualized employee information in a more standardized format. Although such systems are often subroutines of broader administrative systems, stand-alone systems are also available.

2. *Financial projection systems.* These assist employees in selecting options by providing summaries of other benefits for which they are eligible.

3. *Interactive programs.* These can tap into plan and compensation databases to provide employees with information on their current status and benefit eligibility, project future benefits and costs, and permit employees to engage in "what if" scenarios or conduct online enrollment. Although these systems are generally more common in financial security-type plans (e.g., pensions), as compensation and benefit decisions become more closely interwoven (especially with flexible benefit plans), such systems are becoming more important for welfare benefit plan administration and communication.

Q 6:69 In buying or leasing an administrative computer system, what other features should a plan sponsor look for?

All systems arrive with potential, but that is no guarantee that the user will derive any value from them. To avoid a costly mistake, potential system buyers should look for the following:

1. A free trial period or money-back guarantee;
2. A formal training period for personnel;
3. Systems and software support, especially when the system must interact with other systems—someone must be sure they are all properly connected;
4. A complete set of user documentation (i.e., a manual);
5. Phone support for answers to questions; and

6. An ongoing service contract that provides for updates as laws or any other external factors that influence the system's operation change.

Prior to purchase, consider visiting a seasoned user of the system to gauge user friendliness, as well as the quality of the support.

Q 6:70 Is it becoming practical to use the Internet/Intranet for employee benefit administration and communication?

Yes. A 1997 Society for Human Resource Management survey found 83 percent of organizations make the World Wide Web available to employees.

With a large and increasing number of employees having Internet access, it becomes practical to use e-mail or a web site to communicate with employees regarding benefits. It also becomes possible to allow employees to enroll and re-enroll via the Internet.

Q 6:71 Are benefit professionals using the Internet/Intranet to communicate benefit information?

According to a 1998 survey by the International Foundation of Employee Benefit Plans, 29 percent of benefit professionals are already using the Internet (or an Intranet) and 95 percent plan to add more functions in the future. A survey of its members by the International Society of Certified Employee Benefit Specialists found that 60.8 percent said that evaluating, implementing, or expanding the use of Internet/intranet applications was one of their top five benefit priorities for 2000.

Q 6:72 What are the primary functions on the Internet/Intranet?

A 1998 survey by the International Foundation of Employee Benefit Plans found that 71 percent of respondents reported having their SPDs online, 50 percent reported having posted answers to frequently asked questions, and 44 percent reported having links to other web sites.

Q 6:73 What are the advantages of electronic communication?

According to a survey by William M. Mercer, Inc., 72 percent of the respondents cited "deliver information faster" as an advantage of electronic communication. "Ease of updating information" was named by 61 percent of the survey participants. Other advantages include:

- Lower cost (27 percent)
- More flexibility (23 percent)
- Easier to find correct information (19 percent)
- Easier to customize for employee groups (12 percent)

A 1998 survey by the International Foundation of Employee Benefit Plans reported the following primary benefits of using the Internet or an Intranet:

- Increased speed of information transfer and feedback (74 percent)
- Reduced reliance on print (67 percent)
- Reported improved cost-effectiveness (54 percent)
- Reported improved efficiency (51 percent)

Q 6:74 What are the different types of outsourcing?

Buck Consultants explains the different types of outsourcing as follows:

1. *System outsourcing.* A company uses an outsourcing organization's systems (either on a time-share basis or through an in-house installed system), but continues to use its own staff to perform administrative functions.
2. *Staff outsourcing.* A company continues to maintain its own systems, but uses an outsourcing organization's staff for benefit administration.
3. *Partial outsourcing.* A company uses an outsourcing organization's systems and/or administrative staff for certain services (such as flex plan enrollment), while other administration continues in-house.

Q 6:74   **Health Insurance Answer Book**

4. *Full outsourcing.* A company uses an outsourcing organization for all employee benefit plan administration. Most staff and administrative system functions are provided by the outsourcing organization, including administrative systems and operations, day-to-day telephone contact with the company's current and former employees, interaction with third-party vendors (such as health claim payers and pension check printers), and storage and retrieval of source documents. Even in a full outsourcing arrangement, several administrative functions typically remain with the company's senior benefits or human resources staff, including financial management of the plans, benefit design changes, and decisions regarding administrative situations for which there are no clearly documented procedures or guidelines.

Chapter 7

Managing Health Insurance Costs

As health insurance costs have increased, insurers and plan sponsors have redesigned their plans to include cost-containment features. This chapter explores the reasons behind rising health care costs and explains some of these cost-containment features, how they work, and how they apply today.

Factors Affecting Costs	7-1
Health Care Data	7-14
Utilization Review and Case Management	7-24
Medical Savings Accounts	7-37
Coordination of Benefits	7-44
Additional Cost-Management Strategies	7-49
Billing Codes	7-57
Impact of AIDS on Insurance	7-58
Rationing Health Care	7-62
The Employer's Role	7-65

Factors Affecting Costs

Q 7:1   What is the single most important factor affecting group health insurance in recent decades?

From the late 1970s through the early 1990s, the most significant factor affecting group health insurance was the rapid escalation of health care costs. Increases in medical costs exceeded the increases in the consumer price index. In addition, total health care spending (including public and private expenditures for personal health care, medical research, construction of medical facilities, administrative and health insurance costs, and government-sponsored public health activities) increased at double-digit rates for years. Healthcare spending is over $1 trillion.

The increases in costs led to greater sharing of costs with employees, new types of health care delivery systems, and greater emphasis on wellness and preventive medicine.

Health benefit costs have started rising again. According to the Mercer/Foster Higgins annual survey, employers' average costs for health benefits in 1999 rose 7.3 percent, following an increase of 6.1 percent in 1998. In 1997, costs rose only 0.2 percent after costs in 1996 rose 2.5 percent. In 1995 costs rose only 2.1 percent; and in 1994 average health benefit costs fell 1.1 percent.

Q 7:2 Are health care costs coming under control?

According to the Bureau of Labor Statistics, the annual rate of increase in health care costs was as follows during the 1990s:

Year	Cost Increase (%)
1990	9.6
1991	7.9
1992	6.6
1993	5.4
1994	4.9
1995	3.9
1996	3.0
1997	2.8
1998	3.2

The 2.8 percent increase in 1997 was the smallest increase since 1965, when medical costs also rose only 2.8 percent.

Costs appear to be increasing again. Health premiums for the Federal Employees Health Benefit Program, the largest group health insurance plan in the country, increased by 10.2 percent in 1999 and 9.3 percent in 2000. Health premiums for the California Public Employees Retirement System, the second largest group health insurance plan, increased an average of 9.7 percent for 2000 and would have increased 8.6 percent for 2001, but increases in copays cut the increase in premiums.

Q 7:3 What are some of the factors that influenced the rise in medical costs?

Many factors contributed to the increase of health care costs. Some of these factors are still present or may recur. Some of these factors are easily addressed by any employer; other factors may be only indirectly applicable or not work at all. Regardless, an employer should carefully examine and assess all factors. The factors are:

- Proliferation of new and expensive technology
- Overprovision of medical services
- Inappropriate use of medical services
- Oversupply of medical professionals and facilities
- Defensive medicine
- Adverse selection
- Aggressive marketing of some services, such as substance abuse treatment
- Fraud and abuse
- Cost shifting from plans that pay very little, such as Medicaid
- A leveraging effect if plans do not increase deductibles and out-of-pocket limits
- Aging population
- Insulation of consumers from cost exposure for medical services
- Lack of medical understanding on the part of consumers
- Lack of communication by employers
- Inappropriately designed plans
- Mandated coverage

- Lack of evidence as to what is the best course of treatment for a particular condition.

These factors account for increases in addition to underlying inflation.

Q 7:4 Which of the factors contributing to the rapid escalation of health care costs are to some extent under control?

Factors over which an employer may exercise some control include the following:

1. *Excessive use of medical services.* This situation has been fostered in part by too much medical insurance. Without facing a meaningful cost element, employees may lack incentive to refrain from using medical services. Managed care plans have controlled excessive use of medical services, but have been accused of denying necessary care as well.

2. *Defensive medicine.* Physicians may view performing costly multiple tests as a defense against very expensive malpractice suits being brought against them for an unsuccessful medical outcome, in which failure to perform sufficient tests may be cited as a factor. Controls in managed care plans have largely offset the added costs of defensive medicine.

3. *First dollar coverage medical insurance.* The practice of eliminating the deductible further insulates employees against an awareness of the cost of medical care. By switching to comprehensive major medical, increasing deductibles, and implementing managed care plans, employers have overcome this problem.

4. *Fraud.* Fraudulent practices by care providers include billing for services not provided, code gaming, unbundling of services, and waiving of copayments. Physicians, medical testing laboratories, hospitals, and others have experienced declining revenues and increased operating expenses. To compensate for loss of income, some providers of medical services have resorted to these unethical or fraudulent practices.

Q 7:5 How does the proliferation of new and expensive medical technology contribute to rising medical costs?

The most commonly cited example of this phenomenon is expensive machinery such as computerized axial tomography (CT) scanners and magnetic resonance imaging (MRI). When it was originally developed, the CT scanner was expected to replace the X-ray machine. Similarly, with the invention of the MRI, the CT was supposed to become obsolete. In reality, none of the machines is used to replace another; each is used in addition to the others. Less widely reported is that similar redundancies exist in other diagnostic and testing procedures. When a new blood test, for example, will tell a physician more than an older version, although perhaps not precisely the same data, both tests will regularly be ordered, despite the fact that the newer test was intended to replace the prior version. Admittedly, blood tests cost substantially less per case, but they are performed with much greater frequency.

Q 7:6 What effect do legal liability issues have on health care costs?

Medical malpractice insurance rates are one of the major factors behind the inflation of professional medical fees. The prevalence of lawsuits that have awarded billions of dollars in damages over recent years has forced health plans and physicians to pay exorbitant liability premiums, which are, in turn, passed along to the consumer. (See also Q 7:14 regarding defensive medicine.)

Q 7:7 What is cost shifting?

Cost shifting is the term used to describe how one patient's health care is subsidized by the charges made to another for the same services. It occurs when the first patient's insurer has an arrangement, established by law or negotiation, that allows for reimbursement at less than the normal full charge. Medicare and Medicaid are examples of cost-shifting arrangements created by law. Hospitals and physicians are faced with what they believe is less than adequate reimbursement for a large number of patients, which must be made up elsewhere. The providers shift costs to other patients, thus inflating the charges for the care delivered. HMOs have created a similar situation through negotiation.

Q 7:8 How do higher claims affect health insurance costs?

Health insurance premiums are based in part on the expected number and cost of claims that will be filed during a plan year. If the actual number and cost of claims exceed the expected level, the insurer will probably increase future premiums to reflect the higher claims experience.

Q 7:9 How does overprovision of medical services contribute to the problem?

Medical providers usually receive a direct financial benefit from providing services. This leads them in the direction of overprovision of services, as does their need to practice defensive medicine (Q 7:12). Patients motivated to receive only the most cost-efficient service may be the best line of defense an employer has in holding down this aspect of health care costs. Patients can, and should, understand every procedure being performed in the course of their treatment. They should also have an active, decision-making role in determining what does and does not get done. If, say, one additional procedure will reduce the chances of something "bad" happening, the patient should clearly understand what that means. Is it a danger of misdiagnosing a cancer? Or is the provider talking about a minor non-invasive condition? And will the chances be reduced from 90 percent to 20 percent, or from 10 percent to 5 percent? Further, will that take another day in the hospital, and perhaps a (minor) operation? The patient has a right to know what is involved, and should make the decision whether to proceed.

Q 7:10 Why do health care providers deliver unnecessary care?

Most physicians and other practitioners do not set out to provide unnecessary care to their patients; however, they—as well as the facilities they practice in—are encouraged to do so because

1. Demand for care is not driven by price.
2. Patients traditionally do not question treatment.

3. Care deemed unnecessary by one physician may be deemed appropriate by another.

It should not be surprising that when no one questions the price or the quantity of care provided, and the quality of care is subjective, more care, rather than less, is "bought" and "sold." In any market, increased demand increases price. In the health care market, price increases have not, until recently, resulted in a corresponding decrease in demand for services.

Q 7:11 Why have consumers not purchased less care, as prices have increased?

Insurance companies reimburse individuals for health care expenses with relatively few restrictions on the price of the care received. Although, in reality, consumers are the payers, they fail to see it that way because they continue to receive care while sharing little in the cost. Further, consumers feel entitled to medical care. An increase in price, even if passed directly to consumers, does not result in the same relative decrease in demand that occurs in simpler markets.

Q 7:12 How does the inappropriate use of medical services exacerbate the problem?

Having been covered for many years by high-yielding medical benefit plans, too many employees have gotten used to the practice of going to a doctor's office, or worse, an emergency room, for virtually any medical reason, no matter how slight. To a great extent this has been fostered by the fact that it costs the employee virtually nothing to receive the services (after being reimbursed by the plan), coupled with the fact that for many years employers encouraged or ignored the practice because the cost to the employer was not high enough to worry about. Medical plans were continually expanded to cover more and more items at greater levels of coverage, which further conditioned employees to think that the use of any medical service was fine, and indeed desirable, because it shortened the period of illness and led to a quicker recovery.

These factors have created an attitude, perhaps even a dependency, that must be addressed.

Q 7:13 How does the oversupply of medical professionals and facilities contribute to the problem of rising medical costs?

Normal free-market economics and the operation of elasticity of demand dictate that an oversupply (assuming no change in the level of demand) will result in a price drop; however, there has not been a reduction of prices—another indication of the degree of distortion created by removing price considerations from the purchase decision. In response to a decreasing volume of business resulting from a surplus of capacity, providers increased the per-unit fee to sustain their level of revenue. Because there was no resistance to the increase from consumers (i.e., consumers did not seek lower-cost suppliers), the price increases were sustainable. Re-introduction of price as a factor in the purchase decision will help to create a more realistic pricing structure.

Q 7:14 How does the practice of defensive medicine contribute to the health care cost spiral?

Defensive medicine occurs when medical professionals perform additional testing and procedures, or call for a second opinion for such vague reasons as "just to be sure" and to "not leave any stone unturned." Medical professionals generally do this to protect themselves against possible lawsuits for malpractice. In an attempt to control this practice, it has been suggested that limits be placed on the size of malpractice awards that can be obtained by injured patients. While this might reduce malpractice insurance premiums, it will not improve a physician's defense in a courtroom. Their position will be improved by following validated treatment protocols, or by joining a health maintenance organization or other similar medical network that regularly reviews treatment plans and provides member physicians with medical oversight.

Q 7:15 How does the insulation of consumers from cost exposure for medical services contribute to rising medical costs?

This is one of the prime causes of the problem, or it may be *the* cause. In a letter to *The New York Times,* John C. Goodman of the National Center for Policy Analysis wrote (in part):

> One reason health-care costs are out of control is that when we enter the medical marketplace as patients, we are usually

spending someone else's money. Economic studies—and common sense—confirm that we are less likely to be prudent shoppers if someone else is paying the bill.

Q 7:16 How does consumer lack of medical understanding contribute to the cost problem?

Generally speaking, consumers are not sufficiently educated to know whether they are receiving efficient or wasteful care. Many patients are not willing to question their doctors. Consumer education programs are starting to improve this situation.

Q 7:17 How does lack of communication contribute to the cost problem?

For years, employers have watched medical costs rise and said virtually nothing meaningful to employees about it. Although many employers are now communicating the fact that costs are rising, little effort is being made to explain anything beyond that. When employees grossly underestimate the cost of coverage to an employer, a communication opportunity has been missed. Further, it is unlikely that an employer will gain an employee's understanding, let alone cooperation, when the facts, and the reasons behind them, have not been explained.

Q 7:18 What role do inappropriately designed plans play in the cost problem?

In the past, employer plans were designed to provide ever higher levels of reimbursement and to assume more and more of the costs of medical care. Compounding that, reimbursement often rewarded inefficient patterns of obtaining care (e.g., reimbursement of emergency room treatment at higher levels than office visits, which resulted in employees receiving non-emergency care at the emergency room).

Q 7:19 How does mandated coverage contribute to the cost problem?

The requirements for specific categories of coverage or for specific procedures to be included as a covered expense in group contracts have typically come from state legislatures or state insurance commissioners, usually as a result of lobbying efforts by a special interest group (e.g., chiropractors, who have succeeded in their efforts to be accorded covered status by being mandated in a number of states). Other benefits have been mandated by insurance companies although these mandates do not carry the force of law. An insurance company will mandate a benefit by requiring that a test or procedure be performed as a prerequisite to having other procedures or tests accepted as covered items. One insurance company has even required certain tests to be performed in support of an admission diagnosis.

Q 7:20 Are employers to blame for high health care costs?

The sad truth is that American business unwittingly played a large part in driving up health care costs. Employers helped to create it by designing plans with the wrong incentive structure—although at the time no one foresaw the consequences of actions such as covering 100 percent of hospitalization expenses or of upgrading from fixed-rate surgical schedules to reasonable and customary surgical schedules, or even of not having checks and balances in the system.

Q 7:21 How did employers create the high health care costs we know today?

Employers went along with, and even encouraged, the process of creating ever-richer medical coverage plans. These plans created an improper set of incentives, beliefs, and expectations in employees and the provider community. The development of the problem is outlined as follows:

1. *Most health care decisions are made by doctors.* Few employers or employees have medical backgrounds. We all go to doctors to learn what is making us ill, and to be cured. If a doctor proclaims that a certain test or medication is necessary, most

people do not offer a counter-opinion. Generally, they do not even question the decision or get another medical opinion. If a doctor deems an operation to be necessary, a patient may question the need, but in the long run most recommended operations are performed.

2. *There were few constraints on, or reviews of, the doctor's decisions.* Although there are second surgical opinion (SSO) programs and utilization reviews (URs), these programs are of relatively recent vintage and still do not cover all of the population. By and large, where they are in place, these programs detect and prevent only egregious deviation from the standard. They do not review every detail of a patient's treatment; therefore, even with these programs, the treating physician has wide latitude in the practice of medicine.

3. *Doctors directly control the level of their compensation.* Most physicians in the United States today are still compensated to some extent on a fee-for-service basis; therefore, their compensation is directly proportional to the volume and type of service they perform. To a great extent, physicians also determine the type and number of services they perform. Thus, they can greatly influence the purchasing of their services, and, thereby, their own compensation.

4. *Doctors feel responsible to do more for their patients.* This laudable trait has the unfortunate consequence of adding significant cost to the system. Because there are currently no restraints, doctors require some external influence to act as a damper. The problem is being exacerbated in the court system, where malpractice suits abound. Doctors can and will indulge their sense of responsibility. Doctors face the threat of extraordinary financial liability if a problem develops in a patient under their care. Are they to be blamed if they practice defensive medicine by calling for procedures that may be only remotely necessary, but that will give them a more credible defense if they are called into court?

5. *Doctors' actions are precisely aligned with their customers' desires.* The patient (not at all unreasonably) wants to be cured as quickly and painlessly as possible. If that goal can be achieved with another test, which patient will refuse it? And how many doctors will balk at ordering a test that might help?

Beyond tests, it is not uncommon for a physician to recommend a course of treatment with a lesser likelihood of success than a more painful—but perhaps more appropriate—treatment. It is laudable that a physician might want to spare the patient some discomfort, but the interests of the employer who pays the bill for these services are not taken into consideration. An employer (or anyone, for that matter, who is concerned with the costs being incurred) would likely start asking questions about what the extra test will show or what decision will be facilitated by having the data produced by the test. On the treatment side, they might start asking what the outcome from the suggested treatment has been in similar cases, or they might ask which course of treatment has the best (validated) record for similar conditions. In short, they will try to bring cost efficiencies and validated protocols into the equation.

The consideration of cost has been removed from the purchase decision. Employers have done too effective a job of shielding employees from the costs involved in medical care. Employees approach the purchase decision with no incentive to do anything but buy the best they can find.

In too many instances, patients cannot make a prudent purchase decision. Patient health—or that of their children—is at stake. They are as emotionally involved as one can get. Neither do they have the medical knowledge to evaluate the doctor's decision. How can they possibly measure quality or cost-effectiveness of treatments when getting better is their only yardstick?

Q 7:22 What are some specific, fundamental ways in which an employer's medical costs may be reduced?

The most successful strategy has been switching from a traditional indemnity plan to a managed care plan. For traditional plans, there are two fundamental approaches through which an employer can reduce its medical plan costs: design changes and funding or administrative changes. Under these two main categories, there are further subheadings.

Design changes include actions such as the following:

1. Decrease the percentage of the company's coinsurance (e.g., change from 80 percent/20 percent to 70 percent/30 percent).
2. Increase the employee's deductible amount (e.g., change from $250 to $350).
3. Change from a basic or major medical plan design to a comprehensive plan design (i.e., eliminate first-dollar coverage; require a deductible before any payment is made from the plan).
4. Add a per-confinement deductible (i.e., require a deductible payment, such as $300 or $400, for every period of hospital confinement).
5. Eliminate family deductibles (i.e., require every family member to satisfy an annual deductible).
6. Eliminate deductible carryovers (i.e., do not allow expenses incurred in one year and used to meet a deductible in that year—usually in the last three months of a calendar year—to be used toward the next year's deductible).
7. Change from a "reasonable and customary" to a "scheduled" approach. A schedule of surgical procedures, for example, fixes the maximum dollar amount the plan will pay for each procedure and freezes those amounts until another action is taken to increase the level of payment.
8. Add an emergency room deductible, which is similar to the per-confinement deductible (e.g., require a $50 or $75 payment for every instance of emergency room use).

Funding or administrative changes include the following:

1. Change from a conventionally insured to a self-funded plan (see Chapter 17 for more on this point).
2. If a plan pays any benefits that are determined on a reasonable and customary method, reduce the percentile at which reasonable and customary is determined (e.g., reduce from the 90th percentile to the 80th percentile).
3. If an employer is conventionally insured and is "experience rated" (see Chapter 5), switching carriers may help—particularly if the employer had a "shock" claim during the previous year (see Q 7:94). While the former carrier will be anxious to be repaid for that claim, the incoming carrier will tend to

discount its effect. Be warned, however, that while this tactic may work once or even twice, a pattern of switching carriers every few years will be a red flag to new ones.

4. If an employer is self-insured and is using an insurance company to administer its claims, switching to a third-party administrator (TPA) may help. TPAs generally are slightly more efficient than insurance carriers and tend to be more "bare bones" in the services they offer. If an employer is not utilizing the complete array of services available from the insurance company, it can probably buy just the services it is using from a TPA and thus save fees on unused services. (See Chapter 17 for concerns about stop-loss insurance.)

Health Care Data

Q 7:23 Why have health data become an integral part of many employer cost-management programs?

Health cost management is highly complex. There are many alternative cost-containment situations, and employers are trying to sort out the most effective approaches from among many competing options. Hard data provide a decision support framework. Specifically, good data can help pinpoint the problem areas and the extent of the problems. In essence, managers have an opportunity to focus their efforts. Rather than trying to implement several solutions without any idea which are most needed and will have the greatest impact, they can predict with some certainty the likely results of particular health cost-management programs.

Q 7:24 How can an employer know which programs to implement?

To determine the appropriate cost-management programs, the employer must ascertain the specific problems that are causing the company's costs to rise. This involves analyzing the internal situation—an employers own claim experience—as well as the external situation—the price and quality of care delivered by providers in the local area.

An employer should start by analyzing its claim data. Broad samples can indicate patterns of use. This in turn can lead to general avenues to pursue. Following are four examples:

1. A high incidence of office visits for nonspecific reasons might indicate value in negotiating a capitated arrangement with a managed care plan.
2. High numbers of back injuries or sprains could indicate the usefulness of a training program in the proper way to lift things.
3. Excessive numbers of upper-respiratory ailments might point to the need for a targeted wellness program, aimed at smoking cessation.
4. High numbers of mental health or substance abuse claims should suggest the advantages of a contract for specialized services or a managed mental health network.

Insurers have developed management information systems and reporting and analysis services that can provide employers with many of these cost data. These automated systems also provide the information that will allow insurers to suggest plan redesign and work with employers for direct intervention with physicians and hospitals.

When studying their data and attempting to draw conclusions, employers should remember that, if the database is not large enough, minor variations that are not statistically significant will appear to be much more meaningful than they are.

A small employer might consider forming or joining a coalition of employers for the purpose of negotiating discounts, or sharing data to identify efficient providers.

Q 7:25 Why are employer-specific data helpful?

Employer-specific data can help a company focus its cost-management strategies. For example, data may reveal the need for a smoking cessation program at one plant and an employee assistance program (EAP) at another. Both programs may not be needed at both plants. Or data may indicate that an HMO is working well at one plant while it is causing a problem with adverse selection at another. Comparisons of hospital admission rates among divisions may spur local managers to greater action than a general call for action at the corporate level.

A corporation can use health utilization and cost data to determine plan design modification needs, develop collective bargaining positions, select the right level of deductible or copayment, understand the operation of the health care system, educate employees and managers, evaluate insurance carriers and other plan administrators, evaluate the impact of plan changes and cost-control measures, select HMOs and preferred provider organizations, and identify the need for particular wellness programs.

Q 7:26   What elements are needed to analyze data effectively?

In order for an employer to analyze its claim data effectively the following three elements are necessary:

1. Most importantly, the data must be in usable form. Generally, information will be easiest to use if it is automated so that it can be easily sorted and re-sorted in different ways. If an insurance company or TPA performs the claim payment services, it probably already has the data automated. The employer need only specify what it wants to look at and in what manner.

2. Comparative norms must be used. These are available in both national and regional bases. If regional norms are not available, national norms adjusted to regional norms are acceptable substitutes. An insurance company, TPA, or intermediary should have these available or be able to get them.

3. Employers will need time and, perhaps, assistance. The answers are not always immediately clear; it may be necessary to look at the data in two or three ways before a picture emerges. There are a number of experienced consultants who can assist employers in analyzing the data more quickly than they could on their own.

Q 7:27   What kinds of data are useful to better manage health care costs?

Useful data include several years of claim experience, presenting such detail as charges and allowed payments, broken down by diagnosis and health care provider; however, unless an employer's claim volume is very high for specific conditions and for specific providers, conclusions may be inaccurate. Employers with fewer than 100 employees cannot rely on claim experience to indicate conclusively what type of cost management is appropriate. This is why insurers offer many standard cost-controlling plan design features, even if specific claim problems are not clear.

For employers with fewer than 500 employees, conclusions about providers based on just their own claim analysis can also be dangerous. Additional data regarding provider practice patterns are necessary. These can be obtained from the employer's insurer, third-party administrator, or local employer coalition.

Historically, insurance carriers have furnished companies with two types of data: reports on claim experience and employee coverage information. More recently, interest has developed with regard to claim cost and benefit utilization levels. The following utilization indicators are very helpful:

- Hospital inpatient days per year per 1,000 employees and dependents
- Hospital admission rate
- Average length of hospital stay
- Number of inpatient and outpatient surgeries
- Number of outpatient visits per year per person

In addition, the following cost measures are relevant:

- Total annual payments
- Average annual cost per employee
- Total charges
- Total payments after adjustments
- Total hospital inpatient payments
- Total surgical payments
- Total out-of-hospital payments

Q 7:28 What types of data are most useful for plan redesign purposes?

Utilization data, which identify frequency of use of a particular type of service and cost per unit of service, are the most useful in conjunction with population or covered persons data. In order to analyze utilization data properly, it is also necessary to have the demographics of the population and area norms.

Q 7:29 If an employer wants to analyze claim data without assistance, what specific steps must be followed?

An employer should start by obtaining comparative norms for the categories of coverage or treatment it wants to analyze. For instance, the employer might want to analyze hospitalization claims for its employees. With the norms in hand, the employer should then organize its claim data in the same manner as the norms. For example, in Figure 7.1, admissions data are broken out by county; naturally, the complete set of data (the employer's data and norms) will be considerably more detailed and comprehensive than this simplified example.

If the data show the employer's overall usage to be at or below norms, self-funding may be advisable. If the employer is above norms in one category of usage, it should focus on that category and try to determine why. Wherever a distortion appears, the employer should look at the data in finer and finer slices, refining the question or the sort pattern each time. Answers will begin to point to solutions.

> **Example 7-1.** Using the data shown in Figure 7.1, the employer has the lowest average length of stay; however, the employer's inpatient days per thousand of population are higher than all others, and so are its number of admissions per thousand. This employer should ask: Are my admissions occurring in lieu of outpatient treatment? Do I have a low outpatient payment structure, but a high (perhaps 100 percent) inpatient reimbursement rate? A "yes" may give the employer its answer.
>
> **Example 7-2.** For another employer, the average length of stay was high and the admissions per thousand were good. The figures shown for Midland County are appropriate for this comparison,

so assume Midland County represented the employer's figures and the other data were all norms. Is the average length of stay the result of one or two unusually lengthy stays that drove the average up? Probably not, based on the high incidence of inpatient days per thousand. Those answers might lead the employer to perform a retrospective review of its hospitalizations. Were the lengths of the stays necessary? Should there have been some outpatient planning? Would the availability of hospice care or home health care have been useful? Based on the findings, this employer might consider a few actions. For example, it might want to engage the services of a utilization review firm (if its insurance company does not have this feature) to monitor future admissions for necessity of length of stay and to do discharge planning. If this employer does not already have hospice or home health care, it might want to include these features as well.

Example 7-3. The employer as shown in Figure 7.1 should also look at its emergency room visits. At first glance, it doesn't look outrageous: 422 is lower than any other usage being shown. But look at that number as a percentage of total ambulatory visits: 64

Figure 7.1. Comparative Data—Selected Counties

Service	Bedford	Chessher	Midland	Employer
Admits per 1,000	4.22	3.65	4.05	6.27
Inpatient days per 1,000	852	937	1,021	1,256
Average length of stay (days)	3.68	3.54	4.21	1.93
Ambulatory visits per 1,000	1,327	1,522	1,044	659
Emergency room	526	682	488	422
Doctor's office	576	552	349	207
Other	225	288	207	30

percent of ambulatory treatment is being performed in an emergency room setting. The others are 40, 45, and 47 percent. That calls for further analysis. Some questions to ask here are: Were the conditions being treated actually emergencies? Does the plan provide higher reimbursement for emergency room use?

Q 7:30 How does an employer extract useful information from the data an insurance company or TPA can provide?

The employer is engaged in a process of hunting for clues, then following up on those clues. Some promising clues might lead nowhere. Clues might be readily apparent based on a simple comparison between numbers. On the other hand, it might be necessary to examine the data to discover its implications (as was done in the example in Q 7:29, by looking at data as a percentage instead of as a number). Two additional examples may help.

Example 7-4. An employer, ABC Company, wanted to reduce any excess that might be hidden in its hospitalization charges, but was unsure whether there was significant "fat" and where or how to redesign its program to get at it. Accordingly, ABC requests data from its claim processor in the form of a listing of its hospitalization charges against comparative norms. The data come back in the form of Figure 7.2.

The data in Figure 7.2 reveal that for 1996 and 1997, ABC Company's inpatient charges have exceeded the normal charges against which they were being measured. The outpatient charges are reasonably close to the norm—more importantly, they were below normal for both years. The effort, then, must be concentrated on the inpatient services. Without having any idea specifically where to look, it might make sense to try one more broad cut before looking at specific diagnoses or conditions. Accordingly, the inpatient data should be sorted into the charges paid directly to the hospitals and inpatient charges paid to physicians. Those data come back in the form of Figure 7.3.

These data show that ABC Company is exceeding the expected level of expense for both categories. This should tell ABC Company that it needs to continue to look at both hospital and physician fees. The next step is to slice hospital and physician charges into major

Managing Health Care Costs   Q 7:30

Figure 7.2. Inpatient and Outpatient Charges vs. Comparative Norms

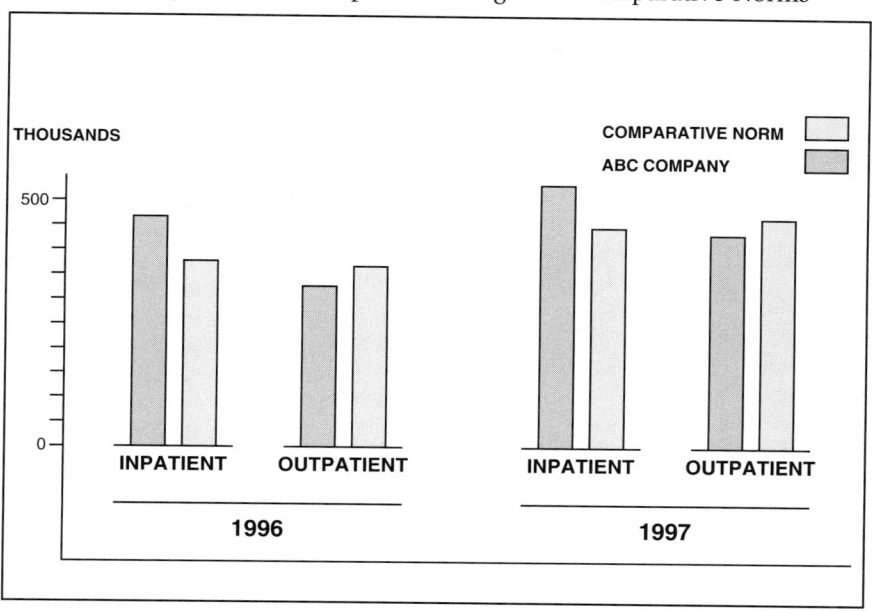

Figure 7.3. Inpatient Hospital and Physician Charges—Compared to Norms

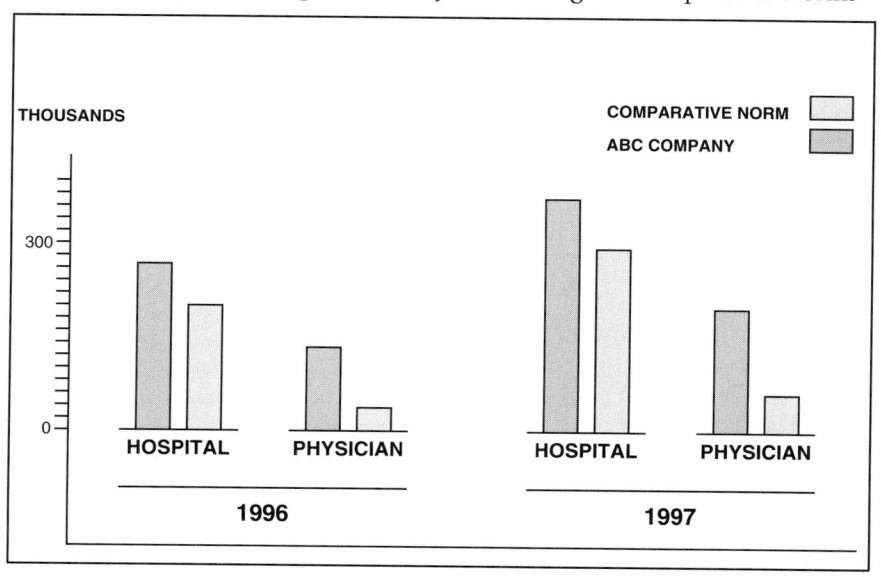

7-21

diagnostic/treatment categories with similar comparisons against normative data. The employer should keep slicing and comparing until more anomalies are found. Inpatient data has been compared and discarded on maternity, skeletal, blood, respiratory, and a half dozen other categories, until only mental, cardiovascular, and pulmonary are left. Those are shown in Figure 7.4.

Figure 7.4 shows that cardiovascular and pulmonary can be discarded. The problem is in the mental services. Presumably, similar results would occur from the physician side. Because physician charges were also above expected, that overage will appear somewhere. Rather than belabor the point, assume it too showed up in mental services.

Having found the source of the excess expense, the questions remain: Why is it happening, and what can be done in response?

Start with the plan design. Is the plan structured to encourage inpatient usage rather than outpatient? So far the analysis illustrated in these three charts has focused only on dollars of expense. The employer needs to know how the usage compares to norms of days per 1,000 of population or to average length of stay.

There are three possible actions for the employer to consider in this situation:

1. Carve out the mental and nervous program from the overall medical plan.
2. Engage the services of a managed mental health network.
3. Use an EAP as a gatekeeper for the mental and nervous program.

Example 7-5. Using data identical to those used in Figure 7.2, arrive at the last set of data, as in Figure 7.5. This time charges for circulatory conditions shown in Figure 7.5 are abnormal. The employer might stop the analysis right here and consider contracting with an HMO or a PPO with a good hospital affiliation. Either an HMO or a PPO would offer the benefit of discounted hospital daily rates; an HMO also offers capitated charges. An alternate course would be for the employer to continue refining its knowledge of the specific causes, narrowing this further and further. For example, it might be useful to find out if the problems can be

Managing Health Care Costs   Q 7:30

Figure 7.4. Inpatient Charges by Type of Service—Compared to Norm

MENTAL
CARDIOVASCULAR
PULMONARY

THOUSANDS

300

0

ABC   NORMS   ABC   NORMS

1996   1997

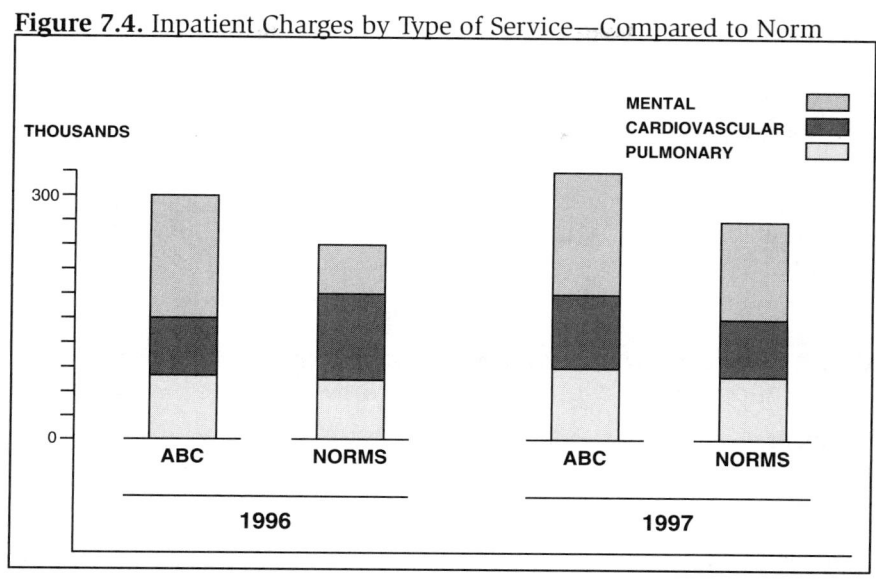

Figure 7.5. Inpatient Charges by Type of Service—Compared to Norm

CIRCULATORY
CARDIOVASCULAR
PULMONARY

THOUSANDS

300

0

ABC   NORMS   ABC   NORMS

1996   1997

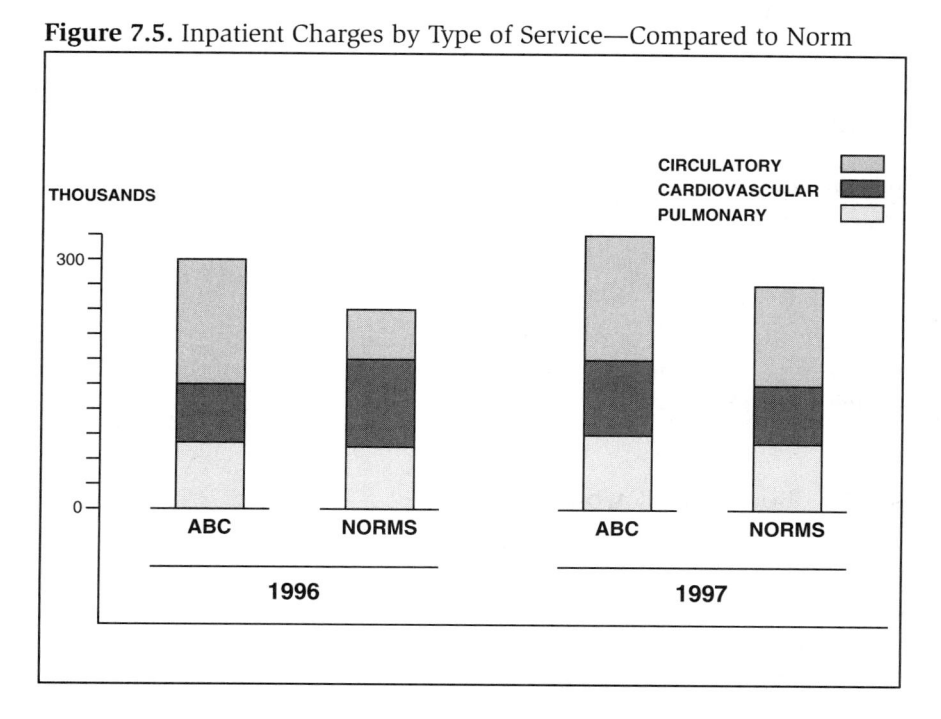

attributed to sedentary lifestyle, smoking, alcohol, stress, high blood pressure, diet, or weight.

All of the preceding are "modifiable" lifestyle issues. If any of these is the root cause of the circulatory abnormality, perhaps a wellness program is the answer. The employer might still want to consider contracting with an HMO, but might look for one with a strong wellness program targeted at the lifestyle behavior to be modified.

Q 7:31 What kinds of plan design features should employers implement, even without conclusive data on problems?

Several specific actions can be taken to help manage costs, such as implementing plan features that do the following:

- Prevent illness and injury
- Increase cost sharing by employees
- Encourage utilization of the most cost-effective care

Utilization Review and Case Management

Q 7:32 What is utilization review?

Utilization review is the system of evaluating the necessity, appropriateness, and course of health care provided at various stages in its delivery. Although UR is often described as an insurance plan feature, it is actually a cost-containment function. The UR process analyzes the health history and current condition of a patient and then determines whether the care prescribed is correct, justifiable, and optimal.

Q 7:33 How does UR work?

Utilization review for a health plan can be handled through an in-house UR department or contracted to an outside UR vendor. The objective of UR is not to replace the physician as the decision-maker, but to monitor and oversee patient care, primarily in situations of chronic or costly conditions. UR procedures should regulate and minimize hospital admissions and prevent unnecessary surgeries. It also provides a retrospective review of care provided to uncover aberrant practice patterns among physicians. For years, insurance companies have audited and reviewed historical claims in order to catch inappropriate charges or services; UR attempts to prevent inappropriate charges or services. UR systems use peer review, that is, medical professionals analyzing the care provided by other medical professionals, before, during, and after prescription and delivery of care.

At most utilization review organizations, the bulk of the first-level review work is done by registered nurses working with commercially developed criteria or sophisticated software for their analysis. Physicians are typically involved only in second reviews and appeals. [US GAO, Document GAP/HRD-93-22FS (Nov 1992)] Among UR organizations, the trend is toward broadening the traditional UR work—which focuses on monitoring the level of care and use of specific resources (such as hospital days)—to include more sophisticated services that assess the appropriateness of medical services and treatment patterns of physicians.

Employers can obtain UR services directly from a UR organization, through a third-party administrator, or through the insurer. Numerous review companies are available from which to choose. Although some are capable of providing more sophisticated services than others, most offer similar basic services. Some of the commonly offered services are:

- Hospital length-of-stay review
- Pre-admission certification
- Concurrent review with discharge planning
- Retrospective review

Other services sometimes offered include review of long-term care, mental health care, and outpatient services, including surgery, diagnostic tests, and visits to specialists.

Q 7:34 Do states regulate utilization review?

Yes. Dozens of states regulate utilization review. Although state laws share many common elements, there are enough differences to present a significant compliance challenge to multi-state UR organizations.

Q 7:35 With the growth of managed care, how is UR changing?

With managed care health plans gaining the lion's share of the market, UR has taken on a somewhat different role. Instead of analyzing a physician's recommended course of treatment for a patient, determining its appropriateness, and deciding whether it should be authorized for insurance coverage or modified, UR in a managed care environment strives to establish clinical pathways, that is, general guidelines for health care providers to follow in common care scenarios (e.g., diabetes, smoking, cardiovascular disease, or breast cancer). The path to be followed is determined once the physician determines the needed level of care. For uncommon care scenarios, the managed care UR system will single out these "exception" cases (unusual, extremely high risk, etc.) for tracking and special attention.

Many of the health plans that had previously contracted with outside UR companies have now incorporated UR as an in-house function. An internal UR unit can be less expensive to operate and can also be used for other purposes, such as case management, quality assurance reporting, and appeals processing. To survive, independent UR companies have had to enhance their systems and services. Many of these companies have undergone extensive computer hardware and software upgrades to maintain compatibility with the health plans and insurance companies. UR companies will often provide on-line reporting (even daily), cost projection and analysis, and historical audit and analysis services.

Q 7:36 What are treatment protocols?

Treatment protocols are also known as practice guidelines, clinical pathways, or standards of practice. Treatment protocols represent the consensus of a group as to how a particular condition should be treated. An increasing number of managed care organizations and UR companies use treatment protocols.

Treatment protocols usually rely on research to indicate the best way to diagnose or treat a condition. Sometimes this is referred to as evidence-based medicine.

The Agency for Health Care Policy and Research has developed a number of guidelines for clinical practice.

Q 7:37 What kinds of utilization review are there?

There are several techniques in use, including:

- Individual case management
- Preadmission certification
- Second opinions—medical and surgical
- Hospital discharge planning
- Retrospective review and audit
- Specialized review for specific services (mental health, podiatric, chiropractic)
- Ambulatory care review

Q 7:38 What is case management?

Case management describes the close supervision a health plan or insurance company provides for chronic and particularly costly cases. Case managers work with health care providers and patients to regulate utilization when possible. The following are examples of costly cases:

- Cardiovascular disease
- Cancer
- Strokes
- AIDS
- Severe traumatic injury
- Degenerative neurological disease
- Long-term psychiatric cases

Case managers are also involved in care situations of excessive duration or when such issues as patient noncompliance arise. Early involvement in any potentially high-cost case is essential to achieve loss control and optimum treatment for the patient.

Q 7:39 How does case management work?

Trained reviewers, usually registered nurses with extensive discharge planning experience and specialized clinical experience, monitor catastrophic cases during the acute hospitalization phase. At a very early stage, they begin to develop a long-term treatment plan to achieve the most efficient use of medical resources and the best patient outcome. These case workers might recommend patient care alternatives to lengthy hospitalization such as home care, hospice care, rehabilitation services, or skilled nursing facilities. They might contact the employer about the employee's ability to return to work or about job modifications that might be required to accommodate the patient's continuing recovery or rehabilitation once he or she returns to work. The process involves flexibility geared toward what is best for the patient and what will be the most efficient use of resources.

Q 7:40 With the growth of managed care, how is case management changing?

Although managed care health plans are designed to protect against excessive losses from the types of cases that warrant the involvement of a case manager, chronic and high-risk patients still require special supervision and assistance. Case managers can be instrumental, for instance, in obtaining patient approval to pursue a less costly route of treatment. Case managers can also provide patient assistance when multiple specialists and facilities are involved in the course of care.

Just as UR companies are adapting to the changing health care marketplace, case managers are enhancing and diversifying their services to maintain and grow their business. An employee assistance program, which may work entirely for one insurance carrier or with multiple plans and carriers, is often staffed by case managers who work with employees on "preventive" measures to avert or minimize disability and illness whenever possible. Case managers are also often looked upon as "data collectors" and provide much of the case history, outcome, and statistical information reported to the health plan.

Q 7:41 Is hospital discharge planning different from individual case management?

Yes. Discharge planning may be used with any hospitalization rather than with only catastrophic cases. Discharge planning is used to ensure that the patient stays in the hospital only as long as is medically necessary, and that once the patient is discharged, any ongoing care is appropriate. The process may include a recommendation that the patient leave the hospital for home care, nursing home care, skilled nursing facility care, rehabilitation services, or other treatment.

Q 7:42 How does preadmission certification work?

An employer that elects UR for its health plan explains to employees and their dependents that before any nonemergency hospital admission, the individual will be expected to contact the UR organization, or the medical care review agent, to obtain preadmission certification. The medical review agent will analyze the situation prior to the prescribed surgery or hospital stay. This watchdog function stimulates the attending physician to prescribe necessary, cost-efficient care and, when questioned, to justify surgical procedures or hospital stays with clear evidence of patient need. Failure by the insured to initiate the process usually results in reduced payment for treatment even if it would have been certified if reviewed. Emergency admissions are to be reported for review usually within 48 hours of admission.

This idea is not new: In the 1950s, several unions asked medical societies to help them conserve dollars in their health and welfare funds by reviewing health care services received by their members. Medicare spawned foundations for medical care in the early 1960s, and, later, 200 professional standards review organizations were created to provide review of all federally financed patient care in acute care hospitals, with plans to extend review to long-term care and ambulatory care services in future years. Recently, private insurers have incorporated UR into their benefit services.

An individual contemplating a hospital admission may not have any contact with the medical review agent after the first call or letter. The agent often deals directly with the attending physician in order to get a clear understanding of the reasons for the admission. The agent confirms the need for the admission; suggests an alternative setting, such as an outpatient facility; or suggests that the surgery or treatment is inappropriate, and that an alternative be explored. A second surgical opinion may be requested. In any situation in which an intake nurse reviews the plan of care and does not agree with it, he or she passes the case to a doctor, who then attempts to reach an agreement with the attending physician as to the appropriate care. If the two physicians disagree, usually a second UR physician reviews the plan of care. If the UR organization still disagrees with the patient's physician after that second review, and the patient goes ahead with the admission, the employer's insurer will either pay the claim as usual, reduce the benefit percentage, or deny the claim. The course of action depends on the arrangement agreed upon when UR is implemented as part of the insurance plan. Employees receive materials explaining the claim payment implication involved before the UR process takes effect.

The review process is fully documented, and the information is provided to the insurer as well as the attending physician and the patient. Most often, the hospital admission is approved and the person is admitted as planned. The review process then continues with concurrent review.

Q 7:43 If hospital admissions are usually certified, why is UR necessary?

UR appears to have a sentinel effect on physicians. That is, physicians who are told by their patients that the hospital admission must be precertified are more likely to suggest an alternative to hospitalization if there is one. United HealthCare has discontinued UR, but does monitor practice patterns retrospectively. See Q 7:53 regarding physician profiling.

Q 7:44 What criteria are used to determine the length of a hospitalization?

Different organizations use different criteria. They may rely on published studies that show the historical experience (nationally or regionally) for a particular condition or procedure. Some allow whatever the average has been, while others allow as much as the time required for much more than the average hospitalization. Others start at the low end, and use concurrent review to decide if a continued stay is necessary. Some organizations do not rely on historical data, but use criteria related to the patient's condition. They may determine the initial need for hospitalization based on condition (such as a surgical procedure), then use factors such as infection or change in medication to conclude whether the patient needs to stay.

Q 7:45 What happens during concurrent review?

Patient care is monitored while the patient is in the hospital. The UR organization may send a nurse on site or communicate with the physician or physician's assistant by telephone to keep abreast of the length of the stay. Less frequently, other procedures and services are audited. Concurrent review is aimed at getting the patient out of the hospital as quickly as possible, with due regard to patient safety.

Q 7:46 How does retrospective review help manage claim costs?

The UR organization typically provides the insurer (or large employer) with periodic reports on physician practice patterns and hospital length-of-stay averages. In areas where there are several providers to choose from, the providers that consistently deliver cost-effective care can be identified, and insureds can be channeled to them. In regions with only one hospital and a handful of doctors, discussions can at least be opened with that institution and those physicians to review patterns of care. Information that will help alter practice patterns may be a sensitive issue, but such discussions are being held frequently, as insurers and employers pursue cost management.

Q 7:47 Do the cost savings produced by UR justify the additional expense for the UR service?

Prior experience with plans that have had UR in effect long enough to evaluate indicates that savings exceed the cost, resulting in a 3 percent to 10 percent reduction in overall premium. Actual cost savings depend on the state (when DRGs are used, UR savings are attributable only to admission avoidance) and the degree of hospital overutilization that exists. Careful analysis of utilization data is necessary to determine the potential savings.

Without a special communication effort, employees will not use the program as intended and savings will inadvertently result from penalties. A review of the source of UR savings is essential in determining the effectiveness of the program.

Q 7:48 What is ambulatory care UR?

Ambulatory care UR is an extension of the UR process into the outpatient setting in an effort to manage the frequency and cost of services that are outside the scope of hospital and surgical reviews.

UR programs forced hospitals to reduce the total amount of inpatient care, but environmental pressures such as diagnosis-related groups and negotiated discounts prevented hospitals from making up the revenue shortfall by raising the price of inpatient services. Hospitals attempted to recoup costs from outpatient services that were subject to less scrutiny and control.

While outpatient care used to be a small-ticket item in many health care plans, the shift of more and more services to the outpatient setting and the increase in costs in order to subsidize inpatient care has eroded much of the savings from inpatient utilization review programs. The result has been a "balloon effect:" As costs are squeezed in one area of the health plan, they expand in another part.

Q 7:49 How is ambulatory care UR different from inpatient UR?

Outpatient or ambulatory care is provided not only in hospitals, but in clinics, doctors' offices, emergency centers, and hospital emergency rooms. The frequency of such services is 40 to 50 times that of hospital admissions; therefore, ambulatory care review requires a different technique and a vastly different type of computer support.

Q 7:50 What techniques are used in ambulatory care review?

Ambulatory care review may only preauthorize certain high-cost diagnostic procedures, such as PET, MRI, and CAT scans, or it may also include referrals to specialists or rely on retrospective review of claims. A few claim administrators and some commercial software vendors have developed programs that screen current cases by diagnosis and identify those where excessive or unusual care might be taking place. Those claims are reviewed by medical personnel, and the treatment plan may be discussed with the physician. While the patient's physician is always in charge of care under a traditional indemnity plan, the treatment plan may be voluntarily adjusted, or the claim administrator may adjust future benefits (no adjustment for claims already incurred). Managed care plans may deny coverage if authorization and referral procedures are not followed.

Q 7:51 How prevalent is ambulatory care UR?

Ambulatory care UR is gaining popularity. There are many vendors, not all of whom are able to integrate with every claims system. Few, in fact, have the capability of "physician profiling," the element most likely to produce solid cost savings over time. At present, cost-effective ambulatory UR is mostly limited to insurance carriers and UR organizations that manage large physician networks, HMOs, or PPOs.

Q 7:52 How much can ambulatory UR save?

Estimates are that savings of 5 percent to 8 percent of total health costs may be available from an efficient ambulatory UR program.

Q 7:53 What is physician profiling?

Physician profiling is the process of systematically recording a physician's practice patterns. This would include tasks like tracking the usage frequency of items such as test or diagnostic procedures for various illnesses or conditions. It would also consider treatments given, by condition or illness. The entire process is intended to create a general picture—a profile—of how the physician practices his or her profession. By comparing each physician to other physicians treating the same condition, or by measuring the physician against treatment protocols developed by recognized experts in the treatment of that condition, it is possible to categorize the physician under review as one who follows recognized, cost-efficient procedures or as one who uses certain diagnostic tools excessively.

With a valid profile of a physician's practicing techniques or biases in hand, a reviewing physician or panel can more readily spot potential areas of cost reduction or areas where the physician can be counseled and guided into more efficient and effective methods of providing care.

Q 7:54 How much can physician profiling save?

Physician profiling can save a considerable amount of money. One study found that savings for just a few selected expenses can exceed 13 percent. The study compared PPO claim data of network providers (who were selected by the PPO for their practice style) to non-network providers and found that network physicians used laboratory services 31 percent less frequently and X-rays 13 percent less frequently than their non-network counterparts did. It also found that when network providers did use X-rays and lab services, their average cost per use was lower. In the final analysis, the total savings for lab work, X-rays, and related office visits amounted to 13.7 percent for 1992. [Zalta, "The Case for Economic Profiling of Physicians," *Managing Employee Health Benefits* (Winter 1993)]

Q 7:55 What is a second surgical opinion program?

Second surgical opinion programs encourage individuals to have a second evaluation of a medical condition for which elective surgery has been recommended. The decision to elect or reject surgery still remains with the patient.

Insurance reimbursement for an SSO has been available through many plans for years, but managed care procedures are making it obsolete.

Q 7:56 Which procedures should require second opinions?

Each insurance carrier or UR vendor uses a list, called a "focus list," of procedures that it considers to be the most appropriate. The lists vary by region because of different physician practice patterns.

Most plans pay for the required second opinion (and related tests) in full, so the cost of the program may outweigh the demonstrable savings from surgery avoided (although resulting in better medical care). With the widespread inclusion of UR programs, the need for focused lists has been questioned. The most cost-efficient programs now require a second opinion only when the clinical information suggests the probability of nonconfirmation. The UR vendor decides when an opinion is necessary, saving employee time and plan resources.

Q 7:57 What is the difference between self-referral and referral by an SSO panel?

Self-referral means that the original physician who recommended surgery refers the patient to another physician for the required second opinion. There are no restrictions on who can perform the second opinion consultation; for example, it can be the first physician's associate, someone in another specialty, or the assistant surgeon. Such self-referral programs are ineffective in achieving the goals of an SSO program and may actually add to plan costs.

Panel referral is the only method that will achieve both objectives of an SSO program—cost-effectiveness and quality medical care. With panel referral, the second opinion must be obtained from a select group of specialists who have agreed (1) to fixed fees for the consultation, (2) not to perform additional tests unless strictly necessary, and (3) not to perform the surgery. The patient is given a list of three or four physicians from which to choose, and the administrator of the panel (carrier or UR vendor) arranges the appointment and the reporting of the results

Q 7:58 How do mandatory SSO programs work?

There are two types of mandatory SSO programs. The first requires only that an employee obtain a second opinion in order to receive regular plan benefits. Failure to obtain an opinion when required results in benefit reduction. Benefits may be reduced as little as 10 percent, or payment may be denied altogether, with a 50 percent cutback the norm. If the opinion does not confirm the need for surgery, the employee may still proceed without penalty.

The second type is called "mandatory-affirming" and requires that a second opinion (or third opinion, called a "tiebreaker") affirm the need for surgery. If no affirming opinion is obtained and surgery is elected, penalties apply.

When used in conjunction with preauthorization programs, second opinions are required on a case-by-case basis only when the clinical information suggests the probability of nonconfirmation. This approach is more cost-effective than spending $150 to $500 (including additional testing) to review all surgery on a certain list.

Some employers are uncomfortable with programs that inhibit their employees' free choice or penalize them for choosing a certain type of care. Some states do not permit programs that reduce benefits unless a confirming opinion is obtained, although reduction is permitted for failure to obtain a second opinion. Studies have shown that second opinion programs that leave the choice of physician for the second opinion entirely up to employees are not as effective as programs that require employees to choose a consultant from a list of physicians provided by an SSO panel. The panel approach, combined with a preauthorization program that determines whether a second opinion is necessary, is the acknowledged state of the art today.

Q 7:59 What is the current thinking regarding second surgical opinion programs?

Many utilization review organizations have sharply curtailed the list of procedures for which a second opinion is required. Plans with pre-surgical review components determine the need for a second opinion on the basis of case-specific clinical data rather than a predetermined list. Aetna Life Insurance Company found that dissenting opinions occurred in only 3 percent of cases referred for a second opinion and advised its clients that a second opinion program appears to cost employers more than it saves.

Medical Savings Accounts

Q 7:60 What is a medical savings account?

Medical savings accounts (MSAs) are an approach to controlling health care costs by placing more responsibility on consumers. In most instances, an MSA would be set up for and owned by an employee, with funds provided by the employer. The employee would draw on the funds to pay for unreimbursed medical expenses.

Q 7:61 How do MSAs differ from flexible spending accounts?

In a flexible spending account (FSA), funds remain the employer's property and any unused amounts revert to the employer under the IRS "use it or lose it" rule. With an MSA, the money would belong to the employee and any unused funds may earn interest and be carried forward to cover future expenses. Under an FSA the entire balance is available throughout the year. With an MSA, the balance would build over time.

Q 7:62 How would an MSA save money?

MSAs would usually be used in conjunction with a health plan that has a higher deductible than is common today, such as $2,000. The higher-deductible plan would cost less than the old plan, which is one source of account funding. Employers would deposit all or part of the savings into MSAs for each employee. Because employees would have to judge whether to spend money on health care now or save it for potentially more serious health care needs, proponents argue that MSAs will make employees better health care consumers.

Q 7:63 Why do some people oppose MSAs?

Opponents argue that MSAs undermine the progress made in controlling health care costs through managed care, by luring healthy workers out of managed care plans. Opponents also contend that MSAs help the healthy at the expense of the sick.

Q 7:64 Who is eligible for a medical savings account?

Under HIPAA, beginning in 1997, MSAs are available to employees covered under an employer-sponsored high-deductible plan of a small employer and to self-employed individuals. Other people may benefit from state laws that provide tax breaks for MSAs. Unless extended by Congress, no new MSAs may be created after 2000. Chapter 10 describes MSAs available to Medicare beneficiaries.

Q 7:65 What is a small employer for MSA purposes?

Under HIPAA, an employer is a small employer if it employed, on average, no more than 50 employees during either the preceding or the second preceding year. In determining whether an employer is a small employer, a preceding year is not taken into account unless the employer was in existence throughout that year. If an employer was not in existence throughout the preceding year, the determination of whether the employer has no more than 50 employees is based on the average number of employees that the employer reasonably expects to employ in the current year. For purposes of determining the number of employees of an employer, employers under common control are treated as a single employer.

Q 7:66 What happens if a small employer grows to have more than 50 employees?

If a small employer with an MSA exceeds the 50-employee limit, the employer or its employees can continue to make contributions to MSAs, including contributions for new employees and employees who did not previously have MSAs until the year following the first year in which the employer has more than 200 employees. After that time, the employees with MSAs can continue to make contributions (or have contributions made on their behalf).

Example 7-6. Employer A has 48 employees in 1995 and 1996 and 205 employees in 1997 and 1998. A would be a small employer in 1997 and 1998 because it had 50 or fewer employees in the preceding or the second preceding year. Employer A would still be considered a small employer in 1999; however, in years after 1999, Employer A would not be considered a small employer (even if the number of employees fell to 50 or below). In years after 1999, only employees who previously had MSAs could continue to make contributions (or have contributions made on their behalf).

Q 7:67 Which employees are eligible for MSAs?

Under HIPAA, for an employee of an eligible employer to be eligible to make MSA contributions (or to have employer contributions made on his or her behalf), the employee must be covered under an employer-sponsored high-deductible plan and must not be covered under any other health plan (other than a plan that provides certain permitted coverage).

Q 7:68 Can both employees and employers make contributions to an MSA?

Under HIPAA, either—but not both—the employee or the employer can make contributions to an MSA.

Q 7:69 What other coverage is permitted for MSA participants?

Employees can have any of the following types of insurance (or self-funded coverage) that may provide some type of medical benefits, and can still be eligible for an MSA:

- Medicare supplemental insurance
- Liability insurance
- Insurance for a specified disease (e.g., cancer) or illness
- Insurance that provides a fixed payment for hospitalization
- Accident insurance

- Disability insurance
- Dental insurance
- Vision insurance
- Long-term care insurance

Q 7:70 How much can be contributed to an MSA?

The maximum annual contribution that can be made to an MSA is 65 percent of the deductible under the high-deductible plan for people with individual coverage or 75 percent of the family deductible for people with family coverage. No other dollar limits or maximums apply. The annual contribution limit is the sum of the limits determined separately for each month, based on the individual's status and health plan coverage as of the first day of the month.

Q 7:71 What is a high-deductible plan?

A high-deductible plan is a health plan with an annual deductible of at least $1,550 and no more than $2,350 for individual coverage and at least $3,100 and no more than $4,650 for family coverage. In addition, the maximum out-of-pocket limit (including the deductible) must be no more than $3,100 for individual coverage and $5,700 for family coverage. (These are 2000 amounts.) Starting in 1999, the dollar amounts were indexed for inflation in $50 increments based on the consumer price index. If state law prohibits a deductible for preventive care, a plan can still qualify as a high-deductible plan.

IRS Revenue Ruling 97-20 [1997-1 CB 77] explained the IRS position regarding family deductibles for MSAs. Unlike traditional health insurance where an individual deductible applies to each person with an overall family limit on deductibles, for MSAs, no individual deductible applies when there is family coverage. If two people have family coverage and only one is sick, that person has a deductible of between $3,050 and $4,600.

Q 7:72 What is the deadline for MSA contributions?

Contributions for a particular year can be made until the due date for the individual's tax return for that year (without regard to extensions).

Q 7:73 Are there nondiscrimination requirements that apply to employers with MSAs?

Yes. If an employer provides high-deductible health plan coverage and makes contributions to MSAs, the employer must make available a comparable contribution on behalf of all employees with comparable coverage during the same period. Comparable contributions can either be the same dollar amount or the same percentage of the deductible. The comparability rule is applied separately for part-time employees (defined as employees who are customarily employed for fewer than 30 hours per week). No restrictions are placed on the ability of the employer to offer different plans to different groups of employees.

> **Example 7-7.** An employer maintains two high-deductible plans: Plan A with a deductible of $1,550 for individual coverage and $3,100 for family coverage and Plan B with a deductible of $2,000 for individual coverage and $4,000 for family coverage. The employer offers an MSA contribution to full-time employees in Plan A of $500 for individual coverage and $750 for family coverage. In order to satisfy the comparability rule, the employer would have to offer full-time employees covered under Plan B one of the following MSA contributions:
>
> 1. $500 for individual coverage and $750 for family coverage; or
> 2. $645 for individual coverage and $968 for family coverage.

Different contributions, or no contributions, could be made for part-time employees covered under either plan.

Q 7:74 What happens if an employer fails to comply with the comparability rule?

Employers who do not comply with the comparability rule are subject to an excise tax equal to 35 percent of the aggregate amount contributed by the employer to MSAs for that period. An employer is deemed not to fail the comparability rule if the employer is precluded from making contributions for all employees with high-deductible plan coverage because the employer has more than 200 employees or because of the limit on the number of people with MSAs.

Q 7:75 Who has jurisdiction over high-deductible plans?

States have oversight over high-deductible plans issued in conjunction with MSAs and could impose additional consumer protections. The legislative history makes it clear that Congress expects the National Association of Insurance Commissioners (NAIC) to develop model standards for high-deductible plans that individual states could adopt.

Q 7:76 What rules govern distributions from MSAs?

Distributions from an MSA for the medical expenses of the employee and his or her spouse or dependents generally are excludable from income; however, in any year for which a contribution is made to an MSA, withdrawals are excludable from income only if the individual for whom the expenses were incurred was eligible to make an MSA contribution at the time the expenses were incurred. This rule is designed to ensure that MSAs are used in conjunction with a high-deductible plan and that they are not used by individuals who have other health plans.

> **Example 7-8.** In 2000, individual A is covered by a high-deductible plan and A's spouse (B) is covered by a health plan that is not a high-deductible plan. A makes contributions to an MSA for 2000. Withdrawals from the MSA to pay B's medical expenses incurred in 2000 would be includible in income and subject to the 15 percent additional tax on nonmedical withdrawals because B is not covered by a high-deductible plan.

Distributions that are not for medical expenses are includible in income. Such distributions are also subject to an additional 15 percent tax unless made after age 65, death, or disability.

Q 7:77 What happens to an MSA when an employee dies?

Upon death, any balance remaining in the decedent's MSA is includible in his or her gross estate. If the employee's surviving spouse is the named beneficiary of the MSA, then after the death of the employee, the MSA becomes the MSA of the surviving spouse. If the MSA passes to a named beneficiary other than the decedent's surviving spouse, the MSA ceases to be an MSA as of the date of death and the beneficiary is required to include the value of MSA assets in gross income. The amount included in income is reduced by the amount used within one year of death to pay qualified medical expenses incurred prior to death. If there is no named beneficiary for the MSA, the MSA ceases to be an MSA and the value of the assets in the MSA are includible in the decedent's gross income for the year of death.

Q 7:78 What are medical expenses for MSA purposes?

Medical expenses are defined under the itemized deduction for medical expenses, except that medical expenses do not include expenses for insurance. There is an exception that allows MSAs to be used to pay for long-term care insurance, premiums for health care continuation coverage, and premiums for health care coverage while an individual is receiving unemployment compensation.

Q 7:79 What is the limit on the number of people with MSAs?

HIPAA created MSAs as a four-year experiment. In general, the number of people with MSAs is limited to 750,000. There are complex rules for determining when the maximum is reached.

Q 7:80 Have MSAs been popular?

No. According to IRS Announcement 99-95 [1999-42 IRB 520], the number of tax returns for MSAs has not come anywhere near the number needed to trigger an early cutoff of the pilot project.

Q 7:81 Why haven't more people adopted MSAs?

One reason may be communication; some people just don't know about MSAs or what makes them advantageous. Another reason is state requirements that conflict with federal law. MSAs must be linked to high-deductible health insurance policies. Some states require first dollar coverage or low deductibles for certain benefits. For example, Connecticut prohibits deductibles of more than $50 for home health care. That means MSAs cannot attain tax-favored status in Connecticut.

Q 7:82 What happens at the end of the MSA pilot project?

After December 31, 2000, no new contributions may be made to MSAs except by or on behalf of individuals who previously had MSAs and employees of participating employers. To be considered a participating employer, an employer must have made MSA contributions at some time or at least 20 percent of the employees covered under a high-deductible plan must have made contributions of at least $100 in the year 2000. Proposals have been introduced in Congress to extend MSAs past 2000 and to allow any employer to offer an MSA.

Coordination of Benefits

Q 7:83 What is coordination of benefits?

Coordination of benefits (COB) provisions were developed during the 1950s to eliminate the potential for employees to obtain dual reimbursement for medical expenses when they had multiple coverage. Without COB, an individual might receive more than 100 percent of the cost for medical care. For example, assume that an employee has an 80/20 copay plan, and her spouse also has an 80/20 copay plan. She has a claim, and her employer pays 80 percent of the bill. She might collect another 80 percent under her husband's plan if there were no coordination provision. This results in a 60 percent profit on the medical service. At a time of high health care costs, this kind of windfall is not affordable.

Q 7:84 How does COB help manage claim costs?

COB is a process by which insurers that cover the same individual for similar kinds of health care expenses coordinate their payments so that the insured is reimbursed for no more than the amount of the expense. When a claim is submitted and the insured is entitled to benefits for the same expense from more than one source, the benefits are coordinated among insurers. The employee usually cannot receive coverage for more than 100 percent of health care expenses. COB was initiated years ago, as a result of the rapid increase in overinsurance. COB used to save between 4 percent and 9 percent in claim costs, but duplicate coverage is less common today because of managed care. Standard COB provisions are included automatically in almost all group health care plans.

Q 7:85 Which plan pays first when there is coverage under more than one plan?

The NAIC has promulgated a standard hierarchy that has been adopted by nearly every state and insurance company. Plans without a COB provision always pay first. With minor exceptions, the sequence is as follows:

1. The plan covering the individual as an employee pays first.
2. The plan covering the individual as a dependent pays second.
3. If both plans cover the individual as a dependent, the plan of the employee whose birthday occurs soonest in the year pays first. This rule ("the birthday rule") applies only if both plans have adopted the birthday rule.
4. If either plan has not adopted the birthday rule, the plan of the male parent will pay first.
5. If the parents are divorced, the plan awarded primary responsibility by the court will pay first.
6. If the parents are divorced and there is no court-determined primary, then the following order will be used:
   a. The plan of the parent with custody of the child will pay first.
   b. The plan of the spouse of the parent with custody will be second.
   c. The plan of the parent without custody will be third.
   d. The plan of the spouse of the parent without custody will be last.
7. The plan covering an individual as an active employee will pay first; the plan covering that individual as an inactive

employee (such as a retiree or laid-off employee) will pay second.

8. The plan covering an individual as a COBRA continuee will be secondary to a plan covering that individual as an employee, a member, or a dependent.
9. If none of the preceding rules results in a determination, then the plan covering the individual for the longest period of time will pay first.
10. If both plans have covered the individual for an equivalent period of time, expenses will be split 50/50 between the two plans.

Q 7:86 Are coordination of benefits rules controlled at the federal level by ERISA?

No, they are not federally controlled. The COB rules must be adopted at the state level. In addition, before a state adopts the rules, individual insurance companies or plans can choose to follow the rules or not. Fortunately, however, there is a high degree of compliance with these rules. Failing to adopt them serves little purpose, and it has already been determined that no plan may be established as secondary to any and every other plan.

Q 7:87 Have all states adopted the rules exactly as written?

No, there are exceptions. Insurance carriers should know which rules apply in each state.

Q 7:88 What is maintenance of benefits?

Many employers are using an alternative COB approach called maintenance of benefits (MOB), which limits the total reimbursement from all sources to the amount one plan would have paid in the absence of other coverage. The objective is to pay in total only what the most generous of the plans would normally pay.

Under this approach, employees with coverage under two plans do not receive 100 percent reimbursement. For example, if an employee has an 80/20 copay plan and his spouse has a similar plan with her employer, he could collect the 80 percent from his employer but not an additional 20 percent from his wife's company plan as he would be able to do under COB. Using another example, if the spousal plan had a 90/10 copay, and the employee's plan had an 80/20 copay feature, he could collect 80 percent from his plan and another 10 percent from the spouse's plan.

MOB, also called "carve out" and "nonduplication," was approved at one time by NAIC but is no longer part of the model COB rules. MOB is included in many self-funded plans.

Q 7:89 What are the forms of coordination available and what are the differences among them?

The two most common forms are:

1. Standard COB;
2. Maintenance of benefits.

The differences affect only how the secondary payer computes its payment. In either case, the primary payer must determine its payment; then the secondary payer computes its payment under one of the approaches. Briefly stated, the concepts are:

1. Standard COB will permit reimbursement to the employee of up to 100 percent of total allowable expenses.
2. Maintenance of benefits aims to limit the total reimbursement from all plans to no more than what the secondary plan would have paid, had it been primary. Under this concept, overall reimbursement is limited to the normal liability of whichever plan would pay the higher amount.

Example 7-9. A dependent incurs $5,000 in expenses, all of which are eligible under both plans. Deductibles have been met, and the primary plan paid $3,500. The secondary plan would pay as follows:

Total Allowable Expenses

$5,000 eligible expenses
− $3,500 paid by primary
= $1,500 paid by secondary, because it will allow up to 100%

Total Allowable Expenses, with Coinsurance

      $5,000 eligible expenses
×   80%
= $4,000 combined target
− $3,500 paid by primary
= $ 500 paid by secondary

Maintenance of Benefits

      $5,000 eligible expenses

      $3,700* amount secondary plan would have paid had it been primary

− $3,500 paid by primary plan
= $ 200 amount paid by secondary
     ($3,700−$3,500 = $200)

*Had this amount been $3,500 or less, the secondary plan would have paid $0. The amount the secondary plan would have paid is based solely on that plan design; the method of determining that amount is not pertinent to this example.

Q 7:90 May an employer elect to use any form of COB?

If the employer is self-funded, yes; however, insured plans are generally limited to standard coordination of benefits. Some allow secondary payers to preserve coinsurance.

Q 7:91 What is the birthday rule?

Historically, the plan of the father was considered primary; however, with a new awareness of fairness and a climate of nondiscrimination, NAIC has developed guidelines to eliminate any appearance of discrimination. When a child is covered by both parents, the primary plan will be the plan of the parent whose birth date falls earlier in the year.

Q 7:92 Have companies tried any other COB innovations?

As health cost management becomes increasingly important, companies are experimenting with all sorts of innovative approaches.

Some companies are requiring COB against a spousal plan even if the spouse does not participate in the plan. Mere eligibility for the plan triggers coordination. This is called coordination with a "phantom plan," which is prohibited in many states.

When the wife and husband work for the same employer, the company might not pay both an employee benefit and a spousal benefit. Each can collect as an employee, but cannot collect in both capacities.

In an effort to avoid duplicate coverage, J.C. Penney went all the way to the U.S. Supreme Court to win the right to deny dependent coverage to an employee who was not the head of household or the highest paid earner in a family. Other employers have conditioned dependent coverage on lack of availability of any other group coverage.

Additional Cost-Management Strategies

Q 7:93 How does conventional insurance give an employer a predictable cash flow?

The cash flow will be predictable for at least the duration of the employer's contract. Once the premium rate is agreed upon, the employer is protected against unexpected bills arising from medical claims.

Q 7:94 How does conventional insurance give an employer protection against shock claims?

A shock claim is an unusually large claim. When a claim reaches shock size is entirely subjective and is dependent on the employer's ability to absorb the hit. Aside from the uneven cash flow that can result from normal claims, just think what a single claim of $500,000 or $750,000 would do to most employers' financial health. If an employer believes that the results of this kind of claim could be devastating, it needs stop-loss or conventional insurance.

Q 7:95   If an employer determines that plan design features alone will not manage costs sufficiently, what other options are available?

A wide variety of techniques other than plan design features have been implemented to reduce the cost of health insurance plans. The most common of these are educational programs, hospital audits, negotiated arrangements with health care providers, UR, and some form of self-funding.

Q 7:96   How does education contribute toward health care cost control?

One fundamental message must be communicated to all employees: Medical plan costs ultimately come back to the employer. This is true whether the employer is self-insured or conventionally insured. The only difference between these two employers is the length of time it takes for the costs to return. (This is true for experience-rated groups, but not prospectively rated groups. See Chapter 5.)

Once employees are educated in these basic concepts, the relationship between their actions and the employer's ability to maintain a medical program becomes evident. It might then become possible to control the rising costs of medical care.

Q 7:97   What is a hospital bill audit?

Hospital bill audits take two forms: audits done by an insurer or a professional bill review organization hired by the insurer, and audits by patients themselves. Professional bill audits involve retrospective review of all charges billed by a hospital to ascertain whether all services for which charges are billed were delivered and whether the charges are reasonable. Many hospital bills have errors, and insurers have found significant cost savings in questioning them. Audits are generally performed on larger bills, and the claimant and the hospital are put on notice that an audit is being performed, so that late payment is not an insured's problem.

Employee bill audits have been implemented recently at some companies. Employees are encouraged to review their own hospital bills, just as they would review car repair bills, before they pay them or submit them to their insurer for payment. Financial incentives help; some insurance companies will pay the person who discovers an error half of the amount of the billing error, up to a maximum amount per year. These programs may be worthwhile not only in helping insurance companies find billing errors but also in educating individuals on the substantial costs of care.

Q 7:98 How can negotiations with providers contribute toward cost management?

A more complex approach to cost management involves negotiations between insurance companies and health care providers. Large self-insured employers may become directly involved with providers (direct contracting), but most employers work through their insurers or TPAs.

Preferred provider organizations are groups of health care providers—doctors, allied health practitioners, and hospitals—that contract with insurers (or large employers) to provide specified health care, usually at discount rates and always with strict utilization review. This contrasts with traditional insurance arrangements in which insurers did not negotiate prices with the providers; they simply paid the charges for the services performed in accordance with the contract.

Typically, employers looking for cost management purchase a health care plan that gives employees an unlimited choice of health care providers, but when individuals use a "preferred provider," they are reimbursed at a more generous rate than they would have been had they been treated by a nonpreferred provider. Health care costs are managed for the employer in two ways: (1) the price for a plan that includes preferred providers is less expensive than one without, because the health care prices have been discounted; and (2) the preferred providers are contractually bound to give appropriate care. Utilization review is an integral part of preferred provider arrangements. (PPOs are discussed in detail in Chapter 8.)

Q 7:99 What are centers of excellence?

Centers of excellence are specific providers selected to perform certain low-volume procedures because of their expertise and the fact that they are willing to offer discounts for increased volume. By

Q 7:100   Health Insurance Answer Book

referring all of the specified procedures to a single provider, the health care management organization or insurer obtains high-quality services and the economies of scale; however, the location of the centers may not be convenient for the patient's family, and the treatment team may be unfamiliar to the patient.

Q 7:100 What types of procedures are usually referred to centers of excellence?

Procedures referred to centers of excellence are typically high-cost, very complex, and relatively uncommon. Center of excellence programs originally focused on organ transplants, but today have been expanded to include other complicated procedures such as cardiac surgery.

Q 7:101 How does using centers of excellence cut costs, and what are the resultant savings?

The cost savings come from several sources. First, the employer (or insurer) can negotiate a discount with the center of excellence because it can offer the facility all of the specified procedures plan participants will need. Increasingly, negotiations are aimed at setting a "global" fee—one agreed-upon fee for each procedure that covers most of the services involved. For example, a global fee for an organ transplant might include the standard preoperation procedures and tests, the transplant, and a certain amount of postoperative care, all in one price. Negotiations may save employers 30 percent or more over the normal cost of some procedures.

Another source of savings is the quality of care itself. Patient outcomes for complicated procedures are generally better when the procedures are performed by experienced teams at facilities that handle a high volume of such cases, and better patient outcomes mean fewer complications and shorter hospital stays, both important factors in high-risk operations.

Q 7:102 Can employers be held liable for poor quality of care delivered as a result of health care cost control efforts?

Although employers and providers can always be sued, whether or not they can be held liable depends on the circumstances and previous legal rulings in the jurisdiction. For example, a distinction is emerging relative to the type and degree of employer involvement in establishing the cost control program. An employer that utilizes a "canned" program available from its insurer and merely authorizes its use will be seen as having less involvement (and therefore less liability exposure) than an employer that directly contracts with providers and participates in the creation of the cost control techniques. Similarly, an employer that exercises reasonable due diligence in selecting an HMO will have greater immunity from a medical malpractice claim filed against an HMO physician than would an employer that directly contracted with specific physicians in constructing a PPO network.

Several states have passed legislation specifically allowing HMOs to be sued for medical malpractice. In 1999, the U.S. House of Representatives approved a proposal that would allow HMOs and employers to be sued.

Legal counsel should be consulted if there is any question regarding a particular design element.

Q 7:103 Are any cost control actions taken by an employer less risky than others?

Yes. For example, suppose an employer engaged the services of one doctor and required all employees to utilize his or her services in order to have their medical expenses covered. In this circumstance, if the doctor were guilty of malpractice, the employer would very likely be swept into any damage settlement because it selected the doctor and presumably endorsed his or her qualifications and expertise. On the other hand, if an employer established a requirement that any proposed medical procedure necessitated approval by a second physician of the employee's choice, the employer's chances of being brought into a suit are diminished because it had no part in selecting the second doctor.

As a second example, consider an employer's position in selecting an HMO or a managed care network from an insurance company. In this circumstance, the employer selects the vendor, not the doctor. The employer has an obligation to select the vendor with diligence. The employer should check that the HMO is qualified or that the managed care network administrators have a credentialing requirement, and that they follow it. In performing these actions, the employer is not endorsing the physicians or their qualifications, but simply validating that the vendor has performed its functions. It is the vendor who is making the determination as to the skills and abilities of the doctors; however, the employer can still be brought into the suit and, accordingly, should consider getting "hold harmless" agreements from the vendor. (These are agreements whereby the vendor agrees to defend the employer and to pay the employer's legal fees and awards, if found against the vendor or employer.)

Q 7:104 How do direct contracting arrangements between employers and health care providers work?

Only the largest employers contract directly with providers rather than with an organization representing providers. Enormous due diligence efforts are required before entering into such contracts in order to establish specific objectives and measures. Direct contracting without the assistance of specialized professionals is not recommended. The costs reflect the unique services being contracted, and small and medium-sized employers are typically better served by participating in an existing structure and obtaining economies of scale.

Q 7:105 What are coalitions?

Employer coalitions are groups of employers that have joined together primarily for purposes of gathering and sharing data on health care. Although the establishment of a useful health care database was initially the chief priority, coalitions have been instrumental in applying pressure to gain the release of data historically withheld by providers and HMOs.

Today, coalitions in most states are actively addressing issues in health care such as mandated benefits, quality assurance, and delivery systems.

Q 7:106 Who participates in health care coalitions?

Although primarily made up of local business firms, coalitions include as members and advisors various provider representatives (medical society, hospital association), consumer organizations, health systems agencies, and insurers. Most function on a county or regional basis, although a dozen large cities are serviced by their own coalitions. All provide member education through publications, workshops, and seminars.

Q 7:107 How can existing health care coalitions be located?

The National Business Coalition on Health can provide specific information concerning health care coalitions. The International Foundation of Employee Benefit Plans maintains a database of coalitions with multiemployer plans. See Appendix A.

Q 7:108 What is value-based purchasing?

According to Irene Fraser, Ph.D., director of the Center for Organization and Delivery Studies at the Agency for Health Care Policy and Research (AHCPR), value-based purchasing is defined by the following characteristics:

1. Employers focus on quality as well as cost.
2. Plans and providers compete on quality.
3. Employers reward good plans and providers, often by urging employees to select the best performers.
4. Employers use their market power to improve value.

According to the Midwest Business Group on Health, common activities of value-based purchasers include efforts to identify and contract with the plans and providers that adopt the best clinical practices and demonstrate high-quality care, educate employees and their families about quality, encourage enrollment in those plans or provider organizations that deliver the best care, and provide incentives for plans and providers to improve their care and service over time.

Q 7:109 Why might an employer consider requiring the use of an HMO?

HMOs, whether independent practice association or staff model, require the use of a certain group of doctors and hospitals. Well-managed HMOs can help an employer control its costs over the long run. Because requiring the use of an HMO impinges on the employee's ability to make choices, this would have been heresy a few years ago. Recently, however, the need to cut costs has led some employers to cancel their indemnity plan and replace it with an HMO or a choice of HMOs.

Q 7:110 What are claim audits?

Claim audits are conducted to evaluate the level of service provided by a TPA, insurer, health maintenance organization, or other vendor or provider. Claim audits can focus on a specific problem, such as coordination of benefits claims or adjustments, or evaluate overall services. The audits can include staffing and systems issues as well as whether performance guarantees are being met. Audits can be structured to show how quickly claims are paid and how frequently the claim office makes errors by selecting random claims to be audited. Stratified sampling techniques allow a plan sponsor to determine, with a relatively high degree of confidence, how well a claim office is handling its money. Without a claim audit, if claims are consistently underpaid or overpaid, the plan sponsor could be found to have breached its fiduciary responsibility for managing the plan.

Q 7:111 What are performance guarantees?

Many insurers, third-party administrators, and even HMOs are now agreeing to return a portion of their fees if they fail to meet negotiated performance standards. The rationale is that employers assume a certain level of accuracy and timeliness from the vendor; if performance does not live up to that standard, the employer is entitled to a partial refund. Standards can be negotiated to cover any number of categories, such as accuracy (which can be defined in various ways and should be specified in the contract), turnaround time for claim processing, generating reports, producing identification cards and summary plan descriptions, or anything else the vendor should do on a timely basis. Savings, such as those from coordination of benefits, utilization review, and managed care discounts, also are frequently guaranteed.

Q 7:112 What are the most common performance standards and performance guarantees?

According to a 1999 survey by Deloitte & Touche, claim turnaround time is the most common performance standard, used by 84 percent of employers using at least one standard. Claim turnaround time is also the most common performance guarantee, with 47 percent of employers using at least one standard putting fees or premiums at risk. Claim financial accuracy is the second most common in each category, with 69 percent and 45 percent, respectively. Phone response and/or abandonment rate standards and guarantees are the third most common at 60 percent and 35 percent respectively. The fourth most common in each category is claim coding accuracy at 51 percent and 33 percent. The next most common is ID card distribution at 37 percent and 15 percent.

Billing Codes

Q 7:113 What are medical billing codes?

Medical billing codes are complex billing systems required by Medicare and private insurers that assign a code number to each specific medical procedure.

One prominent coding system, current procedural technology (CPT), was developed by the American Medical Association to categorize several thousand different medical procedures, each of which is represented by a 5-digit code.

The complexity of billing codes leads to incorrect billings, either as a result of ignorance of the correct code to apply, or as a result of deliberate manipulation of the coding system, or "code gaming."

Q 7:114 Why do providers engage in code gaming?

Incorrect codes are deliberately used in billings generally either to increase the provider's income, or to qualify a patient for reimbursement for which he or she would be ineligible if the correct code were used.

Q 7:115 What kinds of code gaming are there?

There are four main methods of code gaming:

1. *Upcoding (also known as "code creep")*. This involves reclassifying or redefining a procedure so that it falls into a category that qualifies for a higher rate of reimbursement.
2. *Exploding*. Itemizing a group of tests performed on the same specimen as individual procedures.
3. *Unbundling*. Itemizing each step of a procedure and billing each separately, such as billing for the surgical incision as a procedure separate from an appendectomy.
4. *Visit churning*. Charging for the same visit more than once. For example, a doctor who meets a patient in the emergency room and accompanies him when he is admitted may bill the emergency room visit and inpatient time as separate visits.

Q 7:116 How can code gaming be detected?

Code gaming can only be detected by experienced, diligent claim administrators. Some use specially designed software to improve their ability to identify potential gaming situations. Actual gaming is difficult to prove, and specifically flagged providers may be screened more rigorously than others. No claim administrator can afford to screen all providers and all claims.

Impact of AIDS on Insurance

Q 7:117 What is the impact of AIDS on health benefits?

The cost of treating Americans infected with the human immunodeficiency virus (HIV), the virus that causes acquired immune deficiency syndrome (AIDS), has stabilized. The Health Insurance

Association of America (HIAA) says the demographics of the nation's AIDS population are changing. Increasingly, people with AIDS contracted the virus through intravenous drug use or sexual contact with an IV drug user. Many people in those risk groups do not have group insurance.

Q 7:118 How much do AIDS claims actually cost?

According to the Employee Benefit Research Institute, the lifetime costs of treating a person with HIV disease range from $71,143 to $424,763. Employment-based costs are heavily influenced by the type of benefits provided by the employer. The estimate was calculated by using the expected medical, disability, employee replacement, life insurance, and pension costs to a business for an HIV-infected employee.

A relatively new combination of drugs shows evidence of success in driving AIDS into remission. A new class of medicines known as protease inhibitors, when used in combination with drugs based on AZT, is proving effective. Treatment costs $12,000 to $16,000 a year, and each patient will probably receive treatment for years. Despite the high cost, early studies indicate that the new treatment reduces total costs. One study found a 57 percent reduction in hospital days for patients using protease inhibitors.

More new treatments are on the way. On November 25, 1998, the Pharmaceutical Research and Manufacturers of America reported that 113 medicines for AIDS and AIDs-related conditions were being tested.

Q 7:119 Why will the medical costs be so high?

The reasons for the high level of expense and the variation include:

1. *Expensive drugs.* Because most drugs used in the treatment of AIDS are still new, they are also very expensive. The cost of providing protease inhibitors in combination with AZT to an AIDS patient may be $12,000 to $16,000 a year.

2. *Lengthening life expectancy.* The average life expectancy of a person with AIDS has been increasing. Successful treatment means longer life, which in turn means longer periods of care and more prescription drugs, all of which translates to higher costs.

3. *Lengthy hospital stays.* Although more and more AIDS care is being provided at home, in nursing facilities, and through volunteers—all of which reduce the cost of caring for AIDS victims—there can still be long periods of care in some sort of medical facility.

Q 7:120 Are there restrictions on the information that may be requested to identify a person at risk for AIDS?

Yes. Although laws vary from state to state, some jurisdictions prohibit or restrict employers and/or carriers from basing coverage decisions on such things as blood/HIV antibody tests, questions about former AIDS tests, and life-style questions, particularly those surrounding sexual preference. Contractual AIDS exclusions are also prohibited.

Q 7:121 Would all forms of care for AIDS patients be covered under an employer's health insurance program?

Not necessarily. Insurance policies tend to be quite specific about the nature of treatment covered. Because care for AIDS patients may be of an experimental nature, or may be provided through an alternative facility that is not staffed by "licensed practitioners," it may fall outside policy definitions.

Also, the plan may limit reimbursement to "actual treatment of illness or injury," which would not extend to custodial care, often the largest single cost item for AIDS patients. A considerable portion of such care is provided through home health care, residential facilities, or hospices. Plans that provide hospice coverage would pay for these types of expenses.

Q 7:122 What legal protections have been extended to persons with AIDS?

AIDS as a cause for dismissal is not acceptable now for reasons beyond the humane; such an action is considered discriminatory under the ADA. Persons with AIDS or who are HIV-positive are considered disabled under the ADA. The Supreme Court upheld the EEOC's position in this regard in the case of *Bragdon v. Abbott.* [US No 97-156, June 25, 1998]

Many states and local agencies also classify AIDS as a handicap under their fair employment laws.

Q 7:123 Is testing for AIDS permissible?

According to the Equal Employment Opportunity Commission's (EEOC's) Technical Assistance Manual on the employment provisions of the ADA, "If a test screens out or tends to screen out an individual with a disability or a class of such individuals on the basis of disability, it must be job-related and consistent with business necessity." Therefore, testing for AIDS would usually (if not always) be prohibited.

Q 7:124 How does the Americans with Disabilities Act affect persons with AIDS?

AIDS is classified as a disability under the Americans with Disabilities Act, which makes it illegal to discriminate against people with AIDS or HIV infection as to terms and conditions of employment. If an individual is qualified for a job, he or she may not be denied a position because of a disability. An employer may describe the essential functions of the job and inquire as to the applicant's ability to perform them, but may not inquire about the origins of any impairment or the prognosis for the impairments. The applicant's ability to perform marginal, as opposed to essential, job functions may not be considered.

Post-hire physicals for such illnesses as AIDS (or HIV infection) are prohibited unless (1) the employer can demonstrate that they are job-related and a business necessity, (2) they are mandated by the government, or (3) they are purely voluntary, with the results kept confidential.

The Equal Employment Opportunity Commission issued interim guidance outlining the enforcement of the ADA in terms of employer health insurance plans, and this guidance essentially prohibits employers from excluding or limiting coverage for specific conditions considered disabilities (as is HIV infection) unless the exclusion or limitation is based on reasonable actuarial principles or relevant experience. The guidance includes as an example of an illegal disability-based distinction a health plan cap for AIDS-related illness that is lower than for other illnesses. (For a more complete discussion of the ADA, see Chapter 4.)

Q 7:125   How should an employer respond to AIDS?

An employer should first establish a corporate policy on AIDS that goes beyond financial concerns to address the social environment of the workplace, and should include a program of education for other workers. Other appropriate actions include:

1. Planning for the reasonable accommodation of persons with AIDS, with special attention to those working in sensitive areas such as food service, health care, laboratory, and other kinds of work that are encompassed by guidelines established by the Centers for Disease Control. Special precautions or reassignment might need to be considered.
2. Making arrangements for job modifications, or alternative work assignments on a part-time or temporary basis, that would allow the individual with AIDS to continue working as long as possible.
3. Contacting community agencies that will help both the employer and the person with AIDS.
4. Reviewing existing insurance arrangements to see what forms of coverage are provided.

Rationing Health Care

Q 7:126   Is there objective evidence of the existence of illogical practice patterns?

Yes. Studies have repeatedly shown geographical variations in practice patterns that are not justified by the outcomes. One example of this is that the rate of cesarean sections performed in Detroit is twice that of Minneapolis.

Another example can be found in a study performed by the Rand Corporation. In sampling cardiovascular procedures, the study found that one-third of operations for clogged neck arteries were inappropriate and another one-third were borderline. In looking at coronary artery bypass operations, the study found that only 56 percent of those operations were clearly appropriate.

Variations in age, sex, or health status did not account for the differences. Analysis of the populations receiving the greater amount of medical services established no correlation to outcomes or to overall health status. The prevailing medical treatment patterns involved in the local communities proved to be the most significant factor.

Two of the most commonly performed operations in the United States are tonsillectomies and hysterectomies. Broad-based studies of these operations have concluded that 20 percent of those performed are not medically necessary.

Q 7:127 Is anyone considering rationing health care?

Yes, this is happening, and it has occurred in employers' plans for years in one form or another. In its most basic form, the mere setting of a limit is rationing. Limits have been commonly set on things such as mental and nervous conditions, alcohol and drug abuse treatments, maximum number of days in a hospital during a plan year, and maximum dollar amount of major medical benefits. This type of rationing is almost universal and has been refined by tactics such as pre-certification requirements.

Q 7:128 What further developments have taken place concerning rationing?

According to a Louis Harris poll in 1994, more than nine out of ten Americans believe that "everybody should have the right to the best possible health care—as good as the treatment a millionaire gets," even if the cost of an individual's care exceeds $1 million. The spread of expensive technologies has increased the incidence of high-cost procedures. It is no longer unusual to have programs of treatment, some of which may be regarded as experimental, running into hundreds of thousands of dollars.

Some years ago, bioethicists began asking disconcerting questions about this and other traditional assumptions regarding health care availability: Does it make sense for society to underwrite the cost of all of these expensive procedures? Would it be better if this money were channeled to other types of care that would provide valuable benefits to a wider range of people? Should there be formal mechanisms for weighing the benefits of various procedures against their costs, and refusing to pay for those that do not meet specified cost/benefit standards?

The state of Oregon asked these questions about its Medicaid program. By cutting off high-cost procedures that benefit relatively few residents, the state hopes to expand health coverage generally and provide at least some health care services to every resident living below the federal poverty level.

In public hearings held around the state, those attending supported preventive care services over costly life-saving procedures. Based upon the findings of these hearings, as well as a telephone survey, a "quality of well-being scale" was developed that ranked how an average person might feel after receiving treatment for a particular ailment. The scale takes into account the cost of a procedure and the number of years an average person might live after receiving the treatment. The final outcome is a cost-to-benefit ratio that allows each of 745 procedures to be ranked, with those having the highest ratio receiving Medicaid reimbursement and those ranked lower being denied reimbursement. As a result, those ranked below 581 will be denied reimbursement. The Oregon approach has already drawn protests from groups representing beneficiaries such as organ transplant recipients.

Before proceeding with implementation, Oregon needed to receive federal approval for the program. Based on legal concerns, the Bush Administration denied approval. In response, the state modified the design somewhat and on March 19, 1993 received permission from the Clinton administration to proceed. The permission (which is actually a waiver from federal requirements) began on January 1, 1994 and ran for a five-year period. As approved, the waiver contained certain terms and restrictions, not the least of which is the requirement that any revision to the list of procedures and services must receive approval from the Health Care Financing Administration before taking effect. Even though the waiver has expired, nothing has changed, pending an extension from HCFA.

A 1999 survey by the Oregon Department of Human Resources showed that two-thirds of the Medicaid recipients in managed care plans would recommend their plan and that only 9 percent would not. Respondents generally said that access to health care had improved since a 1995 survey.

The Employer's Role

Q 7:129 What are some actions individual employers can take to manage health care costs?

The problem is like a snow storm. Taken individually, each snowflake is fragile; together they can create a blizzard. Similarly, just as no one employer created this problem, no single employer will solve it; however, actions by individual employers, when they are repeated by other employers, will have enough cumulative effect to control the problem.

An employer should examine its medical plan and study the other contributing factors discussed in Q 7:3. The employer can then begin to decide which factors will likely yield the greatest or quickest return. Taking action on any one of these issues will have an effect on the problem. The more steps an individual employer takes, the faster results will begin to develop, not only for that employer but for others as well. As employers individually take steps to address the issues, a momentum will build (as it already has), encouraging other employers to take similar steps.

Q 7:130 Can an employer make cuts in its plan without hurting itself competitively?

Yes. In fact, an employer should make cuts in its plan if it wishes to remain competitive. Anything that contributes to an employer's overhead costs adds to the cost of goods or services the employer is selling. Higher overhead costs must eventually result in a higher selling price; higher selling prices will put the employer at a competitive disadvantage to lower-cost producers. While it remains true that employees expect employers to provide medical coverage, the level of coverage in competitive plans is receding.

The question then becomes not whether to cut, but which cuts to make. Today's health insurance market is complex and challenging. Employers may choose from a wide array of cost-cutting and redesign options, only some of which will be helpful to a specific employer.

Q 7:131   What steps can employers take to help reduce costs associated with new and expensive medical technology?

1. Encourage employees (either through plan design incentives or through education) to question the need for multiple tests such as an X-ray plus an MRI. Or, if multiple blood tests are being prescribed, encourage the employee to press for a clear explanation of what each test is intended to reveal and why each one is necessary. A classic response to this type of questioning is "just to be sure." Suggest to employees that they continue the questioning with inquiries such as: "How much more knowledge or certainty will the test add?" "Will the additional data determine a course of action?"

2. Set aside the question of whether an MRI test is necessary and accept that it indeed is a powerful and necessary diagnostic tool. An employer should question, however, how many of these machines are necessary in a given geographic area. Each hospital or local physician group with such a machine will need many patients to justify its expense. A joint MRI (or CT) facility shared by two or more hospitals may make much more sense economically. An employer can make its views known by active participation in, or formation of, a local health care coalition, or by sitting on a hospital board or advisory committee. The local Chamber of Commerce or similar organization may have a health care committee an employer can join.

3. Be cautious of a physician-owned testing facility of any kind. Once purchased, the facility (or machinery) must be amortized. The more tests are run, the sooner the enterprise will be on a sound financial footing. This could lead a physician to order tests more out of economic than medical necessity. A tightly managed utilization review program or physician profiling could identify instances of this nature, which would then suggest further action.

Q 7:132 What can employers do about the overprovision of medical services?

An employer should make sure the employee is motivated to receive only cost-efficient treatment. The employee must be educated about his or her rights and responsibilities in receiving medical treatment. Patients should no longer feel they are there for the physician's benefit, or that they have no financial stake in the proceedings.

Q 7:133 How can employers combat the inappropriate use of medical services?

Employees must be motivated to seek medical services only when the services are truly necessary. Education is the key in determining when services are necessary, and acquiring the ability to use appropriate home-treatment is something that can be learned. Insurance companies, hospitals, and other medical providers have educational services available to assist employers in this effort. Some of the assistance is available for a fee; other assistance is free.

One such source of assistance is a fee-based program put out by Optum (a wholly owned subsidiary of United HealthCare). This program includes a book intended for distribution to employees and their families called *Take Care of Yourself*.

In part, the book lists common injuries, emergencies one might encounter in the home, and other illnesses and symptoms. For each injury, illness, or symptom listing, there is a brief section of text describing the condition followed by an explanation of appropriate home treatment. There is also a logic-tree format that asks pertinent questions, and, based on a yes or no answer, instructs the patient to "See Doctor Today," or "Make Appointment with Doctor," or "Apply Home Treatment."

A report in the *Journal of the American Medical Association* describes a randomized study in which some people (drawn by lot) in Woodland, California, were given *Take Care of Yourself.* Four-hundred-sixty families were given the book, and 239 were not. The number of visits to doctors by those who were given *Take Care of Yourself* was reduced by 7.5 percent as compared to those who were not given the book. Visits to doctors decreased 14 percent for upper respiratory tract infections (colds).

Q 7:134   How did employees' expectation of receiving benefits add to the problem of escalating costs for benefits?

The normal balance of free market competitive dynamics was severely distorted by removing the price of services from consideration by the purchaser. By interposing the employer as the payer, the buyer became a consumer without the normal restraints imposed by cost considerations. An analogy popularly used today is to say that if employers, instead of providing 80 percent or 90 percent reimbursement for medical services, had instead provided automobile purchase reimbursement plans providing the same level of coverage, every employee would be driving a Mercedes or BMW, and it would cost as much as a Rolls-Royce.

Removal of price considerations led also to lack of incentives for providers to practice cost-efficient medicine. Inherently inflationary reimbursement practices, such as fee-for-service reimbursements, added to the imbalance of the system and created the crisis in medical costs in the 1980s. Other factors, such as the lack of communication to employees about actual costs and an attendant lack of employee understanding about the basis of the cost problem and their part in it, defensive medicine, and the expansion of technology, did not themselves create the current cost problem, but they greatly increased its pace of growth.

Chapter 8

Managed Care Plans

Employers and other health care plan sponsors have experimented with a variety of methods to manage health care costs. One cost-management option available to employers is to reorganize the way employee health care services are provided and funded. This chapter discusses managed health care delivery systems such as HMOs and PPOs.

Introduction	8-1
Health Maintenance Organizations	8-4
Adverse Selection	8-16
Legal Standards	8-18
Evaluating HMOs	8-24
Preferred Provider Organizations	8-29
Managed Care Backlash	8-47

Introduction

Q 8:1 How has the traditional reimbursement system in this country contributed to the escalating cost of health care?

Retrospective reimbursement guarantees revenue to doctors and hospitals. There are few financial incentives for providers to reduce the amount of care or to deliver it more efficiently; in most traditional plans, payment and reimbursement are on a fee-for-service basis. More care generally means more revenue. Patients have allowed this to occur because they have been insulated from the cost of care through their insurance plans. There are minimal financial barriers to getting as much care as desired.

Broad insurance coverage encourages employees to use medical care with little regard for price. Demand for care does not drop as price increases, and insurance companies have passed along the costs of increased utilization and cost of care to employers in the form of premium rate increases.

Q 8:2 What is managed care?

Broadly speaking, managed care is any health care delivery system in which a party other than the physician or the patient influences the type of medical care delivered. A managed care system actively manages both the medical and financial aspects of a patients care. A managed care system may limit benefits to its customers but will actively manage those limitations.

Q 8:3 What caused the shift toward managed care in the health care marketplace?

Years ago, health insurance coverage provided reimbursement to insured members for a portion of any medical expenses incurred. The insured member could go to the doctor as many times as he or she wanted and could choose any doctor to provide care. If the insured member wanted to visit a specialist or undergo expensive testing of some sort, those charges were paid, submitted to the insurance carrier, and reimbursed. No questions were asked, no penalties for overuse or misuse were assessed, and unlimited access was available. These uncontrolled claims, combined with skyrocketing medical inflation, resulted in high loss ratios for insurance companies which, in turn, caused them to increase health plan premiums significantly. These increased rates for coverage, of course, were not well received by employers, who paid a large share of these premiums, or by the purchasing public in general. The need to lower and control costs in order to maintain health care affordability moved to the top of the industry's priority list.

Q 8:4 How are insurers and providers merging their services?

Employers and their insurers—the government, Blue Cross/Blue Shield (the Blues), and private insurers—all agree that too much money is being spent on health care. Insurers cannot simply restrict reimbursement and shift costs to insureds in order to reduce costs. Furthermore, providers, particularly hospitals, are experiencing decreasing demand for their services because alternative care facilities and insurance plans exist that can channel patients to the least expensive care sites. As a result, insurers began working with providers to reorganize the delivery of care. Providers and insurers are exchanging roles. Insurers are becoming involved in defining reimbursable health care, and providers are entering into risk-sharing and profit-sharing arrangements with insurance companies. Two well-defined models of integrated delivery systems are health maintenance organizations (HMOs) and preferred provider organizations (PPOs).

Q 8:5 How many people are enrolled in the largest managed care plans?

The following rankings by Employee Benefit News include people in HMOs, PPOs, and Medicaid plans.

Rank	Organization	Enrollees
1	Aetna US Healthcare	21.0M
2	United Health Group	14.3M
3	CIGNA Healthplan	10.8M
4	Kaiser Permanente	8.0M
5	Humana Health Care Plans	5.9M
6	Blue Cross of California	5.3M
7	PacifiCare Health Systems	4.0M
8	Regence Group	3.0M
9	Alliance BlueCross BlueShield	2.2M
10	HealthNet	2.2M

Health Maintenance Organizations

Q 8:6 What is an HMO?

An HMO is an organization that provides comprehensive health care to a voluntarily enrolled population at a predetermined price. Members pay fixed, periodic (usually monthly) fees directly to the HMO and in return receive health care service from the HMO's network of providers as often as needed. Out-of-pocket expenses are typically limited, as long as the member uses providers in the HMO's network. Some HMOs pay a fixed monthly fee to primary care physicians (PCPs) to provide routine care. This payment structure is known as "capitation." These primary care physicians often act as a gatekeeper, managing referrals to specialists and hospitals.

HMO revenues increase only when enrollment increases, not when services increase. If monthly payments from members exceed the funds the HMO expends on care, the HMO profits. If revenues are less than the cost of care, the HMO loses.

Q 8:7 When were HMOs developed?

The concept of pre-paid group health care central to HMO plans first appeared around the turn of the century. Employers in remote mining and lumber regions deducted fees from workers' wages and in turn provided them with health care clinics and physicians.

Organized medical care on a pre-paid, comprehensive basis was first introduced to more populated areas in 1929. The Los Angeles City Department of Water and Power contracted with two physicians to arrange for all medical and hospital care for 2,000 of their employees and families in exchange for a fixed premium. The health plan, the Ross-Loos Medical Group, named after the founding physicians, continues today as part of a larger HMO.

Although HMOs have existed since 1929, the real impetus to their development came in the 1970s. It was then that the federal government, as part of an evaluation of the health care delivery system, recognized that the concept of pre-paid health plans might correct structural, inflationary problems with fee-for-service health care.

The government was impressed with the health care plan created by the Kaiser organization. The plan was a combination insurer-provider for workers building the Grand Coulee Dam. The government was interested in the approach because Kaiser was providing its workers with quality health care for considerably less than it cost under traditional plans. The reduced costs were attributable in part to a decrease in utilization. The rate of hospitalization at that time was 349 days per 1,000 members per year, compared with a national average of 1,149 days per 1,000. The plan's emphasis on preventive care and its pre-payment basis concept, which the government believed would encourage physicians to be more cost-conscious in their delivery of care, seemed to be working.

Congress passed the HMO Act of 1973 to encourage the development of HMOs. It set requirements for federal qualification and provided for grants and loan guarantees for planning, development, and initial operating costs for those HMOs that met the qualifying standards. The act also encouraged enrollment among a skeptical public by establishing criteria for HMOs seeking federal qualification.

Q 8:8 Who develops and sponsors HMOs?

HMOs have several different types of sponsors. Some have been developed and sponsored by employers or labor unions. Others have been started by medical schools, hospitals, or medical clinics. Some insurance companies have also been involved in establishing their own HMOs or have invested capital or in-kind expertise in existing or developing organizations.

Q 8:9 How many people are enrolled in HMOs?

Nationwide, HMO enrollment was estimated at 81 million Americans in 1999, according to InterStudy. The number in HMOs increased by 2.6 percent from 1998. This was the smallest percentage increase of the 1990s. See the tables that follow for statistics on the number of HMO enrollees annually for the last ten years and the top ten HMOs by size.

HMO Growth

1990	34.7
1991	36.5
1992	38.8
1993	42.1
1994	47.3
1995	53.4
1996	63.3
1997	73.1
1998	78.8
1999	81.0

Top Ten HMO Chains by Size

	Enrollment in Group Plans	Total Enrollment (including Medicare and Medicaid)
1. The Blue Cross and Blue Shield System	7.8M	13.9M
2. Kaiser Foundation	NA	8.5M
3. United Health Group	1.6M	6.4M
4. Aetna US Healthcare	3.6M	5.9M
5. Foundation Health Systems	2.3M	4.0M
6. PacifiCare	2.5M	3.8M
7. CIGNA Health Care Inc.	2.2M	3.4M
8. Humana	1.7M	2.9M
9. Prudential	2.6M	2.9M
10. WellPoint Health Networks	1.0M	1.8M

Source: 30 InterStudy

Q 8:10 What are the trends in HMO enrollment?

According to InterStudy, there were 81 million people enrolled in HMOs as of July 1, 1999. That represents an increase of only 2.6 percent since July 1, 1998.

According to the Mercer/Foster Higgins National Survey of Employer-Sponsored Health Plans, the percentage of large employers offering at least one HMO fell slightly from 57 percent in 1995 and 1996 to 54 percent in 1997 and 52 percent in 1998 and 1999. Despite the decrease in the percentage of employers offering HMOs, HMO enrollment held steady at 32 percent, essentially unchanged since 1995.

Q 8:11   Are there any reasons for the geographic differentials of HMO acceptance?

The differential is not explained by quality of service differences, but seems to be based on slowly growing word-of-mouth acceptance.

The high acceptance rate found in the western United States may result from the fact that this is the region where HMOs started. The Ross-Loos Medical Group of Los Angeles (now part of CIGNA) was formed in 1929. The Kaiser Health Plan was created in the 1930s to serve the workers building the Grand Coulee Dam, revived during World War II to serve shipyard workers, opened to the public in California after the war, and has grown nationwide since that time.

Q 8:12   Do physicians own HMOs?

Most HMOs require too much development and working capital to be owned exclusively by physicians. HMOs are owned by private insurance companies, hospitals, and various investors. Physicians typically have "pieces of the pie" under profit-sharing arrangements or partial ownership of the corporations. As an exception to the rule, the California Medical Association formed its own HMO (which filed for bankruptcy in 1998). Such HMOs should be inclined to provide the most cost-effective care. This contrasts with physicians in the traditional fee-for-service delivery system, who can increase their income by delivering more care. The American Medical Association is providing resources to physicians who want to form their own HMOs. The Balanced Budget Act of 1997 created new options for Medicare beneficiaries, one of which is enrollment in a provider-sponsored organization (PSO). PSOs are essentially HMOs owned by providers. As of press time, only a few PSOs had applied to be part of Medicare.

Q 8:13 How are HMOs organized?

HMOs are organized on a physician basis. There are five basic organizations of HMO physicians (definitions provided by InterStudy, the leading HMO analysis organization):

1. *Group model.* Contracts with one independent group practice to provide health services, with care usually billed to the HMO on a fee-for-service basis.
2. *Staff model.* Delivers health services through a physician group that is controlled by the HMO. The physicians, in effect, are employed and paid by the HMO.
3. *Network model.* Contracts with two or more independent group practices (no solo practices) to provide health services.
4. *Independent practice association (IPA) model.* Contracts with physicians from various settings (individual physicians or a mixture of solo and group practices) to provide health services.
5. *Mixed model.* Combines elements of the above categories.

Q 8:14 What is the most popular type of HMO today?

Early HMOs were "staff models." Staff model physicians are employees of the HMO. Typically, they practice out of a central location, which created the impression of a "clinic" in the minds of some customers. Most HMOs today are IPA models, which are more easily organized and marketed. IPA physicians practice out of their own offices, treating HMO and private patients. Few physicians are willing to sign exclusive contracts and give up private patients, a situation typical of non-IPA HMOs. The IPA structure permits HMOs to sign quality specialists for their panels.

Q 8:15 What is an IPA?

IPA stands for individual (or independent) practice (or physician) association. It is a loosely affiliated group of physicians organized to contract with HMOs and other managed care organizations. The doctors may be paid on a fee-for-service basis or may be capitated.

Q 8:16 How is a capitated payment structure different from a fee-for-service payment structure?

Health care providers—which include individuals (e.g., medical doctors, dentists, osteopaths, psychiatric social workers, physical therapists, and chiropractors) and institutions (hospitals, clinics, surgicenters, skilled nursing care facilities, and hospices)—have historically been compensated on a fee-for-service basis. For each unit of service provided, an associated fee is billed. A doctor examines a patient complaining of back pain and is compensated for that examination. A hospital provides emergency room care to a heart attack victim and is paid for the treatment provided.

Under a capitated payment structure, health care providers are paid a fixed amount per member per month regardless of which services (if any) are performed. This pre-paid arrangement is analogous to a person buying an annual maintenance warranty without knowing whether the washing machine will ever need repair.

Q 8:17 What factors typically affect capitation payments?

To determine the appropriate amount of capitation, primary care services must be defined. Capitations are frequently adjusted for age and gender. Capitation amounts also may be adjusted for higher-cost categories of patients.

Q 8:18 Do employers pre-pay for health care services in traditional plans?

In a sense, employers pre-pay for expenses their employees will incur by agreeing to pay fixed monthly health care premiums to an insurer. Although premiums are pre-paid, providers are still paid on a fee-for-service basis. This means that the risk is assumed by an intermediary, the insurer. With HMOs, it is the care provider itself that assumes the risk.

Q 8:19 Do employees pre-pay for health care through their payroll deductions for traditional plans?

To a degree, employees do pre-pay for their medical care. Many employees perceive their health care costs to be on a pre-paid basis, because their monthly contributions are fixed payroll deductions; however, in most plans, employees do share in the cost of each service as it is provided (through deductibles and coinsurance), in addition to the monthly premiums paid. HMOs typically require much smaller copayments.

Q 8:20 Does enrollment in an HMO entitle an individual to unlimited health care?

HMO plans are comprehensive and include both physician and hospital services. Enrollment in an HMO entitles the individual to as much future health care service as the HMO physician deems necessary and appropriate. There are limitations, just as there are restrictions on the care allowable under other health plans. For example, cosmetic surgery would generally not be covered by an HMO plan unless required to correct a congenital condition or in connection with accidental injury.

Q 8:21 What is a gatekeeper?

A gatekeeper is a primary care physician. Many HMOs, some POS plans, and some EPOs require patients to obtain referrals from their PCPs in order to see a specialist.

Q 8:22 Do HMOs require a deductible that patients pay before care is provided?

Typically, HMOs require a small per-visit deductible known as copayment or copay, or a charge for certain services, such as tubal ligations, in addition to the membership payments.

Q 8:23 What happens when an individual who is enrolled in an HMO needs to be hospitalized?

Some HMOs lease or own hospitals to provide care to their members. Most simply negotiate arrangements with hospitals to provide the HMO members with hospital services. The patient must be admitted to a hospital with which the HMO has such arrangements in order for the care to be covered.

Q 8:24 Is an employee reimbursed for care received outside the HMO area?

If an HMO member receives emergency care from a non-HMO provider, usually the member's HMO will pay the cost of that emergency care. If an individual elects to receive nonemergency care from a non-HMO provider, the cost of this care is not reimbursable.

Under the 1988 amendments to the HMO Act, federally qualified HMOs have the option of developing benefit offerings that reimburse fee-for-service care from physicians who are not part of the HMO panel. The amount of out-of-panel care that can be reimbursed under the "self-referral option" is limited to 10 percent of all basic health services, and such services can be subject to traditional deductibles and coinsurance typically found in indemnity plans.

Q 8:25 When can employees enroll in an HMO?

Employees can enroll in an HMO immediately upon employment instead of enrolling in the employer's plan. Otherwise, they must wait until the specified period of open enrollment, unless a special enrollment period applies (see Chapter 4).

Q 8:26 How does an employee choose whether to enroll in an HMO or in the traditional health plan?

When deciding whether to choose an HMO or a conventional health care plan, employees weigh the advantages and disadvantages of both. Generally, employees who join HMOs do so for one or more of the following reasons:

1. The credentials and quality of care are well-established.
2. The selection of doctors is broad enough to meet patient needs.
3. The HMO is located near home or work.
4. The HMO's office hours include late evenings and holidays, and it offers a 24-hour emergency on-call service.
5. The individuals are agreeable to being treated for some conditions by a paraprofessional (e.g., a nurse practitioner or other nonmedical doctor whom some HMOs rely on heavily).
6. HMO specialists to whom patients are referred are of high quality.
7. HMOs require no claim forms.
8. The price is comparable to or less than the price of the regular group plan.

Q 8:27 What percentage of employees change plans every year, and why do they do so?

A 1996 survey by CalPERS (the plan for state and local government employees in California) reports that fewer than 4 percent of all enrollees switch health plans during the annual open enrollment. Of those who do change, the most important reasons are:

- Cost (36.6 percent)
- Physician access (20.9 percent)
- Benefits (12.3 percent)
- Health plan quality (10.6 percent)
- Member services (6 percent)

Q 8:28 Would an employee want to enroll in both a traditional plan and an HMO plan?

Employers typically do not allow employees to enroll in more than one plan. Enrolling in two plans would provide duplicate coverage, and the employee would pay premium or membership fees under two plans. If an employee receives free, or low-cost, coverage through his or her employer and his or her spouse's employer, the employee and spouse may have both traditional plan coverage and HMO membership.

Q 8:29 Are HMOs more cost-effective for employees?

Yes and no. Employees usually pay less for care once they are enrolled in the HMO, because there are few or no copayments or deductibles required; however, if employees receive care from non-HMO providers, neither the employer nor the HMO is required to pay their expenses. The HMO physicians determine medically appropriate care, and a member who does not agree with that determination and wishes to receive unauthorized care must pay for all the expenses associated with that care. (See Q 8:24 regarding reimbursement of some non-HMO care.)

Q 8:30 How can an employer achieve 75 percent participation in its conventional plan if employees are allowed to enroll in HMOs?

The 75 percent enrollment required by most insurers uses eligible individuals as a basis. Employees enrolled in an HMO generally are not eligible to participate in the conventional plan. Alternatively, some insurers require that at least 75 percent of eligible employees enroll in one of the available plans.

Q 8:31 Why did enrollment in HMOs increase during the health care cost crisis?

Some employers encouraged their employees to enroll in an HMO in their area if the cost of the HMO would be less than what the employer was spending on conventional plans or if the annual increase in membership payments was likely to be lower than the expected increase in insurance premiums. In addition, HMOs are increasingly attractive to employees who must pay for part of their health care costs. Because employers are increasing deductibles and coinsurance, some employees have found HMOs more attractive. (Although HMOs have cost-sharing provisions, they are generally far less significant than conventional deductible and coinsurance amounts.)

Q 8:32 Why might employers experience lower costs with HMOs than with other health care plans?

HMOs emphasize preventive care, and they minimize hospitalization by treating patients on an outpatient basis whenever possible. The financial structure of HMOs rewards physicians for providing the most cost-effective care. This strategy helps control the rate of hospital admissions and the length of hospital stays.

On average, the number of inpatient days per 1,000 individuals per year is considerably lower in HMOs than under traditional health care plans. Various studies have shown that HMOs' inpatient days per 1,000 members range from 50 percent to 75 percent, of those of traditional fee-for-service group health plans. Hospital costs make up a large part of health care costs, so HMO costs have tended to be lower, in aggregate, than those under traditional health care plans. In addition, there is evidence that HMOs attract younger and perhaps healthier people who would require, on average, less medical care than older persons.

As traditional health plans have changed to provide for cost management, rates of hospitalization and lengths of stay have begun to decrease under those plans as well. Costs of HMOs versus those of other providers may become comparable as additional efficiency is introduced into the traditional health care delivery system, as HMOs cover a broader cross-section of the population, as financially troubled HMOs are forced to accelerate the rate of fee increases, and as HMOs respond to the backlash against managed care plans.

Q 8:33 Do employers offer only HMOs?

Some do, but according to the American Association of Health Plans, 92 percent of employees are offered a health plan with a non-network component, such as a PPO, POS plan, or a traditional indemnity plan. According to a 1998 survey by Deloitte & Touche, 77 percent of employees are offered more than one plan, with the average employer offering four.

Q 8:34 Do physicians treat HMO patients differently than fee-for-service patients?

Some probably do, but there is evidence that physicians tend to treat all patients alike. The February 3, 1999 *Journal of the American*

Medical Association contained an article by researchers from Stanford University who concluded that HMOs have widespread influence on fee-for-service expenditures. The researchers found that Medicare fee-for-service expenditures decreased as the market share of managed care organizations increased. According to the researchers, physicians working in a managed care environment may treat all of their patients with the same managed care mindset.

A 1998 report by the Congressional Research Service indicates that health care quality does not differ because of the type of health insurance coverage. Researchers based this conclusion on an examination of 36,000 patient records from 1,883 physicians.

Q 8:35 What is a self-funded HMO?

Instead of paying for services on a capitated basis, under which the entire risk is passed on to the HMO, a self-funded HMO takes on some attributes of a self-insured indemnity plan. These include paying (1) an administrative fee, typically monthly, which is comparable to an ASO fee, (2) fees for services rendered, such as hospital charges, and (3) specialist fees. The hospital charges paid to the HMO are generally paid in a "pass-through" manner. This means that the employer pays only what the HMO was charged by the hospital. That amount is heavily discounted because of the contractual arrangement between the HMO and the hospital.

Q 8:36 When would converting to a self-funded HMO arrangement be advantageous?

That depends on how an employer is presently paying the HMO. Is the billing on a community-rated basis or a demographically adjusted basis? If the employer is community rated, then it should analyze the characteristics of its employees who have signed up for the HMO against the characteristics of the HMO's total enrollment. If the employer's enrollment is younger and the HMO's population is older, then the employer is likely to benefit from a self-funded or demographically adjusted basis.

Before taking definitive steps to convert to a self-funded arrangement, an employer should perform a detailed study based on utilization statistics of its employees. Most HMOs are developing the capability to produce utilization reports by the employer and are becoming more willing to share the data with employers. Only after studying the data can an employer make an informed decision as to whether the self-funded arrangement would likely be beneficial.

Q 8:37 Are self-insured HMOs different from other HMOs?

No. In fact, in all instances they are the same HMOs that would be used on a conventionally funded basis. The only difference is the manner of funding.

Q 8:38 Can an employer self-fund with a federally qualified HMO?

As part of the qualification requirements, federally qualified HMOs are prohibited from using methods other than community rating. The HMO amendments of 1988 expanded the definition of community rating to allow demographic adjustments. State qualification requirements may or may not present difficulties. While that may seem to exclude federally qualified HMOs from consideration in a self-funded mode, it does not necessarily do so.

In order to attract customers who are interested in the self-funded approach, federally qualified HMOs can set up "mirror image" configurations of themselves and simply not apply for federal qualification on the newly created mirror image. In these instances, the mirror image HMO provides access to the same panel of physicians, hospitals, and administrative staff as the federally qualified version.

Also, there are many excellent independent or local HMOs that, for a variety of reasons, have decided not to apply for federal qualification. Such HMOs are not limited by the community rating requirement and are under no constraints that prevent them from directly entering into a self-funding arrangement with an employer.

Adverse Selection

Q 8:39 What is adverse selection?

Adverse selection, or antiselection, is the tendency for persons with known health problems to elect more insurance, or to incur significantly greater health care expenses, than healthy persons. Insuring a group that is heavily weighted with persons with high health risks is, therefore, more expensive than insuring a group of healthier individuals.

Q 8:40 Does adverse selection occur in the HMO setting?

Yes. In fact, employers sponsoring HMOs are becoming increasingly concerned about the potential impact of adverse selection. Frequently, healthier or younger employees gravitate toward HMOs, leaving sicker or older workers in the insured or self-funded indemnity plan. This adverse selection drives up the cost of the indemnity plan.

Q 8:41 Will the cost of an employer's conventional plan be affected by an HMO plan?

If an employer loses half of its employees to an HMO, the employer's rates on a conventional plan may be higher than if all employees were enrolled. There is some evidence that suggests that younger, healthier employees are more inclined to enroll in HMOs than their older, less healthy counterparts (see Q 8:42). Premium rates charged by insurance companies reflect the characteristics of a group. The size, "average" gender, and average age of the conventional plan group will be affected when certain employees join an HMO. So, for example, if the conventional plan group is older because young employees enrolled in the HMO, the premium rates would be higher.

Ironically, adverse selection is of less concern in the short term to the very smallest employers. Employers with less than 50 employees often buy fully pooled policies. That is, their claim experience does not directly affect their premiums—premiums are set based on the experience of the pool; therefore, employers with pooled policies can offer a choice of plans without suffering any immediate consequences of adverse selection.

Q 8:42 Why might HMOs attract younger, healthier persons?

One reason may be that HMOs require members to receive care from a limited group of physicians. Younger persons are generally less likely to be attached to one doctor. Also, younger persons tend to be less concerned than their elder counterparts about experiencing serious illness, and their choice of medical plans may reflect this attitude.

Q 8:43 Is the adverse selection obvious to employers?

No. Many employers assume that the HMO is a good deal because the cost is usually lower than the cost or premium of the indemnity plan. What they fail to realize is that the adverse selection factor is pushing up the cost of the indemnity plan. In order to measure costs realistically, the company must have adequate data to compare the various plans it offers to employees.

Q 8:44 What can be done about adverse selection?

A company experiencing adverse selection can negotiate a lower rate with the HMO based on actual HMO utilization. Another option is to bring younger, healthier employees back into the indemnity plan by offering certain attractive benefits such as health club membership, dental care, or prescription drug cards in conjunction with the indemnity plan. Another alternative might be to change the contribution levels so that they are more equitable, based on the actual experience with each plan, or by employee age bracket. Amendments to the HMO Act specifically authorize adjustments based on utilization experience, geographic variation, and employee demographics.

Legal Standards

Q 8:45 What is the Health Maintenance Organization Act?

The Health Maintenance Organization Act of 1973 was intended to encourage the spread of HMOs. In addition to establishing standards for federally qualified HMOs, it required employers to make

HMOs available to their employees under certain circumstances (the dual choice requirement). Affected employers were those that are subject to the minimum wage standards of the Fair Labor Standards Act, employ 25 or more full- or part-time employees in the calendar quarter, and offered a health benefit plan.

The Health Maintenance Organization Amendments of 1988 eliminated the dual choice requirement, revised employer contribution requirements, permitted rates to be set on the basis of employer experience, imposed stricter financial requirements for federal qualification, and permitted greater flexibility in benefit offerings.

Q 8:46 What standards must a federally qualified HMO meet?

To be federally qualified, an HMO must be organized and operated and provide health services as prescribed by the law. Basic health services prescribed by law include:

1. Physician services (including consultant and referral services by a physician);
2. Inpatient and outpatient hospital services;
3. Medically necessary emergency health services;
4. Short-term (maximum 20 visits) outpatient evaluative and crisis intervention mental health services;
5. Medical treatment and referral services (including referral services to appropriate ancillary services) for the abuse of or addiction to alcohol and drugs;
6. Diagnostic laboratory services and diagnostic and therapeutic radiological services;
7. Home health services; and
8. Preventive health services, including immunizations, child care from birth, periodic health evaluations for adults, voluntary family planning services, infertility services, and children's eye and ear examinations to assess the need for vision and hearing correction.

A qualified HMO may also make available "supplemental health services" as specified in the law, including:

1. Services or facilities for intermediate and long-term care;

2. Vision care not included as a basic health service;
3. Dental care not included as a basic health service;
4. Mental health care not included as a basic health service;
5. Long-term physical medicine and rehabilitative services (including physical therapy);
6. Prescription drugs prescribed in the course of the provision by the HMO of a basic health service, or of one of the preceding supplemental health services; and
7. Other health services, not included as basic health services, that have been approved by the secretary of the Department of Health and Human Services.

Q 8:47 How prevalent are federally qualified HMOs?

According to InterStudy, fewer than 58 percent of HMOs are federally qualified. In order to be flexible and competitive with respect to benefit offerings and rate structure, many newer HMOs do not seek federal qualification.

Q 8:48 What is a community rating system?

Under a community rating system, one average premium rate is determined on the basis of the entire membership's characteristics and past claim experience. This is different from rate setting on private insurance plans, where a particular group's rates can be partially or fully based on that group's risk characteristics (age, sex, industry) and past claim experience. The 1988 amendments to the HMO Act allow "adjusted community rating." Although HMOs are still not permitted to return surplus or dividends to employers, they are now permitted to establish specific employer rates based on utilization of services prospectively, based on past experience. For groups of less than 100 employees, the adjusted rates cannot be more than 10 percent higher than community rates.

Q 8:49 What was the dual choice mandate?

Under the HMO Act of 1973, certain employers were required to offer HMO coverage if requested to do so in accordance with specific procedures.

The dual-choice requirement was repealed under the Health Maintenance Organization Amendments of 1988. Note that several states have similar dual-choice requirements for state-certified HMOs that are not affected by changes in the federal law.

Q 8:50 Does the HMO Act specify how much an employer is required to pay for HMO coverage for its employees?

Prior to the 1988 amendments, the law required that the employer contribute at least the same dollar amount for an employee who joined an HMO as would be paid for that employee to enroll in the employer's conventional health plan. If the HMO was more expensive, the employee could be required to pay the difference, although there are various employer approaches to this situation.

The 1988 amendments substitute a requirement that the employer not financially discriminate in its contribution for an employee enrolling in a federally qualified HMO. The method for determining the employer contribution must be "reasonable and assure employees a fair choice among health benefit plans." A variety of methods, including equal dollar amount, class rates for both HMO and indemnity plans, equal percentage, or equal employee contributions for each plan, are permitted by existing HMO regulations.

Q 8:51 What are the HMO financial nondiscrimination rules?

HMO nondiscrimination requirements applied to all employers as of October 1995. Until then, the nondiscrimination requirements applied only to HMOs offered as the result of a mandate under the HMO Act of 1973. The HMO Amendments Act of 1988 put a sunset date on the mandate provision. HMOs no longer can require employers to offer an HMO. (In practice, HMOs seldom used the mandate in areas with multiple HMOs.) In exchange for removing the mandate requirement, all employers now must comply with the financial nondiscrimination requirement. The Health Care Financing Administration (HCFA) issued a final rule for employee contributions to HMOs on May 31, 1996.

There are a number of ways an employer can satisfy the financial nondiscrimination requirement:

1. Pay the same dollar amount to an HMO that the employer pays toward the cost of its indemnity plan.
2. Pay the same percentage of the HMO premium that the employer pays toward the cost of its indemnity plan.
3. Pay the same dollar amount to the HMO that the employer pays toward the cost of its indemnity plan, adjusted to account for the demographic differences between the HMO plan participants and the indemnity plan participants.
4. Require HMO participants to pay half (or less) of the dollar amount indemnity plan participants must pay. (This approach can only be used if the HMO coverage would otherwise be available at no or nominal cost.)
5. Have equal employee contributions for all plans.

Employers must retain data used to compute the level of contribution for each plan for at least three years and make it available to HCFA upon request.

Q 8:52 Are HMOs subject to state regulations?

Many states have laws meant to promote HMO development while ensuring the quality of care delivered by HMOs. These laws also provide grievance procedures for enrollees and allow for some form of enrollee participation in the HMO's policy-making body. Also, some states have established financial reserve requirements for HMOs that are similar to those required by insurance companies, or they require state approval of an HMO's rates. These laws vary from state to state.

Many states have based their legislation on the model HMO law prepared by the National Association of Insurance Commissioners in the early 1970s. In recent years, the NAIC has created a series of issue-specific revisions of its original model to reflect what it called "the rapid evolution of the HMO industry." Among the goals of the revisions were the following:

1. Make becoming a licensed HMO more difficult.
2. Improve HMO financial reserves, institute investment guidelines, and tighten cash management of HMOs.

3. Ensure that enrollees are held harmless for HMO debts.
4. Create a mechanism for enrolling members of failed HMOs into new or existing HMOs.

While some of the revised model laws have been adopted by a few states, most states have not yet acted on these issues.

Q 8:53 What is ERISA preemption?

Preemption refers to ERISA's restriction of a state's ability to make laws relating to employee welfare benefit plans. States are still permitted to regulate insurance and are thus "saved" from preemption in this area, but are not permitted to "deem" an employee welfare benefit plan to be an insurance company in an attempt to regulate those plans.

Q 8:54 Are state laws with respect to HMOs preempted by ERISA?

Certain laws that regulate the HMOs themselves are not preempted by ERISA; however, there is evidence that dual-choice requirements of certain states are preempted by ERISA. A California court case involving Hewlett-Packard found such requirements preempted because they sought to regulate employee welfare benefit plans as insurance companies. [Hewlett-Packard Co v Barnes, 571 F2d 502 (9th Cir 1978), *cert denied,* 439 US 831, 99 S Ct 108, 58 L Ed 2d 125 (1978), *aff'g* 425 F Supp 1294 (1977)] The court relied on a letter from an official at the U.S. Department of Labor, stating his opinion that the California HMO dual-choice provisions were preempted by ERISA.

Although the California decision sets a precedent, it is not binding in other jurisdictions; however, an employer seeking to avoid a dual-choice mandate may be able to dissuade an aggressive HMO from taking expensive legal action to enforce the mandate. Alternatively, with the assistance of counsel, an advisory opinion letter could be requested from the U.S. Department of Labor. If an employer does business in more than one state, the request should specify all business locations.

Evaluating HMOs

Q 8:55 How can a company compare costs of health plans?

A company must accumulate demographic information for each plan population in order to analyze the age and gender composition of the employees and dependents in the indemnity plan and those in the HMOs. Next, the company can obtain claim experience data from its insurance carrier and HMOs in order to find out the true cost of each plan and each demographic category. By weighing the relative participation in each plan and comparing the "cost" to the premiums paid for coverage, the company will know whether there is adverse selection and, if so, the extent of it. Then it can elect to take action to bring things back into balance.

Q 8:56 How does the quality of HMO care compare with that of conventionally insured medical care?

Although HMO members see their doctors more frequently than conventionally insured individuals and are admitted to hospitals less often, no conclusion concerning the quality of care can be drawn. Less care does not necessarily mean poorer quality care, and more care does not suggest better care. Other complaints involve physician compensation arrangements, especially those that divide unspent treatment funds among participating physicians. This practice may provide too strong an incentive for doctors to withhold needed care.

Employers that are concerned about HMO quality should carefully review the financial incentives for physicians and be wary of those arrangements that discourage referral to specialists or inpatient hospital confinement.

See also Q 8:34.

Q 8:57 How well do managed care plans score on quality of care measurements?

In its report *The State of Managed Care Quality*, the National Committee for Quality Assurance (NCQA) noted that for eight

(HEDIS) quality measures examined, managed care did as well or better than fee-for-service plans.

Q 8:58 Can changing managed care plans affect the quality of care?

Possibly. A study reported in *The Journal of Family Practice* found that patients who said they were forced to change primary care physicians reported low scores on interpersonal communications with physicians, physician knowledge of the patient, and coordination of care. The report concluded that the benefits of emphasizing primary care are not likely to be realized with frequent forced change in physicians.

Q 8:59 How do HMO participants rate HMO plans?

A 1997 survey underwritten by PacifiCare found that 87 percent of HMO members were satisfied and 91 percent of Medicare HMO members were satisfied, compared with 90 percent of fee-for-service members.

A survey by Aragon Consulting Group reports that 28 percent of people in HMOs are completely satisfied with their health insurance, compared with 36 percent in fee-for-service plans, 27 percent in POS plans, and 22 percent in PPOs.

A 1998 Hewitt Survey found that 87 percent of employees are satisfied with their HMOs.

Q 8:60 Why do some HMOs have financial difficulty?

HMO failures are generally the result of undercapitalization, severe inflation leading to high medical care costs, slow membership enrollment, and inexperienced management. Without a sufficient spread of risk—number of members—a period of uncontrolled inflation can wreak havoc for insurers and health care providers. The HMO, a unique combination of medical care and risk management, is extremely difficult to manage successfully.

Q 8:61 How can a prospective HMO client get more information about the HMO?

Information on HMOs can be obtained from the following sources:

1. The HMO itself, its annual reports, and, for public corporations, SEC filings;
2. Employer health care coalitions;
3. State insurance commissioners and health departments;
4. Accrediting organizations such as the Joint Commission on Accreditation of Health Care Organizations;
5. The U.S. Health Care Financing Administration's Office of Prepaid Health Care; or
6. The National Committee for Quality Assurance.

HMO Evaluation

Evaluating an HMO is a complex undertaking. Things to consider in making an assessment include:

Structure and Organization
- ☐ Type: group, staff, IPA, or network?
- ☐ Ownership: insurer, the Blues, HMO chain?
- ☐ If owned by a larger entity, how much local autonomy?
- ☐ What is management structure?
- ☐ Is it federally qualified?
- ☐ How many members (enrollees, employers)?
- ☐ How are medical personnel and hospitals recruited and compensated?
- ☐ Is the HMO accredited with organizations such as the National Committee for Quality Assurance?
- ☐ Are all providers contracted by the HMO fully licensed or accredited, and supervised by the HMO?

Benefits and Services
- ☐ Basic services: Do they include mental health, dental, and prescription drugs?

- ☐ Are other services, such as substance abuse treatment (smoking cessation) and preventive care (stress management) provided?
- ☐ How is coverage provided outside the HMO area? Is it nationwide? International?
- ☐ What is the HMO's policy regarding nonaffiliated doctors and hospitals?
- ☐ What sort of marketing support does it provide?
- ☐ What other services does it provide (e.g., COBRA administration)?
- ☐ Is there a single account representative for the employer to deal with for questions and resolution of problems?

Rates
- ☐ Will the group be rated by its own experience, community rated, or community rated by class?
- ☐ Can rates be negotiated?
- ☐ What additional charges are there for supplemental services?
- ☐ What charges will enrollees pay in the form of deductibles or per-visit fees?

Financial Status
- ☐ Is it nonprofit or for profit?
- ☐ What is its past profitability, and what are projections for the future?
- ☐ Are enrollees protected from creditors in the event of insolvency?

Data
- ☐ What sorts of reports are provided?
- ☐ Are reports available on a customized basis to employers, or on a standardized basis such as the Health Plan Employer Data and Information Set?

Quality
- ☐ Has the HMO been cited for noncompliance by state or federal regulators?
- ☐ Has it been a defendant in any lawsuits?

☐ What sorts of reviews or surveys have been conducted that would indicate enrollee satisfaction?

☐ Has there been a significant drop or increase in enrollment? If so, why?

Q 8:62 What are indicators of excellence?

The book *Choosing and Using an HMO* (Bloomberg Press, 1998) includes the following "indicators of excellence."

1. A 15- to 20-year history;
2. Nonprofit status, with doctors on staff or in a group;
3. Full accreditation from the Foundation for Accountability;
4. Low heart by-pass and angioplasty rates;
5. High screening rates for cervical cancer and breast cancer;
6. Relatively few cesarean sections;
7. High diabetic retinal testing rates;
8. Excellent follow-up after hospitalization for mental disorder;
9. Available doctors;
10. Highly satisfied doctors; and
11. Highly satisfied members.

Q 8:63 What is a triple option plan?

A triple option plan is an integrated plan offered by a single vendor. The plan offers an HMO and a PPO (which includes two choices: in or out of network) administered by one entity, usually an insurance carrier. Such plans are advantageous only if claim experience from all three options is integrated in the pricing. Otherwise, triple option plans may offer administrative convenience but not cost advantages. If a point-of-service plan is included, it is likely to be referred to as a multiple option plan.

Q 8:64 What are the advantages and disadvantages of a triple option or multiple option plan?

The advantages include:

1. It is possible to base employer contributions on the least expensive option.
2. It provides employees with more choices.
3. It can be used to introduce managed care.
4. It can minimize employee problems with continuity of care.

The disadvantages include:

1. Potentially higher administrative costs.
2. The number of choices can be confusing to employees, which means more staff time is needed to educate and enroll employees.
3. Costs may still increase rapidly if most employees use the option with the least managed care.
4. Employees may perceive the most attractive plan to be too expensive.

Preferred Provider Organizations

Q 8:65 What is a PPO?

A PPO is an organization that arranges contracts between a select group of health care providers (hospitals, physicians) and purchasers of health care (employers, union trust funds), but is itself neither a provider nor a purchaser. Typically, provider fees are negotiated in advance and providers offer discounts in return for rapid reimbursement and a potential increase in market share. Payment is on a fee-for-service rather than a capitated basis. Strict utilization controls are combined with flexibility in benefit design and freedom of choice with respect to providers.

Q 8:66 How did the PPO concept develop?

The preferred provider approach developed initially out of negotiated fee arrangements such as those pioneered in connection with workers' compensation laws in 1911 in the states of Washington and Oregon. In the 1930s, an organization called the California Physicians' Service offered discounted fees and participating physician payment-in-full benefits, which became the basis for the modern-day Blue Cross/Blue Shield. Various "foundations for medical care" proliferated throughout the 1950s, and the concept was adopted by Medicare and Medicaid in 1966.

Modern PPOs—the second generation—combined provider selectivity with discounts for the first time in the early 1980s in California and Colorado. The 1982 revisions to Medi-Cal (the name for Medicaid in California) established contractual arrangements with cost-efficient hospitals for Medi-Cal beneficiaries, and the state of California passed laws permitting selective provider contracting. Although some states had laws that prohibited PPOs, PPOs now operate in every state, plus the District of Columbia and Puerto Rico.

Q 8:67 How does a PPO differ from an HMO?

Under the rules associated with HMOs, the enrollee must stay in-plan and use only the participating physicians/providers in order for any reimbursement to occur. Enrollees who use an out-of-network physician/provider in an HMO must bear full financial responsibility for the expenses incurred. A PPO offers enrollees some reimbursement even if they select an out-of-network provider.

An HMO is an alternative to a traditional health plan and is a separate entity. PPOs exist within the traditional plan structure and are integrated.

An HMO requires that services be rendered by participating providers in order to be covered. Integrated plans such as PPOs typically reimburse services by nonpreferred providers at a lower rate than services by participating providers, but cover, to some extent, all medically necessary services.

HMOs assume risk. An HMO assumes the risk that the cost of services required by members could exceed revenues generated by capitation. PPOs assume no risk and reimburse on a fee-for-service basis; the risk continues to be assumed by the employer, trust fund, or insurance carrier.

HMOs are strictly regulated by federal HMO and various state laws; PPOs remain largely unregulated.

An HMO delivers health care; a PPO facilitates the delivery of cost-effective health care, but is not itself a provider. Rather, it is more of a manager or broker.

Q 8:68 How is the PPO concept different from the Blues and Medicare contracts with providers?

With respect to discounting charges, the PPO concept is not very different. For years, individuals covered under the Blues plans have had the option of receiving care from a participating or a nonparticipating physician or hospital. Charges of participating providers are covered more fully because of agreements between the providers and the Blues and Medicare. Commercial insurers have only recently entered this negotiated price and service arena, in the form of PPOs.

PPOs focus less on price discounts than on managed care. One significant weakness in the old Blues provider-insurer contracts was the lack of utilization review (UR) and case management. Prices for care were discounted to the Blues, but the amount of care was not managed. Thus, providers sometimes sought to make up for the agreed-to discounts by providing more care, on a fee-for-service basis, than might have been necessary; however, PPOs include utilization controls, agreed to by the providers and monitored by the insurance company or other party to the agreement.

Q 8:69 What is a preferred provider arrangement, and how is it different from a PPO?

A preferred provider arrangement (PPA) is an agreement between health care providers and another entity or group of entities (insurance companies, employers, third-party administrators (TPAs)) to provide medical care services at negotiated fees to certain groups in return for prompt payment and increased patient volume. Use of the term PPO typically indicates an actual organization of providers, while the designation PPA suggests simply that a contractual agreement has been made, but there is no other legal entity formed as a result of the agreement. The providers enter into a contract directly with the insurer, employer, or TPA. (The term PPA can be used to describe a PPO arrangement itself, and is sometimes used interchangeably with the term PPO. This text uses PPO as the generic term.)

Q 8:70 What is an exclusive provider organization?

An exclusive provider organization (EPO) closely resembles an HMO and is a type of PPO that requires individuals to use only designated preferred providers. Payment to providers is, however, on a fee-for-service basis.

Q 8:71 What is the difference between an EPO and a PPO?

EPOs are similar to PPOs, but only provide reimbursement for services rendered by network providers. Some EPOs use a primary care physician (PCP) to act as a gate keeper.

Q 8:72 What services are offered by PPOs?

There are two basic types of PPOs: comprehensive and limited. The comprehensive variety typically includes a broad range of physicians in every specialty as well as general and specialty hospitals and support services such as home health care agencies.

It is not, however, uncommon for a PPO to include only hospitals or only physicians. Also in the limited category are specialty PPOs that provide dental, mental health, or substance abuse services, cardiac care, maternity care, vision services, and prescriptions.

In arranging a plan of benefits, one or more specialty PPOs may be more cost-effective in addressing particular utilization concerns and provide a degree of customization and flexibility unavailable through a "one-size-fits-all" comprehensive PPO; however, integrating several PPOs results in additional complexity and administrative cost.

Q 8:73 Who sponsors PPOs?

PPOs are sponsored by a variety of entities and organizations: hospitals, physicians, trust funds, insurance carriers, employers, TPAs, brokers, and other entrepreneurs. In addition, joint ventures between the various entities are common, such as multi-hospital networks and hospital/physician and insurance carrier/entrepreneur joint ventures.

Provider-sponsored PPOs are typically marketed to insurance carriers, trust funds, and self-funded plans, while insurer/TPA-sponsored PPOs are marketed exclusively to clients and policyholders.

Unless provider-based PPOs are operated by independent organizations with strong cost-management abilities, these types of PPOs can become strictly marketing ploys. It is often difficult for a hospital to screen out inefficient physicians who have privileges at the hospital, or to ignore the economic incentive to increase quantity or intensity of service. Employer- and entrepreneur-based PPOs often lack the data to identify cost-efficient providers. Insurance carrier or HMO-sponsored PPOs offer the best chance for effective provider selectivity, which is the basis for long-term savings.

Q 8:74 How prevalent are PPOs?

The growth of PPOs has been explosive. According to the Mercer/Foster Higgins National Survey of Employer-Sponsored Health Plans 1999 report, PPOs are offered by more large employers than any other type of plan. The percentage of employers offering PPOs grew from 59 percent in 1996 to 70 percent in 1999. Enrollment in PPOs grew from 32 percent in 1997 to 39 percent in 1999.

Factors responsible for the rapid growth of PPOs include:

1. Physician surplus and low hospital occupancy rates encourage providers to develop market share through PPO participation.

2. Advances in computer technology permit collection of utilization data and analysis of provider practice patterns.

3. Wider implementation of employee cost sharing allows plan design incentives that channel patients to cost-effective providers.

Q 8:75   **Health Insurance Answer Book**

 4. Growth of purchaser coalitions has resulted in the development of useful community average data with which to measure provider efficiency.
 5. Self-funding creates incentives for employers to introduce more proactive cost-management strategies, including restricting or discouraging access to inefficient providers.

Q 8:75 What are the nationwide PPOs?

According to *Managed Healthcare*, the following companies offer PPOs in all 50 states and the District of Columbia (as of May 1999):

- Aetna U.S. Healthcare
- Blue Cross/Blue Shield Association
- CIGNA Healthcare
- CNA Managed Care
- Community Care Network
- Great-West Life
- Multiplan
- National Preferred Provider Network
- Private Healthcare Systems
- Prudential Healthcare
- United Health Group
- USA Managed Care Organization

Q 8:76 What is involved in establishing a PPO?

No matter who establishes a PPO, certain steps are involved. The complexities of merging medical care with insurance make these alternative delivery systems difficult to develop successfully.

First, an adequate network of health care providers must be determined. The locations of providers selected and the various specialties required will depend on the characteristics of the group for whom PPO care is to be provided. The demographics of the group and past medical care utilization should be reviewed in order to determine the types and numbers of providers that will be needed to meet the needs of that population. For example, if the group health plan covers retirees, several geriatric specialists would be required; if the insured group includes a large percentage of dependent children, the number of pediatricians who should be available as preferred providers must be carefully determined.

Q 8:77 How are PPO providers selected?

Selecting specific providers involves two crucial ingredients for a successful PPO: (1) selecting physicians whose practice patterns are cost-effective and whose abilities are excellent; and (2) providing the right incentives to encourage those physicians to become a part of the PPO. An intense review of practice patterns is usually performed to determine the appropriate physicians, and because of the expertise required to interpret these patterns, experienced health care consultants are normally used to perform this function.

Although the historical practice patterns of the physicians will be expected to continue if they become part of the PPO, it is still necessary to develop the utilization review controls that will help ensure cost-effective medical care from the PPO physicians and hospitals; therefore, as the ideal list of physicians is developed, a UR plan must be developed concurrently. This plan depends on the readiness of the providers (particularly the hospital management involved) to practice by the UR standards, and must be developed jointly with the providers involved. Later, as additional providers become part of the PPO, they will be required to subscribe to the UR, which is a fundamental tenet of the PPO.

In addition to the actual medical practices of physicians, the accreditation, licensure, hospital staff privileges, appropriate liability and malpractice insurance, and other administrative details must be arranged.

Q 8:78 What else is necessary for ensuring cost-effective treatment in a PPO?

Data-processing systems that will allow the care provided to be tracked are absolutely necessary to ensure that the most cost-effective treatment is provided. Hospitals unable to collect and produce these data in a form capable of analysis would not be effective participants in a PPO.

Negotiating the price discounts that physicians and hospitals will provide to PPO participants is also paramount, and is done during the development of the provider network. The financial incentives that will encourage the providers to become involved vary, according to the medical marketplace at that time. A certain hospital may be willing to provide a discount of 10 percent to its per-diem rate for PPO insurers. A hospital with a large number of empty beds and a need to fill them may be willing to discount its surgical fees and its room and board fees.

Developing a mix of providers that will offer high-quality medical care at discounted fees requires a great deal of negotiation and administration. Months of negotiations are usually necessary to get the appropriate providers, a workable UR system, and discounted prices for medical services provided.

Q 8:79 What are the incentives for doctors and hospitals to be preferred providers?

Hospitals and doctors believe that by participating in a PPO they can expect to increase their market share by increasing patient volume. Because competition for patients is fierce, providers are willing to negotiate discounts in return for the prospect of increased patient volume.

Q 8:80 Must a PPO include UR controls?

Each PPO sponsor develops the means of monitoring and controlling participating providers' practice patterns as it sees fit. The effectiveness of the PPO in managing health care costs depends on the incentives for the PPO providers to deliver cost-effective care. Fee discounts alone will not provide this. Cost-effective PPOs must therefore include UR controls.

Q 8:81 Are utilization controls important when using a PPO?

Yes. Any employer contracting with a PPO should spend a considerable amount of time reviewing the utilization controls. Without effective UR, any discount is suspect, because it can be more than offset by increased utilization of services. For example, if a PPO offers a 10 percent discount through its participating providers, but then increases utilization by 15 percent over what it would have been without the PPO, the employer or trust contracting for services is spending more, rather than less, on health care.

UR results should be compared with community norms. It is increasingly common for employers to specify utilization targets, adjusted for their population, and to negotiate performance guarantees with the PPO.

Q 8:82 Who does the utilization review?

Frequently, UR is done by the medical staff of the PPO. In this case, the UR function must be monitored closely in order to make sure that the review is being done effectively. Independent, external review is preferable.

Q 8:83 Are there federally qualified PPOs?

No. The PPO concept emerged from the marketplace with no legislative impetus and, to date, there is no set of national standards for PPOs.

Q 8:84 Do state PPO standards or laws exist?

Yes. Many states have passed or proposed laws. The laws vary from enabling legislation, which simply notes that PPOs are pro-competitive and desirable, to laws that include specific discrimination tests for PPOs. Some states require that benefit payment differences between non-PPO and PPO providers fall within specified variance limits. Other laws include provisions that prohibit discrimination by classes of employees in terms of PPO versus non-PPO benefit payment percentages.

Q 8:85 What types of rate regulations apply to PPOs?

PPOs (and point-of-service plans) are usually regulated as insurance products. Generally, there is a great deal of flexibility in setting rates, but some states require that rates or rating methodologies be filed with (or even approved) by state regulators.

Q 8:86 What antitrust issues affect PPO development and negotiations?

The relevant antitrust issue involved is price fixing. The fact that PPOs may eliminate competition because the same discounted fees are negotiated with many insurers (or employers or TPAs) may be construed as price fixing, which is a violation of antitrust law; however, the current stance among regulatory agencies is to enable PPO activity, mindful of, rather than confined by, the principles of antitrust law.

Q 8:87 What incentives do employers have to include PPOs in their health plans?

PPOs allow employers to provide employees with health care benefits at lower costs than traditional plans, and provide some relief to employers faced with unbridled annual premium increases. The cost savings come from the price discounts and utilization review negotiated with the preferred providers. Discounts can range from 20 percent to 30 percent. Recent surveys have found that many employers believe PPOs to be more effective at controlling health care costs (or at least moderating the rate of increase in those costs) than HMOs or conventional reimbursement plans.

Q 8:88 What kinds of employers can expect the largest discounts from a PPO health plan?

Employers with large concentrations of workers located in areas with strong competition for patients—high physician-to-population ratio and excess hospital resources—have the potential to achieve large discounts. Smaller employers must identify an insurance carrier or association that is achieving large discounts as a result of its ability to deliver market share.

In these instances, the smaller the PPO network, the larger the potential discount. Although large networks are an attractive selling point to employees, they are rarely as efficient in providing care, and the leverage in negotiating discounts is diluted.

Q 8:89 Is an employer that elects a plan with a PPO sacrificing quality care for low cost?

Enough competition exists in many areas to encourage providers to lower their prices while continuing to provide high-quality care. The UR process helps ensure quality.

PPO providers are typically not at risk as are HMO providers, so there is no incentive for PPO providers to skimp on care. Employers must assure, however, that there is sufficient access to employees in terms of location, a full range of medical specialties in addition to primary care, and reasonably located general and specialty hospitals.

Q 8:90 Can any employer include a PPO in its health care plan?

No. To date, formal PPOs have been developed only in areas where there is heavy competition among providers. Many rural areas with only a few physicians and one community hospital do not justify the work involved in establishing a PPO, although providers' practice patterns and costs may be a problem.

In addition, not all insurers offer PPOs. An insurer must have a significant market share in an area in order to justify the effort required to establish a PPO. Some insurers may have other health care delivery arrangements that offer employers similar cost-management techniques.

Q 8:91 How can an employer or trust evaluate a prospective PPO?

PPO evaluation is a complex subject, and the employer or trust is well-advised to seek professional help. There are a number of evaluation areas to consider, including: organizational considerations, scope of services, access, utilization controls, participation incentives, benefits design, data and performance reports, financial considerations, and legal issues.

Employers or unions should take the following steps in negotiating with a PPO:

1. Define scope of services.
2. Develop appropriate employee participation incentives. Select the payment methodology.
3. Include stringent utilization controls.
4. Determine provider selection (and retention) criteria.
5. Determine provider risk-sharing levels.
6. Insist on timely, accurate, and adequate data.
7. Clarify any provisions relating to workers' compensation, continuation of benefits, and subrogation.
8. Review any insolvency and reinsurance clauses.
9. Include a hold-harmless clause to protect employees.
10. Reserve the right to terminate the agreement on short notice.

Q 8:92 How should a PPO be incorporated into an existing program?

There are two basic approaches. The simplest approach is to superimpose the PPO option on the existing plan as a voluntary option; use of preferred providers results in payment in full, while regular plan benefits continue to apply to all other providers. Unless significantly more efficient care is provided through the PPO, this approach may result in higher total plan costs if discounts are insufficient to neutralize the additional cost of in-full benefits.

The second and more successful approach involves integration or complete program redesign incorporating benefits incentives and disincentives, and utilization controls applicable to all providers.

Q 8:93 What types of discounts are available?

The following hospital discounts are available under a PPO:

1. *First dollar.* A percentage discount applies to each dollar of charge, such as a 10 percent discount.
2. *Volume.* After a certain volume of business is directed to a provider, a discount applies.
3. *Scheduled.* Fees are predetermined according to "case" or "per diem."
4. *Case mix.* Similar to diagnosis-related group.

The following physician discounts are available under a PPO:

1. *Percentage of UCR.* A reimbursement is established as a percentile of "usual, reasonable, and customary" charges.
2. *Relative value study (RVS).* An RVS, such as an updated version of the California RVS, or the RBRVS used by Medicare (see Chapter 10) is used to establish the relative intensity of service. A community-sensitive conversion factor multiplied by the value determines the reimbursement amount.
3. *Freeze.* Current fee levels are accepted but frozen to limit future increases.

The discounting methodology used by a PPO is an important factor in determining whether cost savings objectives can be attained. Generally, case mix and freeze approaches attract the most qualified providers.

It is critical to determine the basis of the discount as well as the method. Services should be offered at unit prices below community averages after application of the discount methodology. Independent community average information may be available from local business coalitions.

Q 8:94 When incorporating a PPO into a health plan, what employee education is necessary?

Employers should provide their employees with written material that carefully explains the reasons for the PPO plan, identifies the preferred providers, and explains the differences in reimbursement for preferred provider and nonpreferred provider care. Most employers find that continual written and visual communications are necessary. Employee meetings allow employees to ask questions and learn about the changes occurring in the health care delivery system.

Q 8:95 What other kinds of health care delivery arrangements are available to employers?

PPOs and HMOs represent integration of services, but there are other arrangements as well. A catchall term for these arrangements is "vertical integration." In this case, integration combines all services under one umbrella in order to meet one need—health care. Suppliers, providers, and financiers of services are now joining together in various ways to deliver health care, thereby creating opportunities for increased efficiency, improved services, and lower costs for health care consumers.

For example, insurers are acquiring HMOs and integrating them into their health care plans rather than competing with them. Third-party administrators and claim payment organizations are joining forces with physicians to implement quasi-PPOs for certain large employers that need only claim administration and utilization review. Hospitals are acquiring insurance companies and equipment suppliers. Significant integration will continue.

HMOs vs. PPOs

Both HMOs and PPOs attempt to:

1. Contain costs without relying heavily on participant contributions, or doing away with needed services.
2. Cut back on unnecessary and overly expensive procedures by monitoring treatment, and promoting less expensive modes of treatment.
3. Encourage more price competition among suppliers.
4. Emphasize alternatives to inpatient care, such as outpatient treatment, prevention, and early detection.
5. Provide incentives for providing lower-cost treatment.

HMO Advantages

1. Through capitated pre-payment, HMOs transfer risk from employers directly to suppliers, who are in the best position to control spending.
2. Budgeting is simplified.
3. HMOs offer incentives to suppliers to reduce costs.
4. Through emphasis on prevention and routine care, HMOs forestall major, more costly ailments.

HMO Disadvantages

1. The choice of physicians may be limited, which means that employees joining an HMO may have existing doctor-patient relationships disturbed, or may be faced with additional costs (out-of-panel charges) to keep those relationships intact.
2. Centralized HMO facilities may not be as convenient as a local physician's office.
3. HMO financial incentives might restrict needed care.
4. Institution of an HMO can result in adverse selection.
5. In the past, some HMOs have had a reputation for bad management, poor service, and financial problems.
6. HMOs may not be as effective in controlling employer costs as expected.

PPO Advantages

1. PPOs allow maximum flexibility in benefits program design.
2. Adoption of a PPO does not necessitate a change in the mix of services, which means there is less likelihood that the issue of quality will be raised.
3. PPOs allow a wider choice of physicians.

PPO Disadvantages

1. When the PPO offers only a fee-for-service discount, there has been no shifting of risk from employer to provider.
2. Without adequate controls, providers may offset discounts by revising billing schedules or prescribing increased services.

Q 8:96 What are the advantages and disadvantages of a large network?

A large network has the following advantages:

1. More choices of primary care providers;
2. More specialists means less likelihood of disrupting referral patterns;
3. Redundancy means there will be less impact if any provider or group of providers leaves the network; and
4. Lower costs because a higher proportion of care can be rendered in the network.

Theoretically, the biggest disadvantage to a large network is that limiting the size should allow for lower rates with contracting providers because smaller networks shift more market share. From a practical standpoint, hospitals have been more inclined than physicians to give larger discounts when they are part of a smaller network.

There is also a larger administrative cost to credential, negotiate with, and maintain contracts with a larger group of providers, but this is not a large portion of total costs.

Q 8:97 What are hybrid HMO arrangements?

Such arrangements are also called "leaky HMOs," "point-of-service (POS) HMOs," or "open-ended HMOs." Participants in a hybrid HMO plan may use non-HMO providers at any time they decide to obtain service (the decision is made at the point of service, hence the initials POS) and receive indemnity-type benefits, but with higher deductibles and coinsurance payments than if an HMO physician had provided services.

POS plans can offer as comprehensive an array of benefits as does any other health care plan, with the added feature that the participant has the option of receiving care from panel or non-panel providers at the time medical services are required. The reimbursement for non-panel providers is established by the plan sponsor and is generally lower than that for panel providers. This makes the out-of-pocket costs to the participant, and possibly to the employer, greater than they would have been had all the care been obtained through panel providers.

POS plans are designed to acquaint employees with the use of panel providers without being "locked-in" to the requirement to use panel providers for a long period (generally a year). As patients become comfortable with panel providers, they may be willing to receive most or all of their care through the managed care component of the health care plan. The POS option functions as a phase-in process when introducing managed care.

Q 8:98 What are the advantages and disadvantages of POS plans?

The main advantages of POS plans are that employees are introduced to managed care in a non-threatening way and remain in control of all health care choices.

Among the disadvantages of POS plans are increasing difficulty in predicting claims costs from year to year, depending on how accessible non-panel providers are. (For example, if there are strong financial disincentives for non-panel care, costs are more predictable.) Depending on the vendor, another disadvantage may be that the non-panel care is completely unmanaged (i.e., no utilization review). The costs for the non-panel care would then accelerate like those of any unmanaged indemnity plan.

Q 8:99 What should employers look for when deciding to participate in a POS plan?

Employers should look for an established delivery system and evaluate the panel in the same way as they would any HMO or PPO. The success rests on the panel itself; if employees are not satisfied with panel providers, they will obtain less cost-effective care outside the panel.

Q 8:100 Can an employer be held liable for negligent care provided by an HMO or PPO?

It is possible that an employer could be held liable for negligent care provided in a managed care setting. An injured party might argue that the employer was liable based on legal principles of ostensible agency or corporate negligence, and, depending on the facts and circumstances of the case, might be able to win.

To date, no court has found an employer responsible for a decision made by its managed care program's physician. Employers generally contract with the managed care organization, not with specific providers, so it is the organization that is responsible for ascertaining the credentials of health care providers and the quality of care provided. This would place the burden of potential liability with the managed care organization in most cases.

Employers concerned about their potential liability should consult with legal counsel to prepare specific protections. Generally, the methods for avoiding liability are to ensure that due diligence is exercised in choosing to hire a managed care organization, to include written protections in the contract signed with the managed care organization, and, in some cases, to purchase liability insurance (see Chapter 7).

Several states have passed laws allowing HMOs and other managed care organizations to be sued for malpractice when a denial of medically necessary care leads to adverse impact on a patient's health. At press time, legislation was pending in Congress that would allow employers, HMOs, and other managed care organizations to be sued for malpractice.

Aetna challenged the Texas law, but the U.S. District Court (Southern District) upheld the liability portion of the law. The court struck down another portion of the law giving patients the right to an independent medical review as preempted by ERISA.

Courts in Connecticut and Pennsylvania have ruled patients can sue HMOs for malpractice.

Q 8:101 How prevalent are point-of-service plans?

According to the Mercer/Foster Higgins annual survey, the percentage of large employers offering POS plans held steady at 33 percent in 1997 and 1998 and was essentially unchanged at 32 percent in 1999. Enrollment in POS plans declined from 22 percent in 1997 to 18 percent in 1999.

Managed Care Backlash

Q 8:102 How does the public feel about managed care?

The public seems to feel ambivalent about managed care. There seems to be a backlash against the restrictions of managed care, yet many managed care organizations receive high marks in surveys of their members.

According to a survey by the Employee Benefit Research Institute, 59 percent of Americans think the health care system needs major change. At the same time, 59 percent report they are extremely satisfied or very satisfied with the quality of their current care. The survey found that 56 percent of managed care enrollees state they have never been in managed care.

According to a survey by the Kaiser Family Foundation, 55 percent of people in managed care plans expressed concern that if they were sick their health plan would be more concerned about saving money than about what is the best medical treatment, compared to 34 percent of respondents in traditional plans who felt the same way. Half (51 percent) of respondents said that managed care has decreased the quality of care, while 32 percent believe the quality of care has increased under managed care. Sixty-one percent believe that the amount of time doctors spend with patients has decreased under managed care. Fifty-nine percent of respondents believe that managed care plans have made it harder for people to see specialists. Forty-six percent of respondents say managed care has made it easier to get preventive care.

A 1999 survey by Hewitt Associates showed that 22 percent of consumers were dissatisfied with their managed care plans, up from 17 percent in 1997; however, a survey by the American Association of Health Plans found that only six out of every 10,000 HMO members filed complaints or inquiries with their state insurance departments in 1997.

Q 8:103 How do employers feel about managed care?

A survey released in 1998 by the Washington Business Group on Health found that 42 percent of employers think cost pressures are hurting the quality of care, up from 33 percent in 1997 and 28 percent in 1996.

Q 8:104 How do health care providers feel about managed care?

A survey released in 1998 by the Healthcare Financial Management Association found that 54 percent of health care providers report that cost pressures are adversely affecting quality. Even so, 64 percent of providers said that quality care can continue to be delivered in the future at the same or lower costs.

There are some attempts to unionize physicians. For example, the United Food and Commercial Workers Union filed a brief in January 1999 with the National Labor Relations Board seeking permission to organize doctors. The union is targeting AmeriHealth, a New Jersey HMO. The American Medical Association has also decided to form a collective bargaining unit.

Q 8:105 What form does the managed care backlash take?

Many states have passed anti-managed care legislation. At the federal level, the President appointed a commission to study the issue.

In March 1998, the Presidential Advisory Commission on Consumer Protection and Quality in the Health Care Industry released its proposed Consumer Bill of Rights and Responsibilities.

The commission stated its position on the following eight areas of consumer rights:

1. *Information disclosure.* Consumers have the right to receive accurate, easily understood information and assistance in making informed health care decisions about their health plans, professionals, and facilities.
2. *Choice of providers and plans.* Consumers have the right to a choice of health care providers that is sufficient to ensure access to appropriate high-quality health care. All health plan networks should provide access to sufficient numbers and types of providers to assure that all covered services will be accessible

without unreasonable delay—including access to emergency services 24 hours a day and 7 days a week.

Consumers with complex or serious medical conditions who require frequent specialty care should have direct access to a qualified specialist of their choice within a plan's network of providers. Authorizations, when required, should be for an adequate number of direct access visits under an approved treatment plan.

Public and private group purchasers should, whenever feasible, offer consumers a choice of high-quality health insurance products.

3. *Access to emergency services.* Consumers have the right to access emergency health care services when and where the need arises. Health plans should pay when a consumer visits an emergency department with acute symptoms of sufficient severity—including severe pain—that a prudent layperson could reasonably expect the absence of medical attention to result in placing that consumers' health in serious jeopardy, serious impairment to bodily functions, or serious dysfunction of any bodily organ or part.

4. *Participation in treatment decisions.* Consumers have the right and responsibility to participate fully in all decisions related to their health care. Consumers who are unable to participate fully in treatment decisions have the right to be represented by parents, guardians, family members, or other conservators.

5. *Respect and nondiscrimination.* Consumers have the right to considerate, respectful care from all members of the health care system at all times and under all circumstances. An environment of mutual respect is essential to maintain a quality health care system.

6. *Confidentiality of health information.* Consumers have the right to communicate with health care providers in confidence and to have the confidentiality of their individually identifiable health care information protected. Consumers also have the right to review and copy their own medical records and request amendments to their records.

7. *Complaints and appeals.* All consumers have the right to a fair and efficient process for resolving differences with their health

plans, health care providers, and the institutions that serve them, including a rigorous system of internal review and an independent system of external review.

8. *Consumer responsibilities.* In a health care system that protects consumers' rights, it is reasonable to expect and encourage consumers to assume reasonable responsibilities. Greater individual involvement by consumers in their care increases the likelihood of achieving the best outcomes.

Q 8:106 What are the essential elements in HMO complaint and appeal systems?

The General Accounting Office identified 11 elements that were deemed as important by at least two of the five regulatory, consumer, and industry groups surveyed by the agency: the Joint Commission on Accreditation of Healthcare Organizations (JCAHO), the NCQA, the American Association of Health Plans (AAHP), Families USA (FUSA), and the National Association of Insurance Commissioners (NAIC).

The 11 essential elements in HMO complaint and appeal systems are:

Element	Group Recommended By
1. Explicit time periods	AAHP, FUSA, JCAHO, NAIC, NCQA
2. Expedited review	AAHP, FUSA, JCAHO, NAIC, NCQA
3. Two-level appeal process	FUSA, NAIC, NCQA
4. Member attendance at appeal hearing	NAIC, NCQA
5. Appeal decisions made by medical professionals with appropriate expertise	FUSA, NAIC, NCQA
6. Appeal decisions made by individuals not involved in previous denials	FUSA, NAIC, NCQA

Element	Group Recommended By
7. Written information provided in an understandable manner about how to register a complaint or appeal	FUSA, NCQA
8. Oral complaints accepted	FUSA, NCQA
9. Oral appeals accepted	FUSA, NCQA
10. Appeal right included in notice of denial of care or payment of service	AAHP, FUSA, NAIC, NCQA
11. Written notice provided of appeals denials, including further appeal rights	NAIC, NCQA

Q 8:107 Can managed care systems exclude physicians, hospitals, or other providers?

Generally, yes, but many states have begun to restrict the exclusivity of managed care networks. One of the bases of open-panel managed care (i.e., other than staff-model HMO managed care, where providers are usually salaried) is the concept of guiding plan participants to cost-efficient network providers, and this is inherently exclusionary. Open-panel managed care organizations (e.g., PPOs) contract with specific providers who give the plan discounts on medical care and agree to other terms in return for inclusion in the network and a certain volume of patients. Care provided to plan participants by providers excluded from the network—either because the provider was unwilling to discount or because for some reason the managed care organization did not seek to contract with that provider—is not covered (or, in some hybrid arrangements, is only partially covered) by the plan.

Some states have passed "any willing provider" (AWP) laws, which prohibit managed care organizations from excluding from their networks any providers that are willing to provide care at the prices and under the terms set by the plan. The stated intention of most of these laws is to protect plan participants' freedom to choose their health care providers.

These laws have recently been tested in the courts. In one prominent case in Virginia (a state with a limited AWP law), Stuart Circle Hospital Corporation brought suit against Aetna Health Management for unjustly excluding it from Aetna's managed care network. Aetna argued that it was protected from the state law by ERISA preemption. Although the federal district court in Richmond decided in favor of Aetna, the court of appeals for the fourth circuit reversed the decision, ruling that the law is not preempted by ERISA. The case went all the way to the U.S. Supreme Court, which followed the fourth circuit and let the Virginia law stand. [Stuart Circle Hospital Corp v Aetna Health Management, 995 F 2d 500, 502 (4th Cir 1964)]

More recently, the fifth circuit court of appeals ruled that ERISA preempts a Louisiana AWP statute. The 1992 law prohibited PPOs from excluding any physician who met certain state standards. The court ruled the law "related to" benefit plans and was therefore preempted by ERISA. The court has jurisdiction over Louisiana, Mississippi, and Texas.

During early 1997, AWP laws were struck down in Arkansas and Texas on the grounds they are preempted by ERISA. Later in the year, a U.S. District Court in Boston ruled that ERISA does not preempt a Massachusetts AWP law that bans HMOs from exclusive contracts with retail pharmacies. This marked the first time a federal court has upheld a states AWP pharmacy law. In 1998, the 8th U.S. Circuit Court of Appeals upheld the earlier ruling that the Arkansas law is preempted by ERISA.

Q 8:108 How many states have passed any willing provider laws?

According to the American Association of Health Plans, as of March 1996, 24 states have adopted AWP laws. Most apply only to specialists, such as pharmacists or chiropractors. Only four states have enacted requirements that physicians be allowed to join health plans: Arkansas, Idaho, Kentucky, and Wyoming. Indiana, Virginia, and Utah also have broad AWP laws. [*BNA Pension & Benefit Reporter* (March 18, 1996) at 706] In 1996, Washington repealed its measure.

Q 8:109 Why is exclusion from networks such a controversial issue?

The rapid growth of managed care has meant that a significant portion of the health care market is now controlled by HMOs, PPOs, and other managed care organizations. In many competitive areas, physicians or hospitals must belong to the dominant networks in the market in order to have the kind of patient volume they need to stay profitable; however, the managed care organizations want to keep network size manageable to control administrative costs and to avoid spreading their market share too thin, and so may exclude providers from their networks regardless of a willingness to provide discounts. This may leave non-network providers without sufficient patient volume to stay in business.

Both sides have a point. Providers argue that network exclusions unfairly deny them access to the health care market, limit participants' freedom of choice, and reduce the importance of competence as a criterion for network inclusion. The managed care organizations that sponsor the networks argue, however, that AWP laws limit their ability to negotiate the discounts needed to keep premiums low.

Adding fuel to the fire is the fact that managed care organizations are using increasingly sophisticated systems for monitoring and reevaluating their network physicians. These systems are designed to determine which providers are most cost-effective in order to weed out "inefficient" physicians. As a result, many competent doctors are dropped from networks, often with no warning and sometimes after years of practicing within the network.

Q 8:110 How are doctors responding to these actions by managed care organizations?

Physicians have begun to seek loosening of federal antitrust regulations, which restrict them from collaborating within the health care marketplace. They argue that they need to be able to act collectively when negotiating with insurers and large health care organizations that exercise significant control over the medical market, and that freeing them from the antitrust laws will heighten competition and lower prices. The American Medical Association (AMA) has succeeded in getting legislation introduced in Congress that will provide them the relief they desire.

Lining up against this move by the AMA are a number of consumer organizations, including the powerful American Association of Retired Persons, and the insurance industry. These groups dispute the AMA's arguments, saying that if doctors are allowed to act collectively, they will fix prices and attempt to eliminate non-physician providers from the market. [Rick Wartzman, "Consumer Groups, Insurers Launch Effort to Keep Doctors From Winning Looser Antitrust Laws," *Wall Street J* (May 25, 1994)]

Q 8:111 What is a gag rule?

Gag rules, also known as anti-disparagement provisions, are contractual provisions between managed care plans and physicians that forbid the physicians from making comments that could undermine the confidence of members in the plan. Some physicians complain that these provisions prohibit them from advising patients about treatment options that may not be covered.

Q 8:112 Are gag rules common?

No. The Government Accounting Office reviewed physician contracts from 529 HMOs and found no clauses that specifically restricted physicians from discussing appropriate medical options with their patients.

Q 8:113 What is anti-managed care legislation?

Anti-managed care legislation is a phrase used to describe many types of legislation designed to curb perceived abuses in the managed care industry. Some legislation is intended to be constructive by improving managed care and some is reactionary and intended to prompt a return to the days before managed care. Laws against gag rules generally fall in the former category, but AWP laws generally fall in the latter category. Other examples of anti-managed care legislation include laws that would require HMOs to allow patients to see physicians who do not belong to the network and laws that mandate minimum lengths of stay for certain conditions.

Q 8:114 What are some examples of state managed care legislation?

Maryland has a large number of health care mandates. Among the mandates are:

- Minimum stays for maternity
- Mental health and substance abuse coverage
- Prostate exams for men between the ages of 40 and 75

New Jersey publishes HMO report cards.

Oregon's Patient Protection Act requires health plans to:

- Disclose financial incentives for physicians to control costs
- Give consumers the right to an appeal process
- Allow access to emergency rooms

Texas allows consumers to sue HMOs and insurance companies if they do not use "ordinary care" in denying or delaying treatment. Texas also makes HMO complaint records public.

Q 8:115 What are the categories of consumer protection laws?

Families USA has identified the following 13 consumer protection laws relating to managed care:

1. Establishing a "prudent layperson" standard in obtaining emergency care;
2. Providing access to out-of-network physicians;
3. Allowing specialists to serve as primary care providers;
4. Allowing enrollees to obtain standing referrals to specialists;
5. Requiring direct access to obstetricians/gynecologists;
6. Allowing patients to continue to see the same provider for a specific number of days when their physician leaves a plan;
7. Requiring plans to have a procedure to allow enrollees to obtain nonformulary prescription drugs;
8. Requiring plans to adopt a meaningful independent external review process;

9. Establishing independent statewide consumer assistance programs;
10. Prohibiting plans from preventing the disclosure of treatment options;
11. Prohibiting plans from providing physicians financial incentives to reduce or deny care;
12. Preventing plans from barring enrollee participation in clinical trials; and
13. Enabling enrollees to sue their health care plans for damages.

As of June 1998, Families USA reported no state had enacted all of these laws. Vermont has enacted the most protection laws, with 11; followed by Missouri with nine; and New Mexico, Pennsylvania, and Texas each enacting eight. South Dakota has enacted no consumer protection laws relating to managed care.

Q 8:116 What is expanded liability legislation?

Federal courts have consistently held that ERISA preempts state law with respect to benefit denials under an employer-sponsored plan. Some courts have also held that ERISA preempts malpractice claims against insurers and HMOs for substandard medical care. Expanded liability legislation proposed in Congress would amend ERISA to expose employers, insurers, HMOs, and TPAs to state law personal injury and wrongful death lawsuits. Several states have already passed laws that expose insurers and HMOs in those states to malpractice claims.

Some lower courts have already held managed care organizations liable for either direct liability or derivative liability. Direct liability is for the wrongful actions or inactions of the managed care organization itself. Derivative liability is for the wrongful actions of network providers.

Q 8:117 What are external reviews?

External review (or appeal) programs allow managed care patients to have an independent party resolve disputes. A number of states require external reviews, as does Medicare. Some HMOs, such as Aetna U.S. Healthcare, have voluntarily adopted external reviews.

Q 8:118 Do external reviews usually favor the patient?

No. According to a study by the Kaiser Family Foundation, review programs uphold about half the decisions by managed care organizations. Only 32 percent of Medicare appeals in 1997 were decided in favor of the patient.

Q 8:119 How is the managed care industry responding to the backlash?

Some managed care organizations and industry groups are trying to improve care and safeguard patients. For example, in 1997 the American Association of Health Plans' Board of Directors adopted "Putting Patients First" policies, which include:

1. Member plans cannot require patients to have mastectomies on an outpatient basis.
2. Patients should be fully informed about how the health plan functions and should be able to speak freely with doctors about treatment options.
3. Denials should be clear and appeals should be handled promptly.

Chapter 9
Flexible Benefits

As the name denotes, flexible benefits plans come in all shapes to meet the needs of employees with diverse lifestyles and employers with varied objectives. This chapter covers the basic principles involved in the design and handling of flexible benefits plans, with an emphasis on cafeteria plans as provided for under Section 125 of the Internal Revenue Code. Nondiscrimination requirements are addressed in Chapter 11.

Introduction	9-1
Tax Advantages	9-3
Cost Control	9-7
Types of Plans	9-8
Vacations	9-30
Flexible Benefits Options	9-33
Implementation	9-37

Introduction

Q 9:1 What is a flexible benefits plan?

A flexible benefits plan (flex plan) is an employee benefit plan based on the concept of employee choice. Traditional benefit plans offer each employee the same benefits and the same level of coverage. Under a full flexible benefits plan, employees have the opportunity to select, individually, the type of benefits and the level of coverage desired from a menu of options offered by their employers.

Flexible benefits is a generic name given to an employee benefit plan that offers employees a choice of benefits and coverage options. If the flex plan is designed in accordance with the tax provisions of Section 125 of the Internal Revenue Code (Code or IRC), it is legally known as a cafeteria or Section 125 plan.

Q 9:2 How prevalent are flexible benefits plans today?

According to the 1999 Mercer/Foster Higgins survey, 27 percent of employers offer a full flexible benefits program, unchanged from 1997, but up from 23 percent in 1993. Larger employers are more likely to offer a flex plan: 44 percent of employers with 20,000 or more employees reported offering a flex plan in 1999, compared to 22 percent of employers with 500 to 999 employees.

Q 9:3 How does the Code define a cafeteria plan?

Under Code Section 125, a cafeteria plan is one in which:

1. All participants are employees.
2. The participants may choose among (a) two or more benefits consisting of cash and qualified benefits or (b) two or more qualified benefits.

Q 9:4 What are qualified benefits?

Qualified benefits include the following:

1. Group term life insurance up to, and in excess of, the amount ($50,000) normally excludable from taxable income; [IRC § 79]
2. Accident and health insurance; [IRC §§ 105, 106]
3. Dependent care assistance; [IRC § 129]
4. Cash-or-deferred arrangements (CODAs). [IRC § 401(k)]

Benefits that are not qualified include:

1. Scholarships and fellowships; [IRC § 117]

2. Meals and lodging; [IRC § 119]
3. Van pooling; [IRC § 124]
4. Educational assistance; [IRC § 127]
5. Certain other fringe benefits, such as no-additional-cost services, qualified employee discounts, working-condition fringes, and de minimis fringe benefits defined by Code Section 132.

The Health Insurance Portability and Accountability Act of 1996 (HIPAA) specifies that neither long-term care insurance nor medical savings accounts can be included in cafeteria plans.

Note that the Transportation Equity Act of 1998 allows pretax contributions for parking or transit vouchers, but these must be completely independent of cafeteria plans.

Q 9:5 Is a flexible benefits plan subject to the Employee Retirement Income Security Act of 1974?

No, a cafeteria plan is not an Employee Retirement Income Security Act of 1974 (ERISA) plan. Cafeteria plans act like umbrella benefits plans that encompass the underlying life, health, disability, and 401(k) plans; however, ERISA may, in fact, govern the individual benefits options that are covered by the flexible benefits umbrella.

Tax Advantages

Q 9:6 What are the tax advantages of a cafeteria plan?

An employer's FICA and FUTA contributions (and perhaps workers compensation premiums) are based on its payroll, and an employee's FICA contribution and local, state, and federal tax are based on gross income. Because employee contributions to cafeteria plans are on a pre-tax basis, they reduce the employer's payroll and the employee's taxable income by the amount of the contribution. Consequently, the employer's FICA and FUTA contributions decrease. The employee also benefits, because he or she is able to spend these benefit dollars and not pay taxes on them.

Reducing salary means reducing earnings for purposes of Social Security, unemployment compensation, and perhaps workers compensation. This can result in slightly lower Social Security, unemployment, or workers compensation benefits. The tax savings more than offset any resulting reduction in benefits. If employees use the tax savings to purchase additional disability benefits and save for retirement they will be better off than if they elect not to make salary reductions.

Q 9:7 Can health benefits be provided to an employee on behalf of his or her domestic partner on a pre-tax basis through a cafeteria plan?

Yes, but coverage must be on an after-tax basis, unless the domestic partner is a dependent of the employee. An individual can qualify as a dependent only if all of the following are true:

1. The employee provides more than half the individual's support during the calendar year.
2. The individual has his or her "principal place of abode" in the employee's home and is a member of the employee's household.
3. The relationship between the individual and the employee is not in violation of local law.

If the domestic partner qualifies as a dependent under these rules, coverage may be on a pre-tax basis. Even when coverage is provided on an after-tax basis, reimbursements (claims) are nontaxable. The employee's after-tax salary reduction is the equivalent of a cash election under the cafeteria plan rules.

Q 9:8 Are employee contributions to a cafeteria plan subject to state income tax?

Such contributions are subject to income tax in Puerto Rico as of this writing. Applicability of taxes is based on where the employee resides, not on where the employer conducts business.

In 1997, Pennsylvania enacted legislation to allow pre-tax contributions for life and health plans, but contributions to a dependent care flexible spending arrangement (FSA) are still subject to state income tax.

Until 1995, New Jersey also taxed cafeteria plans. In 1995, New Jersey enacted a limited exception to its taxation. If a plan provides cash to employees who waive medical coverage, New Jersey no longer taxes employees who elect medical coverage. New Jersey still taxes pre-tax premiums and contributions to flexible spending accounts.

Q 9:9 How does the federal government view employee contributions under flexible benefits plans?

The IRS and Department of Labor (DOL) have slightly different views. The IRS believes that salary reductions for before-tax contributions, salary reductions to fund flexible spending accounts, and salary reductions to purchase additional benefits are all converted from employee to employer contributions by virtue of being salary reductions.

The DOL considers all types of employee contributions under cafeteria plans, including salary reductions, to be employee contributions. This means that, technically, employee contributions under cafeteria plans should be subject to the DOL's plan asset rules. While the DOL studies this issue further, it has announced that it will not enforce the proposed plan asset rules for cafeteria plans. Conceivably, the DOL could have decided to enforce its plan asset rules for after-tax contributions to flexible benefits plans, such as under COBRA or the Family and Medical Leave Act (FMLA). Fortunately, in the preamble to its 1996 plan asset regulations, the DOL expressed its view that "the mere receipt of COBRA contributions or other after-tax participant contributions (e.g., retiree contributions) by a cafeteria plan would not by itself affect the availability of the relief provided for cafeteria plans."

Q 9:10 When were flexible benefits plans first introduced?

The first flexible benefits plans were established by large companies in the early 1970s. The Revenue Act of 1978 added Section 125 to the Internal Revenue Code, under which a plan could legally offer a choice between nontaxable benefits and taxable benefits or cash without adverse tax consequences ("constructive receipt") to employees.

Although flexible benefits have been in existence for about 30 years, only recently have they been available to small and medium-sized employers. This was because only large companies had the resources to implement and administer flexible benefits plans; however, technological innovations have decreased the cost and have streamlined the process of administering the plans, and insurance companies have learned to predict the cost and selection of the benefits offered under such plans more accurately. As a result, they are now available to employers of all sizes.

Q 9:11 What is constructive receipt?

Taxpayers must report as taxable income any compensation or earnings realized during the year. This may include amounts not actually paid to or received by an individual if these amounts are deemed to have been "constructively received." A person is in constructive receipt of income or property if he or she has an unconditional right to take possession of it, whether he or she exercises that right or not. There is, however, no constructive receipt if possession is contingent upon surrendering some valuable right (such as the right to continue participating in the plan), or if there are other limitations on the exercise of the option.

Constructive receipt also does not apply if there is a statutory exemption. The Revenue Act of 1978 provided an exception to the doctrine of constructive receipt for cafeteria plans in Code Section 125. Thus, an individual who could have elected cash or some other taxable benefit is not in constructive receipt when choosing a nontaxable benefit instead.

Q 9:12 Why were flexible benefits plans developed?

Flexible benefits plans were developed as a result of two significant trends in the business world: a need to control or manage escalating employee benefits costs (see Chapter 7 on managing health insurance costs) and a changing employee population with changing needs.

Traditional benefit plans were designed in the 1950s, when 60 percent of the workforce consisted of men whose wives did not work. Only 30.5 percent of all wives worked in 1960. In addition only 32 percent of the labor force was comprised of women as recently as 1970.

These demographic changes mean that a standard benefit package is inappropriate for the majority of today's workers. For example, a single person would not need or want as much life or health insurance as an older married person with children. A single parent might need day care or more life insurance. An older worker with no children might need more medical but less life insurance. Thus, different lifestyles give rise to different benefits needs, and workers today are asking for benefits that are more meaningful to them.

Cost Control

Q 9:13 How do flexible benefits help control costs?

Flexible benefits provide a vehicle for separating the level of benefits from the cost of benefits. Employers can:

1. Fix benefits costs as a percentage of payroll.
2. Freeze costs at a set dollar level.
3. Cover increased costs.
4. Increase benefits as productivity or profits increase.
5. Add new benefits without increasing the cost of the benefits program.
6. Manage choices by controlling the price the employees pay for the benefits they select.
7. Control the options employees can select through plan design.

In contrast, the structure of traditional benefit plans mandates cost increases each year, because medical care costs increase each year, and at a rate faster than the consumer price index. A plan designed to cover the reasonable and customary charge for services, as most plans are, becomes more expensive as the cost of the services increases.

An employer with a traditional plan has several options for controlling costs: limiting the coverage provided, increasing the extent to which employees pay for the services provided (through increased deductible and coinsurance requirements), and increasing employees' contributions to the plan, all of which create the impression that the employee is "giving back" benefits.

Q 9:14   How successful have flexible benefits plans been in controlling costs?

Cost containment is frequently cited as a reason for instituting flexible benefits plans. According to the 1998 survey by Mercer/Foster Higgins, 32 percent of employers with flexible benefits were convinced that flexible benefit plans had reduced their benefit costs.

Q 9:15   Are flexible benefits plans expected to increase in popularity?

The decline of the two-parent, one-worker family and the growth in the number of women who work enhance the value and popularity of benefit plans that can be adapted to the needs of particular families.

The increase in new flexible benefits plans may have been slowed as employers waited for the results of the discussion about health reform in 1993 and 1994. The halt in medical increases that followed probably lessened the perceived need for flexible benefits as well. Mercer/Foster Higgins reports that while few employers are adding full-fledged flex programs, many employers have added flexibility to their existing benefit programs by offering additional managed care options or combined paid-time-off banks.

Types of Plans

Q 9:16   Are there different types of flexible plans?

Yes. There are a number of different types of flexible benefits plans:

- Salary reduction premium conversion plans
- Flexible spending or reimbursement accounts
- Modular plans
- Core plus plans
- Working spouse plans
- Total flexible, or full cafeteria, plans

Q 9:17 What is a salary reduction premium conversion plan?

A salary reduction premium conversion plan is a simple plan that permits employees to reduce their compensation by an amount equal to their contributions to a benefit program, such as a medical benefit plan. This has the effect of converting their contributions from after-tax to before-tax.

Q 9:18 What is a flexible spending or reimbursement account?

Flexible spending or reimbursement accounts are accounts funded by employee salary reductions, employer contributions, or both. Amounts placed in these accounts are used to provide reimbursement for expenses incurred by the employee for specified benefits during the year.

Q 9:19 What is a health care reimbursement account?

Health care reimbursement accounts, established under Code Section 105, allow participants to recover expenses on a pre-tax basis for those health care charges not reimbursed by any other source and not claimed on the participant's income tax return. These expenses can include, but are not limited to, medical and dental insurance deductibles and coinsurance; amounts over the reasonable and customary charges not covered by insurance; and other reimbursable expenses permitted as income tax deductions under Code Section 213, such as contact lenses, orthopedic shoes, nursing, prescription drugs, lab tests, and hearing aids. To deduct them on one's income tax, these expenses must exceed 7.5 percent of adjusted gross income; however, the 7.5 percent threshold does not apply to health plans, such as health care reimbursement accounts.

Q 9:20 Have there been any recent changes in what are considered eligible expenses for health care reimbursement accounts?

The last legislative change was when the Omnibus Budget Reconciliation Act of 1990 (OBRA '90) added Section 213(d)(9)(A) to the Internal Revenue Code. This section provided that expenses incurred by taxpayers in connection with elective cosmetic surgery would generally no longer be allowed as a medical expense deduction. As a result of this legislation, employer-provided reimbursement for such expenses, whether through a flexible spending arrangement or any other health plan, is includible in gross income; therefore, such expenses may not be reimbursed with before-tax dollars through a health care reimbursement account.

The Internal Revenue Service (IRS) issued Revenue Ruling 97-9 [1997-1 CB 77] clarifying the tax status of certain substances. In 1996, voters in California and Arizona approved initiatives legalizing the use of marijuana for medicinal purposes. The IRS ruled that the amount paid to obtain a controlled substance in violation of federal law is not a deductible expense under Code Section 213. Code Section 213 governs tax-favored reimbursements under employer-sponsored health plans and cafeteria plans. The IRS ruling stressed that reimbursements under Code Section 213 will not be allowed, even if the state law requires a prescription to obtain and use the controlled substance (such as marijuana).

The IRS also reversed an old position on laetrile (touted by some as a cure for cancer). Revenue Ruling 78-325 [1978-2 CB 124] held that laetrile was deductible if purchased in a locality in which it was legal. The Food and Drug Administration has not approved the use of laetrile, but it is widely available in Mexico. Revenue Ruling 97-9 changed the old position and treats laetrile the same as marijuana and other controlled substances, meaning that group health plans cannot reimburse participants for the purchase of laetrile.

The IRS has also changed its interpretation of whether Lamaze classes are eligible expenses. The IRS now believes Lamaze is for the convenience of the mother and not required for the medical condition; therefore, the IRS now says Lamaze classes are not eligible for reimbursement.

On June 21, 1999, the IRS published Revenue Ruling 99-28, making the cost of smoking-cessation programs and prescription drugs used to alleviate the effects of nicotine withdrawal deductible expenses under Section 213 of the Internal Revenue Code. Over-the-counter medications, such as non-prescription nicotine patches and gum are not deductible expenses.

The ruling does not necessarily change what is covered by a health plan. The ruling makes it permissible for a health plan to cover smoking-cessation programs and prescription drugs to alleviate the effects of nicotine withdrawal, but most plans will have to be amended before such expenses could be covered. Many flexible spending accounts use the Section 213 rules to define what is a covered expense; for those plans, smoking-cessation programs and prescription drugs to alleviate nicotine withdrawal will be covered automatically.

Q 9:21 Are there any exceptions to the rule regarding elective cosmetic surgery?

Yes. Expenses in connection with (1) surgery that is necessary to improve a deformity that resulted from a congenital abnormality, a trauma or accident causing personal injury, or a disfiguring disease or (2) surgery that is medically necessary to restore bodily function and that only incidentally affects the patient's appearance will continue to be deductible.

Q 9:22 What procedures are considered elective cosmetic surgery?

Cosmetic surgery is defined as any procedure that is designed to improve the patient's appearance and does not contribute meaningfully to proper body function or prevent or treat a disease. [IRC § 213(d)(9)(B)]

It is unclear whether orthodontia and tooth capping are to be considered elective cosmetic surgery, and the IRS is not expected to issue guidance in the near future. Employers that allow reimbursement of these expenses should make sure they disclaim tax liability should the taxpayer incur taxes and penalties retroactively.

Q 9:23 What are some examples of medical expenses that are or are not eligible for reimbursement?

1. *Bed wetting alarms* are medical expenses if they relate to a medical condition, but not for developmental reasons.
2. *Breast pumps* are not medical expenses, unless medically necessary for the care of a premature infant.
3. *Exercise clubs* are not medical expenses, unless part of a treatment plan for a specific medical condition.
4. *In-vitro expenses* for a surrogate mother are not eligible for reimbursement, but expenses for the taxpayer, spouse, or dependent are eligible for reimbursement.
5. *Removal of lead paint or asbestos* is not a medical expense, unless required because of a current medical condition.
6. *Sales taxes or surcharges on a hospital bill* are medical expenses.
7. *Smoking cessation and drugs for smoking cessation* are medical expenses. This is a new development under Revenue Ruling 99-28.
8. *Tuition for special schools* is a medical expense, but only if the special school treats a specific condition, such as a school for the blind.
9. *Vitamins* are not a medical expense, unless they are only available with a prescription.
10. *Weight loss drugs and treatment* (even if prescribed by a physician) are not a medical expense, unless related to a specific medical condition.

Q 9:24 What are the average participation rates and contributions for health care reimbursement accounts?

According to the 1999 survey by Mercer/Foster Higgins, among companies that offer health care spending account plans, 19 percent of employees participated in such plans; the average annual contribution to medical spending accounts was $930.

Q 9:25 What is a dependent care reimbursement account?

A dependent care reimbursement account allows for the use of pre-tax dollars to provide benefits for the care of (1) a dependent under the age of 13 for whom a dependent deduction is allowed under the Code or (2) a dependent who is physically or mentally incapable of caring for himself or herself, to enable the benefit plan participant and his or her spouse to work. This benefit works in conjunction with the dependent care deduction available on the participant's income tax return; however, expenses reimbursed through this account may not be claimed for income tax purposes.

These accounts may be used to provide up to $5,000 in dependent care assistance ($2,500 for a married individual filing separately). Amounts provided from a reimbursement account offset amounts available from the tax credit for child and dependent care expenses on a dollar-for-dollar basis. [IRC §§ 21, 129]

Q 9:26 When are dependent care services incurred?

Proposed regulations generally require that expenses must have been "incurred previously during the period of coverage" in order to be eligible for reimbursement under a flexible spending account. Reimbursement is not permitted merely upon execution of a contract. To be "incurred," the service must have already been provided. Reimbursement is permitted before the employee has paid the expense, as long as the services have been provided.

Q 9:27 What are some examples of dependent care expenses that are or are not eligible for reimbursement?

1. *Art supplies* and *field trips* are not eligible for reimbursement if there is a separate charge for these items.

2. *Dependent care expenses* while a taxpayer is sick are eligible for reimbursement as long as it is not a long-term illness. The IRS has not defined "long-term" illness.
3. *Registration fees* are eligible for reimbursement if payment is required to obtain daycare.
4. *School tuition* is not eligible for reimbursement, even for kindergarten. After-school care, even by the same provider, is reimbursable.
5. Specialty camps, such as sports or computer camps, are eligible for reimbursement, as long as they are not overnight, but exorbitant expenses may be challenged by the IRS.
6. *Summer camps* are not eligible for reimbursement if they are overnight. The IRS does not even allow prorating the portion attributable to "day" versus "night."

Q 9:28 What are the average participation rates and contributions for dependent care reimbursement accounts?

According to the 1999 survey by Mercer/Foster Higgins, among companies that offer dependent care spending account plans, 8 percent of employees participated in such plans; the average annual contribution to dependent care spending accounts was $2,997.

Q 9:29 How are these reimbursement accounts structured?

Health care and dependent care reimbursement accounts can be structured through a salary reduction agreement, employer contributions to the plan, or both. The employer sets the maximum amount of contribution allowed for each account at the beginning of the plan year. Each participant may choose to contribute an amount per plan year up to that maximum, and a portion of the total annual contribution elected is then added to the account each pay period. The participant submits expenses to be reimbursed periodically from funds in his or her account. Reimbursement is permitted only for services provided during the plan year.

Until 1990, reimbursement for health care accounts was available generally only up to the amount already accumulated in the individual's account from periodic deposits. Expenses in excess of the accumulated amount were not reimbursed until sufficient funds were available in the account; however, included in the cafeteria plan regulations proposed on March 7, 1989 was a new rule—called the uniform coverage rule—requiring that the maximum reimbursement under health care accounts be available for the entire period of coverage. [Prop Reg § 1.125-2, Q&A 6 & 7] (The IRS has never finalized these regulations but still expects compliance with these rules.) This prevents employers from limiting reimbursement to the amount of salary reduction accumulated in the individual's account, and allows short-service employees an opportunity to use more money than they contribute. While the uniform coverage rule created a real possibility for considerable plan losses, the problem is not as large as it was originally anticipated to be. Reimbursement under dependent care accounts can still be limited to the amount accumulated.

Proposed cafeteria plan regulations stipulate that health care flexible spending arrangements must provide for uniform reimbursement throughout the year. This means that an employee who enters into a salary reduction agreement of $50 a month, or $600 a year, must have the full year's contributions available for reimbursement at the beginning of the year. That is, if an employee incurred $600 of reimbursable expenses in January, the full $600 would have to be made available to the employee at that time.

Employers cannot defer payment to the end of the plan year or until sufficient accumulation exists. In many states, the shortfall cannot be made up from other benefit distributions (e.g., accrued vacation time) or from final pay.

Q 9:30 If an employee terminates employment, what happens to a reimbursement account?

Employees may elect COBRA continuation of health care reimbursement accounts. Contributions continue to be made (on an after-tax basis), and the full amount of the election remains available for eligible expenses incurred up to the end of the coverage period (i.e, the end of the plan year or until participation ceases, whichever comes first).

Q 9:31

The final COBRA regulations limit the circumstances under which an employer must offer continuation of health care reimbursement accounts. An FSA need not be offered to a qualified beneficiary if the maximum amount that the qualified beneficiary could be required to pay for coverage for the remainder of the plan year exceeds the maximum benefit payable during the remainder of the plan year.

If an employee does not elect to continue to participate in the reimbursement account and make the required contributions, only health care expenses incurred prior to termination of employment are eligible for reimbursement.

Q 9:31 What happens if the benefits paid plus administrative costs are less than the total contributions plus interest earnings?

If monies remain after all claims and expenses have been discharged, the plan is said to have an "experience gain." It can be used to reduce future contributions, in aggregate, and to improve current benefits for all participants. The return may not be based on individual claim submissions but can be either an equal amount to all employees or proportional to each participant's contribution as a percentage of total contributions.

Q 9:32 What has been the experience under the uniform reimbursement approach?

When the uniform coverage rule was first announced, many employers feared it would create significant losses for their plans. Some expected to see employees "game" the system by submitting claims exceeding year-to-date contributions prior to terminating employment. The early fears are not being borne out, and continuing indications are that patterns of participation and utilization are relatively unchanged by the availability of full reimbursement, although some employers are more at risk than others.

Furthermore, case studies conducted since the rule went into effect have found that net losses, if any, are generally small. One study found that, on average, plans actually experienced very small gains. This was because losses from reimbursements in excess of employee contributions were more than offset by forfeitures of benefits (since reimbursement accounts are prohibited from carrying leftover funds from one year to the next, any funds remaining in accounts at the end of the plan year are forfeited to the plan). The survey by Mercer/Foster Higgins found the forfeiture rate to be running at an average of 4 percent for 1998.

Planning Pointer. Offering an early retirement window early in the plan year can result in unanticipated reimbursement and higher-than-expected plan losses.

Q 9:33 What steps can an employer take to reduce the risk that reimbursements will exceed contributions?

Employers may take any or all of the following five steps:

1. *Reduce the annual maximum contribution permitted.* Previously, maximums of $5,000 to $10,000 were common; most plans now limit contributions to $2,000 or $2,500 annually.

2. *Increase the waiting period for participation.* Waiting periods of up to one year are common because turnover is typically highest among short-service employees.

3. *Tighten the rules concerning decreases in contributions.* This reduces the occasions when changes in family status allow for a decrease in contributions.

4. *Restrict the types of medical care covered by the plan.* Some types of medical costs are easier to incur voluntarily than others (e.g., new eye glasses), and limiting coverage for these may protect plans from some losses.

5. *Charge employees a small fee to cover the risk of loss.* The plan could impose a small surcharge on employee contributions, which could be used to offset losses. The fee would not accrue to the employee's account. The tax status of such a fee is not clear, and employers considering this option should seek guidance from the IRS.

Q 9:34 Are there any new developments regarding plan changes?

Yes. On March 23, 2000, the Internal Revenue Service issued final and proposed regulations that provide guidance on the circumstances under which a cafeteria plan participant may revoke an existing election and make a new election during a period of coverage. The final regulations generally allow more changes than the 1997 proposed regulations.

The old rules governing changes in family status were very general and only provided examples of the kinds of situations in which a plan could allow a change. The new change in status rules specify that the change must fall into one of the categories specified in Q 9:35.

The final regulations include two principal changes from the temporary regulations. The final rules incorporate a more flexible rule under which any change in the employment status of the employee or a spouse or dependent that affects that individuals eligibility under a benefit plan constitutes a change in status for purposes of permitting a mid-year election change. Under this new, more flexible rule, a strike, lockout, commencement or return from an unpaid leave of absence or a change from salaried to hourly (or vice versa) will be considered a change in status. The final regulations also permit an employee to increase or decrease life or disability benefits as the result of a change in marital or employment status.

The final regulations were developed as part of a package with proposed regulations that were also published at the same time. The proposed regulations address changes in status with respect to dependent care assistance and adoption assistance and changes in cost or coverage for a number of types of benefits.

The final regulations do not prescribe a period of time by which election changes must be made. The preamble to the regulations points out that nothing in the regulations would prevent a plan by its terms from requiring that any election change must be made within a specified period after a change in status.

Under the final regulations, the following events are changes in status:

- Legal marital status
- Number of dependents
- Employment status
- Dependent satisfies or ceases to satisfy eligibility requirements
- Residence

The final regulations clarify that, in the event of a loss of Medicare or Medicaid entitlement by an employee or a spouse or dependent, a cafeteria plan may permit the employee to add health coverage. Termination or reduction in coverage if an employee, spouse, or dependent who is enrolled in a health plan becomes entitled to Medicare or Medicaid is also permitted. The rules specifically apply only to Medicare and Medicaid and not to other governmental programs.

The final regulations do not address when a bona fide termination of employment occurs; however, an example in the regulations provides a practical safe harbor that generally may be applied without regard to other facts and circumstances. Under this example, if an employee terminates and resumes employment within 30 days, the cafeteria plan should provide that the employees election is automatically reinstated. A cafeteria plan (by design) may permit an employee who resumes employment more than 30 days following termination to be automatically reinstated to the prior election, to make a new election or keep the participant out of the plan until the next open enrollment period.

The regulations are applicable for cafeteria plan years beginning on or after January 1, 2001. Until that date, plans may follow the rules in the final regulations, the 1997 proposed regulations, or the 1989 proposed regulations.

The IRS published a set of proposed regulations at the same time as the final regulations. The proposed regulations supplement the final regulations by addressing the situations under which an employee may make a mid-year change in dependent care or adoption assistance elections because of a status change. The proposed regulations also address the circumstances under which an employee may make a mid-year election change under any benefit plan because of a change in cost or coverage.

The change in status rules for dependent care and adoption assistance parallel the change in status rules for life and health plans. One exception is that a change in the number of dependents is a status change for dependent care plans only if the dependent is eligible for dependent care. The other exception is that commencement or termination of an adoption proceeding is a status change for adoption assistance plans.

The expansion of the cost or coverage rules allows employees to make election changes if a new benefit option is offered or if a benefit option is eliminated. The new proposed regulations provide that a cafeteria plan may permit an employee to make an election change corresponding with an open enrollment change made by a spouse, former spouse or dependent; therefore if the spouse makes an election change during open enrollment and that plan has a different plan year than the employee's plan has, the employee can still make an election change to avoid a gap in coverage or duplicate coverage. Under the old rules, the employee had to wait until his or her open enrollment to make a change. Similarly, if the spouse makes an election change because of a change in cost or coverage under the spouses plan, the employee can make a corresponding change in election. Under the consistency rule, if the spouse does not make an election change because of a change in cost or coverage, the employee cannot make a change.

The cost or coverage rules in the new proposed regulations do not extend to health care spending accounts.

The new proposed regulations differ from the 1989 proposed regulations in that they permit election changes for cost or coverage changes under self-funded plans. The new rule allows unilateral changes in employee contributions by self-funded employers.

The new proposed regulations allow an election change when an employee changes dependent care providers. An election change is also allowed if the dependent care provider changes costs. This rule does not apply if the dependent care provider is a relative of the employee.

The new proposed regulations do not specify an effective date, but plans can follow the rules in the new regulations or any applicable prior regulations until the effective date of further guidance.

The regulations include a number of examples that clarify certain points, including the following:

1. If an employee marries during the year, two changes might be consistent with the change in status: the employee could add the new spouse or the employee could cancel coverage if the employee becomes covered under the spouse's plan.

2. In the event of a divorce, the employee cannot cancel his or her own coverage, only that of the spouse (and presumably, any stepchildren who would lose coverage because of the divorce).
3. If an employee terminates employment, then resumes employment in order to change an election, the employee has not had a qualified change in status, other than to cancel coverage during the period of unemployment.

The regulations clarify that if a 401(k) plan is part of a cafeteria plan, the 401(k) rules, rather than these rules, apply to the 401(k) plan.

If the employee, spouse, or dependent becomes eligible for COBRA or any similar state law, the employee may elect to increase payments under the cafeteria plan to pay for the continuation coverage.

Q 9:35 What kinds of changes may an employee make during the plan year?

Tax law requires that an employee's choices in a flexible benefits plan be made in advance of the plan year. This means that after the effective date of the plan, no changes can be made (except as described below) until the next enrollment period. Under the final regulations, changes in choices during the plan year are permitted only if a status change occurs. A status change is defined to include the following:

1. *Legal marital status.* Events that change an employee's legal marital status include marriage, death of spouse, divorce, legal separation, and annulment.
2. *Number of dependents.* Events that change an employee's number of dependents include birth, adoption, placement for adoption, and death of a dependent.
3. *Employment status.* Events that change employment status include a termination or commencement of employment by the employee, spouse, or a dependent; a strike or lockout; a commencement of or return from an unpaid leave of absence; and a change in worksite. In addition, if the eligibility conditions of the plan depend on employment status and there is a

change in employment status (such as salaried to hourly) then that change constitutes a change in employment status.

4. *Dependent satisfies or ceases to satisfy the eligibility requirements.* Events that cause an employee's dependent to satisfy or cease to satisfy the requirements of coverage include attainment of a limiting age, change in student status, or any similar circumstances provided in the plan.

5. *Residence.* A change in the place of residence of the employee, spouse, or a dependent.

If a situation clearly falls into one of these categories, the employee has a change in status. The change in status must affect eligibility for coverage and the election change must correspond to the status change. The employer must judge whether the event and the election change are consistent. For example, if a child loses health coverage upon graduation from college, the cafeteria plan may allow the employee to cease payment for the child's coverage.

Also, if an employee, spouse, or dependent becomes entitled to Part A or Part B of Medicare or Medicaid, a cafeteria plan can permit an employee to cancel coverage.

An election change must be consistent with the change in status. For example, if an employee divorces, it would be consistent to change from "employee and spouse" coverage to "employee only" coverage, but it would not be consistent to drop coverage entirely. Proposed regulations address the circumstances under which a change in cost or coverage can permit a change in elections.

The proposed regulations allow the following changes:

1. *Automatic cost changes.* If the cost of a plan changes during a plan year and, under the terms of the plan, employees are required to make a corresponding change in their payments, the plan may automatically change contributions.

2. *Significant cost increases.* If the cost of a plan increases significantly during a plan year, the plan may permit employees to increase contributions or change options.

3. *Significant curtailment of coverage.* If the coverage under a plan is significantly curtailed during a plan year, the plan may permit

employees to revoke their elections. Employees may elect other options.

4. *Addition or elimination of an option.* If a plan adds or eliminates an option during a plan year, the plan may permit employees to add the new option (or elect another option if an option has been eliminated.)

5. *Change in coverage of a spouse or dependent under another plan.* A plan may permit an employee to make an election change that corresponds with a change made under the plan of the spouse's or dependent's employer if the other employer's cafeteria plan has a different plan year.

Cafeteria plans can also allow mid-year plan changes to comply with the Family and Medical Leave Act (FMLA), the Health Insurance Accountability Act of 1996 (HIPAA), the Consolidated Omnibus Budget Reconciliation Act of 1985 (COBRA), or a qualified medical child support order.

Q 9:36 What changes in status permit participants in flexible spending arrangements to change their elections in mid-year?

Except for the items specified as being in the proposed regulations, the items in Q 9:35 apply to flexible spending accounts. The change in election must be consistent with the status change. For example, if an employee's spouse lost employment and health coverage, it would not be a consistent change to allow the employee to drop FSA coverage.

Q 9:37 Are changes in the cost of medical care options grounds for changing elections in mid-year?

The plan may permit automatic adjustment of employee premium contributions if the terms of the plan require changes in contributions. This adjustment feature must be properly specified in the plan document.

If the third party "significantly" increases the cost of medical coverage, the plan may allow employees to revoke their election and select another "similar" health plan. Regulations do not require the similar health plan to be of the same employer.

The IRS had informally stated that mid-year benefit election changes are not permitted when a self-funded medical plan cost is significantly increased, but the 2000 proposed regulations allow self-funded plans to change contributions on a pre-tax basis.

Q 9:38 If an employer introduces a new benefit mid-year, can participants increase salary reductions to elect coverage under the new benefit for the remainder of the year?

Plan participants may increase their salary reduction election mid-year to elect coverage under a new benefit for the remainder of the year, provided the benefit was not offered before that time.

Q 9:39 Can a cafeteria plan permit a participant to make a mid-year election change if the participant's first election was a mistake?

Mid-year election changes are permitted if there is clear and convincing evidence the first election was a mistake. An election will only be considered a mistake if it was clear from facts available at the time of the election that a participant could not benefit from the coverage chosen. For example, if someone elected dependent care coverage, but had no eligible dependents, the mistake could be corrected. Incorrectly estimating the amount needed in a flexible spending account is not considered a mistake.

Q 9:40 Are mid-year election changes permitted when a day care provider changes its rate?

Yes. Participants may elect new salary reduction amounts if the provider changes its rates.

Q 9:41 Is a mid-year election change permitted when a parent changes day care providers?

Yes, the proposed regulations allow a change in dependent care spending account elections when an employee changes day care providers.

Q 9:42 Is a mid-year election to increase dependent care salary reductions permitted if the participant raises a nanny's salary?

Yes, the proposed regulations allow an increase in dependent care spending account elections because of an increase in salary for a household employee.

Q 9:43 Can a participant who has elected cash in lieu of benefits make a mid-year election to opt into a benefit plan?

Yes, if the participant has a change in status and if the plan document permits mid-year election changes. A plan sponsor could choose to restrict status changes to participants who elect nontaxable benefits at the beginning of the plan year.

Q 9:44 Can medical coverage commence mid-year under a cafeteria plan to comply with a court order?

Yes. The final regulations allow a cafeteria plan to comply with a court order, such as a qualified medical child support order. An employee can also cancel coverage if an order requires a former spouse to provide coverage.

Q 9:45 Can coverage be effective before a participant makes a mid-year election?

No, services cannot be covered under a cafeteria plan before the election of coverage, except in the case of a newborn or adopted child. If the employee enrolls within 30 days of birth, adoption, or placement for adoption, coverage is retroactive to the date of birth, adoption, or placement (as required by HIPAA.)

Q 9:46 What is a modular plan?

Modular flexible plans offer employees a choice of benefit packages. The employer determines combinations of coverage from which employees may choose. The employee selects the benefit package rather than the level of coverage within each benefit. For example,

Plan A might have life insurance equal to three times salary, a comprehensive medical plan with a $200 deductible and 80 percent coinsurance, and disability insurance equal to 50 percent of salary. Plan B might have life insurance equal to two times salary, a comprehensive medical plan with a $400 deductible and 80 percent coinsurance, and disability insurance equal to 60 percent of salary. Plan C might have life insurance equal to salary, a comprehensive medical plan with a $1,000 deductible and 80 percent coinsurance, and disability insurance equal to 60 percent of salary. Each employee could then choose Plan A, B, or C, or, if the employer allows, none of the plans. Employees could not, however, choose only part of each plan. Generally, these plans are only partially responsive to employee needs, but offer moderate control of adverse selection and price stability; therefore, these plans are not common.

Q 9:47 What is a core-plus plan?

Core-plus flexible plans provide a certain level of benefits for all employees participating in the benefit plan, with employees having the option to increase one or all of the coverage. The core level is usually funded by the employer. For example, with this plan, employees would be provided with $50,000 life insurance, a comprehensive medical plan with a $500 deductible, and disability insurance equal to 50 percent of salary. They would then have the option to increase their life, medical, or disability insurance benefits if they so desired, or perhaps add dental, which is not included in the core. These plans are more responsive to employee needs than modular plans. Most flexible benefit plans can be characterized as core-plus plans.

Q 9:48 What is a working spouse plan?

Working spouse plans allow employees to elect a supplemental plan, such as a plan with a 20 percent benefit designed to supplement an 80 percent benefit. Employees would make this election when their spouses are covered by another plan, such as the spouse's employer plan.

Q 9:49 What is a full-menu or total flexible benefits plan?

While there is no industrywide definition or agreement about what constitutes a "full" menu, the term is commonly accepted to mean any plan with more than one category of coverage in which choice is available. The number of choices available within a specific category is not especially relevant, although it is generally assumed to mean more than two choices.

For example, a flexible benefits plan that allowed three, four, or even 10 choices among only medical plans, but no other type of benefit, would not be considered a full-menu plan. In contrast, a flex plan providing, for example, two choices each for medical, dental, life insurance, and long-term disability would be considered a full-menu plan. Most flex plans allow more than two choices within some categories.

Q 9:50 Are full-menu plans restricted to large employers?

Yes and no. The "yes" derives from the administration of the plan. Administering a full-menu plan involves pre-tax deductions from employee paychecks, recordkeeping of various enrollment choices, and myriad other administrative concerns attendant on a flex program. The effort and systems involved are often beyond the capability of many smaller employers, although as systems improve and software prices drop, flex plan administration is becoming feasible even for small employers.

On the other hand, there is no inherent design reason why small employers cannot offer full-menu plans if they should choose to do so. Some authorities may view full-menu plans as inappropriate for small employers predicated on the theory that each option offered must have sufficient participation to provide an adequate "spread of risk"; however, it is perfectly feasible to combine the coverage risk under all options within a category.

When an employer establishes a flex plan, it makes sense to do so only with the intent of offering employees a true economic choice. To offer employees a choice between two plans, where, for example, Plan A pays 100 percent and Plan B pays 50 percent, would, effectively, be no choice if there were no other distinction between them (such as the price the employee pays). Every employee would take Plan A. It is therefore fundamental to flex design that each choice come with a price attached to it. While it is not imperative, it is appropriate that a participating employee's cost bear some relationship to the cost of the plan.

> **Example 9-1.** Employees will pay 100 percent of the actual cost of each plan; the employer will contribute nothing. The total cost of each plan is divided by the number of employees participating in the plan, and each employee pays a proportionate share of whichever plan he or she chooses. The employer need only communicate the cost of each plan and turn it into a paycheck deduction. Presumably, the better plan will cost more because it provides more in benefits; however, if there are not enough employees in one option to provide a sufficient spread of risk (probably Plan B in this example), the option lacks underwriting credibility. The cost of that option, then, might fluctuate wildly from year to year. Perhaps worse, the cost between Plan A and Plan B could invert, with Plan B costing more than Plan A. Naturally, the employer could subsidize either plan with whatever employer contributions were required to prevent either wild fluctuations or inversion of the prices. The result would, however, be the forfeiture of all rationality between the cost of the plan and the employee's contributions.

This undesirable situation can be avoided if the employer is willing to recombine the experience (costs) of Plan A and Plan B, and then to develop a method of apportioning the costs in some equitable manner to become the "cost" of each plan. Aside from the extra work, it does expose an employer to charges of being arbitrary, unfair, and subsidizing one plan with the other. In general, there is nothing wrong with subsidizing one plan with another. The employer should, however, communicate the rationale behind its actions to employees to secure their understanding.

Q 9:51 What are life cycle flex plans?

Life cycle flex plans represent a variation in flex design whereby the changing needs of the employee over different life stages is taken into consideration and, ideally, integrated into a single equitable benefit program. These plans include benefits that are specific to only some periods of an employee's life—such as child care, elder care, home purchase assistance, and long-term illness care—as well as the traditional lifelong benefits such as life and health insurance. The goal of the life cycle concept is to take benefit equity one step further while providing employees with support throughout different phases of their lives, thereby helping to retain them and keep them productive. Some elections are taxable, while others are not.

The life cycle approach is based on recognizing some of the realities of employee benefit needs and utilization. For example, some employees may never need to use child care benefits, but may well need elder care at some time in their lives. By providing both within a flexible plan concept, employers can ensure benefit equity among employees. Another example of a life cycle type of benefit is home purchase assistance. This can be offered on a once-per-career basis, with the amount of assistance prorated to salary or years of service. Other benefits that fit into the life cycle approach include flexible work time, employee assistance programs, legal services, adoption benefits, financial planning, health screening, and various types of leaves of absence.

Q 9:52 What is a life cycle allowance?

Some employers use life cycle allowances as an equitable method of funding life cycle benefits. They function as lifetime benefits spending accounts: Each employee is provided with a fixed amount of benefit dollars to use over his or her career for any of the life cycle benefits on the menu. The amount of the allowance may be adjusted for salary or other factors, may be accrued over service, or may be a flat amount, and there are usually annual spending caps to prevent abuses.

Life cycle allowances give employees flexibility in how they spend their benefit dollars, letting them use them where and when they need them most. In a given year, one employee may use his allowance to pay for child care; another may use hers to pay for home care for her elderly parent; a third may use it on legal services for a divorce; and yet another may hold her allowance in reserve, planning on using it to help purchase a home in another year.

Q 9:53 What types of benefits do cafeteria plans include?

Cafeteria plans include such benefits as:

- Medical benefits
- Dental benefits
- Health care reimbursement accounts
- Dependent care reimbursement accounts
- Life insurance
- Accidental death and dismemberment (AD&D) insurance
- Long-term disability
- Short-term disability
- 401(k) cash-or-deferred arrangements
- Vacation
- Vision care

Vacations

Q 9:54 How common is it to include vacation buying and selling in cafeteria plans?

Most plans do not allow vacation buying and selling because it is considered too complicated and too expensive to administer. The Mercer/Foster Higgins 1998 survey found that vacation buying or selling was an option in 23 percent of the flexible benefits plans.

Q 9:55 What are the tax consequences of letting employees transfer vacation days to other employees?

When employees transfer unused vacation time to other employees or to a leave bank from which employees with emergencies may draw supplemental time off, the IRS has clarified the tax status of donor and donee. [Rev Rul 90-29, 1990-15 IRB 5] Amounts paid to an employee under the leave-sharing plan are treated as compensation received from the employer and are, therefore, taxable. Employees who surrender leave to the employer or to the leave bank realize no income either on the occasion of the surrender or at the time it is used by the other worker.

Q 9:56 What are some advantages of allowing employees to buy or sell vacation days?

For health care planners, the chief advantage is that allowing the buying or selling of vacation days gives employees more flexibility in benefit planning, so that the relative importance of benefits can be reassessed, and the benefit mix rearranged, from one year to the next.

When employees are allowed to sell vacation, they can also avoid "use it or lose it" rules, where only a limited amount of unused vacation time may be carried over from one year to the next; anything in excess of a maximum number of carryover days may be forfeited. Vacation selling means that employees who cannot take vacation because of extraordinary job demands are not punished by losing leave forever (a genuine morale issue), and the company avoids the awkwardness of having to make special exceptions to their leave policies for these workers.

Another advantage is that vacation buying allows employees to match vacation schedules with spouses and children. Families who vacation together need some conformity in available time off. The individual who has two weeks off compared to his or her spouse's three has a way of equalizing available time off if vacations are included in a flex plan. Vacation buying also permits employees to take a big vacation without cutting back in other years.

Overall, flexibility in planning their leisure time makes employees feel less controlled and more in control of their own activities—and both make the job and the employer seem more attractive.

Q 9:57 What are the disadvantages of allowing employees to buy or sell vacation days?

One concern of many companies is that if employees have the option of increasing their vacations, their decisions could complicate scheduling in critical areas at critical times. A key consideration: Does an employee on vacation have to be replaced, or is there enough slack in the system to permit productivity to continue without him or her for limited periods?

Companies must also consider the types of employees who will be buying or selling vacation time. Salaried employees are paid to produce specific results; allowing them to sell can mean paying more for the same amount of work. Another consideration: Will higher-paid employees buy and lower-paid employees sell (or vice versa)? Time-off flexibility is very popular, especially with those types of employees who are hardest to retain: highly skilled people who can move freely and are most likely to consider working for themselves. Does that mean that the program will be essentially a transfer payment from one class of employees to another?

Added cost is another concern. For example, companies with very liberal vacation policies may have found that many employees did not use their full allotment of time off—and lost it when that amount exceeded a pre-set limit (e.g., a maximum of five or ten days carried over from year to year). Such employees would be quick to sell these surplus days if offered the option, thereby creating a new expense for the company.

Finally, cash-out of unused vacation time tends to be an end-of-year problem, creating difficulties with payroll.

Q 9:58 What sorts of restrictions should be placed on vacation buying and selling options?

Availability of additional time off should not interfere with normal rules on scheduling vacations and limits on the number of consecutive days off. Sales can be limited to "extra" days above the minimum number of vacation days that the company requires every employee to take a year. Only days in excess of the minimum may be sold. Also, caps on the total number of days, consecutive and total, to be taken without special permission should be established.

Companies can limit the sale price so that the highly paid do not have an advantage—that is, sell a day or two and buy out the entire benefit package. Other companies limit the buying price to make sure that extra days are available to a wide range of employees.

Flexible Benefit Options

Q 9:59 What medical insurance options are available under a cafeteria plan?

The design of medical options under a cafeteria plan is not restricted; however, offering a base-plus plan as an option is not advisable if cost control is an objective. In fact, a flex plan provides an opportunity for an employer to move its plan from a base-plus to a more cost-effective comprehensive plan, or to increase the deductible on a comprehensive plan, with less difficulty.

Most flexible plans offer several choices of deductibles and out-of-pocket maximums. Some include a catastrophic illness plan with a high deductible and no coinsurance, and may allow an employee to take no medical coverage at all if covered elsewhere. The deductibles are designed with different life situations in mind and combined so that the choices among options are meaningful.

Q 9:60 Can a cafeteria plan reimburse employees for individual health insurance policies they purchase?

A cafeteria plan may reimburse employees for the purchase of individual health insurance policies, subject to the following conditions:

1. The plan document must state that the plan will provide for payment of individual health insurance policies.
2. Reimbursement cannot be from a flexible spending account.
3. The policy must be owned by the employee. This rule precludes reimbursement of premiums paid to the spouse's employer for group coverage.

Q 9:61 Can a flexible plan include an HMO?

Yes, an HMO can be among the medical options offered in a flexible plan; however, evidence indicates that this can adversely affect the cost of the rest of the plan, whether it is insured or self-funded, because younger, healthier employees may be more likely to choose the health maintenance organization (HMO).

Q 9:62 Can a flexible plan include a PPO?

Yes, a preferred provider organization (PPO) can be incorporated into one or more of the medical options offered in a flexible plan. The level of reimbursement for each person will depend on whether the insured uses a preferred provider or not, as well as on the plan option selected for the plan year. The PPO arrangement is the same as it would be for a traditional plan.

Q 9:63 Is all the insurance provided under a flexible plan provided by one insurer, or do insurers bid for pieces?

Plans may be designed and handled either way; however, small employers often prefer to place all coverage and reimbursement accounts with one insurer, because it simplifies implementation and administration.

Q 9:64 What are the advantages of using one carrier?

When using one carrier, integration of all parts of the plan is inherent in its design, and all procedures, including enrollment, are coordinated. This makes installation more efficient. On an ongoing basis, plan administrators deal with one set of procedures, and forms and processes can be streamlined. For example, claims submitted but not covered in full under the medical or dental insurance plan can be automatically transferred for reimbursement from the health care reimbursement account. All of this should add up to lower costs in the long run.

Q 9:65 Does a cafeteria plan allow employees to select cash instead of benefits?

Yes, although the degree to which employees can receive cash instead of benefits varies by employer. Some employers require that employees maintain a level of medical insurance protection (through their spouse's plan, for example) if the employee wants to forgo all benefits and select cash exclusively.

Q 9:66 Can a 401(k) plan be integrated into a cafeteria plan?

Yes. The Miscellaneous Revenue Act of 1980 amended Code Section 125 to allow cafeteria plans to include 401(k) plans, which are "cash-or-deferred" arrangements under which employers can make nontaxable contributions to qualified defined contribution plans. Employees can make similar contributions through salary reduction, thereby deferring taxes on a portion of their incomes. Code Section 401(k) plans are the only deferred-compensation plans allowed in cafeteria plans. Contributions to 401(k) plans are subject to FICA taxes.

Q 9:67 What are the advantages and disadvantages of including a 401(k) plan in a flexible plan?

In addition to the tax advantages to both employers and employees, packaging a 401(k) plan with a flex plan makes administration of the 401(k) plan easier for the employer. The same salary reduction payroll system is used for both plans, and employees make their contributions and coverage choices at the same time. Also, employees may appreciate their benefit package more if they see the total package in an integrated manner. The disadvantage of including a 401(k) plan as part of a flexible benefits plan is that the Code Section 125 nondiscrimination requirements are imposed on the 401(k) plan, in addition to the 401(k) rules. This is most troublesome for small employers, who are more likely to run afoul of the 25 percent concentration test. This disadvantage can be overcome by offering the 401(k) plan alongside a flexible benefits plan. Technically, the employee converts flexible credits to cash, then elects to reduce salary under the 401(k) plan.

Q 9:68 Why would all employees not choose the plan options that offered the best coverage?

The types of benefits provided under each option in a flexible plan are often the same or similar. What differs is the level of coverage offered and the cost of the coverage. For example, an employee can choose one of several life insurance coverage levels—the difference is in the amount of insurance protection the employee elects. With medical coverage under a flexible plan, the deductibles and the out-of-pocket maximums generally are the differentiation factors, although the coinsurance level and benefit features may also vary, especially in a catastrophic option. Although one choice may be "richer" than another, it will cost more. Many employees prefer not to pay this extra cost. They feel that these benefit dollars would be more wisely spent on another insurance coverage for which they have greater need, or they prefer to receive the difference in cash, as deposits to their 401(k) accounts, or as additional paid time off.

Q 9:69 What is the purpose of waivers in a flexible benefits plan?

A key objective of flexible benefits plans is to let employees decide which coverage they need and want and which they do not. If they have a particular type of coverage elsewhere (e.g., through a spouse's plan), it would be costly for an employer to provide the same duplicate coverage. Flex plans let workers eliminate unnecessary or duplicate items from their benefits and add more of those benefits they really need. This means allowing employees to elect more of benefit A and to waive or opt out of benefit B. Some plans provide cash, cash equivalents, or other incentives (such as vacation days) to those who opt for less of a given benefit.

Q 9:70 Why should there be controls on waivers?

Employers will face problems if they permit unlimited waivers. Suppose an employee opts out of needed medical coverage and goes for cash instead, but subsequently incurs an expensive illness or disability. Should he or she be left to suffer the consequences, or should the employer attempt to find some way to help? If the employee changes his or her mind, the cafeteria plan regulations restrict changes.

To avoid complications like these, many flex plans require the employee to show proof of coverage from another source before permitting a waiver. Company policy on rescinding waivers usually varies according to the nature of the benefit. Where adverse selection is a particular problem, especially with long-term disability and group term life coverage, the privilege of opting back in is usually contingent upon (1) the employee's demonstrating that he or she is in good health and/or (2) a waiting period of up to a year.

Q 9:71 What sorts of policies have employers adopted regarding waivers?

The 1998 Mercer/Foster Higgins Health Care Benefits Survey found that 93 percent of flexible benefits plans permitted employees to waive employee medical coverage and fewer than half required proof of other coverage.

A Towers Perrin survey of 212 flexible benefits plan sponsors found that employers are more likely to let employees opt out of health care coverage than the less costly group term life or long-term disability. Those that permit waivers reported that a larger percentage of employees exercised the right to opt out with dental and long-term disability than with medical and group term life.

The insistence on proof of coverage was heaviest with medical coverage, with 51 percent of respondents requiring such proof. At the other extreme, none of the respondents required any proof of coverage from employees waiving group term life. Dental and long-term disability proof of coverage was required by 5 percent and 3 percent of respondents, respectively. Some companies required only a statement from the employee listing the source (the covering employer) of the alternative coverage and a policy number. Others required statements from the other employer, sworn statements from the employee, or photocopies of the insurance card. Of those who required proof, 74 percent required the information to be furnished each year.

Implementation

Q 9:72 How are flexible benefits plans funded?

There are two sources of funding: employer contributions and employee contributions. This is true pertaining to the funding of traditional benefit plans as well as flexible benefits plans.

Flexible benefits plans are typically thought of as Section 125 plans. Under Code Section 125, employee contributions can be made on a pre-tax basis or a post-tax basis. Determining whether benefits will be funded using pre- or post-tax contributions is one of the major aspects of designing a flexible benefits plan.

Q 9:73 What factors should be considered when deciding between using pre- or post-tax contributions?

For medical plans, the overwhelming choice is to use pre-tax contributions. For disability, particularly long-term disability (LTD), the one most often requiring employee contributions, the argument is not cut and dried. If the employer utilizes pre-tax contributions, the benefit will be taxable income to the employee when it is received. Considering that the employee will be disabled at this time, and perhaps not receiving more income than the LTD benefit, it hurts to have to pay taxes on it. Alternatively, if the employee contribution is post-tax, the tax-free benefit will be based on the employee's contribution in proportion to the employer's contribution. That is, if the employee contributes 30 percent of the premium, 30 percent of the benefit will be tax-free when received.

The trade-off is that pre-tax contributions will benefit everyone who signs up for the coverage a little bit. Post-tax contributions will benefit, perhaps greatly, the few who receive the benefit.

Caution: Life insurance can involve complications. If an employer is providing term life insurance, it is okay to use pre-tax contributions; however, if an employer is providing universal life (group or individual), pre-tax money cannot be used. One of the fundamental aspects of universal life is that it cannot be purchased with employer money. For this purpose, pre-tax contributions are considered to be employer contributions and are therefore prohibited.

Q 9:74 Must flexible benefits plans be contributory?

Yes. A flex plan simply would not achieve anything if the benefits were not contributory in one way or another. Flexible benefits plans have been created to give employees choice, often with the underlying intent of channeling employees into the most cost-efficient plan available. (This does not necessarily mean the cheapest plan—it could well mean an HMO or point-of-service plan, even if that plan initially costs the employer more.) Channeling implies that a certain choice will be encouraged, but that employees are free to choose some other plan if they are willing to pay for it. The only way to accomplish this is through varying employee contributions.

The word "contribution" is used here in the broadest sense. It implies that an employee choosing between varying amounts of cash back is the same as an employee choosing between varying amounts to be contributed.

Example 9-2. The employer has three medical plans: A, B, and C. Plan A pays 100 percent, B pays 85 percent, and C pays 70 percent. To purchase one of these plans, the employee has a choice between Scheme 1 or Scheme 2.

	Employee Contribution		
	Plan A	*Plan B*	*Plan C*
Scheme 1	$300	$200	$100
Scheme 2	($100)	($200)	($300)

While Scheme 1 is a self-explanatory concept, Scheme 2 may deserve a word of explanation.

The fact that an employee forgoes receiving an additional $100 or $200 as a consequence of having chosen Plan A over B or C represents real cost. Were this a full-menu plan, the employee would presumably have been able to "spend" the $100 or $200 on, for example, additional life insurance, better dental coverage, more vacation, or cash.

Q 9:75 How does an employer determine its level of contribution to the flexible plan?

Employers can determine their levels of contribution to a flexible plan in a number of ways, such as freezing benefit costs as a percentage of payroll, determining a set dollar amount to spend on employee benefits, or contributing the same amount they did under the traditional benefit plan. All of these options are based, however, on the employer's objectives in establishing a flexible plan. Although these objectives may differ for each employer, they can generally be broken down into three categories, which are not necessarily exclusive:

1. Attract and retain the best employees.
2. Control costs.
3. Reduce costs while maintaining an adequate benefit plan.

The contribution level will differ just as the structure and design of the plan will vary, according to the employer's objectives. If the plan is a tool to attract and retain employees, employer contributions would probably be higher than if the objective were to reduce costs.

Q 9:76 How are employee contribution levels determined?

Employee contributions are determined by the employer at the beginning of each plan year and vary depending on a number of factors, including the cost of the plan, the benefits each employee selects, and the level of employer contributions.

Q 9:77 How are employer and employee contributions made in a full flexible benefits plan?

Employer contributions are commonly made by allocating credits to a "decision pool." Employee contributions consist of pre-tax contributions to the decision pool. A decision pool represents the combined contributions of employer and employee, and is the amount available for each employee to pay insurance premiums for chosen benefits, fund reimbursement accounts, or receive as cash instead of benefits.

Q 9:78 Can small employers self-fund flexible benefits plans?

Small employers can self-fund their flexible benefits plans, but the adverse selection issues discussed at Q 9:80 become more acute for them. If self-funding is desired, employers need a skilled and experienced intermediary to assist with plan design, implementation, administration, and renewal.

Q 9:79 Is purchasing a flexible benefits plan similar to purchasing a traditional plan?

Flexible benefits plans are purchased in much the same way that traditional plans are. The employer, working with its insurance intermediary (broker, agent, or consultant), might survey employees to determine their needs, and must establish its own objectives. The intermediary then solicits quotes from insurers and assists the employer in selecting the benefits based on the needs and objectives.

Q 9:80 How does adverse selection affect flexible benefits plans?

With a flexible benefits plan, employees select a package of benefits that reflects their specific needs. Thus, they are most likely to select benefits they will actually use. This phenomenon is known as "adverse selection." Adverse selection does not actually cause higher utilization of benefits: Employees generally use what they need, and claims remain the same. What does result is that less premium is available from those who do not use their benefits to pay for those benefits that are used.

This means, then, that pricing the benefits in a flexible benefits plan and predicting benefit utilization is a complicated process. Insurance companies and the larger consulting firms have actuarial professionals who can estimate fairly accurately the expected cost of each flexible benefits plan component, and can make demographic predictions of who will elect certain benefits as well as who will use the benefits. In addition, the financial resources of most insurers allow them to absorb the financial consequences of some inaccurate predictions. In the future, as the accuracy of prediction of utilization increases, employers may be in a better position to consider assuming more of the risk of flexible benefits plans. Small employers will still be subject to the volatility of utilization that comes with being able to spread the risk over only a relatively few employees.

For an employer with fewer than 500 employees that is implementing a flexible benefits plan for the first time, insurance is highly recommended, because the financial risk associated with utilization in a flexible benefits plan is greater than with a traditional benefit plan.

Adverse selection is not an issue for very small employers with fully pooled insured plans (although it may be an issue for the insurance company). A small employer can offer employees a flat dollar amount that can be applied to health insurance or other benefits or taken in cash without directly affecting health insurance costs.

Q 9:81 What specific issues should an employer address in contemplating the purchase of a flexible benefits plan?

Most companies adopt flexible benefits plans to meet the needs of a diverse workforce, to attract and retain employees, to manage and control costs, and to achieve tax-effective use of their benefits dollars; however, although these are the basic reasons for purchasing a flexible plan, designing a plan to meet these objectives requires a more precise analysis.

The specific issues that employers should address before designing a plan include whether the company is considering the following:

1. Offering better benefits than companies competing with it for skilled labor;
2. Raising employee morale by offering better benefits;
3. Retaining top-level management;
4. Preventing unionization;
5. Improving the company's image;
6. Increasing equity in benefits among employees, regardless of marital status or income;
7. Increasing employee awareness of the cost of medical care;
8. Separating benefit costs from benefit levels; and
9. Spending no more than a predetermined dollar amount on the benefit package for a specific period of time.

Plan features, including coverage, levels, and costs, can be designed differently to accomplish the objectives of each individual company. For example, if a company wants to offer a more attractive benefit plan than its competition, but still needs to control costs, the flexible plan can be designed so that the employer provides the same level of benefits as under its traditional plan, but gives employees the option to purchase additional benefits through pre-tax salary reduction. For an employer that is interested in cost control and determines, therefore, that it cannot spend more than a certain dollar amount on benefits, the plan can be structured so that the benefits offered remain the same, and the employer's contribution remains the same even if the cost of benefits rises. In such an example, the employee who wanted to maintain the previous level of benefits would assume more responsibility for the purchase of the benefits.

Proper design of a flexible plan requires an analysis of the company's specific situation, the employer's objectives, and the employees' benefit needs.

Q 9:82 How can an employer determine its employees' benefit needs?

Employee needs can be determined by a written survey that should be administered at least six months before the proposed effective date of the flexible benefits plan. When planned and analyzed carefully by the employer, consultant, or insurer, a survey can provide valuable information for designing a flexible plan that will be well-received by employees. Just as employers must determine precisely what their needs are, it is important to determine what employees want in their benefit package.

In addition, an employee needs survey is one tool for having the employees participate in designing the plan. This involvement, in turn, will lead to greater employee acceptance of the flexible plan and the advantages it offers; however, some employers feel a survey is unnecessary. They have other reliable means of knowing employee needs and would prefer not to spend the time to conduct a survey.

Q 9:83 Are there any resources that would be useful in researching flexible benefit plans?

The Employers Council on Flexible Compensation publishes reference material related to flexible benefits plans. For more information, contact:

ECFC
927 15th Street NW, Suite 1000
Washington, DC 20005
Telephone: (202) 659-4300

Q 9:84 How are flexible benefits plans implemented?

Implementation of a flexible benefits plan is generally the same as for a traditional plan: The plan is announced, employees are enrolled and receive information concerning their benefits, and the plan becomes effective. Although the basic outline for plan implementation remains the same, each of the steps involved requires different tactics. For example, the plan announcement requires more communication from the company to the employees in order to explain the new concept of flexible benefits, and the enrollment of employees is more involved.

Q 9:85 How long does it take from the purchase of a flexible benefits plan until it can be implemented?

The preliminary analysis of employer objectives and employee needs can take somewhat longer than for a traditional benefit plan, depending on the size of the employer and the complexities involved in compensation analysis. This analysis will be done before the plan is quoted, as with traditional plans.

The time from the initial quote on the plan design to the actual effective date of the plan is usually at least four months. The first month is spent reviewing the quote for its success in meeting the employer's determined objectives. Actual implementation, once the decision to buy has been made and the final plan design settled on, requires two-and-a-half to three months. Larger employers typically require more time because they have to communicate with more employees and deal with more data.

Q 9:86 What kinds of employee communications are advisable in advance of enrollment?

As the size of the employee group increases, so does the intensity of the communication effort involved in flexible benefits plan implementation. Regardless of size, careful, clear communication is essential. Employers usually use a letter from the chief executive officer or president of the company to announce the flexible benefits plan. Posters may be placed in strategic locations around the company to introduce the concept of flex. Also, in preparation for enrollment, some explanation of the concept of flexible benefits, in easily understood form, should be given to employees. A simple conceptual brochure can serve this purpose. After enrollment, some employers send employees confirmation of their elections. This allows employees to correct mistakes without the need to comply with the rules regarding changes (see Qs 9:34 and following).

Q 9:87 How do employees enroll in a plan and select their benefits?

Because understanding is so critical to making the most appropriate choices, employee meetings are usually held to explain the flexible benefits plan. They may be conducted by the employer, an intermediary, the insurer, or a combination of them. At those meetings, employees are provided with a written explanation of the process and forms on which to make their selections. The forms will typically identify the benefit options and their costs, as well as the amount of benefit dollars provided by the employer. Employees are expected to make choices and calculate their total costs, including the salary reduction that will result if selections cost more than the amount the employer provides. If an employee opts for fewer benefits than his or her benefit dollars cover, the plan might provide that he or she receive the excess as additional taxable income.

To minimize confusion to employees, particularly during the first plan year, enrollment requires a great deal of employee education, even after employee meetings have been held and the materials have been distributed. An employer representative must be knowledgeable and should be available to answer questions during the enrollment period, which is usually at least two months prior to the effective date. This educational effort takes time, but the employer's genuine concern for employee needs is communicated repeatedly, often resulting in increased employee morale.

The enrollment process can result in some dissatisfied employees, especially if previous benefits were extremely comprehensive and some new limitations are being imposed. It is advisable for management to determine what communication of compensation objectives is necessary before the flexible benefits plan is announced, to assure maximum satisfaction.

Q 9:88 Are "default" or "negative" elections permitted in a cafeteria plan?

Yes, but not for an individual's initial election under the plan. If an individual has affirmatively elected an option, the plan can continue the option for that individual in subsequent years, even without a subsequent election, as long as the individual is given notification and time to change the election before each year. A default election is permitted for flexible spending accounts as well as other cafeteria plan options.

Q 9:89 What is enrollment confirmation?

Employees are provided with a summary of their individual benefit choices and the costs associated with them. They may be asked to verify the accuracy of the summary by signing and returning it to the company's personnel accounting department, which in turn directs it to the administrator of the flexible plan. Usually a short period is allowed for employees to change their choices or correct any errors or misunderstandings. Once signed, the summary serves as confirmation that the employee's choices are correct as recorded, and benefits will be paid based on the record.

Q 9:90 How do the cost and pricing of a flexible benefits plan compare with those of a traditional employee benefit plan?

The cost issue has two parts: (1) the cost of the benefits themselves, which incorporates the risk of adverse selection and the potential for cost management inherent in a flexible benefits plan; and (2) the cost involved in developing and implementing the program.

The cost of the benefits, if insured, will be based on the insurer's underlying price structure, which usually applies to traditional as well as flexible benefits plans. Traditional insurance allows insurers to calculate an average rate for the group to be covered and multiply it by the number of employees and dependents enrolled or, for some coverages, such as life and disability, by the volume of insurance elected overall. Insurers' methods for flexible plan pricing vary. They must take into account selection assumptions and utilization rates. The risk of adverse selection is in addition to the utilization risks in a single traditional plan. Such risk may be assumed by the employer or the insurer. An intermediary can help the employer obtain an acceptable pricing agreement with an insurer.

Cost management or cost control is most applicable to medical coverage. Decisions about features such as coinsurance variations, deductibles, and preferred provider arrangements are not inherently different for flexible benefits plan coverage, but a flexible plan, by virtue of the availability of choice, allows an employer to introduce plan features that promise long-term cost control. Furthermore, by establishing the basis for future contributions for the employee benefit plan, an employer can begin the process of long-term cost management.

Depending on who performs the services associated with design and implementation of the plan, the costs of these services may be charged separately or incorporated in the benefit cost. Excellent communication materials and enrollment assistance are available to employers of all sizes at reasonable costs. Ongoing administration costs generally depend on the frequency of the services requested, such as reimbursement account payments and reports.

Q 9:91 How does renewal of a flexible benefits plan compare with traditional employee benefit plan renewal?

Annual reenrollment makes renewal of a flexible benefits plan somewhat more time-consuming. Renewal costs will be based on prior elections and anticipated changes, plan design adjustments, and the insurer's medical care costs in general; however, for some plans, the past experience of the total plan and its options are used separately to compute renewal costs. The process also takes more time than for traditional plans, because there are more alternatives for meeting the employer's objectives, which also may have changed.

Q 9:92 What kinds of reports are necessary to ensure smooth implementation and administration of a flexible plan?

In addition to the standard reports associated with utilization, additions and deletions of employees and dependents, and premium accounting reports, three flexible benefits plan reports are necessary. A salary impact report is usually generated after enrollment confirmation. This identifies the costs of the benefits and the salary reduction or increase associated with each employee's choices. It is the blueprint for changes to the employer's payroll system.

For plans with health care reimbursement or dependent care reimbursement accounts, periodic reports are necessary for employees and the employer to summarize available funds in each account and payments made from them. For plans with 401(k) plans, an individual periodic report showing employee contributions, employer contributions, interest, and fund balances is recommended, as well as an employer summary for the plan.

Q 9:93 How does an employer decide who will administer the flexible benefits plan?

After understanding what is involved in administering a flexible benefits plan, an employer must evaluate the options available. Resources (both systems and people), priorities, and cost should be considered, taking into account the efficiencies of working with one source for the entire plan.

The employer may decide for simplicity's sake to select an insurer that has the ability to administer the plan as well as provide the plan design and coverage options. Insurers that offer flexible plans to small employers will generally also offer administrative support. Some insurers also offer special software packages to small employers for plan administration.

If the employer has the systems necessary to administer the plan or is willing to invest in such areas because of anticipated cost savings, then the employer could administer the plan itself. Third-party administrators are also an option, as are brokers and consultants who have the systems available. Thus, many options are available to the employer for administering the plan.

Q 9:94 What type of billing arrangement is used: self-accounting or home office?

Complete records of each employee's current choices must be kept, regardless of how a flexible benefits plan is billed. Generally, the first bill would identify each employee and the costs associated with his or her selections. Subsequent bills can reflect only the changes to choices as a result of the addition of new employees, termination of employees, or changes in family status. This is somewhere between what is commonly referred to as self-accounting and home-office billing by insurance companies.

Q 9:95 What special rules apply to cafeteria plans under FMLA?

On December 21, 1995, the Internal Revenue Service published proposed regulations on the effect of the Family and Medical Leave Act on the operation of cafeteria plans, also known as Section 125 plans or flexible benefits plans. Some of the rules were expected, but others were not. The most noteworthy items were:

1. An employee taking FMLA leave may revoke group health plan coverage, including coverage under a flexible spending arrangement, for the remainder of the coverage period.

2. A cafeteria plan may, on a nondiscriminatory basis, offer one or more of the following payment options: pre-pay, pay-as-you-go, and catch-up.

3. Under the pre-pay option, a plan may permit an employee to pay premiums before the start of the leave. Under FMLA regulations, this cannot be the only option offered. The new rule makes it clear that if FMLA leave spans two cafeteria plan years, employees cannot pre-pay premiums for the second year. Contributions under the pre-pay option can be made on either a pre-tax or after-tax basis.

4. Under the pay-as-you-go option, employees may pay on the same schedule as payments would be made if the employee were not on leave, under the payment schedule used for COBRA premiums, or any other system voluntarily agreed to between the employer and the employee that does not violate these rules. Pay-as-you-go contributions are generally after-tax, but pre-tax contributions may be made from taxable compensation, such as vacation days. The employer is not required to continue coverage for an employee who fails to make premium payments while on FMLA leave. If the employer chooses to continue coverage, including FSA coverage, for an employee who fails to

make premium payments, the employer is entitled to recoup these payments. If the pay-as-you-go option is offered to employees on non-FMLA leave, the pay-as-you-go option must also be offered to employees on FMLA leave.

5. If an employee elects the catch-up option, contributions can be either after-tax or pre-tax, even if the leave spans two years. The catch-up option can be the sole option offered to employees on FMLA leave only if the catch-up option is the sole option offered to employees on non-FMLA leave.

6. In addition to these options, employers can voluntarily waive employee contributions, on a nondiscriminatory basis, for employees on FMLA leave.

7. If an employee elects to terminate FSA coverage while on FMLA leave, the employer cannot require the employee to reinstate coverage upon return from FMLA leave. If an employee elects to reinstate FSA coverage, the employee's coverage for the rest of the year is prorated for the period during which no premiums were paid, less prior reimbursements.

Q 9:96 If a company with a cafeteria plan is acquired by another company, what happens to the cafeteria plan?

One option is to terminate the cafeteria plan as of the date of the acquisition. Many companies find this option unattractive because participants will forfeit unused balances in flexible spending accounts. This problem can be avoided by having the acquiring company adopt the cafeteria plan and maintain it until the end of the original plan year. If the acquiring company also maintains a cafeteria plan, the acquired cafeteria plan would be a separate plan. If the acquired cafeteria plan includes other plans (HMO, PPO, etc.) as well as FSAs, it is possible to maintain only the FSA portion while terminating the other plans.

Chapter 10

Medicare

Medicare is an important consideration for employers planning health insurance programs. This chapter explains who is covered by Medicare, the benefit coverage provided, how that coverage affects any other coverage, and how companies must coordinate these benefits.

The Basics	10-1
Medicare Order of Benefit Determination	10-8
Medicare Cost Containment	10-14
Medigap	10-18
Operation Data Match	10-20
Medicare+Choice	10-23

The Basics

Q 10:1 What is Medicare?

Medicare is a system of federal reimbursement for medical care to certain eligible elderly and disabled individuals. Medicare consists of a hospital benefits plan (Part A) and supplementary medical insurance (Part B). Part A covers individuals for expenses incurred at hospitals, extended care facilities, hospices, and some home health care. Part A is automatic at no fee to eligible individuals. It is funded by a hospital insurance tax that is part of the Federal Insurance

Contributions Act (FICA)/Self Employment Contribution Act (SECA) taxes.

Part B helps pay for physicians' services and other medical services not paid for under Part A. Participation in Part B is voluntary and requires premium contributions by the individual. Participation in Part A means automatic enrollment in Part B, but Part B participation is terminated if the individual files a notice withdrawing from Part B participation or fails to pay a premium within the three-month grace period.

Q 10:2 Who is eligible for Medicare coverage?

The following individuals are eligible for Medicare:

1. Individuals who are eligible for monthly Social Security or Railroad Retirement benefits, including retirees over the age of 65, dependents, or survivors;
2. Individuals, including those who are under age 65, who have been entitled to receive social security disability income for two years, or receive treatment for end-stage kidney disease; and
3. Persons 65 or older who are not eligible for Social Security or Railroad Retirement benefits, but who have qualified for hospital benefits by paying a monthly premium and enrolling in Part B.

The Consolidated Omnibus Budget Reconciliation Act of 1985 (COBRA) extended Medicare coverage to state and local government employees for services provided after March 31, 1986.

Q 10:3 How many people are covered by Medicare?

According to the Employee Benefit Research Institute, in December 1998 there were 39.7 million individuals enrolled in Medicare.

Q 10:4 What services are covered under Part A?

The following services, when provided by an approved provider of services, are covered for eligible individuals:

- Bed and board in a semiprivate room
- Hospital physician and nursing services
- Special care (e.g., intensive care)
- Drugs in a hospital
- X-rays and radiation therapy
- Hospital laboratory tests
- Operating room costs (including anesthesia)
- Recovery room costs
- Some home health services
- Inpatient rehabilitation (e.g., physical therapy or occupational therapy)

Q 10:5 What services are covered under Part B?

Part B covers:

- Services provided by medical doctors and osteopaths, including surgery, consultation, and visits, whether at home, in the office, or at a medical care institution
- Outpatient physician and hospital care, including drugs that cannot be self-administered
- Certain dental surgery
- Diagnostic x-rays and laboratory tests
- X-ray and radiation therapy
- Ambulances, if required by the patient's condition
- Costs of surgical devices, durable medical equipment, and prosthetic devices
- Colostomy supplies
- The first three pints of blood
- Some home health services

Q 10:6 What types of care are not covered by Medicare?

Medicare does not cover:

1. Private room in a hospital or nursing home (unless medically required);
2. Private nurse;
3. Routine physical checkups;
4. Dental services and dentures;
5. Custodial care;
6. Most services provided by optometrists, psychologists, and chiropractors;
7. Cosmetic surgery;
8. Personal comfort items, such as hospital TVs;
9. Most services provided outside the United States (except certain emergency inpatient care), services required as a result of war, and services covered by workers' compensation;
10. Orthopedic devices; and
11. Services or devices that are not reasonable and necessary for the diagnosis or treatment of illness or injury or to improve the function of a malformed part of the body.

Q 10:7 Does Medicare cover transplants?

Yes. The Health Care Financing Administration (HCPA) has said that lung and heart-lung transplants will no longer be considered experimental and will be covered by Medicare. Other transplants already covered by Medicare are heart, liver, and kidney transplants, and bone marrow transplants for treatment of leukemia and aplastic anemia.

Q 10:8 What preventive services are covered?

The Balanced Budget Act of 1997 expanded coverage of a number of preventive services under the traditional Medicare fee-for-service program. The new services include mammography, pap smears, pelvic exams, prostate cancer screening, colorectal screening, diabetes screening, and bone mass measurement. The bill also extended the vaccine outreach program for flu and pneumonia vaccinations.

Q 10:9 What is the Part A hospital deductible?

The deductible changes annually. For 2000 it is $776 per "benefit period." A benefit period is the time that begins on the first day of hospitalization and ends 60 consecutive days after the beneficiary has not been an inpatient in either a hospital or skilled nursing facility. For example, if Mr. A is hospitalized on February 22, is transferred to a skilled nursing facility on March 18, and is discharged from there on May 22, this benefit period for Mr. A would end on July 21.

There can be more than one benefit period per calendar year, and the deductible will apply for each benefit period.

Q 10:10 What are the new indexed coinsurance requirements?

The indexed coinsurance requirements for benefit periods in 2000 are as follows:

Category	Period	Coverage
Inpatient Hospital	First 60 days	Fully paid by Medicare
	61st–90th day	$194 per day
	Lifetime reserve	$388 per day (if used)
Skilled Nursing	First 20 days	Fully paid by Medicare
	21st–100th day	$97 per day

Q 10:11 Is there a maximum dollar out-of-pocket limit on the 20 percent coinsurance payable for Part B (physician) expenses?

No.

Q 10:12 What are the Part B deductible and coinsurance amounts?

The deductible is $100 per calendar year. The coinsurance is 20 percent of the Medicare-approved amount.

Example 10-1. Mrs. Jones receives medical services from Dr. White, totaling $400. This is the first claim of the year for Mrs.

Q 10:13   Health Insurance Answer Book

Jones, so no deductible has yet been paid, and Medicare approves the entire amount. Payment would be $240 from Medicare.

That is calculated as follows:

$400 total claim
− $100 deductible
= $300
× 80% Medicare payment
= $240

Q 10:13   What are the new Medicare premiums?

Part A does not require a premium payment from persons eligible for coverage under Social Security or Railroad Retirement benefits. The payments required are just the coinsurance and deductibles previously mentioned. For persons not automatically entitled to coverage in 2000, Part A may be purchased for $301 per month if they have less than 30 quarters of coverage or $166 if they have 30 to 39 quarters of coverage. Persons purchasing Part A coverage must also purchase Part B coverage.

The Part B premium for 2000 is $45.50 per month. Part B also requires coinsurance, as previously mentioned.

Q 10:14   What is the current Medicare payroll tax?

The Omnibus Budget Reconciliation Act (OBRA '93) repealed the $135,000 wage limit on the Medicare payroll tax. The tax rate is still 1.45 percent of wages, and as of January 1, 1994 applies to all wages. The employer and employee each pay 1.45 percent of wages.

Q 10:15   How much does a typical Medicare beneficiary spend on health?

An analysis by the American Association of Retired Persons showed that, on average, Medicare beneficiaries spent a fifth of their income on health in 1997. The low-income elderly spent a much higher percentage.

Beneficiaries spent an average of $2,149 on medical bills, including prescription drugs and Medigap policies, but not counting long-term care. Medicare beneficiaries living below the poverty line spent 35 percent of their annual income on medical expenses.

Q 10:16 When can someone enroll in Medicare?

People who want coverage as of the first of the month in which they turn age 65 should contact the Social Security Administration four months before they reach age 65. If someone rejects Medicare, they may enroll or re-enroll in January through March of any year, with coverage effective July first. Premiums for people who rejected coverage will be higher than for other beneficiaries, unless they were covered by a group health plan.

Q 10:17 Are there any plans to extend Medicare to more people?

Yes. President Clinton supports a bill that would help an estimated 300,000 people. This bill would allow the "near elderly," early retirees age 62 through 64 and laid-off employees age 55 through 64, to buy into Medicare.

Q 10:18 Are there any proposals to add benefits to Medicare?

Yes. Both President Clinton and Republicans have proposed adding a prescription drug benefit.

The National Bipartisan Commission on the Future of Medicare discussed adding prescription drug coverage to Medicare. The Commission disbanded without issuing a report because it could not achieve a super majority of members in favor of any proposal.

Q 10:19 What is balance billing?

This is a practice whereby nonparticipating physicians charge full fees, then bill the patient for that portion of the bill not reimbursed by Medicare. Under the current rules, nonparticipating physician fees cannot exceed 115 percent of Medicare allowable costs.

Balance billing is not permitted for those whose Medicare premiums are paid by Medicaid or Medicare beneficiaries below the federal poverty level.

Q 10:20 What are the federal Medicare balance billing limits?

The limit now stands at 115 percent. This means that physicians are prohibited from charging Medicare recipients fees greater than 115 percent of the amount listed in the reduced Medicare fee schedule.

Q 10:21 Are there any state balance billing requirements that affect employers?

Yes. Several states have enacted separate Medicare balance billing limits that differ from the federal limits.

Medicare Order of Benefit Determination

Q 10:22 How are Medicare benefits integrated with employer-provided benefits for older active employees?

Several different pieces of legislation have changed the "order of benefits." Originally, Medicare eligibles received primary benefits from Medicare; any employer-provided benefits were additional. To avoid duplicating Medicare benefits, employer plan benefits were "integrated," which means that Medicare benefits were taken into account before determining supplemental benefits in one of three ways:

1. Benefits payable under the employer's plan were reduced by the benefits payable under Medicare. Generally, the employer's plan covered the same benefits as Medicare, but employer-provided benefits were reduced by the Medicare payments. This is known as "carve out."
2. Benefits payable under the employer's plan "wrapped around" Medicare: The employer plan was specially designed to pay for

expenses that Medicare did not cover, called "Medicare Supplement."

3. Benefits payable under the employer's plan were combined with Medicare benefits using a coordination of benefits provision, which allowed the insured to be reimbursed for up to 100 percent of expenses allowable under either plan.

During the first 15 years of the Medicare program, Medicare was the primary payor for all Medicare-covered services, with the sole exception of services covered under workers' compensation. Beginning in 1980, Congress passed a series of amendments to make Medicare the secondary payor for services covered by other types of insurance. In general, Medicare is now secondary to all of the following:

1. All forms of liability insurance.
2. Automobile and non-automobile no-fault insurance.
3. Group health plans (GHPs) that cover end-stage renal disease (ESRD) patients (during the first 30 months of Medicare eligibility or entitlement). Effective August 5, 1997, group health plans are primary for Medicare beneficiaries with end-stage renal disease for 30 months, instead of 18 months. This apparently applies to anyone whose 18-month period expires August 5 or later, not just people beginning Medicare coverage August 5 or later.
4. GHPs that cover aged individuals who have current employment status with an employer of 20 or more employees and aged spouses of individuals of any age who have current employment status with an employer of 20 or more employees.
5. Large group health plans (LGHPs) that cover disabled individuals if the individual or a member of the individual's family has current employment status with an employer.

The result in almost all cases is that the employer's plan continues to be primary coverage, and older employees defer eligibility for Medicare benefits to retirement. Employees have, however, the right to reject their employer's plan and elect only Medicare coverage.

The Omnibus Budget Reconciliation Act of 1990 (OBRA '90) prohibited employers and other entities from offering Medicare beneficiaries incentives not to enroll or to terminate enrollment in any group health plan that would otherwise be primary to Medicare. There is a $5,000 penalty for each violation. In a letter ruling on this issue, the Health Care Financing Administration has said that an employer will not be in violation of this rule merely by virtue of the fact that under a valid cafeteria plan a Medicare-covered employee can elect a benefit in lieu of the health plan.

Q 10:23 Can a group health plan be designed to exclude workers over age 65?

No. Employees over age 65 must be given continuing coverage under the employer's plan if they wish to receive it. Employees must be given a choice between (1) the employer's plan being primary with Medicare being secondary and (2) Medicare as the sole provider, with no employer coverage. The employer cannot offer to pay for Part B, provide a Medicare supplement, or in any way encourage the employee to elect Medicare. Moreover, an employer cannot designate its group health plan as secondary to Medicare.

Q 10:24 Is Medicare primary for retirees with end-stage renal disease?

Probably not, but there is much confusion and uncertainty over this issue. The HCFA initially interpreted OBRA '93 as requiring employers to be primary for retirees who develop ESRD. After protests from employers and insurers, HCFA reversed its position in 1995. A dialysis center sued to block HCFA from enforcing its revised interpretation. In January 1998, a District Court in Washington ruled that HCFA cannot retroactively enforce its interpretation that Medicare is primary. Whether HCFA should be allowed to enforce its regulations prospectively is still in litigation. [National Medical Care, Inc. et al. v. Shalala 1995 WL 465650 (DDC)]

Q 10:25 Is there any guidance regarding Medicare secondary rules?

The HCFA issued final regulations clarifying a number of issues regarding Medicare secondary rules:

1. Employers must offer the same coverage to rehired retirees, as well as to their spouses who are over the age of 65, as they do to nonretirees; however, this means that if the rehires are part of a class of employees where active workers do not receive health care benefits, the rehires need not receive them either. So Medicare would be the primary payer.
2. The rules are intended to apply to self-funded plans as well as to insured ones.
3. Self-employed persons are affected only if they had at least $400 in net earnings from self-employment in the preceding year. Self-employed clergy are included only if their churches pay FICA taxes for them.

The regulations also spell out rules for recovering payments made by Medicare that should properly have been made by the employer plan.

Q 10:26 How have the secondary payor rules been enforced?

Starting in late 1991, questionnaires were sent to 800,000 employers by the U.S. Department of Health and Human Services (HHS) in an effort to recover payments made by Medicare that should have been made by employer plans. The goal is to recover between $600 million and $1 billion from employer plans that should have been the primary payers of claims incorrectly paid by Medicare.

Targeted firms were those that filed 20 or more W-2 forms and employed Medicare beneficiaries or their spouses between January 1987 and December 1989. There were two questionnaires: The first asked if the employer sponsored a group health plan at any time since January 1, 1983 and whether it employed 20 or more persons during that period. For those employers that answered yes, a follow-up questionnaire identified and asked Medicare beneficiaries whether they were covered by the employer's group health plan.

HHS has enforcement clout in the following three ways:

1. It can levy fines for failure to supply information (up to $1,000 per employee).
2. It can impose a 25 percent excise tax on plans that fail to comply.

3. It has the potential to sue for damages for nonconformance.

Q 10:27 What are the rules for the disabled?

Medicare is secondary to large group health plans that cover disabled individuals if the individual or a member of the individuals family has current employment status with the employer sponsoring the LGHP. The Balanced Budget Act of 1997 made this rule permanent.

Q 10:28 Is there a penalty for failure to comply?

Yes. The penalty for noncompliance is 25 percent of the employer's annual contribution to noncomplying health plans. Depending on the number of persons affected, this could be a steep price to pay for failure to comply. In addition, an individual or the government may file for damages in the case of a noncomplying employer. The claim can be for double the actual damages.

Q 10:29 How long must an employer plan provide primary benefits for individuals with end-stage renal disease?

Employers are primary for 30 months after Medicare entitlement (a maximum period of 33 months, which includes a three-month waiting period for Medicare coverage). Thereafter, Medicare is primary for all individuals with end-stage renal disease, whether active, disabled, or dependents of active or disabled employees.

Q 10:30 Who is considered disabled for Social Security purposes?

Disability under Social Security means that the individual is so severely impaired, either mentally or physically, that he or she is unable to perform any substantial gainful work. This condition must be expected to last at least 12 months, or result in death. To qualify for benefits, there is a five-month waiting period during which the individual must have been continuously disabled.

In determining whether an individual's impairment is sufficient to qualify for disability benefits, claims adjudicators at the Social Security Administration (or a state agency that performs this function for the SSA), take into account such things as:

1. Current gainful employment (earning $500 per month would disqualify the person from being considered disabled).
2. The severity of the impairment or impairments. If the impairment is severe and is listed in the schedule (Appendix 1) of the regulations, then the person is deemed to be disabled. If not, additional factors are considered, such as residual functional capacity, age, education, and work experience.

The person who is unable, based upon these factors, to do the type of work performed in the past 10 years, and is equally unable to perform any other types of work because of age, education, and experience is considered disabled.

Q 10:31 What special rules apply to Medicare secondary requirements for disabled individuals?

In order for the secondary rules to apply, the individual must still be an "employee" under HCFA regulations.

OBRA '93 defined the term "current employment status" as an individual with an employer if the individual is an employee, is the employer, or is associated with the employer in a business relationship.

According to HCFA final regulations published August 31, 1995, the inclusion of individuals whose relationship to the employer is based on business rather than on work demonstrates that Congress intended to give the term current employment status the broadest possible application.

According to the regulations, current employment status encompasses not only individuals who are actively working but also individuals under contract with the employer whether or not they actually perform services for the employer, such as attorneys on retainer, tradespeople, and insurance agents. For example, an independent insurance agent who is licensed to sell insurance for a particular insurance company has current employment status with that company by virtue of that "business relationship." If an agent age 65 or older has plan coverage through that company based on this current employment status, the coverage is primary to Medicare (unless specific statutory exceptions apply, such as the 20-employee rule—see Q 10:22) without regard to the extent to which the agent is presently selling policies on behalf of the company should the "business relationship" with the employer be severed. Medicare would, however, be the primary payer, if the company imposes earnings thresholds or other requirements for qualifying for health benefits that the agent does not meet based on this "current employment status."

Q 10:32 What other individuals are covered under the Medicare secondary rules?

The Medicare secondary rules apply to disabled dependents and self-employed individuals as well as to employees.

Q 10:33 What is a large group health plan?

Large group health plans are those sponsored by employers who employed at least 100 employees, full-time or part-time, on at least half of their regular business days during the previous calendar year. Plans maintained by more than one employer are affected if at least one employer meets the 100-employee test.

The rules apply to most employers, including nonprofit, government, and religious organizations.

Medicare Cost Containment

Q 10:34 What steps has Medicare taken to limit costs?

The HCFA began implementing a prospective payment system (PPS) for Medicare in 1983. (Some state Medicaid administrations have also implemented prospective payment systems.) Hospitals can expect a fixed reimbursement for each patient discharged, based not on the number and kinds of services delivered, but on the diagnosis of the patient. The old cost-plus system encouraged providers to deliver more care. In contrast, PPS eliminates the incentive for hospitals to deliver unnecessary care.

Another initiative is the resource-based relative value scale (RBRVS). The net effect of RBRVS is that the Medicare reimbursement structure no longer heavily reward costly specialty services and providers. Instead, reimbursement to those providers has been toned down, while reimbursement for generalized services is being increased. The initial reallocation of fees was not intended to reduce total Medicare expenditures, but to reapportion the same amount of expenditures. While not intended to do so, it is likely to start reducing expenditures, as more doctors are expected to enter the generalized arena in response to increased reimbursements being directed there.

Medicare also allows beneficiaries to elect coverage under a health maintenance organization (HMO).

Q 10:35 Why is Medicare cost containment important?

From its creation in 1965 through fiscal 1994, the Medicare hospital insurance trust (for Part A) built a surplus of $129 billion. In 1995, the trust lost money for the first time. On June 5, 1996, the trustees released a report estimating that the trust would go broke in early 2001.

The Congressional Budget Office estimated that changes made by the Balanced Budget Act of 1997 would sustain the trust fund until 2007. Because of these changes, Medicare spending declined for the first time in fiscal 1999.

Each year, the trustees of the Medicare trust fund report in detail on the trust fund's financial condition. The report describes the current and projected financial condition within the next ten years (the "short term") and over the next 75 years (the "long term"). Because the future cannot be predicted with certainty, three alternative sets of economic and demographic assumptions are used to show a range of possibilities. The intermediate assumptions reflect the Trustees' best estimate of future experience. Under the intermediate assumptions, the report released in March 2000 indicated that the Hospital Insurance (HI) Trust Fund will be exhausted in 2023; a later statement indicated that there was a computational error and that Medicare should remain solvent until 2025.

Q 10:36 What did Congress do about the impending bankruptcy of Medicare?

The Balanced Budget Act of 1997 called for $115 billion in Medicare savings over five years.

The act was intended to modernize Medicare by providing new health plan choices and reforming payment methodologies for home health agencies, skilled nursing facilities, and HMOs. Most of the savings come from reducing payments to hospitals and other health care providers. The cuts were even more extensive than Congress intended. The bill also raised Medicare Part B premiums.

Language creating a bipartisan Medicare commission was included in the legislation enacting the budget deal. Many lawmakers wanted a commission to restructure Medicare because of the large number of baby boomers expected to retire starting in 2010. The commission failed to reach consensus of changes.

Q 10:37 How are payments determined on the basis of diagnosis?

In 1975, Yale University introduced a system of diagnosis-related groups (DRGs) for 467 diagnoses. Initially, these DRGs were meant to be used as a management and planning tool for the health care system. But because of the need for cost management, the federal government decided to apply them as a reimbursement method. Payment schedules for all DRGs were developed. Patients' conditions were translated to a DRG, and the allowable charge was determined based on the payment schedule.

Q 10:38 If the care delivered costs a hospital less than the DRG-allowed sum, does the hospital retain the difference?

Yes. It is hoped that DRGs will encourage cost-effective care. Conversely, if the care provided costs the hospital more than it is reimbursed under DRG, the hospital must make up the difference.

Q 10:39 Is Medicare the only plan that uses the DRG reimbursement system?

No. There are other situations in which insurers have agreed to reimburse on a DRG basis through a private insurance arrangement at a particular hospital. Some states had required all reimbursement by insurers to be based on DRGs; New York was the last such state and ended DRG reimbursement in 1996.

Q 10:40 What is the RBRVS payment system?

The resource-based relative value scale RBRVS system is used to determine the level of Medicare payments to physicians. RBRVS pays doctors the lesser of their actual charge, or a fee calculated using the following three factors, or relative value units:

1. The amount of work, measured by time and intensity, of the service provided
2. Practice expenses, such as office rent and employee compensation
3. Malpractice expenses

There will be adjustments to the practice and malpractice components, as well as to a portion of the work component, based upon geographical location. About 60 percent of the fee will be subject to geographical adjustments determined for urban and rural areas of each state.

Q 10:41 What is the difference between usual, customary, prevailing, and reasonable payments and RBRVS payments?

The customary, prevailing, and reasonable (or usual, customary, and reasonable) system bases reimbursement on actual levels of physician charges. While the payor may not reimburse the physician for the entire charge, fees are increased over time, and benefit payments track those increases. The RBRVS system is based on the value of the service rendered as calculated by the resources that went into providing the service. It is an attempt to compensate physician "work" instead of basing payments on the physician-controlled marketplace.

Q 10:42 What effect has RBRVS had on physicians' fees?

Some fees were lowered and some increased. Generally, those fees charged by high cost specialists such as anesthesiologists, surgeons, radiologists, and the like came down, while those charged by internists and family practitioners went up.

Anesthesiologists and registered nurse anesthetists are now paid for actual time worked, rather than time units (15 to 30 minute minimum increments) as was the practice.

Medicare procedures are often copied by commercial insurers; therefore, the RBRVS system could ultimately become the standard of payment for employer-sponsored plans as well.

Q 10:43 How does Medicare reimburse ambulatory surgery centers?

Medicare maintains a list of ambulatory surgery center (ASC) procedures. Every procedure falls into a payment group. Medicare reimburses the center at the rate specified for the payment group, and updates the rates annually based on a survey of actual costs or an automatic inflation adjustment. The ASC payment group concept is similar to the concept behind DRGs.

Medigap

Q 10:44 What are the rules regarding Medigap policies?

OBRA '90 directed the National Association of Insurance Commissioners (NAIC) to develop up to 10 standard Medicare supplement policies. These 10 packages of benefits replaced all previous individual insurance plans for the elderly.

Medigap policies must conform to one of ten standardized benefit packages, designated as plan "A" through "J." State requirements may be more restrictive than the federal requirements, but each state must allow the sale of the core plan "A."

The Balanced Budget Act of 1997 added two high-deductible Medigap standard policies with benefit packages that are the same as plans "F" and "J." The high deductible amount is indexed, starting at $1,500 for 1998 and 1999 ($1,530 for 2000). States do not have to allow the high deductible plans, even if they allow the standard versions of plans "F" and "J."

The Balanced Budget Act of 1997 prohibits any other Medigap policies for people who elect medical savings accounts.

Medigap policies must be issued without evidence of insurability to anyone who applies within six months of reaching age 65, or certain other events. Preexisting conditions exclusions under Medigap policies must be reduced by the length of creditable coverage.

Employer-sponsored policies for retirees or union-sponsored policies for members are not considered Medigap policies. Medicare + Choice plans are not considered Medigap policies.

Q 10:45 What do Medigap policies cover?

All 10 policies cover 20 percent of physician charges (Part B) and the hospital daily copayment from the 60th to the 90th day. Beyond that, each policy adds coverage for certain additional services. The most comprehensive policy offers coverage for the inpatient hospital deductible, the Part B deductible, physicians' charges in excess of Medicare-approved charges (up to the balance billing limits), foreign travel emergencies, home health care services, prescription drugs, and preventive care.

Costs for these policies vary substantially. Under the law, insurers have to return 65 cents on every premium dollar in the form of claim payments, an increase from the old average of 60 cents.

A 1996 report by Families USA found that a female age 65 purchasing the basic Medigap Plan A would pay $280 annually for a Blue Cross/ Blue Shield plan in New Mexico and $876 in Ohio. The more substantial Plan F would cost $711 in Iowa and $1,531 in Florida.

A 1998 survey by Weiss Ratings Inc. found large variations in cost by insurer. For example, a 65-year-old male in the Tampa Bay area could buy a no-frills Medicare supplement policy for as little as $550 a year or could pay more than twice that much. For a comprehensive plan that includes prescriptions, premiums ranged from a low of just over $2,000 to more than $2,700.

Operation Data Match

Q 10:46 What is Operation Data Match?

Operation Data Match is a nationwide effort by the HCFA to identify retroactively all payments made erroneously by Medicare and to bill industry for those payments. Its name derives from its primary method of identifying overpayments, which is through the comparison of data from the IRS, Social Security Administration, and the HCFA itself. Congress originally authorized the Data Match program through September of 1995, then extended it through 1998, and finally made it permanent.

Q 10:47 What were the causes of Operation Data Match?

HCFA has been attempting to shift costs away from Medicare and to private industry for many years. In some instances, this attempt was based on clearly defined laws and regulations. For the working aged (those over age 65 continuing to work and covered by an employer's plan), the employer's plan was clearly primary. In other circumstances, HCFA issued interpretations that were generally regarded as having gone beyond the empowering legislation, and that therefore received sporadic compliance from industry. The numerous attempts by HCFA to define an employee—particularly its attempts concerning disabled former employees—comprised the most contentious issue.

Whether from lackluster compliance because of good faith disagreement with HCFA's definition, from ignorance of the general requirements of the Medicare as Secondary Payor (MSP) program, or from improper processing by Medicare, many claims were erroneously paid by Medicare as primary. The GAO estimated that Medicare overpayments were between $400 million and $1 billion per year. HCFA estimates that, through Operation Data Match, it stands to recoup $600 million to $1 billion from industry.

Q 10:48 What is an employer's responsibility in Operation Data Match?

Generally speaking, the employer's role is to wait until HCFA contacts the employer; the employer need not take any action until then. If the HCFA (or one of its Medicare contractors, mostly insurance companies) identifies a claim, it sends out a demand letter with a bill to the appropriate party—third-party administrator (TPA), insurer, or employer.

Originally, it appeared that the burden to disprove a claim would be on the employer in cases where there was some dispute. The demand letters mailed by the HCFA or its contractors threaten interest charges, penalties, and lawsuits if the bills are not paid and require the recipient to produce explanations and evidence if the billing is in error; however, in a recent case between Provident Life and Accident Insurance Company and the HCFA, [Provident Life and Accidental Insurance Co v US, DC E Tenn, No CIV-1-89-190, May 28, 1993] a U.S. District Court ruled that the burden of proof was on the HCFA. The case was ultimately settled, with the government receiving $27 million (the initial claim was for $223 million).

The burden of proof issue is significant. Many of the demands for reimbursement are for relatively small amounts, so defending each case—from either side—with litigation is not often cost-effective. Until the *Provident* case, most employers and insurers were advised to pay small claims they could not easily disprove; however, if the HCFA is required to prove every claim, it may have to decide not to pursue small claims.

In the case of *Shalala v. Health Insurance Association of America* [US Sup Ct, No 94-919, Feb 21, 1995] the Supreme Court refused to review a lower court decision. In that case, the lower court ruled that HCFA could demand reimbursement from employers if claims were not filed within the time limit specified by the plan. The lower court also ruled that TPAs cannot be held liable for claims under self-funded plans. The Balanced Budget Act of 1997 overturned this decision by giving Medicare three years from the date medical services are rendered to seek repayment from group health plans.

Q 10:49 What is the process involved in Operation Data Match?

HCFA began by cross-checking Medicare payments with tax records to see if the Medicare recipients were employed. If they were, HCFA contacted their employers to determine if they were covered under the MSP program. The first mailing was sent to approximately 800,000 employers, who together covered nearly eight million workers. As a result of this mailing, HCFA weeded out companies with fewer than 20 workers, because such companies are exempt from the MSP program. Then HCFA started to collect information about nonexempt employers' group health plans, and lists of their employees.

In this ongoing process, a Data Match questionnaire is sent to an employer for each employee who might have been covered by the employer during a time that employee received Medicare benefits. The first part of the questionnaire asks, "Did you offer a health plan to full-time employees, part-time employees, or self-employed individuals at any time since January 1, 1983?" A "no" answer here ends the employer's involvement in Operation Data Match.

An employer answering "yes" must provide further information about its plan, the length of time the plan has been in effect, and specific information about named individuals and whether they, their spouse, or dependents were covered by the employer plan. The completed form is returned to HCFA. HCFA then determines if it made an overpayment or an improper payment and how much the employer owes if errors were made.

HCFA now says it will limit new overpayment demands to 1990 and later. It has also increased its threshold from $50 to $1,000 (but reserves the right to pursue smaller claims later).

Q 10:50 What was the Medicare and Medicaid Data Bank?

OBRA '93 established the Medicare and Medicaid Coverage Data Bank and set into place rules requiring employers to report certain employee medical benefit information to the bank. Employers would have been required to file the information annually along with their

W-2 forms beginning in 1995. Congress never funded enforcement before repealing the requirements in 1996.

Medicare+Choice

Q 10:51 What is Medicare+Choice?

The Balanced Budget Act of 1997 created a new, Part C of Medicare, also known as Medicare + Choice. The Medicare + Choice program is an alternative to the traditional Medicare Parts A and B.

Medicare + Choice was intended to allow beneficiaries access to a wide array of private health plan choices in addition to traditional Medicare. It was also intended to enable Medicare to utilize innovations that have helped the private market contain costs and expand health care delivery options. Medicare + Choice includes HMOs (with or without point-of-service options), preferred provider organizations, provider-sponsored organizations, and private fee-for-service plans. Medicare + Choice also includes a pilot Medicare medical savings account (MSA) program, similar to the one enacted as part of the Health Insurance Portability and Accountability Act for small employers.

Q 10:52 Has Medicare+Choice been successful?

Not yet. As of press time, only about a dozen new plans had been approved, none of which were MSAs or private fee-for-service plans. Basically, Medicare + Choice consists of the HMOs that had been available before the Balanced Budget Act of 1997.

Q 10:53 How are HMOs paid under Medicare?

The Balanced Budget Act of 1997 narrowed the differences in payments to capitated Medicare risk plans. Previously there were wide variations between counties. The law now bases payments on a blend of local and national costs and sets a floor for low-cost areas. This should encourage development of Medicare risk HMOs in rural areas. The Balanced Budget Act of 1997 also called for risk-adjusted

Q 10:54 Health Insurance Answer Book

payments to HMOs based on the health status of enrollees. HCFA will begin phasing in the risk adjustment in the year 2000.

Even though Congress mandated a blend of local and national costs, with a floor for low-cost areas, it also mandated budget neutrality. Unfortunately, that combination was impossible to achieve, so HCFA basically increased all HMO payments by 2 percent. Many HMOs have dropped out of the Medicare program in rural areas.

The General Accounting Office reported that a "variety of factors" contributed to the pullout of HMOs from Medicare. The GAO said payment level was one factor influencing where plans offer services, but noted that withdrawals were not limited to counties with low payments.

Q 10:54 Are Medicare beneficiaries happy with HMO coverage?

Most likely. In 1996 only 3 percent of Medicare beneficiaries disenrolled from an HMO and returned to the fee-for-service system. Another 10 percent changed HMOs; 87 percent stayed with the HMO they selected.

A 1997 survey conducted jointly by CareData Reports, Inc., Towers Perrin, and 39 large employers that provide retiree health benefits found that 71 percent of retirees are extremely satisfied or very satisfied with their Medicare HMO plan. Among respondents, 60 percent rate the HMO as better than traditional Medicare and 20 percent rate it the same, with 20 percent preferring traditional Medicare.

Q 10:55 How many Medicare beneficiaries receive coverage through an HMO?

As of March 2000, 6.22 million Medicare beneficiaries received coverage through a Medicare + Choice HMO. This was down from 6.35 million in December 1999, the first decline in enrollment since HMOs were first offered to Medicare beneficiaries. Low reimbursement from HCFA has led many HMOs to drop out of Medicare + Choice. Despite widely publicized withdrawals of HMOs from Medicare, slightly more Medicare beneficiaries had access to managed care plans in 1999 than in 1998 primarily because of new HMOs.

Surveys by the American Association of Health Plans indicated that HMOs dropped Medicare coverage for over 250,000 Medicare beneficiaries in 2000 and are planning to drop more than 700,000 in 2001. Many of these beneficiaries were able to enroll in another HMO, but some were not.

Chapter 11

Nondiscrimination Rules

This chapter address the nondiscrimination rules that apply to health plans. While not considered "health plans," group term life and dependent care assistance plans are often included in cafeteria plans; therefore, information on the nondiscrimination rules applicable to such plans is included in this section.

Accident and Health Plans	11-1
Group Term Life Plans	11-5
Cafeteria Plans	11-8
Dependent Care Assistance Plans	11-11
Voluntary Employees' Beneficiary Associations	11-13
Nondiscriminatory Classification	11-14

Accident and Health Plans

Q 11:1 Is discrimination in health plans permitted?

With respect to insured accident and health plans, the only federal rules regarding benefit discrimination are those applicable to cafeteria plans (see Qs 11:20–11:28). Employers must still abide by discrimination statutes that are not specifically benefit-oriented and any requirements specified by a particular insurance company.

Self-insured health plans (including medical, dental, and vision) must not discriminate in favor of highly compensated individuals.

The plan must meet at least one of three eligibility tests and a benefits test.

The distinction between insured and self-insured is not as obvious as it might seem. The use of an insurance company for claim administration does not suffice to render a plan insured. Plans underwritten by insurance companies, such as minimum premium plans, or prepaid health care arrangements such as HMOs and PPOs, may be considered partially self-insured unless there is a meaningful shifting of risk.

Q 11:2 Which types of self-insured accident and health plans are not subject to discrimination testing?

The nondiscrimination rules apply only to the self-insured portion and only to the employer-provided portion of plans. Furthermore, the rules do not apply to disability plans (including accidental death and dismemberment (AD&D) and travel accident plans). Plans that cover employees but not dependents for diagnostic procedures only, such as annual physical exams, are also exempt.

Q 11:3 What is a highly compensated individual?

The Small Business Job Protection Act (SBJPA) of 1996 simplified the Internal Revenue Code (Code) Section 414(q) definition of highly compensated employees (HCEs), allowing plan sponsors to choose one of two definitions. An employee is considered to be highly compensated if he or she is one of the following:

1. A 5 percent owner (in the current or prior year) or earned more than $80,000 (indexed) in the prior year; or

2. A 5 percent owner (in the current or prior year) or earned more than $80,000 (indexed) in the prior year and was in the top-paid 20 percent of all employees.

Most employers will choose not to use the top-paid 20 percent rule because fewer than 20 percent of their employees earn more than $80,000. Employers with a large proportion of highly paid employees will use the top-paid 20 percent rule because it will make it easier to pass the nondiscrimination tests.

The requirement that the highest-paid officer be treated as a highly compensated employee regardless of his or her compensation was repealed.

The family aggregation rules have also been eliminated. Family members will be considered non-highly compensated employees unless they are 5 percent owners or earned more than $80,000 in the prior year.

The attribution rules for ownership have not changed. If an employee's spouse owns more than 5 percent of a corporation, the employee will also be considered to own more than 5 percent and will be a highly compensated employee.

A retiree who was highly compensated prior to retirement is considered to be a highly compensated individual. [IRC § 105(h)]

IRS Notice 97-45 provides guidance on the changes to the definition of HCEs enacted by the SBJPA. The employer can elect to use the top-paid 20 percent rule without notifying the IRS. If elected, the rule must be used for all retirement and welfare plans. An employer can switch from using fiscal-year data to calendar-year data to determine HCEs, provided the switch applies to all plans. These elections will apply until changed. If a plan document defines HCEs, it must be amended to reflect the new SBJPA definition as well as the employer's elections.

Q 11:4 What are the eligibility tests applicable to self-insured accident and health plans?

A plan will be considered nondiscriminatory if it meets one of the following three eligibility tests:

1. It benefits at least 70 percent of employees.
2. It benefits at least 80 percent of those eligible, provided 70 percent or more are eligible.
3. It benefits a nondiscriminatory classification of employees.

Planning Pointer. If the plan is part of a cafeteria plan it must also meet the nondiscrimination requirements of Code Section 125.

Q 11:5 What employees are excluded in applying the eligibility tests?

In applying these tests, the following five types of employees are excluded:

1. Employees with less than three years of service;
2. Employees under the age of 25;
3. Part-time or seasonal employees (generally those working not more than 25 hours per week or seven months per year. This group could also include those who work less than 35 hours per week or nine months provided other employees doing essentially the same job work substantially more hours or longer periods as in the case of seasonal employees);
4. Employees who are members of a collective bargaining unit that has bargained in good faith with respect to benefits provided under the plan; and
5. Nonresident aliens with no income from U.S. sources.

Q 11:6 What is the benefit test applicable to self-insured accident and health plans?

All of the benefits that are available to highly compensated employees must be made available to all other employees. The plan may not discriminate as to type or amount of benefit. Provided benefits are equally available to all participants—the fact that highly compensated individuals actually receive greater benefits, because they submit higher claims or have more dependents, is of no consequence. Different waiting periods or participation costs apparently would, however, result in the plan being deemed discriminatory.

Q 11:7 What is the penalty for discrimination in a self-insured accident and health plan with respect to eligibility or benefits?

The penalty imputes additional income to the participants for tax purposes, resulting in additional income taxes. The penalty is assessed to "highly compensated" individuals to the extent of the employer-provided "excess reimbursement" benefits.

Q 11:8 How is the penalty determined?

Determining the additional taxable income for a highly compensated individual depends on the nature of the discrimination. If the plan fails the benefits test because it provides a benefit to highly compensated employees that it does not provide to other employees, the entire amount of the reimbursement not available to all participants is includible in taxable income.

If the plan fails one of the eligibility tests, the portion of the reimbursement determined by applying the following fraction is includible in income for all highly compensated individuals:

$$\frac{\text{Total reimbursements for all highly compensated individuals during the plan year}}{\text{Total reimbursements during the plan year}}$$

The amount is based on reimbursement/claim payments, not the "premium" or cost.

Q 11:9 Are all self-insured accident and health plans aggregated for the purpose of applying eligibility and benefit tests?

Employers must aggregate all plans in the controlled group of employers.

Q 11:10 Are retiree plans subject to the same rules?

Yes, but IRS regulations are unclear on how to define a retiree, how to apply the eligibility tests, and how to treat benefits that are a function of service. It does appear, however, that the benefit test applies separately to retiree plans.

Group Term Life Plans

Q 11:11 What does Code Section 79 say?

The value of employer-provided group term life insurance in excess of $50,000 is taxable.

Q 11:12 Who is a key employee under Code Section 416(i)?

A key employee is any employee who, in the current year or any one of the four preceding plan years, was:

1. A 5 percent owner;

2. A 1 percent owner earning more than $150,000;

3. An officer earning more than over 50 percent of the Code Section 415 defined benefit pension limit (50 percent of $135,000 or $67,500 in 2000); or

4. One of the 10 highest paid owners earning more than the Code Section 415 defined contribution pension limit ($30,000).

Note. The number of officers who will be considered key employees will not exceed 50, or, if fewer, 10 percent of employees (but not fewer than three).

Q 11:13 What nondiscrimination tests are applicable to group term life insurance?

Group term life insurance plans must meet one of several eligibility tests and a benefit test in order to demonstrate that the plan does not discriminate in favor of key employees.

Q 11:14 What are the eligibility tests applicable to group term life insurance plans?

A group term life insurance plan will be considered nondiscriminatory if it meets one of the following four tests:

1. It benefits at least 70 percent of employees.

2. At least 85 percent of plan participants are not key employees.

3. It benefits a nondiscriminatory classification of employees.

4. The plan is part of a cafeteria plan and it meets the Section 125 nondiscrimination requirements.

Q 11:15 What employees may be excluded in performing these tests?

The following four types of employees may be excluded from testing:

1. Employees with fewer than three years of service;
2. Part-time or seasonal employees (generally those working not more than 20 hours per week or five months per year);
3. Employees who are members of a collective bargaining unit that has bargained in good faith with respect to benefits provided under the plan; and
4. Nonresident aliens.

Q 11:16 What is the benefit test for group term life plans?

The benefits test requires that all of the benefits available to key employees be available to non-key employees. The plan may not discriminate as to type or amount of relative benefit. The IRS does, however, permit differing benefit amounts when the benefit is based on a uniform relationship to employee compensation expressed similarly for all employees. The same definition of pay (e.g., basic, total) must be used for all employees. A plan that provides a common multiple of pay benefit (such as "two times pay") would not be considered discriminatory.

Q 11:17 Are all group term life insurance plans combined for testing purposes?

All plans that cover a common key employee must be tested together. This includes individual term policies which are considered group insurance for purposes of Code Section 79.

Q 11:18 What is the penalty for discrimination under group term life?

Normally the first $50,000 of group term life insurance benefit in a nondiscriminatory plan is exempt from taxation. Amounts in excess of $50,000 in a nondiscriminatory plan are taxed based on income imputed according to a table published by the IRS known as the Uniform Premium Table, or Table I. If the plan is discriminatory, the value of the first $50,000 of employer-provided group term life insurance on key employees will be included as income for tax purposes and the total value imputed as income will be based on actual cost or the Table I rates, whichever is higher.

Recently, the IRS has stated that the higher of actual cost or Table I rates would apply to amounts in excess of $50,000 for all employees even if the group term life insurance plan was nondiscriminatory, if the plan was part of a cafeteria arrangement. (Note: This contradicts current statutory language and may not be legally defensible).

Q 11:19   Are group term life benefits for retired and former employees subject to nondiscrimination rules?

Yes. The eligibility and benefit tests are applied separately to retired and former employees; however, not all such employees need be taken into account. There are complex "grandfathering" provisions under the Deficit Reduction Act of 1984.

Cafeteria Plans

Q 11:20   What are the nondiscrimination rules for cafeteria plans?

They are an eligibility test, a benefit test, a contribution test, a concentration test and a health benefit test. In order to avoid constructive receipt, the plan must not discriminate in favor of highly compensated individuals, either as to eligibility or as to contributions and benefits. The definition of highly compensated individuals is different for cafeteria plans than for self-insured health plans.

Q 11:21   Who is a highly compensated individual for the purpose of cafeteria plan nondiscrimination rules?

Under Code Section 125(e), highly compensated individuals are defined as either employees or participants who are one of the following:

- Officers
- More than 5 percent shareholders
- Highly compensated based on facts and circumstances
- Spouses or dependents of one of the preceding

Note that the IRS uses circular logic, by defining a highly compensated individual as someone who is highly compensated.

Q 11:22 What is the eligibility test for cafeteria plans?

The plan may not favor highly compensated individuals as to eligibility to participate. That is, it should provide coverage to a reasonable classification of employees (see Q 11:40). The nondiscriminatory classification rules for qualified retirement plans may be considered a safe harbor in satisfying this test. If the safe harbor is used and the waiting period is less than three years, employees who have not satisfied the waiting period may be excluded for the purpose of this test.

Q 11:23 Which employees may be excluded for purposes of this eligibility test?

Employees who have fewer than three years of service may be disregarded, provided:

1. They are ineligible for the plan; and
2. Newly eligible employees become eligible to participate not later than the beginning of the plan year following their third anniversary of employment.

This means that all eligible classes of employees must be subject to the same three-year wait. That limits the utility of this rule for most plans.

A plan will not be considered discriminatory if it is maintained under a collective bargaining agreement.

Q 11:24 What are the benefit and the contribution tests for cafeteria plans?

There are two parts to these tests. The first part is a facts and circumstances test; the plan must not favor highly compensated individuals with respect to benefits available or contributions. The second part requires that the benefits actually selected do not favor the highly compensated.

Q 11:25 What is the concentration test?

The concentration test states that a plan that provides key employees with more than 25 percent of the total nontaxable benefits will be considered discriminatory.

Q 11:26 What is the health benefit test?

Health benefits are not discriminatory if employer contributions for each participant equal 100 percent of the cost of the majority of highly compensated individuals who are similarly situated (for example, have families). Alternatively, health benefits are not discriminatory if employer contributions for each participant are at least 75 percent of the cost of the most expensive coverage selected by a similarly situated participant.

If employer contributions exceed these amounts, the plan will still be nondiscriminatory provided the contributions are uniformly proportional to participant compensation.

Q 11:27 What is the penalty for discrimination in cafeteria plans?

Section 125 of the Internal Revenue Code protects employees who are offered the choice between taxable and nontaxable benefits from being deemed to have received the taxable benefits irrespective of their actual selection, i.e., constructive receipt. The protection is only available in nondiscriminatory plans. If a cafeteria plan is discriminatory, the applicable favored group (highly compensated if the eligibility or benefits test is failed, key employees in the case of concentration test failure) will be taxed on the highest aggregate value of all available taxable benefits.

Nondiscrimination Rules   Q 11:31

Q 11:28 Does a plan that is part of a cafeteria plan have to satisfy more than one set of discrimination rules?

Yes. Plans must satisfy the rules applicable to the particular section of the Code as well as those for cafeteria plans.

Dependent Care Assistance Plans

Q 11:29 What are the nondiscrimination rules for dependent care assistance plans?

Those rules require an eligibility test, a benefit test, and a concentration test (see Chapter 9, Q 11:33 and following, and Q 11:44 for details).

Nondiscrimination tests for dependent day care plans may be applied on a separate-line-of-business basis, determined in "good faith" until regulations or additional guidance become available.

Q 11:30 What is the eligibility test for dependent care assistance plans?

The plan must not discriminate in favor of highly compensated employees as defined in Code Section 414(q). The eligibility test is satisfied if benefits are provided to a nondiscriminatory classification of employees (see Q 11:40).

The test is based on employees to whom the plan is available if the plan is part of a cafeteria arrangement. If, however, the plan is a stand-alone plan, the test is applied to employees actually receiving benefits.

Q 11:31 Who is a highly compensated employee with respect to dependent care assistance plans?

Any employee who, during the current year or the preceding year

1. Was a 5 percent owner; or

2. Received compensation in excess of $80,000 ($85,000 for 2000) for the preceding year and (if the employer elects) was in the top-paid 20 percent of the group for that year.

The Small Business Job Protection Act of 1996 simplified the definition of "highly compensated."

Q 11:32 What employees are excluded for purposes of nondiscrimination testing with respect to dependent care assistance plans?

The following groups of nonparticipants may be excluded from testing:

1. Those who are less than age 21 and have not completed one year of service (if these are conditions for participating in the plan); and
2. Members of a bargaining unit.

If the dependent care assistance plan is provided through salary reduction, for purposes of the average benefits test only, employees earning less than $25,000 may also be excluded.

Q 11:33 What is the benefit test for purposes of dependent care assistance plans?

The benefit test requires that employer-provided benefits or contributions must not favor highly compensated employees.

Q 11:34 What is the concentration test for dependent care assistance plans?

The concentration test prohibits more than 5 percent owners from receiving more than 25 percent of the employer-provided benefits, including salary reduction. This is in addition to the cafeteria plan concentration test applicable to key employees when the dependent day care plan is part of a cafeteria plan arrangement.

Q 11:35 What is the average benefits test for dependent care assistance plans?

The average benefits test provides that non-highly compensated employees must receive an average benefit that is at least 55 percent of the average benefit of the highly compensated. Nonparticipants, except excludable employees, are included in this test, although employees earning less than $25,000 may be excluded in salary reduction plans.

Q 11:36 What is the penalty for discrimination with respect to dependent care assistance plans?

If any one of the tests is failed, highly compensated employees are taxed on their total dependent day care benefits.

Voluntary Employees' Beneficiary Associations

Q 11:37 What are the nondiscrimination requirements for VEBAs?

Voluntary employees' beneficiary associations (VEBAs) are subject to the nondiscrimination requirements of Code Section 505, unless the particular benefit provided by the association has its own nondiscrimination requirements under the Internal Revenue Code, such as the Section 79 requirements for group term life insurance.

The nondiscrimination rules for VEBAs do not apply to nontaxable benefits that are subject to other nondiscrimination rules; however, a benefit included in a VEBA that fails its own nondiscrimination tests would result in the loss of the VEBA's tax-exempt status with the result that previously tax-free earnings would become taxable.

The VEBA nondiscrimination rules apply to all other benefits funded through the VEBA, whether taxable or nontaxable, employer paid, or employee pay all.

Code Section 505 requires the following:

1. Each class of benefits provided by the VEBA is provided to a class of individuals set forth in the plan, and does not discriminate in favor of highly compensated individuals (who are

determined under rules "similar" to those for "highly compensated employees" as defined in Code Section 414(q)).
2. The benefits themselves do not discriminate in favor of highly compensated individuals (this does not rule out life insurance, severance pay, disability benefits, or supplemental unemployment compensation benefits that are higher for higher paid employees, provided they bear a uniform relationship to total compensation).

For purposes of applying these tests, employees with less than three years of service, who are less than 21 years old, who are seasonal or half-time, who are covered by a collective bargaining agreement for which the benefits in question were the subject of bargaining, or who are nonresident aliens who receive no compensation from U.S. sources, may be excluded.

Q 11:38 Are there limits on compensation?

Yes, for purposes of calculating benefits, no more than $150,000 in annual compensation (adjusted for inflation—$170,000 in 2000) may be taken into account. If the provided benefits are group term life insurance that must meet the Code Section 79 nondiscrimination requirements, the dollar cap does not apply.

Q 11:39 What are the penalties for discrimination in a VEBA?

As previously mentioned, the inclusion of a discriminatory benefit in a VEBA eliminates its tax-exempt status. Employees still receive nondiscriminatory nontaxable benefits tax free and are subject to the penalties described for each discriminatory benefit.

In addition, an employer who provides discriminatory postretirement medical or life insurance through a VEBA is subject to a 100 percent excise tax on the amount of the discriminatory benefits.

Nondiscriminatory Classification

Q 11:40 What is a nondiscriminatory classification of employees?

Section 410(b) regulations describe the nondiscriminatory classification test. These regulations apply to Section 125 plans and may apply to Section 129 dependent care plans. The key to passing the test is the relationship of two ratios:

1. The percentage of non-highly compensated employees who benefit under the plan as compared to the percentage of highly compensated employees who benefit; and
2. The percentage of non-highly compensated employees to total employees (less excludable employees).

After determining these ratios, they are compared to the following table of acceptable ratios:

Safe Harbor and Unsafe Harbor Percentage at Each Non-Highly Compensated Employee Concentration Percentage

Non-Highly Compensated Employee Concentration Percentage	Safe Harbor Percentage	Unsafe Harbor Percentage
0–60	50	40
61	49.25	39.25
62	48.50	38.50
63	47.75	37.75
64	47	37
65	46.25	36.25
66	45.50	35.50
67	44.75	34.75
68	44	34
69	43.25	33.25
70	42.50	32.50
71	41.75	31.75
72	41	31
73	40.25	30.25
74	39.50	29.50
75	38.75	28.75
76	38	28
77	37.25	27.25
78	36.50	26.50
79	35.75	25.75

Safe Harbor and Unsafe Harbor Percentage at Each Non-Highly Compensated Employee Concentration Percentage (cont'd)

Non-Highly Compensated Employee Concentration Percentage	Safe Harbor Percentage	Unsafe Harbor Percentage
80	35	25
81	34.25	24.25
82	33.50	23.50
83	32.75	22.75
84	32	22
85	31.25	21.25
86	30.50	20.50
87	29.75	20
88	29	20
89	28.25	20
90	27.50	20
91	26.75	20
92	26	20
93	25.25	20
94	24.50	20
95	23.75	20
96	23	20
97	22.25	20
98	21.50	20
99	20.75	20

Q 11:41 How does the nondiscriminatory classification test work?

If an employer with 500 nonbargaining employees has 300 non-highly compensated nonbargaining employees (excluding those who do not meet age and service requirements), the employer has a non-highly compensated employee concentration percentage of 60 percent. The table in Q 11:40 shows that at that concentration percentage the safe harbor is 50 percent and the unsafe harbor is 40 percent. If all 200 highly compensated employees participate in the plan, at least 150 of the 300 non-highly compensated employees must participate in order to meet the safe harbor. If fewer than 120 participate, the plan is discriminatory. If more than 120, but fewer than 150, participate, the relevant facts and circumstances will determine whether the plan is discriminatory.

A Comparison of Privileged Groups

Highly Compensated Individuals [IRC § 105(h)(5)]

A highly compensated individual is defined as one of the following:

- One of the five highest-paid officers
- A shareholder who owns more than 10 percent of the employer's stock
- One of the highest-paid 25 percent of all employees

Highly Compensated Participants/Individuals [IRC § 125(e)]

Highly compensated participants and highly compensated individuals are defined as either employees or participants, respectively, who are the following:

- Officers
- More than 5 percent shareholders, in terms of voting power or value of all classes of stock
- Highly compensated employees
- Spouses and dependents of one of the above

Highly Compensated Employees [IRC § 414(q)]

This category includes any employee who during the current year or the preceding year fits one of the following criteria:

- Has been a 5 percent owner
- Received compensation from the employer in excess of $80,000 (adjusted for inflation—$85,000 in 2000) and (if the employer elects) was in the top-paid group of employees (i.e., the highest-paid 20 percent)

Key Employees [IRC § 416(i)]

A key employee is an employee who, at any time during the plan year or any of the preceding four plan years is:

- An officer earning more than 50 percent of the defined benefit pension plan limitation (that is, earning more that $67,500 in 2000); the total number of officers will not exceed 50, or, if fewer, 10 percent of employees (but not fewer than three)
- One of the 10 employees who own the largest interests in the company and who earn more than $30,000 a year
- A 5 percent owner
- A 1 percent owner earning more than $150,000

Chapter 12

Dental, Vision, and Other Benefits

This chapter looks at some of the other benefits provided to employees and the challenges they present to employers. These include dental, vision, life insurance, wellness, and health promotion programs.

Dental Benefits	12-1
Vision and Hearing Benefits	12-6
Life Insurance Benefits	12-8
Disability Benefits	12-10
Disability Management	12-16
Health Promotion and Wellness	12-20

Dental Benefits

Q 12:1 Do health insurance plans cover dental care?

Proper dental care was considered a budgetable expense, so traditionally it had not been included in group health insurance plans. In the 1970s, as its cost increased, dental care was added to employee benefit plans. Some plans include dental coverage as part of the medical plan; others include dental coverage as a separate plan. Many health insurance plans do provide coverage for non-cosmetic dental work necessitated by an accident. Some plans include limited coverage for hospital room and board expenses related to dental procedures, such as removal of impacted wisdom teeth, performed in a hospital.

Q 12:2 How common are dental benefits?

According to Web MD in 1999 about 156 million Americans had dental coverage. The 1999 survey by Mercer/Foster Higgins found that 95 percent of large employers offer dental benefits, with 8 percent offering preventive benefits only, but 87 percent providing a comprehensive plan. According to a Tillinghast-Towers Perrin survey, about 50 percent of the U.S. population has dental insurance.

Q 12:3 How are dental benefits provided?

Self-insured plans have been most prevalent among larger companies, which frequently have administrative services only (ASO) contracts with commercial carriers for claim processing and review. Dental coverage through HMOs and PPOs is also available.

A substantial number of employers that offer dental coverage provide it through a managed care program. According to the 1999 survey by Mercer/Foster Higgins, 37 percent offer a dental PPO and 20 percent offer an exclusive provider organization (dental HMO). According to the National Association of Dental Plans, 23.9 million people were covered by dental HMOs in 1996, up from only 7.8 million in 1990. Managed dental care is not evenly distributed; 60 percent of enrollees are in five states: California, Florida, Texas, Pennsylvania, and Illinois. California has 31 percent of the managed dental enrollment.

The number of dentists participating in prepaid plans is also increasing.

Q 12:4 What is direct reimbursement for dental care?

Direct reimbursement is a non-insured dental program in which an employer agrees to pay for a specified percentage or amount of receipted dental expenses. It has been used by smaller employers as a way of avoiding the costs associated with an insured plan and the administrative complexity that often accompanies insurance company programs. And, because dental expenses are more predictable than medical expenses—seldom involving emergencies or catastrophic expenses—the risk to employers is considerably smaller.

Q 12:5 What dental services are typically provided?

Dental services fall into a number of categories, as follows:

- Diagnostic
- Preventive
- Restorative
- Oral surgery
- Endodontic
- Periodontic
- Prosthodontic
- Orthodontic

Q 12:6 Are all types of dental services covered by insurance?

Usually not. Dental services are often divided into different coverage levels. Level I services include semiannual examinations, semiannual cleaning, x-rays, and diagnosis. Most plans cover at least preventive and diagnostic care. Level II (basic services) includes simple restoration (fillings), crowns and jackets, repair of crowns, extractions, and endodontics (root canals and internal pulp treatment). Level III (major services) includes dentures, bridges, and replacement of bridges and dentures. In order to emphasize prevention, many plans cover the Level I services at higher reimbursement levels than Level II or III services.

Q 12:7 What cost-management features are built into dental plans?

Dental plans in general tend to have more cost-effectiveness built into their design. The reason is that the insurance industry learned a lot from its experience with medical plans. Dental plans had the benefit of this experience and have cost management as an integral

Q 12:8

part of plan design. Cost-effective features include precertification and an emphasis on prevention as well as deductibles and copayments. There may also be maximum limits on outlays for services during a year, including separate maximums for orthodontic benefits, and the exclusion of orthodontic benefits altogether for persons over a certain age, such as 19.

There is something of a trend away from reasonable and customary reimbursement toward scheduled allowances to protect plan costs from the effects of inflation. Benefits remain fixed until the employer decides to increase the allowances. There is also a trend toward managed dental plans.

Q 12:8 Is evidence of insurability required to become covered under a dental plan?

Even though the Health Insurance Portability and Accountability Act of 1996 (HIPAA) rules prohibiting evidence of insurability in group plans do not apply to most dental plans, it is typical to cover any active employee without any evidence of insurability. Some plans do require a longer waiting period before being covered for major dental services than for preventive and basic services.

Q 12:9 Why is orthodontics often treated as a special coverage category?

Orthodontic problems are usually not the result of a disease, generally involve no acute symptoms, and are often more a matter of aesthetics (akin to cosmetic surgery). Some form of malocclusion (faulty spacing or meeting of teeth) occurs in large numbers of people. To provide all of these people with time-consuming and costly orthodontic corrections would be prohibitive for most plans. These problems can rarely be categorized as emergencies, so controls such as special dollar limits and prospective review are appropriate for orthodontics.

Q 12:10 Are there special cost-control considerations for dental plans?

Given the usual nature of dental expenses, yes, special considerations should apply. Dental treatments are generally not emergencies;

they are, for the most part, routine, predictable, and postponable. Employees can measure that against the cost of participating in the plan. If they have the choice of joining or not joining the plan, an employer should expect that employees will schedule their dental work to occur while they have coverage and drop coverage as soon thereafter as they can. In flex plans, this expectation has led to restrictions such as the "one up/one down" rule. This rule states that an employee cannot move more than one level up or down at each enrollment. This works for plans that have more than two levels of coverage.

A level of coverage refers to a choice. A dental plan might, for example, provide coverage at 50 percent, 60 percent, 70 percent, or 80 percent. By offering four choices, each providing a different amount of reimbursement, the plan is said to offer four levels of coverage. Under the one up/one down rule, an employee with 60 percent coverage would be permitted to move only to either 50 percent or 70 percent at the next enrollment cycle.

Plans with only two levels of coverage might instead impose a rule stating that a decision will be in effect for two years from the date it is made. That is, an employee who chooses to join the plan must retain (and pay for) coverage for at least two years. Similarly, the employee who chooses to opt out of the plan will be out of the plan for no less than two years. For the purposes of rules restricting movement between levels, opt-out (no coverage) is considered an option or level of coverage.

Q 12:11 What are dental plan incentives, and how do they work?

Dental plan incentives are designed to foster cost-effective benefit utilization. They are intended to encourage preventive services that are less costly than restorative services and that will reduce the need for restorative services in the future. For example, a plan may specify that Level I services will be reimbursed at 100 percent, while Level II services will be reimbursed at only 80 percent. Level III services, such as bridges, may be limited to 50 percent of their usual and customary charges. (See Q 12:6 for a more detailed explanation of Level I, II, and III services.)

Another form of incentive is structured to provide payment at a higher level if the services are used regularly. For example, a plan might cover Level I services at 100 percent and Level II services at 100 percent if Level I services had been used in each of the preceding two or three years. Had Level II services not been used regularly as required by this design, then they might be reimbursed at a lesser level, perhaps 70 or 75 percent.

Q 12:12 What is precertification?

Dental plans have used precertification or predetermination for years. Precertification or preauthorization of services involves three steps:

1. The dentist examines the patient and proposes a course of treatment.
2. A precertification form is completed by the dentist and the patient, and the form is submitted to the insurer or self-insured plan administrator for review prior to commencement of treatment.
3. The insurer considers the proposed treatment plan and approves it, denies it, or approves it with some modification.

Usually the precertification requirement applies to any amount over a specified level—often $200 or $300. Thus, excess paper work is not generated for minor or low-cost items. This allows the employee to reconsider or prepare to pay for nonapproved treatment.

Q 12:13 Are some dental services excluded from coverage?

Yes. Many plans exclude all cosmetic services. Plans also may not cover work in progress that is not completed within a specified period (say 60 to 90 days) of termination of coverage. Other plans limit costs by excluding adult orthodontia or any orthodontia. Another area of controversy involves temporomandibular joint syndrome (TMJ). Many plans limit the benefits for TMJ and periodontia.

Vision and Hearing Benefits

Q 12:14 How is vision care covered?

Most health insurance plans provide coverage for medical care related to eye injury or disease but do not cover the costs of periodic eye examinations or corrective lenses. Like dental care, vision care is a relatively new employee benefit, offered by employers that can afford to expand their employee benefit plans to include additional fringe benefits previously considered budgetable. Vision care is most often covered on a scheduled basis that pays a fixed dollar amount for examinations, lenses, and frames. Vision care is almost universally noncontributory because of the potential for biased selection.

Q 12:15 How prevalent is vision coverage?

According to the U.S. Department of Labor, 24 percent of full-time employees in medium and large establishments had vision coverage in 1995.

The 1999 Mercer/Foster Higgins survey found that 46 percent of large employers offered vision benefits, up from 36 percent in 1997. The survey found that vision benefits are much more common in the West, where 67 percent of employers offer vision benefits.

Q 12:16 What are the different types of vision care delivery systems?

There are three types of vision care plans offered by employers:

1. Indemnity plans,
2. Managed vision care plans, and
3. Discount plans.

Vision expenses can also be reimbursed through a flexible spending account. Many HMOs include vision benefits.

Q 12:17 How do indemnity vision plans work?

Typically, indemnity vision plans are scheduled benefits that pay up to a fixed amount for each covered service, regardless of the provider used.

Q 12:18 How do managed vision plans work?

Just as with medical plans, there are HMO-type vision plans and PPO-type vision plans. Managed vision plans function much the same way as managed medical plans.

Q 12:19 How do discount vision plans work?

Discount vision plans typically offer 20 percent to 30 percent discounts when using certain providers. There is often a monthly membership or administration fee of $3 or less. The plan sponsor can pay the membership fee or simply offer the plan on a voluntary basis. People needing vision services simply present their ID card and pay the discounted fee. There are no claim forms, deductibles, or copayments.

Q 12:20 Is coverage available for hearing evaluations and hearing aids?

While still not broadly available, hearing care plans are becoming somewhat more prevalent than they used to be. A 1997 survey by Hewitt Associates found that 12 percent of large employers provide hearing coverage. Where they are available, they typically provide a fixed dollar amount toward the cost of a hearing exam and some payment toward the purchase of a hearing aid. Both of these payments are also commonly restricted to once every two years. Hearing expenses can also be reimbursed through a flexible spending account.

Life Insurance Benefits

Q 12:21 Why would survivor benefits be included in a group health insurance program?

Small group health insurance policies offered by many insurers carry an option to provide life insurance benefits. Some insurance companies require such coverage as a condition for issue of a group health policy.

Q 12:22 What form do these death benefits take?

Under Internal Revenue Code (Code) Section 79, group term life insurance benefits must be offered to a group of employees on the basis of factors that preclude individual selection. This means that coverage is based on such things as age, years of service, compensation, and position.

The coverage may not discriminate in favor of key employees. Common nondiscriminatory formulas include flat benefits, with all covered employees entitled to identical death benefits, and earnings-based benefits, with each employee covered up to some multiple of compensation, commonly 1, 1½, or 2 times pay. Another formula, the position schedule, provides different levels of coverage to different classes of employees, with senior employees typically receiving the greatest benefits. This arrangement is most likely to produce discriminatory benefits and additional taxable income.

Q 12:23 How are these death benefits taxed?

Under Code Section 79, the cost of providing the first $50,000 of these benefits is tax-free to non-key employees. Key employees receiving "discriminatory benefits" also pay tax on the value of the first $50,000 of benefit. Amounts in excess of $50,000 result in taxable income to all employees. The value of imputed income is determined as the greater of actual cost or IRS Table I cost. Taxable life insurance benefits are also subject to FICA withholding.

Death benefits under an insured group term or AD&D (accidental death and dismemberment) program are not taxable income to the beneficiary. Self-funded death benefits are treated as ordinary income to the beneficiary. Before passage of the Small Business Job Protection Act of 1996, up to $5,000 in self-funded death benefits could be provided tax free.

Q 12:24 Does taxation differ depending on who pays for the coverage?

Yes. If the employer pays for the entire amount of coverage, the employee is taxed on the total cost. If the employee pays for any part of the coverage, the amount paid by the employee may be deducted. This is true whether the employee contributions are toward the purchase of optional or basic coverage. The amount of taxable income generated by life insurance is calculated as shown in the following example:

> $60,000 employer-provided life insurance
> \+ $20,000 employee purchase life insurance (if any)
> = $80,000 total amount of life insurance
> − $50,000
> = $30,000
>
> This amount is multiplied by the appropriate Section 79 rate (or actual cost, if greater). For example, the Section 79 rate for a person age 55 to 59 is $5.16 per year per $thousand of coverage.* The rest of the calculation is:
>
> 30 thousands of dollars of coverage
> × $5.16 annual rate
> = $154.80
> − $100 employee contributions (if any)
> = $54.80 taxable amount

---

*The rate chosen for this example, $5.16 (.43/mo) per thousand dollars of coverage is correct for persons age 55 to 59.

Q 12:25 Are employer contributions for group term life insurance subject to state income tax?

Employer contributions attributable to amounts in excess of $50,000 are taxed in most states.

Disability Benefits

Q 12:26 How much of employers' payroll is used to pay disability benefits?

According to a 1999 survey by the Washington Business Group on Health, direct costs alone total 6.3 percent of payroll; the components are:

1. Workers' compensation (2.5%),
2. Sick pay (1.7%),
3. Long-term disability (0.6%),
4. Short-term disability (1.5%).

The same survey found the average indirect costs of disability, including overtime, replacement employees and workstation or job accommodation, to be 8 percent of payroll.

The annual cost of lost time is about $5,000 per employee.

Q 12:27 How pervasive are disabilities in the United States?

According to a study by the Social Security Administration, 19 percent of working males and 15.3 percent of working females will lose some amount of work time by age 60 because of disability.

Q 12:28 How do employees become disabled?

According to a study by Aetna, the most frequent causes of disability claims are:

1. Pregnancy,
2. Respiratory problems,
3. Back disorders,
4. Bone fractures and joint sprains,
5. Bone and joint problems not caused by accidents,
6. Stomach and intestinal disorders, and
7. Mental illness.

Q 12:29 What programs are available to compensate employees for disability?

There are a number of public and private programs. Public programs include Social Security, workers' compensation at the state level, and nonoccupational temporary disability plans in some states. Private programs include individual disability plans, short-term disability (STD), long-term disability (LTD), accidental death and dismemberment, and disability pension benefits.

Q 12:30 What is a short-term disability plan?

Short-term disability plans are designed to provide income to employees during temporary periods of disability. Although this period may extend up to two years, the most common period is six months. An STD program may be made up of two types of plans:

1. A sick pay plan that pays employees according to their credited sick days, which are accrued ratably over the employee's period of service; and
2. An accident and sickness plan that provides for full or partial replacement of income following a waiting period of a specified number of days (such as seven), up to a maximum number of weeks, generally ranging from 13 to 52, at which time LTD benefits would commence.

Sick pay plan payments are generally made from general company accounts; accident and sickness plan payments are usually insured or self-funded.

Q 12:31 Must employers provide short-term (nonoccupational) disability benefits?

Five states—California, Hawaii, New Jersey, New York, Rhode Island—and Puerto Rico mandate temporary, nonoccupational disability benefits. The requirement for coverage is based on the state of employment, not the state of residence. Provisions vary from state to state.

Q 12:32 What is a long-term disability plan?

A long-term disability plan is a program that provides income to employees who are disabled for significant periods of time, generally from six months to life.

Q 12:33 How is disability defined?

Long-term disability plans may define disability as the inability to perform the duties of any occupation, or the inability to perform the duties associated with one's own occupation. Some plans use the latter definition for the first two or three years to allow time to adapt to a new occupation, after which the first definition becomes operative. Still other definitions tie disability income payments to the inability to perform the duties (or any, every, or material duties) of one's own occupation (or any other occupation for which one is qualified by education, training, or experience) and a loss of some income. Partial disability benefits could be payable if the employee is unable to perform some functions of his or her job and has experienced a loss of some portion (e.g., 20 percent) of his or her income.

Q 12:34 What are other important components of an LTD plan?

Long-term disability plans have the following components:

1. *Eligibility period.* Employees may be required to complete a minimum period of service with the company, which may be as much as a year but is generally less.
2. *Preexisting conditions.* Disability benefits may not be payable if the disability results from a condition the employee suffered or for which he or she was receiving treatment during a specified period (e.g., 3 to 12 months) preceding coverage. When benefits for such a disability are payable, they may be contingent upon a continuous period of coverage, for example, a full year.
3. *Elimination period.* LTD benefits become payable a specified number of months after the disability commences—usually 6 to 12 months. STD payments are usually payable in the interim.
4. *Integration with other benefits.* To prevent pyramiding of disability income payments, LTD plan benefits are generally offset by payments from other sources such as pension plans and Social Security.
5. *Payment period.* Although some plans provide lifetime disability income payments, most are payable up to age 65 or 70, at which time payments from other sources, such as pension plans

and Social Security, would commence. In order to comply with the Age Discrimination in Employment Act, payment durations may be tied to age at the time the disability commences—equal premium costs translating to shorter payment periods for older workers.

6. *Cost-of-living adjustments (COLAs).* COLAs may be either a fixed percentage or a floating percentage tied to an index such as the consumer price index.

Q 12:35 How much do disabled workers receive from disability plans?

Typically, an STD plan will pay anywhere from 50 percent to 100 percent of salary, with 50 percent to 67 percent of salary being the most common. LTD plans generally provide from 50 percent to 67 percent, with 70 percent at the high end.

Q 12:36 How are employees taxed on disability benefits?

Employer contributions to accident or health plans are not includible in employee income under Code Section 106. Benefits received by employees from a noncontributory employer plan are generally taxable, except for those unrelated to absence from work that constitute payment for loss of a bodily function or permanent disfigurement. [IRC § 105] Other accident and health insurance payments (i.e., those attributable to employee contributions, or employer contributions that were included in the employee's income) are not part of an employee's taxable income. [IRC § 104]

Individuals under age 65 with limited incomes who are retired because of permanent and total disability (that is, inability to engage in any substantial gainful activity by reason of a medically determined physical or mental impairment that can be expected to result in death or that has lasted or can be expected to last for at least 12 continuous months) are entitled to a tax credit. The credit is 15 percent of an "initial amount" ranging from $3,750 to $7,500 (depending on the tax filing status of the recipient) and adjusted for pension, Social Security, veterans, or other disability payments; and 50 percent of adjusted gross income in excess of specified levels (ranging from $5,000 to $10,000, again depending on tax filing status). [IRC § 22]

Q 12:37 Is an employee who leaves the service of his or her employer as a result of a total disability entitled to exclude certain payments from his or her qualified retirement plan from taxable income?

Code Section 105 permits such exclusions if the payments are received from accident and health insurance or an employer-sponsored accident and health plan. Retirement plans are clearly not designed to be accident and health plans; their primary purpose is to provide retirement income benefits. It is possible, however, for a retirement plan to serve a dual function, providing both retirement and disability benefits. In order for a retirement plan to be deemed an accident and health plan, it must meet certain criteria, as follows:

1. It must be clear from a reading of the plan that it is intended to be an accident and health plan; and
2. In order for payments to be excluded from gross income, it is necessary that the distributions:
   a. Constitute payment for the permanent loss or loss of use of a member or a function of the body, or the permanent disfigurement of the taxpayer; and
   b. Be computed with reference to the nature of the injury without regard to the period the employee is absent from work.

Few qualified retirement plans meet these requirements. Most, if they cover disability at all, provide for accelerated vesting and full payment of benefits upon total disability. In such instances, payments are perhaps offset or delayed by disability benefits from other sources. The Internal Revenue Service has denied dual-purpose status in the past, when it has found the plan provisions to be insufficient to establish clearly the dual nature of the plan. Examples are:

1. Plan provisions that determined the size of the payment as a function of employee compensation and length of service (and perhaps company profitability, as with a profit sharing plan) rather than the nature of illness or disability,

2. Plan provisions that provided for vesting only on permanent and total disability and not for any other level of disability or illness, and

3. A plan amendment that permitted the company to make discretionary distributions for prolonged illness and other non-health-related emergencies, as it was viewed as a trigger for distributing vested benefits and not specifically as a health plan feature. [Ltr Rul 8753011]

Those employers or retirement plan sponsors who might choose to restructure their plans to meet the dual-purpose tests have some guidance from the Sixth Circuit Court of Appeals as to how to go about it. A ruling spelled out some "clear indicia" for identifying a plan as a dual-purpose deferred compensation/accident and health plan. These criteria include the following:

1. A statement indicating that the plan is intended to be dual-purpose, as well as a statement that benefits are intended to be excludable under Code Section 105(c);

2. A plan provision that indicates that benefits include amounts spent for medical care, and that limits benefits to legitimate medical expenses; and

3. Provisions for compensation of specific injuries or illnesses, comparable to those found in accident and health plans.

Even with these provisions, benefits must still be computed on the basis of the nature of the injury or the expenses incurred. Simple payment of the employee's vested benefit, without variance for the nature or severity of the disability or illness, would fail to meet the requirements of Code Section 105(c)(2). [Berman v Commr, No 90-1356 (6th Cir 1991)]

Disability Management

Q 12:38 How can employers achieve effective disability management?

There are two fundamental approaches to disability management: prevention/wellness and rehabilitation.

Q 12:39 How does an employer, union, or insurer put a disability prevention program in place?

There are nine steps to effective disability prevention:

1. Collect adequate data.
2. Use preemployment physicals.
3. Screen employees and prospective employees for health risks.
4. Correct on-the-job health hazards.
5. Educate employees and prospective employees about health risks.
6. Educate employees about job-related health hazards.
7. Develop employee assistance programs (see Chapter 22).
8. Identify and treat lifestyle-related problems with education and behavioral modification programs.
9. Optimize employee health benefit design.

Q 12:40 What is an independent medical examination?

Independent medical examinations (IMEs) are a way to control long-term disability plan costs by making sure disability benefits go to those who are entitled to benefits, but not to malingerers. An IME is an impartial third-party evaluation of an employee's condition by an independent physician—a specialist in the appropriate medical field who has not treated or examined the claimant. IMEs are used to determine if someone is truly disabled according to plan provisions.

Q 12:41 How does rehabilitation fit into disability management?

One aspect of managing disability program costs is that of returning the employee to work as soon as possible, consistent with good medical practice. A well-designed rehabilitation feature will allow an employee to return to the job site and begin receiving a paycheck, without causing all disability benefits to cease or without causing the employee to face a new elimination period should the disability worsen and the employee be unable to continue the rehabilitation program.

Q 12:42 How does the rehabilitation benefit interact with pay?

The rehabilitation benefit is intended to be an incentive to return to work (see Q 12:47). As such, the employee should not see a one-for-one reduction of disability benefit when the paycheck resumes. Typically, for every $2 of pay, the disability benefit is reduced $1.

Q 12:43 What portion of the disabled can actually be rehabilitated?

Most of the disabled can and do return to work, and certain groups are more likely to return than others. For example, one study showed that those at higher income levels and with more education are most likely to return. Income, education level, and head-of-household status are factors in the likelihood of a disabled employee returning to work.

Q 12:44 Are some people better candidates than others for disability rehabilitation?

Yes. It may help to ask the following questions as part of the disability assessment process:

1. Is the disabled employee motivated to come back to work?
2. Does the company want the employee back?
3. How close is the employee to retirement?
4. Was this a good, bad, or excellent employee before the disability?
5. Can the job be modified if necessary?
6. Is there a potential for a gradual return to work?

Q 12:45 What ingredients go into a rehabilitation program?

The following six ingredients have proven to help program success:

1. Specific program objectives;
2. Use of a team approach;

3. Rapid disability assessment;
4. Professional evaluation of return-to-work potential;
5. Flexibility with regard to treatment and job functions; and
6. Well-informed management.

Q 12:46 Who staffs a rehabilitation team?

The following seven people need to be involved:
1. Rehabilitation coordinator;
2. Registered nurse;
3. Vocational specialist;
4. Claims adjustor;
5. Company health and safety manager;
6. Treating physician; and
7. Supervisor.

Q 12:47 What is a return-to-work program?

A return-to-work program actively involves the employer in finding ways for the employee to get back on the job as soon as possible. The program usually consists of the following:
1. A monitoring system that keeps a current list of disabled employees, their treatment, condition, and estimated return-to-work date;
2. A rehabilitation program that offers physical and psychological therapy; and
3. A job accommodation program that tailors work to the abilities of the employee as much as possible, including special arrangements for light duty, modified low-stress work, or a new job altogether.

Q 12:48 What is an independent living program?

An independent living program (ILP) helps disabled persons live as independently as possible. Often run or managed by disabled persons themselves, ILPs develop job training programs, teach job skills, provide housing assistance, and coordinate worksite modifications. They also provide assistance to disabled workers who are returning to work, or workers who are helping to care for a disabled person.

Q 12:49   What percentage of employers coordinate their overall approach to disability?

A 1999 survey by the Washington Business Group on Health found that 43 percent of respondents said they coordinate their overall disability approach, up from only 26 percent in 1997.

Health Promotion and Wellness

Q 12:50   What is health promotion?

Health promotion and wellness are often used synonymously. Some specialists in the field make a distinction, with wellness being related to preventive medicine and diagnostics and health promotion meaning behavioral modification programs to improve lifestyle. Among the latter they include nutrition, weight reduction, diet, smoking cessation, stress management, high blood pressure control, exercise, accident prevention, and EAPs.

Wellness and health promotion programs are most common among larger companies. A 1999 survey conducted by Hewitt Associates found that 93 percent of companies sponsor some sort of health promotion program, up from 88 percent in 1994.

Q 12:51   Which types of health promotion activities are most common?

A 1999 survey by Hewitt Associates found that 93 percent of employers have some type of health promotion program, up from 89 percent in 1996 and 64 percent in 1992. The survey found that the most common programs are:

1. Health screenings—81 percent of employers indicate they currently use screenings. Most administer screenings for high blood pressure or cholesterol via on-site health fairs, mobile units or through their health plans.
2. Special health promotion programs—76 percent offer programs such as flu vaccinations, well-baby/child care and prenatal care.
3. Education or training—72 percent offer programs that range from seminars and workshops to counseling for lifestyle habits that contribute to chronic or acute conditions.
4. Financial incentive and disincentive programs—40 percent of employers offer incentives or disincentives. The most common incentives employers offer are gifts or monetary awards for employees who participate in health appraisals or screenings. Examples of disincentives include employers charging an employee a higher life insurance premium if he or she is a smoker or providing lower medical benefits if he or she was not wearing a safety belt or was under the influence of alcohol or drugs while involved in a car accident.
5. Health risk appraisals—27 percent of employers administer questionnaires as a way to analyze an employee's health history and promote early detection of preventable health conditions. These appraisals make employees more aware of behaviors they may need to change and sometimes provide suggestions for modifying lifestyles to lessen the risk of health problems. Employers are evenly divided as to whether they use appraisals annually or periodically.

Q 12:52 Why would an employer offer health promotion programs?

One obvious reason is high health care costs. Such programs are one of many strategies that companies use to get a handle on health costs. But there are other reasons as well. Health promotion program objectives include the following:

- Improve employee morale
- Foster better employee relations

- Reduce absenteeism
- Reduce benefits costs
- Enhance recruitment efforts
- Lower disability claims and days of disability
- Lower workers' compensation claims
- Reduce the number of grievances
- Reduce turnover
- Promote more effective use of the health care system

Some insurers offer discounts for healthy life styles; passing along discounts is one way of promoting wellness.

Q 12:53 Are there advantages to offering health promotion programs at the worksite?

Yes, the worksite offers several advantages. First, the worksite is convenient, so people do not have to travel in order to benefit from the program. Second, the coworker peer group serves as a support group, which helps the success rate of programs. This is particularly important for such programs as smoking cessation and weight reduction. Third, there is an organizational structure and a financial sponsor (the company) with a vested interest in the outcome, which also augments success rates.

Q 12:54 How does a company select a health promotion program?

There are a few ways to choose among health promotion programs. For example, a company might conduct an employee survey to gauge interest among its employee population. A review of health and disability claims may suggest environmental problems, such as safety, that should be addressed. Another way to select a health promotion program is with the life-style cost index (LCI).

Q 12:55 What is the life-style cost index?

The LCI is a methodology developed to pinpoint specific health problems at a given employer location. LCI was developed by the National Center for Health Promotion in cooperation with the School of Public Health at the University of Michigan. Essentially, LCI uses a combination of company-specific health claims experience and health risk factor analysis to determine which life-style-related health problems should be addressed at any given company.

Q 12:56 Why is interest in health promotion growing?

The nature of illness has changed dramatically. Because of improvements in the detection and treatment of acute infectious disease, most of our health problems are related to lifestyle issues. Cardiovascular disease, cancer, and strokes account for more than 60 percent of all deaths in the United States. These can all be affected by wellness-based interventions. Some predisposing risk factors include high cholesterol, obesity, smoking, substance abuse, lack of exercise, high blood pressure, diabetes, and exposure to toxic substances.

Q 12:57 Are employees satisfied with the information employers are providing?

A large minority are not. A survey sponsored by Intracorp found that 46 percent of employees were dissatisfied with the health information they were getting at work. The survey also found that 44 percent of employees reported their employers provide no health education.

A 1997 survey by Care Data found that fewer than 44 percent of health maintenance organization members considered care to be adequate for smoking cessation, chiropractic care, weight loss, drug and alcohol rehabilitation, and osteoporosis.

Q 12:58 What is preventive care coverage?

Preventive care coverage provides for expenses incurred in the prevention, rather than the treatment, of illness or injury. It is sometimes referred to as "well care." Some preventive care expenses have traditionally been covered, such as diagnostic tests, to ascertain whether additional medication is required to control high blood pressure to prevent a stroke, and well baby care—nursery care and immunizations at birth. Routine checkups for early detection of problems have not usually been covered.

Q 12:59 What kinds of benefits does preventive care coverage provide when it is part of a health care plan?

Preventive care coverage can include a variety of benefits, ranging from routine checkups, immunizations, and Pap tests to health risk appraisals (HRAs) and wellness programs.

Q 12:60 How often are routine checkups usually covered under a preventive care plan?

There is some difference of opinion in the medical profession concerning how often routine physical examinations should be conducted and how useful they are; therefore, there is a lack of uniformity regarding how often such exams are covered. Some plans cover them annually; others cover routine physicals as well as diagnostic tests and X-rays periodically, based on the insured's age.

Q 12:61 What is the current trend with regard to routine physicals?

The trend is away from routine physicals and toward screening for particular risk factors related to age and sex, along with individual health history and status. Rather than being examined on a periodic basis (such as annually) for all health problems, each individual is profiled for particular screening. Examples would be mammograms for women based on age and history and prostate examinations for men over 50.

Q 12:62 What has caused the move away from the traditional physical?

The change has to do with both quality and cost. From a qualitative standpoint, specific screening geared toward age, gender, health history, and health status is simply more targeted and likely to produce more accurate results. Moreover, specific screening is not as expensive as a comprehensive physical.

Q 12:63 Are there any specific guidelines available for health screening for particular risk factors?

Recently, the Blue Cross and Blue Shield Association and the American College of Physicians issued guidelines for medical tests to be scheduled over an adult's lifetime. The tests, which are designed to detect disease when there are no symptoms, typically would not be covered by most health plans because of the absence of a diagnosed illness or injury. Most HMOs are an exception to that rule because of their greater emphasis on wellness programs.

Blue Cross/Blue Shield plans nationwide are now offering coverage for the recommended screening tests, and other insurers have indicated a willingness to use these guidelines as well. The Health Care Financing Administration is currently working to develop screening guidelines for the Medicare program.

Q 12:64 Are there guidelines on how frequently women should have mammograms?

Yes, both the National Cancer Institute and the American Cancer Society have issued guidelines. They are similar, but not identical. The American Cancer Society urges women to have annual mammograms beginning at age 40. The National Cancer Institute says women in their 40s should get mammograms every year or two if they are at average risk for breast cancer.

Q 12:65 What tests are recommended in the preventive care program?

The recommended tests are: blood pressure screening, cholesterol tests, sigmoidoscopy for colorectal cancer, pap smear for cervical cancer, and mammography. The schedule suggests frequencies based on age ranges and also suggests certain immunizations and boosters.

Q 12:66 Will providing preventive care coverage save money?

When health problems are found early, they can be treated more successfully and more economically. Providing preventive coverage may result in increased productivity, improved quality of life, and perhaps even longer lives. Screening will also detect other, less threatening conditions that might never have been treated, and longer lives require more medical care; therefore, it is likely that preventive care benefits will increase health care costs.

During the 1995-1996 flu season, CIGNA vaccinated nearly 3,000 employees. Only 10 percent of the vaccinated employees reported flu symptoms, compared with 30 percent the year before among employees without vaccinations. Employees with flu shots reported an average of 0.7 days of absence because of colds and flu, compared to 2.1 days the prior year when they did not receive vaccinations. Savings to employers from decreased absenteeism and reduced productivity are likely to outweigh additional costs.

Q 12:67 What is a wellness program?

The most recent trend in preventive care is insurance coverage for HRAs and for exercise, nutrition, smoking cessation, and stress management programs. Because the programs encourage employees to achieve or maintain good health and well-being, they are commonly referred to as wellness programs.

Wellness programs are sometimes covered by insurance in larger companies whose claim experience significantly affects their health insurance premium rates (or when the employer is partially or fully self-funding the plan). Some smaller employers are also being offered wellness insurance coverage as part of their plans.

Q 12:68 What are some advantages and disadvantages of wellness programs?

If properly designed and focused, wellness programs can help cut costs, but there are limitations. Wellness programs are cost-effective, returning anywhere from $2 to $6 per $1 invested; however, that return is achieved over time. An employer with high turnover may find that its employees become healthy just in time to save their next employer a few dollars. Another limitation is that it is not possible to get every employee, spouse, and dependent into a wellness program, so the savings are restricted only to those who participate. Furthermore, not all diseases are related to lifestyle—a wellness program may, for example, cut heart disease costs, but will not affect costs for accident-related injuries.

Q 12:69 What types of wellness programs are there?

Wellness plans may consist of one or more activities that fall into one of the following categories:

1. *Health audits or health risk appraisals.* A health risk appraisal may uncover nascent ailments that can be treated early, thereby heading off more serious and costly complications later. Audits may also show that an employee's health has been affected by environmental factors for which the company could be held liable if an employee becomes ill and sues.

2. *Fitness programs.* Aerobics is one example. Cardiovascular fitness is another. Programs may range from organized gym exercise to special machinery to a fully equipped gym with attached analytical program and trained attendants—from the very cheap to the very expensive. They may also extend to corporate sponsorship of athletic competition. One criticism is that these programs tend to attract people who are health-conscious anyway and who would pursue a similar program elsewhere (at their own expense) if the company did not provide one. Still, they are popular and most are not particularly expensive.

3. *Habit-breaking programs.* Programs to stop smoking and alcohol abuse, prevent stress, and lose weight fall into this category. There is conflicting evidence as to the long-term benefits of such programs for employers.

4. *Education and promotion.* Rather than concentrating on a target population through intensive counseling, as in the habit-breaking programs, these programs reach out for the broadest range of employees through: poster promotions, company-wide screening (e.g., blood pressure testing), and orientations (e.g.,

a company health fair with participation from local health agencies).

As most smaller companies are not expert in health matters, they need to turn to outside professionals who can provide support at reasonable cost. Local hospitals and universities, health clubs, health associations, and charitable groups can supply many of the elements of a successful program. A more ambitious program may require a specialist in wellness plan design.

Q 12:70 What are typical components of wellness programs?

Wellness programs can be grouped into three major categories: education, screening, and fitness.

Some typical education programs are the following:

Smoking cessation. It has been demonstrated beyond question that stopping smoking is the single most healthful thing people can do for themselves. From the employer's standpoint, there is an impressive body of evidence showing that smokers incur higher health care costs than nonsmokers. A number of studies have shown that smoking employees can cost an employer as much as $4,500 per year more than nonsmoking employees. To add insult to injury, recent studies have linked smoking to artery disease (clogging of the carotid artery) in people inhaling second-hand smoke as well as the persons actually smoking; therefore, the cost to the employer is not only direct—in that smokers are sick more often and absent longer when they are sick—but also indirect in that they are affecting their nonsmoking coworkers too.

Prenatal care. Prevent one premature birth and this program will have paid for itself for many, many years. The March of Dimes offers many free and low-cost prenatal wellness services.

Other education programs include nutrition/weight reduction, stress management, injury prevention, back care, self-care, and AIDS education.

Typical screening programs include health-risk appraisals (HRAs), blood pressure, cholesterol, diabetes, glaucoma, and cancers (breast, cervical, colon, prostate, and skin).

Typical fitness programs include exercise facilities, exercise classes, paid or subsidized health club membership, and flexibility training.

Q 12:71 What are some characteristics of effective prenatal care programs?

Successful prenatal care programs include the following:

1. Access to prenatal health education materials, videos, and programs in the workplace;
2. Incentives to participate, including savings bonds, pregnancy calendars, Baby's 1st Year calendars, and prenatal care books;
3. Guest speakers who discuss pregnancy and health-related issues;
4. Health care benefits structured to cover prenatal care services at 100 percent; and
5. Mandates that employees seek early and regular prenatal care from a healthcare provider.

Q 12:72 How can monetary penalties and rewards be used to enhance a wellness program?

Some plans go further than simply making wellness promotion services and activities available. Lifestyle plans establish a monetary tie between wellness and the company health care plan, rewarding employees who pass physical evaluations in certain key areas (similar to the nonsmoking discounts given by life insurers).

The theory is that health care costs are not spread evenly among the workforce. A disproportionate share of the employer's health care dollar goes to pay the costs of treating illnesses that are in some measure preventable. The reward system goes at least part of the way toward encouraging unhealthy employees to change their ways, thereby ultimately reducing costs, or realigning premiums so that those who choose to be high risks pay for their choice.

Companies such as Johnson & Johnson and Adolph Coors are trying similar approaches to provide individuals with unhealthy lifestyles an incentive to change their health habits. U-Haul had a similar program, but dropped it after HIPAA was enacted.

Employers need to consider penalties and rewards carefully in light of HIPAA's prohibition against using health status to determine eligibility, contributions, or benefits. For example, an employer could offer a premium discount to participants who adhere to a cholesterol-reduction wellness program if individuals could qualify for the discount based on adhering to a physician's dietary recommendations. On the other hand, requiring enrollees to achieve a cholesterol count under 200 would discriminate impermissibly because some enrollees may be unable to achieve that level as a result of a health status-related factor.

Despite potential legal problems, a 1998 Hewitt Associates survey found that 18 percent of employers had higher contributions for medical plans for high-risk individuals. Furthermore, 6 percent of employers had lower medical coverage for high-risk individuals. Additionally, 19 percent of employers granted additional credits under flexible benefit plans to employees meeting specific criteria.

Q 12:73 How prevalent are wellness programs?

According to the Bureau of Labor Statistics 1997 survey, 36 percent of full-time employees were offered wellness programs such as physical fitness, smoking cessation, and stress management.

Q 12:74 Do wellness plans work?

A study reported in the *Journal of the American Medical Association* found that a dollar spent on hypertension control programs can return between $1.89 and $2.72 in reduced health care claims, although it takes several years to realize savings.

A two-year study of blue-collar workers at Du Pont reported in the *American Journal of Public Health* showed that a health promotion program consisting of health-risk assessment, counseling, and classes on such things as general fitness, diet, smoking cessation, and stress management was successful in reducing costs. Results include the following:

1. Absences from non-job-related illnesses dropped by 14 percent at job sites where the program was offered, versus 5.8 percent where it was not.

2. Reduced absentee costs represented $1.42 for each dollar spent on the health promotion program. The first year's relative return was only $1.11, in part a reflection of high first-year start-up costs, but the return jumped to $2.05 in the second year.

Q 12:75 How can the effectiveness of wellness plans be measured?

Computers can help evaluate the effectiveness of wellness plans. One program from the University of Pittsburgh Graduate School of Public Health, PREVIEW (Prevention: Risks and Expected Values of Intervention for Employee Welfare), employs national risk-prevalence averages and data from employer health risk appraisals or employee physicals to help employers estimate savings and make cost projections. Once the program is in place, it uses participation and dropout rates as well as behavioral statistics to measure actual savings. It is designed to evaluate programs for smoking cessation, hypertension control, cholesterol reduction, and seat belt usage.

According to a survey by William M. Mercer Inc., 53 percent of employers reported that the inability to measure results was an obstacle to the success of the wellness program.

Q 12:76 In addition to behavioral modification and preventive programs, in what other ways can a company enhance health?

A company can develop specific policies allowing employees time to participate in health programs, create optimum health benefit design, institute smoking policies, and support employee-management communication and EAPs. Companies can also provide nutritious food in their cafeterias and institute noise abatement programs and quality-of-worklife programs.

Q 12:77 Why would an employer want to include preventive care or wellness programs in a group insurance plan?

Some state laws mandate coverage, such as well baby care. A typical benefit covers nursery care for a fixed number of days and specific tests routinely done within 48 hours of birth. Some employers include other preventive care benefits because it is often cheaper to prevent an illness or injury than it is to treat it. Thus, by investing in programs that are designed to prevent illness, employers may realize future cost savings.

Another reason for including preventive care has to do with employees' increasing concern with their health. Employers looking to provide meaningful benefits for their employees can do so by providing preventive care coverage.

Q 12:78 Where can an employer obtain more information on wellness programs?

The Wellness Councils of America offers a book called *The Small Business Source Book* describing wellness programs. Contact WELCOA, 9802 Nicholas Street, Suite 315, Omaha, NE 68114. Call them for membership information at (402) 827-3590.

Q 12:79 Are wellness or health promotion programs usually insured?

No. Most health promotion programs are free-standing programs rather than part of the insurance package. Some preventive services are a required part of an insurance package. For example, some states mandate coverage for well baby care or alcohol and substance abuse, but most programs are optional for the employer. By offering these programs on a free-standing basis, the company has more flexibility. A company may want to offer one or two programs, but not everything; a large company may want to offer certain programs at one location and other programs at other sites.

Q 12:80 What is a health risk appraisal?

A health risk appraisal describes an individual's chances of death, illness, or injury in the future. A typical HRA asks the individual questions about his or her sex, age, family and individual health history, specific health practices, and lifestyle (smoking, drinking alcohol, exercise, stress, seat-belt usage). Depending on the HRA, questions concerning the individual's reactions to everyday work and social situations may be included.

Q 12:81 How does the HRA fit in with health promotion?

Many companies start with the HRA as another way to determine which programs to offer employees. The HRA is an inexpensive way to uncover employee needs. The process usually involves the HRA followed by distribution of some educational materials. At this point, a combination of HRA results, an employee interest survey, and the lifestyle cost index can help the company decide on a course of action. The next step often involves implementation of one or more behavioral modification programs.

Q 12:82 Would an employer use an HRA to determine the components of its group health insurance plan?

Yes. By combining each employee's HRA scores, a total health risk profile of all employees can be produced. The employer will acquire significant information concerning the general health of the employee population in aggregate. Based on the information, the employer may decide to institute health programs or provide certain preventive care benefits. This will help employees improve their health, and may lead to cost savings to the extent medical care utilization is reduced.

Q 12:83 Are HRA results used to set the price for health insurance coverage?

As more and more employers become aware of the link between employees' lifestyles and their medical costs, the concept of using HRAs to influence employee contributions is inevitable. The initial efforts are tentative in nature. In the vast majority of instances where HRAs are reported to be in use, they are being utilized as positive, rather than negative, incentives. As discussed in Q 12:72, negative incentives may be prohibited by HIPAA.

Positive incentives are most often used to reward compliance. "Compliance" can mean either participation in the program or attainment of predetermined goals.

Rewards might include the following:

1. Additional credits, which may be used to purchase coverage in a flexible benefits design;
2. Employer contributions into the employee's spending account;
3. Direct cash payment; and
4. Awards or prizes such as T-shirts, or a day off.

Participation in a program might be defined as:

1. Completing and returning an HRA;
2. Taking a blood pressure, cholesterol, or other screening test and receiving the results;
3. Attending a smoking cessation class;
4. Attending a prenatal class (for expectant mothers); or
5. Agreeing to wear a seatbelt while in a car.

Achieving predetermined goals could be:

1. Having an acceptable serum cholesterol level;
2. Being at or below a specified weight (based on sex and height);
3. Having blood pressure at desired levels; or
4. Being tobacco-free for six months or a year (for quitting smokers).

Q 12:84 Which works better as an incentive, participation or achievement?

The answer depends on the goal and the specific program being considered. To cause modifications in lifestyle behavior, rewarding achievement—not just participation—may be required. This is a tough stance to take and may not sit well with employees, unions, or, in some instances, the government. But if, for example, an employer wants its employees to quit smoking, rewarding attendance at nonsmoking clinics might not be enough, as employees might attend just to receive the reward, with no serious intent to comply with the program. On the other hand, many people will argue that the first step is to get the smoker into the clinic (perhaps using rewards) in order to have any hope of success in modifying the smoker's behavior.

Other things, such as completing an HRA, might be sufficient unto themselves to merit a reward.

Because HIPAA prohibits using health status to determine eligibility, contributions, or benefits, it is safer to base incentives on participation than achievement. Prizes (such as T-shirts) for achievement are not prohibited by HIPAA.

Q 12:85 Which work better, positive or negative incentives?

It is too soon to tell. The concept of using either type of incentive to modify employee behavior is probably better categorized as experimental than as proven technology. A psychologist interviewed for this question suggested, as a broad generalization, that to cause someone to do something, positive incentives are better than negative, and that to cause someone to stop doing something, negative incentives are better. Of more importance than whether the incentive is positive or negative is the matter of magnitude: Is the incentive being utilized sufficient to influence behavior?

As discussed in Q 12:72, penalties may no longer be possible, but rewarding one behavior may be the same as penalizing the opposite behavior.

Q 12:86 What are the arguments for positive incentives?

Employees have become conditioned to expect only positive incentives. Historically, employers have feared that if too many negative incentives were imposed, employees would organize, quit, or reject the employer's program; therefore, employers have tended to utilize positive reinforcement to achieve their goals.

Q 12:87 When might the government take issue with the use of incentives?

While rewarding voluntary participation will probably not be an issue, rewards for achievement (or penalties for its lack) could open the employer to governmental charges of discrimination or of violating HIPAA or the Americans with Disabilities Act (ADA).

The critical consideration is whether the employee has the ability to achieve the goal established by the employer. An employee's inability may not result from lack of desire or of effort, but may be beyond his or her control. Achievement goals must be limited to lifestyle behaviors that can be modified, and the employer must be prepared to deal with situations where modification is not possible. For example, some individuals have genetically linked high cholesterol levels. Because such individuals will not be able to attain a marked reduction in their cholesterol levels no matter what they do, applying a penalty to them will be unfair. Withholding a reward from them based on their failing to attain the goal is also a penalty, so the employer could be accused of discrimination or of unfairness in this circumstance.

The Health Insurance Portability and Accountability Act of 1996 prohibits group health plans from basing any benefits or premiums on health-related factors. Even so, the legislative history makes it clear that plans can establish premium discounts or rebates or modify deductibles or copayments based on adherence to health promotion or disease prevention programs.

Q 12:88 Do insurance companies provide financial incentives to companies to adopt preventive care programs?

Some insurance carriers provide financial incentives for purchasing preventive care programs. This can take the form of lower premium payments for employers that have the programs in place. Others provide deductible and coinsurance percentages related to employee health. For example, employees who control their weight and blood pressure, wear seat belts, do not smoke, and have periodic physical exams may have their annual deductible waived. Some insurance companies also provide for partial reimbursement for individuals who attend health or exercise programs.

Chapter 13

COBRA

COBRA continuation of health care coverage can be an administrative nightmare. Plan administrators face a host of detailed technical requirements and a body of law that is constantly changing as a result of legislative and case law developments. In addition, many critical aspects of the law have not been adequately clarified by the courts or regulatory agencies. This chapter provides advice to readers at all levels of expertise.

The Basics	13-1
Covered Employers	13-8
Covered Plans	13-13
General Requirements	13-20
Notification Requirements	13-23
Premiums	13-30
Election and Grace Periods	13-35
Qualified Beneficiaries	13-39
Miscellaneous	13-43

The Basics

Q 13:1 What is COBRA?

COBRA is an acronym for the Consolidated Omnibus Budget Reconciliation Act of 1985. COBRA grants employees, their dependents, and certain others (see Q 13:56) the right to continue receiving coverage under the employer's health care plan(s) at the employer's group rate. The law requires employers to make the extended coverage available on a uniform basis, without regard to the health status of the person to be covered.

The law has been amended from time to time, either to revise it because of widespread criticism of some aspect of it, to make technical corrections, or to amplify on certain provisions that were unclear or incomplete in their original form and caused misinterpretation or other confusion. Amendments have come from the Tax Reform Act of 1986 (TRA '86), Omnibus Budget Reconciliation Act of 1986 (OBRA '86), Technical and Miscellaneous Revenue Act of 1988 (TAMRA), Omnibus Budget Reconciliation Act of 1989 (OBRA '89), Omnibus Budget Reconciliation Act of 1990 (OBRA '90), Health Insurance Portability and Accountability Act of 1996 (HIPAA), and the Small Business Job Protection Act of 1996 (SBJPA). Additionally, COBRA was affected by the Family and Medical Leave Act of 1993 (FMLA) and the Omnibus Budget Reconciliation Act of 1993 (OBRA '93). Employers researching questions on COBRA are cautioned to look further, not only at the basic law, but at the various amending laws as well.

Q 13:2 What are the highlights of the new COBRA regulations?

On February 3, 1999, the IRS issued final regulations governing the group health plan continuation rules of COBRA. The long-awaited final regulations contain no blockbuster developments, but they do clarify dozens of elements of COBRA processing and will require every plan sponsor subject to COBRA to change its procedures. For the most part, the regulations are reasonable and will be welcomed by plan sponsors and administrators alike.

The IRS also published proposed regulations governing aspects of COBRA not addressed under the final regulations.

The final regulations do the following:

1. Limit the application of COBRA for most health care flexible spending accounts (FSAs);
2. Eliminate the requirement that group health plans offer qualified beneficiaries the option to elect only core (medical) cover-

age under a group health plan that otherwise provides both core and noncore (vision and dental) coverage;
3. Give employers and employee organizations significant flexibility in determining, for purposes of COBRA, the number of group health plans they maintain;
4. Prevent plans from terminating COBRA coverage for "insignificant" underpayments of COBRA premiums; and
5. Require plans to continue COBRA for up to 29 months for the family of a disabled qualified beneficiary, even if the disabled qualified beneficiary does not elect COBRA coverage.

The new proposed regulations would do the following:

1. Clarify which entity has responsibility for COBRA in the event of a sale of stock or assets;
2. Address COBRA obligations in connection with the withdrawal from a multiemployer plan; and
3. Provide guidance on the interaction of FMLA and COBRA.

Q 13:3 When were the regulations effective?

The final regulations applied with respect to qualifying events occurring in plan years beginning on or after January 1, 2000.

Q 13:4 Where are the coverage continuation requirements found in federal law?

COBRA added Section 162(k)—later changed to Section 4980B—to the Internal Revenue Code (Code) and amended the Employee Retirement Income Security Act of 1974 (ERISA) and the Public Health Service Act, which covers state and local government employees.

Q 13:5 What terminology is added to the employee benefits lexicon?

In alphabetical order, here are some of the terms related to COBRA:

After-acquired dependent. An individual who was not covered under the medical plan when coverage terminated, but who later becomes covered under the plan as a dependent of a qualified beneficiary. An after-acquired dependent may be a spouse or a child. Note that, other than newborn or adopted children of a former covered employee, after-acquired dependents are not qualified beneficiaries, so, for example, if the qualified beneficiary dies, they are not entitled to further coverage.

Applicable premium. The cost to the plan for the period of the continuation coverage, for similarly covered beneficiaries who have not had a qualifying event. The cost to the plan is determined without regard to whether the employer, the employee, or both, are paying toward the cost. In its simplest form, for an insured employer, this would be the premium paid to the insurance company for the coverage, regardless of whether employees contribute. Premium payments required from a (non-disabled) person electing continuation coverage may not exceed 102 percent of the applicable premium. Disabled persons availing themselves of the additional time permitted for a disabled qualified beneficiary may be charged not more than 150 percent of the applicable premium for the months in excess of the 18-month initial period.

Bundled plans (or bundled coverage). The treatment of all of an employer's welfare plans as a single unit for purposes of election under continuation rights. That is, a decision to elect one plan for continuation compels that same response for all plans (i.e., the decision to continue dental coverage cannot be made affirmatively while simultaneously rejecting medical coverage).

Continuation coverage. Coverage that is being made available for continuation.

Continuation period. The period of time during which a qualified beneficiary may continue coverage under the employer's plan. The maximum continuation period resulting from termination of employment or a reduction of work hours is 18 months. For all other qualifying events (e.g., death of employee, divorce), the maximum period is 36 months. Note that in the event of multiple qualifying events, the continuation period is measured from the date of the initial event. For example, an employee is terminated, thereby triggering an 18-month continuation period. Then, a second qualifying event occurs (before the expiration of the 18 months), such as the death of the employee. The second continuation period (the 36 months resulting from the death of the employee) will be measured from the date of termination, not the date of death. Note that a reduction in hours followed by termination is not considered to be two qualifying events and only 18 months of coverage has to be made available.

Note. There is a general exception to the 18-month maximum continuation period resulting from termination if the qualified beneficiary is disabled: The maximum period for such a person increases to 29 months.

Continuee (also COBRA continuee). Any person, entitled to receive continuation of coverage, who has elected to do so.

Covered employee. Any individual who is or was covered by a group health plan provided by the employer on the basis of the performance of services for the employer. Specifically included in this definition are self-employed individuals, agents, independent contractors, and directors.

Disabled qualified beneficiary. The conditions that must be met in order to qualify for the extension of continuation coverage to 29 months are:

1. The covered person must be disabled at the time the covered employee's employment is terminated or hours are reduced. HIPAA expanded this rule to allow 29 months of COBRA if the person was disabled at any time during the first 60 days of COBRA coverage. This rule was effective January 1, 1997, regardless of the date of the qualifying event.

2. There must have been a determination of disability under either Title II or Title XVI of the Social Security Act (old age, survivors, and disability insurance and supplemental security income, respectively).

3. Notice of the disability determination must be provided to the employer (or COBRA administrator) within 60 days of the determination and before the end of the 18-month continuation period.

Note. The final regulations make it clear that the disability extension applies to all qualified beneficiaries affected by the same qualifying event, not just the disabled qualified beneficiary.

Loss of coverage. Taken in the context of a qualifying event, loss of coverage means loss of coverage or becoming covered under different terms and conditions than had been the case on the day prior to the qualifying event.

Example 13-1. An employee is terminated and is provided with a three-month continuation of medical coverage. Because (presumably) the plan would have provided medical coverage indefinitely prior to the termination, a loss of coverage or qualifying event has occurred because after the event the individual is covered under different terms and conditions (i.e., the coverage is no longer indefinite). It is important to recognize that "true" loss of coverage and the qualifying event need not occur on the same day. In this example, the qualifying event occurred when the employee was terminated. Note also that periods of continuation entitlement are measured from the date the qualifying event occurs.

Multiple qualifying events. This is the occurrence of two or more qualifying events, with later qualifying events occurring during the initial continuation period. For example, the covered employee retires and loses active employee coverage, thereby triggering a qualifying event. Within the 18-month continuation period following the first event, the employee and spouse divorce, triggering the second event. When there are multiple qualifying events, additional periods of continuation will be triggered; however, in no case, regardless of how many qualifying events occur or in what sequence, will the maximum period of continuation exceed 36 months, beginning with the date of the first qualifying event. In all cases where there are multiple qualifying events, the period of continuation for any of the events will be measured from the date of the first event (see note under Continuation period for a possible exception).

Qualified beneficiary. Any person entitled to elect to receive continuation coverage. A qualified beneficiary is any individual who was covered under an employer's group medical plan on the day before a qualifying event occurs, and who lost medical coverage as a result of the qualifying event. Qualified beneficiaries will have been covered under an employer's plan as a spouse, or as a dependent of the covered employee. A covered employee may also become a qualified beneficiary if the qualifying event causes loss of coverage to the employee. HIPAA expanded the definition of qualified beneficiary to include a child born to or placed for adoption with a covered employee during COBRA continuation.

Qualifying event. One of the legally specified events that results in a loss of coverage and is intended to trigger eligibility for the right to continuation coverage. These events are:

1. Death of the employee;
2. Termination of employment for any reason other than gross misconduct;
3. Reduction of work hours below the level necessary to have coverage;
4. Divorce;
5. Legal separation; and
6. Dependent child no longer meeting the dependency requirements.

Occurrence of any of these events would not be deemed a qualifying event if "true" loss of coverage (see definition of Loss of coverage) does not take place within the appropriate continuation period. For example, an employee is terminated and is granted a two-year period of continuing medical coverage. Because the end of the maximum COBRA continuation period (18 months in this case) occurs sooner than will the actual loss of coverage, there is no occurrence of a qualifying event.

Similarly situated (employees or individuals). Individuals covered under the same plan, under the same terms and conditions, and with the same options as the qualified beneficiary, who have made the same choices. The law itself refers to similarly situated beneficiaries. The regulations generally refer to similarly situated non-COBRA beneficiaries, but in some places refer to similarly situated active employees.

Unbundled plans (or unbundled coverage). Each welfare plan is treated as a separate plan for the purposes of its election under continuation rights; that is, continuation of each plan is elected separately. For example, the decision to continue dental is totally independent of the decision to continue medical.

Covered Employers

Q 13:6   Which employers are covered under the COBRA requirements?

As a practical matter, any employer with 20 or more employees is bound by the law. The measurement of headcount is taken over the preceding calendar year.

Example 13-2. In Year 1 an employer normally employs 19 employees on a typical business day. During Year 2 the employer normally employs 20 employees on a typical business day. In Year 2, Joe retires. The employer is not required to provide COBRA notices to Joe, nor to make continuation coverage available. In Year 3, Sally retires. The employer is required to provide COBRA notices and to make continuation coverage available to Sally, but not to Joe. In Year 3 the employer again reduces its headcount to fewer than 20 employees on a typical business day. In Year 4, Mabel retires. Neither Joe nor Mabel is entitled to COBRA, but Sally continues to be eligible, and must be afforded continuing access to the plan until the expiration of the 18-month continuation period. Continuing eligibility for access to the plan would also accrue to any other beneficiaries who gained COBRA rights during Year 2. This would include surviving and divorced spouses, who would remain entitled for 36 months from the date of the qualifying event.

Small employers that normally employ fewer than 20 employees on a "typical business day" are excluded from the requirements. For those employers whose employee headcount fluctuates under and over 20, the regulations require that an employer look at its level of employment during more than 50 percent of its business days. The regulations also allow employers to count pay periods, rather than each day. While taking headcount for this purpose, seasonal, or part-time employees should be counted as fractions of full-time employees. Temporary or part-time help who are obtained through agencies or other sources and who are not employees need not be counted. Self-employed persons within the meaning of Code Section 401(c)(1) are not counted as employees; therefore, partners and owners would not be counted. If other persons are eligible for the medical plan, such as agents, independent contractors, and their employees, they do not need to be counted.

A cautionary note may be appropriate here. The Age Discrimination in Employment Act of 1976 (ADEA) also uses a 20-employee cutoff for its coverage requirements; however, that law phrases the measurement quite differently. ADEA addresses those employers who have 20 or more employees on each working day in 20 or more weeks in either the current or prior calendar year. Despite the apparent commonality stemming from the use of 20 employees as the measurement standard in each case, the phrasing of each law's requirement is so different that it is not clear that rulings or interpretations on this issue arising from one law can be used as guidance for the other.

For information on certain other plans that are also excluded, see Q 13:16.

Q 13:7 Who is an employer for COBRA purposes?

For the purpose of determining whether the coverage continuation rules apply, "employer" means the employer as well as any other entity that is a member of a controlled group as described in Code Section 414(b), (c), (m), or (o).

Q 13:8 If an employer grows to more than 20 employees, when does COBRA apply?

The answer depends on how and when the growth occurred. If the growth occurred in the typical manner of adding employees to payroll over time, the employer would become subject to COBRA at the beginning of the calendar year following the year in which it no longer met the requirements for the small-employer exception, as discussed in Q 13:6. In contrast, if an employer acquires another company that is not exempted because the acquired company has employed more than 20 employees, the rules become effective immediately for the acquiring company. This rule probably does not apply if one small employer acquires another small employer. In the case of an acquisition of a "large" employer, not to make the rules immediately effective would take away their protection, although admittedly for a relatively short period of time, until the first of the next year or the following year. It is unlikely that the IRS would permit a situation under which protection was suspended, however short the period of suspension might be.

Presumably, as the marriage of two small employers would not create the condition of taking away rights from some group of employees, a different answer is permissible. This event could reasonably be viewed as merely adding employees, which would subject the employer to COBRA continuation rules at the beginning of the year following the year during which the small-employer exemption was lost.

It is also important to note the date on which the growth to more than 20 employees occurred. The regulations point to COBRA becoming effective at the first of the year following the year in which the small-employer exemption is lost; however, remember that the small-employer exemption is a two-part test. The exemption is lost only after the employer has: (1) employed more than 20 employees and (2) done so for more than 50 percent of its typical business days. (The final regulations allow employers to count pay periods, rather than days.) This means that an employer could postpone the effective date for an entire year by timing its hiring or acquisition carefully.

> **Example 13-3.** RST, Inc. is a small business that maintained an insured group health plan for its 10 employees in 1998 and 1999. Mary H., a secretary with six years of service, leaves in June 1999 to take a position with a competing firm that has no health plan. She is not entitled to COBRA coverage with the plan of RST, Inc. because the firm had fewer than 20 employees in 1998 and is not subject to COBRA requirements. Because she had at least 18 months of coverage, she is entitled (under HIPAA) to purchase an individual health insurance policy.

> **Example 13-4.** An employer is employing 19 persons and determines it needs to add another. With the addition of the 20th person, the headcount portion of the small-employer exemption will be lost, leaving the determination of the percentage of typical business days as the final decision point. Exactly half of the employer's

typical business days occur before July 1, 2001. If the employer hires the 20th person on June 30, or earlier, it will be subject to COBRA on January 1, 2002, because the year in which the hire occurs will be the year it loses the small-employer exemption. Alternatively, if the employer postpones the hire until July 1 or later, COBRA will not be required until January 1, 2003, because at the year of hire the employer would still have been eligible for the exemption because it did not have the requisite number of employees for more than 50 percent of that year. The year following the year of hire will be the year during which the exemption is lost (assuming no further changes in headcount). In other words, if the 20th employee is hired in the second half of the year (July 1, in this example) as opposed to the first half (June 30), the plan can avoid COBRA for an additional year.

Q 13:9 How are separate employers who are members of a controlled group of corporations treated with respect to the 20-employee threshold?

If two or more employers, each normally employing fewer than 20 employees in a typical calendar year, together maintain a plan and together exceed the 20-employee exemption limit, they are treated as a single employer covered under the requirements of COBRA.

Q 13:10 Does the small-employer exemption apply to an employer in a multiple employer welfare arrangement?

Yes, so long as an employer meets the small-employer exemption, the fact that coverage is being obtained through a multiple employer welfare arrangement (MEWA) is not relevant. That continues to apply even if there are other employers in the MEWA to whom the small-employer exemption does not apply. Similarly, if another employer in the MEWA violates COBRA, the failure of the offending employer does not taint the remaining employers.

Q 13:11 When a company is sold, does the buyer or seller have the responsibility to comply with COBRA?

On February 3, 1999, the IRS issued proposed regulations concerning COBRA obligations in cases involving a sale of stock in an employer that causes the employer to become a member of another controlled group of corporations (a "stock sale"), or a sale of substantial assets by an employer (such as a plant or division) to another employer outside the controlled group (an "asset sale").

The new proposed regulations provide, for both sales of stock and sales of substantial assets such as a division or plant, that the seller retains the obligation to make COBRA continuation coverage available to existing qualified beneficiaries. In addition, in situations in which the seller ceases to provide any group health plan to any employee in connection with the sale and thus is not responsible for providing COBRA continuation coverage, the new proposed regulations provide that the buyer is responsible for providing COBRA continuation coverage to existing qualified beneficiaries. This secondary liability for the buyer applies in all stock sales and in all sales of substantial assets in which the buyer continues the business operations associated with the assets without interruption or substantial change.

The new proposed regulations make clear that the parties to a transaction are free to allocate the responsibility for providing COBRA continuation coverage by contract, even if the contract imposes responsibility on a different party than would the new proposed regulations. As long as the party to whom the contract allocates responsibility performs its obligations, the other party will have no responsibility for providing COBRA continuation coverage. If, however, the party allocated responsibility under the contract defaults on its obligation, and if, under the new proposed regulations, the other party would have the obligation to provide COBRA continuation coverage in the absence of a contractual provision, then the other party would retain that obligation. The party with the underlying responsibility under the regulations can insist on appropriate security and, of course, could pursue contractual remedies against the defaulting party.

A particular type of asset sale raises issues for which the new proposed regulations do not provide any special rules. Thus, the general rules in the new proposed regulations for business reorganizations would apply to this type of transaction. This type of asset sale is one in which the buyer continues to employ the employees of that business and continues to provide those employees exactly the same health coverage that they had before the sale (either by continuing coverage or by establishing a plan that mirrors the old one). The application of the rules in the new proposed regulations to this type of asset sale would require the seller to make COBRA continuation coverage available to the employees continuing in employment with the buyer (and to other family members who are qualified beneficiaries). Ordinarily, the continuing employees (or their family members) would be unlikely to elect COBRA continuation coverage from the seller when they can receive the same coverage (usually at much lower cost) as active employees of the buyer.

Covered Plans

Q 13:12 What type of plan is covered under COBRA?

COBRA is aimed solely at group health care plans. Health care for this purpose includes dental, vision, in-house medical facilities (but not first-aid facilities), and health care spending accounts (Section 125 plans), along with indemnity, health maintenance organization (HMO), and preferred provider organization (PPO) medical plans. Employee assistance plans (EAPs) that provide only resource and referral services are probably not group health plans, but EAPs that provide a specified number of visits probably are.

Specifically not included for this purpose are plans maintained solely for purposes of complying with workers' compensation laws or disability insurance laws. Long-term care plans are also excluded.

If the employer provides medical care at a facility located on its premises, the proposed COBRA regulations would not treat it as a group health plan, but only if:

1. The medical care consists primarily of first aid that is provided during the employer's working hours for treatment of a health condition, illness, or injury that occurs during those working hours;
2. The facility may only be used by the employer's current employees; and
3. Use of the facility is free.

Note. Employers should understand the COBRA consequences of how they design an on-site medical facility program. For example, if retirees can obtain coverage from such a facility, or if there is a nominal charge for using the facility, the entire arrangement could become subject to COBRA.

Q 13:13 What are the new rules regarding COBRA and flexible spending accounts?

A flexible spending account (FSA) need not be offered to a qualified beneficiary if the maximum amount that the qualified beneficiary could be required to pay for coverage for the remainder of the plan year exceeds the maximum benefits. Even if an FSA must be offered initially, enrollment for future years is not required if the FSA qualifies for the exception under HIPAA. (FSAs that are funded solely or primarily by salary reduction qualify.)

Q 13:14 How is the term "group health plan" defined?

Any plan maintained by an employer to provide medical care (including the payment or reimbursement thereof) is a group health plan. Medical care is defined as the diagnosis, cure, treatment, mitigation, or prevention of disease or related undertakings for the purpose of affecting any structure or function of the body. Transportation primarily for and essential to the medical care is also included in the definition.

This definition applies whether the services are provided through insurance (including MEWAs) or self-funding, directly provided, or directly reimbursed. It applies to group policies or individual policies that are arrangements to provide medical care to two or more employees. It applies regardless of whether the plan is offered as part of a cafeteria or flexible benefit approach, or whether the plan is provided without choice by the employer. "Without choice" refers to choices among alternative forms or plans for medical coverage; it does not refer to whether the employee has the choice to join one plan. It applies to all plans, whether contributory, fully paid for by the employer, or fully paid for by the employee. (However, see Qs 13:16–13:18.)

Further, COBRA applies to group health plans maintained by states, political subdivisions of the state, and any agency or instrumentality of either the state or a political subdivision of the state, including local governments and agencies, provided the state received funds under the Public Health Service Act (PHSA). It is irrelevant to the inclusion of local governments and agencies that the local government or agency did not itself receive funds under the PHSA. So long as the state received such funds, the inclusion applies.

Q 13:15 What kinds of services are excluded from the term "group health plan"?

Anything that is merely beneficial to general health or well-being is not included. As such, wellness, health promotion programs, swimming pools, exercise facilities, fitness centers or programs, and health clubs are excluded. Weight reduction, smoking cessation, and cholesterol reduction programs are all also excluded.

Annual physical or health examination programs deserve special attention. While they might have been covered under an employer's medical plan as a reimbursable expense, they do not fit the description of providing "relief or alleviation of health or medical problems" because they are "accessible to and used by employees without regard to their physical condition or state of health," so they will not be considered a group health plan and as such are not subject to COBRA. Employers are not, however, precluded from allowing these plans to be continued under COBRA; they are just not required to do so.

Other employer-provided programs are not as clear cut. One example is discount programs. Suppose two employers each have employee discount programs for their employees. One employer is a pharmaceutical supply house and the other a drug store. If the pharmaceutical supply house sells prescription drugs or supplies used solely in the "relief or alleviation of health or medical problems," its discount program would be covered under COBRA as a medical plan. In contrast, if the drug store, which makes similar products available at discount, also sells products such as perfumes, toiletries, candy, and other nonmedical goods at discount, its discount program's status as a medical plan might be questioned.

Another similar situation, and probably a more common one, is that of counseling programs. In their earliest incarnation, these programs were typically limited to drug and alcohol problems and counseling. Limited to that, clearly they constitute a medical plan as contemplated under COBRA, and their services would need to be extended to continuees; however, more common today are counseling programs that include counseling on financial, family, legal, and other problems.

In this case, it can be argued that the program meets the requisite definition of being covered and excluded simultaneously. The problem-solving techniques of King Solomon would enable an employer to make the medical aspects of the program available to continuees, while withholding the nonmedical aspects. Even assuming that it is administratively feasible, it raises the thorny issue of determining the continuee's premium for the bifurcated program.

Q 13:16 Are any group health plans excluded from COBRA?

In addition to small-employer plans (see Q 13:6), also excluded by statute are church plans and plans maintained by the federal government. (The Federal Employees Health Benefit Program does have similar temporary continuation of coverage rules.) Similarly, plans maintained by the District of Columbia, any territory or possession of the United States, or small governmental units that normally employ fewer than 20 employees, are exempted from compliance.

There is also a broader exclusion for employee-pay-all plans that are not maintained by the employer and in which the employer has no involvement.

Q 13:17 When is a plan maintained by an employer?

Under COBRA, a plan is deemed to be maintained by an employer if it meets any of the following four criteria:

1. It is a plan sponsored by the employer (i.e., if the employer is identified as the sponsor in the summary plan description (SPD)).

2. The employer contributes to the plan either directly or indirectly.
3. The employer participates in, or has any "involvement" with, the operation of the plan.
4. The coverage is not available to terminated employees at the same cost.

A closer look at each of these points yields some surprises.

Criterion 1 holds no surprises. If an employer announces that it is providing health care coverage in the form of one plan and is actively engaged in enrolling employees into the plan—perhaps assisting with claim filing, and almost certainly contributing toward the cost—that employer is clearly "maintaining" a plan. Most employers will fit that description. Conducting any one of those activities is sufficient to qualify an employer as maintaining the plan.

There is a possible pitfall in criterion 2 in the context of making indirect contributions. Directly contributing to the plan is self-evident: The employer contributes some of its money toward the cost of the plan to make it more affordable or even free to employees. At the moment, there is no clear indication as to what "indirect contributions" might be.

In criterion 3, the scope of what constitutes having "involvement" in the plan might surprise more than one employer. Take, for example, a situation where a plan is sponsored by a union, with the cost of the plan being fully paid for by general revenues of the union, with the general revenues coming in whole or in part from membership dues. In this case, having the membership dues deducted from employees' paychecks might constitute employer involvement. Taking payroll deductions earmarked toward the cost of the plan would constitute involvement. Other points of involvement might be maintaining a supply of enrollment forms to provide to newly hired employees and collecting the filled-in forms to return to the union. Employers with such plans should closely scrutinize their payroll deductions for union dues or plan contributions along with any administrative activities they may be performing; such activities might constitute involvement.

Concerning criterion 4, note the provision in the currently proposed regulations that states that a plan will be deemed to be maintained by the employer if the benefits are not available to employees who terminate employment with the employer at the same cost as they were through the employer. To quote from the final regulations:

> Thus, a group health plan is maintained by an employer or employee organization even if the employer or employee organization does not contribute to it if coverage under the plan would not be available at the same cost to an individual but for the individual's employment-related connection to the employer or employee organization.

Read literally, this statement would cause every plan, including employee-pay-all schemes, to be construed as maintained by an employer. Because it is virtually impossible for two different plans to have identical coverage, coverage under the plan cannot be achieved at any cost outside of the employment-based program. Further, if one were to find identical plans from separate sources (or even the same source), achieving the same cost would be all but impossible because of the differences in administrative efficiency created from a group plan.

Q 13:18 Are there special rules or exceptions for union plans?

Under the final regulations issued February 3, 1999, there do not appear to be any exceptions for union plans.

Q 13:19 What are the requirements if there is more than one covered plan?

Each plan maintained by an employer must be treated separately. (For this purpose, family coverage versus single coverage does not constitute a separate plan for each.) Qualified beneficiaries have the right to make decisions for each plan they may be covered under, independently of other elections they might make (see Q 13:21).

Q 13:20 Do the rules about core and noncore plans still apply?

No. The 1987 proposed regulations include detailed rules requiring that qualified beneficiaries generally be offered the option of electing only core coverage or both core and noncore coverage. The IRS decided not to include any such requirement to offer core coverage separately in the final regulations. This is good news for some employers who offer combinations of medical plus dental or vision coverage. If the dental and vision plans are separate plans, each plan must still be offered separately.

Q 13:21 Can an employer make continuation of one plan dependent on another?

The answer depends on how the benefits are offered to active employees. If active employees are allowed to pick and choose among the array of benefit plans being offered (the "unbundled" approach), then COBRA continuees must be given the same choices. In short, the continuee cannot be granted less freedom to choose than is permitted for active employees.

If active employees are presented with a fully "bundled" choice (they are required to accept a package of all coverages—or no coverage), COBRA continuees may need to be treated differently. They must be presented with more choices if the plans are separate plans.

The new proposed regulations provide guidance, for purposes of the COBRA continuation coverage requirements, on how to determine the number of group health plans that a plan sponsor maintains. Under these rules, the plan sponsor is generally permitted to establish the separate identity and number of group health plans under which it provides health care benefits to employees. Thus, if a plan sponsor provides a variety of health care benefits to employees, it generally may aggregate the benefits into a single group health plan or disaggregate benefits into separate group health plans. The status of health care benefits as part of a single group health plan or as separate plans is determined by reference to the documents governing the plan. If it is not clear from the documents whether the benefits are provided under one plan or more than one plan, all health care benefits (other than those for long-term care) provided by a single entity constitute a single group health plan.

Q 13:22 Does COBRA apply to employees or plans in Puerto Rico?

Yes. COBRA and all other federal laws apply in Puerto Rico.

General Requirements

Q 13:23 What are the general requirements of COBRA?

The broadest intent of the law is to guarantee the availability of medical coverage for specified periods of time, on a group basis and at group rates, to persons who are losing such coverage (from an employer) for any one of a number of reasons. The law requires that these persons be treated the same as similarly situated beneficiaries (except for contributions) in that they must receive the identical coverage, rights, and entitlements.

The law stipulates that all employees and covered dependents must be notified of their COBRA rights both at inception of their coverage as an active employee and upon termination of their coverage (i.e., upon inception of their COBRA rights). The law also imposes on employees and dependents the responsibility to exercise or retain their rights and to provide input, where necessary, to enable an employer to carry out its responsibilities.

Penalties are imposed for failure to meet the requirements of the law or for failure to show good faith in attempting to comply. Employers should note that, under the original law, employers were liable only for their own violations, such as failure to provide notice. Under the amended provisions, employers are responsible for their own violations, plus any violations committed by their administrators (e.g., HMOs, insurers). Employers are cautioned that while it is common practice for administrators to be charged with facets of COBRA administration, employers should take steps to assure the administrator's rigorous fulfillment of its responsibilities.

In addition to penalties under ERISA, the IRS can impose excise taxes for failure to comply with COBRA. In certain circumstances the excise tax can also be imposed on entities other than the plan sponsor, such as an insurer providing benefits under the plan or a third-party administrator processing claims under the plan, but the employer does not escape liability for penalties.

Q 13:24 How was the continuation of benefits under COBRA affected by OBRA '93?

OBRA '93 included only one small provision that affects COBRA continuation regulations: It amended ERISA by adding a rule that prohibits the reduction or elimination of coverage for pediatric vaccines. Under this rule, coverage must be maintained at the level provided as of May 1, 1993. [ERISA § 609(d)]

Q 13:25 If benefits are changed or eliminated for active employees, what must an employer offer to COBRA continuees?

If coverage for the similarly situated nonCOBRA beneficiaries is changed or eliminated, the 1987 proposed regulations required that qualified beneficiaries be permitted to elect coverage under any remaining plan made available to the similarly situated active employees. The final regulations provide that the general principle—that qualified beneficiaries have the same rights as similarly situated nonCOBRA beneficiaries—applies in this situation. Nevertheless, if a plan sponsor providing more than one plan eliminates benefits under one plan without giving the similarly situated nonCOBRA beneficiaries the right to enroll in another plan, benefits would still have to be made available to qualified beneficiaries if the employer continued to maintain a group health plan.

Q 13:26 If a qualified beneficiary in an HMO moves outside the HMO's service area, what must an employer offer?

The 1987 proposed regulations provided that qualified beneficiaries moving outside the area served by a region-specific plan must be given the right to obtain other coverage from the employer maintaining the region-specific plan. The rule conditioned the right to other coverage on the employer having employees in the area to which the qualified beneficiary is moving. The final regulations eliminate the condition that an employer have employees in the area to which the qualified beneficiary is moving and instead require that coverage be made available to the qualified beneficiary if the plan sponsor can provide coverage to the qualified beneficiary under one of its existing plans. Generally the coverage that must be made available is that

Q 13:27   Health Insurance Answer Book

made available to the similarly situated nonCOBRA beneficiaries. If, however, the coverage made available to the similarly situated non-COBRA beneficiaries cannot be made available in the area to which the qualified beneficiary is moving, then the coverage provided to other employees in that area must be made available.

Q 13:27 What disclosures must a plan make to health care providers inquiring about coverage for qualified beneficiaries?

The final regulations require that a plan make a complete response to any inquiry from a health care provider regarding the qualified beneficiary's right to coverage under the plan during the election period. Thus, if the qualified beneficiary has not yet elected COBRA continuation coverage but remains covered under the plan during the election period (subject to retroactive cancellation if no election is made), the plan must so inform the health care provider. Conversely, if the qualified beneficiary is not covered during the election period prior to her or his election, the plan must inform the health care provider that the qualified beneficiary does not have current coverage but will have retroactive coverage if COBRA continuation coverage is elected. The final regulations also include similar requirements with respect to inquiries made by health care providers during the 30- and 45-day grace periods for paying for COBRA continuation coverage.

Q 13:28 What is the relationship between COBRA and USERRA?

The Uniformed Services Employment and Reemployment Rights Act of 1994 (USERRA) gives certain members of the military reserves the right to have up to 18 months of continuation coverage when they are called to active duty. The final regulations clarify that USERRA coverage runs concurrently with COBRA and not consecutively (that is, only 18 months of coverage is required, not 18 plus 18.)

Q 13:29 If an employer withdraws from a multiemployer plan, what happens to that employer's COBRA continuees?

The new proposed regulations address COBRA obligations in connection with an employer's cessation of contributions to a multiemployer group health plan. The new proposed regulations provide that the multiemployer plan generally continues to have the obligation to make COBRA continuation coverage available to qualified beneficiaries associated with that employer. (There generally would not be any obligation to make COBRA continuation coverage available to continuing employees in this situation because a cessation of contributions is not a qualifying event.) Once the employer provides group health coverage to a significant number of employees who were formerly covered under the multiemployer plan, or starts contributing to another multiemployer plan on their behalf, the employer's plan (or the new multiemployer plan) would have the obligation to make COBRA continuation coverage available to the existing qualified beneficiaries.

Q 13:30 When does COBRA apply for someone on FMLA leave?

The new proposed regulations set forth rules regarding the interaction of the COBRA continuation coverage requirements with the provisions of the Family and Medical Leave Act of 1993 (FMLA). The rules under the new proposed regulations are substantially the same as those set forth in IRS Notice 94-103. The qualifying event is deemed to occur on the last day of the employee's FMLA leave, and the maximum coverage period generally begins on that day. The new proposed regulations provide a special rule for cases where coverage is not lost until a later date and the plan provides for the optional extension of the required periods. In the case of such a qualifying event, the employer cannot condition the employee's rights to COBRA continuation coverage on the employee's reimbursement of any premiums paid by the employer to maintain the employee's group health plan coverage during the period of FMLA leave.

Notification Requirements

Q 13:31 What are the COBRA notification requirements?

In the broadest terms, qualified beneficiaries—employees, spouses, and dependent children—must be notified by the group health plan (which, in practice, may be the employer) of their right to continue coverage. This initial notice must be given when the plan becomes subject to the provisions of COBRA, or for plans already subject to the law, when new employees are added to the plan. Additionally, affected qualified beneficiaries must be provided with a notice when a qualifying event occurs. Finally, the plan administrator (who may be the employer) must be notified when certain other qualifying events occur.

Q 13:32 Who is responsible for complying with the notification requirements?

The regulations, and many privately written documents offering instructions on COBRA compliance, take pains to identify who is responsible for sending various notices. Typical language is: "the Plan Administrator must send" or "the Plan is responsible for providing." Timing requirements that are germane to compliance will be dealt with as they arise; however, such definite allocation of responsibilities has been specifically avoided in this work for the following reasons:

1. The law permits delegation of action among various entities, including the employer, the plan administrator, and the insurer.
2. The essential point is that the action be properly accomplished; who accomplishes it is irrelevant.
3. The employer is responsible for compliance, regardless of who has been assigned to perform that task.

Q 13:33 When must employees receive notice of their right to continue coverage?

Qualified beneficiaries must receive notice of their right to continue coverage on two occasions. The first occasion (the initial notice) is their entry into the plan's coverage, and the second occasion is their exit from the plan's coverage (i.e., upon the occurrence of a qualifying event). There is no specific timing requirement for provision of the initial notice other than the law's wording, "at the time of commencement of coverage under the plan."

Notice following the occurrence of a qualifying event must be provided within 44 days of the occurrence of one of the following:

COBRA Q 13:34

1. Death of the covered employee.
2. Termination of employment of the covered employee.
3. Reduction of hours of the covered employee sufficient to cause loss of medical coverage.
4. Bankruptcy of the employer.
5. Divorce or separation.
6. A child ceasing to be a dependent.
7. The employee becoming entitled to Medicare. (This is true when the loss of the dependent's coverage is caused by the employee's Medicare entitlement, even thought the employee does not lose coverage as a result of the entitlement.)

The law stipulates that the employer must notify the plan administrator within 30 days and that the plan administrator must notify the qualified beneficiary within 14 days. When the employer is the plan administrator (which is the case for most single-employer plans), the Department of Labor has informally indicated that the limits can be combined for a total of 44 days; however, the judge in a recent case ruled that an employer that was also plan administrator did not need 30 days to notify itself. [Goodman v. Commercial Labor Services Inc., N.D.N.Y., No. 98-CV-1816, Feb. 11, 2000]. Multiemployer plans must abide by the separate limits of 30 and 14 days. An employer should, however, establish a system to provide the necessary notifications as quickly as reasonable, and not take advantage of the maximum permissible time in the hope that the qualified beneficiary will find other coverage within that time. The IRS could interpret the employer's artificially delaying the process as an attempt to avoid complying in good faith and, therefore, levy fines or penalties. Plan administrators must provide a notice of COBRA rights within 14 days of receiving notification of a divorce, legal separation, or loss of eligibility by a child.

Q 13:34 Does a group health plan need to notify a spouse of an employee of COBRA rights both initially and after a qualifying event?

Yes. A group health plan was fined $36,500 for failing to provide a spouse of an employee with a notice of her rights under COBRA at the time of a qualifying event. The case of *Underwood v. Fluor Daniel, Inc.* was decided by the Fourth Circuit U.S. Court of Appeals. The employee elected COBRA continuation coverage, but stopped paying premiums. His suit attempted to reinstate coverage on the grounds of improper notice. Instead, the court ruled that Mrs. Underwood knew her rights and that she was not harmed by Fluor Daniel's failure to provide the notice. Even so, the employer was fined $100 per day for a full year for failure to provide the notice. The employee was given a notice at work, but the company never sent a notice to his wife. Please note that the ERISA penalty is now $110 per day and that the IRS can add an excise tax of $100 per day.

Q 13:35 Who must receive notification?

The initial notice must be provided to each employee and spouse; therefore, simply posting the notice or handing one to each employee will not suffice. The employer should send the notice to the employee's home by first-class mail, unless the employer has knowledge that the spouse resides elsewhere. In that case, a second notice should be mailed to the other address. If the employer knows of no other address, the last known address is sufficient. Notice mailed to the employee is not sufficient to include the spouse. Notices should be addressed jointly. Notice to the spouse will be sufficient to include eligible dependents—again, unless the employer has knowledge that the notice will not be received by a dependent at that address and has a second address to use.

Q 13:36 What must be included in the notification?

The Department of Labor has provided a model notice (reproduced in Appendix B) that may be used for the initial notice. The DOL has stated that it will consider use of this notice as evidence of good-faith compliance on the part of either the employer or plan administrator. The law has been amended since the DOL released the model notice, and it has not reissued the model notice to incorporate the amendments. Because the DOL has never proclaimed the model notice as being required, or as being the only method of showing good-faith compliance, employers should feel free to modify the notice as they see fit, in order to provide the most current and correct information they can. A sample revised notice is reproduced in Appendix C. The revised notice has been amended to include changes stemming from amendments and regulations, but not to improve clarity or readability. The author encourages employers who find the DOL model or the updated version in Appendix C to be lacking in readability to improve upon it.

Q 13:37 Can the initial notice be placed in the summary plan description?

Yes, as required by ERISA Section 606. An employer must keep in mind that this does not replace nor does it satisfy the requirement for providing either the initial notice to the spouse or the notice upon the occurrence of a qualifying event. The initial notice must be provided to the spouse as well as to the employee; therefore, it is safest to mail the SPD to the employee's home, addressed to both the employee and the spouse.

Q 13:38 Are there notice requirements that apply to employees, spouses, or dependents?

Yes. An employee or spouse must notify the plan administrator of the occurrence of any of the following:

- Divorce
- Legal separation
- Cessation of dependent's eligibility (i.e., loss of dependency status)

The employee or beneficiary has 60 days in which to notify the plan administrator of the qualifying event. Should the qualified beneficiaries fail to provide timely notification, their continuation rights are forfeited. Notice from one qualified beneficiary is sufficient to preserve rights for all beneficiaries. The final regulations place the start date as the later of the date of the qualifying event or the date on which coverage would be lost as a result of the qualifying event.

In a footnote in the preamble to the final regulations issued February 3, 1999, the IRS notes that the DOL has advised the IRS that, if a covered employee or qualified beneficiary has not been adequately informed of the obligation to provide notice in the case of divorce, legal separation, or a dependent child losing eligibility, the covered employee's or qualified beneficiary's failure to provide timely notice to the plan administrator will not affect the plan's obligation to make continuation coverage available upon receiving notice of the event.

Note. The qualified beneficiary is obliged to notify the plan administrator if a qualifying event has occurred, and the plan administrator has 14 days in which to respond upon notice.

The COBRA continuee has 60 days in which to notify the plan administrator when the Social Security Administration approves a Social Security disability claim. If the Social Security Administration determines that a continuee is no longer disabled, the continuee has 30 days to notify the plan administrator.

Q 13:39 What response must a plan administrator provide, once notified of a qualifying event?

Detailed requirements for this notice have not yet been issued in final, or even proposed, regulations. Pending definitive guidance, employers are expected to make a good-faith effort toward compliance, which means that an employer should provide information in a clear and readable form, giving as much information as a beneficiary might reasonably need. Toward that end, the following items are suggested for inclusion in a response to the qualified beneficiaries:

1. The date on which coverage terminated (or will terminate);
2. A listing of the plans that the beneficiary may select to continue;
3. The cost of continuing each plan, specified by rating groups (e.g., single coverage, employee and spouse, employee and children, full family);
4. The date of the notice and the date by which the beneficiary must respond in order to obtain continuation coverage;
5. The date at which continuation coverage will cease;
6. The name and address of the person or office to which the choice of continuation coverage should be sent by the beneficiary;

7. The date by which the first premium payment must be received, and the frequency thereafter at which premium payments must be received; and

8. Instructions as to how the beneficiary should proceed to obtain continuation coverage (e.g., complete and return the enclosed form).

A sample notice is shown in Appendix D. Employers are encouraged to modify the sample to suit their own writing style and specific plan design communication needs.

Q 13:40 Must an employer send bills or payment reminders to continuees?

No, that is not required. As indicated in Q 13:39, an employer should clearly spell out for the continuee the payment requirements such as due date and ongoing frequency. Once having done that, the employer has no continuing obligation to send reminders for payment. (It is not even required that the continuee be notified if coverage is because of nonpayment.) If the employer's plan contains a conversion feature, the employer is obligated to advise the continuee by sending a conversion notice or form.

Note that state laws may require billing for state continuation requirements.

Q 13:41 If an employer chooses to administer COBRA, what should the employer look for in a COBRA administration software package?

In general, a good COBRA administration system should do the following:

1. Produce notices and form letters for qualified beneficiaries.
2. Calculate premium amounts and billing notices.
3. Keep track of qualified beneficiaries, their payment records, and status.
4. Keep track of all transactions and produce a report that can be audited.
5. Generate management reports.

The employer should have a manual that summarizes COBRA rules for ready reference, keying legal requirements to menu items in the system. The system vendor should keep the system current with changing regulations and interpretations. If the IRS conducts an audit, the IRS will want to review a copy of the procedure manual.

Premiums

Q 13:42 How frequently may an employer change COBRA rates to a continuee?

The law itself is not clear on the point of determining or defining the period an individual beneficiary should be allowed to continue paying a particular premium rate, and when it may be changed. The intent of the Conference Committee was fairly evident: The premium for each beneficiary would be determined when that beneficiary's coverage commenced and would remain unchanged for the next 12 months. Unfortunately, for larger employers with greater numbers of persons electing COBRA, such an interpretation would certainly result in a plethora of rates and an attendant administrative nightmare.

The final regulations indicate that the premium would be determined once each year, such as on a date coincident with the plan year, and that rate would be used for all continuees who elect continuation coverage. The law did not intend employers to become insurers. The intent was to allow continuees access to group plans at group rates, not employer-subsidized group rates. That raises the issue of mid-year premium increases. As long ago as mid-1989, IRS officials indicated an "inclination" to allow the pass-along of independent third-party imposed rate increases to qualified beneficiaries. Unfortunately, the final regulations do not permit an increase in the applicable premium during the 12-month determination period.

Q 13:43 How is the COBRA premium (or the applicable premium) determined?

The law states: "The determination of any applicable premium shall be made for a period of 12 months and shall be made before the beginning of such period." It appears then, taken exactly as written, that an employer can select any 12-month period as the "determination period." Further, the applicable premium can only be changed at the end of a successive determination period. Once selected, the determination period must, however, be used consistently from year to year, and cannot be changed at whim.

For fully insured plans, the group premium levied by the insurance company for "similarly situated" individuals, plus the 2 percent administration charge permitted by the law, would be the easiest answer to the question of how much to charge qualified beneficiaries. Determining who is similarly situated is somewhat more nettlesome. Probably the most common rating structure among medical plans is the simple, two-step "single" and "family" rate. In most cases, the family rate presumes the inclusion of the employee. In the case of a divorce, with a spouse and child electing continuation coverage, the employer would have little choice but to charge the family rate to the newly formed two-person family.

It can be conclusively demonstrated that there are valid and reliable cost differences among finer distinctions of covered individuals. For starters, differences can be found among members of the same sex at different ages, between different sexes at the same age and at different ages, and between adults and children. Certainly, no plan would attempt to develop rates for such subgroups as "males age 25 to 30" or "females," but finer distinctions than simply "single" and "family" would make sense. If asked to do so, an actuary engaged by the employer, or on the insurance company's staff, can readily produce rates for children. Doing so would give the employer a more equitable basis for not only paying premiums, but to use for COBRA rates also. A reasonable structure might look something like this:

Category of Coverage	Premium Charged
One adult	Single rate
Two adults	Twice the single rate
One adult and child(ren)	Single rate plus child rate
Two adults and child(ren)	Twice the single rate plus the child rate

Naturally, it would also be possible to determine a single child rate and use that rate multiplied by the number of children being covered as beneficiaries. Such further precision is certainly laudable, but probably will be more than is needed. At this time, COBRA regulations do not require an employer to determine the actual cost for each type of individual or group in the plan; however, an employer that makes the effort to obtain and use a more equitable rating structure will be one step closer to demonstrating a "good-faith attempt" at compliance.

Individuals need not be medically identical to be categorized as similarly situated. In determining appropriate groupings, employers should keep in mind that they cannot define groups so as to increase the cost of continuation coverage "inappropriately" to rank-and-file employees. Additionally, employers should be sure they do not create groups that would violate the Equal Pay Act, the Americans with Disabilities Act, or any other such law. Pending the issuance of regulations that might clarify this issue, employers should take steps to determine which individuals are similarly situated and how they are to be treated (or rated for premium purposes). In so doing, employers should not only define these groups, but also document the determinations in the plan, even by a plan amendment. An employer that reserves unto itself the authority to interpret the plan (which should be done as a general action, anyway), and has not created groups arbitrarily or capriciously, greatly reduces the risk of having a court decide for it which groups are similarly situated.

Q 13:44 How should a self-funded employer determine the COBRA rate?

COBRA provides two methods an employer may use. First, rates may be determined by an actuarial process, taking into account such factors as the Secretary of the Treasury may prescribe by regulation. To date, the Secretary has not prescribed any factors, or given further guidance as to how the rating is to be accomplished. Second, rates may be determined on the basis of actual prior cost. This method is invalidated if there has been a significant change in coverage or in the number of employees covered.

Absent formal guidance or regulations, it is left to employers, actuaries, and other professionals in the field to determine what is reasonable. An actuarial estimation would take claims for the prior year (or years) as a natural starting point. Particularly if only one year is used, this raises the question of whether "paid claims" or "incurred claims" should be used (see Chapter 5). COBRA is concerned with determining the "cost" of providing coverage during a particular period; therefore, the use of incurred claims would appear to be the more accurate measure of cost during a specific period of time. It seems reasonable that a realistic estimation of trend is also an appropriate factor for consideration.

Part of providing coverage to persons situated similarly is the mere fact of administering the plan. Administration adds significant cost to the plan and should therefore also be considered as a factor. Employers should be advised that the cost of administering COBRA itself cannot be included in the determination of either historical costs or the prospective COBRA rate. COBRA administration expenses are dictated by statute and are limited to 2 percent.

If the plan were fully insured, things like margin and risk charges would be built into the premium rate, and as such would be fully passed on to COBRA beneficiaries as part of their premium. Whether these same charges could be included in a self-funded employer's rate is still murky. Part of the reason an employer becomes self-funded is to avoid these and other insurer-imposed charges. Having successfully avoided them, it becomes somewhat self-serving to then include them in a charge to someone buying the coverage from the employer.

If an employer does not wish to obtain an actuarial estimation of costs, the employer may base the calculation on the prior cost method. Using this method, an employer would take the plan's cost for similarly situated beneficiaries for the preceding 12-month period and adjust the costs using the change in the implicit price deflator of the gross national product. The deflator used is for the 12-month period ending on the last day of the sixth month of the preceding determination period. That means, for example, the premium cost for calendar year 2001 would be calculated by adjusting the cost for 2000 by the percentage increase or decrease in the price deflator for the 12-month period ending June 30, 2000. The change in the price deflator is basically a recognition of inflation. To the extent that medical costs increase more rapidly than the rate of general inflation, the use of the GNP deflator will understate the true impact that (medical) inflation is having on the plan. Further, other normal elements, such as trend and margin, cannot be taken into account through this method.

Q 13:45 Has the IRS provided any guidance regarding applicable premiums?

Very little. On January 22, 1996, the IRS published Revenue Ruling 96-8 in the Internal Revenue Bulletin. This revenue ruling provides guidance on premium issues under COBRA. If an employee had family coverage before a qualifying event and only the spouse elects COBRA coverage, the plan must charge the spouse the individual rate, not the family rate. The ruling does not mention the possibility of charging the difference between the individual and family rates (the spousal increment); therefore, it is safest not to use that approach.

The revenue ruling includes an example the meaning of which is not totally clear, but could be interpreted as follows: Assume a plan has fully insured rates of $150 for an individual and $400 for a family. Further assume any two members of a family with a qualifying event make separate COBRA elections. The IRS guidance suggests that the plan may charge 102 percent of the $400 family rate, rather than 102 percent of $150 for each of the two individuals.

Q 13:46 What should an employer do if the premium paid is less than the amount due?

The final regulations establish a mechanism for the treatment of payments that are short by an insignificant amount. Either the plan must treat the payment as satisfying the plan's payment requirement or it must notify the qualified beneficiary of the amount of the deficiency and grant a reasonable period of time for the shortfall to be paid. The final regulations provide that, as a safe harbor, a period of 30 days is deemed to be a reasonable period for this purpose. Unfortunately, the regulations do not define "insignificant."

Election and Grace Periods

Q 13:47 How do the time periods specified in COBRA work?

The 60-day election period. Once a qualifying event occurs, the beneficiaries must be sent a notice describing their various rights and options (see Q 13:39; and see Appendix C for a sample notice). The notice must be dated, and must specify exactly when the medical coverage will end. The election period starts at the later of the date of the qualifying event or the date of the notice and extends for 60 days from that date.

> **Example 13-4.** Suppose the notice of termination of coverage was sent (dated) on October 12, and specified that coverage had been terminated as of September 30. The 60-day clock would start running as of October 12. Conversely, had the notice been sent on the same day, but instead specified that coverage would terminate on October 31, the 60-day clock would start running on October 31.

This election period is intended to give the beneficiaries time to decide whether to avail themselves of COBRA.

The 45-day grace period. The beneficiary is permitted to decide to take advantage of the coverage at any time during the 60-day period described. To activate their decision, they must sign a form or in some manner notify the employer or plan administrator of their election to continue coverage. Assuming they are required to sign a form and return it, the "grace period" is activated when they sign the form. From the date of their signing the form (or whatever response is required), they then have 45 days in which to make the first premium payment.

> **Example 13-5.** Using the October 31 coverage termination date in example 13-4, assume that on December 30, with zero days remaining in the election period, the beneficiary signs the form and notifies the employer, evidently by fax to achieve instant delivery of his or her decision to take the COBRA coverage. The 45-day grace period for payment will end on February 14. The beneficiary will have until that date to deliver the first premium payment to the employer.

The 45-day period is in addition to the 60-day election period discussed earlier.

The 30-day grace period. Once the qualified beneficiary is established in the employer's records as a COBRA continuee, he or she must make continuing periodic payments to keep the coverage in force. The most common cycle for this is through monthly premium payments. The regulations stipulate a 30-day minimum grace period for periodic payments. This is achieved in most cases by establishing the first of the month as the payment due date for that month's coverage and then setting the 30th of the month as the expiration of the grace period for that month.

If the employer has a longer grace period with any insurer, the longer grace period applies to all continuees. For example, if an employer has a 60-day premium delay, the 30-day grace period for COBRA becomes 60 days.

Q 13:48 What is the date of an election or a payment?

The final regulations clarify that payment is considered made on the date it is sent and COBRA elections are considered made on the date sent. This means that COBRA administrators should keep envelopes to retain proof of the postmark if they will deny COBRA because of a late election or terminate COBRA because of a late payment.

Q 13:49 What should an employer do if the monthly payment is postmarked one day after the grace period has expired?

An employer should refuse to accept it, and return it. The law requires employers to allow, at minimum, a 30-day grace period for payment. An employer may allow a longer period, but may not be arbitrary or discriminatory in administering such an extension (or any other provision of the coverage.) To allow a longer period for one person, but deny that same length of time as a grace period to another person, is potentially arbitrary. The net effect is that once an extension is allowed for one person, the plan is effectively modified to a 31-day grace period (or 46- or 61-day period). If sometime thereafter another check arrived "one day late," and, on the 32nd day was accepted, an employer would have extended the grace period to 32 days, and so on. Consistency is the key.

Q 13:50 Must an employer provide coverage during these grace periods?

The answer depends on the type of coverage the employee had. For indemnity style coverage, the answer is, effectively, no. The coverage cannot be canceled, but claims need not be processed either. To the extent possible, the coverage on current claims should be held in abeyance, with claims pending until either the grace period expires, at which time the coverage can be canceled and claims denied, or the payment is received and claims can be processed. Claims dating from an earlier period, which were incurred while the continuee had coverage in full effect, will have to be processed, even if the coverage is canceled for lack of payment. Employers should be careful in setting up procedures with their claims payer or insurance company, to be sure that claims do not get processed and improperly denied during a grace period.

Not all medical plans are indemnity style, and placing coverage in abeyance will not work for HMOs, or an in-network point-of-service claim. Qualified beneficiaries who request services from HMOs are presumed to have elected COBRA and should pay applicable premiums.

Q 13:51 Could this arrangement allow continuees to receive coverage without paying for it?

Conceivably, it could. An employer would potentially be vulnerable in two instances. In the first instance, a 30-day period of financial exposure exists. This situation could be created by a continuee who was enrolled in an HMO or a point-of-service plan. Under these plans, the continuee could be treated by an HMO or point-of-service doctor during a month for which he or she had not yet made payment. Because no claims are filed for receipt of this type of service, there is nothing for an employer to pend. By not making payment by the end of the month, the continuee will have obtained "free" service, but at the expense of forfeiting any additional months of continuation eligibility he or she might have had remaining.

The second instance, which caused a great deal of uproar when COBRA was first announced, is somewhat more dangerous to an employer, at least theoretically. This instance pertains to the combination of the 60- and 45-day grace periods together, creating a 105-day window of exposure for an employer. In the situation of a continuee who was enrolled in an HMO, or a point-of-service plan, the circumstances are identical to the 30-day exposure mentioned previously, except for a longer period of time. In this situation, the beneficiary need only wait to the last possible minute to sign the acceptance of COBRA before returning it to the employer, thereby obtaining the additional 45 days, during which the employer must wait before being able to take any action. The "continuee" can be receiving services throughout the entire period, with no intention of ever paying a premium. Theoretically, the employer can treat the action of receiving services from an HMO as a positive election for coverage by the beneficiary; however, certain timing issues will elapse between the point at which the service is performed, to when the employer is notified, to when the employer sends a bill to the beneficiary, to when the employer realizes the beneficiary is not responding, and so forth.

Q 13:52 How is the amount of the first payment due from a continuee determined?

Notwithstanding the possibility a beneficiary will apparently sign up for coverage with no intention of paying for it, as discussed in Q 13:51, the continuee is obligated to pay for all months during which he or she receives coverage. Simply put, when the continuee begins to make payment, the first payment must cover the period from the inception of the continuee's obligation to pay through the end of the month in which he or she makes the first payment.

Q 13:53 What should an employer do if a qualified beneficiary elects COBRA but does not specify whether the election is for family coverage?

If a covered employee or the spouse of a covered employee elects COBRA continuation coverage and the election does not specify whether the election is for self-only coverage, the final regulations state that the election is deemed to include an election of COBRA continuation coverage on behalf of other qualified beneficiaries.

Qualified Beneficiaries

Q 13:54 What class of individual may be a qualified beneficiary?

In its original form, the law identified three classes of individuals to whom the scope of the law applied:

1. Covered employees;
2. Spouse of a covered employee; and
3. Dependent of a covered employee.

Shortly after the law became effective, an employer that was filing for Chapter XI bankruptcy protection took steps to terminate its retiree health care coverage, stating that it was too costly for the company to afford. Congress viewed this as an undesirable result and passed stopgap legislation to prevent it from happening. Ultimately, both the bankruptcy laws and COBRA were modified to provide additional protection to retirees. Now, loss of coverage because of bankruptcy is recognized as a standard COBRA event that triggers lifetime continuation. Hence, bankruptcy created a fourth class of individuals to whom the law applies: covered retirees and their dependents.

Employers should take note that the law does not intend to create new classes of individuals to whom coverage is to be extended (however, see Q 13:56), and is, therefore, explicit in extending coverage to those individuals who were covered under the plan on the day before a qualifying event. No employee, spouse, or child can therefore become a qualified beneficiary who was not a beneficiary under the plan when coverage terminated.

The Health Insurance Portability and Accountability Act of 1996 (HIPAA) expanded the definition of qualified beneficiary to include a child born to or placed for adoption with a covered employee during COBRA continuation, creating a fifth class of individuals to whom the law applies: children born to or placed for adoption with a covered employee during COBRA continuation.

> **Note.** Children born to or placed for adoption with any other COBRA continuee (such as the child of a child) do not become qualified beneficiaries and, as such, are not entitled to certain privileges, such as continuing coverage in the event of the qualified beneficiary's death.

The final regulations add a provision clarifying that if an individual is denied coverage under a group health plan in violation of applicable law (including HIPAA) and experiences an event that would be a qualifying event if the coverage had not been wrongfully denied, the individual is considered a qualified beneficiary.

Reductions or terminations of coverage in anticipation of an event are disregarded in determining whether the event results in a loss of coverage. This rule applies in cases where a covered employee discontinues the coverage of a spouse in anticipation of a divorce or legal separation. In such a case, upon receiving notice of the divorce or legal separation, a plan is required to make COBRA continuation coverage available, effective on the date of the divorce or legal separation (but not for any period before the date of the divorce or legal separation).

The maximum coverage period for a newborn or adopted child is measured from the date of the qualifying event and not from the date of birth or placement for adoption. Thus, the child's maximum period of COBRA continuation period ends at the same time as the maximum period for other family members.

Q 13:55 Are there any persons who, although covered under the employer's plan, may not be qualified beneficiaries?

Yes, there are. Nonresident aliens, their spouses, and dependents cannot become qualified beneficiaries of the plan pertaining to the nonresident alien. This will not preclude the spouse or dependent from becoming a qualified beneficiary under plans covering them as an employee or as the dependent of an employee who is not a nonresident alien.

Anyone who is not the employee or the employee's spouse or dependent child is not generally a qualified beneficiary. The most common example is domestic partners, although many employers that choose to extend coverage to domestic partners also choose to make COBRA continuation coverage available.

Q 13:56 If a qualified beneficiary gains a dependent, can that new dependent be covered as a qualified beneficiary?

Yes and no. This is one of the most contentious and controversial aspects of COBRA, the infamous "after-acquired dependents" rules. These rules are particularly galling to many employers because they can require more generous treatment than would be accorded to active employees. Although after-acquired dependents have to be covered, they do not gain the status of "qualified beneficiary." Therefore, they have no rights unto themselves; they have only the rights afforded to the qualified beneficiary who acquired them.

HIPAA expanded the definition of qualified beneficiary to include a child born to or placed for adoption with a covered employee during COBRA continuation.

There are three basic categories of after-acquired dependency rules: after-acquired children, after-acquired spouses, and prior decliners.

After-acquired children. Children born to qualified beneficiaries other than the covered employee during a continuation become after-acquired dependents, as do children adopted by a qualified beneficiary other than the covered employee, or stepchildren resulting from a marriage by a qualified beneficiary (including the employee). They do not become qualified beneficiaries, and, being infants, they can neither make independent decisions for themselves nor cause some of the perturbations other after-acquired dependents can that make the rules so controversial.

After-acquired spouses. Most plans allow for the addition of spouses, usually within 30 or so days after the marriage. Continuees must be accorded the same rights as similarly situated active employees; therefore, they too get to add spouses to their coverage. Two examples illustrate this:

Example 13-6. Bob is a single employee who voluntarily terminates employment, and elects COBRA coverage. While in his continuation period, Bob marries Sally and adds her as a covered spouse. Sally is covered through Bob, but is not a qualified beneficiary.

Example 13-7. Mary is the covered spouse of Peter. Peter quits his job and elects COBRA for himself and Mary. While still in the continuation period, Mary and Peter divorce, and a week later Mary marries Fred. Because the plan allows active employees to add new spouses immediately, that right is extended to continuees (that is, qualified beneficiaries—in this case, Mary, who immediately adds Fred). Even though Fred never had any employee or dependent relationship with the employer, he becomes covered, but is not a qualified beneficiary himself.

A common provision in medical plans is that dependent status ends when a child marries. Under COBRA rules, loss of coverage resulting from marriage becomes a qualifying event and affords the (married) child qualified beneficiary status. This means that the married child has the same rights as an active employee, including the right to add a spouse to the coverage. Further, any children resulting from this marriage (during the continuation period) will be eligible for coverage also, but, like the new spouse, will not be qualified beneficiaries. In this case, the employee's grandchildren are being covered, which is a benefit not normally accorded to active employees.

Prior decliners. Qualified beneficiaries have the 60-day election period during which to decide whether to avail themselves of COBRA coverage. Once having declined, at the end of the election period they forfeit status as a qualified beneficiary; however, they can still be added to coverage at some later date, usually at an open enrollment opportunity. If someone waives COBRA in writing, but revokes the waiver within the 60-day election period, coverage is effective as of the date of election (revocation of the waiver).

Example 13-8. Herman is a married employee and terminates his employment. He elects COBRA coverage for himself, but not for his wife, Morticia. Assuming she does not elect it for herself, either, at the conclusion of the election period, she is no longer a qualified beneficiary; however, at the next open enrollment, Herman can elect to add Morticia as a dependent spouse. Even though Morticia again becomes a beneficiary under the plan, she does not reacquire qualified beneficiary status. In the event of a subsequent divorce or the death of Herman (assuming either event occurred during the continuation period), Morticia could not elect COBRA continuation coverage in her own right, as she is not a qualified beneficiary.

Despite the apparent illogic and poor underwriting principles displayed in the after-acquired rules, employers should keep two things in mind. First, attempts by employers to minimize their exposure to requirements less advantageous to them will not be seen as good-faith efforts at compliance. Second, an employer's exposure is somewhat mitigated by the fact that the universe of qualified beneficiaries is generally closed on the day before a qualifying event occurs. Therefore, the after-acquired spouses will be covered for a relatively short period of time.

Q 13:57 If a qualified beneficiary is eligible for the extension of COBRA as a result of a disability, can the other family members also extend COBRA?

Yes. The disability extension applies to all qualified beneficiaries affected by the same qualifying event, not just the disabled qualified beneficiary. The plan may require payment of 150 percent if a disabled beneficiary experiences a second qualifying event during the disability extension.

The final regulations require plans to continue COBRA for up to 29 months for the family of a disabled qualified beneficiary, even if the disabled qualified beneficiary does not elect COBRA coverage. The plan can charge 150 percent of the applicable premium if the disabled individual is covered, but just 102 percent if only nondisabled qualified beneficiaries are covered.

Miscellaneous

Q 13:58 When does COBRA begin, at the qualifying event, or upon the loss of coverage?

The plan administrator can choose whether to use the date of loss of coverage, rather than the date of the qualifying event, as the starting date for COBRA, but must be consistent. These dates might be different when, for example, a plan provides for an automatic continuation of coverage for some period of time. For instance, a layoff might guarantee the affected employee a six-month period of continuing medical coverage following the beginning of the layoff. Employers should note that COBRA "clocks" do not start running until the later of the qualifying event (or loss of coverage) or the date of notice to the qualified beneficiary. These paradoxical statements can be reconciled thusly: Provide the COBRA notices as soon as can be done, even before the date of the event, if at all possible. That starts the 18- or 36-month "clock" running at the date of the event, if the plan has chosen to use the date of the qualifying event, rather than the date of loss of coverage.

If an employer provides continuing coverage while providing a period of employer-paid coverage, the employer should clearly communicate to the employees not only what is happening, but what the employees' obligations are, what they must do, and when they must do it in order to maintain their rights. For instance, the employer should pointedly bring to the employee's attention the fact he or she is being required to sign a document within the normal 60-day period, which indicates the intention to purchase COBRA coverage when the "free" COBRA period runs out. In doing this, the employer should clearly indicate when the first payment will be required from the employee. This is permissible because an employer cannot require payment sooner than 45 days after the intention to purchase coverage is signed. The employer may extend far beyond the 45-day minimum on a nondiscriminatory basis if it chooses to do so.

Q 13:59 Can an employer minimize its financial exposure by reducing the medical plan benefits before a qualifying event occurs?

The final regulations address, and attempt to prevent, this tactic. Were an employer to do this, the regulations stipulate that the plan in effect before the reduction in benefits took place is the plan that will be offered under COBRA. The regulations do not indicate any precise timing, or provide a safe harbor that would enable an employer to do this. Each case will be viewed on its own merits, based on the specific facts and circumstances of the situation. Simply put, the government will not make it easy for an employer to get away with this ploy.

The regulations also prohibit an employee from denying COBRA coverage to a soon-to-be-ex-spouse by dropping the spouse's coverage during open enrollment before the divorce or legal separation triggers a qualifying event. If an employee drops coverage in anticipation of a divorce or legal separation, the ex-spouse is still entitled to 36 months of coverage, starting with the date of the qualifying event, which means there is a gap in coverage.

Q 13:60 What is gross misconduct?

There has been no guidance on this point from the IRS. This silence can be interpreted as a message in itself. Once guidance is provided, employers will know how far they can go, and many will attempt to step as close to the line as possible without crossing it. By not offering specific guidance, the government is in effect telling employers not to attempt to use this avenue freely. Employers should reserve use of this reason to deny COBRA eligibility to only the most blatant cases.

Q 13:61 What are the penalties for failure to comply?

Originally, COBRA provided that any violation, no matter how minor, would result in a loss of tax deductions for all employer contributions, whether paid or incurred, to all group medical plans maintained by the offending employer. Further, any violations could cause any amount contributed on behalf of highly compensated individuals to be deemed as taxable income to all such persons employed by that employer. Because these penalties were so Draconian, they were the subject of severe criticism from all parties, including those who supported the law. It was not therefore considered likely that they would be imposed—certainly not for minor violations. Regardless, technically they remained in effect for violations occurring prior to December 31, 1988.

Excise taxes on employers. The Technical and Miscellaneous Revenue Act of 1988 provides sanctions for plan years beginning after December 31, 1988. The sanction for a group health plan's failure to comply is an excise tax of $100 per day of noncompliance per individual, with a $200-per-day family maximum. The period of noncompliance begins on the first day of the failure and ends on the earlier of (1) the day the failure is corrected, or (2) six months after the employer's responsibility to provide COBRA continuation ends.

There is a maximum tax equal to the lesser of $500,000 or 10 percent of the employer's expenses for health plans in the prior year. This maximum applies to a single employer, providing the failure is not caused by willful neglect.

These sanctions will not apply if the failure is corrected within 30 days, or if it had a reasonable cause.

Excise taxes on individuals. Individuals who are responsible for the administration of COBRA may also be liable if their actions contributed to, or caused, the failure. For these persons, the aggregate tax that may be imposed for all plan failures in a year is $2 million. The IRS retains the right to reduce or waive any or all penalties, especially if the penalty would be viewed as excessive relative to the magnitude of the violation.

Penalties under ERISA. ERISA also contains penalties, and as COBRA is incorporated into ERISA, those penalties apply to COBRA violations as well. An injured qualified beneficiary may file suit against an employer for relief. The Department of Labor may also file suit against an employer for ERISA (including COBRA) violations. Any violation of ERISA Title I can carry criminal penalties of up to $5,000 in fines and up to one year in jail for an individual. Employers can be fined up to $100,000. Further, a plan administrator who failed to provide any COBRA notice may be directly liable to the individual who failed to receive such notice, of up to $110 per day, starting from when the notice was first due.

Remedy. A general remedy is available, known as a corrected failure. This provision allows a failure to be rectified, if "such failure is retroactively undone to the extent possible, and the beneficiary is placed in a financial position which is as good as such beneficiary would have been in had such failure not occurred."

Q 13:62 May each qualified beneficiary make independent elections?

To a certain extent it depends on who the qualified beneficiary is. There is a hierarchy in the decision path, which moves from the employee to the spouse to the dependents. The employee is the primary decision maker for the family, and the employee's decision to purchase COBRA is binding on all of the employee's beneficiaries. Should the employee decline coverage, that decision is not binding on the spouse and beneficiaries, and responsibility for making the decision is passed to the spouse.

The spouse has the same "authority" as the employee, once he or she receives the decision-making responsibility. The spouse's decision will bind dependent children in the same manner as would the employee's, had it been exercised. Only in the event that the spouse declines coverage for dependents will the dependents be allowed to make an independent decision. Once the decision is in their hands, each dependent must be given the full array of options that the employee and spouse had, but only if the legal guardian of the child is someone other than the employee or spouse.

Q 13:63 May qualified beneficiaries change their minds about electing coverage?

During the 60-day election period, qualified beneficiaries may change their minds as often as they wish; however, doing so may not be a "free" choice. Assuming there has been no waiver or denial of coverage, upon electing to buy coverage, the qualified beneficiary's coverage will be retroactive to the date of coverage cancellation. Had the beneficiary waived coverage and then, still within the election period, revoked the waiver, coverage need only begin as of the date of the revocation. Of course, under these circumstances, the requisite premium due may not be for any period of time earlier than the revocation, and claims incurred between the coverage cessation date and revocation of the waiver will not be covered.

Beyond the 60-day election period, only one change can be made: to cease further coverage. Once coverage is "not in effect" after the end of the election period, that status is final, at least as far as being a qualified beneficiary is concerned. A spouse can be added as a dependent after previously turning down coverage as a qualified beneficiary (see Q 13:56).

For rules relating to flexible benefit plans, see Q 13:72.

Q 13:64 Can an employee pay the COBRA premium for a spouse or dependents?

Yes. Actually, as long as the premium is paid on time anyone can pay it. It is reasonable that a dependent child could lose dependency status, and the employee-parent assume responsibility for paying the COBRA premium, perhaps even through payroll deductions. It is conceivable that in a divorce situation, the employee-spouse might agree to make the payments, again through payroll deduction. In either of these events, it remains the continuee's responsibility to assure the timely payment of the premium. Should the premium not be paid for any reason, the employer would be well-advised to terminate the COBRA continuation.

COBRA premium payments have been made by state Medicaid plans and even other employers. In the latter instance, a new employer may have a waiting period before coverage under its plan begins, and in attempting to recruit a particularly valuable employee, the wait for medical coverage may become a sticking point in the negotiations. To resolve the problem, the new employer might agree to finance the premium payments for as long as the waiting period. The final regulations clarify that it does not matter who pays the COBRA premiums.

Q 13:65 Can an employer require evidence of insurability from a qualified beneficiary?

No. Coverage must be made available to all qualified beneficiaries without restriction or conditions.

Q 13:66 Can an employer create and offer a plan specially designed for COBRA continuation only?

Qualified beneficiaries must be offered the same coverage they had before the qualifying event occurred, assuming it is still available to active employees. If the employer's plan is changed for all similarly situated persons, the qualified beneficiaries must be offered that plan, not something created just for them. This does not prevent the employer from offering the specially designed plan in addition to the plan offered to active employees who are similarly situated.

Q 13:67 If an employer offers retirees coverage, does COBRA still have to be made available to retiring employees?

Yes, unless the plan offered to retirees is identical to that offered to active employees.

An employer can, however, offer retiree coverage as an alternative, and if the retiree elects the alternate coverage, that will suffice. This remains true even if the retiree coverage is notably "less rich" than the COBRA coverage. If an employer offers retiree coverage as an alternative to COBRA, the choice should be clearly explained to retirees and clearly recorded.

Q 13:68 What steps should an employer take if retiree coverage is offered as an alternative to COBRA?

The single most significant point of difference between retiree coverage and COBRA coverage is the expected duration of the coverage. COBRA will last for 18 months (or 36, with a surviving spouse extension), whereas retiree coverage is nominally expected to last for a lifetime. While an employer would be ill-advised to state that the retiree coverage is promised for life, the point can still be made. For example, the materials given to an employee or retiree describing the retiree coverage might point out the following:

> COBRA will definitely end after a maximum period of 18 [or 36] months. Alternatively, the retiree coverage is expected to continue without modification for an indefinite period. While the employer reserves the right to modify or cancel the plan, it has no plans to do so in the foreseeable future.

The employer should require a clear rejection of COBRA coverage in the process of enrolling for retiree coverage. To protect itself against adverse selection (see Chapters 8 and 9), an employer may not allow a retiree to decline retiree coverage immediately upon retirement, and to return at a later date to begin the coverage. With that concept in place, an election form patterned on the following might be used:

> Retiree Medical Coverage
>
> I have received, read, and understand the materials provide by [employer name] describing the medical coverage available to me as a retiree. I also understand the rights I have to a limited

period of continuation of my current coverage under the provisions of COBRA. Effective on [date of retirement], I elect to receive medical coverage as follows:

☐ I elect coverage under [company name] medical plan for retired employees, and I reject COBRA coverage.

☐ I reject coverage under [company name] medical plan for retired employees, and may choose to elect coverage under COBRA.

The choice I have made above applies to:

☐ Myself only

☐ Myself and my eligible dependents

Signature _____ Date _____

The purpose of phrasing the rejection of company medical coverage with the qualified phrase "may choose to elect coverage under COBRA," is to avoid running afoul of the 60-day decision period required under COBRA. By phrasing the election form this way, the employer can insist on an immediate decision regarding the employer's medical plan, yet preserve the employee's rights under COBRA.

Q 13:69 How are deductibles handled under COBRA continuation policies?

The 1987 proposed regulations required that in the event of a divorce, legal separation, or a dependent child's loss of coverage, each resulting family unit be credited with all the expenses incurred by the entire family before the qualifying event. Under the final regulations, in computing deductibles and limits for the family unit receiving COBRA coverage, the plan is required to take into account only those expenses incurred before the qualifying event by family members who are part of the resulting family unit after the qualifying event.

> **Example 13-9.** The Jones family, consisting of husband Fred, spouse Robin, and dependents Billy, Janie, Greg, and Mary, is in the employer's plan as a family unit, which requires a deductible of $100 per person, with a $300 family deductible. Prior to the qualifying event, the family deductible was met, $100 by Fred and Billy and $50 by Robin and Janie. After a divorce, Robin elected coverage under COBRA, and has $50 toward her deductible.

Q 13:70 How are pay-based deductibles computed?

In the event of termination of employment or the employee's death, the deductible calculated at the time of the qualifying event will become frozen and will be used for the remaining portion of the first year of continuation, and then will be unchanged for each subsequent period. For other qualifying events, the employer can choose to freeze the deductible or continue to base it on the employee's pay.

Q 13:71 How are plan limits handled in a continuation policy?

Plan limits, such as for out-of-pocket expenses, number of days available for treatment, dollar maximums for a specific treatment, annual dollar maximum or lifetime maximum, and copayment limits, are treated in the same way as are deductibles (see Q 13:69). That is, the level of attainment achieved before the qualifying event for an individual must be carried forward for that individual after the qualifying event. If Robin Jones had satisfied $800 toward a $1,000 out-of-pocket maximum, she would be deemed to have met $800 until she incurs more expenses or the next year begins a new accumulation period.

Q 13:72 Do flexible benefit plans create any unique or special considerations under COBRA?

With the exception of flexible spending accounts, there are no particularly unique requirements under a flexible arrangement as opposed to a nonflexible program. The overriding consideration is that a qualified beneficiary who elects continuation coverage may not be treated any less favorably than a similarly situated active employee or spouse would be treated.

An employer should remember also that COBRA does not require the extension of coverage that a beneficiary does not have on the day before a qualifying event occurs. In a flexible plan, this translates into two operating principles:

1. The employee who opted out of coverage, and was not receiving health benefits from the employer's plan at the time the qualifying event occurs (even if the employee was receiving other, nonhealth benefits), never becomes a qualified beneficiary and need not be offered continuation coverage upon the occurrence of what would otherwise be a qualifying event. If the employee's spouse or dependents were similarly not covered, they too will not attain the status of qualified beneficiary and need not be offered continuation coverage.

2. The employee who is receiving health coverage under one of the employer's health options must be allowed to continue to receive coverage under that same option until the next open enrollment. At the next open enrollment, the employee must be given the opportunity to select among all of the health options he or she would have been given to choose among had the qualifying event not occurred.

Q 13:73 Do flexible spending accounts have any unique features in general?

Flexible spending accounts, which are empowered under Code Section 125, enable an employee to set aside pre-tax dollars from compensation and to use those dollars to pay for a broad list of medical goods and services that are not covered under the employer's plan.

Once there is no longer an employee's paycheck from which to acquire pre-tax contributions for the account, a qualified beneficiary's contributions must be made with after-tax dollars. Using after-tax dollars to pay for medical services through a flexible spending account is no different than paying for those services directly.

There is at least one scenario in which continuing to fund a flexible spending account, even with post-tax dollars, makes sense. For example, an employee may have contributed significantly to his or her account in anticipation of a large expenditure, but was terminated (or lost coverage in any manner that triggered COBRA) before the expense was incurred. Assuming he or she had no other eligible expenses to use against the account, the employee would either have to forfeit the account balance or continue funding it with post-tax dollars. It would make sense to keep the account "alive" until the expenditure is made and then file the claim against the spending account.

An FSA need not be offered to a qualified beneficiary if the maximum amount that the qualified beneficiary could be required to pay for coverage for the remainder of the plan year exceeds the maximum benefits. Even if an FSA must be offered initially, enrollment for future years is not required if the FSA qualifies for the exception under HIPAA. (FSAs that are funded solely or primarily by salary reduction qualify.)

Q 13:74 To offset the additional time and expense, can an employer receive extra compensation for administering a flexible spending account?

To rationalize the requirement that an employer be liable for 100 percent of the requested value of the flexible spending account from the moment it is started, and not limit the employer's liability to the amount contributed into the account by the employee (as happens with dependent care spending accounts), the IRS determined that these accounts were "insurance," and that the employee contributions were "premium" payments. The COBRA rules allow an employer to charge up to 2 percent more on the premium to continuees for precisely the purpose of offsetting the additional expenses of administering COBRA. An employer can then require that the continuee pay $1.02 for every $1 of contribution into the flexible spending account.

Q 13:75 If COBRA coverage is better and less costly than a conversion policy, should an employer advise all terminating employees to take COBRA?

Definitely not, for reasons including the following:

1. Under some circumstances a conversion policy would be preferred to a COBRA continuation. If an employer advises an employee to take the COBRA continuation—and it works to the employee's detriment—that employee would have grounds for a lawsuit against the employer.

2. Unless an employer is fully insured, the claims generated during the period of the continuation will be charged against the employer's experience. Note that the people most likely to take COBRA continuation may be those who have an expectation of using it and, as such, would represent a higher risk.

3. COBRA continuation is generally limited to either 18 or 36 months, while conversion policies are not limited in duration. Conversion policies usually may be retained until age 65 if the insured wishes to continue paying premiums for that length of time. COBRA continuees can elect conversion policies during the last 180 days before the end of the maximum COBRA duration, but that option may not apply to all continuees, either because the plan ceases offering conversions or because the continuee loses COBRA before the last 180 days. This is less of an issue now that HIPAA requires that people exhausting COBRA can obtain individual health insurance policies without evidence of insurability.

Q 13:76 Under which circumstances may an employer terminate COBRA earlier than at the conclusion of the 18-, 29-, or 36-month periods?

COBRA coverage can be terminated prior to the expiration of the maximum times for the following reasons:

1. The qualified beneficiary fails to pay the required premium within the grace period.

2. The qualified beneficiary becomes entitled to Medicare (i.e., entitled means actual enrollment in Medicare, not just eligibility to enroll). (See Q 13:77.)

3. The qualified beneficiary becomes covered under another group medical plan that does not contain a preexisting condition exclusion applicable to that person.

4. The employer terminates all medical plans and no longer covers any employees.

5. A qualified beneficiary who is receiving an additional 11 months of coverage as a result of a disability ceases to be disabled, as determined by the Social Security Administration. The qualified beneficiary is obligated to notify the plan within 30 days of the determination.

6. A COBRA continuee loses coverage because of fraud, such as where an HMO member gives an ID card to a neighbor to obtain medical treatment.

Q 13:77 What is Medicare entitlement?

COBRA itself does not define Medicare entitlement. The final regulations clarify that being entitled to either Part A or B is sufficient for a plan to discontinue COBRA continuation coverage (assuming that the entitlement to Medicare benefits first arises after COBRA continuation coverage has been elected).

Most individuals are automatically "entitled" to premium-free Part A Medicare benefits, which generally means that they will not have to file an application for Part A coverage. Certain other individuals will be required to file an application for premium-free Part A benefits, and others will be required to pay for Part A coverage. With respect to Medicare Part B, certain individuals are required to file an application for such coverage, and all individuals are required to pay premiums for Part B coverage.

Q 13:78 If an employer makes an error that results in COBRA coverage being terminated prematurely, what steps should that employer take to rectify the situation?

An employer should determine why or how the error occurred and take positive steps to ensure it does not happen again. Then the employer should analyze who was adversely affected by the error and take steps to alleviate any damage caused. It is important to take whatever actions are necessary to rectify the error, such as paying any bills that would have been paid had coverage correctly been in place. This should be done even if the employer must pay the bills because the insurance carrier will not. Such payment would be required as part of any government-imposed settlement. If an employer has shown good faith in attempting to remedy the failure, it may be possible to avoid penalties.

Q 13:79 Is Medicaid or CHAMPUS/TRICARE considered another group plan?

No. According to IRS Notice 90-58, employers subject to COBRA regulations are obligated to offer COBRA to reservists and their family members in order to be in compliance. If an employer does not discontinue medical coverage for reservists or their families, COBRA need not be offered.

Q 13:80 If Medicare entitlement does not cause an immediate loss of coverage, when is the 36-month "starting point" if employer coverage is subsequently lost for the spouse?

This situation could arise if an employee reaches age 65, enrolls for Medicare and continues to work, keeping Medicare as secondary coverage, then retires sometime in the future. The law is specific that COBRA coverage is measured from the date of the employee's Medicare entitlement and extends for 36 months thereafter. As an example, assume that this employee retires one year after attaining age 65. The spouse would be eligible for 24 months of COBRA continuation.

Another scenario is that an employee retires less than 18 months before becoming entitled to Medicare. In that case, the 36-month period would begin as of the date of retirement.

Q 13:81 If a COBRA continuee is covered simultaneously by a new employer's plan with a preexisting condition exclusion and the old employer's plan, which plan pays for which conditions?

While the law clearly states that a continuee faced with a preexisting condition exclusion must be allowed to continue COBRA coverage, the law does not state that the continuation be for the preexisting condition only; therefore, the COBRA coverage should remain in force for any and all conditions it would normally cover for any other person. Coordination of benefits guidelines published by the National Association of Insurance Commissioners (NAIC) resolve such dual coverage issues by naming as primary the plan covering the individual as an active employee. The NAIC rules go on to state that if the two plans conflict, the plan covering the employee for the longer period of time (the COBRA plan) becomes the primary plan. This is a standard tiebreaking rule used by NAIC.

Employers should take note that self-funded plans are not automatically covered under the NAIC rules; self-funded plans can choose whether they will be covered under the rules and, if so, which ones. A self-funded plan could therefore name itself as secondary in all cases under which it provides COBRA coverage and another group plan comes into the picture. The tactic may or may not be successful.

Given the restrictions on preexisting conditions and exclusions contained in HIPAA, dual coverage situations should occur less frequently and last for shorter periods than in the past.

Q 13:82 May an employee covered under another employer's plan switch COBRA coverage from family to single in order to maintain protection for a spouse with a preexisting condition?

Yes. Given the emphasis in the final regulations that each qualified beneficiary be allowed to choose independently based on his or her own right to coverage, this change would be interpreted as the employee being removed from COBRA continuation because the other coverage exists, and the spouse independently making an election to continue as single.

Q 13:83 How does state legislation integrate with COBRA?

Despite being federal law, and part of ERISA at that, COBRA does not supersede state continuation requirements. As the two sets of law coexist, there is not necessarily a conflict between them, either. COBRA is aimed at employers. Notable for the purpose of differentiating between these two sources of law, and highlighting the fact that they do not conflict, is the 2 percent additional premium an employer is allowed to charge to help offset the cost of administration. State laws are aimed at insurers, and, despite the added administrative burden that may be placed on insurers for the continuation, no similar additional premium is permitted under some state laws.

To the extent that there is a perceived or actual conflict between state law and COBRA and to the extent that decision-making authority is given to an employer to formulate compliance rules or procedures, prudence would dictate following the more generous of the two laws. The following states have enacted laws with provisions more generous than COBRA.

1. *Arkansas.* For insured groups not subject to COBRA, divorce or legal separation triggers a maximum of 120 days of continuation coverage. Job termination also triggers a maximum continuation of 120 days, if continuously covered for at least three months before termination. Other terminations of membership in a group also trigger continuation coverage.

2. *California.* Insurers and HMOs must offer employees older than age 60 who have worked for the employer for at least five years the same coverage for the employees and their dependents after separation from employment and until age 65. This law allows insurers to charge up to 213 percent of the applicable premium, following the end of COBRA continuation. If an employee divorces or dies during the continuation coverage, the former spouse can continue coverage for up to five years, subject to payment of 102 percent of the applicable premium. Cal-COBRA, enacted in 1997, extends continuation to groups of 2 to 19 employees.

3. *Colorado.* For insured groups not subject to COBRA, an employee's termination of coverage for any reason except termination of a group policy triggers up to 18 months of continuation coverage, if the employee was covered continu-

ously for at least six months. Death, divorce, or legal separation also trigger up to 18 months of continuation.

4. *Connecticut.* Notice of the option to continue must be sent within 10 days (not the 14 or 44 days permitted by COBRA) to the covered employee, dependents, or qualified beneficiaries if the loss of coverage resulted from death, total disability, or termination. Connecticut also allows up to 104 weeks of continuation coverage when an employee terminates. For insured groups not subject to COBRA, Connecticut requires 156 weeks (three years) of continuation following death, divorce, or legal separation.

5. *Florida.* Continuation applies to companies with fewer than 20 workers, provided they pay premiums of up to 115 percent of the group rate.

6. *Georgia.* Continuation for up to three months applies to groups of less than 20 employees. Groups subject to COBRA must allow surviving spouses and divorced spouses older than age 60 to continue coverage, subject to payment of 120 percent of the applicable premium, until the divorced or surviving spouse is eligible for Medicare.

7. *Hawaii.* If an employee is prevented from working because of sickness, the employer must pay for three months of continuation coverage.

8. *Illinois.* Continuation until entitlement for Medicare (as contrasted to the 36-month maximum under COBRA) is required for divorced or widowed spouses aged 55 or older at the time of the qualifying event. Coverage may be terminated as under COBRA (i.e., for nonpayment of premium or coverage under another group plan). For divorced or widowed spouses younger than age 55 covered by insured groups not subject to COBRA, two years of continuation is available.

9. *Iowa.* For insured groups not subject to COBRA, death, divorce, legal separation, or annulment triggers a maximum of nine months of continuation coverage. Termination of membership in a group also triggers up to nine months of continuation coverage, if covered continuously for at least three months before termination.

10. *Kansas.* Any loss of coverage, including discontinuance of a group policy, triggers entitlement to continuation of up to six months. Employees must have been covered continuously for at least three months before termination.

11. *Kentucky.* For insured groups not subject to COBRA, death, divorce, legal separation, or a dependent child reaching the maximum age triggers up to 18 months of continuation coverage. Job termination also triggers up to 18 months of continuation coverage, if the employee had been covered for at least three months before termination.

12. *Louisiana.* The surviving spouse has 90 days to elect coverage (not 60 as established by COBRA) if the qualifying event is the employee's death. Continuation until the earlier of entitlement to Medicare, remarriage, or obtaining other group coverage is required for widowed spouses aged 50 or older at the time of the qualifying event. For insured groups not subject to COBRA, termination of employment triggers up to 12 months of continuation coverage, if covered continuously for at least three months before termination.

13. *Maine.* For insured groups not subject to COBRA, continuation of up to six months is required if termination is casued by layoff or a work-related condition, if the employee was covered for at least six months before termination. If the employee is totally disabled, coverage can be continued for one year.

14. *Maryland.* For insured groups not subject to COBRA, death, divorce, legal separation, or termination of employment triggers up to 18 months of continuation coverage, if continuously covered for at least 30 days before termination.

15. *Massachusetts.* Continuation until the earlier of remarriage, termination of employee's coverage, or the date specified in the divorce decree is required for divorced or widowed spouses. Only 100 percent of the applicable premium can be charged.

    Divorced or separated spouses are eligible, without additional premium, for coverage as long as the group member is covered, until such time as provided in the divorce decree or until either spouse remarries. For insured groups not subject to COBRA, death of the employee entitles dependents to 39 weeks of continuation coverage, a plant closing entitles the family to 90 days of continuation coverage, other involuntary terminations entitle the family to 39 weeks of continuation coverage, voluntary terminations entitle the family to 31 days of continuation coverage, but the length of continuation cannot exceed the length of coverage prior to termination.

16. *Minnesota.* Surviving dependents have until the 90th day after the election to make the first premium payment (as contrasted to the 45 days COBRA permits). Continuation until the earlier of remarriage or termination of employee's coverage is required for divorced or widowed spouses. (*Note:* If the qualifying event is the employee's death, continuation will be permitted until the employee's coverage would have terminated.

    If coverage is being terminated, written notice of the fact must be mailed to the surviving dependents 30 days in advance of the intended termination date. Disabled employees receive continuation until the employee's coverage would have terminated, had the employee not been disabled. Rules similar to COBRA apply to smaller groups.

17. *Mississippi.* For insured groups not subject to COBRA, death, divorce, or legal separation triggers entitlement to 12 months of continuation coverage. Termination of an employee's membership in a group entitles the family to up to 12 months of continuation coverage, if the employee was continuously covered for at least three months before termination.

18. *Missouri.* Qualified beneficiaries are entitled to nine months of continuation coverage in the event of death, divorce, or legal separation, even if the event occurs during the 36-month COBRA period. For insured groups not subject to COBRA, termination of an employee's membership in a group triggers up to nine months of continuation coverage if covered continuously for at least three months before termination.

19. *Nebraska.* Notice of the option to continue must be sent within 10 days (not the 44 days permitted by COBRA) to the covered employee, dependents, or qualified beneficiaries, if the loss of coverage resulted from death, total disability, or termination. For insured groups not subject to COBRA, death of the employee entitles dependents to up to one year of coverage and

termination of employment entitles the family to up to six months of continuation coverage.

20. *Nevada.* Requirements similar to COBRA apply to employers with fewer than 20 employees. Additionally, for small employers dependents are entitled to 36 months of continuation in the event of termination or reduction of hours. The employee and dependents must be covered continuously for at least 12 months before termination.

21. *New Hampshire.* Continuation until the earlier of entitlement to Medicare, remarriage, or obtaining other group coverage is required for divorced spouses aged 55 or older at the time of the qualifying event. Requirements similar to COBRA apply to employers with fewer than 20 employees. A divorced or separated spouse may continue coverage until remarriage.

22. *New Jersey.* Disabled employees receive continuation until becoming reemployed or becoming eligible for other group coverage, whichever is earlier. For insured groups not subject to COBRA, termination of employment triggers continuation coverage if covered continuously for at least three months before termination.

23. *New Mexico.* For insured groups not subject to COBRA, termination of membership in a group triggers up to six months of continuation coverage.

24. *New York.* Requirements similar to COBRA apply to employers with fewer than 20 employees.

25. *North Carolina.* For insured groups not subject to COBRA, termination of membership in a group triggers up to one year of continuation coverage, if covered continuously for three months before termination.

26. *North Dakota.* Dependents are entitled to 36 months in the event of annulment. For insured groups not subject to COBRA, divorce only entitles the former spouse to continuation coverage if the divorce decree requires it. Termination of an employee's membership in a group triggers up to 39 weeks of continuation coverage, if covered continuously for at least three months before termination.

27. *Ohio.* Annulment also triggers continuation coverage. For insured groups not subject to COBRA, termination of an

employee's membership in a group triggers up to six months of continuation coverage if continuously covered for at least three months before termination. Spouses and dependents of reservists called to active duty may extend coverage up to 36 months if the reservist dies.

28. *Oregon.* Continuation until the earlier of entitlement to Medicare or eligibility for other group coverage is required for divorced or widowed spouses aged 55 or older at the time of the qualifying event.

29. *Rhode Island.* Continuation until the earlier of remarriage, termination of the employee's coverage, or the date specified in the divorce decree is required for divorced spouses. For insured groups not subject to COBRA, death of the employee triggers up to 18 months of continuation coverage. Involuntary terminations of employment trigger up to 18 months of continuation coverage.

30. *South Carolina.* An insurer cannot terminate coverage of the former spouse unless the divorce decree so stipulates. For insured groups not subject to COBRA, termination of an employee's coverage triggers up to six months of continuation coverage, if covered continuously for at least six months before termination.

31. *South Dakota.* Rules similar to COBRA apply to employers with fewer than 20 employees.

32. *Tennessee.* If coverage ends during pregnancy, continuation is required until six months after the conclusion of the pregnancy. For insured groups not subject to COBRA, death, divorce, or legal separation triggers up to 15 months of continuation coverage, but premiums must be paid in three-month increments. Termination of an employee's coverage triggers up to three months of continuation coverage if covered continuously for at least three months before termination.

33. *Texas.* For insured groups not subject to COBRA, death, divorce, or legal separation triggers up to three years of continuation coverage, if covered continuously for at least one year before the qualifying event. An employee's termination of coverage triggers up to six months of continuation coverage, if covered for at least three months before termination. An

insurer can offer a conversion policy in lieu of continuation coverage.

34. *Utah.* For insured groups not subject to COBRA, termination of coverage triggers up to six months of continuation coverage.
35. *Vermont.* For insured groups not subject to COBRA, death of an employee triggers up to six months of continuation coverage for dependents. Termination of employment triggers up to six months of continuation coverage if the employee was covered for at least three months before termination.
36. *Virginia.* For insured groups not subject to COBRA, termination of employment triggers up to 90 days of continuation coverage, if covered continuously for at least three months before termination.
37. *Washington.* Insurers must offer policyholders the option to include continuation coverage for any person becoming ineligible for any reason.
38. *West Virginia.* For insured groups not subject to COBRA, involuntary termination of employment triggers up to 18 months of continuation coverage.
39. *Wisconsin.* Notice of the option to continue must be sent within five days (not the 44 days permitted by COBRA) to the covered employee, dependents, or qualified beneficiaries if the loss of coverage resulted from death, total disability, or termination.

The surviving spouse has 90 days to elect coverage (not 60 as established by COBRA) if the qualifying event is the employee's death. Annulment also triggers continuation coverage. Rules similar to COBRA apply to employers with fewer than 20 employees.

An employer should check with its insurer, legal counsel, or benefit consultant in these or other states to ensure that the most current knowledge is available for decision making and interpretation of existing laws.

Q 13:84   Why were the continuation requirements stemming from an employee's disability included in the preceding list, when that is not a COBRA qualifying event?

While perhaps not immediately, most employers would eventually terminate employment of disabled employees, thereby ending medical coverage for those employees. Because termination of employment is a COBRA event, relevant state requirements were included in the list.

Q 13:85   What has been the impact of COBRA on employers?

COBRA has done the following:

1. Imposed significant administrative burdens;
2. Increased health care costs; and
3. Made employers vulnerable to both civil lawsuits and penalties under ERISA.

The Charles D. Spencer & Associates 1999 COBRA survey showed that COBRA continuees have average claims 56 percent above the claim cost for active employees. The same survey showed that only 20 percent of those entitled to COBRA actually elect COBRA. Clearly, the higher claim costs result from adverse selection (sick people are much more likely to elect COBRA than healthy people).

Chapter 14

Form 5500

Most pension and welfare benefit plans must file the Form 5500 series of reports annually. This chapter concentrates on the requirements as they pertain to welfare—primarily health—plans.

Introduction	14-1
Plan Years	14-3
Administration	14-6
Completing the Form	14-16
Electronic Filing	14-17

Introduction

Q 14:1 What is a Form 5500?

The Employee Retirement Income Security Act of 1974 (ERISA) established the requirement for annual reporting to the IRS of data relating to the conduct and operation of employee benefit plans. The Form 5500 series of reports is the mechanism created to implement the administration of that requirement.

Q 14:2 Which welfare plans do not have to file a Form 5500?

The following plans are excluded from filing a Form 5500:

1. A welfare benefit plan that covered fewer than 100 participants as of the start of the plan year and is unfunded, fully insured, or a combination of insured and unfunded. An unfunded welfare benefit plan is one that has its benefits paid as needed directly from the general assets of the employer or the employee organization that sponsors the plan. Any plan that maintains separate funds, such as a trust, cannot be considered unfunded. Any plan that receives after-tax employee contributions cannot be considered unfunded.
2. An unfunded or insured welfare benefit plan whose benefits go only to a select group of management or highly compensated employees.
3. Plans maintained only to comply with workers compensation, unemployment compensation, or disability insurance laws.
4. A welfare benefit plan maintained outside the United States primarily for nonresident aliens.
5. A church plan.
6. A governmental plan.
7. A welfare benefit plan that participates in a group insurance arrangement that files a Form 5500 on behalf of the plan.
8. An apprenticeship or training plan that meets certain conditions.

Note. Cafeteria plans of any size or any sponsor are not exempt from filing a Form 5500. This is because the cafeteria plan filing requirement is part of the Internal Revenue Code, not ERISA.

Q 14:3 What does filing forms in the 5500 series accomplish?

The primary goal of the reporting requirement is to provide a self-reporting method by which the government can monitor compliance with IRS and Department of Labor (DOL) regulations. The reports also provide a substantial database of information for other purposes, including enforcement, research, detection of trends, and disclosure of information to the public.

Q 14:4 Are these reports considered confidential or privileged in any way?

No, quite the contrary. Except for specific exceptions, the filings are intended to be accessible by the public and must be made available to the employer's employees if they so request. Employees must be allowed to view copies of 5500 forms at an employer's offices. They may also receive copies of 5500s at a nominal charge (or free, at the employer's discretion), or they may request copies (for a nominal charge) directly from the government by writing to:

United States Department of Labor, Public Disclosure Room, N4677, Pension and Welfare Benefits Administration, 200 Constitution Avenue, NW, Washington, DC 20216.

The specific exception is Schedule SSA, which is not available to the general public.

Q 14:5 When must 5500s be filed?

An initial filing must be done for each plan when it is established by the plan sponsor. The plan sponsor must indicate the initial filing by checking box B(1), at the top of the form. Similarly, when the plan sponsor is terminating a plan, box B(3) must be checked to indicate this fact. In between establishment and termination, 5500 forms must be filed no less frequently than annually. For any of these filings, the 5500 is due at the last day of the seventh month following the close of the plan year, unless an extension is obtained. [ERISA § 104(a)(1)(A)]

Plan Years

Q 14:6 When must 5500 forms be filed more frequently than annually?

There are two instances that require filing more often than annually. The first occurs when the plan is being terminated, and it is being terminated before the end of the current plan year. Under this circumstance, two filing requirements will be triggered in less than the space of an elapsed year.

Example 14-1. A calendar-year plan is terminated April 5, 2001, the date all liabilities for which benefits are payable are satisfied (paid or transferred to another entity). One 5500 is due at the end of the seventh month following the close of the plan year prior to the final plan year (e.g., seven months after December 31, 2000, or July 31, 2001). The second 5500 filing is due at the end of the seventh month following the termination date, or November 30, 2001.

The second instance occurs when the plan sponsor changes the plan year.

Example 14-2. Assume the same facts as stated in Example 14-1 except that the plan does not terminate, but instead, changes the plan year to end April 5. The filing requirements will be identical to those in Example 14-1. Following the year of change, the 5500 filing will be due each November 30.

Generally, changing the plan year for a welfare benefit plan does not require prior IRS approval. [See IRC § 412(c)(5), and Rev Proc 87-27, 1987-1 CB 769, for an explanation of automatic approval of a change in plan year.]

Q 14:7 What is a plan year?

A plan year is any 12-month period chosen by the plan sponsor. Most plan years are calendar years, although there is no inherent reason they need to be, other than providing the convenience of being coincident with other events, such as the employer's accounting year. Also, while not imperative, many plan years are coincident with the insurance contract or renewal cycle.

Q 14:8 What is a short plan year?

A short plan year is any plan year that is less than 12 months in duration. During normal plan operation, a plan year must be the same 12 months, year after year. There are, however, three "normal" circumstances that might cause the occurrence of a short plan year:

1. The inception of a plan;
2. The termination of a plan; and
3. A change in the plan year.

Form 5500   Q 14:8

At the inception of a plan, an employer might have decided to implement a new benefit plan and is ready to do so in the middle of a calendar year. Assuming this employer wants the plan to operate on a calendar-year cycle, there are two options available: the employer can wait until the end of the calendar year before implementing the plan, or it can begin the plan immediately, designate the plan's operating year as a calendar year, and operate the plan for the first few months (until the end of the calendar year) as a short plan year. Under this circumstance, the 5500 filing requirements for the first plan year will generally be identical to a plan that has been in operation for a full year. Financial, participation, or claim data being reported will necessarily be based only on the months the plan has been in operation.

Assuming the plan referred to here is a fully insured medical plan, a Schedule A must be included as part of the 5500 filing. Schedule A is "Insurance Information" and is prepared, for the most part, based on data supplied by the insurance company (see Q 14:17). Obtaining this information on a timely basis should not present a problem so long as the insurance company has been advised of the requirement beforehand and is prepared to produce the necessary accounting data. Normally, an insurance company will expect the contract to renew annually, meaning 12 months after its inception, and will therefore expect to produce Schedule A data on this same cycle; however, an employer operating the plan for a short year will need the first Schedule A based on those first few months. Although the insurance company will comply, it will probably want to view the event as a short renewal cycle. While this is reasonable, the employer and the insurer should clarify at the beginning whether the first-year renewal will allow the insurance company the opportunity to adjust rates. If the insurer suggests doing this—particularly after a very short period of time—the employer should not agree. Although holding rates unchanged for longer time periods is more difficult, most insurance companies will be willing to extend the first rating period, without requiring a rate adjustment, for more than 12 months, providing they have been alerted to the necessity at the outset. Regardless of the outcome of the rate negotiations, most employers will find it worthwhile to have the plan year (and the insurance contract renewal cycle) running coincident with its other accounting and reporting cycles—often calendar year.

Q 14:9 Rather than operating a short plan year, may an employer operate a long plan year?

No, operating a plan year in excess of 12 months in duration is not permitted.

Administration

Q 14:10 Who is the plan sponsor?

For single-employer plans, the employer is almost always the plan sponsor. The plan sponsor is the person or corporate entity that has established the plan. Benefit plans may also be sponsored by two or more employers working in conjunction with each other, forming a multiple employer plan. In this instance, the sponsor would likely be a joint committee composed of representatives from the participating employers. An employee organization may also establish and sponsor a plan for its members. It is also possible for any combination of two or more of each of these to sponsor a plan. That is to say, one or more employers plus one or more employee organizations could jointly sponsor a plan. When employers and a union establish a plan under the terms of a collective bargaining agreement, it is referred to as a multiemployer plan.

In any instance, the identification of the plan sponsor should be clear and specific. It should enable an uninvolved third party to conclude correctly who the plan sponsor is. For example, the "Employer Coalition of Machinists of Memphis, Tennessee" is more enlightening than the "Employer Coalition of Memphis."

Q 14:11 Who is the plan administrator?

In many, if not most, instances, the plan administrator and the plan sponsor are one and the same. This is particularly true for smaller employers. The plan administrator is the person or group of persons formally charged by the plan sponsor, or named in the plan document, as having the responsibility, and given the authority, of overseeing the operation of the plan. It is important to note that employees who may be performing the actual administration on a day-to-day basis are not necessarily the plan administrator, unless that designation has been formalized by the plan document or stated in writing by the plan sponsor. Specifically, the benefit manager and his or her staff may run the plan on a daily basis. Without a formal designation, such as the plan document identifying the benefit manager as the plan administrator, the benefit manager will not be the plan administrator for Form 5500 or other purposes. The plan administrator will likely be the ultimate recourse for appeals pertaining to, for example, claim denials or plan operation. The plan administrator will also probably be the person or group responsible for ensuring the plan's compliance with relevant law and regulations, including the filing of 5500s. In many cases, the plan administrator delegates the actual performance of these functions to other individuals, such as the benefit manager.

If the plan administrator is a single individual, the designation is best made by job title rather than by named individual. That is to say, the plan administrator would be, for example, the "Vice President of Human Resources," not "John Doe, Vice President of Human Resources." This way, in the event of a personnel change in the named position, it will not be necessary to obtain a new identification number. Further, in the event of a lawsuit claiming benefits, an individual would not be named as defendant. If the plan administrator is a group of individuals acting as a committee or as trustees, that should be reflected in the name. For example, the plan administrator might be named "The Benefit Plans Committee of XYZ Corporation" or "Trustees of the QRS Company Medical Plan."

If the plan administrator is different from the plan sponsor, the plan administrator must have a separate and unique employer identification number (EIN) for reporting purposes. If the plan administrator does not have an EIN, one must be applied for using Form SS-4. This is true even if the plan administrator is an individual.

Q 14:12 How are plan numbers assigned?

Plan numbers are assigned by the plan administrator. Numbers are assigned to all plans belonging to the same plan sponsor for which 5500 reporting is required. The number to be assigned is chosen first by determining into which one of two general categories the plan belongs—either welfare or pension. Pension plans start with the three-digit sequence 001. Welfare plans start with 501. The plan administrator then assigns numbers sequentially for each plan within the general group. Numbers should not be chosen randomly, nor should numbers be skipped. If a plan is terminated, the number assigned to the terminated plan cannot be reused by another plan.

To illustrate this process, assume that a plan sponsor (an employer) has a variety of welfare plans, as follows:

1. A medical benefits plan covering all salaried employees, at all locations;
2. A medical benefits plan covering hourly employees located in Cincinnati, Ohio;
3. A dental benefits plan covering hourly employees located in Mobile, Alabama; and
4. A medical benefits plan covering hourly employees located in Mobile, Alabama.

At the outset, the employer will have to determine whether to report each of these as a separate, freestanding plan, or whether to combine any of them together. For example, it might make sense for this employer to combine the medical and dental plans for the Mobile employees into one. Assuming the employer chooses to keep each separate, it would file four Form 5500s, numbered 501, 502, 503, and 504. Which number attaches to which plan is not material; however, once the number is assigned, it must be used consistently thereafter on all filings and correspondence with IRS and DOL, as long as that plan remains in existence.

Although there are no legal or regulatory requirements governing the assignment of plan numbers, reuse of a plan number could cause great confusion if the plan were audited.

Q 14:13 How does an employer decide whether or not to combine plans?

Welfare benefit plans tend to be less formal than pension plans. Unfortunately, welfare plans frequently lack a plan document. Often the structure for a welfare plan is merely an insurance contract and a summary plan description (SPD). Other employee communication materials, written by the insurance company or by the employer, may also exist.

Note. A formal plan document should exist for every plan. Every benefit plan that is subject to the fiduciary responsibility requirements of ERISA must be administered in accordance with its written plan document. An employer lacking such a document should take steps to create one. (See Q 6:21 concerning the use of the SPD as the plan document.)

An employer has a great deal of liberty to decide what constitutes the scope of a plan. For example, an employer can easily arrange with an insurance company to provide more than one type of benefit (such as medical, dental, or disability) to more than one group of employees, with differing levels and designs of coverage for each group of employees, all within one insurance contract. Despite being subsumed into one insurance contract, the employer can have the insurance company separately rate coverages or groups of employees, track claims, and otherwise administer the groups independently. One insurance contract then could support more than one plan. With one contract, all financial data covering all groups is reflected on one Schedule A and used for a single plan filing on one Form 5500.

It is permissible (and in some instances required, see Q 14:14) to append more than one Schedule A to a single plan's filing. For example, if the employer illustrated in Q 14:12 wanted to combine the Mobile hourly benefits into one plan, but had the coverage underwritten by two insurance companies (one for medical, the other for dental), each insurance company would issue its own Schedule A for attachment to the single 5500.

Q 14:14   When is more than one Schedule A required?

More than one Schedule A is required when insured benefits are provided by more than one carrier. This occurs most commonly when an employer has a basic employer medical plan, such as an indemnity plan, and also offers one or more HMOs as an alternative source of coverage. The 5500 for the medical plan must contain a Schedule A for each HMO or insurance company providing coverage to the identified group.

Note. It is not correct to file a separate 5500 for each HMO, if each provides benefits under the same plan.

Q 14:15 Could an employer combine all its plans into one filing?

Taking the question literally, the answer is most probably no. Most employers' plans are too diverse to make such a combination possible. For instance, combining welfare, educational reimbursement, and pension plans cannot be done. On the other hand, an employer that had only welfare plans could possibly combine them into one filing, as long as they all had the same plan years.

Q 14:16 What steps would an employer have to take to combine all its welfare plans into one filing?

If the employer has been filing a variety of plans separately, the plans must be combined on a number of levels:

1. *Plan document.* A plan document must be created or amended to combine the various plans as one.
2. *Employee communications.* All employee communications would need to reflect the benefits as one plan. A single SPD would have to contain all aspects of the one plan (e.g., medical, dental) and would reference only one plan number. The SPD could refer to more than one insurance carrier in order to identify properly the source of benefits, claim processor, and so forth.

    Note. Select one plan number from those assigned to the existing plans or assign a new plan number.

3. *Accountants; Insurance companies.* Depending on how the plans being combined are funded and administered, coordination may be needed among all involved parties. For instance, if there are multiple insurance companies, using different renewal cycles, bringing these into one cycle will greatly simplify matters. This is particularly true if employee contributions are based on premiums charged by the various providers. Regardless, short plan-year filings must be prepared if any of the plans operate on different plan years, which will require the relevant insurance company(s) to produce the necessary Schedule A(s).

Q 14:17 What attachments are included with a 5500 filing for plan years beginning in 1999 or later?

The new form is much shorter and only includes identifying information and a checklist to indicate which schedules are being filed.

The new form calls for 13 schedules: five pension schedules, seven financial schedules, and one fringe benefit schedule.

A variety of schedules may be necessary. Whether a specific schedule must be included depends on the individual circumstances of the 5500 being filed. Not all schedules are required by all 5500s. Further, there are requirements for additional information that must be provided in a manner other than on a schedule. With a brief explanation as to their use, the schedules are as follows:

Schedule A—Insurance Information. This schedule has been revised. If premiums are paid to, and claims are paid by, an insurance company or an HMO, Schedule A is filed to report the financial results ending with or within the employer's plan year. If a plan is self-funded and an insurance company is being used to process claim payments, but has no insurance liability, payments to the insurance company in this circumstance are fees, not premiums, and are not reported here, but are instead reported on Schedule C.

On line 10(b)(3) of Form 5500 the filer is instructed to check the box if any Schedule As are attached and indicate the number of Schedules A attached as part of the filing. Whatever number is entered represents the number of Schedules A to be attached to the filing.

The law does not require the insurance company or HMO to complete a Schedule A, although some will do so as a convenience to their customers. Carriers do have an obligation to provide the necessary data per ERISA Section 103 (a)(2)(A) within 120 days of the end of the plan year, without any requirement for the administrator or sponsor to request the data first but, according to the Department of Labor, it is the plan sponsor's responsibility to request the Schedule A information. ERISA does not give the Department of Labor any enforcement power over insurance companies that fail to provide Schedule A information. If the employer cannot obtain the information required for completion of the Schedule A from the insurance company or HMO on a timely basis, the filing of the 5500 should not be delayed. Instead, the employer should file the 5500 on time, attach the Schedule As completed as best as possible, and include a cover letter noting that the data was not provided. Do not omit Schedule A when required or the filing will be rejected.

There have been a number of changes to Schedule A, including:

1. Line 1(b) is new and requests carrier EIN (previously, this was only requested for terminated carriers reported in Schedule C).
2. Line 1(c) is new and requests the (NAIC) code of the insurance carrier. Enter zeroes if the code is not provided.
3. Question 2 now requires reporting fees or commissions paid to anyone other than an agent or broker, in addition to those of agents and brokers.
4. Item 4, due but unpaid premium no longer reported (welfare only, pension still reports this).
5. Rate information is no longer required in Part III.
6. Question 7 asks for more slightly detailed information about the type(s) of benefits insured.

Please note:

1. Fees and commissions are reported based on the policy year, not the plan year.
2. In response to question 1(e), some carriers report the total number of employees and dependents; however, the Department of Labor only wants an estimate of the number of covered employees (not dependents.)

Schedule C—Service Provider and Trustee Information. Schedule C has also been revised. Only large plans (100 or more employees) are required to file a Schedule C. There are three circumstances that require the completion of a Schedule C. A Schedule C must be filed if, during the plan year being reported:

1. Any service providers individually received payment of more than $5,000;
2. An accountant was terminated; or
3. An actuary was terminated.

Schedule C has been simplified in that it no longer requires reporting the termination of the:

- Insurance carrier
- Custodian
- Administrator
- Investment manager
- Trustee

Please note:

1. Only complete line 1 if line 2 is completed.
2. If there is no contract administrator, leave the first set of 2(a) through 2(g) blank and begin completing line 2 with the second set.

Schedule D, Participating Plan Information. This is a new schedule. If a group insurance arrangement, such as a multiple employer welfare arrangement (MEWA), completes a 5500 and Schedule D, the participating plans are relieved of the responsibility to do so.

Schedule F, Fringe Benefit Plan Information. This schedule has no material changes. This schedule must be completed only for Section 125 cafeteria plans, Section 127 educational assistance programs, and adoption assistance programs under Code Section 137.

Schedule G, Financial Transaction Schedules. This schedule has been revised. Most of the schedules have been moved to Schedule H. Schedule G is required if something went wrong, such as a default or a prohibited transaction.

Schedule H, Large Plan Financial Information. This is a new schedule for large plans. This schedule now consolidates financial reporting questions from the old 5500 and the old Schedule G into one schedule. The name and employer identification number of the accountant is now required.

Please note:

1. Part I of Schedule H may not agree with the Schedule As because of differences in policy and plan years.
2. If the answer to 4a is "Yes," Part III of Schedule G must be completed.

3. Unfunded or fully insured plans do not need to complete Schedule H. Even if an employer uses a separate account for transactions related to the plan, if the account is still part of the employer's general assets, it is considered an unfunded plan. Plans that receive employee contributions or use a trust are not unfunded.

Schedule I, Small Plan Financial Information. This is a new schedule and is basically an abbreviated version of Schedule H. Form 5500-C/R is eliminated, and small plans must report the same information each year.

Accountant's Report. Large plans generally must attach an accountant's report if Schedule H is required. Plans filing 5500s are generally required to engage the services of an independent public accountant, pursuant to ERISA Section 103(a)(3)(A). Some plans are specifically exempted from this requirement. The exemptions apply if the plan:

1. Is a welfare benefit plan and is unfunded, or fully insured, or a combination of the two; or

2. Has elected to defer the accountant's opinion for the first of two plan years, one of which is a short plan year consisting of seven or fewer months.

Q 14:18 Is a Schedule A required if an employer's assets include a GIC?

Somewhat surprisingly, yes. The DOL views a guaranteed investment contract (GIC) as insurance, presumably because GICs are issued only by insurance companies. There are look-alike products issued by financial institutions, but these technically are not GICs. Schedule A is required even if the GIC is held strictly as an investment. Employers should be careful to distinguish between two conditions. If the employer directly holds the GIC, then a Schedule A is required; however, if, for example, the employer contributes to a GIC fund, or invests in a pooled account that holds GICs as part of the portfolio, but the employer does not directly hold the GIC, then a Schedule A is not required.

Q 14:19 What are some of the common errors made on Form 5500?

One that may catch many employers by surprise is simply doing business as usual and answering questions on Form 5500 the same way as was done in prior years. This will trip up employers for two reasons. First, the questions change from time to time, perhaps only slightly, yet significantly. Also, an employer's situation might have altered, requiring changes in more than one of the answers. A careful reading of all the questions is essential. Second, questions may not be answered with "N/A" or "see attached," because filings are scanned by computerized scanning equipment that will reject either of those two answers. In the majority of instances where an employer might be inclined to answer with N/A, the correct answer is no. For example, question 4c, Schedule H, asks: "Were any leases to which the plan was a party in default or classified during the year as uncollectable?" An employer might reasonably think that, because the plan in question did not hold leases, the entire question does not apply and should therefore be answered N/A. The correct answer is "no."

Other common errors include the following:

1. Omission of necessary information;

2. Failure to answer multiple-part questions completely;

3. Attaching supplemental information to the forms instead of completing the necessary line items;

4. Improper completion and labeling of any accompanying financial schedules; or

5. Failure to attach an accountant's opinion when required with Form 5500.

An obvious area of noncompliance has been failure to file Form 5500, particularly by state and local government plans. These entities are exempt from filing Form 5500 for their retirement and welfare benefit plans, but are not exempt for cafeteria plans.

The IRS reports that 90 percent of all Schedule Fs either report incorrect costs or omit costs. Many plans only report salary reductions, but employer contributions should also be included.

Completing the Form

Q 14:20 Why should some schedules not be completed?

All Series 5500 schedules will not apply to all plans. If applicable, large plans would complete Schedules A, C, F, G, and H and attach an accountant's report. If applicable, small plans would complete Schedules A, F, and I.

Q 14:21 Can a private delivery service be used to file a Form 5500?

Certain private delivery services designated by the IRS can be used to meet the "timely mailing as timely filing/paying" rule for tax returns and payments. The IRS publishes a list of the designated private delivery services each year. The list published in August 1999 includes only the following services:

1. Airborne Express (Airborne): Overnight Air Express Service, Next Afternoon Service, Second Day Service;
2. DHL Worldwide Express (DHL): "Same Day" Service, DHL USA Overnight;
3. Federal Express (FedEx): FedEx Priority Overnight, FedEx Standard Overnight, FedEx 2 Day; and
4. United Parcel Service (UPS): UPS Next Day Air, UPS Next Day Air Saver, UPS 2nd Day Air, UPS 2nd Day Air A.M.

The private delivery service can explain its procedures for obtaining written proof of the mailing date.

Q 14:22 Does a third party administrator have to hire its own auditor?

No, but third party administrators (TPAs) may choose to comply with the American Institute of Certified Public Accountants' Statement of Auditing Standards (SAS) 70 to facilitate audits of plans they serve.

SAS 70 provides an alternative method of examining the internal controls of a service organization, such as a TPA. Under this method, a TPA can hire its own auditor to evaluate and make a report on its internal control structure. That report is made available to the plan's independent qualified public accountant, who can use the report as a basis for evaluating the plan's internal control structure.

Q 14:23 Is a Schedule A needed for a stop-loss policy?

The instructions in the 1999 Form 5500 booklet waive reporting stop-loss contracts paid for out of general assets.

Q 14:24 How can a plan get an extension of time to file Form 5500?

If the plan year and the plan sponsor's tax year are the same and if the plan sponsor applies for an extension to file its taxes, there is an automatic extension for the Form 5500. Otherwise, the plan needs to file Form 5558.

In Announcement 99-37 [1999-15 IRB 9], the IRS stated that all applications will be automatically approved if Form 5558 is filed on or before the standard due date of the Form 5500. Extensions are for up to $2\frac{1}{2}$ months.

Because the extension is automatic, the IRS will stop returning approved copies of Form 5558 for the filer to submit with the Form 5500. Filers simply need to attach a photocopy of the completed and signed Form 5558 to Form 5500.

Electronic Filing

Q 14:25 What is EFAST?

EFAST is a computerized processing system that is designed to simplify and expedite the receipt and processing of the Form 5500 by relying on computer scannable forms and electronic filing technologies.

Q 14:26 Why was EFAST developed?

The Department of Labor, the IRS, and the Pension Benefit Guaranty Corporation (PBGC) created the new EFAST system in conjunction with the development of computer-scannable versions of the Form 5500 in order to streamline the forms and the methods by which they are filed and processed.

Q 14:27 What are the computer-scannable forms?

The 1999 Form 5500 is available in two computer scannable formats: "machine print" and "hand print" (the questions are the same; only the appearance is different).

Under the machine print format, filers use computer software to complete the forms which can be printed out on computer printers. The hand print format is printed on special paper with special green ink and must be completed by hand or typewriter.

Informational copies of the hand print forms and the machine print forms are available at www.efast.dol.gov. These copies are for viewing purposes only and are NOT acceptable for filing.

Q 14:28 Where can a copy of the software for the forms be obtained?

Commercial software developers market approved filing software. Software developers that chose to participate were given the necessary specifications by the Pension and Welfare Benefits Administration to develop their own products and market "approved" software.

The EFAST website lists approved software developers.

Q 14:29 Why use Form 5500 software for filing?

Filers using the software will assist the government by reducing paper to be processed and eliminating the need for data entry. This reduces data entry errors and should result in a savings of staff hours and money.

The software will also assist the filer. Most software should provide many error-checking functions that can prevent filers from making common mistakes. This may prevent a filing from being rejected.

Q 14:30   How are the machine print forms filed?

There are two options for filing:

1. Using the approved computer software, the Form 5500 can be submitted by modem transfer by approved EFAST transmitters. Or a computer diskette, CD-ROM or magnetic tape can be mailed.
2. Approved computer software can be used to print out the form, which can then be filed by mail.

Q 14:31   How is the hand print format different from the machine print format?

The EFAST system uses optical character recognition technology to scan the hand or typewritten data entries on the specially designed green drop-out ink forms that enable the computer to "read" the hand or typewritten entries.

Once printed out with approved software, the machine print form will include a 2D bar code that will appear on every page of the filing. Its purpose is to encrypt the data on that page and allow for easy capture of the information submitted on the Form 5500. Because the bar code will not include any handwritten additions made after printing, it is important that the form be complete when printed.

Also, while the machine print form can be filed by mail or electronically, the hand print form can be filed only by mail.

Q 14:32   How can one become an EFAST electronic filer or an EFAST transmitter (authorized transmitters of forms via modems)?

The individual who signs the Form 5500 needs an EFAST electronic signature to file electronically via modem, magnetic tape, floppy diskette, or CD-ROM. That individual must apply for an EFAST electronic signature by submitting a completed Form EFAST-1 signed by that individual.

Also, a company, trade, business, or other person applying to be an EFAST transmitter must submit a completed Form EFAST-1 signed by an authorized representative. An EFAST Transmitter is any company, trade, business, or other person that sends Forms 5500 for filing via modem, magnetic tape, floppy diskette, or CD-ROM in compliance with EFAST electronic filing procedures.

Q 14:33 Will EFAST perform edit checks on the Form 5500?

Yes. All Form 5500 filings are subject to preliminary computerized edit checks for things such as completeness, accuracy, timeliness, internal consistency, missing schedules or attachments, and failure to answer mandatory questions.

Q 14:34 What happens when a filing fails one or more edit checks?

When errors are identified, a filer may receive a deficiency letter from EFAST regarding the error and requesting that corrections be made. In prior years, the IRS performed these tests and would send out these deficiency letters. A filer's refusal to resolve filing errors can still result in the rejection of the filing and exposure to assessment of civil and other penalties.

Q 14:35 Should any payments owed be included with the filing?

Do not submit any payment with the Form 5500 unless under the Delinquent Filer Voluntary Compliance program. Payments due should be made directly to the appropriate government agency, in accordance with any applicable rules or procedures.

Q 14:36 What is the Delinquent Filer Voluntary Compliance program?

Under the Delinquent Filer Voluntary Compliance program for Form 5500 filers, plan administrators who file late may pay reduced civil penalties for voluntarily complying with annual reporting requirements under ERISA.

Chapter 15

Retiree Health Benefits

Accounting rules have given much greater visibility to retiree benefits in recent years. This chapter explores retiree benefits including such new approaches as defined dollar benefits and Medicare+Choice HMOs.

Determining Eligibility and Responsibility	15-1
Determining and Allocating Costs	15-5
Retiree Medical Liabilities	15-7
Pre-Funding	15-15
Medicare Solutions to Retiree Challenges	15-24
Regulatory Issues	15-32

Determining Eligibility and Responsibility

Q 15:1 Why are retiree health benefits becoming a key area of focus for employers?

The cost of providing retiree health benefits is rising considerably, making it a high priority for employers seeking to manage health care benefit costs. In addition to inflation, many other factors have contributed to rising costs. People are retiring earlier and are living longer, often with chronic diseases such as cancer, heart disease, and respiratory ailments. At the time of this writing (2000), the over-65 age group represents just 12 percent of the population. By 2020, the percentage is expected to grow by one-third to over 16; this growth will increase health care costs for this population exponentially.

In addition, Financial Accounting Statement (FAS) 106, *Employers Accounting for Postretirement Benefits Other Than Pensions,* requires employers to accrue liabilities for retiree health benefits, rather than record the cost as benefits are paid. For this reason, most employers are conscious of the need to manage retiree health benefit expenditures in a way that will prevent a significant impact on the bottom line.

Despite the fact that companies must account for their retiree medical liabilities in much the same way they account for their pension liabilities, companies cannot pre-fund retiree medical liabilities effectively. Pre-funding of nondiscriminatory health costs is permitted on a tax-deductible basis while employees are working, but investment income on the funds is taxable. This means that although contributions to the plan for coverage in future years are tax-deductible, the income earned on those contributions through investment is taxable. This situation makes pre-funding benefits less attractive.

The logic behind not allowing effective pre-funding of retiree medical liabilities is that companies retain the right to terminate retiree medical plans, but court decisions have restricted the right of employers to reduce or modify postretirement benefits for already retired employees.

Q 15:2 How many employers provide health care benefits for their retirees?

Many employers provide medical coverage for at least some of their retirees, although many employers require retirees to pay for some or all of the cost of their medical coverage. The 1999 Mercer/Foster Higgins survey found that 35 percent of large employers (500 or more employees) provided medical benefits to retirees under age 65, and only 28 percent provided benefits to older retirees. There has been a slow but steady decline in the number of employers offering retiree health benefits. In 1993, 46 percent provided medical benefits to retirees under age 65, and 40 percent provided benefits to older retirees.

Larger firms are more likely to offer health care benefits to their Medicare-eligible retirees. According to the 1999 Mercer/Foster Higgins, Inc. survey, 15 percent of all companies with fewer than 500 employees offered health benefits to their retirees, while 63 percent of employers with 20,000 or more employees provided health benefits. Nearly 30 percent of Medicare beneficiaries have some form of employer-provided health insurance to supplement their Medicare coverage.

Q 15:3 What are some factors an employer should consider before providing retiree coverage?

If an employer allows coverage for retirees, the employer's coverage can be secondary to Medicare. Of course, that is only true after employees become covered under Medicare. Prior to Medicare eligibility, the employer's plan will be primary for early retirees.

Also, the Financial Accounting Standards Board has issued a Statement (No. 106) that details elaborate accounting rules on how the cost of providing retiree coverage is to be recognized on the employer's books. In short, the most prevalent method used, the pay-as-you-go method, is no longer permitted. Now the expected expense attributable to all retirees, and to all active employees who will become retirees, must be projected and booked in a process similar to pension accounting.

Keep in mind too that although employers are not legally required to provide retiree coverage, it is difficult to reduce or eliminate the coverage once it is established. Negative employee and retiree reaction will almost certainly develop and may result in a lawsuit. Most employers who lost such lawsuits lost because of a poorly written booklet that stated or implied that coverage would be in place without change for the recipient's lifetime. Almost equally as dangerous is a rash verbal promise by a manager or supervisor. Although an oral statement would likely not prevail against a clearly written summary plan description contradicting it, in the absence of clearly written material to use as a defense, an employer would probably have little recourse but to accede to the terms of the verbal promise.

Taking care with communications can be crucial in preserving an employer's right to make changes to retiree coverage, as the following cases illustrate:

1. *Eardman v. Bethlehem Steel* [DC WNY, 1981, 5 EBC 1985] established that the employer was prevented from later changing the conditions of its plan because its plan documents and other written material specified that coverage would be for life; the employer had failed to preserve its right to change the plan unilaterally.

2. *Hansen v. White Motor Corp* [CA 6, 1986, 7 EBC 1411] (also known as White Farms, the subsidiary from which this case developed) established that an employer could terminate a retiree medical plan. In this case, there was clear preservation of the employer's right to amend or terminate the plan, and there were no contradicting issues such as oral statements or a union to negotiate with.

3. In *Musto v. American General Corp* [DCM Tenn 1985, 6 EBC, 2071], although the employer clearly communicated in writing its right to change and amend the plan, contradictory oral and written communications to retirees stated that coverage would be for life. Oral representations by management personnel were deemed to have provided a basis of material reliance to the retiring employees. The court determined that the company had forfeited its right to make unilateral changes.

Q 15:4 How do companies determine who is eligible for retiree health benefits?

Eligibility criteria for retiree health benefits vary by company. Most employers set eligibility requirements based on length of service (usually at least ten years), participation in the company's health plan before retirement, and a minimum age.

Q 15:5 How are these benefits generally structured?

Most employer-sponsored plans offer identical coverage to their working and retired populations. The majority of these plans require some sort of deductible and copayment by the plan enrollee. Coverage generally includes hospital, physician, laboratory, and x-ray services; skilled nursing facility care; home health and hospice care; and prescription drugs.

Medicare becomes the primary payer when the retiree reaches the age of 65. Coverage then is usually in the form of payment of premiums for a supplemental policy, which covers all or part of the expenses not covered by Medicare.

In some industries, comprehensive retiree health benefits have been regarded almost as an entitlement; however, FAS 106 and the increasing cost of health benefits are causing this to change. Annual surveys by Charles D. Spencer and Associates found that 41 percent of employers amended their retiree plans from 1992 through 1994, but after 1995, few companies made radical changes in their retiree health care plans, as opposed to ongoing, incremental efforts to contain health care costs.

Q 15:6 Does HIPAA apply to retiree medical plans?

Probably not. The Health Insurance Portability Act of 1996 (HIPAA) does not apply to plans with fewer than two participants who are "current employees"; therefore, a stand-alone retiree medical plan is probably exempt from HIPAA's requirements.

Determining and Allocating Costs

Q 15:7 Are costs shared among companies and retirees?

According to the 1999 Mercer/Foster Higgins national survey, 19 percent of employers provide free individual coverage to retirees under age 65 and 42 percent provide no contribution to payment of the health care premium. For Medicare-eligible retirees, 22 percent provide free individual coverage and 40 percent ask the retiree to pay the full amount.

Q 15:8 What is the annual cost of retiree health care versus health care for active employees?

According to the 1999 Mercer/Foster Higgins survey, the average cost of health care per active employee for large employers is $4,320 per year. The average cost of the employer-sponsored Medicare supplemental coverage per beneficiary is only $2,160 (much of which is for prescription drug coverage). The cost for early retirees is $5,470.

Medicare + Choice plans can offer substantial premium savings for employers.

Q 15:9 What is the cost difference between retirees younger than 65 and those older than 65?

Employers usually pay the same cost for premiums for retirees under the age of 65 as they do for their active employees. Mercer/Foster Higgins found that in 1999 the average cost for an early retiree was $5,470, compared to $2,160 for retirees over age 65. Premiums can be as little as $10 per month for Medicare + Choice health maintenance organization (HMO) plans, which vary based on geographical area and any employer upgrades to the core benefit plan (see Qs 15:44 and 15:45).

Q 15:10 What are employers doing to reduce the cost of retiree health care?

Employers use several techniques to reduce retiree health care costs. Often, employers choose to:

1. Increase the amount of the retiree's contributions to health care expenses by raising deductible and copayment amounts, decreasing the number of services covered, reducing the duration of the coverage, or decreasing the percentage of reimbursement for medical services.

2. Replace the open-ended medical benefit with a defined dollar benefit or defined contribution benefit.

3. Phase out employer contributions to the retiree medical plan so that the plan will ultimately be funded by retirees themselves.
4. Carve out prescription drugs and other benefit programs from the retiree health benefit plan.
5. Eliminate retiree health benefits. (The Mercer/Foster Higgins survey shows that companies have been terminating health benefits for retirees.)
6. Contract with Medicare + Choice programs to manage retiree benefits and reduce the employer's financial obligation.

Retiree Medical Liabilities

Q 15:11 What are FASB's rules governing accounting for retiree benefits?

On December 21, 1990, the Financial Accounting Standards Board announced its accounting rules for nonpension retiree benefits. Since first proposed, these rules have focused considerable attention on the size of corporate retiree health care obligations and upon a variety of approaches toward financing and otherwise coping with these obligations.

Financial Accounting Statement 106 requires corporations to make entries to their financial statements reflecting the present value of future retiree benefit liabilities, as well as the value of any assets set aside to meet those liabilities. While these FASB rules apply to all nonpension benefits, including such items as life insurance, legal assistance, tuition reimbursement, and housing assistance, the major cost element by far is retiree health care.

The rules provide standards for valuing liabilities and for allocating costs to periods in which they accrue. The intent of the rules is to make financial statements more complete, and more reflective of the actual liabilities the corporation faces. These rules are also intended to make the financial statements of one company more comparable to financial statements of other organizations.

Q 15:12 What do the rules require?

Employers must determine the present value of future benefits of their substantive plans (see Q 15:13) and allocate the costs over the working lives of employees. The liability is to accrue ratably over a period extending to the date the employee is eligible to receive full benefits, regardless of when he or she is expected to retire or actually retires. In the process, the employer must display unfunded obligations as well as the portion of the obligation charged as an annual expense on corporate financial statements.

Q 15:13 What is a substantive plan?

The substantive plan is the plan as it is understood by both the employee and employer. This means that, in addition to provisions contained in the formal written document, historical practices and employer policies must also be reflected in the projection of liabilities. This would require adjustments for such things as future changes in retiree contributions, deductibles, and copayments if there is a history of such changes in the past and similar changes may be reasonably anticipated in the future.

Q 15:14 How does the employer determine the costs that must be reported?

The employer must determine the expected postretirement benefit obligation (EPBO), which is the present value of all employer-provided postretirement benefits. Part of the EPBO represents benefits associated with employees' future service—benefits that have not yet been earned. A second part represents those attributable to past service—benefits that have been earned—known as the accumulated postretirement benefit obligation (APBO). The unfunded, unrecognized APBO in existence when the FASB rules are first applied is called the transition obligation; it may be recognized immediately or amortized over a period equal to the longer of an employee's average remaining length of service or 20 years.

From these figures the employer calculates the amount to be expensed each year (the net periodic postretirement benefit cost), which consists of the following:

1. Present value of benefits that can be allocated to employees' service during the current year (service cost);
2. Interest on the APBO (that is, on benefits already accrued);
3. Return on plan assets for plans that are funded;
4. Amortization adjustment for that part of the transition obligation that is expensed during the year;
5. Amortization of any benefit increases or decreases resulting from changes to the plan; and
6. Amortization of gains and losses on plan assets (if any) or other experience that varies from those assumed.

Income statements must recognize the net periodic postretirement benefit cost as an expense. Balance sheets must recognize a liability equal to the cumulative expense, less any amounts funded or benefits paid.

Q 15:15 What additional disclosure requirements are there?

The following are additional disclosure requirements:

1. A description of the substantive plan, which includes employee groups covered, benefit formula, types of assets, funding policy, and other "significant matters" that would affect the comparability of the data;
2. The plan's funding status, including changes in the benefit obligation and plan assets during the period; and
3. Significant assumptions underlying the assumed discount rate and the effect of a 1 percent increase or decrease in the health care cost trend.

Q 15:16 Does FASB specify particular actuarial formulas?

No. Employers have considerable leeway in their use of actuarial assumptions, although FASB has identified key types of assumptions to be used in valuing the health care obligation, specifically:

1. Per capita claims by age;

2. Health care cost trend rate, which considers future medical inflation, technological change, and changes in utilization patterns;

3. Medicare reimbursement level;

4. Discount rate; and

5. Probability of payment, which incorporates such factors as life expectancies and turnover.

While employers are expected to use the projected unit credit method, FASB has indicated that estimates, averages, and other shortcuts are permissible so long as the resulting figures are not materially different from those that would be produced by a more precise calculation.

Q 15:17 What were the effective dates of the FASB rules?

The rules took effect for fiscal years beginning after December 15, 1992, although companies outside the United States and those with fewer than 500 employees did not have to comply until fiscal years beginning after December 15, 1994.

Q 15:18 Have employers found any ways to minimize the impact of FAS 106 without simply eliminating benefits for retirees?

Yes. Employers that provide medical benefits for retirees may find Medicare + Choice HMO programs attractive. An employer can reduce its cash expense of providing medical benefits to its Medicare-eligible retirees if the retirees enroll in Medicare + Choice HMO programs because the premium charged by HMOs is frequently less than the employer's indemnity claims cost. The employer may reduce its liability and expense under FAS 106 because the lower cost of HMOs may generate an actuarial gain. For these reasons, many employers are exploring the idea of integrating Medicare + Choice HMO programs with their retiree medical plans. In some parts of the country, Medicare + Choice HMOs are free to enrollees and include benefits not covered by Medicare, such as prescriptions.

Q 15:19 How have companies responded to FAS 106?

A 1996 survey by the Employee Benefits Research Institute found that 51 percent of responding employers had either modified or considered modifying their retiree medical programs in response to FAS 106. The study found that:

- 29 percent modified cost-sharing provisions
- 22 percent placed caps on company contributions
- 4 percent were considering phasing out company contributions

Annual surveys by Charles D. Spencer and Associates found that after 1995, companies made incremental efforts to contain health care costs, as opposed to radical changes.

Q 15:20 Have there been any changes to FAS 106?

Yes, on February 12, 1998, FASB issued new rules intended to streamline disclosures about postretirement health benefits. FAS 132 is effective for fiscal years beginning after December 15, 1997. The new standard is known as "Employers' Disclosures about Pensions and Other Postretirement Benefits."

The new standard is designed to simplify and standardize the footnote reporting requirements of FAS 106, governing postretirement health benefits. The statement reduces disclosure requirements for nonpublic entities and multiemployer plans.

Certain disclosures from FAS 106 have been eliminated, but new requirements have been added. According to FASB, most or all of the additional information required should be available in actuarial or accounting calculations.

The more important changes include the following:

1. Requiring disclosure of changes in the benefit obligation and plan assets during the period;
2. Eliminating disclosure of weighted-average health care trend assumptions;
3. Expanding sensitivity analysis of trend assumptions by requiring reporting of the effects of both a 1 percentage point increase

and a 1 percentage point decrease in the trend assumption for each future year.

Q 15:21 Do these accounting rules apply to government entities?

Not exactly. Governmental entities are subject to rules issued by the Government Accounting Standards Board (GASB), not FASB. GASB Statement No. 12 requires state and local government employers that provide postemployment benefits other than pensions to make certain disclosures on their financial reports. GASB is expected to release an exposure draft of rules similar to FAS 106 by May 2001, with a final standard by April 2002.

Q 15:22 Does FAS 106 apply to multiemployer welfare plans?

No, but Statement of Position (SOP) 92-6 does. In August 1992, the American Institute of Certified Public Accountants (AICPA) issued its SOP 92-6. In SOP 92-6, the AICPA amended the welfare plan financial statement disclosure requirements in its audit and accounting guide to require welfare plans to account for and report postretirement benefit obligations. SOP 92-6 was effective for multiemployer plans for plan years beginning after December 15, 1995.

In March 1997 the Department of Labor's (DOL) Pension and Welfare Benefits Administration (PWBA) proposed a relaxed enforcement policy under which the agency would not reject a Form 5500 filed by a multiemployer plan solely because the accountant's opinion was "qualified" or "adverse" as a result of a failure to account for postretirement benefit obligations. In the November 25, 1998 issue of the *Federal Register*, the PWBA issued a notice that it had decided not to adopt a proposed relaxed enforcement policy regarding postretirement benefit obligations of multiemployer plans.

The reporting relief for multiemployer plans continued to apply to the 1998 and 1999 plan years. This was intended to ensure that multiemployer welfare benefit plans had adequate opportunity to prepare their financial recordkeeping and other related systems so that financial statements could be prepared to comply with SOP 92-6. Form 5500s for multiemployer plans filed for plan years beginning on or after January 1, 2000 may be rejected by the DOL if there is any material qualification in the accountant's opinion because of a failure to comply with the requirements of SOP 92-6.

Q 15:23 How should a company respond to FASBs accounting rules?

Employers must reexamine their philosophy regarding medical benefits for retirees while keeping in mind that those companies that have terminated their medical plans for retirees have had such terminations overturned by the courts. Revisions to the plan that fall short of termination are, therefore, a logical consideration.

Q 15:24 How can a company limit its retiree health care benefit liability?

Once the size of the liability is determined, the next step is to find a way to reduce it. Some of the avenues to consider include the following:

1. Integrating the plan with Medicare. See Q 15:43 for more details.
2. Changing age and service requirements for eligibility (e.g., requiring a minimum of 10 years of service), or changing the way the commitment accrues, so that those with longer service receive larger benefits and those who retire early receive reduced benefits, much like a defined benefit pension (at the same time breaking any link between pension eligibility and health care eligibility).
3. Reducing the level of benefits, including curbs on benefits for dependents. Companies with pension surpluses may consider accompanying the reduction with an increase in pension benefits, to get around restrictions on transferring funds to 401(h) accounts. Unfortunately, this trades a taxable benefit for a nontaxable one. It is also difficult to target the pension dollars and gear pension increases so that they make up the difference for retirees who are not eligible for Medicare while not providing a windfall for those who are Medicare eligible.

4. Increasing the employee/retiree's share of health care costs by such means as increasing the level of participant contributions, reducing or eliminating employer subsidies for dependents, and indexing deductibles.

5. Considering pre-funding arrangements such as voluntary employees' beneficiary associations (VEBAs) and 401(h) accounts.

6. Defining the employer's commitment to retiree benefits in terms of a specified number of dollars to be contributed toward the premium for health care, rather than in terms of providing a specific plan of benefits (a defined contribution approach, rather than a defined benefit approach).

7. Considering another defined contribution approach to retiree health care benefits; that is, for the employer and/or employee to contribute specified amounts to a fund that can be used to pay health care expenses, with no commitment to the ultimate size of the fund, to the amount of money that will ultimately be available, or to the sufficiency of the fund to purchase the necessary coverage or services.

8. Instituting the same types of cost control techniques used for limiting active employee costs, such as:

   - Preadmission review and testing (non-Medicare eligibles only)
   - Utilization review
   - Preferred provider options
   - Discounted prescription drugs
   - Case management

Some companies have applied these cost-saving techniques selectively to avoid legal complications, for humanitarian reasons, or to avoid political complications within the company. For example, benefits for those persons who have already retired may be left untouched; those for persons close to retirement (say within five years of retirement age) would be subject to modest adjustment; those for new hires or persons who have a specified number of years before retiring might be substantially altered or terminated altogether.

Q 15:25 What is a defined dollar approach?

Because it is difficult for companies who offer traditional indemnity plans to predict their long-term future financial liability for retiree health care expenses accurately, some companies prefer to define their actual financial commitment in advance.

With a defined dollar benefit, the employer defines a certain maximum annual dollar amount that will be applied toward the cost of retirees' annual medical coverage. Retirees are responsible for paying for any additional health care expenses incurred or can purchase additional health care coverage elsewhere.

With the defined contribution benefit, the employer provides an annual contribution to an account set up for each active employee, who may or may not become a retiree of that company. The money is invested, and, at retirement, can be drawn for the purchase of health care services or coverage.

The plan might provide for $100 per month to be applied to the payment of a retiree's health insurance premiums. As the retiree must make up the difference between $100 and the actual premium, it is his or her share that is open-ended. Or the plan may pay differing amounts for different participants. The size of the payment may vary depending upon whether or not the retiree is over 65, or may be larger for participants with more years of service. In any case, the amount is fixed and does not fluctuate with changes in the level of medical expense or insurance premium. The employer is, of course, at liberty to increase the amount of contribution it chooses to make.

Pre-Funding

Q 15:26 Do the FASB rules require companies to pre-fund retiree benefits?

No. The rules do not require funding, so companies are free to continue to provide for retiree health care on a pay-as-you-go basis, as most have done in the past. The FASB rules would, however, require the liability to be booked annually on an accrual basis, regardless of whether it was actually funded, and regardless of when the expenses of providing the benefits are actually incurred.

Q 15:27 What options are available to an employer that wants to pre-fund for retiree health benefits?

There is no method for advance funding retiree health plans that offers tax benefits comparable to those available for retirement income (pension) plans. Currently the best alternatives are a VEBA, or Section 501(c)(9) trust, or a separate medical benefits account under Code Section 401(h). The combination of a VEBA with stop-loss insurance may also be effective. Corporate-owned life insurance (COLI) and trust-owned life insurance (TOLI) are also used.

Q 15:28 What are the rules governing VEBAs?

Since 1984, the tax advantages associated with VEBAs have been limited. [IRC § 419A] The maximum annual deductible contribution for postretirement medical and life insurance benefits is:

1. The level annual contribution spread over the working lives of covered employees necessary to fund a reserve for such benefits (determined actuarially using reasonable assumptions); or
2. An annual "safe harbor" of 35 percent of the preceding year's medical costs, not including insurance premiums.

The projected cost of medical benefits (adjusted for health cost inflation) may not be taken into account in determining the annual deductible amount. Because health costs have historically increased at faster rates than the medical consumer price index, this is a significant restriction.

Other shortcomings of the VEBA approach include the requirement that contributions for "key employees" be paid from a separate account; such contributions offset contributions to retirement plans. In addition, earnings on assets for postretirement benefits are taxable as unrelated business income. The taxable income problem may be overcome, however, by investing in tax-deferred vehicles such as annuities.

For more details on VEBAs, see Chapter 17.

Q 15:29 How does the combination of a VEBA and stop-loss insurance work?

The IRS has issued a favorable private letter ruling involving a VEBA that purchases stop-loss insurance from an offshore group captive. A captive insurance company is a subsidiary of a non-insurance corporation. The captive primarily writes insurance on its parent and the parent's other subsidiaries, although unrelated business may be solicited. Captives are usually domiciled offshore for tax reasons. The ruling was obtained by Energy Insurance (Bermuda) Ltd. [Ltr Rul 9752061] Prior to the ruling, at least one utility had been using a VEBA to buy stop-loss insurance from Energy Insurance to pre-fund retiree health liabilities. Even though the ruling only applies to a particular set of facts, it could have broad application.

The IRS said that reserves established for stop-loss policies are not subject to the unrelated business income tax, which is usually the case in a VEBA holding reserves for postretirement benefits.

Offshore captives are not subject to state premium taxes and generally have lower overhead than commercial insurers. DOL rules make the use of a single-parent captive for employee benefits ineffective. So called "rent-a-captive" insurers can be used tax effectively.

Q 15:30 How does COLI work to pre-fund retiree medical liabilities?

With COLI, the policies name individual employees as insureds, but the employer owns the policies. With a typical investment, earnings are taxed. Earnings on reserves for retiree medical benefits are taxed, even if funded through a VEBA. The way life insurance is priced and taxed, there is tax-free buildup of investment income.

When employees die, the proceeds are used to pay for retiree medical claims. In many states, employers must disclose to employees that even though they are insured, their families will not receive the benefits. This can create an employee-relations problem. COLI is not specific; the life insurance proceeds from one retiree's death are not connected to that retiree's medical claims in amount or timing. An employer may establish an account into which all proceeds are deposited and from which all claims are paid, or the employer may pay claims out of corporate assets and deposit insurance proceeds into corporate accounts.

Cash flow is also a problem, because the corporation must pay the retiree medical claims before the life insurance proceeds are available. For a large enough group, cash flow is only a short-term problem. After the first few retirees die, the proceeds will cover the claims. The entire scheme is predicated on favorable tax treatment, but that has been eroding. For example, HIPAA restricted loans on COLI.

Q 15:31 How does TOLI differ from COLI?

The primary difference between TOLI (trust-owned life insurance) and COLI (corporate-owned life insurance) is ownership—with TOLI, policies are owned by a trust, not a corporation. There are tax-free buildup of investment income, disclosure issues, and cash-flow differences with both. Whereas COLI has been the target of recent legislation removing tax advantages, TOLI has escaped Congressional notice so far.

Q 15:32 What is a 401(h) account?

Code Section 401(h) permits medical benefits for retirees and their spouses and dependents to be funded through a separate account of a pension plan, provided:

1. The benefits are subordinate to the retirement income (pension) benefits provided by the plan—that is, aggregate contributions for the purchase of health and life insurance benefits cannot exceed 25 percent of the aggregate contributions made to the plan as a whole since the medical benefits account was established. (There is an exception to the 25 percent rule pertaining to contributions to fund past service liabilities, but the precise meaning of this loophole is unclear.)
2. Company contributions are reasonable and ascertainable.
3. No part of the account is diverted for purposes other than for expenses of administering the medical benefit plan.

4. Assets remaining after all liabilities are satisfied are returned to the employer.
5. Benefits for key employees are accounted for separately.

Q 15:33 What are the terms for Section 401(h) transfers?

Code Section 420 allows annual transfers from pension surpluses to 401(h) accounts, but only for current-year retiree medical expenses. The provision lapses in the year 2000.

Employers may apply excess pension assets to fund health care benefits for retirees, as long as that the following six provisions apply:

1. Only one such transfer to a 401(h) account is made each year.
2. Transferred assets are used only to pay for qualified current health costs for retirees in that year (which makes the rule of limited help in meeting the accounting requirements of FAS 106).
3. The level of benefits for retiree health is maintained for five years, beginning with the year of transfer.
4. The transfer would not reduce the level of pension assets below the full funding limitation (generally 125 percent of current pension liabilities or projected benefit obligations).
5. The employer does not tap any of the pension money until all potential beneficiaries are fully vested, which means that in order to tap the surplus, participants must be immediately vested in 100 percent of their benefits (as if "the plan had terminated immediately before the qualified transfer").
6. The transferred assets are not used for the benefit of key employees.

The restrictions (especially the immediate vesting and the current-year cost rule) make the prospects for these transfers a good deal less exciting than they might have been. Still, many employers were paying for retiree benefits on a pay-as-you-go basis anyway, so pension assets that could be applied to this year's costs represent found money.

The Retirement Protection Act of 1994 also changed the rules for employers that contribute to a Section 501(c)(9) trust in addition to

Q 15:34   Health Insurance Answer Book

a 401(h) account. Under the new rule, the amount of the transfer is reduced by the ratio that the assets previously set aside bears to the present value of the retiree health liability.

Q 15:34 What are the Department of Labor notice requirements for 401(h) transfers?

The Department of Labor has issued notice requirements for pension plans transferring excess assets to 401(h) retiree health benefits accounts. [Tech Rel 91-1, May 8, 1991] The notices are required under ERISA Section 101(e) (added by the Omnibus Reconciliation Act of 1990 (OBRA '90)) and must be provided not later than 60 days prior to the date of the transfer to:

1. Participants and beneficiaries, notifying them of:
    a. The amount of excess pension assets;
    b. The portion of those assets to be transferred to the 401(h) account;
    c. The amount of health benefit liabilities to be covered by the transferred assets; and
    d. The amount of the participant's pension benefits that are nonforfeitable immediately after the transfer.
2. The IRS and the DOL, notifying them of:
    a. The name, address, and identification number of the employer;
    b. The name, identification number, and plan number of the plan;
    c. The amount of the transfer;
    d. A detailed accounting of the assets held by the plan before and after the transfer; and
    e. The filing date and the date on which the transfer is intended to take place.

Q 15:35 Are there any other approaches to financing retiree health care?

Yes. While the foregoing methods were "benefit" approaches, there is growing interest in a "contribution" orientation to funding for postretirement health care. The difference is that under a benefit arrangement, the employer is assuming an open-ended future commitment to provide coverage for whatever medical costs might be incurred (less any costs assumed by the participant). The contribution approach, on the other hand, defines the employer's commitment in terms of a current annual contribution. Each year, that contribution is invested in a fund that is available at retirement for a medical insurance premium subsidy or long-term care insurance premiums, or to reimburse the retiree directly for any medical expenses incurred.

This approach has the advantage of making company outlays precisely predictable (and far more controllable). Its appeal to employers, like that of 401(k) plans as alternatives to defined benefit plans, is understandable. It has found some adherents in Congress who favor special tax benefits for such plans. The obvious shortcoming is, however, that there is no connection between the size of the fund and the magnitude of retiree health care costs, so the accumulated assets may be inadequate to the task.

Q 15:36 What types of defined contribution approaches are there?

The basic approaches involve financing retiree health care benefits through:

1. A profit sharing plan (which includes 401(k) plans);
2. A leveraged stock plan, known as an HSOP; or
3. Employee savings accounts.

Q 15:37 How may profit sharing plan accounts be used to provide health benefits?

The balances in profit sharing accounts may be used to provide current health benefits or may accumulate as a reserve to be applied to the costs of health benefits at retirement.

Although a profit sharing plan should be "primarily a plan of deferred compensation . . . the amounts allocated to the account of the participant may be used to provide him or his family incidental life or accident or health insurance." [Treas Reg § 1.401-1(b)(1)(ii)] "Incidental" means that premiums for health and accident insurance, when combined with those for life insurance, may not exceed 25 percent of the cost of providing all of the benefits under the plan. Put another way, the total expenditure on these premiums may not exceed 25 percent of the employer contributions and forfeitures allocated to a participant's account. [Rev Rul 61-164, 1961-2 CB 99] There is no restriction on the amount of employee voluntary contributions that may be applied to health insurance premiums [Rev Rul 69-408], nor is there any restriction on the use of funds that are distributable under the terms of the plan (e.g., upon attainment of a stated age, such as 50) or because the funds have been accumulated for a fixed number of years (at least two).

Unlike employer contributions to postretirement health insurance in pension plans, or to regular accident and health insurance plans, which are not taxable to employees, a profit sharing plan's costs for an employee's health care are deemed to be taxable distributions. This is true whether the expenditures are for current health and accident insurance premiums [Rev Rul 61-164] or represent direct payouts to the employee to reimburse him or her for incurred medical expenses. [Rev Rul 69-141]

Q 15:38 How can a company stock plan be used to provide retiree health care benefits?

Employee stock ownership plans (ESOPs) may be established as either stand-alone plans or as receptacles for employer contributions to 401(k) plans. An ESOP may consist of a stock bonus plan or a combination of a stock bonus plan and a money purchase plan. [IRC § 4975(e)(7)] At retirement, dividends on stock can be applied to Medigap insurance, or stock taken in cash can be applied to insurance or medical bills.

Q 15:39 What is an HSOP?

A variation on the standard use of ESOP accounts for health care expenses is the HSOP. This concept combines a leveraged ESOP with a 401(h) account. While most of the discussion of 401(h) accounts has centered on defined benefit plans, the HSOP applies the concept to defined contribution plans. The plan sponsor enjoys the benefit of pre-funding retiree health care benefits on a tax-deductible basis, and the HSOP pays out benefits in the form of nontaxable medical benefits instead of taxable cash or stock. As in a conventional leveraged ESOP, stock is purchased with the proceeds of a loan and held in a suspense account as collateral. As the loan is paid off, shares are released from the suspense account into participant accounts. The difference is that, with the HSOP, shares are allocated to two participant accounts: a regular retirement account and a retiree medical account. The expectation is that the value of the shares will appreciate and that the growth in stock value will cover the increasing cost of health insurance.

Q 15:40 What is the position of the IRS on HSOPs?

A lot of excitement about HSOPs was stirred up when several major firms (most notably Procter & Gamble) announced that they would establish these plans. Subsequently, the IRS announced that it would put a hold on further approvals of the concept, following the issuance of an approval letter by a District Office to Procter & Gamble. While the IRS's concerns are not known for certain, one issue could be the subordination question: May contributions of 25 percent to a health care account be truly subordinate to the retirement benefits? (This would be new ground, as the 25 percent level has been a threshold for subordinate benefits, including health care and insured death benefits, for decades.) Another problem may be the potential loss of tax revenue.

Q 15:41 How can employee savings accounts be used to finance retiree health benefits?

Under this option, while the obligation to accumulate a fund to pay for medical coverage during retirement is still transferred to employees, the employer assists them in saving for it. After-tax contributions may be invested in tax-deferred instruments (such as annuities) and then applied to a group policy sponsored by the employer (with any potential savings attached to the group policy rather than to individual policies under the annuities), or simply turned over to employees at retirement for application to their own health care expenses. An employer may choose to boost the employee's savings with matching contributions of its own.

Q 15:42   What are the advantages and disadvantages of the defined contribution approach?

Advantages of the defined contribution approach include the following:

1. It eliminates the open-ended nature of the employer's obligation to fund retiree health care.
2. It forces the employee to deal with the prospect of allocating limited resources to solve his or her own health care problems, thereby reinvolving the consumer in monitoring utilization and fees in a way that no amount of education and exhortation possibly could.

There are also disadvantages, including the following:

1. A given employee or retiree's costs must be satisfied by an account balance that will probably be a function of that employee's career earnings and length of service, the employer's profitability, and the earnings of the funds invested. None of these is in any way related to the ultimate cost of the retiree's medical benefits. Thus, when the time comes to pay for the benefits, the retiree may still not have the money to do it.
2. If the accumulation of funds is to be tied to the company's qualified retirement plan (qualified profit sharing plan accounts may be used to provide current health benefits or may accumulate as a reserve to be applied to the cost of health benefits at retirement), the purchase of health benefits necessarily results in a direct reduction in retirement income (unless profit sharing contributions are correspondingly increased).

Medicare Solutions to Retiree Challenges

Q 15:43   How can a retiree health plan be integrated with Medicare?

There are three commonly used methods for integrating retiree health care plans with Medicare. All three pay at least as much as would have been payable without Medicare, and benefits may be larger under the first two. The methods are as follows:

1. *Coordination of benefits.* Under this method the first step is to calculate what the plan would have paid if there were no Medicare payments and the plan were the sole provider (Answer 1 in the following example). The plan then pays either the calculated amount or the amount that Medicare does not pay (Answer 2 in the following example), whichever is smaller. This means that the retiree may be left with no copayment or deductible, providing him or her with the greatest total benefit.
2. *Exclusion or integration.* Under this method, eligible expenses are totaled first, Medicare payments are subtracted, and then deductibles, copayments, and so forth are applied to determine the amount payable by the plan.
3. *Carve out.* This method calculates benefits as if there were no Medicare and the plan were the sole provider. It then applies deductibles, copayments, and so forth and subtracts Medicare payments to determine the net amount payable by the plan. As copayments and the like are applied to a larger base, this method tends to produce the largest proportion of participant cost sharing and the lowest level of company cost—hence its popularity.

To illustrate the three different methods of calculation, and the varying result produced by each method, review the following examples. For each, assume the following:

- Total expenses: $5,000—all expenses are eligible under both the employer's plan and Medicare
- Medicare payment: $3,500
- Employer plan provisions require a $200 (annual, not yet met) deductible, and pay 80 percent of the remainder

Example 15-1. *Coordination of benefits*

Step 1:

    $5,000 eligible expenses

 − $200 annual deductible

 = $4,800

× 80% copayment percentage
= $3,840 payment plan would make in absence of Medicare (Answer 1)

Step 2:
$5,000 eligible expenses
− $3,500 paid by Medicare
= $1,500 not paid by Medicare (Answer 2)

Step 3:
Compare Answer 1 to Answer 2 and pay the lesser amount. In this example, that would be $1,500.

Example 15-2. *Exclusion or integration*
$5,000 eligible expenses
− $3,500 paid by Medicare
= $1,500 gross amount to be paid by employer's plan
− $200 annual deductible
= $1,300
× 80% copayment percentage
= $1,040 net amount to be paid by employer's plan

Example 15-3. *Carve out*
$5,000 eligible expenses
− $200 annual deductible
= $4,800
× 80% copayment percentage
= $3,840 gross amount to be paid by employer's plan
− $3,500 amount paid by Medicare
= $340 net amount to be paid by employer's plan

Q 15:44 What is a Medicare+Choice HMO?

Medicare + Choice HMOs have now replaced Medicare-risk HMOs, but most aspects of their operational aspects are the same.

Starting in 1982, the Health Care Financing Administration (HCFA) contracted with certain HMOs and competitive medical plans (CMPs) to provide health care services to Medicare beneficiaries under various arrangements, including risk contracts. Risk contracts required HMOs to assume full financial risk for all Medicare-covered services, as do Medicare + Choice contracts.

Under the contract, the government agreed to pay the Medicare-risk plan a fixed monthly amount (calculated at 95 percent of the amount the government would spend on average on beneficiaries in that geographical area, a figure known as the AAPCC or adjusted average per capita cost). This is the same arrangement for Medicare + Choice HMOs initially, but payments will be risk-adjusted in the future.

Using managed care techniques, Medicare + Choice plans are able to offer more health care services than are available through traditional Medicare coverage. Added benefits may include some prescription drug coverage, vision care, and dental care. Employers may save significant costs by contracting with, and encouraging enrollment in, Medicare + Choice plans. This is because the premium per member per month and inflation trend is significantly less than that of the average Medicare supplement policy; therefore, the impact on employers' long-term liability under FAS 106 is exponentially reduced.

Q 15:45 How is the adjusted average per capita cost calculated? What effect does this have on employer premiums?

Health plans that had risk contracts with HCFA were capitated prospectively at 95 percent of HCFA's AAPCC, which is based on the county and class (meaning such variables as the age, sex, disability status, and institutional status) of each Medicare beneficiary. In other words, the AAPCC is the average per-person amount HCFA estimates it would pay on a fee-for-service basis in the coming year, adjusted for the expected savings from managed care and the risk characteristics of the population served.

Depending on the AAPCC, some Medicare-risk plans offered expanded services with little or no premium cost. Because the regulations intended to prevent plans from profiting excessively on Medicare and its beneficiaries, HCFA required the plans to distribute to beneficiaries any actuarial surplus that resulted from the difference between their average reimbursement rate and the actual cost of services. Commonly, plans did so by reducing premium rates and copayments or by providing additional health benefits. Additionally, Medicare+Choice plans may, and often do, charge a premium to enrollees if the actuarial value of the benefit plan is greater than HCFA's reimbursement. The premium cost depends on a number of factors, including whether the employer purchases individual coverage for each retiree or negotiates a package to cover all retirees. In addition, the specific geographic region covered, the design of the health care benefit plan, and the ability of the senior plan to manage cost and quality can all affect the premium cost. Most HMOs with senior plans will work with employers to tailor a program for their retirees, including early retirees.

In addition to lowering the cost of premiums immediately by using Medicare+Choice HMOs, employers can significantly lower their FAS 106 liability in the long term, saving on actual cost as well as minimizing long-term debt.

HMOs and competitive medical plans transitioned into the Part C Medicare+Choice program beginning January 1, 1998. They are now paid under a new Medicare+Choice payment methodology, rather than the AAPCC method.

Q 15:46 How many employers are using Medicare+Choice programs to manage retiree benefits?

According to the 1999 Mercer/Foster Higgins, survey, 39 percent of employers offered at least one Medicare+Choice plan to their Medicare-eligible retirees, an increase from only 7 percent offering Medicare-risk plans in 1993. Only 12 percent of Medicare-eligible retirees were enrolled in an HMO, according to the 1999 survey, up from 10 percent in 1998.

Several consulting firms, such as Towers Perrin and William Mercer, as well as others in the private sector, are attempting to increase the enrollment of retirees in Medicare+Choice programs through initiatives focused on large firms.

Q 15:47 How do Medicare+Choice HMOs reduce the cost of care?

Like commercial HMOs, Medicare + Choice HMOs use a variety of techniques to reduce cost. The most common is the use of a primary care physician (PCP) who manages patient care. The PCP is aware of every aspect of his or her patient's care, so overmedication and duplication of services can be avoided. Primary care physicians refer patients to specialists if specialized services are required, preventing unnecessary and costly self-referrals by patients.

Managed care also rewards physicians for prescribing the right amount of care in the right setting at the right time. For example, skilled nursing or home care may be more appropriate for the patient's medical needs, as well as less expensive, than hospitalization. Managed care also encourages preventive care such as adult immunizations during the flu season. Most plans conduct utilization review or analyze practice patterns and use the data to improve the delivery of health care to their members.

Q 15:48 What are the disadvantages of Medicare+Choice HMOs?

For employers, there may be some practical reasons why Medicare + Choice HMOs are not appropriate for retiree populations. Retirees who travel extensively, or who reside for more than 90 continuous days in another state that is not covered in the HMO's service area, may not be able to join the plan. (At the time of this writing, relatively few HMOs have reciprocity agreements so that members can be served by local HMOs in different states.) Medicare + Choice allows point-of-service and preferred provider plans that could meet the needs of Medicare beneficiaries. These plans would allow greater flexibility as well as out-of-state provider choice, enabling plans to better serve today's more mobile retirees.

Retirees' personal physicians may not be included in the HMO network, depending on the size and scope of the senior HMO. This may cause some resistance to managed care among older employees who are accustomed to indemnity plans or fee-for-service health care coverage and who have well-established relationships with physicians.

Retirees who have spouses who are not yet eligible for Medicare may cause some administrative complexity for employers to consider; however, in most cases, plans will offer the younger spouse the option to enroll in the commercial plan until they are eligible for Medicare benefits when they reach age 65. This is known as a split enrollment. Other options include using specialized pre-65 companion benefit plans or limiting the Medicare + Choice HMO to retirees with Medicare-eligible spouses.

Q 15:49 What about prescription drug coverage?

Most Medicare + Choice HMOs limit prescription drug coverage for their individual plans to a maximum dollar amount between $500 and $3,000, depending on the service area. Plans will, however, work with employers to upgrade coverage of a greater proportion of prescription drug costs. Plans can be upgraded to match whatever benefits are offered to retirees through supplemental policies, almost invariably at a lower cost than indemnity plans.

Q 15:50 What criteria should be used in selecting a Medicare+Choice HMO?

Employers should consider the following criteria when selecting a senior HMO to offer to their retiree population:

1. *Scope and size.* How much experience does the plan have in delivering health care to seniors? How comprehensive is the provider network? Is it likely to include physicians who already have relationships with retirees? Does the service area cover the majority of retirees?
2. *Reputation.* What do current customers say about the plan? What are the results of member satisfaction surveys? What is the rate of disenrollment?
3. *Quality.* Is the plan accredited by the National Committee for Quality Assurance? Does the plan contract with quality providers?
4. *Cost.* Will the plan reduce premium costs significantly?
5. *Plan design.* Does the plan have enough flexibility to match existing benefit plans?
6. *Added value.* Does the plan offer richer and more varied benefits than competitors do? Are there additional programs,

such as wellness or fitness programs, that add value to the product? Does the Medicare + Choice plan currently offer Medicare + Choice on a group basis? How much experience does the plan have in this area?

Q 15:51 How can employers persuade retirees to join Medicare+Choice HMOs?

Communication and education are crucial in successfully transitioning retirees from a traditional indemnity plan to a Medicare + Choice HMO. Many retirees may be suspicious of managed care because it is unlike the health care benefit programs that they have had in the past; however, especially at a time when retirees are being asked to contribute more and more to the costs of their health care, they may be willing to accept this option because of the reduced out-of-pocket expenses these plans offer.

To help their retirees become more familiar with Medicare + Choice HMOs, some employers hold meetings and workshops, develop videos on Medicare + Choice HMOs, conduct health fairs, distribute brochures and written materials, and set up toll-free information lines. Regular, honest communication is extremely important.

To take full advantage of the cost savings, some employers offer a Medicare + Choice plan as the only health care benefit option for their retirees or provide enrollment incentives to encourage them to join the HMO. The design and price of the benefit plan is important in attracting retirees to the program. Financial incentives, such as lower copays and premiums, as well as added benefits, are usually the most persuasive methods to encourage retirees to join senior HMOs. Some employers pay senior HMO members a percentage of the company's premium savings, while others may pay the retirees' portion of their Medicare Part B premiums as an incentive.

Q 15:52 Are there any special enrollment procedures for Medicare+Choice plans?

The key difference between Medicare + Choice enrollments and those for active employees is the requirement that retirees complete the HMO's HCFA-approved enrollment form in addition to any form the employer might require. Most important, the HMO enrollment form requires the retiree's signature on what is typically called the "lock-in" agreement. This provision essentially certifies that the retiree understands that he or she is a member of an HMO and is not covered for non-urgent services provided outside the HMO's network. Another difference is that HCFA requires a lead time of at least one month and one day (although more is recommended) to process these applications after they are received from the HMOs. Given these requirements, employers are well-advised to plan ahead. For example, a January 1 effective date means enrollment needs to be completed in late October or early November. Employers also need to decide which method of enrollment works best. In other words, should the enrollment be coordinated by the HMO or by the employer? Keep in mind, however, that while January 1 effective dates for active employee benefit plans are almost universal, few employers find any real advantage to first-of-the-year retiree enrollments. [JJ Martingale and KS Berkowitz, *Managing Employee Health Benefits* (Winter 1996)]

Q 15:53 What if retirees want to switch back to traditional Medicare and the supplemental plan?

Employers may want to consider allowing retirees who choose coverage under a Medicare + Choice HMO plan to be able to return to traditional Medicare and the employers retiree plan if they do not like the HMO plan. Flexibility may also be in the employer's best interest as options for retiree health care are constantly changing. To date, disenrollment from most Medicare + Choice plans is low. Historically, few Medicare beneficiaries in HMOs have elected to return to traditional Medicare.

Medicare + Choice rules will restrict the ability of Medicare beneficiaries to return to traditional Medicare in the future.

Regulatory Issues

Q 15:54 How are retiree health benefits regulated?

Employer-sponsored retiree benefits are typically subject to the same regulations as health insurance for active workers. Legal decisions affecting employer-provided retiree health benefits have been made in response to lawsuits brought by retirees whose benefits have been threatened. Employers should carefully examine the wording in their employment contracts to determine whether changes in retiree benefits will inspire legal action against the company. In some cases, employers are bound by the provisions of previously negotiated contracts. Legal consultation is advisable early in the process of restructuring of retiree benefits.

Q 15:55 Are there limitations on a company's ability to alter retiree benefits?

Yes. Attempts to curtail retiree benefits, or to increase the cost of those benefits to retiree participants, have frequently been challenged in court. Although the results in these cases have been mixed, the right of employers to make such changes has generally been upheld by the courts (especially at the appellate level) when they had expressly reserved the right to make those changes without the consent of plan participants. This is accomplished through inclusion of clear and unambiguous language to that effect in the plan document.

Courts will look beyond the plan document itself to employee communications, if the plan document is ambiguous or representations to employees have been clearly misleading, fraudulent, or made in bad faith. Employee communications include the summary plan description, company newspapers, films, pamphlets, brochures, letters, and presentations. Special attention has been focused on language promising lifetime benefits at no cost.

For example, the Sixth Circuit U.S. Court of Appeals has held in *Sprague, et al. v. General Motors Corp.* [133 F 3d 388] that GM was not required to provide free lifetime health benefits to retirees. GM had provided free lifetime health coverage to salaried retirees from 1964 to 1988, at which time GM imposed deductibles and coinsurance. Retirees filed a class action suit alleging GM violated ERISA when it reduced benefits. In 1991, a district court ruled that medical benefits do not vest automatically under ERISA. The court went on to say that GM may have entered into separate contracts with early retirees. This issue was in the courts for several years. A January 1998

15-33

ruling held that an acceptance of an early retirement offer did not supersede plan language reserving the right to change coverage. In June of 1998, the U.S. Supreme Court denied a petition to review the decision.

Chapter 16

Pharmacy Benefit Management

Jeffrey D. Herzfeld, PharmD, MBA

Before 1994, the use of managed prescription drug programs had grown slowly. But in 1994, growth in these plans boomed as more employers recognized the value of managing the cost and delivery of prescription drugs. The proliferation of such plans has been accompanied by the development of more sophisticated benefit options for workers and by significant changes in the prescription drug marketplace.

The Basics	16-2
PBM Growth	16-5
Cost Control	16-7
Prescription Drug Management	16-19
Ensuring Quality	16-26
Prescription Drug Plans	16-29

The Basics

Q 16:1 What is a prescription drug plan?

Until the late 1980s, the term "prescription drug plan" was most often used to describe a specific benefit within a plan that covered prescription drugs. This approach, also known as "cash-carry and reimburse," defines the traditional method for purchasing prescriptions. The patient or beneficiary pays for prescriptions out of his or her own pocket and is then reimbursed by a third party, such as an insurance company or a preferred provider organization. Such programs are largely unmanaged and have been one of the contributors to rising health care benefit costs.

Q 16:2 What is a pharmacy benefit manager?

As prescription drugs became more expensive, and as more employees and beneficiaries began to demand that health plans offer the benefit, employers and insurers began to look at ways to manage prescription drug plans more effectively. At the same time, managed care was entering the market. Soon prescription drug plans began to incorporate managed care principles into their benefit design. Today, many employers are incorporating managed pharmacy programs into their health care benefits. Pharmacy benefit managers (PBMs) are the entities that administer the managed pharmacy programs. They are defined as the application of programs, services, and techniques designed to control costs associated with the delivery of pharmaceutical care by:

1. Streamlining and improving the prescribing and dispensing process;
2. Educating the health care consumer; and
3. Controlling the cost of prescriptions dispensed.

Q 16:3 What options do PBM prescription drug plans offer?

To meet clients' needs, most pharmacy benefit managers offer a variety of services that can be used as stand-alone elements or in any combination. It is best to look at the broad spectrum of services a

PBM offers and to ensure that the PBM has the capabilities to meet the needs of plan members. Typical services PBMs offer include the following:

- Claim processing
- Prescription drug card program
- Filling prescriptions by mail
- Development of a network of pharmacy providers
- Formulary development
- Drug utilization management, including prospective, concurrent, and retrospective review programs, as well as reporting capabilities
- Strong educational components for patients and physicians

Q 16:4 What questions should a purchaser ask a PBM?

The first and most important question is not, "How much money can you save me?" but, rather, "How can you make my prescription drug benefit better meet the needs of my enrollees in a cost-effective manner?" Cost will obviously be a factor, but focusing only on pricing could damage the overall effectiveness of the plan over time. Other specific questions should be asked:

1. What kind of network of providers will the PBM be able to develop?
2. What kind of reports does the PBM offer? (Most will offer prospective, concurrent, and retrospective reporting programs.)
3. Is drug utilization review (DUR) conducted in-house? Can the PBM provide electronic DUR edits? (Such edits are conducted during the dispensing process so that the prescription may be changed if needed.)
4. How does the PBM work with physicians to educate and modify prescribing patterns?
5. What type of educational programs are offered to enrollees?
6. If the company has disease management programs, how are the programs designed? Do they emphasize more than prescription drugs?

Q 16:5   Health Insurance Answer Book

7. What types of ancillary services are provided? Are claims processed in-house? Does the PBM have its own mail service capability, or does it subcontract that service?

Q 16:5 What questions should a purchaser ask a PBM's current clients?

Current clients of a PBM can provide information to prospective purchasers about its services. The following questions may be useful in the selection process:

1. Are the PBM's reports submitted in a timely manner?
2. Do the reports provide the type of information needed to improve management of the prescription benefit?
3. What type of customer service does the PBM offer? Are enrollees treated courteously, and are their questions answered promptly?
4. Do enrollees experience difficulty in getting prescriptions filled because of technical problems, such as computer system downtime?
5. What is the PBM's reputation with physicians?
6. What kind of therapeutic interchange protocol rate does the PBM use?
7. What kind of cost savings has the PBM produced for its clients?
8. Has the PBM enhanced its clients' prescription benefit programs?

Q 16:6 Should the ownership of the PBM be a concern for employers?

Within the past four years, three of the largest pharmacy benefit managers were purchased by major prescription drug manufacturers. Many analysts foresee no problems with such consolidations. They believe that manufacturer-owned PBMs will be better able to negotiate volume discounts, create outcomes studies, conduct research, and test new prescription medications. Critics are concerned, however, that such consolidations could lead to PBMs giving preferential treatment to their parent company's prescription drugs. Articles featured in major newspapers and trade publications appear to lend some credibility to this concern. Employers should carefully review each PBM before making a final selection. This has become less of a problem because two of these PBMs have since been sold.

In January 1998, the Food and Drug Administration (FDA) issued guidelines for regulating PBMs. The FDA's first effort at regulating managed care reflects concern over PBMs acquired by drug companies and potential adverse reactions to drug switches. The proposal was opposed by PBMs, and the FDA has said it will change the proposed rules.

Q 16:7 What educational programs for enrollees do PBMs offer?

If the PBM is attached to an HMO or other managed care organization, educational programs can be customized to suit the specific needs of the employer, as part of the managed care organization's health care educational programs. In addition, many PBMs distribute monthly newsletters to enrollees offering information on specific disease states such as asthma or diabetes.

PBM Growth

Q 16:8 Are many people enrolled in PBMs?

PBMs and industry analysts use different methods to determine the number of people covered under their programs. Some reports estimate the number of people enrolled in some type of pharmacy program—whether managed or simply a claim processing or prescription card service—to be as high as 130 million. Some analysts believe these figures and others are inflated. One point is clear: Within the past decade, the number of people enrolled in PBMs has increased about 50 percent. According to a 1997 survey by William M. Mercer, 33 percent of active employees receive pharmacy benefits through a PBM.

Q 16:9 Is nationwide service important for a PBM?

Employees who participate in a PBM are required to have their prescriptions filled by a network pharmacy (except in emergencies) in order to receive benefits. If the plan sponsor and its enrollees are located in one area, a nationwide network may not be necessary. On the other hand, nationwide service can be quite beneficial for large employers who have employees in multiple locations, or whose employees are frequently transferred or who travel often.

Pharmacies join networks and provide services at reduced rates in exchange for volume business: A tight network of pharmacy providers allows PBMs to control costs and quality better. The PBM should design a network that meets the needs of enrollees and offers convenience, although obviously not every pharmacy can be in a network. The strategy of developing tightly controlled networks of pharmacies is being limited, however, by legislative action in many states. Twenty-four states have adopted "any willing provider laws," which require PBMs to allow any pharmacy that meets the PBM's requirements to participate in its network. Many other states are considering implementing such willing provider laws. Even though this type of legislation limits some of the effectiveness of selective network contracting in many areas, PBMs are still able to provide cost savings to plan sponsors.

Q 16:10 Why are prescription benefits a growing concern for health insurance planners?

Prescription drug prices have increased consistently in the past decade. Today, they represent anywhere from 9 percent to 15 percent of an employer's overall health care benefit costs; therefore, prescription drug costs are a significant area to target for better outcomes and lower costs. According to the Employee Benefit Research Institute, prescription drugs represent 7 percent of total national health spending. Selecting a marginal PBM or not knowing how to optimize the services a PBM offers can cost a health plan sponsor considerable money.

Q 16:11 Why are prescription drug costs increasing?

The overwhelming majority of the increases in expenditures on prescription drugs are attributable to the increased volume, mix, and availability of pharmaceutical products. Prescription drugs are a substitute for other forms of health care. More appropriate utilization of prescription drugs can potentially lower total health care expenditures and improve the quality of care. For example, by taking the right medicine an asthmatic patient might be able to avoid emergency room visits and hospitalizations.

Direct-to-consumer advertising has increased the demand for many drugs. Demographics are also driving increased costs as the population ages.

Q 16:12   How much are prescription drug costs increasing?

A report by Express Scripts says average wholesale drug prices increased 5.1 percent in 1998, compared to only 2.4 percent in 1997. Drug costs for insurers and HMOs could increase by 13 percent to 17 percent a year if health plans do not control drug usage aggressively. The 1998 Mercer/Foster Higgins survey found that prescription drug increases averaged 15.6 percent.

Q 16:13   How much do PBMs charge for their services?

PBM prices can vary dramatically by region, age of enrollees, type of industry the plan covers, overall health of beneficiaries, and, most specifically, by the elements the plan sponsor wants or does not want to include. Administrative and prescription costs combined can range anywhere from $20 to $25 per member per month to as low as $9 to $10 per member per month for an aggressively managed plan. The PBM administrative fees are typically 3 or 4 percent of total prescription plan costs.

Cost Control

Q 16:14   What factors influence the cost of the prescription benefit?

The cost of a prescription benefit depends on a variety of factors. The prescription drugs themselves as well as utilization of the program need to be considered. In addition, the cost of the PBM or plan administrator can sometimes include dispensing fees and administration costs. Other major factors influencing the cost of a prescription drug plan are fraud and prescription misuse.

Q 16:15 What can employers and health plans do to control pharmacy costs?

Merck-Medco Managed Care recommends the following:

1. Review the design of the pharmacy benefit and how it fits into the overall medical program.
2. Analyze prior experience to identify areas needing better management.
3. Use the following pharmacy management tools and techniques:
   a. Retail pharmacy networks,
   b. Mail service,
   c. Generic drug substitution,
   d. Formulary management,
   e. Utilization management,
   f. Physician profiling,
   g. Health management.
4. Communicate to plan members.
5. Anticipate the financial impact of new drugs and therapies.

Q 16:16 What is the role of utilization review in a managed prescription program?

Utilization review (UR) allows an employer access to information about its employees' uses of the prescription drug plan and thus helps determine whether it is meeting their needs. Under UR, pharmacists review claims data and physician records. With the help of sophisticated software, many PBMs can provide a comprehensive picture of a prescription drug plan's utilization patterns.

Utilization information can help a PBM to tailor a program specifically to meet the needs of the employer's plan. For example, if enrollees are older and show a high volume of maintenance prescriptions, the PBM might suggest that the employer offer a mail service component. Or if a number of enrollees use antihypertensive medicine, some PBMs, particularly those associated with managed care organizations, might develop a program to encourage lifestyle changes incorporating a healthier diet and exercise.

Q 16:17 What is a formulary?

A formulary is a list of drugs approved by a health plan. The formulary is based on the most effective method of treatment. Some health plans require that physicians prescribe only drugs on their formulary; others allow more flexibility.

Q 16:18 What is the difference between an open and closed formulary?

An open formulary allows plan enrollees to receive the agreed-upon reimbursement within the plan for any prescription drug prescribed for them. Open formularies traditionally have been quite popular with physicians and patients, as they perceive that open formularies offer freedom of choice; however, as most physicians are familiar primarily with only the handful of prescription medications they use most often, formularies—which typically include hundreds of possible medications and several options per category—actually give physicians and patients the chance to make better-informed choices.

Closed formularies are often met with resistance by plan enrollees. Yet many PBMs have found that, with proper education before incorporating a closed formulary, introducing it gradually, and including the most popular and necessary branded medications, closed formularies will be accepted. A closed formulary need not be restrictive or limited to generic medications. If a plan sponsor works closely with its PBM, the formulary can be designed to include everything from contraceptives to the latest ulcer medications or other new therapies. Closed formularies do not necessarily mean that an enrollee cannot elect to use a certain prescription drug simply because it is not on the formulary. Rather, a plan can refuse to cover the nonformulary drug or require enrollees to pay a higher share of its cost. Such a structure might be called an incentive formulary.

Closed formularies are typically created by a panel of physicians, pharmacists, and, sometimes, representatives from the plan sponsor. When tailored for a plan, closed formularies are created after careful review of a plan's utilization records, the needs of the plan enrollees, and the goals of the plan sponsor.

Q 16:19 Where are open and closed formularies most commonly found?

Open formularies are more prevalent in self-funded plans, while closed formularies are more frequently used in health plans such as HMOs and PPOs. The use of closed formularies in both categories is growing.

	Health Plans with a Closed Formulary	Employers Using a Closed Formulary*
1994	35.3%	10.5%
1995	47.2%	18.4%
1996	62.0%	21.1%

*Data SourceTrends & Forecasts Survey, Emron, Inc., 1996.

Q 16:20 Are there any advantages to a closed formulary?

Contrary to popular belief, a closed formulary need not be restrictive or limited to generic medications. The formulary can be designed to include everything from contraceptives to the latest ulcer medications or other new therapies.

Q 16:21 Are there any disadvantages to a closed formulary?

One of the primary drawbacks to closed formularies, as stated in Q 16:18, is that they are often met with resistance by plan enrollees. Yet, many PBMs have found that if the enrollee is properly educated about closed formularies before incorporating a closed formulary, and if it is incorporated gradually and includes the most popular and needed branded medications, closed formularies can and will be accepted.

Q 16:22 What role do generic drugs play in a prescription drug plan?

Generic drugs are nonbranded medications. They contain components identical to those of their name brand counterparts. Generics are produced by a variety of manufacturers and can typically save the buyer 20 percent to 50 percent of the cost of branded drugs.

Major pharmaceutical firms spend millions of dollars developing new drugs. Once created, drugs are patented and become the sole property of the company. Drugs are typically patented for an average of 17 years. By the end of the year 2002, about 40 drugs with $16 billion in sales in 1996 will lose their patents. Those drugs will then be available to other drug manufacturers to produce as nonbranded or generic drugs. PBMs frequently use generics to help manage the cost of prescription drug plans.

Q 16:23 What influence do PBMs have over formularies?

PBMs have a great deal of influence over the development and management of formularies. A progressive PBM has a team of physicians and pharmacists who determine which pharmaceutical products should be included on the formulary. This group is typically known as the pharmacy and therapeutics (P&T) committee. The decisions of the P&T committee are based on safety, efficacy, utilization, prescribing patterns, and cost.

Q 16:24 Which drugs are typically excluded from formularies?

It is important when answering this question not to confuse benefit coverage with formulary coverage. Typically, certain types of drugs are completely excluded from benefit coverage, including drugs used for cosmetic purposes (e.g., Rogaine for hair loss), over-the-counter products (e.g., Tylenol), and drugs classified as experimental by the Food and Drug Administration. In addition, products such as vaccines and other injectables may be covered under a medical benefit rather than a separate prescription benefit.

Formularies may overlap benefit coverage depending on the type of formulary being used. In an open formulary, drug products not listed on the formulary may still be considered a covered benefit, perhaps with a higher share of the cost borne by the beneficiary. In a closed formulary, drug products not listed are typically not part of the benefit coverage. If the physician prescribes a nonformulary product, the beneficiary would be responsible for the entire cost of the medication.

Q 16:25 How do PBMs get physicians to support a formulary?

Patients continue to look primarily to their personal physicians to recommend prescription drugs. The physician can help to enlighten a patient about a change in prescription drugs recommended by a PBM, or the physician can choose not to communicate appropriately and possibly instill fear and bewilderment in the minds of patients when drugs are changed; therefore, it is imperative that PBMs place a great deal of emphasis on developing a cooperative relationship with physicians.

In the past, some physicians have had a reputation for having an antagonistic attitude toward PBMs and formularies. This attitude seems to be fading as the two groups begin to work together more closely, particularly when the PBM endeavors to educate rather than to force and to listen rather than to demand. One of the most effective tools to encourage physicians to support formularies is called a therapeutic intervention protocol (TIP—see also Q 16:32). Under this program, pharmacists contact prescribers to discuss more cost-effective therapeutic alternatives. Often, the TIP is combined with visits from pharmacists and educational seminars.

Q 16:26 Are formularies usurping the role of physicians in prescribing medicine?

Unfortunately, under some managed prescription programs the answer is yes. Physicians and pharmacy managers must work together for a prescription drug program to provide optimal results. A well-managed formulary does not dictate what drugs a physician can and cannot prescribe. Instead, the PBM works with the physician to help educate him or her about the myriad prescription drug options available and the cost associated with each. For example, a medication that manages high cholesterol levels can cost 40 percent to 50 percent more than a therapeutically equivalent drug. Often, physicians are unaware of this cost. Giving physicians all the facts about a particular prescription medication helps them make reasonable and appropriate prescription decisions for their patients. In addition, many formularies will encourage physicians to return to previous medications if desired results are not being achieved with a newly suggested drug.

Q 16:27 Are there ways to manage costs even without a closed formulary?

Plan sponsors are finding that closed formularies can provide therapeutically equivalent results at a much lower cost; however, for a variety of reasons, some plans sponsors opt not to use formularies as a method of cost containment. They may prefer to use options such as mail service, utilization review, and a tight network of providers to manage prescription drug costs.

Q 16:28 Why are formularies so controversial?

Formularies are typically met with resistance because plan sponsors, enrollees, and physicians mistakenly believe that they are being asked to sacrifice therapeutic efficacy in order for the plan sponsor to save money; however, such beliefs are frequently overcome through education and dialogue.

Recent consolidations and acquisitions of PBMs by drug manufacturers have also caused concern among consumer advocates, physicians, and the pharmaceutical industry in general. The Federal Trade Commission has voiced strong concern over alleged improprieties by drug manufacturers, which involve promoting the manufacturer's own brands on the formularies of PBMs that they own. Plan sponsors and formulary development panels should ensure that specific drugs included on formularies are balanced, keeping the needs of enrollees and the goals of the plan sponsor in mind.

Q 16:29 How do new drugs affect formularies?

There were 92 new drugs released in 1996 and 1997. Many of the new drugs treat illnesses that would otherwise require lengthy hospital stays or were previously untreatable. Some of the newly released drugs are simply targeted to take market share away from a leader. Drugs considered breakthrough drugs should be included on a formulary to provide quality patient care and possibly control costs. Drugs added to formularies should clearly benefit the covered population.

Q 16:30 Is Viagra covered?

A great deal of controversy has surrounded coverage of this new drug to treat impotence. Unless a plan has an exclusion that would apply, Viagra should be covered when medically necessary. Someone with a history of treatment for impotence should clearly be considered to have demonstrated the medical necessity. Someone who merely wishes to improve stamina should not be considered to have demonstrated any medical necessity. Many people will fall between these two extremes and should be evaluated individually.

Another difficult question is how large a supply of the drug should be prescribed. According to a June 12, 1998 article in the *Boston Globe*, Harvard Pilgrim Health Care has reduced its allotment from ten pills a month to four. Tufts Health Plan and Fallon Community Health Plan also pay for four pills a month. Blue Cross and Blue Shield of Massachusetts allows twelve pills a month. One Health Plan (a subsidiary of Great-West Life) has announced it will cover six tablets per month.

Kaiser Permanente has decided to exclude coverage of drugs for treatment of sexual dysfunction. Kaiser claims that if it covered ten Viagra tablets per month, Viagra alone would account for 10 percent of Kaiser's pharmaceutical budget.

In July 1998, Prudential HealthCare and Humana announced that they would not pay for Viagra. Both cited safety concerns, despite the FDA's approval of the drug.

In October 1998, Health Net (a California HMO) announced that it would cover six tablets per 30 days for men with organically caused sexual dysfunction. PM Group also covers six pills a month, but with no prior authorization required.

Q 16:31 What are lifestyle drugs?

The term "lifestyle drugs" is applied to prescription products that do not necessarily cure illness but can be used to improve daily life by boosting psychological attitudes, energy levels, sexual performance, and body image. Viagra may be the prime example of a lifestyle drug.

Other examples are Prozac and Zoloft, drugs for clinical depression that are now being used by many people for simple anxiety and stress.

Some lifestyle drugs, such as Propecia and Rogaine, which are baldness treatments, have become over-the-counter medications and no longer require a prescription.

In some cases, the same drug, perhaps in a different dosage, may be a lifestyle drug and a medically necessary treatment for a different condition.

Q 16:32 What are therapeutic interchange protocols?

Typically a number of alternative prescription drug products are available to treat a particular health condition and grouped together in a therapeutic class. For example, Tagamet, Zantac, Pepcid, and Axid are all drugs used to treat gastric ulcers. Each of those products has a different chemical composition but has the same therapeutic effect in the body.

Therapeutic interchange protocols are documented procedures for substituting one therapeutically equivalent product for another, with a goal of a more cost-effective medical outcome. The protocols are generally developed by a multidisciplinary group of physicians, pharmacists, and nurses. Therapeutic interchange protocols, when properly developed, executed, and communicated to physicians and patients, can be quite successful. Some PBMs have achieved close to a 90 percent success rate in moving patients to lower-cost therapies with TIP programs.

Q 16:33 What is the FDA's position on generic drugs?

In a statement released January 28, 1998, the FDA stated: "To date, there are no documented examples of a generic product manufactured to meet its approved specifications that could not be used interchangeably with the corresponding brand-name drug." This statement was apparently issued in response to concern expressed about therapeutic interchange protocols, and provides reassurance to plan sponsors that encourage generic drugs over brand drugs.

The FDA uses guidelines on pharmaceutical equivalence, bioequivalence, and therapeutic equivalence to ensure generic drugs are interchangeable with brand-name drugs. Pharmaceutical equivalence means the generic drug has the same active ingredient or ingredients, is in the same dosage form (tablet, liquid, etc.), and is identical in strength as the brand-name drug. Bioequivalence means the generic drug is absorbed into the bloodstream at the same rate and extent as the brand-name drug. Therapeutic equivalence is achieved when a generic drug is proven to be safe and effective and is both pharmaceutically equivalent and bioequivalent.

Q 16:34 What is a MAC?

For multisource generic drugs, most PBMs have a maximum allowable cost (MAC). The MAC is derived from many sources, including data from proprietary databases and the Health Care Financing Administration.

Q 16:35 What are disease state management programs?

Disease state management (DSM) programs were developed to measure and manage all health care costs associated with a particular disease (e.g., asthma) across the entire continuum of health care delivery. Costs associated with treating and managing many diseases include physician visits, emergency room visits, hospitalization, lab expenses, and pharmacy expenses. The goal of disease management is to decrease the total costs associated with treatment of the disease. This can be accomplished by managing the individual component costs, such as hospital or pharmacy services, that affect the total cost. DSM programs may indicate that, for example, increasing expenses for drug therapy helps to decrease emergency room visits, which results in an overall decrease in health care costs. According to a 1997 survey by William M. Mercer, 51 percent of employers plan to implement or expand disease management programs.

Q 16:36 Can disease management offer real value to plan sponsors?

Disease management became one of the most popular health plan design options of the 1990s. Whether focusing on diabetes, cancer, maternity, or cardiology, a growing number of drug manufacturers work with PBMs to target enrollees with certain diseases. The strategy behind disease management is that, by concentrating on specific diseases with targeted medications, the PBM will be able to lower costs and improve outcomes. Although disease management holds promise, it is important to ensure that the program does more than simply target prescription drugs to treat the disease. To function optimally, disease management should focus on the full spectrum of treatment options available to treat the disease, not just prescription drugs.

According to the MEDSTAT Group, nine diseases (asthma, breast cancer, diabetes, heart failure, hypertension, ischemic heart disease, low back pain, otitis media, and peptic ulcer) make up about 20 percent of all health costs.

PCS Health Systems reports that after introducing an information program aimed at physicians and patients, emergency room usage declined 58 percent for asthma and 27 percent for diabetes. Inpatient hospital costs for asthma also declined 38 percent, but costs for diabetes only declined 1 percent.

Q 16:37 Can proper drug usage reduce other costs?

Yes. According to an article in the *American Journal of Industrial Medicine*, employees using sedating antihistamines purchased over the counter to treat allergic rhinitis have a significantly higher risk of injury than employees taking prescribed nonsedating antihistamines. In addition to adding to workers' compensation costs, the sedating antihistamines contributed to lower productivity, at an expense projected to be greater than $4 billion for all employers.

Q 16:38 How are employers and health plans using disease management to cut prescription drug costs?

Employers and health plans are working with PBMs to introduce programs that will help manage health care costs related to a disease by optimizing the use of pharmaceuticals available. DSM programs offered through PBMs may increase, decrease, or have no effect on prescription benefit costs. The important measure of a DSM program is its effect on total costs related to the disease.

Medication compliance programs are an ideal way to help patients get the most benefit from the medication prescribed for them. It is estimated that $100 billion in annual health care costs can be attributed to patients seeking care in emergency rooms, physician offices, and operating rooms as a result of not taking prescribed medication or of taking it improperly. In addition, working directly with physicians, PBMs can provide pharmacoeconomic information to physicians that can assist them in prescribing cost-effective medications.

Q 16:39 How can a purchaser evaluate disease state management programs?

Writing in the *Journal of Managed Care Pharmacy*, Craig S. Stern, R.Ph., Pharm.D., President of ProPharma Pharmaceutical Consultants, suggests the following evaluation tools:

1. Emphasize health care, not therapeutics.
2. There must be provider network support.
3. Programs should include member education and motivation elements.

4. The delivery system should be integrated.
5. There should be a clearly defined system for organization and management.
6. There should be well-defined contractual criteria, including performance criteria.
7. A program for information management should be included.
8. There should be a well-defined program for measuring outcomes.
9. The economic impact must be well-defined.
10. Any risk sharing should be based upon an actual risk assessment.
11. There should be a clear understanding of whether the program is a strategic partnership or a service offering.
12. There should be a clear evaluation of the total quality management (TQM) impact as an expectation or added value.
13. There must be performance audits and service guarantees, if applicable.

Prescription Drug Management

Q 16:40 What role do prescriptions by mail play in the prescription drug plan?

A mail service component in a prescription drug plan allows patients to obtain prescription drugs by mail. Mail service prescriptions are typically used for drugs used for daily or routine health needs, such as high blood pressure or diabetes (known as "maintenance" medications). This service saves patients time and money and is a popular addition to the benefit design. Mail service pharmacies (MSPs) are staffed by a full complement of pharmacists and technicians, who ensure quality control and a high level of service. Mail service can typically save as much as 35 percent of the cost of traditionally delivered prescription drugs. In addition, most PBMs offer a toll-free customer service line (some with up to 24-hour coverage) to answer enrollees' questions about their prescription drugs. Many enrollees prefer this option to the traditional method of receiving medications from a busy pharmacist in a retail setting, who often does not have time to counsel patients. Prescriptions by mail also typically include newsletters or brochures about the specific diseases or conditions for which the medications were prescribed.

Q 16:41 Why are mail service pharmacy programs underused?

Typically, mail service programs are underused because enrollees are not familiar with their mail service benefit or are not sure how to access the service. Once enrollees are introduced to the convenience, simplicity, and safety of an MSP program, most express a high level of satisfaction with the plan. Industry analysts and the managed care pharmacy industry expect the mail service industry to experience tremendous growth in the next few years. They believe that, as millions of aging baby boomers begin to need more prescriptions, they will want to take advantage of the convenience offered by mail service. According to the American Managed Care Pharmacy Association (AMCPA), in 1994, about 64 million of the 120 million prescriptions filled by PBMs were dispensed by mail service pharmacies. The AMCPA estimates that 1995 sales for mail service prescriptions were $8 billion and projects that, by the year 2000, sales will exceed $20 billion.

The 1998 Mercer/Foster Higgins study found that 73 percent of point-of-service plans and 65 percent of HMOs include mail order, up from 63 and 51 percent, respectively, in 1996. The same survey found that the median mail-order copayment for all types of plans was $5 for generic drugs and $10 for brand-name drugs, except for PPOs, where the median copayment for generic drugs was $7.

Q 16:42 Have any studies been done on the effectiveness of mail service pharmacies?

The AMCPA cites numerous studies that conclude that managed care mail service programs reduce overall prescription costs while maintaining and improving quality. A study by the benefit consulting firm William M. Mercer concluded that MSPs reduce a plan sponsor's total gross costs, despite minor increases in the use of their prescription drug program. The Boston Consulting Group obtained similar results. It found that, "at the unit-cost level, [mail service pharmacy] plans offered savings of 30 to 35 percent on maintenance drugs over card and [major medical] plans." Another study by FIND/SVP observed a 26 percent difference in cost between a mail order prescription and a prescription reimbursed through a standard major medical plan. The international benefit consulting firm Wyatt Company compared costs under managed care mail service pharmacies with prices in unmanaged retail environments. Managed care pharmacy operations (best suited for maintenance medications) generally charged 13 percent below the average wholesale price (AWP), plus a $2.50 dispensing fee. Pharmacy preferred-provider organizations prices are about 10 percent below AWP, plus a $2.75 dispensing fee. Unmanaged retail stores charge 8.25 percent above AWP, plus a $4 dispensing fee.

Q 16:43 How does a health care purchaser know if an MSP is right for its insured population?

Mail service programs are developed for any health care purchaser whose insured population uses maintenance medications. The greater the percentage of the population on maintenance medications, the greater the cost savings. Mail service programs offer convenience for beneficiaries and cost savings to plan sponsors. Good mail service pharmacy programs should also offer programs that add value for the sponsor and patient. The programs may include toll-free counseling with pharmacists, drug information mailed with every prescription, and health and wellness information as part of disease management programs.

Q 16:44 Are prescriptions by mail safe?

Error rates in mail-service pharmacies are at least equal to, or, in may instances, below the level of most retail pharmacies. A handful of leading PBMs offer state-of-the-art technology designed to improve efficiency and ensure safety. Among the techniques used to ensure safety are radio-controlled totes, a conveyor system that routes prescriptions to various stations; and intensive quality-control programs that ensure that prescriptions are filled efficiently and accurately. Yet another key to the quality and safety measures in mail service pharmacies is an imaging application that shows pharmacists via a computer screen the national drug code (NDC) number and an "image" of what the prescribed drug must look like. By carefully comparing the ready-to-ship product with the image on the screen, the pharmacist can confirm the content and thus ensure accuracy during filling operations.

Q 16:45 Is it common for a plan to have incentives to use a mail-order program?

Yes. Some plans have lower copays for mail-order drugs; other plans offer a larger supply for the same copay; still others offer larger supplies for lower copays. The backlash against managed care is having an affect on mail-order programs. For example, in 1997, Missouri passed a law that bars HMOs from using benefit incentives to favor mail-order drugs.

Q 16:46 How is pharmacoeconomic research being used to cut prescription drug costs?

Pharmacoeconomic research can be used to determine the cost-effectiveness of pharmaceuticals, to design formularies, disease management programs, and pharmacy benefit programs. Such research can show plan sponsors which prescription drugs provide optimal therapeutic and cost values, with the goal of decreasing overall health care costs. For example, research may demonstrate that using a relatively expensive drug may be justified given its ability to decrease surgical treatment. Pharmacoeconomic research may result in a decrease or an increase in actual prescription drug expenses, but it can contribute to a decrease in overall health care costs.

Q 16:47 What is a prescription drug card plan?

A member in a card program presents his or her prescription to a participating pharmacy. By using an online computer network, or telephone database, the pharmacist can answer a number of questions including whether the patient is eligible and what other drugs the patient may be taking. The member typically pays a fixed copayment, and the payor is billed at a prenegotiated discount rate. Prescription drug card plans, while convenient, are typically loosely managed. As such, there has been, and will continue to be, a great potential for fraud. The 1998 Mercer/Foster Higgins survey found that the majority of plans included a prescription drug card plan.

Q 16:48 What are the disclosure limitations in HMO pharmaceutical plans?

In the vast majority of cases, HMO pharmaceutical plans provide full disclosure of the medications they do or do not cover. Some HMOs will not cover drugs for behavioral modification therapy, such as nicotine patches and diet pills. Plan sponsors should carefully review all elements of the plan to be certain that they are aware of any specific drugs that the HMO does not cover.

Q 16:49 How can employers protect themselves from HMO nondisclosure?

The best advice to protect against surprises in the pharmacy benefit plan is carefully to review all elements of the plan. Do not simply listen to what someone says the plan will cover; be sure to read it personally.

Q 16:50 What is the most important element to look for when considering a PBM?

The most important would be utilization management, which includes prospective, concurrent, and retrospective review programs. Specifically, the PBM should:

1. Have resources available to work with physicians, prospectively, prior to the prescribing process, to modify prescribing behavior.
2. Provide electronic drug utilization review edits, which are conducted concurrently, during the dispensing process, so that the prescription may be changed if needed.
3. Offer utilization reports to analyze utilization data retrospectively, after the prescribing process, to provide a better compre-

hension of the benefit expenses and allow the plan sponsor to modify the prescription benefit plan as needed.

Q 16:51 What kinds of reporting should a purchaser seek from a PBM?

Perhaps the single most important report a PBM should offer is a review of utilization. Utilization review information can be broken down in whatever manner the sponsor prefers—by region, sex, age, and so forth; however, some PBMs provide utilization data in one report, claims data in another, and reports from different regions covered by the plan sponsor in yet another. For a complete analysis of the PBM's activity, it is preferable to have one integrated report that provides an overview of all elements of the pharmacy program; the reports should be available semimonthly, quarterly, and year-to-date. Reports can be used to identify and manage trends, as well as to answer specific questions, and are of critical importance in the day-to-day management of a successful PBM program.

Q 16:52 What is integrated claims information processing?

Integrated claims processing provides a plan sponsor with information on utilization, claims, cost analysis, and the like, in one easy-to-read report rather than in several different reports spread throughout the year. This allows the plan sponsor to monitor the performance of the PBM over any time period. Integrated reports should be offered by any PBM selected by a plan sponsor. Additional reports, such as reports that further detail the information in the integrated report, are also beneficial.

Q 16:53 How are PBMs compensated?

PBMs traditionally generate profits in three ways: (1) charging payers an administrative fee per transaction based on the number of prescriptions or employees; (2) retaining rebates negotiated with manufacturers; and (3) securing discounts through a contracted network of pharmacies.

Discounting involves an agreement between purchasers and manufacturers to secure significant reductions in the cost of prescription drugs. The savings are passed along to employers, who receive average discounts of 9 percent to 11 percent on prescription drugs. In the past, manufacturers would discount solely based on utilization; however, today manufacturers are often insisting on an increase in market segment before giving discounts.

With rebates, drug manufacturers reward PBMs that are able to encourage a significant percentage of enrollees to switch to the company's key products. At the end of a predetermined period, the PBM and the manufacturer review utilization. If the goals agreed upon were met, the PBM receives a rebate that varies from 5 percent to 30 percent and averages about 16 percent of the cost of the drug. In some cases, the savings are passed on to the PBM's client. Rebates are becoming increasingly more controversial because manufacturers primarily offer them only to large HMOs and PBMs that can provide greater market share, and not to independent pharmacies that have a minimal ability to shift market share.

Q 16:54 What role does capitation play in pharmacy benefit management?

The success of capitation in other managed care settings has encouraged some plan sponsors and PBMs to explore it as a method of payment for PBMs. Capitation involves an agreement between a payer and a PBM to provide prescription benefits for a predetermined amount per covered life, regardless of the cost of the prescriptions actually dispensed. Theoretically, this causes the risk for providing the prescription benefit to become the responsibility of the PBM and not the payor; however, many industry analysts caution that PBM capitation is still new and poses risks for employers: They may be overcharged because, without satisfactory historical utilization data, actual costs are difficult to predict. Critics also fear that PBMs would limit potentially beneficial medications to meet capitation goals. If capitation is to be successful, further utilization data will need to be available to determine mutually beneficial and equitable capitation rates.

A better alternative to straight capitation may be a "risk sharing" arrangement, in which the PBM and plan sponsor share accountability for the pharmacy benefit costs. Risk sharing better aligns goals and incentives and avoids many of the pitfalls seen in either pure capitation or fee-for-service arrangements.

Ensuring Quality

Q 16:55 How do PBMs identify duplicate prescriptions?

Pharmacies submit prescription claims electronically at the time the prescription is filled. A PBM's data center, or central clearing house, compares the submitted prescription with the patient's prescription profile. If a duplicate prescription exists, the pharmacy is notified immediately before the prescription is dispensed.

Because PBMs use some of the most advanced and sophisticated software programs available, it is becoming increasingly easy to track duplicate claims and prescription abuse. Software programs are available that identify duplicate Social Security numbers, patient identification numbers, and physician identification numbers.

With the support of retail pharmacists using this software, duplicate dispensing can be prevented, and prescription abusers can be stopped.

Q 16:56 What error detection and reporting programs are available?

As part of the drug utilization review process conducted by PBMs on behalf of their clients, a variety of clinical monitoring criteria or "edits" are applied to each submitted claim. An example would be a drug-to-drug interaction edit. If a potential harmful drug-to-drug interaction exists, the pharmacy is notified online and must override the communication, or the prescription will not be processed. Identifying these potential problems is very important: between 10 and 25 percent of all hospitalization are estimated to be caused by drug therapy problems. PBMs will typically provide clients with reports documenting the number of edits that were executed on behalf of these clients. The reports are helpful in identifying physicians who might not be properly reviewing a patient's history before prescribing medications.

Q 16:57 How is electronic data interchange being used to review prescriptions?

In today's environment, approximately 99 percent of all prescriptions paid for by third parties are processed electronically. The pharmacy enters vital patient and prescription information into the computer and transmits the information to a data center typically operated by a PBM. The PBM applies a variety of criteria in evaluating the prescription submitted, including drug-to-drug interaction review, duplicate therapy review, refill-too-soon analysis, and appropriate-dose review. Information is transmitted back to the pharmacy that allows the pharmacist to fill the prescription or that informs the pharmacist of a potential conflict.

Q 16:58 What is point of dispensing?

Point of dispensing allows doctors to dispense certain drugs from their offices. The drugs dispensed are the most frequently prescribed medications that can be conveniently stocked.

Typically, a computer provides the physician access to a variety of information, allowing the doctor to check for allergies, duplicate therapies, and drug interactions, while verifying that the product is on the formulary.

Q 16:59 Can PBM enrollees go anywhere to have their prescriptions filled?

No. To receive coverage, employees participating in a PBM typically must have their prescriptions filled by a network pharmacy, except in emergencies. Pharmacies join networks and provide services at reduced rates in exchange for volume business. It is up to the PBM to design a network that meets the needs of enrollees and is convenient and acceptable. A tight network of pharmacy providers allows PBMs to control costs and quality effectively.

Q 16:60 Can any size of company participate in a PBM?

Almost any size company can participate in a PBM plan. Until recently, only large self-funded companies, HMOs, and trust funds had the number of members that PBMs needed to negotiate discounts and develop appropriate programs; however, with the growth of coalitions, companies with fewer than 500, 100, or even 50 employees can usually find a way to enjoy the benefits of a PBM.

Q 16:61 Besides lower costs, how can the quality of a PBM be measured?

In addition to cost savings, plan sponsors should work with their PBM to develop specific, attainable goals for prescription drug plans. An example of a goal is a reduction in the utilization of anti-inflammatory medications (such as Motrin or Naprosyn) and the increased use of therapeutically equivalent over-the-counter medications. An increased focus on enrollee educational programs such as exercise and smoking cessation, which can help diminish dependence on prescription drugs, may be another goal. Employers and other health plan sponsors should become actively involved in all elements of the pharmacy benefit to ensure optimal results.

Q 16:62 Are PBM satisfaction rates a valid way to measure the quality of services offered by a PBM?

Surveys of satisfaction rates can be quite subjective. The results can depend on variables such as wording of questions, recent changes in benefits design, and how often prescription benefits are used. For example, a 1995 study conducted by CareData Reports, Inc., a managed care information company, reported that 70 percent of 10,272 employees at 81 companies in 5 regions nationwide were "extremely" or "very satisfied" with their prescription drug benefits. A similar study, also published by CareData Reports, reported, however, that seniors in Medicare risk programs had a much higher satisfaction rate. These seniors, who used their prescription benefit much more often than the consumer population, were "extremely" or "very satisfied" with their prescription benefit 85 percent of the time. This is not to say that plan sponsors should not expect their

PBMs to provide customer satisfaction surveys as a measure of quality service; however, it may be best to develop customized questionnaires specifically tailored to the needs of the plan sponsor and to update them periodically as the plan matures. In most cases, satisfaction rates increase as enrollees become familiar with the parameters of their plan. If the satisfaction rates do not rise, benefit administrators should discuss ways to improve the level of satisfaction with the benefit with their PBMs.

Prescription Drug Plans

Q 16:63 What is the typical cost of prescription drug coverage?

Prescription drugs typically account for approximately 10 percent of major medical plan costs, but are increasing at higher rates than other components—15.6 percent from 1997 to 1998, according to a survey by Mercer/Foster Higgins. Annual drug costs per person averaged from $330 to $376. According to a 1997 survey by The Segal Co., the average annual per-employee cost of drug claims in 1997 was projected to be $430, a 17.5 percent increase over 1996. According to a survey by Express Scripts/Value Rx, drug usage grew 4.5 percent in 1997 to 7.33 prescriptions per member per year.

Q 16:64 Are all prescription drugs covered under health care plans?

Generally, only prescription drugs that treat an illness or injury are covered, subject to applicable deductibles and coinsurance. Many plans do not cover contraceptive prescription drugs, for example, or nicotine chewing gum prescribed for smokers who are trying to quit.

Q 16:65 Will some plans cover contraceptive prescription drugs?

Yes. In fact, most prescription drug plans offer plans "with or without contraceptives."

Q 16:66 Why would an employer have a separate prescription drug plan?

There are a number of reasons for having separate plans:

1. Employees may not realize that their medical plan covers medications.
2. High deductibles may preclude reimbursement for medication because many people do not meet the deductible.
3. The use of a card eliminates claim forms.
4. Year-end claim submission is reduced, which facilitates processing by the insurer.

Q 16:67 Why would an employer avoid a free-standing drug plan in favor of covering medication under a major medical or comprehensive health plan?

Quite simply, a free-standing plan encourages greater utilization of the benefit. At a time when cost management is so important, emphasis is on covering long-term care, catastrophic illness, and other big-ticket items rather than budgetable items such as medications. Moreover, abuse of the benefit as well as overutilization has occurred under the card approach to prescription drugs.

Q 16:68 Who offers drug plans?

Prescription medication plans originate through many sources, including commercial insurance carriers, Blue Cross/Blue Shield plans, trust funds, HMOs, and, in some instances self-funded employers or other organizations.

Q 16:69 What are the largest PBMs?

According to *Managed Health Care,* the following organizations are the largest PBMs:

Organization	Covered Lives
PCS Health Systems	56,000,000
Merck-Medco Managed Care	51,000,000
Express Scripts	47,000,000
Advance Paradigm	27,000,000
Argus Health Systems	20,000,000
WellPoint Pharmacy Management	18,000,000
Eckerd Health Services	15,000,000
Aetna US Healthcare	10,000,000
First Health Services	8,000,000
National Prescription Administrators	7,000,000

Q 16:70 Is a flat copayment more common than coinsurance for prescription drugs?

Yes. According to the Pharmacy Benefit Management Institute's 1996 Prescription Drug Benefit Cost and Plan Design Survey Report, 76 percent of respondents had a flat copayment and 32 percent have coinsurance. Coinsurance is down from 36 percent in 1995. Of those that have coinsurance, 70 percent have a member share of 20 percent. Of all respondents, 66 percent have a lower copay for generic drugs, with $5 being the most frequent difference. The survey found that 90 percent of mail-order plans have copayments.

According to the 1997 Mercer/Foster Higgins survey, fewer than 10 percent of card plans require a deductible and over 90 percent require a copayment. In traditional indemnity plans, 19 percent require a deductible and 79 percent require a copayment.

Q 16:71 What are average prescription drug copays?

According to data released by the Pharmacy Benefit Management Institute, the average brand-name copay in 1997 was $10.33 and the average copay for a generic drug was $5.70. According to the 1998 Mercer/Foster Higgins survey, the median copayment is $5 for generic drugs and $10 for brand-name drugs.

Q 16:72 What is a three-tier copay?

A three-tier copay has the lowest copays for generic drugs and the highest copay for off-formulary products, with on-formulary brand-name drugs in the middle.

Chapter 17

Self-Funding

Since the 1980s, more employers have realized the enormous potential of self-funding their benefit plans. By self-funding, many businesses can create plans that fit employees' needs better than traditional insurance plans can while helping to reduce health benefit costs for employers and for workers. Self-funding is not, however, for every company.

Introduction	17-2
Reasons for Self-Funding	17-4
Decision to Self-Fund	17-10
Administration	17-13
The Marketplace	17-17
Effect of Self-Funding on Regulations	17-24
Stop-Loss Insurance	17-28
Voluntary Employees' Beneficiary Associations	17-37

Introduction

Q 17:1 What is self-funding?

Self-funding is the self-retention of risk in lieu of transferring the risk to a third party, such as a traditional insurer.

Q 17:2 How long has self-funding been in existence?

Self-funding has existed ever since "risk" has existed. Virtually all employers (and individuals) are in fact self-funded for at least those risks that are too costly to insure or excluded under traditional insurance contracts. Thus, the practice of self-funding, also called self-insurance, is older than the traditional insurance industry itself. Perhaps that is one reason self-funding is the funding vehicle of choice in risk assumption.

Q 17:3 What types of employers self-fund health insurance?

Thirty years ago, almost all health insurance was offered through fully insured health plans. But today, many U.S. employees are covered by self-funded plans. The Employee Benefit Research Institute estimates that 48 million workers (39 percent of covered workers) were covered by fully or partially self-funded plans sponsored by nongovernmental employers. This is the same as in 1995, despite the shift to managed care plans, where self-funding is less common. Self-funding is increasing, however, in managed care plans. A survey by Mercer/Foster Higgins of employers with at least 500 employees found that 70 percent of preferred provider organizations (PPOs) were self-funded in 1999, down from 73 percent in 1998. The survey also found that 50 percent of point-of-service plans were self-funded in 1999, down from 55 percent in 1998. The same survey found that 10 percent of health maintenance organizations (HMOs) were self-funded in 1999, the same as in 1998. Indemnity plan self-funding increased to 72 percent in 1999 from 68 percent in 1998.

Among the employers that self-fund are most of the Fortune 500 companies, many state governments, and the federal government. Virtually all employers, regardless of size, can participate in some form of self-funding. Self-funding is commonplace for employers with more than 1,000 employees and is popular among employers with fewer than 500 employees. The greatest percentage growth in self-funding is among employers with fewer than 100 workers.

Q 17:4 What is a fully insured health plan?

Unlike self-funding, a fully insured health plan is one in which the employer pays a premium to an insurer for employee health coverage. The insurance premium is due in advance of the coverage and is actuarially projected to cover anticipated claim costs and the insurer's overhead, commissions, reserves, various risk charges, and taxes. In exchange for the premium, the insurer assumes the risk of providing health coverage and performs various tasks such as printing employee booklets.

Q 17:5 What law makes self-funding possible?

The Employee Retirement Income Security Act (ERISA) of 1974 established the right of ERISA plans to fund risk without the need to purchase traditional insurance. Because ERISA exempts self-funded plans from ambiguous and often contradictory state laws, it creates a uniformity of law that helps employers—particularly multi-state employers—to reduce administrative expenses. ERISA also made it clear that employers that self-fund ERISA plans are not in the business of insurance; therefore, state laws regulating insurance do not apply to ERISA plans. Other forms of self-funding, such as workers' compensation, are regulated at the state level and, in some cases, a combination of state and federal laws apply.

Q 17:6 What laws govern self-funded plans?

Depending on an employer's line of business and size, the federal laws applicable to health plans are ERISA, the Consolidated Omnibus Budget Reconciliation Act (COBRA), the Americans with Disabilities Act, the Pregnancy Discrimination Act, the Age Discrimination in Employment Act, the Civil Rights Act, the Family and Medical Leave Act, the Health Insurance Portability and Accountability Act, the Newborns and Mothers Health Protection Act, the Mental Health Parity Act, the Women's Health and Cancer Rights Act, and, various budget reconciliation acts, such as the Tax Equity and Fiscal Responsibility Act, the Deficit Reduction Act, and the Economic Recovery Tax Act.

Q 17:7   Why do employers self-fund health insurance?

Employers self-fund to create plans that fit employees' needs better than traditional insurance, Blue Cross/Blue Shield (the Blues), or HMOs. Self-funding helps to reduce health benefit costs for employers and workers. In addition, managing health plans directly enables employers to be more responsive to employee health care needs, further reducing costs; therefore, the primary reason employers self-fund is to control the management and financing of their health insurance programs.

Reasons for Self-Funding

Q 17:8   Why do employers consider self-funding?

Employers invest millions of dollars each year in insured employee benefit plans. To control rising costs, employers are examining ways to economize and improve cash flow without sacrificing coverage. Budget considerations, bargaining agreements, geography, and plan design each have an effect on the way a health plan is funded. Many employers with as few as 25 employees and a stable benefit history believe the best alternative is self-funding.

Because employer-provided health care costs have risen dramatically over the past 25 years, self-funding could be an attractive method of paying for employee benefits at significantly lower cost, particularly for an employer facing large health plan premium increases.

Q 17:9   What other reasons do employers have for self-funding?

Health care costs constitute an increasing proportion of total corporate budgets, and these costs often exceed companies' net earnings; therefore, many employers have begun to view the funding of their medical expense benefits as a corporate financing tool rather than simply as an insurance arrangement. For many businesses, decision-making responsibilities pertaining to employee benefit plan funding choices, including insurer selection, have moved from the personnel and human resource divisions to risk management and corporate finance departments. In recent years, companies have examined the feasibility of a wide range of alternative risk-financing arrangements in an attempt to curtail double-digit increases in medical plan costs. Self-funding has proved to be a valuable financing alternative.

Q 17:10 What should an employer consider in deciding to self-fund?

The decision to self-fund should be made after considering both financial and nonfinancial implications. Large increases in health premiums could be a function of plan design or administration as well as funding. If self-funding is feasible, long-range planning and decisions about plan design, administration, investment of funds, and plan documentation should be made before the employer takes over the plan's funding.

Insurance companies charge money to assume risk; the more risk they assume, the more they charge. Because there are real savings in self-funding, employers that can manage their own risks should consider this option.

Q 17:11 What is a self-funded health plan?

A self-funded (or self-insured) health plan is one in which the employer assumes some or all of the risk for providing health care benefits to employees. The employer takes control of the assets of the plan, invests them to the employer's advantage, and eliminates insurer charges. The employer can redesign the plan completely. When deciding to self-fund its health plan or plans, employers usually review their insurer's quality of administration. If the employer is not satisfied, this is the time to change administrators.

Q 17:12 Does a distinction exist between self-funding and self-insurance?

An important terminology issue relates to the question of whether "self-funding" and "self-insurance" constitute a single approach to risk financing and whether these terms should be used interchangeably. In the marketplace, these terms are routinely substituted one for another; however, purists generally present a case that important differences exist between self-funding and self-insurance. Their argument is based on the assumption that ". . . true self-insurance differs significantly from mere failure to buy insurance. A self-insurer establishes a scheme for handling risk that is fundamentally the same as insurance," according to James L. Athearn, S. Travis Pritchett, and Joan T. Schmit in *Risk and Insurance.* [West Publishing Co, St Paul, MN, 1989].

Q 17:13 How does self-funding work?

The four basic steps to self-funding are:

1. *The employer decides on a plan of employee benefits with the help of an insurance agent or broker, employee benefit consultant, or a third-party administrator (TPA).* This plan is often similar to the plan currently provided on an insured basis.

2. *Stop-loss insurance is arranged to protect the plan against extreme losses.* The amount of risk to be insured will be a function of the employer's size, the nature of the business, location, plan of benefits, financial resources, prior experience, and tolerance for risk.

3. *A plan document is prepared.* The plan document contains all the provisions of the plan, including those regarding eligibility, coverage, and termination. Typically, a TPA assists an employer in preparing employee benefit descriptions, identification cards, and other materials necessary to administer the plan and for the employers' legal counsel to review.

4. *The TPA manages the plan on behalf of the employer.* Operating the plan includes advising the employer of the amount of funds required to be on deposit so claims can be paid, adjudicating claims, preparing special claims reports and other required data

for the plan and the stop-loss insurer, and assisting in the preparation of any required government reports. The TPA also bills and collects any premiums and other administrative fees for the plan.

Q 17:14 What are the advantages of self-funding?

Employers often find the following advantages when operating self-funded programs. Keep in mind that these benefits overlap, but they all may affect any employer:

1. *Elimination of most premium tax.* With a self-funded plan, an employer does not pay state premium taxes, which usually range from 2 percent to 3 percent of the monthly insurance premium. Every state taxes insurers on the premiums they collect. In turn, insurers pass these costs to employers. In a self-funded plan, there's no insurer, no premiums, and no state jurisdiction; therefore, there are no premium taxes to pay, according to a decision of the U.S. Supreme Court. In some jurisdictions, employers do pay a premium tax on stop-loss insurance.

2. *Improved cash flow.* An employer does not have to pre-pay coverage, thereby improving cash flow. Insurance premiums are due in advance. Self-funded plans pay claims as they are presented to the claims administrator, usually 60 to 90 days after medical services are received; therefore, during the first year of self-funding, an employer pays for only nine to ten months of claims.

3. *Lower cost of operation, no risk charges, commissions, or retention charges to insurers.* Employers frequently find that administrative costs for self-funded programs through TPAs are lower than those charged by their previous insurer. An insurer charges several fees to insure and to administer a health plan. Many of these, such as booklet printing costs or actuarial fees, must be paid no matter how the plan is funded or who administers it. But some charges, such as risk and retention charges and costs for overhead and profit, are not applicable to self-funded plans. Insurers charge for an array of services that an employer may

17-7

not need. By self-funding, an employer effectively unbundles administrative fees and only pays for the desired services.

4. *Effective claim processing.* The TPA's success depends on providing accurate, controlled claim processing for each employer.

5. *Cost and utilization controls.* The TPA may audit hospital bills and provide access to a preferred provider organization, among other programs offered through a variety of sources, such as a second surgical opinion program, outpatient surgery, and large case management. Such programs allow employers to select the best services available, rather than having to use only an insurer's in-house programs.

6. *Employer control over health plan reserves.* The employer retains control over its health plan reserves, enabling it to maximize interest income. When the employer decides to self-fund and all claims have been paid under the former insurance contract, the employer recaptures any reserves that are left (unless the group is prospectively rated—see Chapter 5). Usually the employer then invests this money and receives the interest income. Insurers traditionally credit an employer much less than the actual interest income received from the employer's reserves. The difference between what the insurer credits an employer and what that employer can earn with its own investments is another advantage of self-funding.

7. *Fewer regulations.* Insurers are subject to state regulation, but self-funded plans are subject only to federal regulation. As a result, employers have almost total control over plan design. This preemption of state regulation saves the most money in self-funding, more than is saved in having no premium taxes, no insurer risk and retention charges, or commissions. Most states have numerous laws requiring myriad coverages for insurance company plans. A self-funded plan does not have to comply with these state laws; therefore, an employer can customize its health plan design by focusing on employee needs and on cost savings. For example, if a state mandates that hair transplants must be a covered expense and cannot have a maximum lower than $50,000 a year, then every fully insured plan written in that state must abide by this law. A self-funded plan does not have to abide by this law, and if an employer wanted a lower annual maximum, it could have one.

Q 17:15   Have any challenges to these benefits been launched?

Yes. The California Board of Equalization and General Motors went to court to determine if premium tax was due on the portion of a minimum premium plan that covers the claim fund. The board won. There was some concern that this concept might spread from minimum premium plans to self-funded plans if the employer has purchased stop-loss coverage, but this has not happened. The tax is payable by the insurer (not the group directly), so some insurers add wording in their policies to protect against having to pay back taxes.

Q 17:16   What other advantages are available with self-funding?

In addition to the advantages cited previously, an employer can contract with the managed care system that saves the plan the most money, not just the managed care system owned by the insurer. Also, a self-funded employer pays only for benefits based on its employees' histories, not on someone else's employees, as is common when insurers use a community rating. In all but the largest of health plans, an insurer pools the experience of its clients; therefore, an employer often pays for the poor histories of other employee populations. In self-funding, each employer pays only for its own employees' benefits.

Q 17:17   What are the benefits of self-funding to employees?

Employers tailor the benefit program to meet the needs of their employees, maximizing benefits for workers. Claim payment is speedier, reporting procedures are easier, employees benefit from cost efficiency, better service, and broader benefits. Employees also enjoy less cost when the cost to fund the plan is shared by the employer and employee.

Q 17:18   What are the disadvantages of self-funding?

Self-funding is not appropriate for every employer. To gain the advantages of self-funding, the employer must be willing to exercise discipline over eligibility for benefits, over the actual payment of claims, and in incurring expenses. Even then, self-funding may not reduce costs every year—or at all. In addition, the employer must be willing to deal with these potential disadvantages:

1. *Risk assumption.* The employer assumes the risk between the level of normally anticipated claims and the level of stop-loss coverage.
2. *Provision of services.* The employer must provide the services the insurer normally provides. This is generally accomplished by contracting with a TPA.
3. *Asset exposure.* The employer's assets are exposed to any liability created by legal action against the self-funded plan. While specific and aggregate stop-loss protection limits maximum employer liability, some risk is not transferred to the stop-loss insurer (see Qs 17:56, 17:58, and 17:62–17:64). The employer must be willing to trade the complete security (and associated cost) of a fully insured plan for the possibility that actual cost will exceed what the fully insured plan would have cost.

Decision to Self-Fund

Q 17:19 Is self-funding for all companies?

No. The major difference between an insured plan and a self-funded one is that in self-funding the employer assumes the risk for the claims and these claims should be somewhat predictable; therefore, if the employer is small, self-funding is not recommended. Although there are companies as small as 25 employees that do successfully self-fund their health plans, an employer this size should seek expert consulting advice as to the viability of self-funding. Also, if the work force is volatile, making future claims difficult to predict, self-funding may not be an option. The volatility of future claims can be smoothed out to a great extent by the purchase of excess-risk (stop-loss) coverage.

Q 17:20 Is self-funding primarily for large companies?

Historically, larger employers have self-funded, while smaller employers were relegated to traditional insurance coverage; however, in recent years, many smaller employers have learned that they can enjoy the benefits of self-funding. Many of these arrangements are sponsored by national trade and professional associations.

Q 17:21 What criteria should a small employer meet if considering self-funding?

Before committing to self-funding, any employer should consult with a benefits expert, such as a third-party administrator or employee benefit consultant. These experts can assist the employer in determining the level of liability that the employer can fund without undue hardship on cash flow. In addition, any employer considering self-funding should conduct a comprehensive cash flow analysis and compare all costs associated with self-funding and traditional insurance costs.

Q 17:22 Can self-funding work for any small employer?

Yes, it can, provided the employer is not a partnership.

Q 17:23 Why would self-funding not work for a partnership?

Current law allows employees to receive medical benefits tax free. Partners are not employees; therefore, they usually pay their own medical premium using after-tax dollars. This allows them also to receive medical benefits tax free; however, this is true only if the benefits are provided by a third-party insurer. The employer (or partnership) acting as an "insurance company" is not a third party and so cannot provide the tax-free medical coverage to partners even if they pay the premium using after-tax dollars. Because they would be taxed on the benefits, self-funding for a partnership would lose significant appeal.

Q 17:24 What should an employer that self-funds expect in the first year?

Many employers that self-fund find the following:

1. Self-funding results in a large first-year savings through the lack of premium taxes and various insurer charges, and a first-year claims lag.
2. Employers can, and should, save considerable money through new plan designs that take advantage of the latest cost containment strategies.
3. Self-funding does not affect the plan from the employees' standpoint. There does not have to be any noticeable change in the plan unless the employer so wishes.
4. The employer receives interest from reserves.
5. Every aspect of plan administration becomes subject to competitive market pricing, thereby saving money on such items as claims administration and the printing of the summary plan descriptions.
6. Stop-loss coverage is available to insure the employer against unforeseen adverse claims experience.

Q 17:25 What is stop-loss coverage?

Stop-loss (also known as excess-risk) coverage is insurance sold to employers that offer self-funded health plans to guard against unacceptable losses. The two types of stop-loss coverage are:

1. Specific coverage that insures against a single catastrophic claim that exceeds a dollar limit chosen by the employer and agreed to by the stop-loss insurer. For example, specific coverage would come into play if one covered participant were in a catastrophic accident and had claims that exceeded the agreed-upon dollar limit. In this case, the specific coverage would reimburse the employer for the covered expenses beyond that dollar limit.
2. Aggregate coverage that insures against the total of all claims paid during a specified period—but not covered by the specific coverage—in excess of the dollar limit chosen by the employer and agreed to by the stop-loss insurer. If all the claims payable exceed the agreed-upon dollar limit, aggregate coverage would reimburse the employer for the excess. Stop-loss coverage protects the employer against unforeseen catastrophic claims

that would cost more than is budgeted in the plan and place undue financial burdens on the employer.

Q 17:26 Does an employer that self-funds need to redesign its existing health plan?

Not at all. Self-funding does not require a change in existing group coverage. Some employers have become comfortable with certain plan designs and decide to leave the plan as is for at least the first year of self-funding. Others find that the existing plan is needlessly expensive because of an overly generous design or onerous administrative requirements. Employers redesign these plans to meet employees' needs, to save money, and to simplify their plans.

Q 17:27 How does self-funding affect payroll deductions for health care?

Any payments made by employees for their coverage or coverage for their dependents are still handled through the employer's payroll department; however, instead of being sent to the insurer as premium payments, they are put in a tax-free trust controlled by the employer.

Q 17:28 Does self-funding affect group term life insurance coverages?

No. Life insurance and other benefit plans are separate from health plan benefits and as such would be unaffected.

Administration

Q 17:29 What organization takes the place of the insurer as administrator of the plan?

A self-funded employer can administer the plan itself, convert the present "insured" arrangement to an administrative services only (ASO) arrangement with its present insurer, or have an independent TPA administer the plan. TPAs are specialized administration compa-

Q 17:30   **Health Insurance Answer Book**

nies that have come into being because of the growth of self-funding over the past 25 years.

Few employers have the resources to self-administer; therefore, employers typically contract with TPAs or contract with an insurer that offers ASO services.

Q 17:30   Are there advantages in using a TPA versus an ASO arrangement?

The only business of a TPA is the administration of benefit plans. TPAs do not insure. They deal only with administration of services. TPAs are entrepreneurial in nature, responding to each client's needs individually.

In contrast, the primary business of insurers is insurance. Insurers that offer ASO contracts may not provide the level of flexibility desired; however, insurers generally have more resources, e.g., legal, medical, and number of examiners. Employers should also consider price, service, and staffing levels. (For more information on TPAs, see Chapter 18, *Third-Party Administration*.)

Q 17:31   What services do TPAs and ASOs offer?

Services offered by TPAs and ASOs include the following:

- Plan design consulting
- Cafeteria plan design
- Contracting for stop-loss coverage
- Claims administration
- Contracting with managed care and utilization review companies
- Assistance in completing government forms, such as Form 5500
- Assistance in writing and printing summary plan description booklets and plan documents for counsel review
- Employee communications programs
- COBRA compliance assistance
- Client reports
- Record keeping

Q 17:32   How are self-funded plans classified?

Possibly the most fundamental regulatory issue pertaining to self-funding of medical expense plans—one that is often overlooked—is the determination of what actually constitutes a self-funded plan. Should self-funding be defined broadly to include, for example, experience-rated group insurance contracts and various insurer offerings designed to enhance corporate cash flow? Or should the definition of self-funding be limited to include only those risk financing approaches in which the employer is ultimately (and completely) responsible for the payment of claims, where any excess insurance simply reduces an employer's overall financial risk?

In classifying risk financing arrangements as either insured plans or self-funded plans, it is clear that the key issue is not what entity actually performs the claims payment function. Rather, the distinguishing factor should be which entity bears the ultimate financial responsibility for the payment of eligible claims. If the employer is obligated to pay all promised plan benefits, then the plan is self-funded regardless of the existence of (excess) insurance purchased by the employer to reduce the company's financial risk. In contrast, if a commercial insurer, in exchange for a premium paid by the employer, assumes full responsibility for the payment of plan benefits, then the plan should be classified as an insured plan despite the existence of modifications to the group insurance contract that permit employers to enhance their cash flow positions.

Consistent with these views, ASO contracts issued by insurers and similar arrangements administered by TPAs or through employer self-administration, where the employer retains full liability for the ultimate payment of plan benefits, are classified as self-funded plans. Similarly, premium-delay and reserve-reducing agreements, experience-rated and retrospective-premium agreements, and minimum-premium (and similar) arrangements are classified as insured plans. An important feature common to all of these approaches is that a commercial insurer is ultimately responsible for the payment of plan benefits and must establish reserves for claims that have been incurred but not reported, called run-out claims. Further, under all of these arrangements, the insurer is ultimately responsible for the funding of claims incurred during the period covered by the contract, even though the plan sponsor becomes bankrupt and is unable to meet its financial commitment to the insurer (including any unremitted premiums under a conventional contract and any outstanding bank account liability under a minimum premium arrangement).

Q 17:33   What are the existing approaches to financing employer medical expense plans?

A continuum of alternative risk financing arrangements exists for funding employer-sponsored medical expense plans. At one end of the spectrum is the conventional, fully insured plan under which annual employer costs are fixed at an amount equal to the sum of the monthly billed insurance premiums. At the other end is the fully self-funded plan in which the employer bears the ultimate financial responsibility for the payment of all plan benefits, and in which annual employer costs are likely to vary considerably from year to year. In moving along the continuum from no risk and fully insured to full risk and fully self-funded, employers are presented with many risk financing choices, including opportunities to participate in favorable plan experience and to improve corporate cash flow.

Q 17:34   What are the distinguishing characteristics of a conventional, fully insured plan?

A conventional, fully insured group medical expense plan possesses a number of distinguishing characteristics. Foremost among them is that the employer's total funding costs are a predetermined, fixed amount per employee (and family unit) for the period of the insurer's premium rate guarantee (usually either 6 or 12 months). Regardless of actual claim experience during the plan year, the employer's total costs equal the paid premiums for the year. Because the financial responsibility for claim payments is transferred entirely to the insurer, an employer's actual costs for a given plan year are unaffected by either favorable or unfavorable claims experience. As part of the fully insured arrangement, employers with favorable experience, through the loss-spreading mechanism of insurance, subsidize employers with unfavorable claim experience. Historically, large employers whose health claim experience was consistently better than average had a significant financial incentive to enter into an alternative arrangement whereby they assumed some, or all, of the risk associated with the financing of medical plan benefits.

The Marketplace

Q 17:35   How have traditional insurers modified their conventional products to meet employer demand for self-funding?

Many employers have entered into modified insurance arrangements, or established self-funded plans, in an attempt to control their medical plan costs. In response, commercial insurers and the Blues have developed a number of contractual modifications to their conventional group contracts to provide employers with a wider range of risk financing options.

Several modifications may be viewed simply as constituting minor changes to the conventional approach, providing employers with the opportunity to enhance their corporate cash flow without altering the basic risk-sharing agreement. Examples include the following:

- Agreements that allow 60- or 90-day premium delays
- Incurred-but-not-reported (IBNR) reserve reduction arrangements
- Extended plan year accounting

Q 17:36   What are experience-rated plans?

An amendment commonly added to group medical expense insurance contracts permits employers to share in any favorable claim experience of the plan. Called experience-rated contracts, these plans allow an employer to receive a year-end refund if the actual claim experience is below the level assumed in the premium calculation. On the other hand, if claim experience is unfavorable, the insurance (risk transfer) feature limits the employer's maximum cost for the plan year to the paid premium. This adverse experience (carryover) will be used, however, to determine premiums for the subsequent policy period, resulting in higher premiums.

A potential disadvantage to employers is that experience-rate refunds are determined under an insurer-controlled formula. In addition, payment of any refunds is deferred until after the close of the plan year, at which time a final accounting is undertaken by the insurer. Experience-rated contracts have played an important role in the evolution of alternative approaches to the risk financing of medical expense plans. These arrangements provided many employers that currently self-fund their medical expense plans with their first exposure to what may be viewed as a limited version of risk retention.

Q 17:37 How do retrospective-rating agreements work?

Similar in approach to experience-rated contracts, retrospective-rating agreements reduce an employer's initial billed premium by some percentage, such as 10 percent, in return for a contractual promise requiring the employer to remit this additional amount at year-end if incurred claims, plus the insurer's retention, exceed the paid premium. For regulatory purposes, experience-rating and retrospective-rating agreements are deemed to be insurance contracts, primarily because the insurer is ultimately responsible for the payment of plan benefits to covered employees and their beneficiaries.

Q 17:38 What is a minimum-premium product?

Minimum premium is a generic name applied to risk financing approaches under which only a modest premium (possibly 8 percent to 10 percent of the standard premium) is paid to the insurer. In return, the insurer performs the claim administration function and bears the ultimate financial responsibility for the payment of eligible claims. Minimum-premium plans are often viewed by employers (and others) as self-funded, or partially self-funded approaches to risk financing; however, traditional group insurance contracts are generally used in these arrangements, with the minimum-premium agreement simply attached as an amendment, or a rider, to the underlying group insurance contract. Further, as is the case with fully insured, experience-rated, and retrospective-rating contracts, state insurance regulation requires that insurers offering minimum premium arrangements establish IBNR reserves on their balance sheets to pay for claims after contract termination.

The most notable feature of a minimum-premium plan is that a special bank account, established by the employer, is used to finance normal and expected levels of medical claim payments. The bulk of the required "premium" (typically 90 percent to 92 percent) is paid into this account. The remainder is paid to the insurer to cover administrative costs, profit, and a charge for assuming the risk of large losses. Claims can be paid directly by the insurer out of this account. More commonly, claims are paid from the insurer's own funds, and the insurer then exercises its contractual right to obtain reimbursement from the employer's bank account. If aggregate claims exceed the employer's bank account liability (to the insurer), the insurer is financially responsible for the payment of excess claims from its own funds. In addition, even if an employer defaults on its contractual obligation to the insurer with regard to funding the bank account, the insurer is still liable for the payment of promised plan benefits to covered participants.

Q 17:39 What approaches are used for self-funding?

Self-funded medical expense plans may be administered by commercial insurers, the Blues, TPAs, and employers themselves. Insurer involvement in self-funded approaches is generally through agreements commonly referred to as ASO contracts. Under these contracts, insurers are hired by employers essentially to perform the claim administration function and to provide actuarial services, advice with regard to plan design, and cost-containment features, claim analysis and reporting, and selected other administrative services.

The administration of a large number of self-funded plans is performed by TPAs. These TPAs may be independently owned, or they may be subsidiaries of commercial insurers (including the Blues). The types of services performed by TPAs on behalf of self-funded plans are similar to those performed by commercial insurers; however, any stop-loss coverage or conversion policies must be contracted for separately, because TPAs are not licensed insurers.

Q 17:40 Do any employers administer their own claims?

A number of large employers have elected to administer, in-house, their medical expense plans. Employees are hired and trained to perform the claim administration function. Selected administrative services, such as actuarial and cost containment, may be purchased from outside vendors.

Q 17:41 Is a separate trust required when employers self-fund the medical expense benefits?

Unlike the regulatory environment surrounding qualified pension plans, a separate trust is not required when employers self-fund their medical expense benefits, except when employee funds are collected (unless employees make pre-tax contributions to the plan); however, Section 501(c)(9) trusts are often an integral part of a self-funded plan. The primary advantage of Section 501(c)(9) trusts is that they permit employers to take a current tax deduction for contributions to trust reserves up to maximums prescribed by federal tax law. These trusts are generally used in conjunction with a voluntary employees' beneficiary association and, as such, must meet several regulatory requirements.

Q 17:42 What is the primary characteristic of a self-funded plan?

Whether an employer selects an ASO contract, third-party administration, or in-house administration, the primary characteristic of all self-funded plans is that the employer bears the ultimate financial responsibility for payment of covered medical benefits on behalf of plan participants and beneficiaries.

Q 17:43 Are covered employees affected by an employer's decision to self-fund?

Generally, covered employees and their dependents are unaffected by an employer's decision to self-fund unless the employer also decides to alter the plan's benefit structure, including a change in the level at which "reasonable and customary" determinations of eligible expenses are made. Employees are not legal parties to either group insurance contracts or self-funding arrangements; in most instances, they are unaware of the risk financing approach actually used by the employer in funding the medical expense benefit plan. Of course, employers must inform their employees of the coverage and benefit provisions of the medical expense plan and the process by which eligible claims are submitted for payment, as well as the funding mechanism.

Q 17:44 How does self-funding help an employer avoid cost shifting?

Under conventional, fully insured arrangements, the medical expense claims of a specific employer are pooled with the claims of other similar groups insured by the same insurer. To the extent that one or more insured employers consistently have worse claim experience, on average, these excess costs are shifted to, and spread among, the other employers in the pool. Employers that routinely enjoy better-than-average claim experience will likely object to this cost shifting over time. Many employers are also concerned about possible cost shifting that might arise to indemnity plans because of cost reductions that PPOs and HMOs have negotiated with medical care providers. In addition, under an experience-rated insured plan, losses (deficits) incurred by the insurer when total claims and expenses for the plan exceed the paid premium are usually carried forward into the next year, either in the form of higher insurance premiums or higher claim charges in the experience rating formula. Thus, over time, it can be argued that employers essentially "pay their own claims" under experience-rated insured plans. When claim amounts are such that large deficits are carried forward into the next contract year, employers are provided with an incentive to either switch insurers or to change to a self-funded plan.

Q 17:45 How does self-funding help an employer get a reduction in risk financing costs?

A primary objective among employers that self-fund is to retain a greater amount of risk in the financing of their employee benefit programs. In return, employers expect a corresponding reduction in long-term financing costs of the benefit programs because the risk charges otherwise assessed by the insuring organization would be eliminated.

Q 17:46 How does self-funding help an employer get more choices in claim administration?

Insured medical expense plans, by definition, involve contracts underwritten by commercial insurers and Blues plans. Under these contracts, the insurer assumes both the transfer of financial risk associated with funding the promised benefits and the responsibility for claim administration and other plan-related services; however, in self-funded plans, the risk-bearing function and the claim administration function typically are separated. The unbundling of the risk component from the service component provides employers with a wider range of options from which to select an entity to provide claim administration services on behalf of the employee benefit plan. The self-funding employer can still select a commercial insurer (including a Blues plan) to perform the necessary claim administration functions, but the employer also can choose from hundreds of TPAs or it can employ salaried personnel to perform the claim administration activities.

This increased choice likely also results in a corresponding increase in the level of competition in this market, thereby offering the possibility of lower overall plan administration costs to the employer. A 1999 survey by Mercer/Foster Higgins of New York showed that 38 percent of responding employers used TPAs for traditional indemnity plans (up from 36 percent in 1998); 57 percent used commercial insurers, including Blue Cross/Blue Shield plans, to administer their self-funded plans (unchanged from 1998).

The same survey found that 44 percent of PPOs were administered by TPAs, while 49 percent were administered by commercial insurance carriers or Blue Cross/Blue Shield plans. Seven percent of employers self-administer their PPO plan.

Q 17:47 What effect does greater control over claim administration have?

Greater control over claim administration means greater control over medical expense costs. The separation of the risk-bearing and claim administration functions makes it possible for sponsoring employers to exert greater influence over claim payments. This objective is especially important in an environment in which health care costs are considered out of control. Self-administration, or the hiring of a TPA, usually provides self-funding employers with an opportunity to design their own claim administration system to provide customized claim reports. A criticism frequently leveled at commercial insurers is that they are relatively inflexible and often unwilling to modify their claim administration software programs to accommodate the special administrative and reporting needs of different employers. TPAs seem better positioned and more willing to offer customized claim administration and reporting activities.

Of course, self-administration provides employers with ultimate flexibility in the design of customized claim administration and reporting systems. The ability to administer medical expense plans in a way that is totally consistent with employer objectives, together with the capacity to analyze medical expense claims to identify areas of overutilization and other high-cost areas, allow employers to examine possible benefit changes under "what if" scenarios.

Q 17:48 How does self-funding affect cash flow?

As part of its total financial responsibility for claim payments, the self-funding employer retains all funds used to meet the claim obligations under the medical expense plan. As a result, the sponsoring company's cash flow position may be enhanced considerably. The extent that this improved cash flow leads to greater employer profits depends on the plan sponsor's ability to earn a rate of return on these funds that is higher than the interest amounts otherwise credited by an insurer in its premium calculations and experience rating formula.

This should be viewed cautiously in the case of trade- or professional association-sponsored plans. Because of larger pools of funds and a staff of investment specialists, insurers can generally earn greater gross rates of return than would be possible for association groups whose funds are more limited. An association group will not benefit from the improved cash flow under a self-funded plan unless the group can earn higher net returns than the net investment returns credited by insurers in their premium calculations and experience rating formula.

Improved cash flow to the plan sponsor can also be achieved through other risk-financing arrangements, including deferred premium and reserve reduction agreements, retrospective premium arrangements, and minimum premium (and similar) plans. To a large extent, employer interest in selecting a risk-financing arrangement that enhances the company's cash flow varies according to the level of market interest rates. This fact was clearly demonstrated in the late 1970s and early 1980s when interest rates spiked to unusually high levels. During this period, many employers shopped for alternative risk-financing arrangements that would yield higher cash flows.

Q 17:49 What is a stop-loss intermediary?

A stop-loss intermediary is a managing general agent, known in some states as a general agent. Many stop-loss carriers choose to market through intermediaries. Typically, the intermediary handles product development, marketing, underwriting, issuing policies, service, claim, and auditing. For all practical purposes, except for risk, the intermediary is the carrier.

Q 17:50 What is a producer-owned reinsurance company?

A producer-owned reinsurance company is a reinsurance company owned by an agent or broker. The insurance company accepting the business acts as a "front" and reinsures some or all of the risk with the producer-owned reinsurance company. Producer-owned reinsurance companies are usually based in Arizona, which has low capitalization requirements, or offshore in a lax regulatory environment.

Effect of Self-Funding on Regulations

Q 17:51 What is the effect of self-funding on premium taxes?

State legislatures generally assess a tax on insurance premiums collected within the state. Quite often, the state premium tax is in lieu of a corporate income tax. The premium tax is applied to life and non-life insurance premiums, and the tax on property-casualty premiums is frequently higher than that on life-health premiums. A typical state tax on life and health insurance premiums is 2 percent. Commonly, Blues policies are subject to a reduced premium tax, or they are exempt from premium taxation in light of their special treatment under separate enabling legislation enacted by the states. Because funds used to finance claim payments and administrative costs under fully self-funded plans are not "insurance premiums," these amounts are exempt from state premium taxation. Potentially, large employers that self-fund may save tens (or even hundreds) of thousands of dollars in premium taxes each year. To the extent that stop-loss insurance is purchased by a self-funding employer, premiums for this coverage are subject to state premium taxes.

Q 17:52 How does self-funding help employers with mandated benefit rules?

Under ERISA's preemption provision, self-funded health care plans are exempt from state-mandated benefit provisions that apply to group medical expense insurance contracts. Relieved of the constraints imposed by state mandates, self-funded employers can design their medical expense plans in ways that meet employee needs and overall corporate objectives.

Today, there are over 1,000 state-mandated benefit requirements, and every state has at least one mandated health insurance requirement. States may mandate that specific types of benefits be provided, such as coverage of newborns and treatment for alcoholism and mental and nervous disorders. Additionally, state mandates may specify that the charges of certain providers of medical services (such as chiropractors, psychologists, and optometrists) be eligible for reimbursement under the insurance plan.

Although many states mandate important and useful benefits to be included in an insured plan, other state-mandated benefits serve only special interest groups. In addition, historically, many large employers have routinely provided coverage for a majority of the mandated benefits under their medical expense plans, irrespective of whether the plans were insured or self-funded. Conventional wisdom suggests that, for the most part, only small employers are truly affected by these state mandates. For these companies it is frequently argued, however, that the collective costs of the various benefit mandates discourage small employers from offering medical expense insurance to their employees. In other instances, employers replace an insured program with a self-funded plan, thus avoiding the reach of the mandated benefit provisions.

One important study on the effect of state-mandated benefits concluded that state health insurance mandates:

1. Adversely affect total health care costs, particularly for small employers;
2. Do not apply equitably to all employers that provide medical expense coverage to their employees; and
3. Do not close the gaps in medical expense benefits for private or public employers.

Q 17:53 Does self-funding play a role in health plan revisions?

The right of self-funded plans to make revisions under ERISA has been upheld many times in the courts. In fact, in one case in 1995, *Curtiss-Wright Corp. v. Schoonejongen* [115 S Ct 1223], the U.S. Supreme Court affirmed the right of the plan sponsor to make revisions. Writing in the journal *Managing Employee Health Benefits* [Panel Publishers, New York, Summer 1995], Kenneth F. Phillips, president of Employee Communications Services, consultants in Natick, MA, said the case is instructive because—although the court affirmed the plan sponsor's right to revise the plan—the issue of how the revisions were made was sent back for a rehearing in a lower court. In this case, the U.S. Supreme Court overturned two lower-court decisions regarding medical plan termination for retirees. Phillips writes:

> In 1976, when Curtiss-Wright Corp., a defense contractor in Lyndhurst, NJ, established its health benefit plan, it included in its summary plan description (SPD) the statement that "the company reserves the right at any time and from time to time to modify or amend, in whole or in part, any or all of the

provisions of the plan." The SPD statement also reserved "the right to terminate the plan for any reason at any time." Such language is common in SPDs.

In 1983, the company modified the plan so that medical coverage for retirees and their dependents would end if the company closed a facility where the employees worked before retirement. This modification was included in an amended SPD distributed to all plan participants early in the year. Later that year, the company closed its plant in Wood-Ridge, NJ, and terminated the health benefits of the retired workers at that facility. Following the plant closing, 520 retirees filed suit to regain their medical benefits.

The case was filed in the U.S. District Court for the District of New Jersey, and, on appeal, was brought before the Court of Appeals for the Third Circuit, in Newark, NJ. Both the District Court and the Court of Appeals agreed that Curtiss-Wright's statement reserving the right to make revisions did not satisfy the requirements of ERISA section 402(b)(3), and therefore declared the amendment eliminating retiree benefits invalid. The District Court also awarded the retirees $2.6 million as compensation for the value of their lost medical benefits. The appeals court upheld this award.

On appeal, however, the U.S. Supreme Court unanimously agreed that the primary purpose of 402(b)(3) was only "to ensure that every plan has a workable amendment procedure." In making its ruling, however, the court also ruled that medical plan termination amendments could be voided if Curtiss-Wright did not follow its own corporate procedures when it terminated the plan in 1983. It sent this issue back to the Third Circuit Court for a decision. In its decision, the U.S. Supreme Court emphasized that, while this ruling generally gives benefit plan sponsors latitude in how they describe to workers their procedures for revising plans, employers also are obligated to follow specifically whatever internal administrative rules they have established. Employers that have language allowing them to revise their plans should carefully audit their by-laws and internal procedures to be sure that the delegation of authority to implement plan amendments is stated clearly and is consistent with generally accepted corporate law principles. Also, employers should determine that their by-laws and internal procedures are followed rigorously each time a plan is amended in any way.

Stop-Loss Insurance

Q 17:54 How does stop-loss coverage affect medical expense plans?

A common concern associated with self-funding of medical expense plans is the risk of catastrophic claims and the potential inability of the sponsoring employer to pay for such losses within a relatively short time. This problem is of special importance to small employers and other companies with limited capital. Stop-loss coverage is an attractive option for employers concerned about the risk of catastrophic claims but that wish to sponsor a plan that retains the essential elements and characteristics of self-funding.

Specific (or individual) stop-loss and aggregate stop-loss coverage are commonly purchased by employers to reduce the financial risk associated with the self-funding of their medical expense plans. In essence, stop-loss insurance covers the financial risk that the employer will have to pay out more claims, with respect to a given plan year, than had been anticipated. It is important to understand that stop-loss coverage insures employers against excess claims for which they are responsible according to the benefit provisions in the medical expense plan; stop-loss insurance does not insure employees (and their dependents) against large medical claims. Also note that stop-loss insurance makes payments only to the employer (or the plan), whereas a group medical expense insurance contract pays benefits directly to insured employees or to their health care providers.

The use of aggregate stop-loss insurance is limited to self-funded plans administered either in-house, by TPAs, or by insurers and the Blues under ASO contracts. In contrast, specific stop-loss insurance is commonly used in minimum premium (and similar) arrangements and self-funded plans.

Q 17:55 How does specific stop-loss coverage work?

The purchase of specific stop-loss insurance limits the employer's financial risk that arises from unusually large claims incurred by any one individual (employee or dependent) covered under the medical expense plan.

The specific stop-loss limit, or attachment (trigger) point, is often referred to as a self-funded retention; the attachment point is an amount mutually agreed to by the plan sponsor and the insurer. The specific stop-loss deductible represents the financial risk borne by the plan sponsor for eligible claims in excess of the covered employee's (or dependent's) out-of-pocket maximum, which is the plan self-funded retention plus any cost sharing (coinsurance) up to the limit at which the coinsurance is capped.

Example 17-1. Consider a $50,000 specific stop-loss deductible. Under this arrangement, an employer is financially responsible to pay all eligible medical claims for each participant over and above any plan deductible (e.g., $200) and coinsurance (e.g., 20 percent of eligible expenses to as much as $5,000); however, once the $50,000 deductible (attachment point) is reached, the stop-loss insurer becomes obligated to reimburse the employer for any eligible claims above this amount up to any overall maximum (such as $500,000 or $1 million) stated in the stop-loss agreement.

Some observers have suggested that specific stop-loss deductibles be set at approximately 100 times the number of plan participants. Another rule of thumb is that the specific stop-loss trigger point be set at 5 to 10 percent of expected aggregate claims for the plan.

The 1999 survey by Mercer/Foster Higgins found that 81 percent of self-funded traditional indemnity plans purchase stop-loss insurance, typically for both aggregate and specific. The same survey found that 90 percent of self-funded PPOs purchase stop-loss. Of those, 58 percent have both kinds.

Q 17:56 What types of specific stop-loss plans are available?

Two fundamentally different types of specific stop-loss plans are available in the marketplace, depending on whether claims above the stop-loss attachment point are covered on an "incurred" or "paid" basis. Variations of each approach also exist as follows:

1. *Incurred in 12 months, paid in 12 months.* Under this agreement, charges reimbursed by the stop-loss insurer include only those claims incurred in the policy (contract) year and paid in the same year.

2. *Incurred in 12 months, paid in 15 months.* This arrangement requires the stop-loss insurer to reimburse the employer for claims incurred in the policy year that are paid during the policy year or within three months after the end of the policy year. Specific stop-loss agreements of this type can be designed to extend the payment period beyond three months after the end of the policy year for a slight increase in the stop-loss premium.

3. *Paid in 12 months.* Under this agreement, the stop-loss insurer reimburses the employer for all eligible claims above the attachment point paid by the employer in the policy year. Thus, claims incurred in a prior policy year are eligible for reimbursement if paid in the current policy year. To minimize the potential for employers to "game" the system, i.e., delay payment of a claim in order to collect stop-loss insurance applicable after a particular date, eligibility for this type of stop-loss agreement is usually limited to renewal situations for groups that have been covered continuously by the stop-loss insurer and transfer groups that had similar "paid" arrangements with previous insurers.

4. *Incurred in 15 months, paid in 12 months.* This is a common variation of the basic "paid" agreement. This agreement limits the stop-loss insurer's coverage of run-in claims to those incurred within 90 days prior to the inception of the policy year. Other limits on run-in periods may also be used under a "paid" stop-loss agreement.

Q 17:57 What does the term "incurred claim date" mean exactly?

It is also important to note that an "incurred claim date," as defined in the stop-loss agreement, generally refers to the specific date on which the service was rendered. This is in contrast to the typical group insurance contract that treats an entire hospital confinement as "incurred" on the participant's date of admission. For example, under specific stop-loss insurance, two stop-loss deductibles will apply to hospital confinements that extend over two policy years when the stop-loss contract is written on an "incurred" basis rather than on a "paid" basis.

Q 17:58 How does aggregate stop-loss work?

Aggregate stop-loss insurance is used by employers to limit their total financial risk with respect to covered medical claims for the total group in a given plan year. When total eligible claims of all covered participants exceed the attachment point, the aggregate stop-loss insurer becomes obligated to reimburse the employer for all eligible claims exceeding this limit, subject to any overall maximum reimbursement limit specified in the stop-loss agreement. The aggregate stop-loss limit, typically applied on an annual basis, is expressed as a percentage of total expected claims. This percentage generally ranges between 105 percent and 160 percent. Self-funding employers commonly select 120 percent or 125 percent.

When specific stop-loss insurance also is purchased, only those claims paid by the plan sponsor below the specific stop-loss attachment point are credited toward the aggregate stop-loss attachment point. During the first plan year the aggregate stop-loss contract is in effect, the contract generally is written to cover eligible claims "incurred and paid" in that contract year. In subsequent years, the contract usually is written on a "paid" basis which then provides reimbursement for claims incurred but not paid in a previous contract year. When the total dollar amount of claims is unusually large, employers are often faced with cash flow problems under a conventional aggregate stop-loss contract, because the insurer reimburses the employer for excess claims only at the end of the contract period. To alleviate this problem, many aggregate stop-loss insurers are willing to include a monthly claims cap provision in their contracts that limits (on an accumulated basis) the employer's monthly "out-of-pocket" claim costs.

Q 17:59 Does stop-loss coverage affect the employer's responsibility to its workers?

Regardless of stop-loss arrangements, the employer is ultimately responsible financially for paying all covered medical claims to plan participants, even though the stop-loss insurer reimburses the employer for excess claims above the attachment point. Because the stop-loss insurer has no financial obligation for the direct payment of medical claims to employees and beneficiaries, the establishment of any reserves for claims that have been incurred but not reported is the sole responsibility of the employer.

Q 17:60 How do stop-loss contracts differ with respect to the reimbursement of claims?

Typically, claims are paid from employer funds, and the employer's account is reconciled at the end of the plan year. Stop-loss insurance indemnifies the employer against claim amounts in excess of contractual limits; it does not reimburse employees for claims. This means that the employer must have adequate cash flow to pay catastrophic claims unless prior arrangements have been made to reimburse excess employer fund payments before the end of the plan year.

Note. A contract providing for the immediate reimbursement of claim payments beyond the "trigger points" is useless if the claim administrator cannot provide the stop-loss carrier with regular individual and aggregate claim totals.

In addition, contracts differ on how soon after the reconciliation reimbursement will actually be made to the employer's claim fund. The reconciliation and the reimbursement itself may vary in the first plan year and in a termination year. It is important to understand and have in writing the carrier's detailed procedure and the basis on which the carrier may deviate from that procedure.

Q 17:61 How do stop-loss contracts differ with respect to benefit period?

Typically, stop loss is provided for claims "incurred and paid" in a specific period. The standard is known as a 12/12: Only those claims incurred in a 12-month period and paid in the same period are subject to stop-loss protection. This means that the employer is responsible for claims presented after the plan year unless the employer purchases an extended contract for an additional premium.

A 12/15 covers claims incurred in a 12-month period but paid up to three months after the close of the plan year; 12/18, 12/24, and 12/36 policies are less widely available and can be more expensive than they are worth. Employers who desire complete "run-out claims" security are perhaps better off in fully insured programs.

Q 17:62 How are claims incurred prior to the benefit period under the contract paid?

When switching from an insured to a self-funded plan, there are effectively no "prior incurred" claims, because the fully insured plan guarantees to pay all claims incurred during its existence, and establishes funded claim reserves for this purpose. When switching from one stop-loss carrier to another, there are, however, claims that are not automatically covered by either the successor carrier or the predecessor carrier. The employer can make special arrangements, to the extent necessary and desirable, to limit risk. Carriers offer 15/12 contracts, which cover claims incurred within the three months prior to the benefit period but paid within the 12-month benefit period.

Q 17:63 Why are stop-loss provisions problematical?

Stop-loss insurers are often not in the health insurance business; therefore, their contracts do not mirror standard employee benefit provisions. It is not uncommon for stop-loss contracts to limit reimbursement for any one individual's claims to $1 million even though the employee benefit plan provides unlimited coverage. Some stop-loss carriers exclude coverage for mental and nervous conditions or automobile accidents, for example.

Careful analysis of the actual policy, not just of a proposal, is important in order to identify areas in which the employer is actually not covered by stop-loss insurance policies or is "going bare" before entering into a stop-loss contract.

Q 17:64 Can stop-loss policies be terminated mid-year?

Usually, no. And even if the policy allows for mid-year termination and the employer formally cancels the policy and transfers coverage to another carrier, the employer remains liable for the full year's premiums. Furthermore, there is usually a window for notifying the carrier that coverage is not being renewed. Often the renewal premium increases are not delivered in a timely enough fashion to permit an employer to shop for new coverage and still make the window. Termination provisions should be reviewed carefully, and the employer should insist on a contractual right to review the renewal for at least 60 days.

Q 17:65 How has the regulatory environment affected employers' efforts to self-fund?

Employer efforts to self-fund their medical expense plans are often hindered by the regulatory treatment accorded special insurance arrangements, which are important to the successful operation of the majority of self-funded plans. Probably the most serious problem is that the regulatory treatment varies considerably from one state to another. The most notable problem is the disparate regulatory treatment of stop-loss insurance, including the determination of permissible insurers of this coverage. Both specific and aggregate stop-loss insurance are vital to thousands of employers that have decided to self-fund their employee medical expense benefits. It is important that self-funded employers have available to them a competitive and stable market, free of unnecessary regulation, for stop-loss coverage. In the absence of such an environment, these employers are likely to face even larger health care cost increases in the future. Employers then may be forced to cut the benefits in their medical expense plans, exacerbating the problem of inadequate access to health care in this country.

Q 17:66 What does the National Association of Insurance Commissioners say about self-funding?

On September 11, 1995, the National Association of Insurance Commissioners (NAIC) adopted model legislation that defines stop-loss insurance. The model law defines any policy with an attachment point of less than $20,000 as being a health insurance policy subject to state laws.

States often adopt model legislation as passed by the NAIC; however, states also often make changes to the model laws. For example, some states could decide to define stop-loss as being a much higher amount, which would constitute an attempt to regulate many self-funded plans. Expect a court challenge to any state's attempt to subject self-funded plans to state legislation. The U.S. Court of Appeals for the Fourth Circuit originally ruled that Maryland's regulations were preempted by ERISA. In 1999, the Maryland legislature passed a law prohibiting stop-loss policies with attachment points of less than $10,000. The same judge ruled that ERISA did not preempt legislation regulating stop-loss insurance. A circuit judge in Cole County, Missouri, ruled that Missouri's regulations were preempted by ERISA. The Kansas Supreme Court upheld actions by the insurance commissioner to regulate a stop-loss policy as a health insurance policy.

The American Legislative Exchange Council, a national association of state legislators, voted in March 1996 to oppose the NAIC Stop-Loss Model Act.

Q 17:67 Do states regulate stop-loss insurers?

An argument can be made that stop-loss insurance should be regulated by the states as to policy form and contract language and any necessary reserves that should be held by the stop-loss insurer. The purchase of stop-loss insurance, by itself, should not however subject the benefit structure of a self-funded plan to state-mandated benefit laws that otherwise apply to insured plans.

Q 17:68 Is there any alternative to stop-loss that provides similar protection?

Yes, there is. This alternative entails combining self-funded coverage for the "front end" with fully insured coverage for the "back end." Under this alternative, an employer would purchase fully insured coverage with high deductibles—for example, $5,000 or $10,000 per person—and self-fund up to that amount. The employer could, but need not, focus on the existence of the high insurance deductible when communicating the plan to its employees. The employer would want to design and describe the plan in terms of the benefit as it appears to employees, not necessarily in terms of how the plan is funded. That is to say, there might be a $200 deductible before the plan begins to make payment, and there may or may not be coinsurance on the amount being paid. Once the deductible has been satisfied (see advantage (4), as follows), the employer makes payment as a self-funded plan.

There are a number of advantages to this concept, including the following:

1. *Lower cost.* This design provides what is essentially individual stop-loss at the chosen level—$10,000, for example. Stop-loss insurers would consider that level to be low, and would therefore price coverage beginning at that level quite high. In contrast, medical insurers would view a $10,000 individual deductible as extraordinarily high and would price their coverage appropriately lower.

2. *Certainty of stop-loss payment.* Under a normal stop-loss arrangement, the stop-loss insurer may disagree with the medical insurer as to the eligibility of items that have been paid, and, refusing to accept as covered expenses some that have been paid, the stop-loss carrier might deny (some) payment on the basis that the trigger has not been reached. Because the medical insurer is acting as the stop-loss insurer in this design, there can be no disagreement.

3. *Improved cash flow from the stop-loss carrier.* Although an employer might face a lengthy delay before receiving reimbursement from the stop-loss carrier, under this arrangement the employee will receive funds by the normal claim processing period, perhaps ten to 14 days.

4. *Ease of administration.* Normally, when employers self-fund, one of the considerations they must face is whether to self-administer (impractical for most small or mid-size employers) or to engage the services of a claims payer. Under this arrangement, while an employer could certainly engage a TPA to process the self-funded portion, there is little need to do so. In fact, doing so may be more cumbersome than not doing so. Under this arrangement, the employer would be better off submitting all claims to the insurance company as they occur. Even though there is no expectation the insurance company will make payment until the deductible has been reached, the insurance company will still review the claim and apply its

normal techniques to determine if the expenses are covered. Once that determination is made, the insurer will issue an explanation of benefits (EOB) delineating which expenses were not covered and, most importantly, which were covered and were applied toward the deductible. The employer then need only issue payment to the employee from the self-funded portion of the plan, based on the determination made as shown by the EOB. Naturally, if there is a deductible or coinsurance to be satisfied by the employee, that would need to be taken into account when making payment to the employee.

Q 17:69   What is the difference between pooling and stop-loss insurance?

Both pooling and stop-loss insurance involve the same concept: protection for the employer against large losses in set time periods. Pooling is used to exclude large claims from an employer's claim experience so that when renewal rates are developed, fluctuations are not counted. Employers pay a pool charge to avoid this fluctuation and the resulting fluctuation in rates. Without pooling, the insurer would pay the claims and would also apply them toward the employer's loss ratio.

Stop-loss insurance is a term used in many different contexts; it is also used as a synonym for out-of-pocket maximum by some insurers. Technically, it refers to a contractual agreement involved in most alternative funding arrangements. The protection requires the insurer to pay for claims in excess of predetermined limits. Without stop-loss insurance, the employer would have to pay for all claims.

Voluntary Employees' Beneficiary Associations

Q 17:70   What is a voluntary employees' beneficiary association?

A voluntary employees' beneficiary association (VEBA) is an association established for the purpose of providing "life, sick, accident or other benefits" [IRC § 501(c)(9)] to employees, their dependents, and beneficiaries. It is the primary self-funding method for establishing reserves to pay for these benefits.

Q 17:71 What tax benefits do VEBAs confer?

Provided the VEBA complies with the requirements of Code Sections 501(c)(9), 505, and 419A, employer contributions to VEBAs are tax-deductible, the VEBA pays no tax on earnings, and income is not taxable to association members.

Q 17:72 What other benefits can be provided through a VEBA?

VEBAs may be used to provide benefits similar to life, sick, or accident benefits that are intended to safeguard or improve the health of a member or beneficiary, or protect against a contingency that would reduce a member's income. Such benefits include the following:

- Vacation benefits and facilities
- Recreational activities such as sports leagues
- Child care facilities
- Supplemental unemployment benefits
- Severance benefits
- Education or training benefits
- Workers' compensation
- Legal service benefits
- Emergency loans
- Job readjustment and economic dislocation payments

Q 17:73 What benefits cannot be provided by a VEBA?

VEBAs may not be used to provide the following five types of benefits:

1. Deferred compensation benefits, or any other form of compensation that is dependent upon the passage of time rather that the occurrence of an unanticipated event. This prohibition extends to pensions, savings plans, stock bonus plans, and the like.
2. Accident or homeowners insurance.
3. Non-emergency loans.

4. Malpractice insurance.

5. Miscellaneous employment expenses such as commuting costs.

Q 17:74 What are the requirements for establishing a tax-exempt VEBA?

The four requirements for establishing a VEBA are as follows:

1. The organization must be an employees' association: It must be an entity such as a trust or corporation that is independent of the employer or its employees.

2. Membership must be voluntary: It involves some sort of affirmative act on the part of the employee, or is required as a result of a collective bargaining agreement, or is conferred as a result of employment provided there is no detriment to employees (such as a mandatory contribution).

3. Substantially all of its operations must be devoted to providing life, sick, or accident benefits to employees and their beneficiaries.

4. No part of the organization's net earnings may inure to the benefit of any private shareholder or individual, except for the payment of life, sick, and accident benefits.

Q 17:75 How does a VEBA obtain tax-exempt status?

A VEBA gives notice to the IRS that it is applying for tax-exempt status as a VEBA by submitting Form 1023, "Application for Recognition of Exemption under Section 501(c)(3) of the Internal Revenue Code." The application must be filed within 15 months (plus extensions) of the end of the month in which the association was organized.

Q 17:76 May a VEBA be established to benefit only one person?

No. It must be for the benefit of a group of employees.

Q 17:77 May a VEBA benefit persons who are not employees?

Yes, provided they share an employee-related common bond. Employee-related common bond means that they are employees of a single employer, employees of several employers who are members of a controlled group or an affiliated service group as defined by Code Section 414, members of a collective bargaining group, or employees of several companies in the same type of business in the same geographical area.

Membership may be extended beyond actual employees to other individuals who are not employees but otherwise share the common bond, such as owners of a business whose employees are VEBA members. Where the VEBA benefits such individuals, it will still be considered to be an "employee" association, provided 90 percent of the total membership of the association (on one day of each quarter) consists of employees.

Q 17:78 Who is an employee for VEBA purposes?

An individual who is an employee for employment tax purposes or under a collective bargaining agreement is considered to be an employee for VEBA purposes. Temporary, part-time, and retired employees, surviving spouses, and dependents also qualify.

Q 17:79 What restrictions on VEBA membership are permissible?

Membership may be restricted on the basis of employment-related criteria such as geographical area, length of service, maximum compensation, full-time employment status, or reasonable classification of workers. In addition, VEBAs may exclude individuals who are members of another employer-funded association that provides comparable benefits, employees who are subject to a collective bargaining agreement or those who refuse to make required contributions, and those who do not meet a reasonable standard for health condition. The Health Insurance Portability and Accountability Act of 1996 prohibits the use of health status to determine eligibility for benefits under a health plan. Health status can still be used to determine eligibility under other plans, such as life and disability plans.

Q 17:80 Who controls a VEBA?

In order for the organization to be considered a voluntary association of employees, the employees' interests must be represented by one of the following three:

1. Member employees;
2. An independent trustee such as a bank; or
3. Trustees, at least some of whom are designated by or on behalf of the member employees.

Q 17:81 Is there a limit on deductible contributions to a VEBA?

The amount that may be set aside for an exempt purpose in a VEBA may not exceed the qualified direct costs determined under Code Section 419, plus certain additional amounts for reserves determined under Code Section 419A.

Qualified direct costs are the amounts that the employer could have deducted if the benefits were provided as direct cash payments to employees.

Code Section 419A sets limits on additional assets that may be "set aside" to provide future disability, medical, supplemental unemployment or severance, or life insurance benefits. The basic limits are (1) the amount reasonably and actuarially necessary to fund the cost of claims that have been incurred but unpaid, plus the administrative cost of processing those claims; and (2) certain limited additions to reserves for the payment of post-retirement medical and life insurance benefits.

Q 17:82 What are the restrictions on funding for post-retirement medical and life insurance benefits?

The two maximum funding limits are (1) the level annual contribution, spread over the working lives of the covered employees, that is necessary to fund such benefits fully upon retirement, using reasonable actuarial assumptions; and (2) a nonactuarially calculated safe harbor of 35 percent of the preceding year's medical costs, not including insurance premiums.

Each year's limit must be determined on the basis of current medical costs; projected inflation may not be taken into account.

Q 17:83 What are the special rules regarding VEBA contributions for key employees?

Contributions made on behalf of "key employees" as defined in Code Section 416 must be made to a separate account, and key employee benefits must be paid from that account. These contributions are treated as annual additions to a defined contribution pension plan for purposes of applying the overall limits on annual pension contributions.

> **Planning Pointer.** Although the contribution to the post-retirement medical benefit reserve is deductible, the income on that reserve constitutes "unrelated business income."

Q 17:84 What is unrelated business income?

Certain VEBA income is deemed to be unrelated business income (under Code Section 512), which means it is not entitled to exemption from tax and is taxed at corporate rates. Amounts set aside and used for purposes other than for providing benefits are unrelated business income. The earnings on reserves for post-retirement medical benefits are also unrelated business income. Some VEBAs circumvent this problem by investing in tax-deferred investment vehicles such as annuities.

Q 17:85 Are there special nondiscrimination rules for VEBAs?

Yes. See Chapter 11 for a complete discussion of the nondiscrimination rules applicable to VEBAs.

Chapter 18

Third-Party Administration

Just as self-insurance has grown in the past decade, so has the importance of third-party administrators (TPAs). TPAs process the vast amounts of paperwork and claim payments for employee benefit plans. But they do much more than simply push paper. The best ones act as counselors and advisors to their employer clients.

The Role of the TPA	18-1
Performance Standards	18-6
Legal Issues	18-8
The TPA Market	18-12

The Role of the TPA

Q 18:1 What is third-party administration?

There is no single definition or description in federal statutes or regulations of the term third-party administration. In the broadest sense, the term "third party" refers to any individual or organization that pays medical bills on behalf of a patient. Most commonly, third-party administrators are third-party payors on behalf of their clients' employee benefit plans. The National Association of Insurance Commissioners (NAIC) has recognized the role of TPAs and has devised a model law that some states have adopted to oversee TPAs. Some TPAs manage property-casualty insurance claims and some

TPAs specialize in employee benefits, such as pensions or disability, and health coverage (also known as welfare plans). For the purposes of this chapter, we focus on TPAs servicing health and related employee benefit plans.

Q 18:2 What is a third-party administrator?

In the strictest sense, a third-party administrator is the individual or organization that actually does the third-party administration, but the terms "third-party administration" and "third-party administrator" are used and misused in the health insurance field to describe everything from insurance agents who help clients fill out applications and claim forms to large and small companies that provide comprehensive benefit administration and management services to client employer plans. The terms also are used to describe insurance companies and Blue Cross/Blue Shield plans (the Blues) that offer administrative services only (ASO) contracts to benefit plans. Moreover, government sources often confuse the term third-party payor with third-party administrator, but the term third-party payor implies that the third-party payor has responsibility for the payment itself (funding).

Q 18:3 What is the role of TPAs?

TPAs play a role much like that of a certified public accountant (CPA) hired to handle the masses of paperwork involved with filing taxes. Even though the CPA completes all the forms, may handle all tax paperwork, and generally manages the business of paying taxes and complying with tax law, the taxpayer—and not the CPA—is ultimately responsible to the government for the taxes and accuracy of the tax forms. Likewise, TPAs are hired to handle varying amounts of the paperwork and processing of client employee benefit plans while the plan official, sponsor, administrator, or trustees remain legally responsible. The TPA may be recognized under the Employee Retirement Income Security Act of 1974 (ERISA) as a "knowing participant" or "cofiduciary," but legally the TPA is just a paperpusher. All power and responsibility rest with the official "plan administrator," which is usually the sponsoring employer or a board of trustees of the plan.

Q 18:4 What is the history of using TPAs for employee benefit administration?

The TPA concept has its roots in the jointly administered Taft-Hartley multiemployer union-management benefit plans, codified in the federal Taft-Hartley Act of 1946. Such plans typically are composed of several employers whose workers belong to a single union. The concept is especially beneficial to workers in trades that have frequent turnover. For instance, a carpenter may belong to one local construction union and work two weeks on one project, a few days for another employing contractor, and so on. Under a Taft-Hartley plan, the worker is covered by a health and pension plan jointly sponsored by his or her union and the various employers.

The Taft-Hartley plans are careful to give equal representation to union and management interests, and both sides are represented equally on the board of trustees of the independent jointly sponsored employee benefit plan. Not surprisingly, these Taft-Hartley plans are called multiemployer plans. Such multiemployer plans are not to be confused with multiple employer welfare arrangements (MEWA) (see Q 18:5).

It was a natural progression for the independent benefit plan to seek the services of an independent TPA to administer the plan and process the paperwork to pay claims. Thus, many of the earliest and largest TPAs have a long record in the administration of Taft-Hartley employee benefit plans.

Although there is no clear reason for the trend, most of the early growth of the TPA industry was centered in the western United States. This geographic trend continued until the early 1980s, when employers across the country began using TPAs.

As early as the 1950s, some TPAs began to specialize in serving plans sponsored by single employers providing health care benefits for their own workers. Thus, firms that offer TPA services to Taft-Hartley plans are usually well versed in the administration of pension plans (because most Taft-Hartley plans include pensions), while most TPAs that serve single-employer corporate plan sponsors specialize in health coverage, disability options, and flexible benefits.

Q 18:5 What are multiple employer welfare arrangements?

Another type of employee benefit plan administered by TPAs is called a multiple employer welfare arrangement. They are also called multiple employer trusts or association plans. In such plans, a group of employers with a common business interest (such as a trade association) forms a single employee benefit plan to cover the employees of all the members of that group. This provides not only the personalization, cost, and efficiency advantages of a TPA-administered plan, but also the advantages of a larger group: lower overall rates. Like multiemployer plans, multiple employer plans function best when they have a central independent plan administration office.

Not all MEWAs are desirable. Unfortunately, a lack of consistent government oversight of MEWAs has drawn some unscrupulous people to design MEWAs to be little more than "get-rich-quick" schemes.

Q 18:6 What are the regulatory differences between multiemployer plans and multiple-employer plans?

The important distinction in regulatory authority is the following: Taft-Hartley jointly administered plans (characterized by more than one employer and one or more unions) are known and defined under ERISA as multiemployer plans. The distinction is important because virtually all Taft-Hartley multiemployer plans are considered to be covered by ERISA. Thus, they are usually exempt from regulation and taxation by state laws, under the preemption provision of ERISA Section 514.

Conversely, multiple employer plans are not, by themselves, covered under ERISA and its preemption provisions even though they must file ERISA Form 5500 and are subject to ERISA's fiduciary requirements.

Q 18:7 When selecting a TPA, what characteristics should an employer seek?

When selecting a TPA, an employer should keep in mind that it is hiring a whole firm, not one person. But because the employer's relationship with the TPA is based heavily on trust, cooperation, and partnership, an important factor for future success is that the employer and main contact at the TPA have a solid working relationship. Just as in selecting an attorney, accountant, or other business consultant, the employer's goal should be to match the employer's needs with the TPA's offerings.

Specifically, each employer should consider these five factors:

1. *Cost.* Can the TPA help the employer to minimize both claim costs and administrative costs? TPAs have been pioneers in reducing claim costs and in developing efficient plan design, and TPAs typically cost less in administration than insurance companies or self-administration. Employers should be sure, however, to review more than the TPA fee in making such a selection. Each employer should understand all services the TPA would provide and know the costs of each.

2. *Flexiblity in plan design and service.* Third-party administration is a service industry, and the client's wish should be the TPA's command (within the limits of law, common sense, and any extra costs incurred). Normally, an employer should be able to reach a professional at the TPA firm who can answer its question, solve its problem, or begin the appropriate research within minutes. The interaction between the employer and the TPA should not be a distant and impersonal relationship.

3. *Legal compliance.* This issue should be the most important area of consideration because it represents the employer's biggest liability. Each year, there are about 1,500 new laws, regulations, and official opinions issued by about 150 different governmental entities regarding employee benefit plans. Given these numbers, there is a good chance that many would conflict in letter or spirit. Moreover, only about 33 percent are ever explained adequately, even in the best technical trade press. Most of these new laws, regulations, and opinions are the legal responsibility of the employer, not the insurance company or the health maintenance organization or any other entity. Neither the state nor the federal government ever issues any final, comprehensive regulatory guidance on how to comply with 99 percent of these new laws, regulations, and opinions, yet the government has designed penalties that would cripple an

employer that failed to comply, even if noncompliance was unintentional. Recognizing this dilemma, TPAs started 20 years ago with the specific goal of being highly informed on how to guide clients through the legal maze. As a result, the professional staff at some TPAs spend about 40 percent of their time on government compliance for client plans, a cost that should be factored in when pricing the TPA's services. Potential administrators should also be queried as to how they stay up to date on new laws, regulations, and opinions, and what role the TPA will play in ensuring that the employer complies fully with all government requirements.

4. *Hardware, software, personnel, capacity, and experience.* Does the TPA have the ability to handle the needs of the employer in question? The employer should ask such questions as: How fast does the TPA pay claims? What is its error rate? The employer also should walk through the operation, if possible, and should ask whether the TPA has other clients of similar size and needs. If so, meet with those employers or discuss these issues with those clients over the phone.

5. *Performance guarantees.* Many employers may want to ask a TPA about some form of performance guarantee, based on speed and accuracy of processing claims. Although doing so may sound logical, some employers have found performance guarantees for turnaround time to be counter productive—the TPA may sacrifice accuracy for timeliness. As noted in item 3 here, 99 percent of government requirements come with no comprehensive guidance on how to comply, and the penalties for unintentional noncompliance could cripple an employer. Does the employer want to urge its TPA to move quickly through such a minefield?

Performance Standards

Q 18:8 What examples are available regarding performance standards or guarantees?

Standards can be negotiated to cover any number of categories, such as accuracy (which can be defined in various ways and should be specified in the contract), turnaround time, report generating, ID card production and summary plan descriptions, or anything else a vendor could do on a timely basis. Savings—such as those from coordination of benefits (COB), utilization review, and preferred provider organization (PPO) discounts—are also frequently guaranteed.

A common guarantee calls for a 2 percent penalty if financial accuracy is less than 99 percent, 4 percent if it is less than 98.5 percent, 6 percent if it is less than 98 percent, and 8 percent for anything less than 97 percent. Another variation is for the client to be reimbursed 0.5 percent of the fee for each 0.2 percent reduction in financial accuracy below 99 percent. Alternatively, the penalty could be a fixed dollar amount, such as $500 for each 0.2 percent reduction in financial accuracy, or $15,000 if financial accuracy is between 98.0 percent and 98.9 percent, and an additional $10,000 if accuracy is below 98 percent. The contract should specify the formula to be used, including how the numerator and denominator are defined. For example, financial accuracy could be defined as calculated by dividing the dollars paid, minus the sum of the overpayments and underpayments, by the total payments.

Another typical guarantee calls for 80 percent of claims to be processed within 10 days, with a 1 percent penalty if turnaround time is 75 percent to 79 percent, a 2 percent penalty if it is 70 percent to 74 percent, and a 5 percent penalty if it is less than 70 percent. Another variation would be 85 percent of claims should be paid in 15 calendar days and a $15,000 penalty will be levied if turnaround time is between 80 percent and 84.9 percent and an additional $10,000 penalty will be levied if timeliness falls under 80 percent. For this type of guarantee a claim needs to be defined, as do the start and ending points for measurement and whether the standard is calendar days or working days.

Many telephone systems today can track the speed with which calls are answered. Therefore, another common guarantee is to answer telephone calls within 45 seconds, or to have an abandonment rate of less than 5 percent. Again, terms of the guarantee need to be defined, such as whether it is 100 percent of calls within the time specified, or an average within that time. Sample penalties are

1 percent if the average is 46 to 50 seconds, 2 percent if it is 51 to 60 seconds, and 5 percent if it is over one minute.

Q 18:9 In lieu of performance standards or guarantees, do employers use bonuses and incentives for good service?

Bonuses or incentives for good service are acceptable as long as any additional payment comes from the client's corporate (nonplan) assets. If the bonus is taken from plan assets, the normal fee plus the bonus must not be excessive given the services provided. This type of bonus often arises when an employer or plan encounters a new complex government compliance issue or cost-containment program and the TPA puts forth extra effort to make it work. In effect, the bonus is simply payment for extra services and is best designated as such.

Legal Issues

Q 18:10 What are the penalties for noncompliance with ERISA?

The federal government enforces the rules governing ERISA with civil and criminal penalties, including jail time if necessary. Most relationships between TPAs and their clients are covered under ERISA's fiduciary responsibility requirements, which provide much tougher consumer protections than any state insurance or even any standard business law. The TPA's fiduciary responsibility means that each TPA must always do what is in the best interest of the plan. In fact, many TPAs will occasionally chastise their clients to ensure that the employers stay in strict compliance with their primary fiduciary responsibilities as the plan sponsor.

Q 18:11 Should employers expect legal opinions from TPAs?

Most TPAs do not issue legal opinions, even on new or emerging government laws, regulations, or opinions. Because most of the requirements that employers must follow either have no precedent or are subject to conflicting court decisions, common sense and experience are usually more useful.

Q 18:12   What laws govern TPAs?

Self-funded plans and those sponsoring and administering self-funded plans (see Chapter 17) are regulated by ERISA and other federal laws. ERISA was created to be the ultimate consumer protection law, and so the requirements and limitations on those involved with ERISA plans are often far more stringent than they are on state-regulated insurance plans. To avoid conflicts with state laws regulating health insurance, Congress included in ERISA a broad preemption of state law.

Q 18:13   What is ERISA fiduciary responsibility?

Many books have been written to describe ERISA fiduciary duty and to stipulate those subject to it. Meanwhile, state and federal courts have stumbled over each other trying to define it. When asked, the U.S. Department of Labor (DOL) has answered: Fiduciary responsibility depends on the facts and circumstances of each situation. Thus, there is no shortage of precedents and anecdotes that lawyers and other professionals have collected on the subject. But a short answer may be as follows: ERISA was passed to be the ultimate consumer protection law. Its protections and prohibitions are far stronger than and different from those provided in insurance law or normal business practice.

ERISA's requirements regarding fiduciary responsibility are in sections 404 and 405 of Title I. These sections state that each transaction involving the plan or the individuals covered under the plan must be handled with maximum prudence and each person involved with the plan will be judged on each transaction individually. "Prudence" is best described as maximizing the size and security of payments to legitimate, eligible plan participants. In other words, the person being paid must be eligible and the benefit to be paid must be covered under the plan language. Moreover, fiduciaries are expected to maximize the security and size of plan assets (including, of course, minimizing expenses). The penalties can be both civil and criminal in nature, and the government can seek to prosecute both the corporation and actual individuals involved in decision making.

Q 18:14 Why are ERISA's fiduciary requirements tougher than state insurance and normal business consumer protections?

Many health insurance companies require health plans to buy their more profitable life insurance products or other services, such as utilization review. Such mandatory or automatic portions of those requirements could be a criminal offense (under the self-dealing regulations that govern self-funded ERISA plans). The law does not forbid plans from buying such packages of services. The plans must be able to prove that doing so is a prudent action on behalf of plan participants and that such decisions are made consciously and carefully by the official plan sponsor, administrator, or trustees.

Doing what is best for the whole plan often requires making difficult decisions in favor of the greatest number of participants, even if some participants would suffer. For ERISA sponsors, administrators, or trustees, doing so might mean reducing the number or scope of benefits or doing whatever else is prudent to keep the whole plan alive. In addition, ERISA requires that the wording in the plan be followed exactly. For example, if the plan language says that a particular service is not covered or is limited to certain participants, it would be a breach of fiduciary duty to give benefits for that service to a participant or someone not designated to be covered, regardless of the good intentions behind such a move.

Q 18:15 How does an ERISA fiduciary judge whether a deal is prudent?

Every transaction regarding an ERISA plan is judged individually. Thus, the plan's payments to the TPA for purely TPA services would be one transaction that could be reviewed. A regulator will ask: Does the payment represent a good deal for the plan for the range of services rendered? Any payments to brokers also would be scrutinized. The regulator will want to know whether the amount paid to a broker is justifiable given the value of the services the broker actually provides to the plan. For example, saying, "Add $3 per person" for a particular service would be inadequate justification for an investigator from the DOL. Selecting appropriate stop-loss coverage would be another transaction to be evaluated. The DOL would want to know whether each penny was spent on the most prudent service at the most prudent price.

Q 18:16 Who is subject to fiduciary duty?

There are two classes of fiduciaries:

1. *The named fiduciary.* This is the person or entity named in the plan document, usually the plan administrator or the plan sponsor, that is the employer for a single-employer plan or the trustees for a multiemployer plan. This administrator is not to be confused with the TPA, who has the legal role of a contract service provider only.

2. *Other fiduciaries.* This is the group of people and entities that are also subject to fiduciary duty, depending on the amount of decision-making power they can exercise. This group includes anyone who knew or should have known about the operations of the plan. Thus, this group may include executives and employees of the TPA or utilization reviewers. All could be pursued by DOL investigators. Predicting whom the DOL will pick as its main target is difficult, so all parties need to be scrupulously prudent. For example, in a situation in which a preferred provider organization was careless, the DOL targeted the employer fiduciary, charging the official administrator with not exercising enough care in the selection of the PPO and not exercising enough care in the oversight of the PPO's services.

Q 18:17 What are the risks for fiduciaries?

The charges can be both civil and criminal. A jail sentence is possible, especially in cases in which an individual received personal gain from a nonprudent activity. Prosecution also goes beyond the corporate veil. The DOL can pursue individuals' personal assets for fines and restitution. Using such excuses as "Everyone does it," and "I've always done it that way," is worthless.

The TPA Market

Q 18:18 What do TPAs charge?

Fees vary widely, as does the basis for fees. Some TPAs charge a set amount per covered employee each month. Others charge for each claim or transaction. Some charge a percentage of the amount paid (although this is prohibited in some states). Others use different approaches or combination of approaches. While various numbers can be generated, they are not applicable to the industry as a whole. Because no two TPAs operate in the same way, and most use different definitions of common statistical terms, the same question can produce widely differing answers, depending on which firm is asked. In careful cross-examination by people exceptionally familiar with TPAs, it was discovered that one firm defined a "claim" as any occasion that the TPA had to enter its database for a client (thus an operation or medical treatment might generate 100 different bills, checks, or "claims"). Another TPA considered all bills for the same treatment as one claim for one person.

Most TPAs are privately held and are protective of their privacy. In computing their income, some count only their administrative fee, some list a fee for comprehensive services, and others list separate bills for special services. Some include commission, consulting, and other income, and some include every penny that they ever receive.

Q 18:19 How many individuals are served by TPAs?

Again, calculations of the number of individuals covered vary widely. Some plans and TPAs only count the employee. Others count the employee as one and count the "family" as another participant. Others count each individual in the family. Thus, a husband and wife with 10 children might be reported as one, two, or 12 covered lives. Numbers are further skewed by insurers and other organizations that do some TPA or ASO work and tend to include those figures in their own corporate statistics rather than showing them as having been part of the TPA function all along.

Q 18:20 Why has the market for TPAs grown?

The market has grown for a number of reasons. Among the most significant are the following:

1. *Lower cost.* Independent studies have shown that TPAs typically cost less than comparable coverage from private insurers or the Blues. While large insurers and the Blues have the advantages (the most efficient computer and processing costs), they also have high overhead.

2. *Service.* ERISA and self-funding allow a plan to be tailor-made specifically for the workers of that employer, so the plan itself tends to be more personalized than those under state regulation, which must include about 1,000 state-mandated benefits, including such medically unnecessary items as toupees in one state and hair implants in another. There is another reason: TPAs have a direct interest in keeping their customers satisfied because their clients can simply leave and start with another TPA the next day. Unlike the situation of starting with a new insurer or Blues plan, in which a new application, underwriting, preexisting condition exclusions, and a new policy would be required, a self-funded employer can keep his or her plan intact and simply find a new TPA with minimal hassle.

3. *Government compliance.* Each year, there are about 1,500 new laws, regulations, interpretations, opinions, and major court cases emanating from about 150 major government offices. Not all apply to every plan, but the plan must be aware of each to determine whether it applies. Only about 30 percent of these new requirements are announced publicly, and only about 1 percent of the requirements come with any official comprehensive compliance guidance.

4. *Underserved segments of the market.* As the insurance companies and Blues underwent multiple massive marketing strategy shifts in the past 20 years, huge segments of the market were abandoned, hit with high premiums, or limited in coverage offered. Most of the underserved markets were small employers and various industries that insurers and the Blues had deemed undesirable. The burst of growth of TPAs and self-funding filled those market niches. The protections in the Health Insurance Portability and Accountability Act of 1996 (HIPAA) mean that

insurers and the Blues can no longer refuse to offer coverage to small employers.

Q 18:21   Have there been any discernible patterns of growth in the TPA business recently?

Most firms have been started fairly recently and serve single-employer corporate clients and multiple employer plans sponsored by associations. They also seem to prefer only health, cafeteria, and disability plans. The tremendous growth of new firms has been seen in every area of the country, not just the traditional TPA strongholds in the far west. Most of the executives starting these new firms have entered the business laterally; thus, they have had several years of experience in employee benefits as brokers, agents, insurance executives, or in a similar specialty. Many of these firms report that the idea to form a TPA was initiated by one or more of their insured clients. In fact, a fairly common scenario seems to reoccur among new TPAs. An agent or broker goes to one or more of his or her major insurance clients with the policy renewal. The client balks at the new higher insurance premium and announces his or her intention to look for other coverage. Then the client says, "What about this self-funding or independent administration I keep reading about?" The agent or broker researches the idea and realizes that he or she could provide better service and savings to the client, and a TPA is born.

Q 18:22   What are the major markets for TPAs?

There are seven major market segments for TPAs:

1. Plans for about 67 percent of the workers in the Taft-Hartley union-management multiemployer plans are administered directly or indirectly by independent TPAs.

2. As small employers have met increasingly higher costs from traditional insurers, and as stop-loss insurance became more flexible, the role of self-funding and TPAs has grown for small plans (even plans as small as two-person plans). The small-employer market has grown through single-employer plans and multiple employer welfare arrangements, such as those spon-

sored by trade associations for member employers and by commonly owned groups of employers.
3. There has been tremendous growth among TPAs serving government plans, such as local school districts, and city and state employees.
4. Branch offices and subsidiaries of large companies have been a market that has had slow but steady growth for TPAs because of the local attention a TPA can bring to that branch or subsidiary.
5. For many years, insurers including the Blues have farmed out the administration of some of their fully insured customer plans to TPAs. This market has grown slowly but steadily.
6. A new and fast-growing market is being developed as medical facilities, including health maintenance organizations, preferred provider organizations, and hospitals, seek to develop relationships with TPAs to foster growth in market share. These providers also have sought to acquire TPAs.
7. New entities, such as physician-hospital organizations and other medical provider-based health plans, are evolving and seeking TPAs to manage their employer-client business.

Q 18:23 What changes are underway in the TPA business?

Because the roots of the TPA concept started with multiemployer and multiple employer plans, some TPAs have been experimenting for many years with health insurance purchasing cooperatives and with serving health maintenance organizations. The results of these experiments have not been universally successful, but clearly, there is a role for TPAs in these arrangements. Neither the medical personnel nor the employers want to do the mountains of administrative work necessary to process and to pay claims for that many people. Because TPAs thrive on administrative processing, this is a good fit.

Q 18:24 What is the future of the TPA business?

All current efforts to reform the health care system and to cut costs require much greater administrative red tape from all employers (not just those who currently offer benefits). Thus, there will be more administration for more people from more employers and for more plans per employer.

Q 18:25 What types of services do TPAs provide?

A recent survey of independent TPAs found that the most common services provided by TPAs include:

- COBRA administration (89 percent of respondents)
- Data management and reporting (79 percent)
- Prescription drug cards (78 percent)
- Managed care plans (75 percent)
- Precertification (75 percent)
- Consulting (74 percent)
- Employee communications (71 percent)
- Case management (70 percent)
- Hospital concurrent review (61 percent)
- Discharge planning (59 percent)
- Government reporting (59 percent)
- Cafeteria plan administration (56 percent)
- Second opinions (55 percent)
- Hospit audits (50 percent)
- Computer facilities (49 percent)
- Psychiatric case management (49 percent)
- Electronic claims (36 percent)

[Charles D. Spencer & Associates, Inc., Independent Third Party Administrative Statistics for Year Ending Dec. 31, 1998]

At the start of their business arrangement, the plan sponsor and TPA sign an agreement that outlines the services and authority of the TPA. If the plan is only partially self-insured, most insurance companies reserve the right to approve the employer's TPA appointment.

TPAs are also providing a new service to assist employers with the selection of managed care providers. TPAs that provide this service are known as managed care TPAs.

Q 18:26 What is a managed care TPA?

With the growth of managed care as a health insurance cost control strategy, some TPAs have begun to offer sophisticated health care management services that go far beyond the traditional TPA functions. These TPAs are known as managed care TPAs. Some, referred to as managed care affiliates, are even directly allied with managed care organizations such as HMOs or PPOs.

Among the services managed care TPAs supply are provider profiling, utilization review, provider network development, risk contracts, and clinical protocols. They also focus on the implementation of new administrative technologies, such as automation of their capitation and referral authorization processes and use of computer programs that automatically rebundle tests and procedures that providers have unbundled into separate billing codes. [Charles J. Singer & Co., The Singer Report on Managed Care Systems and Technology (Dec. 28, 1992)]

Q 18:27 What is the value of using a managed care TPA?

Using a competent TPA may afford an employer some legal insulation from negligence claims and other types of liability. This is particularly an issue for self-insured plans, where the employer itself is directly funding employee medical benefits.

The clearest potential legal threat that use of a TPA may help mitigate is in managed care plans. In a managed care setting, employees are typically limited to using only health care providers chosen by the plan. If one of those providers is sued for malpractice by an employee, the employer sponsoring the plan may face liability for its role in choosing that provider. Interposing a TPA between employer and provider will limit the employer's role in actually managing care, and may thereby limit the employer's exposure to liability.

In the end, the best way for employers to avoid legal exposure is to use prudence and caution in all aspects of their plan, and this includes the process of hiring a TPA. Employers should ensure that the TPA they hire is competent, experienced in administering the intended plan type, and appropriately licensed or accredited (as the case may be) for the jurisdiction.

Q 18:28 How prevalent is the use of TPAs?

The Self-Insurance Institute of America estimates that there are approximately 1,500 TPAs operating in the United States, serving more than 196,000 plan sponsors. In 1998, TPAs administered plans covering approximately 17 million participants and paid about $14 billion in claims. [Miriam Basch Scott, "TPAs Paid $14 Billion in Claims in 1998," *Employee Benefit Plan Review* (July 1999)]

The current trend in the industry seems, however, to be toward consolidation. Where once the vast majority of TPAs were relatively small, localized, and privately owned operations, today many smaller TPAs are being purchased by national or regional organizations.

Chapter 19

Quality Assurance

Convinced that in the long run the best quality health care will be the least costly, many employers put greater emphasis on quality of care than on cost. This chapter describes a number of ways organizations measure quality, including report cards, accreditation, HEDIS, and outcomes measurement.

Quality Measures	19-1
Report Card Movement	19-13
The Joint Commission and HEDIS	19-16
Outcomes Measurement	19-17

Quality Measures

Q 19:1 What does quality mean in a health care context?

Webster's Dictionary will tell you that the word "quality" describes a degree of excellence. This basic definition of quality holds true in health care. As medical technology advancements, treatment specialization, and product, practice, and plan expansion continue to evolve in the health care industry, the issue of quality becomes more and more important. Buyers of medical services and health plans are looking for value, as determined by the quality of care, plus the quality of service, divided by the cost. To determine quality, buyers want data. They want to know how the care provided at one hospital compares to the care provided at another; they want to know if a new treatment, surgery, or medication is effective, and if so, how effective; they want a way to evaluate their available health care alternatives just as they want consumer information and comparisons when they look for a new car, purchase a home appliance, or select a financial institution for their mortgage.

According to United HealthCare, a large managed care organization in Minneapolis, Minnesota, quality means that a health care service:

1. Is appropriate—it's the right care for the patient at the right time, and supported by current medical standards;
2. Is performed well—that is, with the necessary level of skill and tools to optimize success; and
3. Achieves results that improve the health or functioning of the patient.

Q 19:2   What are quality measures?

Quality measures are benchmarks used in determining quality on many levels: quality of care, service, and health care facilities; credentials of health care providers; effectiveness of procedures and treatments; and efficiency of health plan administration, among others.

The quality of a health plan is evaluated by comparing it against national norms, using performance measures such as medical loss ratios, the utilization ratio of eye exams among diabetics, annual pap smears for female members, hospitalizations of children with asthma, mammography rate, childhood immunizations, and annual disenrollment rates. To standardize and centralize these measures, or quality assurance indicators, the National Committee for Quality Assurance (NCQA), an independent nonprofit organization, was founded during 1979 in Washington, D.C. NCQA makes health plans accountable for the quality of care and service they deliver in two complementary ways: by evaluating the health plan's internal quality processes through accreditation reviews, and by developing measures to gauge health plan performance.

The NCQA evaluates health plans in five key areas:

1. Access and service,
2. Qualified providers,
3. Staying healthy,
4. Getting better, and
5. Living with illness.

Q 19:3   What is the NCQA?

The National Committee for Quality Assurance is a nonprofit organization based in Washington, D.C. working in partnership with purchasers, consumers, and the managed care industry to improve the quality of patient care and the performance of health plans. NCQA is also the nation's leading accreditor of managed care plans. Its accreditation designations are: excellent, commendable, accredited, provisional, and denied.

Q 19:4   Why are quality measurements of health plans important to employers?

Quality measurements of health plans are important to employers for these reasons:

1. *Assurance of high quality and service among plans.* Enrollee satisfaction information from employees can be useful in identifying and correcting problems with current plans. Information about other plans can assist an employer in selecting the plan most likely to provide superior satisfaction.

2. *Reduced costs.* By comparing multiple plans, employers can identify less costly plans that have high employee-satisfaction ratings and avoid weak plans that have low satisfaction ratings. For employers that do not pay the entire cost of employee and dependent care, it has been shown through research that when employees are more satisfied with their health plan, they are more willing to contribute higher amounts toward the cost of care. Satisfied employees can help in cutting administrative costs by minimizing enrollment changes among plans and reducing the number of complaints. Large employers that have

concentrated their workers into a few high-quality plans have reported savings of as much as 20 percent.

3. *Improved employee relations.* Information about the specific areas of a plan's performance may help guide employees toward plans that will best meet their needs. The simple act of surveying employees on their satisfaction with health plans demonstrates an employer's concern for the workers' well-being.

4. *Fiduciary responsibility.* According to a letter written by the Department of Labor's Office of Interpretation and Regulations, a fiduciary's failure to take quality of services into account in selecting a health plan provider would constitute a breach of fiduciary duty under ERISA. According to the DOL letter, quality of services could include the qualifications of providers available to participants, ease of access to providers, ease of access to information concerning the operations of the provider, the extent to which internal procedures provide for timely consideration and resolution of patient questions and complaints, enrollee satisfaction statistics, and rating or accreditation by independent agencies.

Q 19:5 How prevalent are quality measures?

Although implementation of quality measurement systems is spreading, the health plans and employer groups that use performance reporting remain the exception rather than the rule. Hospitals have pioneered much of the quality measuring standards and contribute greatly to widespread reporting. About half of all health maintenance organizations (HMOs) have been accredited by NCQA.

Among the health plans and hospitals that are accredited and have adopted quality measurement programs, several have produced performance reports for marketing purposes. Some of these plans have focused on publishing the information that reflects favorably on their key indicators when compared to national averages. For instance, MEDICA's 1994 performance report showed a 74.4 percent pediatric immunization rate versus the national average figure of 61 percent and a cesarean-section birth rate of 17 percent, nearly 5 points below the 21.8 percent rate representing all health plans combined.

Additionally, several employers have formed coalitions, such as the Pacific Business Group on Health (PBGH), to set guidelines, mandate reporting, and make recommendations to health plans. They have joined together to obtain and share data on health plan performance levels and to wield influence via their combined purchasing power.

The 1999 Mercer/Foster Higgins national survey found that 67 percent of large employers require their HMOs to be accredited by either NCQA, the Joint Commission on Accreditation of Healthcare Organizations (the Joint Commission), or both, up from 46 percent in 1996. Most employers (89 percent) report quality is a very important criteria in evaluating a managed care plan. Thirty-eight percent request HEDIS data or other outcomes data, up from 23 percent in 1996.

Q 19:6 How do employers and health plans collect quality assurance data?

There are still limited resources for comprehensive quality assurance information; however, an increasing amount of information is available on the Internet. NCQA began regular and full disclosure to the public on the accreditation status of all health plans. The accreditation status list is available at NCQA's web site (at http://www.ncqa.org), which will allow an information search by health plan or geographic locality.

According to NCQA:

> Accreditation is a rigorous and comprehensive evaluation process through which NCQA assesses the quality of the key systems and processes that make up a health plan. Accreditation also includes an assessment of the care and service plans are delivering in important areas such as immunization rates, mammography rates and member satisfaction. NCQA began accrediting managed care organizations (MCOs) in 1991, in response to the need for standardized, objective information about the quality of these organizations. NCQA's accreditation program is voluntary, and has been embraced by purchasers, consumers and health plans as an objective measure of the quality of these organizations.

NCQA also makes available a national database of comparative information on the quality and performance of managed care plans. Quality Compass is available only on CD-ROM. Quality Compass is the first publicly available, national database of information about health plan quality.

Although NCQA has pioneered much quality data collection, other organizations and individuals contribute to this process:

1. *Health plan-driven data-collection efforts.* Hospitals and health plans often have dedicated quality assurance units staffed by medical professionals and operational personnel.

2. *Employer-driven data-collection efforts.* Some large employers have been working alone or in groups to collect data on health plan performance. Efforts by employers and employer coalitions are having a profound effect on the quality of care delivered in their markets, in part because buyers have significant market clout and in part because they are paying their health plans based on the results of their data-collection efforts. In other words, those health plans that get the best quality scores are given more business or more money in the form of higher reimbursements. After several years of experience, these efforts are paying dividends.

3. *Market-driven data-collection efforts.* Recognizing the need for health care cost data as well as quality data, a number of vendors have developed proprietary data-collection systems. Some systems have been contracted by and designed for a specific employer. Other data have been gathered through independent health plan participant surveys. Survey results are compiled, analyzed, and summarized, and then sold to employers. There is no shortage of consultants, systems vendors, and researchers seeking a greater share of the health plan data-collection market.

Q 19:7 Are any results available from Quality Compass?

Yes. NCQA releases an annual report entitled "State of Managed Care Quality." The report is based on detailed surveys of managed care plans that participated in Quality Compass.

Quality Assurance Q 19:8

The national averages for clinical measures were:

- 62.5 percent of smokers age 18 and older received advice to quit from a health care professional.
- 72.2 percent of the pertinent health plan population received breast cancer screening.
- 40.9 percent of diabetics received retinal exams.
- 64.8 percent of children received the appropriate immunizations.
- 67.4 percent of patients hospitalized for mental illness received follow-up care.
- 83.6 percent of pregnant women received prenatal care during the first trimester.

Q 19:8 What can employers do to ensure that their health plans offer high quality services?

At the very least, employers should require their health plans to provide them with current, ongoing data on quality assurance measures, and health plans should do so at no additional cost to the employer. Employers should also consider the following:

1. *Report cards.* Before contracting with any health plan, ask the plan to provide a report card on the results of its quality initiatives. If a plan does not issue a report card, ask the local representative from a national health plan such as United HealthCare to send its report card, and ask a prospective health plan to give similar numbers for comparison.
2. *Accreditation.* Employers should require health plans to seek accreditation from NCQA or the Joint Commission.
3. *HEDIS.* Request the health plan regular data collection and reporting using the latest version of HEDIS. Most HMOs are already producing modified HEDIS report cards for marketing purposes. Purchasers should request employer-specific HEDIS data, usually available at no additional cost to any employer with at least 1,000 plan participants (see Q 19:24).
4. *Customer satisfaction surveys.* Conduct satisfaction surveys among plan participants. Some employers use the results of

such surveys to raise or lower health plan reimbursement levels. Distribution of survey results to the plan participants will enhance enrollment in the best-rated plans. Both measures foster competition among health plans to improve quality.

5. *Absenteeism.* Employers should compare absenteeism rates between health plans. A health plan that keeps its premiums low by avoiding treatment costs may be costing the employer a lot in absenteeism and disability. A health plan that treats employees properly and promptly may be more cost-effective even if its premiums are higher.

In 1998, the ERISA Industry Committee released a policy statement on health care quality and consumer protection that included the following:

> One key to successful market-driven reform is the effective marshaling of market forces to motivate groups of health care providers to compete for blocks of business on the basis of clinical quality and cost-effectiveness. In particular, health care providers must be accountable to third-party payers and individual consumers for both the quality of their clinical performance and the cost-effectiveness of the services provided. This means forging new economic relationships among sellers, third-party payers and individual consumers that depends on:
>
> **Linking the scope of health care coverage to practice protocols, outcomes measurement and other means of defining appropriate care** (e.g., coverage of appropriate care would exclude reimbursement for unnecessary, ineffective and unproven treatments).
>
> **Defining provider performance standards and patient satisfaction standards, as well as measuring actual outcomes, performance and satisfaction.** Thus, selection among competing providers can be made on the basis of the measured quality of their performance in addition to the price charged for their services.
>
> **Federally-sanctioned mechanisms for group purchasing to assure that small groups and individuals have a choice among competing high quality and cost-effective coverages.** Together with large-employer purchasers, small employer purchasing groups will be able to hold providers accountable for their clinical performance as well as drive better bargains on the price of health care services.

Applying market-driven reforms equally to public as well as private coverage.

Q 19:9 Are any new systems available for employers to use in measuring and ensuring the quality of care offered through health plans?

Currently, one of the most significant efforts to measure health plan quality is being conducted by the Foundation for Accountability (FACCT). FACCT is a nonprofit organization dedicated to helping Americans make better health care decisions. FACCT's board of trustees is made up of consumer organizations and purchasers of health care services and insurance representing 80 million Americans.

FACCT believes that America's ability to create a more responsive health care system depends on informed, empowered consumers who help shape the system, hold it accountable for quality, and act as partners in improving health.

To achieve this goal, FACCT creates tools that help people understand and use quality information, develops consumer-focused quality measures, supports public education about health care quality, supports efforts to gather and provide quality information, and encourages health policy to empower and inform consumers.

Under the Balanced Budget Act of 1997, HCFA is required to provide comparisons of HMO quality to Medicare recipients. HCFA granted $150,000 to FACCT to develop a framework. FACCT's framework sorts data into five broad categories:

1. The Basics,
2. Staying Healthy,
3. Getting Better,
4. Living with Illness, and
5. Changing Needs.

Consumers will be able to use the framework to determine what kind of coverage will best meet their needs.

The Dartmouth Atlas of Health Care in the United States is another tool that can help focus efforts to improve health care quality. The atlas shows variations in health care practice patterns in local areas and regions. The atlas is produced by the Center for the Evaluative Clinical Sciences at Dartmouth Medical School and published by the American Hospital Association. Dr. John E. Wennberg leads the atlas research team.

In May 1998, three accreditation groups announced they would work together to coordinate their performance measurement activities. The three groups are the NCQA, the Joint Commission, and the American Medical Association's American Medical Accreditation Program (AMAP). They have created a new Performance Measurement Coordinating Council.

Q 19:10 What is the American Medical Accreditation Program?

The American Medical Accreditation Program was a voluntary, comprehensive accreditation program to measure and evaluate individual physicians against national standards, and criteria in five areas: (1) credentials, (2) personal qualifications, (3) environment of care, (4) clinical performance, and (5) patient care results. In 2000, the American Medical Association announced it was discontinuing AMAP.

Q 19:11 What is URAC?

The American Accreditation HealthCare Commission/URAC is a nonprofit organization that was established in 1990 to establish standards for the managed care industry. URAC's broad-based membership includes representation from all the constituencies affected by managed care—employers, consumers, regulators, health care providers, and the workers' compensation and managed care industries. Member organizations of URAC participate in the development of standards.

URAC offers ten different accreditation programs for managed care organizations:

1. Case management organization standards,
2. Credential verification organization (CVO) standards,
3. Health call center standards,
4. Health network standards,

5. Health plan standards,
6. Health utilization management standards,
7. Network practitioner credentialing standards,
8. Workers' compensation network standards,
9. Workers' compensation utilization management standards, and
10. External review standards.

Since 1991, URAC has issued over 1,600 accreditation certificates to over 300 organizations doing business in all 50 states. URAC-accredited organizations provide managed care services to over 120 million Americans.

Because of URAC's broad-based standards and accreditation process, purchasers and consumers look to URAC's accreditation as an indication that a managed care organization has the necessary structures and processes to promote high quality care and preserve patient rights. In addition, regulators in over half of the states recognize the URAC's accreditation standards in the regulatory process.

URAC's quality mission also has diversified and expanded in recent years. For example, URAC is engaged in several research projects to assess and identify new approaches to improve performance measurement in a variety of health care settings.

Q 19:12 Is quality important to employees when they choose a health plan?

According to a 1998 survey by the MEDSTAT Group, choice of providers was the most important category to consumers. Confidence that the plan will provide needed services was second most important. The third most important factor was the attentiveness and listening skills of the physicians and other healthcare professionals.

A 1998 survey of Massachusetts employees by researchers at Brandeis University found the five types of information rated as essential in choosing a health plan were:

1. Specific benefits,
2. Average out-of-pocket costs,

Q 19:13   **Health Insurance Answer Book**

3. Quality of primary care physicians available,
4. Premiums, and
5. Lists of participating physicians and hospitals.

Few employees consider customer satisfaction results or ratings by independent experts to be essential. The researchers concluded that consumers may be "willing to make quality comparisons among providers and plans but are skeptical about the reliability of outside evaluators." Consumers may need more exposure to this type of information before considering it essential. The "key to getting employees to use such information may be a function of the clarity of the presentation." This conclusion is consistent with the results of a 1998 study by researchers from the University of Oregon who found that consumers tend to disregard quality information that they do not understand.

Q 19:13   Are employers really concerned about quality?

According to a 1997 survey by the Washington Business Group on Health, 51 percent of employers said they look for quality in their definition of value, up from 45 percent in 1996. The survey also found that 51 percent mentioned cost as a definition of value in choosing a health plan, down from 59 percent the prior year.

Q 19:14   What is being done to help employees understand the quality issues?

In April 1998 a new employer program, the Employer Quality Partnership (EQP), announced a campaign to help employees become more aware of quality in their health plans.

EQP is a coalition of leading employer groups, including the following:

- The Business Roundtable
- Association of Private Pension and Welfare Plans
- The ERISA Industry Committee
- National Association of Manufacturers
- National Association of Wholesalers-Distributors

- National Federation of Independent Business
- The U.S. Chamber of Commerce

The EQP's first activity was a brochure for employees entitled "Navigating the Health Care System." It was designed to help employees both understand their health plans and deal with problems as they happen. Included are topics such as understanding a health plan before joining it; how and when to find a second opinion; consumer rights and responsibilities; how to appeal unpaid claims; and how to contact help when questions arise.

Other activities of the EQP program include preparing information for consumers about selecting health coverage and advice for small and medium-sized employers about choosing health care coverage for employees. The coalition's booklets are available to the general public through its web site: www.eqp.org.

Q 19:15 Are cost pressures affecting quality?

According to a survey released in 1998 by the Healthcare Financial Management Association, 54 percent of health care providers report that cost pressures are adversely affecting quality.

Report Card Movement

Q 19:16 Does the report card movement among managed care plans affect health care quality?

To date, the results of the quality assurance and "report card" movement are widespread, and marked improvements have occurred in the quality of care throughout most health plans. Challenging accreditation standards have forced health plans to focus on continuous improvement. Dissemination of this information has created external and internal motivators. Externally, health plans and hospitals compete for market share; internally, health care professionals (i.e., physicians, nurses, assistants, administrators) gain awareness and education and strive for more optimal contribution to overall plan performance.

Health plans use report cards to demonstrate their level of performance, to drive market share, and to fend off criticism of managed health care. Self-reported statistics on levels and results of care delivered to plan participants become a useful tool over time in documenting patterns and trends as well as in pinpointing problem areas. For example, if the percentage of women aged 50–74 receiving annual mammograms declines, the health plan is made aware of a patient education and recommendation need.

Q 19:17 What criticisms have been leveled against managed care report card efforts?

The three major criticisms of managed care report card efforts are that: (1) the report card data can be suspect because they are self-reported by health plans; (2) the data are not audited or validated by independent third parties; and (3) the ability of employers to compare plans is limited because only a portion of the total number of available health plans have incorporated quality assurance and report card procedures.

Q 19:18 Are customer satisfaction measures included on report cards?

Yes. One example is the report card used by the Buyers HealthCare Action Group in Minneapolis. Employees are given the following patient satisfaction results for each provider:

- Overall satisfaction with the clinic
- Satisfaction with overall quality of care and service from the clinic
- Satisfaction with ease of seeing doctor of choice
- Satisfaction with amount of time doctor spends with patient
- Satisfaction with attention paid by doctors and staff to what patients say
- Satisfaction with explanations of medical procedures and tests

Q 19:19 How common are patient satisfaction studies?

A 1998 survey of health care executives by KPMG Peat Marwick found that 67 of 70 organizations surveyed have done at least one patient satisfaction study. A surprising 51 of the 70 surveyed report advanced consumer satisfaction activities, such as linking compensation to survey results.

Q 19:20 Are there any national report card projects?

There are two noteworthy evaluation programs: HEDIS (see the following section) and Consumer Assessment of Health Plans (CAHPS). The CAHPS project is sponsored by the Agency for Health Care Policy and Research in a cooperative effort with the Harvard Medical School, the Rand Corporation, and the Research Triangle Institute.

Q 19:21 How satisfied are people enrolled in managed care?

According to the NCQA's Quality Compass report, which uses HEDIS data, 57.08 percent of members nationally are "completely" or "very" satisfied with their current managed care plan.

Q 19:22 What are some examples of report cards in use?

According to the *Report on Report Cards* by the Economic and Social Research Institute, there are cases where employers and employees are using report cards to help make good choices, such as:

1. Faced both with information ranking health plans on cost and quality and with financial incentives to select a good plan, General Motors' salaried employees are migrating to the better-performing plans.
2. The California Public Employees Retirement System (CalPERS), serving about one million state and local government employees and their dependents, has produced three rounds of useful report cards and uses feedback from consumers to improve them each year.

3. CalPERS and The Alliance in Colorado, which represents business purchasers, have both tied a portion of premiums to the plan's ability to meet performance targets.
4. In December 1999, New Jersey's State Health Benefits Program (the sixth-largest public employee benefit plan in the nation, announced it would use data from the 2000 report card as a tool to set rates. The program will cut administrative fees by 5 percent if a plan fails to reach statewide averages on at least 70 percent of the customer satisfaction and performance measures.

The Joint Commission and HEDIS

Q 19:23 What is the Joint Commission?

The Joint Commission on Accreditation of Health Organizations examines the quality of health care workers. The Joint Commission's criteria for health care worker evaluations include professional experience and the type and amount of education and training received. It also reviews policies and procedures used by health care providers. The Joint Commission makes a provider's accreditation status a matter of public record; however, it will not make publicly known the reason a provider is placed on conditional accreditation. Joint Commission representatives contact plan participants to obtain customer feedback and report views and recommendations to the health plan.

Q 19:24 What is HEDIS?

The Health Plan Employer Data and Information Set (HEDIS) is the most widely used tool for evaluating health plan performance. Initiated in the late 1980s by employers seeking uniform measures of HMO performance, HEDIS has evolved through several versions under the leadership of the NCQA.

HEDIS is a set of standardized performance measures designed to ensure that purchasers and consumers have the information they need to compare reliably the performance of managed health care plans. The performance measures in HEDIS are related to many significant public health issues such as cancer, heart disease, smoking, asthma, and diabetes. HEDIS also includes a standardized survey of consumers' experiences that evaluates plan performance in areas such as customer service, access to care, and claim possessing. HEDIS is sponsored, supported, and maintained by NCQA.

Using information from NCQA's accreditation program (an evaluation of how managed care plans are organized and how they operate) in combination with HEDIS data provides the most complete view of health plan quality available to guide choice among competing health plans. HEDIS provides purchasers and consumers with an unprecedented ability both to evaluate the quality of different health plans along a variety of important dimensions, and to make their plan decisions based upon demonstrated value rather than simply on cost.

Q 19:25 Does the NCQA use HEDIS data as part of its accreditation process?

Traditionally, NCQA's HEDIS and accreditation programs were separate. Starting in 1999, HEDIS measures became part of the accreditation process. NCQA gives 75 percent weight to site visits and 25 percent to HEDIS measures. Although site visits normally occur every three years, NCQA will be able to evaluate HEDIS data annually.

Q 19:26 Does HEDIS include financial measures?

Yes. HEDIS addresses three categories of financial measurement: performance, liquidity, and efficiency indicators. Measures include total revenues, net income, overall loss ratio, administrative loss ratio, medical loss ratio, days cash on hand, ratio of cash to claims, and days in unpaid claims.

Outcomes Measurement

Q 19:27 What is outcomes measurement?

Once employers have gained experience in collecting data on quality, they usually find they want more detailed data. They want details on the health status of workers as well as information on the results of care, also called "outcomes" data. Outcomes measurement identifies the effects of health services on patients, that is, whether a patient's health has improved as a result of the treatment rendered. It includes establishing mechanisms to identify effects, creating data collection and reporting mechanisms to evaluate whether services fulfill purchaser and patient expectations, and developing information for patients about what to expect as a result of care.

Q 19:28 What type of system is need to measure outcomes?

Proponents of establishing outcomes measurement systems say that medicine needs a common language to describe the effects of medical services and other factors on patients. At the same time, they say, medical practice needs to evolve into an ongoing observational study, tracking and measuring patients' well-being and quality of life. To accomplish this, ideal systems would:

1. Measure a patient's functional status and quality of life over time, using terms readily understandable by patients and providers.
2. Document changes over time in a patient's clinical condition as a result of therapy.
3. Ensure that data are collected in a common format, using widely accepted public domain protocols across a large number of sites.
4. Maintain data collected from multiple sites in a single repository, allowing comparisons of patient outcomes.
5. Incorporate standardized and valid methods of accounting for health care organizations' effects on health and quality of life.

Advocates say that such an extensive data base would help eliminate some of the variation in quality found commonly in medicine today. Providers could use the system to evaluate and to choose therapies, to counsel patients about expected outcomes and side effects, to follow the progress of health conditions, and to estimate the necessary resources that would be expended on treatment. Employers could use the system to predict the cost of medical care, to select from among various providers, and to redesign employee health insurance benefits.

Q 19:29 How can employers reduce the cost of obtaining outcomes data?

Collecting outcomes data likely may require the efforts and financial resources of more than one employer. Consider the following steps:

1. Join a coalition of employers and push for a data-collection effort. Some coalitions already have extensive outcomes and quality data-collection programs in place. Depending on the services available through the coalition and the size of the insured population, coalitions may charge roughly $250 to $5,000 annually for membership. Contact the National Business Coalition on Health for information on local coalitions.
2. Join the Foundation for Accountability to get population-based and condition-specific outcomes measures.
3. Have a consultant develop an outcomes data-collection system, and share the cost with employer health plans. The cost to develop such a system could be in the millions of dollars, depending on the employer's needs.

Q 19:30 What is a quality improvement organization?

A quality improvement organization (QIO) is a regional corporation that develops programs in quality improvement and evaluation for Medicare, Medicaid, and a variety of other private and public payers. QIOs have expertise in the clinical application of statistical analysis of health care data.

Chapter 20

Home Health Care and Long-Term Care

An increasing amount of health care is now being rendered at home. Long-term care is also a growing concern. This chapter introduces alternative approaches to chronic care, including hospice care, and discusses such issues as home health care fraud.

Home Health Care	20-1
Home Health Care Fraud	20-12
Long-Term Care	20-14
Subacute Care	20-21
Hospice Care	20-24

Home Health Care

Q 20:1 What is home health care?

Home health care provides services in the home, rather than in a hospital or facility. Home health care services usually include the services of registered nurses, licensed practical nurses, certified nurse's aides, and other specialty services provided by individuals such as physical and occupational therapists. Sometimes home health care agencies are confused with homemaker agencies, which provide nonmedical services such as light housekeeping, shopping, meal preparation, laundry service, and companionship. Some agencies offer both types of services.

Q 20:2 What is the history of home health care?

The first home care program was organized in the United States by the Boston Dispensary around 1800. It was developed in response to wealthy patients' preference for home health care over hospitalization. In the late 1800s, voluntary home nursing services were organized; they later became visiting nurse associations. With improved sanitation and living conditions, the focus of patient care shifted from communicable diseases to long-term illnesses. In addition, the lack of available care caused by the shortage of hospitals was alleviated by the increase of home care programs.

In the 1940s, the need for home health services expanded so quickly that government agencies, hospitals, voluntary health associations, and private insurance companies all offered home health services. With the enactment of the Medicare program in 1965, home health care began to change rapidly. Medicare stipulated that for an agency to participate in the Medicare program, the agency had to meet the criteria specifically outlined in Section 1861(o) of the Social Security Act as well as comply with federal regulations.

During the 1970s and into the 1980s, most home health care was provided by nonprofit agencies, such as the Visiting Nurse Association. By the early 1990s, most home health care was provided by for-profit corporations.

Q 20:3 Is the market for home health care growing?

Home health care services are continuing to grow in popularity and complexity. This can be attributed to the growth of the aging population, the advancement of medical technology, and an increasing focus on controlling health care costs. Services and treatment that previously required hospitalization can now be offered in the patient's home. In addition, providing services in the home setting is usually less expensive, and lower cost is attractive to health care payors. Reimbursement tied to diagnosis-related groups (DRGs) has resulted in earlier discharge from hospitals for even medically complex patients.

Total home care spending in the United States in 1994 was estimated to be $40.1 billion, according to a recent study conducted for the U.S. Department of Health and Human Services by Lewin VHI Inc. According to the U.S. Bureau of Statistics, the fastest growing occupation is that of home health aide.

Agencies themselves have also undergone change. Traditionally provided primarily by voluntary, nonprofit organizations with strong community ties, the provision of home health care services has begun to shift to private, for-profit organizations.

Q 20:4 Who provides home health care?

The Omnibus Budget Reconciliation Act (OBRA) of 1980 changed the ownership patterns of home health agencies. OBRA removed the restriction barring certification of proprietary home health agencies in states without home licensure laws and liberalized the conditions under which Medicare would reimburse home care. Now, home health care is provided by institution-based agencies, proprietary agencies, nonprofit agencies, and government organizations.

Visiting nurse associations (VNAs) and private nonprofit agencies. VNAs are nonprofit agencies that are run autonomously by members of local communities. They are generally older agencies and often provide more supportive home health services than do proprietary agencies. In addition to VNAs, there are also private nonprofit agencies. Like VNAs, they are tax-exempt and have a board of directors that is responsible for the agency's management and operation. These agencies commonly merge with hospitals or other agencies to ensure survival—many VNAs and nonprofit agencies are even forming for-profit ventures with hospitals, durable medical equipment providers, and others in the health care marketplace.

Government agencies. These agencies are gradually declining in number. Increased competition with for-profit agencies has often left these agencies to care for a high percentage of indigent patients. In addition, there has been a decrease of available funds because many government programs have been cut. Government agencies are strongest in rural areas and in states that have certificate of need (CON) programs that limit the number of licensed home health agencies. These laws vary from state to state.

Institution-based agencies. An agency affiliated with an institution, such as a hospital, may have organizational and resource benefits that can be beneficial to both staff and patients. These type of home health agencies can be for profit or nonprofit. Hospitals began providing home health care in the 1980s to keep patients within their systems, to provide a comprehensive network of health care services, and to increase revenues. The majority of home care referrals come from hospitals; therefore, these agencies have an advantage over other types of agencies.

Proprietary agencies. Proprietary, or "for-profit," agencies now constitute the majority of Medicare-certified home health agencies. They may be independently and locally owned, part of a chain, a locally owned franchise, or part of a national or international organization. These agencies are investor-owned and must pay taxes on profits. Usually they do not provide the amount of charity services that nonprofit agencies do.

Q 20:5 Who uses home health care?

The primary users of home health care are people over 65. Of this population, those over age 85 and people in their last years of life have the greatest utilization, as they are more likely to lose their independence and require supportive and skilled health care services. The pediatric population also has a high rate of home health care utilization. Technology is allowing increasingly greater numbers of children with serious health problems to be discharged and treated at home. The goal of home health care is to promote independence and to provide an alternative to institutional care no matter what age group is being served.

Q 20:6 What are the advantages of home health care?

Home health care can be used to avoid hospitalization for the patient altogether or to shorten the length of stay. Obviously, the cost savings potential for health care services provided in the home is enormous. Based on government figures, average hospital charges per day in 1992 were $1,459, skilled nursing facility charges were $264 per day, and home health care charges per visit were $75. Estimates for 1994 were $1,756, $284, and $83, respectively.

Equally important, however, is that by providing care in the patient's own home setting, his or her social support system can also be easily incorporated into a program of care. Studies have shown that the home environment promotes recovery faster than the long-term-care setting. Finally, providing health care in home settings reduces the possibility of contracting an infectious disease.

Q 20:7 What kinds of services can be provided in the home?

Not all home health agencies provide the same services. An agency that is Medicare-certified must provide skilled nursing, physical therapy, occupational therapy, speech therapy, and social services. Agencies employ licensed professionals such as registered nurses, therapists, and physicians, and offer some or all of these services and equipment needs:

1. Skilled nursing services:
   - Oxygen
   - Oximetry
   - Ventilator services
   - Suction equipment
   - Apnea monitoring
   - Nasal C-PAP, Bi-PAP
   - Hand-held nebulizers
   - Asthma programs
   - Respiratory medications
   - Kidney dialysis
   - Medication administration
   - Infusion therapy
   - Phototherapy
   - Uterine monitoring

2. Professional services
   - Occupational therapy
   - Physical therapy
   - Speech therapy
   - Skilled nursing
   - Respiratory therapy
   - Social work
3. Home medical equipment and durable medical equipment:
   - Hospital beds and specialty beds
   - Wheelchairs, walkers, and bedside commodes
   - Hoyer lifts
4. Social or custodial services (usually provided by unlicensed personnel such as certified nurse's aides, home health care aides, or companions):
   - Transportation
   - Personal care
   - Meal preparation or delivery
   - Housekeeping
   - Shopping
   - Companionship

Q 20:8 How are the frequency and the duration of services determined?

The frequency and duration of services provided to the patient are determined by a physician's orders and, to some extent, what the patient's health care plan will cover. The physician's orders are received when the agency begins care for the patient. The physician then continues to work with the agency's licensed professionals, seeking their recommendations as he or she issues further orders.

Q 20:9 How can employers foster the use of home health care?

Employers can foster the use of home health care by providing coverage for these services as a part of health care benefit plans.

Employers can opt to contract directly with the home health care provider or use existing contracts negotiated by their benefit administrators. A generous benefit plan would cover all medically necessary home health care services. A less liberal plan might offer reimbursement for a specific number of visits from registered nurses, certified nurse's aides, physical therapists, occupational therapists, and other health care professionals each calendar year.

Q 20:10 Who monitors home health care agencies?

Home health care agencies are typically monitored by state and federal governments and private organizations.

Most states require licensing and perform some sort of review to monitor performance. Any agency accepting Medicare patients must comply with extensive rules set forth by the Health Care Financing Administration. Copies of the Medicare Survey Report are available to the public through the agency or any Social Security office.

The National League for Nursing and the Home Care Accreditation Program, a division of the Joint Commission on Accreditation of Healthcare Organizations (the Joint Commission), both accredit home health care agencies (see Q 20:17).

Q 20:11 Does coverage for extended care facilities and home health care help an employer manage health care costs?

The average cost for a day in a hospital varies from region to region and hospital to hospital, but it is almost always higher than for a day in an extended care facility. Many individuals can recuperate just as quickly and safely at a skilled nursing center.

Home health care can be even less expensive. In addition, some patients find that recuperation at home is more comfortable and faster than in a hospital. Further, the possibility of contracting an infectious disease increases the risk of extended stay at a hospital.

Q 20:12 How much can home health care save?

In some instances, quite a bit. Although extensive data covering a broad spectrum of employers and situations over a lengthy period of time are not available, the data that are available show promise. The U.S. government estimated that average hospital charges per day were $1,549 in 1992, while skilled nursing facility charges were $264 per day, and home care was $75 per day. In 1994, those same estimates were $1,756, $284, and $83, respectively.

Q 20:13 Are there reasons an employer should not include home health care coverage as part of its medical plan?

There is growing evidence that home health care coverage should be included. Home health care coverage has shown enormous potential for reducing costs. There are, however, ample opportunities for excessive or unnecessary use of home health services, and abuses of this benefit could lead to cost increases, not savings.

To any plan administrator faced with the possibility of trading off a $500-per-day hospital room for a $200-per-day visiting nurse service charge, the decision may seem obvious; however, the question is: Could the treatment be administered on an outpatient basis, either at the hospital or at the doctor's office? On that basis, the charge might have been $50 or $75 per day.

In choosing among inpatient, home care, and outpatient options, the critical factor is the quality of the controls (such as utilization review) available to the administrator. What decision processes are in place (or can be put in place) to assure that each case is looked at fairly? What processes will be used to evaluate the range of options available, and how will it be determined that home health care is the most appropriate health care method available?

Q 20:14 Is home health care coverage commonly found in medical plans?

This coverage has become widely available. As employers come to recognize the benefits of home care and its cost-effectiveness, more are making the option available. In fact, it is now highly unusual for an employer of any size not to reimburse for home health coverage.

Q 20:15 Which home care services are most employers providing?

Most employers cover professional services such as skilled nursing and therapy (physical, occupational, and speech). Also commonly covered are medical equipment and supplies, especially high-tech equipment, which is very expensive in a hospital but less so in the home. Coverage for visits by aides and physicians is not uncommon, but is not as universal as is skilled service coverage. Almost no contracts cover custodial and social services.

Q 20:16 What is the procedure for installing home health care coverage?

An employer must decide whether to contract directly for in-home services or to make use of already existing contracts that the employer's insurance company may have negotiated with providers. It is much more common to use the latter approach, because it is likely that a health maintenance organization (HMO) or insurance carrier has already secured such services for other clients.

Whether the services are contracted directly or indirectly, the employer should pay particular attention to accreditation. Two major home health care accreditation agencies are: (1) the National League for Nursing; and (2) the Joint Commission. Addresses for both organizations are listed in Appendix A at the end of this book.

Q 20:17 What kinds of information does accreditation provide?

Both the National League for Nursing and the Joint Commission examine the quality of the workers, including their experience and the type and amount of training they have received. The agencies also review the policies and procedures used by the providers.

The National League for Nursing goes further, requiring that the providers perform criminal background checks of their home care workers. They also contract with consultants to perform a financial and management review of the providers.

The Joint Commission makes a provider's accreditation status a matter of public record; however, it will not make publicly known the reasons for placing a provider on "conditional accreditation." The National League for Nursing also makes its accreditation status known; however, it does not have a "conditional" status.

Each agency treats the issue of customer references slightly differently. The National League for Nursing demands that providers release names of former customers, while the Joint Commission calls current customers for their views and recommendations.

Q 20:18 What information cannot be learned through accreditation?

Accreditation is specific and limited to the area of expertise for which the accreditation was granted. That means, for example, that a firm accredited for providing intravenous medications and physical therapy is not necessarily accredited for skilled nursing. Instances have been found in which home care companies have misrepresented their accreditation as being all-encompassing when in fact it was limited. Some providers have even falsified having certification.

Q 20:19 What is the best procedure to follow in dealing directly with the home care agency?

First, an employer should obtain feedback from people who work with the agency or agencies being considered. Some sources include: other employers in the area; doctors, nurses, or other direct health services providers; discharge planners; and equipment providers.

When obtaining information from the home care agency itself, the following points may be used to lead the discussion:

1. Is the agency accredited? If yes, for what? Be as specific as possible (see Q 20:17).

2. If the agency is not accredited, why not? Has it been refused accreditation? If it was, why? Is it currently seeking accreditation?

3. Does the state in which the employer—or the agency—is located require licensing? If yes, is the agency licensed? If not, why not?
4. Is the agency certified by Medicare? If yes, the agency has met certain federal minimum requirements. Check with a local Social Security office and ask to see the Medicare Survey Report.
5. How long has the agency been in business?
6. What are the professional accreditations, skills, and backgrounds of the principals of the agency?
7. What are the minimum skills, experience, and training requirements for their employees? Does the agency check references and licensing status?
8. How does the agency select employees?
9. Does the agency train employees after they are hired (e.g., in the use of new technology or techniques)? Is there a formal or informal training/recertification program for employees?
10. How does the agency evaluate employees? Does it perform site evaluations? Are the evaluation criteria and standards written? If so, ask for a copy.
11. How frequently does the agency evaluate employees?
12. Will an employer be allowed to audit and review the agency's files to ensure compliance with the answers they have just provided?
13. How is the plan of care determined? Does the agency interview the patient's family, physician, or hospital records?
14. Who creates the plan of care? Is it done by a registered nurse, therapist, or doctor?
15. Is the plan of care in writing? May the employer review it?
16. How does the agency handle medical emergencies?
17. How does the agency handle patient care during natural emergencies, such as snowstorms?
18. Has the agency ever been sued? If yes, what was the suit about? What was the outcome?
19. How does the agency assure confidentiality of patient records?

20. How does the agency handle complaints from the patient? Who reviews the complaint and the response? Does the employer/purchaser have any say in the resolution?
21. If the agency uses advanced technology and machinery, how does it assure its proper functioning, care, and maintenance? Is the machinery inspected/calibrated/oiled on schedule? Are the batteries replaced on a regular basis?

Home Health Care Fraud

Q 20:20 Why is home health care frequently cited as ripe for health care fraud?

Fraud includes any intentional deception or misrepresentation that an individual knows to be false and that can result in an unauthorized benefit to himself or herself or some other person. In home health care, such activities include billing for services not rendered, kickbacks, deliberate duplication for duplicate reimbursement, using unlicensed or untrained staff, falsifying plans of care, forging doctors' signatures, and false or misleading entries on cost reports.

Sometimes incidents or practices are not fraudulent but may directly or indirectly cause financial losses to the health benefit payer, or to beneficiaries or recipients. Providing unnecessary services to the patient is an example of this type of activity, and is often difficult to detect because the physician or utilization review nurse seldom actually visits the patient receiving services. The patient's care is overseen by these professionals but is actually provided by other licensed professionals under their direction. It is therefore difficult for a third party to determine what services are necessary. The duration of services can also be an opportunity for fraud and abuse. Because the agency usually determines how often and how long the patient should receive services, it can increase length of services provided beyond what is medically necessary.

Other abusive practices include, but are not limited to, the breach of assignment (contract for payment) agreement, failure to maintain adequate records or accounting to substantiate costs, and excessive compensation to patient referral sources.

Some agencies have different pricing for private pay patients and those covered by a health plan. Finally, if the services are provided by a specialty company, or shared by two home health care agencies, duplication of services and billings can occur.

Q 20:21 Who pays for home health care fraud?

Taxpayers and consumers bear the greatest burden for home health care fraud. Medicare payments for home health care reached $18 billion a year in 1996, an increase of more than 500 percent from 1990. Unfortunately, a portion of these increased costs can be attributed to fraud. The General Accounting Office estimates that rampant fraud and waste in home health care claims is costing the Medicare program billions of dollars annually.

Q 20:22 What is being done to stop home health care fraud?

In May 1995, an initiative that targets fraud, waste, and abuse in home health care, nursing home care, and durable medical equipment began. Led by the U.S. Department of Health and Human Services (HHS) and the White House, the project involves the HHS Office of Inspector General (OIG), the U.S. Justice Department, several state attorneys general, and state health authorities. Developed as a two-year demonstration project, it targets fraud in California, Florida, Illinois, New York, and Texas, which together account for 40 percent of the nation's population of Medicare and Medicaid recipients. Under the Ethics in Patient Referrals Act (also known as the Stark Bill), referrals by a physician to a clinical laboratory in or with which the physician has a financial interest or relationship are expressly prohibited. Effective December 31, 1994, under an amendment to the Stark Bill, the prohibition was extended to cover home health care (as well as numerous other health care services) in addition to clinical laboratory services.

The Health Insurance Portability and Accountability Act of 1996 (HIPAA) included a number of provisions intended to reduce fraud, including home health care fraud. For example, physicians who give false certification of the need for home health care services are subject to penalties.

Long-Term Care

Q 20:23 What is long-term care?

Long-term care refers to the services that would be required over an extended period of time by someone who has a chronic illness or disability. Patients who require long-term care are generally individuals who are functionally disabled because of a chronic or long-term nonremediable physical or mental condition. An individual who cannot perform some or all of the activities of daily living (ADLs) is considered functionally disabled. HIPAA defines ADLs as the following: bathing, dressing, toileting, eating, continence, and transferring from a bed or chair.

The types of care provided could range from home health care to hospitalization; however, the emphasis is on custodial and skilled nursing care, and attendant outpatient services. It can also include such things as meals-on-wheels, respite care, home health aides, and visiting nurses.

Q 20:24 What are the different levels of long-term care?

There are three basic levels of long-term care:

1. *Skilled nursing care.* Care is provided by skilled medical personnel under the supervision or orders of a doctor. (Medication administration alone does not usually qualify as a need for skilled services.) This includes daily nursing or rehabilitative care at a skilled nursing facility, which is usually licensed by the state and approved by Medicare/Medicaid to provide skilled care.
2. *Intermediate care.* Nursing care on an occasional basis is provided by skilled medical personnel. The care must conform to a doctor's orders.
3. *Custodial care.* Assistance is provided in meeting such personal needs as bathing, dressing, and eating. It can be provided by

skilled or nonskilled medical personnel in skilled or intermediate nursing facilities or, in less demanding circumstances, through a program of home health care.

Q 20:25 What are the special issues connected with long-term care?

According to the National Council on Aging, there is a 45 percent to 60 percent probability that some age 65 eventually will be admitted to a nursing home. Because of the mobility of the population and varying life styles, family support systems have been reduced, and more institutional care will therefore be necessary. Generally, neither group insurance plans that continue after retirement nor Medicare provides coverage for long-term care, except in a facility that provides skilled medical care. Even then, coverage is usually for only a limited period of time.

For most of the elderly disabled, the greater need is for intermediate or custodial care. Insurance companies have begun to respond with individual policies that address the special needs of elderly former employees.

Q 20:26 What are the advantages of long-term care?

Skilled or intermediate nursing facilities are a useful alternative to prolonged hospitalization. The cost of care in a nursing facility is much less than that in an acute care hospital. Many individuals can recuperate just as quickly and safely at a skilled nursing facility. Extended care is usually an option when the patient is not safe at home and does not have the support systems available for home health care. Therapies and medical regimens also might not be available in the home setting.

Q 20:27 How expensive is long-term care?

Nursing home costs can range from $30,000 to $80,000 or more a year, depending on geographic region and level of care provided. Minimum home health care five days a week can cost $10,000 a year—more for skilled assistance. In 1997, *The Wall Street Journal* reported that nursing home costs had risen roughly 20 percent in three years to an average of $46,000 a year and that assisted-living facilities ranged from $20,000 to $48,000. According to *Financial Services Online*, the average cost in New York City is $81,000.

According to a 1998 study by MetLife, the average cost of a nursing home is $140 per day ($51,100 annually). It ranges from $90 per day in Louisiana ($32,850 a year) to $413 per day in Alaska ($150,745 annually). The second most expensive state is Connecticut at $202 per day ($73,730 a year). The average nursing home stay is two and a half years, so the average cost per nursing home confinement is $127,750.

Q 20:28 What long-term care benefits does Medicare provide?

Medicare pays less than 5 percent of the nation's total annual nursing home expenses and provides home health or nursing home care only in limited circumstances. Coverage for medically necessary skilled nursing care is available for up to 100 days per "spell of illness" (with some limitations and exclusions) and requires a copayment of $95.50 per day after the first 20 days. To be eligible, a person must be admitted within 30 days of a three-day hospital stay. In some circumstances, part-time skilled home health care may be available.

Q 20:29 What long-term care services are covered by Medicaid?

Unlike Medicare, Medicaid pays substantial benefits for nursing home care, accounting for over 40 percent of all nursing home payments. As a federally funded program administered by the states, Medicaid can vary in coverage. Medicaid coverage for long-term care is actually a form of public assistance, designed to supplement an individual's monthly income to pay for care. Participants must meet specific income and assets requirements before becoming eligible for Medicaid benefits. The patient pays as much as he or she is able each month, and the balance is paid by the Medicaid program. Medicaid reimbursement rates are usually less than what would be charged to a private patient. HIPAA includes criminal penalties for fraudulent disposition of assets in order to obtain Medicaid.

Q 20:30 How prevalent are employer-sponsored long-term care plans?

According to the Health Insurance Association of America (HIAA), 1,532 employers sponsor long-term care plans in the United States. That number is growing by about 22 percent a year. HIAA reports that participation rates vary from 1 percent to 37 percent; the average is 6 percent. The average age of participants is 43 years. According to the National Association of Life Underwriters, the average age of purchasers of individual coverage is 63. A survey by the Gallup Organization for Intracorp found an average participation of 17 percent. Now that the Health Insurance Portability and Accountability Act of 1996 has clarified the tax status of long-term care plans, most observers expect rapid growth in the number of employer-sponsored plans. A 1996 survey by Hewitt Associates found that 25 percent of major employers offered long-term care insurance, up from 5 percent in 1990. According to the Bureau of Labor Statistics, less than 10 percent of full-time employees were offered long-term care insurance in 1997.

Q 20:31 Do employers contribute to the cost of long-term care policies?

Generally, no. A William M. Mercer Inc. survey of 66 employers with long-term care benefits found only one that contributed to the cost. This is likely to change in the future.

Q 20:32 What does a typical long-term care benefit cover?

A typical plan might provide for skilled, intermediate, and custodial care in state-licensed nursing homes, as well as home health care from Medicare-approved or state-licensed providers. Benefits are often based on a stated dollar amount for skilled nursing care. The dollar benefit is usually an option chosen at the time the policy is written. A survey by William M. Mercer Inc. found a range from $30 to $260 a day. Lesser types of care, such as adult day care, are usually covered at a percentage of the skilled nursing benefit (e.g., 50 percent of the skilled nursing benefit).

A 1997 survey by William M. Mercer, Inc. of over 50 employers with long-term care policies found that 100 percent cover nursing home care, 92 percent cover skilled home health care, 91 percent cover adult day care, 74 percent cover unskilled home personal care, and 74 percent cover respite care.

The survey also found that 98 percent of the policies offer coverage to spouses of employees, 96 percent offer coverage to parents of employees, 91 percent offer coverage to parents of spouses of employees, 73 percent offer coverage to retirees and their spouses, and 23 percent offer coverage to grandparents and grandparents-in-law of employees. Two employers reported that they offered coverage to domestic partners of employees.

Most plans offered choices of three or four daily maximum benefits, but some only offered one, and one offered 18 choices.

Q 20:33 Are benefits adjusted for inflation?

Although some policies make adjustments for inflation in the level of daily benefits over time, many do not. Those that do may not fully adjust for changes in the cost of living. For example, some policies provide a flat dollar increase (e.g., $5 a day) after a specified number of years (e.g., five). To be qualified under HIPAA, inflation protection must be offered.

Q 20:34 What is the tax status of custodial care?

HIPAA clarified the tax status of long-term care insurance. Long-term care insurance is now clearly treated as an accident and health insurance policy. This means employers can provide long-term care insurance to employees and the employees will not be taxed on either the value of the coverage or the benefits received. For policies that pay a flat per diem benefit, rather than reimbursing actual expenses, benefits in excess of $190 per day (in 1999) are taxable (this amount is indexed by the medical component of the consumer price index).

The IRS issued final regulations on long-term care policies on December 10, 1998. HIPAA provides that a contract issued before January 1, 1997 is treated as a qualified long-term care contract if it met the requirements of the state in which it was issued at the time it was issued. For purposes of this grandfather provision, any material change is considered a new contract.

Q 20:35 Who provides long-term care insurance?

Long-term care insurance is fairly widely available from commercial insurers. In addition, HMOs, preferred provider organizations, nursing home chains, and continued care retirement communities provide long-term care plans.

Q 20:36 How much does long-term care insurance cost?

The cost varies, depending on age at purchase, level of benefits elected, and normal variability from one insurer to another. Individual premiums may be as low as $250 annually, and can range up to $8,000 or more. The annual premium for a long-term care policy with good inflation protection can run as much as $2,000 for someone age 65.

According to a survey by the Health Insurance Association of America, a 50-year-old would pay $364 annually for a daily nursing home benefit of $100. A 65-year-old would pay $980 for the same policy. Adding a 5 percent automatic annual increase to the benefit raises the premium for the 50-year-old to $802 and $1,829 for the 65-year-old.

According to the American Council of Life Insurance, the average annual premium for a person age 65 to 69 desiring an individual policy that will cover a five-year stay in a nursing home is $2,400. For someone age 75, premiums are more than $5,300 a year. For someone age 35 to 39, the cost is only $507.

Q 20:37 What considerations should be taken into account in evaluating long-term care insurance policies?

These nine factors should be considered when evaluating long-term care policies:

1. *Premium.* Premiums are generally determined on an entry-age level basis. An older person buying long-term care insurance would pay more than a younger one, but a given individual's premium does not increase as he or she gets older. Many

policies offer a premium waiver, which continues the policy in force if the owner is unable to continue payments. Another consideration is how long the rate is guaranteed; group policy premiums are often adjusted annually.

2. *Coverage ages.* Most policies have minimum and maximum coverage ages, generally ranging from age 45 to age 50 at the low end and from age 75 to age 80 at the high end.

3. *Duration of benefits.* Policies may impose limits on the duration of care in a nursing facility (e.g., a maximum of five years of nursing home coverage). There may be a limit for each confinement, and a lifetime overall limit, which may apply to utilization or maximum reimbursement amounts. Limits for custodial care and home health care may also be expressed separately. Of course, the longer the period covered, the higher the premium.

4. *Elimination periods.* Policy benefits may not cover the initial period of care, and may require a specified stay, such as 30 days, before any benefits are payable. In this example, benefits would be payable commencing with the 31st day.

5. *Exclusions.* Long-term care insurance generally does not provide coverage for preexisting conditions (from three to six months before, and from six to 12 months after, the effective date of coverage), self-inflicted injuries, alcoholism, mental illness, or treatment outside the United States. One problem area is an exclusion for mental illness and nervous disorders; sometimes these disorders are further broken down into organic and nonorganic. Special care should be taken that these exclusions do not encompass Alzheimer's disease and related impairments, because patients with these illnesses frequently require nursing home care. HIPAA requires qualified long-term care plans to provide benefits for people with severe cognitive impairments.

6. *Renewability.* The policy should be guaranteed renewable and noncancelable. HIPAA requires qualified long-term care policies to be guaranteed renewable.

7. *Care levels.* Some policies are specific in covering only certain types of care, such as skilled nursing care only. Because long-term care expense is associated with custodial care, this

should be avoided. Preconditions (such as prior hospitalization) for home care should be avoided as well.
8. *Facilities.* Some policies, while covering all levels of care, restrict coverage to certain facilities, such as skilled nursing facilities approved by Medicare; however, because custodial care, which is often provided in an unskilled setting, is crucial, such restrictions should be avoided.
9. *Benefit levels.* Few policies gear benefits to actual costs incurred; instead, they pay a stated daily benefit determined by the level of care provided. Some sort of adjustment that increases the daily level over the life of the policy is necessary to keep the value of the policy from being overtaken by rising costs.

Q 20:38 Where can an employer obtain additional information on long-term care?

The HIAA offers a free "Consumer's Guide to Long-Term Care." Contact HIAA, 555 13th Street, N.W., Suite 600 East, Washington, DC 20004-1109, (202) 824-1662.

Subacute Care

Q 20:39 What is subacute care?

According to the American Subacute Care Association (ASCA), subacute patients are those who "are sufficiently stabilized to no longer require acute care services, but are too complex for treatment in a conventional nursing center." As defined by the Joint Commission

> subacute care is comprehensive inpatient care described for someone who has an acute illness, injury, or exacerbation of a disease process. It is a goal-oriented treatment rendered immediately after, or instead of, acute hospitalization, intended to treat one or more specific, active, complex medical conditions or to administer one or more technically complex treatments, in the context of a person's underlying long-term conditions and overall situation.

Subacute care is generally more intensive than traditional nursing home care and less intensive than acute care. It requires daily or weekly patient assessment and review of the treatment plan. Most of the subacute settings have been developed in nursing homes, but they can be free-standing or hospital-based. Katherine Reilly, RN, BS, ARCC, as reported in *The Broadcaster Newsletter*, profiled the average patient in subacute care:

- Age: 50
- Length of stay: 7 to 25 days
- Discharge status: return to home
- Payer: managed care benefit plan
- Daily charges: $225–$550 per day
- Rehabilitative therapy provided: up to four hours per day
- Patient care approach: patient education and instruction for self-care
- Physician visits: one to three times per week
- Patient care conference frequency: weekly
- Nursing care hours required per day: three to 5.7 per day

Q 20:40 What are the standards for assessing the quality of subacute care?

Both the Joint Commission and the Commission on Accreditation of Rehabilitation Facilities (CARF) have developed standards for subacute providers. The Joint Commission's standards for subacute care are based on its current accreditation standards for long-term care providers, while CARF's standards are focused more on the rehabilitation model. While there are no federal regulations that govern the level of care subacute agencies provide, individual states have passed regulations about licensure.

Q 20:41 Are there different levels of subacute care?

The International Subacute Healthcare Association specifies various levels of subacute care, including:

1. *Transitional subacute.* This level of care offers an alternative to continued hospitalization for stabilized medically complex patients. The patient's length of stay is usually five to 40 days.
2. *General subacute.* Often found in community-based nursing facilities, this level of care is typically appropriate for geriatric patients and patients needing rehabilitation rather than traditional subacute nursing care. The average length of stay is ten to 30 days.
3. *Chronic subacute.* This care level is appropriate for chronically ill patients such as those who are ventilator dependent.
4. *Transitional hospital.* A transitional hospital is usually licensed as a specialty hospital and is considered an acute long-term hospital. The average length of hospitalization stay is greater than 25 days. Most patients are technology dependent and require daily physician monitoring. Transitional hospitals often have an intensive care unit but are not equipped to provide emergency room, maternity, or other services offered by an acute care hospital.

Q 20:42 What are some of the objections to using skilled nursing facilities to provide subacute care?

It is becoming increasingly common for patients who are medically stable, but do not yet have the functional independence to return home safely, to be transferred from acute care hospitals to skilled nursing facilities for short-term subacute rehabilitative care. Despite this growing trend, patients are not always eager to receive care and treatment in skilled nursing facilities, traditionally known as nursing homes, because of the stigma they attach to them. A good nursing facility will be interested in working with the health benefits payer and the patient to make placement in a skilled nursing facility an acceptable alternative for short-term subacute care. Many skilled facilities will place the patient with another patient with a similar functional status and a goal of returning home, as well as encourage family members to visit the facility frequently.

Q 20:43 How is subacute care paid for?

Payment for subacute care includes private insurance, managed care contracts, Medicare, and Medicaid, and varies from state to state (although some states do not recognize subacute care). Many traditional insurance plans cover subacute care based on the setting in which it is provided. For example, the daily benefit payable for services rendered in a transitional hospital may be higher than the daily benefit for care in a skilled nursing facility.

Hospice Care

Q 20:44   What is a hospice?

A hospice provides palliative care, intended to relieve pain or symptoms rather than actually cure disease, for terminally ill patients with a limited life expectancy. An interdisciplinary team works with patients and their families, dealing with their physical, emotional, and social needs at a time when a curative approach is no longer available. Hospice care is appropriate for terminally ill patients:

1. Who do not want aggressive life support measures implemented;
2. Who reap no benefit from curative measures (aggressive disease treatment is no longer effective or appropriate); and
3. Who make an informed choice for hospice care.

A physician's order is required for patient participation in a hospice program. Hospice care can be provided in the patient's home, in a nursing facility, or in a dedicated hospice facility.

Q 20:45   Who pays for hospice care?

Medicare offers a comprehensive benefit for hospice patients who are eligible for Medicare Part A when services are rendered by a licensed, Medicare-certified hospice program. To be Medicare-certified, the hospice must have inpatient beds available for its patients, located either in a nursing facility or a dedicated hospice facility. The program pays for Medicare-approved services such as medications, medical supplies, and equipment related to palliative care of the patient. While the program does not allow curative-oriented therapies for the terminal illness, patients continue to be eligible for treatment of preexisting conditions other than the terminal illness through traditional Medicare coverage.

Traditional health care plans cover expenses for necessary medical care aimed at curing illness or injury. Hospice care, conversely, does not cure disease; therefore, clear-cut contractual coverage for palliative care is necessary for insurers to cover hospice care expenses.

Q 20:46 Is hospice care effective at controlling costs?

Hospice care has been shown to cost much less than confinement in an acute care hospital, where many chronically ill individuals spend much of their last months. Many factors contribute to the reduced costs of caring for terminally ill patients using a hospice program, including the following:

1. The nature of hospice care, aimed at managing the patient's symptoms and pain, is inherently less costly than the aggressive treatment of a terminal disease.

2. Room and board expenses are eliminated for hospice patients who are managed in a home setting, and are substantially less for patients in nursing facilities or dedicated hospice facilities.

3. Many hospice programs offer a full range of supportive services, such as homemaker services, caregiver support, and bereavement counseling, at little or no cost to hospice patients and their families. Many hospice programs have strong volunteer programs that assist in providing nonmedical services.

Hospice care is palliative, intended to relieve pain or symptoms rather than actually cure disease. It is provided to individuals with diseases that are incurable or have progressed to untreatable stages. Most hospice care benefits pay for additional home care, hospice facility care, palliative drugs and therapy, family counseling, and respite for family members caring for the patient.

Because hospice care does not technically cure disease, clear-cut contractual coverage for palliative care is necessary in order for insurers to cover hospice care expenses.

Chapter 21

Communication

The best benefit plan in the world will not deliver value to the employer without good communication. This chapter addresses strategy, principles, open enrollment communications, event-based communications, benefit statements, periodic benefit reports, and interactive systems.

Developing Communication Strategies	21-1
Benefit Statements	21-5
Periodic Benefit Reports	21-6
Interactive Systems	21-7
Online Services	21-9
Communicating Employee Benefits	21-11

Developing Communication Strategies

Q 21:1 Why do employers focus on employee health care benefit communications?

Health care benefit communication, like other benefit communication, should do more than inform. It should educate employees about how to use benefits intelligently. The idea of informing and educating employees is not just an altruistic goal for employers. The more that employees come to know and understand their benefits, the better they will appreciate the value that the benefits add to their overall compensation. This is best accomplished by a continuous rather than a one-shot communications effort.

Q 21:2 What makes a communication effort successful?

There are three steps to successful employee benefit communication. First, the employer should develop a strategy. This, in turn, establishes the boundaries for the employer's second step: the selection and development of media. After implementation, the employer should evaluate the communication effort in order to further hone the communication plan.

Q 21:3 How is a communication strategy developed?

First, objectives should be clearly identified. This includes deciding what employees need to know and what they will be expected to do with the information. The employer should be aware of the balance between too much information and not enough, not only when news is good and benefits are good, but also when benefits are reduced, eliminated, or changed in any way.

Next, the distinct audiences within the workforce should be identified. Messages can then be addressed to employee groups according to factors such as age, position, education, sex, marital status, length of service, and location, if appropriate to the information being conveyed. Employers should note that the constituents of these audiences change as employees join or leave the company, are promoted, or retire. In addition, some health benefit information will need to be explained only to employees who are affected.

Determining employees' familiarity with the subject matter is another important consideration in developing a communication strategy. Are employees knowledgeable about the benefit being communicated? Is the primary source of their information reliable? Information gathered through surveys or focus groups will be helpful in finding the correct level for the communication.

If time permits, employers should begin with a basic message without details, perhaps merely announcing the news and telling employees what to expect over the coming months. The idea is to create an awareness and to set the stage for more detailed communication. Next, they should provide the promised information, using examples wherever possible, especially to illustrate formulas or dollar amounts. If data cannot be personalized, it should be as relevant as possible for each audience in the workforce.

Depending on the complexity of this information, reinforcement may be in order in the form of group meetings, audiovisuals, or more lengthy written pieces. Finally, as the follow-up to an education or information effort, employers should reinforce the messages sent, perhaps by highlighting key points that require action and the deadline for response.

Q 21:4 What should an employer consider when selecting communications media?

The appropriateness of the communications media is an important consideration. There is a tendency to want to communicate benefits with "exciting" and expensive products such as four-color booklets, interactive computer programs, or videotapes. It is easy to forget that there are advantages and disadvantages to these media and that sometimes one format is more appropriate than another. Some options for communicating include letters, newsletters, brochures, handbooks, summary plan descriptions (SPDs), telephone voice response systems, telephone hotlines, meetings, counseling sessions, posters, and benefit statements. One rule about media choices always applies: The most successful campaigns use a variety of media, so that messages can be repeated and reinforced without becoming stale.

Q 21:5 What is an average budget for a communication campaign?

Generally, the overall communications budget should fall between 1 percent and 3 percent of the total annual benefits budget. While these percentages provide a good guideline for average to large size companies, smaller organizations (500 or fewer employees) may need to spend more. The budget for communicating a particular change should bear some relationship to the importance of the benefit and the company's style of communicating with employees.

Q 21:6 When should employers communicate changes in benefit plans?

When a benefit change is required because of a regulatory change or legal decision, it is unwise to communicate before the company has determined the full effect on its benefits. A more common mistake is, however, to react too slowly. Time lags leave employees to rely on other sources of information, eventually making it that much more difficult to communicate the company's message. When planning the communication budget, employers should anticipate the likelihood that pending benefit legislation or regulations will be passed, and judicial decisions will be handed down.

Anticipating benefit developments is just one aspect of timing. For employer-directed changes, employers should involve those responsible for benefit communication in the early discussions about plan changes or new benefits, rather than addressing benefit communication only after decisions are made. This gives communicators a head start on developing a strategy and pace for communications. The release of information should be paced over time so that employees are not overwhelmed by receiving too much information at once.

Q 21:7 Which is more effective for benefit communication, written or human resources?

Ideally, communication channels should include written and human resources. Under the Employee Retirement Income Security Act (ERISA), employers have a legal obligation to prepare written benefit information for employees. By law, the average plan participant must be able to understand this written material. "But because communication is, by definition, an exchange of information, ERISA-required SPDs, summary material modifications, and summary annual reports do not, and cannot, fulfill the same function as face-to-face communications. Effective communication elicits and responds to specific questions from employees about their benefits. The opportunity to have questions answered by an expert can take whatever form best matches the corporate culture and budget, from individual or group meetings to telephone hotlines to computer interactive benefit systems.

Q 21:8 What situations are appropriate for using event-based communications?

Event-based communications can be used to make general communications material more useful to employees in different stages of their life cycles. For example, information included in the SPD can be organized to address life-cycle events such as marriage, birth, divorce, and retirement. This approach underscores the employer's interest in employees as individuals and saves employees time by making pertinent information easier to find.

Another approach to event-based communications is to undertake communication campaigns targeted to specific groups of employees. For example, pregnant employees and their spouses could receive videos on prenatal care or printed information on nutrition and exercise during pregnancy. They could also be provided with information about family and medical leave, dependent care assistance plans, and flextime. Targeted communication campaigns also show that the employer recognizes and is concerned about employees' different benefit needs. Although these materials can be expensive to develop for relatively small groups, using existing products from vendors can help to minimize program costs.

Benefit Statements

Q 21:9 Why do employers issue benefit statements?

ERISA regulations require employers that sponsor defined benefits to provide retirement plan accrued and vested benefit statements to employees on request, no more than once a year. No such statement requirement exists for health insurance coverage. Many employers recognize, however, the advantages of going beyond ERISA's requirements and providing comprehensive benefit statements to every employee. Benefit statements allow employees to see exactly what benefits their employer provides and help to generate a sense of appreciation for employer-provided benefits. Typically, the statements list each benefit's monetary value to the individual and summarize the total package for which the employee is eligible, so employees can see that their compensation goes well beyond what they bring home in a paycheck.

Q 21:10 Do employees find benefit statements useful?

Employees generally rate benefit statements as one of the most popular forms of employer-provided benefit communication because they are personalized. Employees need no special equipment (as opposed to videotapes or computer programs) or skills (such as those of an actuary or an accountant) to read the statements. Well-designed, concise benefit statements are much easier to understand than SPDs and are therefore more likely to be read, especially when they are sent directly to an employee's home.

Periodic Benefit Reports

Q 21:11 What is a periodic benefit report?

A periodic benefit report is most easily described as the benefit version of the corporate annual report: It provides the key information participants in the plans need to know, including costs to the employer and the employees. It is an extremely flexible benefit communication tool that can accomplish multiple communication objectives. Periodic benefit reports can be produced annually or less frequently and can be a simple brochure or a more elaborate book.

Q 21:12 How can periodic benefit reports communicate the value of benefits to employees?

In a periodic benefit report, average benefit expenditures can be expressed as a percentage of average total compensation, as well as in dollar terms, so that employees can see the value of their benefit package in relation to their earnings and the company's revenues. These reports are also an excellent way to highlight accomplishments. Employers can underscore the success of a particular program, for example, the total and average weight lost by employees who participated in a wellness exercise program over the last year. In addition, comparisons can be made with groups of employers in the same industry or region to show that a benefit package is competitive or on the leading edge.

Q 21:13 What types of information are typically included in a periodic benefit report?

Periodic benefit reports are a cost-effective way for employers to emphasize the value of the total benefit package, reinforce employees' understanding of the need for any changes, and repeat other important messages that relate benefit to the employer's business goals. For example, a periodic benefit report can lay the foundation for forthcoming, potentially unpopular, changes in the benefit program. If health care costs are out of control, an employer could include various aggregate and per-capita data, such as expenditures and lengths of hospital stays, as well as the total cost of several catastrophic cases. Changes that follow the release of the report, such as increases in the indemnity plan's deductibles or the introduction of tighter managed care, should then be easier for employees to accept because they have been informed about the catalysts for the changes. Subsequent periodic benefit reports afford an opportunity to restate why the changes were necessary and to show the effect of implementing the changes on the employer's bottom line. After citing historical data on cost increases once more, the employer could explain how it decided what changes to make, and conclude with preliminary information on the savings that have resulted.

Q 21:14 What risks are associated with using periodic benefit reports as an employee communication tool?

Employers should be aware of these risks associated with periodic benefit reports:

1. Overloading employees with information, a temptation because the format is so flexible; and
2. Raising expectations by failing to tell employees at the time the report is distributed whether and when to expect the next one.

Interactive Systems

Q 21:15 What are the benefits of using interactive systems to communicate with employees?

Interactive systems promote employees' involvement in their benefits. Interactive systems with modeling programs that are either

Q 21:16   **Health Insurance Answer Book**

PC-based or phone-linked make it easy for employees to investigate "what-if" scenarios. Information can be accessed on demand and responses are accurate and consistent. Interactive systems can also be used to communicate in more than one language.

Q 21:16 Why do some employees prefer interactive systems to access benefit information?

Interactive systems protect employees' confidentiality through the use of Social Security numbers and personal identification numbers, or, in the case of a PC-based system, passwords. Employees need not be embarrassed about asking basic questions, because they can obtain answers privately. Interactive systems are also available 24 hours a day and seven days a week.

Q 21:17 What are the administrative advantages of using interactive systems?

Perhaps the most compelling advantage of interactive systems is that they ease plan administration considerably by handling routine tasks more efficiently and accurately. They save time, freeing staff to answer employees' more detailed questions and to work on benefit planning and other strategic issues. The paperwork associated with administration—especially enrollment—also can be reduced dramatically.

In addition, interactive systems facilitate employee feedback, making plan evaluation easier. Reporting mechanisms included in the system help identify recurring problems and benefit misunderstandings. Which benefits employees refer to most and what questions they ask most often can indicate where further communication may be needed.

Q 21:18 Are interactive systems expensive?

Viewed in isolation, the cost of introducing an interactive system can seem high. Commissioning a customized program may cost $10,000 for one simple application, but can be well over $75,000 for a complex arrangement. For larger employers, of course, the per-employee cost of such an expenditure can be quite affordable. Before dismissing this option, smaller employers might, however, want to investigate the savings that an interactive system could yield as a result of spending less time on administration. Interactive systems become more affordable over time precisely because they make it possible to save money on administrative expenses.

Online Services

Q 21:19 Are online systems being used to communicate benefit information?

Benefit managers in a growing number of companies have seized the opportunity to go online with benefit enrollment and communication material. The opportunity involves a substantial savings not only in costs but also in staff time. These efforts involve putting online such information as company policies and the ERISA-required summary descriptions of the company's benefit plans.

Because much benefit information is static, it needs to be updated only when changes occur. This low-maintenance characteristic makes benefit information ideal for online applications.

A survey by the International Society of Certified Employee Benefit Specialists found that evaluating, implementing, and expanding Internet and intranet applications was one of the top five priorities for the year 2000 of 60.8 percent of respondents, up from 47 percent the year before. A 1998 survey by the International Foundation of Employee Benefit Plans found that 29 percent of respondents were already using the Internet for benefit communication.

Q 21:20 Can online technology be used for employee enrollment in benefit programs?

A more exciting use of computer technology involves online enrollment over the Internet or what are called "intranet" sites. An intranet is a nonpublic counterpart to the Internet, the worldwide computer data base open to the public. The advantage of an intranet site is that it can have all the features of a home page on the World

Wide Web, the graphical portion of the Internet, but is open only to company workers.

Using an Internet or intranet system, all company documents can be connected with hypertext links that allow a user to click on a word, phrase, or section heading and jump immediately to more detailed information on that particular topic. For instance, online health plan enrollment forms will contain links that will connect users to health insurers' computers so they can choose a doctor from among that plan's preferred providers. Most companies do not need a sizable systems staff to do this work. In fact, a company developing an intranet site might only need one computer developer.

Q 21:21 What are the advantages for employers of using online services for enrollment activities?

The advantage is that staff members do not need to devote weeks to publishing materials they produce once a year for open enrollment. Instead, they can revise the information as needed. The information is also available to employees at any time. In addition, because online technology eliminates the need to print booklets or workbooks, the cost of putting this information online is about one tenth of the cost of traditional print campaigns.

For example, a company providing benefits to 15,000 workers and dependents might spend $250,000 to $500,000 per year to publish all the required printed information. In contrast, making this same material available online costs only $25,000 to $60,000. Moreover, the cost of updating online material is much lower than in print campaigns.

Obviously, this technology is ideal for companies with a technology-savvy workforce, and the trend is strongest among large companies. But the low cost also makes the technology ideal for many companies, even smaller employers.

Q 21:22 Are there any disadvantages to using online services for enrollment activities?

The disadvantage for many companies is that not all employees have access to a computer and modem. This is becoming less of a concern as more employees gain access to the Internet. For factory and warehouse workers, employers may need to dedicate several computers for employees to use in a specific area or a kiosk with a computer and a videotape player.

Another disadvantage is the concern about security. To guard the privacy of workers' records, appropriate protections must be developed.

Communicating Employee Benefits

Q 21:23 What are some basic principles for successful employee benefit communication?

When selecting a method of communicating benefit information, employers should keep in mind these four basic principles of communication:

1. No one method is suitable in every situation. Vital messages can get lost in periodic benefit reports, which are also inappropriate for exceptionally time-sensitive communications.
2. Any new communication tool should be tested. Using focus groups or surveys to test new methods is especially important before investing in a new system, such as an interactive computerized program.
3. A multifaceted or multimedia approach should be used. Such an approach is most likely to grab employees' attention and drive the message home. Employers may want to experiment with more than one technique.
4. The media should be consistent with the message. For example, employees may react negatively to flashy, expensive videos or glossy booklets explaining the need to reduce benefits to control costs.

Q 21:24 What legal trends are developing in the area of employee communications?

In January 1999, the Department of Labor issued proposed rules that provide a safe harbor for using electronic media to furnish SPDs and other required communications.

Q 21:25 Under what circumstances may a plan administrator rely on electronic media to satisfy disclosure obligations under ERISA?

According to the January 1999 proposed rules, employees must have access at their worksite to documents furnished in electronic form. Participants also continue to have a right to receive the disclosures in paper form upon request and free of charge.

The new rule sets forth criteria that are generally intended to ensure that the system of electronic communication utilized by a plan administrator for distribution of disclosure information results in the actual delivery of such information to participants and that the information delivered is equivalent in both substance and form to the disclosure information the participants would have received had they been furnished the information in paper form.

In general, the rule provides for the utilization of an electronic delivery system that (1) the administrator takes appropriate and necessary steps to ensure results in actual receipt by participants, such as through the use of a return-receipt electronic mail feature or periodic reviews by the plan administrator to confirm the integrity of the delivery system and (2) results in the furnishing of disclosure information that is consistent with the style, format, and content requirements applicable to the disclosure.

The new rule requires notification to each participant, through electronic or other means, apprising the participant of the disclosure documents furnished electronically (e.g., SPDs, summaries of material changes to the plan, and changes to information included in SPD), the significance of the documents (e.g., the document contains summary descriptions of changes in the benefits described in your SPD), and the participant's right to request and receive, free of charge, a paper copy of each such document from the plan administrator. The DOL believes such notification is necessary so that participants who, for example, receive a disclosure document as an attachment to an electronically transmitted message will be put on notice that the attachment contains important plan information.

Participants must have the ability to access at their worksite documents furnished in electronic form and the opportunity at their worksite to convert furnished documents from electronic form to paper form, free of charge. In this regard, the DOL believes that, however effective an electronic system may be for delivering plan disclosures, the critical determination in assessing the adequacy of the system, as a means for communicating to plan participants, will be the extent to which participants can readily access and retain the delivered information.

Q 21:26 What is important to include for enrollment communication campaigns?

First, it is important to determine whether the enrollment will be active or passive. An active enrollment implies that all employees must reelect the benefit coverages that they want to enroll in for the coming year. Passive enrollment offers a default option that enables employees to keep the same coverage elections made in prior years. Passive enrollment campaigns are easier and less expensive to administer because only employees who elect changes need to respond. This, in turn, results in a decreased burden on administrative staff, who will need to update changes only. It is important to keep in mind, however, that if a Section 125 flexible spending account is offered, employees should actively reenroll every year.

If the employer elects passive enrollment, communications sent to employees will need to include:

1. *A concise list of plan changes that will affect benefits for the coming year.* An explanation of how these changes will affect employee contributions should accompany the list.

2. *Enrollment instructions.* An explanation of how and when employees may enroll in the plan should be accompanied by an explanation of default options. This communication is intended to make employees aware of the coverage that is automatically available to them without taking any direct action. This communication should also include pertinent enrollment deadlines and a referral list of individuals who can provide additional information or help.

3. *An individualized enrollment form.* This personalized form outlines the employee's current coverage and shows all available benefit choices and their costs. This enrollment form

provides all the information that an employee needs to make an informed decision.

Q 21:27 What information should be communicated to new employees?

The most critical information for new employees to know is the date their benefits become effective. If the plan has a waiting period, new employees should be informed so that they can elect or cancel any available COBRA coverage. As part of their orientation, new employees should be provided with a general overview of benefits as well as their role in the employee's total compensation. When appropriate, new employees should be given the same enrollment materials provided to other active employees.

There are also a number of legally required notices. The Consolidated Omnibus Budget Reconciliation Act (COBRA) requires that newly covered participants be given an initial notice of COBRA rights. The Health Insurance Portability and Accountability Act of 1996 (HIPAA) requires that employees be notified of their special enrollment rights. There are also notice requirements under the Newborns' and Mothers' Health Protection Act and the Women's Health and Cancer Rights Act (WHCRA). Generally, these notices can be included in the SPD that must be provided to newly covered employees, with three additional requirements:

1. The COBRA notice must also be provided to the spouse.
2. The HIPAA special enrollment rights notice must be provided to eligible employees who do not enroll.
3. The WHCRA notice must be provided annually.

Q 21:28 What information should be communicated to retiring employees?

Maintaining health care coverage is a key issue for retiring employees. At a minimum, retiring employees should be informed about their eligibility for company-sponsored programs before and after they become eligible for Medicare benefits. If the employer provides no health care coverage, employers should clearly communicate this important information well in advance of the employee's retirement.

This allows retirees to plan for their health care coverage in retirement.

Q 21:29 How should "bad news" be communicated?

The way to communicate bad news successfully is to present it in a balanced fashion. The employer should explain the reasons for the negative impact the change in benefits will have and simultaneously acknowledge that, although the employer is aware of the effects, this alternative is the best of many investigated.

Apart from a written communication that describes the reasons for the change, the employer may choose to have a person with significant authority and visibility in the corporation deliver the message. This communicates to employees that the decision-making process was thorough and approved by the highest echelons of management. It also conveys a certain resistance on the part of management to be forced to resort to an obviously unpopular but necessary action. Taking a forthright approach in transmitting unpleasant information tends to produce the best reaction from employees.

Chapter 22

Mental Health

Mental health benefit costs have declined as a percentage of total health care spending in recent years. This chapter reviews some of the trends that have led to the decline, including managed mental health plans and behavioral health carve-outs. This chapter also discusses the impact on mental health plans of the Mental Health Parity Act.

Mental Health Benefits	22-1
Controlling Costs	22-9
Substance Abuse	22-12
Managed Mental Health	22-16
Employee Assistance Programs	22-22
Outcome Measurements	22-29
Americans with Disabilities Act	22-30
Mental Health Parity Act	22-34

Mental Health Benefits

Q 22:1 Are mental illnesses usually covered by health plans?

Although there is much less unanimity regarding diagnosis and treatment of mental health than that of physical ailments, mental health benefits are nonetheless covered under medical plans. This lack of unanimity and the tendency for mental health diseases to require lengthy treatments, often with little evidence of progress, have led to high costs and fertile grounds for abuse. Insurers and plan designers have responded by carving out (segregating) mental health benefits into a specific subset of the health plan (see Q 22:35). As a result, a differing schedule of benefits may be constructed, with the intention of limiting the ultimate financial exposure of the plan or employer.

A subset is currently being defined within mental health: treatment pertaining to substance abuse and addiction. As with mental health benefits, the intent of carving out substance abuse benefits is to define yet another, usually more restrictive, schedule of benefits available.

Q 22:2 What are the concerns of employers in designing mental health benefit plans?

Employers design mental health benefit plans with these goals in mind:

1. Improving the quality of mental health and substance abuse services;
2. Reducing mental health and substance abuse claims costs;
3. Enhancing beneficiary coverage;
4. Achieving employee acceptance and compliance with a managed benefit plan;
5. Improving workplace employee productivity via a behaviorally healthy workplace;
6. Giving more people access to behavioral health treatment;
7. Providing a continuum of care through a comprehensive spectrum of alternatives to inpatient services; and
8. Improving or implementing systems that measure treatment outcomes and the quality of services provided.

Decisions and choices regarding a behavioral health benefit plan should be based on a review of claim experience and costs, and a careful examination of employee and dependent demographics.

Q 22:3 Why have mental health benefits traditionally been structured differently from other health benefits?

Behavioral health benefits have commonly been more limited and carried higher cost-sharing requirements than other medical benefits.

This has largely been because many behavioral health problems were viewed as chronic and recurrent, requiring periodic treatment, often intensive in nature, throughout the lifetime of the individual. As a result of these perceptions, and because of a lack of utilization and outcomes data to better inform them, employer-sponsored behavioral health benefit plan structures tended to promote inpatient care by allowing more generous coverage for hospitalization than for outpatient treatment. [DF Anderson and JL Berlant, "Managed Behavioral Health and Substance Abuse Services," *The Managed Health Care Handbook*, (PR Kongstvedt, ed) Gaithersburg, Md: Aspen Publishers, Inc 1993)]

Q 22:4 Do employers place limitations on mental health benefit coverage?

According to the 1999 Mercer/Foster Higgins survey, most large employers control the cost of mental health coverage through special limitations. The survey found that 76 percent of health maintenance organizations (HMOs) limit the number of days of inpatient treatment that are covered; 80 percent of point of service (POS) plans and patient provider organizations (PPOs), and 81 percent of indemnity plans also limit days of inpatient care. For each type of plan, the median number of days covered is 30 per year. The survey also found that 75 percent of HMOs limit the number of outpatient visits each year, as do 78 percent of POS plans, 76 percent of PPOs, and 82 percent of indemnity plans. The median number of covered visits with HMOs is 20; with 30 for other plans.

In the last 10 years, employers have come to realize that, alone, traditional cost sharing and strict limitations have had an uneven effect on the cost, quality, and value of behavioral health benefits. In response, managed behavioral care has been playing an increasingly meaningful role in the development of behavioral health benefit plans and the delivery of behavioral health treatment services.

Curiously, a common factor found in treatment programs and benefit plan designs is the 30-day limit on treatment length. One might assume that is because treatments last 30 days and that plans were designed up to this limit; however, in actuality, plans arbitrarily imposed this limit, then treatment programs were designed to require that many days. There is not a shred of clinical evidence to support the appropriateness of 30-day treatment programs.

Q 22:5 Have changes in the clinical practices of mental health care changed the design of mental health benefits?

Changes in behavioral health treatment, such as increasingly effective psychopharmacology and an increase in the use of alternative treatment modalities, including short-term, focused therapy, and partial hospitalization programs, have affected treatment delivery systems, and those advances are playing a role in benefit design.

Q 22:6 What mental health benefits do health maintenance organizations typically offer?

According to the 1999 Mercer/Foster Higgins National Survey of Employer-Sponsored Health Plans, HMOs had the following limitations on mental health and substance abuse benefits:

Common mental health/substance abuse benefit limitations in HMOs

Inpatient Limitations		Outpatient Limitations	
Maximum number of days per year		**Maximum number of visits per year**	
Percent of plans with limitation	71%	Percent of plans with limitation	73%
Median number of days	30	Median number of visits	20
Maximum number of days per lifetime		**Higher cost-sharing than medical plan**	
Percent of plans with limitation	8%	Percent of plans	30%
Median number of days	60	**No special limitations**	
Higher cost-sharing than medical plan		Percent of plans	19%
Percent of plans	16%		
No special limitations			
Percent of plans	25%		

Q 22:7 Is there any federal regulation of HMOs that provide mental health care?

The federal government has adopted some guidelines for the utilization of managed behavioral health services. For an HMO to receive a federal contract, it must offer at least 30 days of inpatient treatment per year and 20 days of outpatient treatment per year for adults.

Q 22:8 What benefit coverage should a behavioral health plan include?

At a minimum, comprehensive and effective commercial behavioral health benefit plans should include coverage for the following:

- Inpatient treatment
- Nonhospital residential treatment
- Partial hospitalization or day treatment
- Individual and group outpatient treatment
- Crisis intervention
- Structured outpatient therapies, often for specific treatment issues, such as eating disorders

Below is a fairly typical plan design, showing the difference between network and out-of-network coverage:

Type of Care	In-Network Coverage	Out-of-Network Coverage
Outpatient	100 percent paid by plan, with a $20 copayment per visit, and unlimited visits if approved by MCO	Plan pays 70 percent, $200 annual deductible, no payment after 20 visits
Inpatient	Plan pays 85 percent, with a $250 copayment per episode	Plan pays 70 percent (still requires precertification by MCO), and deductible
Emergency facility visits	90 percent paid by plan	70 percent paid by plan

Q 22:9 Are employers using lifetime maximum amounts for mental health benefits in their plan designs?

Before increasing the use of managed care techniques, most employers controlled mental health and chemical dependency expenses by placing restrictive lifetime limits on care. From time to time, employers were faced with a dilemma when an employee or dependent reached the lifetime limit. With the assurance that care would be managed, some companies liberalized the limits, and others were able to stretch the dollars of their present limits through cost reductions and better use of resources.

The Mental Health Parity Act of 1996 (MHPA) prohibits lifetime maximums for mental health benefits that are less than the lifetime maximum for medical or surgical conditions. This law is scheduled to expire on September 30, 2001. There is an exception for chemical dependency treatment, which means lifetime maximums for substance abuse are still permitted. The act does not apply to employers with 50 or fewer employees, so small employers can have lifetime maximums for behavioral problems as well as alcohol and drug abuse.

Q 22:10 What are some trends in mental health benefit plans?

Like other types of health care, mental health care is constantly in flux. Among other changes, mental health benefit plans are doing the following:

1. Moving away from arbitrary benefits limitations and toward benefit allowances that expand to encourage outpatient care and alternative levels of care;

2. Becoming demonstrably difficult to manage, resulting in increased contracting with specialized organizations;

3. Becoming increasingly accepted by employees participating in managed care, thus promoting easier access to care at less cost to them;

4. Depending on specialty provider networks overseen and managed by expert, clinically driven systems of care and qualified clinicians; and

5. Evolving, as funding arrangements and payor and provider relationships become progressively more circumscribed by capitated contracts.

Q 22:11 Is there disagreement about what constitutes mental health coverage?

Many insurance policies limit benefits for "mental and nervous conditions" but fail to be more specific. Others contractually specify benefit limits for substance abuse treatment. Some disorders that have been previously assigned to the mental health category are now considered to have a physiological basis and courts are now being asked to resolve claim disputes arising from mental health benefit limitations.

For example, a class action suit in U.S. District Court seeks a permanent injunction against insurers that classify manic depression as a mental illness. In an unrelated case, the court ruled that where mental illness was not defined clearly, it should be construed according to "ordinary, not specialized meanings" in line with the Employee Retirement Income Security Act (ERISA) requirement that participants be furnished a plan description in lay language.

Q 22:12 Why has attention focused on mental health care issues?

One reason for the increase in interest is the growing availability of data on both utilization and costs. Many employers have initiated plan redesign as one technique for managing health costs. These redesign efforts include flexible benefits programs and other sophisticated approaches that have focused attention on particular problem areas. Moreover, the use of data has come into its own as a decision support mechanism. As hard data on benefit usage and costs become available to the plan sponsors responsible for cost-management decisions, they are better able to pinpoint specific areas in need of attention, such as mental health care.

According to a 2000 report by the Surgeon General, the annual direct costs of mental disorders is $70 billion and indirect costs are almost $80 billion.

Q 22:13 What contributed to the increased utilization of mental health services?

Several influences have resulted in an increase in mental health service utilization:

1. An increasing awareness of the need for psychiatric and substance abuse treatment. Approximately 52 million people aged 15 to 54 suffer from some form of mental disorder.
2. Growing evidence that behavioral health treatment is effective and can reduce other types of health care expenditures.
3. Focus on early identification and resolution of problem.
4. Behavioral health has become a basic and integral benefit in most employer-sponsored health insurance programs, with over 99 percent of respondents in the 1999 Mercer/Foster Higgins survey reporting that their plans cover mental health treatment.

Q 22:14 Can data from information systems help to coordinate medical care and behavioral care?

Yes. One example is the integration of behavioral health benefit and prescription drug benefit information. As patients enter alternative care facilities or hospitals, drug history profiles that include outpatient information are becoming more frequently available. A routine review of the drug history data base identifies high-risk patients and physicians, whose profiles are sent to case managers for follow-up. Direct patient interventions include educational information sent to the prescribing physician and to the patient.

Q 22:15 What is the primary care physician's role in behavioral health care?

Studies have demonstrated that between 25 percent and 60 percent of all primary care visits include treatment for a behavioral health problem. It has also been noted that communication between behavioral health providers and primary care physicians (PCPs) improves understanding of behavioral health disorders and the need for treatment, as well as the use of new diagnostic instruments designed specifically for use in primary care settings. Managed mental health care vendors are working with PCPs to facilitate referrals to behavioral health providers, to increase communication between PCPs and behavioral health providers, and to assist behavioral health providers in identifying potential medical problems. They are also developing PCP educational programs, which focus on the following:

1. Coordinating behavioral health services and primary care;
2. Using behavioral health services and their relationship to controlling costs of medical care;
3. Teaching PCPs how to direct populations away from expensive emergency care and into appropriate managed care settings;
4. Developing consultation policies with clearly defined procedures, incentives, and outcome measurements;
5. Accessing member information for behavioral health and general medicine; and
6. Giving PCPs a working knowledge of available screening tools for identifying behavioral health disorders.

In some areas, behavioral health providers are available for telephone consultations with PCPs who have questions about behavioral health issues for their patients. Additionally, two-way releases of information between PCPs and behavioral health providers help to assure that members are receiving comprehensive, coordinated care. This is particularly important for members who are receiving psychotropic and other medications.

Controlling Costs

Q 22:16 How much do behavioral health benefit cost employers?

According to a study by the Hay Group, behavioral health benefits cost an average of $69.87 per covered individual in 1998. The amount has decreased steadily from $154.48 in 1988.

Q 22:17 How can mental health services be better managed?

There are a number of ways that an informed employer, union, or insurer can get a handle on mental health services. One way is to improve outpatient services so that only those individuals in need of hospitalization will be admitted. In some cases, people really need to be hospitalized; other patients may be hospitalized unnecessarily because their company benefit packages pay for inpatient care but provide inadequate coverage for outpatient services.

Case management is another effective cost-control technique. Stated simply, case management involves professional review of proposed services by an independent organization that specializes in this field. This independent review checks the diagnosis, prognosis, proposed treatment plan, and other variables in order to determine the most effective treatment.

Q 22:18 What strategies are employers using to control mental health care costs?

One way employers have addressed these problems is with utilization review (UR) managed behavioral health firms specializing in behavioral healthcare.

According to the 1999 Mercer/Foster Higgins survey, only 5 percent of employers have a separate contract with a specialty network to provide mental health benefits. In the past few years, many managed care organizations have signed contracts with specialty networks, which has reduced the need for employers to have separate contracts. The survey found that 20 percent of employers with 20,000 or more employees have carve-out arrangements for point-of-service plans.

Q 22:19 What methods for reducing these costs are employers considering?

Many plans are either raising the employee share of dependent costs or reducing the level of benefits, especially for mental health and substance abuse treatment, which are heavily frequented by dependent adolescents.

Some popular cost-cutting approaches include:

1. *Limiting the length of stay.* While normal hospitalization has no set limitations, many plans limit the length of time they will

cover inpatient mental health or substance abuse treatment. Limits of 30 to 60 days are becoming more common.

2. *Limiting the size of payment.* There may be caps on the per diem rate for inpatient care (such as $1,000). Annual caps (such as $20,000 per year) and lifetime caps (such as a lifetime maximum reimbursement of $50,000) were common prior to the Mental Health Parity Act of 1996. Annual and lifetime limits are still allowed for substance abuse and small groups (50 or fewer employees).

3. *Increasing the coinsurance level.* A common coinsurance for outpatient mental and substance abuse treatment is 50 percent. There may also be no cap on out-of-pocket expenditures. The 1999 Mercer/Foster Higgins survey showed that the median indemnity, PPO and POS plan limits outpatient visits to 30 per year, while HMOs limit the number of visits to 20.

4. *Increasing premiums.* Some plans are shifting some (or even all) of the additional costs for dependents to employees.

5. *Substituting outpatient care or partial hospitalization.* This may be effective for the short term, but outpatient costs are rising as well, and less intensive care may be required for a longer period of time.

Q 22:20 Is there a downside to reducing benefits?

Some studies have found that arbitrary cutoffs of benefits, such as limits on lengths of stay, can ultimately cost more. By limiting the length of time that is reimbursable, or the size of the reimbursement, patients may be deprived of the care they need. By denying the necessary extra days, the patient may be discharged before treatment is complete. Ultimately that may mean additional costs over a longer period of time.

Q 22:21 How does case management of mental health services work?

In most instances, prior approval is needed before treatment commences. In an emergency situation, review takes place as soon as possible. Briefly, the professional representative of the review organization, usually either a psychologist or psychiatrist, contacts the mental health practitioner who is going to treat the patient and discusses the case. This discussion is designed to determine the relevant facts in the case, including diagnosis, clinical condition, severity, proposed treatment, medications, goals of treatment, discharge plans, reasons for admission (if hospitalization is proposed), and alternative treatment possibilities. The independent professional makes an assessment of the case and, if necessary, makes alternative recommendations. When necessary, ongoing monitoring also takes place.

Q 22:22 Is cost sharing an effective strategy?

In an attempt to control utilization, and thereby contain cost, behavioral health benefit plans have traditionally emphasized the importance of cost sharing between payer and beneficiary. Cost sharing can include annual deductibles, coinsurance, copayments, out-of-pocket maximums, per-treatment deductibles, annual and lifetime maximums (for employers with 50 or fewer employees or for substance abuse), penalty provisions, and incentives.

Research by organizations such as the Rand Corporation has repeatedly demonstrated that informed decision making by purchasers of health care services will almost always result in reduced costs; however, while encouraging employees to be prudent in controlling health care costs, cost sharing does relatively little to address issues of quality and appropriateness of care.

Substance Abuse

Q 22:23 Is treatment for alcoholism and other types of substance abuse covered under typical health insurance plans?

Coverage for treatment of alcoholism and other forms of substance abuse is often limited under health plans. The limitations are similar to those for mental illnesses, and are imposed because appropriate treatment is difficult for health care professionals to define, thus making expected claims and an appropriate price for coverage difficult to establish; however, many plans extend additional coverage for treatment as a result of a referral from an employee assistance program (EAP).

According to the 1999 Mercer/Foster Higgins survey, over 95 percent of health plan participants had coverage for substance abuse services.

The Mental Health Parity Act of 1996 has an exception for substance abuse that allows plans to have annual and lifetime limits on treatment for chemical dependency.

Q 22:24 What benefits are typically offered for substance abuse treatment?

Commercial substance abuse coverage typically includes the following:

- Detoxification (inpatient, non-inpatient residential, and outpatient)
- Hospital rehabilitation
- Nonhospital residential rehabilitation
- Structured outpatient rehabilitation
- Individual and group outpatient rehabilitation

Outpatient utilization is encouraged and employees are being encouraged through benefit design to seek structured, intensive outpatient settings, rather than 30-day inpatient treatment programs. Today, more and more employers are wrapping substance abuse treatment into a total package of behavioral health treatment. This trend may be slowed by the chemical dependency exception in the Mental Health Parity Act of 1996.

Q 22:25 How costly is substance abuse to companies and their employees?

Numerous studies reveal that somewhere between 6 percent and 10 percent of any given employee population has a problem with alcohol or another controlled substance. These data hold up whether the population is blue collar or white collar, male or female, young or old. People with substance abuse problems use health care services and other resources at much higher rates than other employees. They are also absent three times as often, are involved in more grievances, and have higher accident rates. Other costs include higher medical costs, more disability claims, more workers' compensation claims, and lost productivity.

Q 22:26 What are some strategies for employers to use when designing substance abuse benefit plans?

Some suggestions for substance abuse benefit plan design include the following:

1. Preserving benefit dollars by favoring outpatient care services, except for patients who have demonstrated that they are incapable of improvement outside of an inpatient setting, or have no family, job, or community support;
2. Promoting treatment of substance abuse care for all of those in need, taking into account the available total dollars; and
3. Combining or closely coordinating mental health and substance abuse benefits within a comprehensive behavioral health benefit plan.

Q 22:27 Why should substance abuse or addiction treatments be restricted?

There is growing acceptance of the theory that too much benefit coverage in this area can be counterproductive. First, the potential for abuse is enormous. Consider the example of an employee who is found to be using drugs and who knows that this will probably cause termination; his or her immediate reaction may be a request for a program of rehabilitation. If the plan specifies nothing to the contrary, the employee can request treatment as many times as he or she is discovered using illegal drugs.

While termination or other disciplinary action may be contemplated as a result of the illegal drug use, these are employee relations or legal issues. From the medical plan standpoint, the plan could be paying for treatment whose sole purpose is to preserve employment for the abuser. In fact, even if the employee is terminated, by electing

COBRA continuation he or she could pay a relatively small premium to receive an expensive course of treatment at the plan's expense.

Second, and perhaps more importantly, prevalent medical and psychological theory indicates that people who are sincere in their desire to become free of drug or alcohol addiction need to know there is a certain finality to the program—that if they resume substance abuse, there may not be a safety net to catch them. One way of achieving this is to provide full coverage for the first course of treatment, and 50 percent or 60 percent if a second treatment is needed, with zero coverage beyond that.

Q 22:28 Why have inpatient benefits for substance abuse treatment historically been more restrictive than for mental health treatment?

Substance abuse benefit programs have restricted inpatient treatment for several reasons. Employers argue that they:

1. Are offering benefit levels that are higher than any they may be required to provide;
2. Want to promote self-reliance rather than service reliance among recovering members;
3. Feel an obligation to provide the opportunity for a substance abuser to get help, but cannot afford to so indefinitely; and
4. Consider that limitations on benefit allowances can in themselves be motivators for a substance abuser to take advantage of treatment while the opportunity is available and mostly or entirely paid for by the benefit plan sponsor.

Furthermore, the public system has traditionally been the payer of last resort for severely mentally ill and chronic patients, and public funding for mental health and substance abuse has been viewed as an entitlement rather than a benefit.

Q 22:29 Is substance abuse considered a treatable illness?

Yes. Drug and alcohol abuse and dependence are classified as treatable illnesses by both standard diagnostic medical manuals: the *Diagnostic and Statistical Manual IV* (DSM-IV) and the *International*

Statistical Classification of Diseases, Injuries, and Causes of Death (ICD-9). These manuals also provide criteria for diagnosing drug and alcohol abuse and dependence that focus on psychological, behavioral, and cognitive symptoms.

Managed Mental Health

Q 22:30 What is a pre-paid mental health plan?

Pre-paid mental health plans offer care through a prescreened panel of mental health care providers who offer their services through discounted negotiated fees. Fees are set in advance, and the plan assumes the risk of providing the benefits for program beneficiaries. These plans may be offered through mental health PPOs, mental health carve-outs, or capitated mental health plans.

Q 22:31 How is managed care affecting mental health and substance abuse benefit programs?

Rising health care costs and health care reform are making mental health and substance abuse benefit plans, increasingly referred to as "behavioral health plans," good candidates for managed care. There are three trends in managed care for these types of services:

1. Managed behavioral care is being successfully used to move patients away from more costly, and often inappropriate, inpatient care settings into carefully selected and monitored alternative treatment modalities.

2. Per-person, fixed-fee compensation schedules, known as capitation, are gradually becoming the rule rather than the exception between payers and providers of care.

3. The laws governing the provision of health care are evolving, as states and the federal government enact reforms—many of which require that mental illness, and often chemical dependency, be treated through specialized managed care plans—thereby taking the first steps in integrating public and private systems of behavioral health care.

Q 22:32 In addition to cost savings, what else is driving the trend toward managed mental health benefits?

Regardless of funding arrangement, payer source, or patient type, four other concerns are driving the trend:

1. While behavioral health care costs have been rising, quality measurements of the value of treatment modalities have been fragmentary or nonexistent in unmanaged settings.
2. A need has been firmly demonstrated for the application of specialized, clinically driven, patient-oriented approaches to the delivery of behavioral health benefits.
3. Data gathered on the use of benefits need to be applied to enhancing service quality and long-term benefits planning.
4. Networks of highly qualified professionals must be sought out, routinely profiled, and assisted by expert managed care clinicians to achieve effective, quality treatment at a reasonable cost.

Q 22:33 What are the benefits of managed behavioral health care?

Large managed behavioral health companies encourage payers to adopt plan designs that are open to the use of alternatives to inpatient acute care and that encourage the use of select network providers. Networks include a wide variety of providers, clinics, health centers, practice groups, hospitals, and other caregivers that have been structurally defined and regionally organized. When using networks, patients often receive treatment without day or visit limits, and usually with a sharply reduced or even nonexistent copayment or deductible. Network utilization allows the company to control costs and more effectively monitor quality. Employees benefit by having much lower out-of-pocket costs for treatment. Employers benefit by receiving the assurance that the money it is spending is going to appropriate and well-managed care.

Q 22:34 What should employers consider when developing a managed care program for behavioral health benefits?

When managed care programs enter into capitated contracts with payers and providers, there are many questions to be answered by all parties, including the following:

Q 22:35   Health Insurance Answer Book

1. What is the service area?
2. Is the plan amenable to short-term treatment?
3. What is its methodology for crisis intervention and short-term evaluation?
4. What criteria does the plan use to determine medical necessity?
5. Who will perform gatekeeping functions?
6. What role will be played by primary care physicians?
7. How will patient self-referrals be handled?
8. What is the number of mental health providers within a plan's network of providers?
9. What are the percentages among disciplines within that pool?
10. Who are the current hospital providers?
11. What problem areas have been identified, such as availability of emergency assessment, hospital overutilization, and poor care quality?
12. Do any state laws affect the ability to enter into capitated contracts?
13. What are the average utilization and cost figures for:
    a. Inpatient mental health treatment?
    b. Inpatient chemical dependency treatment?
    c. Outpatient mental health treatment?
    d. Outpatient chemical dependency treatment?
    e. Average hospital per diem, exclusive of physician's fees, paid in the prior three years?
14. What are the therapist fee schedules and average professional charges paid in recent years?

Q 22:35   What is a mental health carve-out?

A carve-out is a benefit strategy in which an employer separates one portion of benefits from others and hires a managed care company to manage or provide those benefits through its provider network. A behavioral health carve-out program separates the delivery of behavioral health services from a general medical plan. Management of a carve-out program is provided by specialty managed care programs. According to Towers Perrin, a carve-out:

1. Is totally separate (i.e., "carved out") from the medical care plan;
2. Offers a specialty network of behavioral health practitioners and facilities;
3. Offers a comprehensive range of providers and services;
4. Usually offers access to care with a toll-free number staffed by clinicians who will answer questions or make a referral to a network practitioner;
5. Has a triage specifically designed to match patients to appropriate individual providers, programs, and level of treatment;
6. Contains a sophisticated care management process with specialty consultation available;
7. Often has little or no out-of-pocket costs and no claims for beneficiaries who use contracted providers to file; and
8. May be either at-risk or non-risk.

Q 22:36 Why are carve-out plans appropriate for behavioral health care?

Carve-out plans are appropriate for behavioral health care because they improve on historical, unmanaged behavioral health plans by providing:

1. Quality measurements of the value of treatment modalities;
2. The application of specialized, clinically driven, patient-oriented approaches to the delivery of behavioral health benefits;
3. Data to enhance service quality and for informed long-term benefit planning; and
4. Networks of highly qualified professionals, routinely profiled, and assisted by expert managed care clinicians to achieve effective, quality treatment at a reasonable cost.

Research has demonstrated that the centralized assessment function of a managed care plan, coupled with the subsequent fit between client and provider, has important clinical implications and is an independent predictor of treatment completion. Carve-out plans offer an opportunity for specialized case management, ensuring that care is coordinated, that there is a continuum of services utilized, and that attention is paid to the process of care. [*Managed Behavioral Health Carve-Outs* (Towers Perrin, for Behavioral Health Corp of Massachusetts, 1994)]

Q 22:37 Do carve-out plans limit access to behavioral health services?

While nonspecialized managed care has been blamed for placing limits on access to behavioral health services generally, a well-designed carve-out program can improve access. Carve-outs can offer recipients multiple access points. For example, clinicians making referrals use computerized listings of network professionals, specifying their licensure, specialties, and geographic locations, to provide the beneficiary with choices. A standard access point offered by many carve-outs is a toll-free number, staffed 24 hours a day by behavioral health professionals, that can provide immediate and confidential assistance.

Q 22:38 Do carve-outs cover services that traditional mental health and substance abuse plans do not?

Traditionally, behavioral health benefit coverage reimbursed only inpatient and outpatient services. Research has demonstrated that individuals with behavioral health or substance abuse problems can often be treated more effectively in alternative settings. For substance abusers, partial hospitalization, residential treatment, and intensive outpatient therapy with appropriate aftercare often produce better clinical outcomes and fewer relapses than traditional hospital-based treatment. In addition, an expanded range of outpatient services, such as in-home treatment and specialized group treatment, is often included to improve access and outreach capabilities. Under a managed behavioral health program, the delivery system is centered around client needs, and services are used flexibly. Coverage through a carve-out is therefore provided for services historically not reimbursable.

Carve-out vendors also pay significant attention to the multi-disciplinary composition of their network. Provider management is done through individual provider profiling. Profiles reflect different elements of provider performance, such as treatment conceptualization and planning, practice patterns, prescribing patterns, utilization levels, and patient satisfaction, and usually provide comparative network results.

Q 22:39 How do behavioral health carve-outs control costs?

Plan designs under a carve-out program remove stringent benefit limitations and provide generous first-dollar coverage for network-based care. In well-designed carve-out programs, clinical management and reimbursement mechanisms offer the most control.

In response to employer and health plan demands for cost management, carve-outs have devised a two-pronged approach. The first component, negotiated service rates and per diems, is one of the approaches used to reduce cost shifting; historically, the indemnity plan beneficiary bore the brunt of the cost shift. Carve-out beneficiaries are protected against cost shifting by negotiated reimbursement arrangements.

The second and most significant factor in cost management consists of utilization and case management. A carve-out vendor's ability to reduce unnecessary utilization by diverting care to less-intensive, lower-cost treatment alternatives can generate significant cost reductions while actually increasing total utilization.

Q 22:40 What are the advantages of carve-out plans for behavioral health care?

Carve-out plans offer significant advantages over nonspecialized benefit plans, including the following:

- Easy access to care
- Referrals to highly qualified, patient-matched providers
- Specialized clinical oversight for all cases
- The opportunity for cost-sensitivity within enhanced benefit levels

- Customized information systems and data-reporting capabilities
- Behavioral health-specific account management
- Higher patient satisfaction
- Well-planned treatment for improved outcome

Q 22:41 What are the disadvantages of carve-out plans for behavioral health?

Generous benefit levels can result in cost shifting from the HMO plan into the specialty plan. To a certain extent, for a carve-out to be successful, care coordination and administrative functioning can sometimes depend on the ability to coordinate with the medical or surgical plan. This can be problematic in a competitive environment. Proper planning and implementation are critical for a successful carve-out.

Critics claim that carve-outs create divisions between medical or surgical care and behavioral care. On the other hand, these types of care have never been well coordinated.

Employee Assistance Programs

Q 22:42 What is an employee assistance program?

An EAP is designed to help employees cope with problems that not only manifest themselves in poor job performance, but that can often lead to costly medical complications as well. While basic programs stress alcoholism and drug abuse, more ambitious programs offer assistance with problems in the following four areas:

1. Work-related situations such as stress and burnout;
2. Marriage and personal relationships;
3. Legal and financial difficulties; and
4. Day care for children, long-term care for parents, and related matters.

If successful, the EAP should reduce health care costs, increase productivity and retention rates of experienced employees, reduce accidents, improve quality, lower workers' compensation claims, and reduce absenteeism.

Q 22:43 How prevalent are EAPs?

The exact number of EAPs is a matter of dispute, partly because of a looseness of definition. Many companies have some sort of program for dealing with employee personal problems, although the arrangement might not constitute an EAP by professional standards. At any rate, given that EAPs come in a variety of shapes and sizes, the Bureau of Labor Statistics estimates that slightly more than half of U.S. workers had access to an EAP in 1991. The U.S. Congress on Alcohol and Health estimates that there are 5,000 EAPs.

The 1999 Mercer/Foster Higgins survey found that 61 percent of employers had EAPs.

Q 22:44 Is EAP coverage cost-effective?

An EAP can be insured or it can be a stand-alone benefit. It does not have to be expensive. Some employers pay for an initial diagnostic visit to a trained counselor. This person's role is to help the employee or family member determine a course of action. The counselor ascertains the nature of the problem and makes an appropriate referral. This referral may be to a therapist, financial counselor, community organization, or substance abuse treatment center. Some of the treatment may be covered by company insurance, such as medical care. Other treatment may be paid for by the individual. The most important aspect of the program is that it helps get people into the right system where they can obtain the help they need.

EAPs may actually save money. They can increase productivity and reduce job-related accidents, medical expenses, disabilities, absenteeism, and recruitment and training costs. They are also useful in deflecting expensive wrongful-discharge suits. Companies that have formal programs designed to help drug or alcohol addicted employees are in a much better position to show that firing the worker was a last resort after all other efforts were exhausted. Some companies report that their EAPs return several dollars for each dollar spent.

Q 22:45 How can EAPs be financed?

While services such as an EAP are generally considered to be "basic" in nature, and as such are usually paid for directly by an employer, there are ways of defraying costs, such as the following:

1. Counseling and substance abuse treatments may be covered under the employer's health insurance plan, in which case these services may be subject to some degree of cost sharing through any deductible or coinsurance features that may apply.
2. The EAP may coordinate such services as day care referrals, drug counseling, and elder care with local agencies that provide these services at little or no cost.
3. Some states subsidize EAPs.
4. Not all services must be provided free. Financial and legal counseling may carry a small charge to the participant (to defray the services of the local Bar Association referral service, for example), yet still be an extremely valuable service to the employee who simply does not know where to begin.

Q 22:46 Is an EAP an ERISA welfare plan?

If the EAP offers benefits similar to those found under medical plans, it may be viewed as an ERISA welfare plan. For example, a plan that provides for psychological counseling and drug rehabilitation would be subject to ERISA reporting requirements, such as Form 5500 annual reports and summary plan descriptions (SPDs). These requirements could be satisfied by including information about the EAP in the documentation for the employer's regular medical plan. If an EAP only provides referrals to counseling services, it probably is not an ERISA welfare plan.

Q 22:47 Do companies hire in-house counselors or use external resources?

Most companies refer individuals to an external source. This may be a community organization or one of a growing number of commercial organizations that provides EAP services on a for-profit basis. There are reputable organizations of both types. A company can justify having an in-house counselor if it has 1,500 to 2,000 employees or more; this is the volume needed to warrant a full-time staff. The other reason that many companies use an outside resource is to maintain confidentiality. It is important for employees to have confidence in the discretion of the counselor, because EAPs tend to deal with the most personal of problems.

Q 22:48 What components are needed for an effective EAP?

An effective EAP requires a solid foundation, including top management support, training for company supervisors, written company policies, adequate health care coverage, specific disciplinary actions for poor job performance (which lead to the identification of problems), understandable procedures, good counselors, and specified criteria for return to work if treatment requires hospitalization.

Q 22:49 What are the important elements of a well-designed EAP?

The key principle of an EAP is the use of job performance as the basis of intervention and short-term counseling or screening prior to referral to a skilled professional. The message from the company to the employee is: "You are not performing up to standard. Is there a problem you would like to discuss with someone?" The employee is then referred to the EAP counselor, without any attempt on the part of the supervisor to diagnose the specific nature of the problem. It is up to the counselor to make a preliminary determination as to the most appropriate type of professional help.

An effective EAP emphasizes some of the following:

1. *Confidentiality.* There are two reasons for this. One is the tendency of most people to be more willing to divulge personal information to a sympathetic stranger than to a boss or family member. The second reason is that, to secure the employee's cooperation, it is important for an individual to know that everything he or she says is not going into the personnel file

and will be available to the company only on a "need to know" basis.

2. *Management training.* It is the manager's job to spot the problem and steer the employee, who may be reluctant at first, toward the EAP. Managers are most likely to take this initiative when senior management makes it clear that the program has its full support. This support should be clearly communicated through training that includes descriptions of warning signals of employee difficulty and shows the manager how to set the assistance process in motion.

3. *Counseling.* The first job of the EAP counselor is to get as much personal history as possible, covering both on-the-job and off-the-job matters, and to select the most appropriate professional treatment. This calls for a good deal of experience and interpersonal ability. Any EAP service should be prepared to document the qualifications of its counselors, and the sponsoring corporation should be prepared to review them.

4. *Timeliness.* When help is needed, particularly if the employee is emotionally distraught, it should be available right away in the form of counseling that is available 24 hours a day, either through an on-duty intervention specialist or through a telephone hotline.

5. *Monitoring/follow-up.* Once the referral is made, there should be regular and frequent reviews of the treatment program to be sure that it is achieving its objectives. This is the responsibility of the EAP coordinator.

6. *Surveys.* In addition, the program may include an employee job attitude survey. It may be expected that only 7 to 10 percent of the employee group would make use of a broad-ranging program.

7. *Evaluation.* After the program has been in force for a specified period, statistics should be assembled to see if it is having the desired effect on health costs, productivity, employee performance, and so forth, and whether the results justify the expense. If not, the plan should be revised.

While failure to enter into or cooperate in an EAP program has been upheld as grounds for dismissal, the utility of this mandatory approach should be weighed against the potentially greater long-term advantages arising from voluntary participation. These greater advantages will accrue both to individual employees and to the program overall.

Q 22:50 Other than in-house or commercially, how else may EAP services be provided?

Of growing interest to the small employer is the association or consortium EAP, in which several employers join together to sponsor an EAP. Although this can reduce costs when compared with each employer's cost of going it alone, it is important that the companies have similar needs and demographics, and that utilization be carefully tracked so that expenses can be fairly apportioned.

Q 22:51 What role do employee assistance plans play in cutting employers' behavioral health costs?

Employee assistance programs began in the 1950s as no more than counseling services for substance abusers. Since then, they have evolved into the first point of contact for the delivery of behavioral health services, frequently serving in a gatekeeper or "gateway" role. An EAP acting as a gatekeeper can improve quality and hold down costs by treating those people it is qualified to help and referring the others to appropriate resources.

Q 22:52 What are the advantages of using an integrated EAP carve-out?

When a carve-out provides EAP and behavioral health services, a centralized triage function can be established to direct the members to the most appropriate treatment provider, either EAP or network services. In an integrated model, brief-treatment EAP services are considered part of the complete treatment continuum and not a separate system of care.

The linkage between workplace issues and care resources is the cornerstone of an integrated model. Effective management of an integrated EAP and behavioral health program begins with matching a cost-effective EAP and other behavioral health services with participant needs. Because gaps in the linkage of care impede quality care and can cause poor outcomes, EAP case managers oversee patient care and continue to follow their progress after discharge to assure continuity of care and monitor return-to-work issues.

This ongoing monitoring is a key factor in "normalizing" the situation for the patient. The integrated EAP and behavioral health model uses a full array of clinical and nonclinical services to enable patients to return to healthy functioning in the shortest time possible, using the least intrusive, most conservative, and most clinically effective interventions available. It can also result in cost savings over nonintegrated EAP and managed behavioral plan offerings.

Q 22:53 Do employees appreciate EAPs?

Yes. According to a 1998 survey by Aon Consulting, the only benefit that generates greater employee loyalty than an EAP is an employer-paid retirement program.

Q 22:54 Is there evidence that EAPs are cost effective?

A four-year study of mental health treatment alternatives by McDonnell Douglas Corporation compared the results for employees who obtained treatment on their own to those who participated in the company's employee assistance program. The study included medical claims and absentee data for 125,000 employees and reported a significant difference in outcomes. Employees who used the EAP for chemical dependency missed 44 percent fewer workdays and filed lower medical claims than those who did not use the EAP. Only 7.5 percent of those using the EAP for substance abuse left the company during the four years, compared to 40 percent of those who managed their own treatment.

With respect to all types of mental health treatment, the study found that employees who sought treatment from HMOs were several times more likely to terminate employment than those who used the EAP.

Outcome Measurements

Q 22:55 What performance indicators do employers use for behavioral health care programs?

Typical outcomes indicators in managed behavioral health contracting often include demonstrations of the following:

1. Administrative performance:
   a. Patient access: telephone access and appointments
   b. Provider access: initial availability, turnover, and access throughout treatment
   c. Customer service: response time for nonclinical telephone and mail inquiries
   d. Claim payment: coding accuracy, adjudication accuracy, and turnaround
2. Financial performance:
   a. Annual behavioral health care expenses, per-member expenses, and cost savings
3. Clinical performance: Because clinical outcomes are difficult to track and conclusively assess and report in a benefit management environment, a number of proxy measures are designed to indicate clinical outcome, such as:
   a. Relapse rates
   b. Recidivism rates
   c. Volume of appeals and grievances
   d. Patient satisfaction
   e. Provider profiling data

Q 22:56 What other types of outcome measures are used in behavioral health care?

One method is to distribute an outcomes standard to people eligible for treatment services, and have them subsequently provide information on their experiences. The tools that can be used vary in statistical validation, ranging from a simple questionnaire to the more sophisticated Health Status Questionnaire, as well as Global Assessment of Functioning (GAF) and Life Role Functioning Scales.

With this type of reporting mechanism, there is need for a high rate of response (greater than 50 percent), which has proven difficult to obtain with populations that access behavioral services. Employers may want to use incentives, such as gift certificates, to encourage participation.

Americans with Disabilities Act

Q 22:57   Who does the Americans with Disabilities Act protect?

According to information provided by the Program on Employment and Disability, School of Industrial and Labor Relations, at Cornell University, people with past drug or alcohol problems are protected from job discrimination by the ADA, as are people with current alcohol problems who are able to perform their job. The only individuals with drug and alcohol problems who do not have the same rights as others with disabilities are those who currently use drugs illegally.

Q 22:58   Are any employees exempted from protection under the ADA?

The Legal Action Center states that the ADA specifically excludes from the definitions of "individual with a disability" any employee or applicant who is currently engaging in the illegal use of drugs, when the covered entity acts on the basis of such use. This includes individuals who use illicit drugs as well as those who use prescription medications unlawfully. Individuals who use drugs under the supervision of a licensed health care professional, such as methadone, are not using drugs illegally and therefore could be protected against discrimination. Although individuals with current drug problems are not protected, the ADA specifically protects individuals who are participating in a supervised drug rehabilitation program or who have completed a treatment program or have been rehabilitated through self-help groups, employee assistance programs, or any other type of rehabilitation, and are no longer using drugs. According to the Legal Action Center, the ADA protects individuals who are erroneously perceived as abusing drugs illegally, but are not doing so.

Because of societal attitudes about drug abuse, many individuals who have had drug problems in the past are perceived as still being drug-dependent. Similarly, individuals who participate in methadone maintenance programs are also often perceived as drug-dependent, even though methadone is a lawfully prescribed medication and individuals who participate in a methadone maintenance program are able to do every task—even safety-related tasks—that a person who is not receiving such treatment can do. These individuals are protected against discrimination under the ADA.

Invariably, drug tests will inaccurately identify some individuals as drug users. "This occurs because the drug test may be performed incorrectly, substances in an individual's system may be incorrectly identified as a drug, or a prescription medication may be incorrectly identified as an illicit drug," according to Ellen M. Weber, co-director of national policy for the Legal Action Center in Washington, D.C. The ADA prohibits discrimination against individuals who are erroneously regarded as engaging in the illegal use of drugs because of a false positive drug test, but are not engaging in such use.

Q 22:59 Does the ADA apply to employees with alcohol abuse problems?

Individuals with current alcohol impairments are protected against discrimination like any other individual with a disability. Alcohol is not, however, considered a drug under the ADA; therefore, the current abuse of alcohol does not exclude an individual from the ADA's protection. Employees, like any other individual with a current disability, must, however, be able to perform the essential functions of the job to be protected against discrimination. In addition, the ADA specifically permits an employer to hold employees who abuse alcohol to the same performance and conduct standards applicable to all employees, even if that employee's problems are related to the alcohol abuse.

Q 22:60   How is current drug abuse defined?

According to the Legal Action Center in Washington, D.C., the determination of illegal drug use must be "close enough to the time of the employment action to indicate that there is a real and on-going problem." It is not permissible to impose a blanket time limitation, such as 30 or 60 days of abstinence from drugs, as a way to define what is "current" illegal use of drugs. In addition, because the ADA protects individuals who are participating in a rehabilitation program and those who have been rehabilitated (as long as they are not still using drugs illegally), "employers should be careful about reaching back in time and taking adverse actions against individuals for drug use that occurred before they entered treatment," the Center advises.

Q 22:61   What questions can an employer ask a job applicant regarding illegal drug use?

Employers may ask a job applicant about current illegal use of drugs before a conditional offer of employment. They may also ask an employee about current illegal use of drugs at any time without showing that the inquiry is job-related or required by business necessity. Finally, the ADA explicitly states that a test to detect the illegal use of drugs is not considered a medical examination; therefore, drug tests may be given before a conditional offer of employment or at any time in an employee's tenure. Employers must be careful, however, in conducting a drug test before a conditional offer of employment, because the drug test could reveal information about other disabilities that applicants have a right to withhold until after an employment offer.

The ADA does allow employers to make certain that employees are no longer illegally using drugs. Employers are permitted to conduct drug tests and to obtain information from treatment programs to monitor drug use. If an employer has an EAP, it might be the best entity to conduct the follow-up.

Q 22:62   Are there any regulations about employee confidentiality?

According to the Legal Action Center, while the ADA does not impose many restrictions on drug testing, employers are required to use accurate test procedures and to comply with any federal, state, or local law that regulates drug testing. In addition, when seeking information from a drug or alcohol treatment program about an individual's rehabilitation, employers should be aware that federal regulations govern the release of drug and alcohol patient information by virtually all treatment programs. To protect the confidentiality of individuals with drug and alcohol problems, these regulations require the execution of a detailed consent form before employers can receive treatment information and place strict limitations on the employer's use, maintenance, and redisclosure of that information. Because these regulations impose more stringent confidentiality standards than those in the ADA, they supersede the ADA's requirements for protection of drug and alcohol treatment information.

Q 22:63 What accommodations in the workplace might employees recovering from drug or alcohol abuse need?

Accommodation for individuals in recovery from a drug or alcohol problem will vary, depending upon the requirements of their jobs and their length of time in recovery. For example, individuals who have recently completed a rehabilitation program may need to participate in a structured, outpatient continuing care program on a regular basis. Others who have been sober for a long time may participate in self-help groups, such as Alcoholics Anonymous, for the rest of their lives to prevent relapse. Involvement in such continuing care may require some accommodation. Examples of necessary accommodation, according to the Legal Action Center, could include:

1. A modified work schedule to permit an employee to pick up a daily methadone dosage or to attend an outpatient relapse prevention counseling session;
2. Job restructuring to relieve an employee of particular marginal tasks that may compromise recovery or be inappropriate in the early stages of recovery;
3. Temporary reassignment of an employee in a safety-related position to a vacant non-safety-sensitive position while he or she completes treatment.

Individuals with current alcohol impairment are protected against discrimination to the extent they can perform their jobs effectively and safely. Employers are required to consider providing unpaid leave to permit individuals with current alcohol impairment to attend in-patient treatment programs. In addition, if an employer provides paid leave to individuals who are obtaining medical treatment for a disability, the employer must provide the same benefit to an individual who is obtaining treatment for an alcohol problem.

Mental Health Parity Act

Q 22:64 What does the Mental Health Parity Act of 1996 require?

On September 26, 1996, President Clinton signed the Mental Health Parity Act of 1996. It is effective for plan years beginning on or after January 1, 1998 and is scheduled to sunset on September 30, 2001. At press time, there were efforts to extend and expand the Mental Health Parity Act. The legislation prohibits lifetime or annual dollar limits on mental health care, unless comparable limits apply to medical or surgical treatment. The impact of this legislation is likely to be limited. The definition of mental health excludes chemical dependency; therefore, separate limits for substance abuse are still permitted. Plans are not required to cover mental health treatment, but if they do, they cannot have separate lifetime or annual dollar limits. Other types of limits are still permitted. Some plans with a $1,000 annual limit for outpatient mental health treatment changed to a limited benefit of $20 per visit, combined with a limit of 50 visits per year. Informally, the Department of Labor says it views such combinations of limits as prohibited.

Q 22:65 Are there any regulations published regarding the Mental Health Parity Act?

Yes. On December 22, 1997, the Health Care Financing Administration (HCFA), the Pension and Welfare Benefits Administration (PWBA), and the Internal Revenue Service (IRS) published interim regulations in the *Federal Register* governing the Mental Health Parity Act (MHPA) of 1996. The MHPA requires parity in the application of lifetime dollar limits and annual dollar limits between mental health benefits and medical or surgical benefits. The MHPA does not require group health plans to provide mental health benefits. Benefits for substance abuse treatment can be subject to lifetime or annual dollar limits. The MHPA does not apply to employers with 50 or fewer employees.

The MHPA includes a provision exempting plans if the MHPA's rules result in an increased cost of 1 percent or more. The new rules explain how the MHPA's exemption for plans claiming increased costs works. The new rules explain that plans can take advantage of the exemption after complying with the law for six months, if they can document that costs have increased by at least 1 percent as a result of the MHPA.

Before a group health plan may claim the 1 percent increased-cost exemption, it must furnish participants with a notice of exemption. The rules specify the contents of the notice. It is not necessary for plans to obtain prior governmental approval to claim the exemption. The Department of Labor (DOL) must be provided a copy of the notice, and the exemption is not effective until at least 30 days after the notice is sent to participants and the DOL. Upon request, plans must provide the data substantiating the 1 percent increased cost.

Q 22:66 Does the Mental Health Parity Act require mental health coverage?

No. The law only affects health plans that choose to offer mental health benefits. Of course, insured plans are subject to state mandates. According to the National Alliance for the Mentally Ill, 28 states now have some degree of mental health parity.

Q 22:67 Must benefits for mental health treatment be identical to the benefits for medical conditions?

No. The Mental Health Parity Act allows health plans to set higher deductibles and copayments for mental health treatment. The law also allows plans to distinguish between acute conditions and chronic conditions. Plans can still set the terms and conditions (such as cost-sharing and limits on the number of visits or days of coverage) for the amount, duration, and scope of mental health benefits.

Q 22:68 Are any employers exempt from the Mental Health Parity Act?

Yes. Employers with 50 or fewer employees are exempt from the law's requirements. Also, any group health plan that can show that the parity requirements resulted in an increase of 1 percent or more in its health care costs can become exempt.

Q 22:69 How does a plan claim the 1 percent increased cost exemption under MHPA?

The increased cost exemption must be taken based on actual claims data, not on an increase in insurance premiums. The provisions of MHPA must be implemented for at least six months, and the calculation of the 1 percent cost exemption must be based on at least six months of actual claims data with parity in place. In addition:

1. Plans claiming the increased cost exemption must notify the appropriate government agency and plan participants and beneficiaries 30 days before the exemption becomes effective.
2. Plans must use the formula provided in the regulations to calculate the increased cost of complying with parity.
3. A summary of the aggregate data and the computation supporting the increased cost exemption must be made available to plan participants and beneficiaries free of charge upon written request.
4. Once a plan qualifies for the 1 percent increased cost exemption, it does not have to comply with the parity requirements for the life of the MHPA provisions, scheduled to sunset on September 30, 2001 (although at press time there were efforts in Congress to extend or even expand the Mental Health Parity Act.)

Q 22:70 Have many plans taken advantage of the 1 percent exemption?

No. As of late 1998, only four plans had claimed the exemption. Three were in Oregon and one in Ohio.

Q 22:71 Can plans limit the number of inpatient days or outpatient visits for mental health treatment?

Yes. The only prohibitions in the law are annual and lifetime dollar limits.

Q 22:72 Does the Mental Health Parity Act apply to substance abuse treatment?

No. Plans can still impose annual and lifetime dollar limits on substance abuse treatment.

Q 22:73 How much will the Mental Health Parity Act cost employers?

According to one study, it may be only about $1 per employee per year. The study, by an economist at Rand, is based on data from managed mental health plans, so the cost is likely to be higher for unmanaged plans. The study found that removing a $25,000 annual limit would cost about $1, while removing a $10,000 limit would cost about $4 per employee per year. An earlier study by the Congressional Budget Office indicated the cost would be about $100 per enrollee.

Q 22:74 How much would it cost to achieve treatment parity between mental health or substance abuse coverage and medical or surgical coverage?

According to a 1998 study by Mathematica Policy Research, full parity for mental health and substance abuse benefits would increase health insurance premiums by 3.6 percent. PPOs and traditional indemnity plans would face increases of about 5 percent, while HMOs would register increased premiums of only 0.6 percent. Requiring parity for substance abuse treatment alone would raise premiums an average of only 0.2 percent. The study was based on costs in states with insurance laws requiring parity between mental health and other medical benefits.

According to the Office of Personnel Management, providing parity for mental health and substance abuse treatment could raise insurance premiums by between 1 and 2 percent for the Federal Employees Health Benefits Program.

Appendix A

Health Information Resources

The following is a list of resources that can provide information on various aspects of health care and insurance.

Government	A-1
Associations/Organizations	A-4
Accreditation Agencies/HMO Quality Review Organizations	A-12

Government

Agency for Healthcare Research and Quality
Office of Health Care Information
Suite 501
Executive Office Center
2101 East Jefferson Street
Rockville, MD 20852
(301) 594-1360
http://www.ahrq.gov

Bureau of Labor Statistics
Division of Information Services
2 Massachusetts Avenue, NE
Room 2860 Washington, DC 20212
(202) 691-5200
http://stats.bls.gov/

The Center for Substance Abuse Prevention
5600 Fishers Lane
Rockwall II Building
Suite 900 Rockville, MD 20857
(301) 443-0365
http://www.samhsa.gov

Centers for Disease Control and Prevention
1600 Clifton Road, NE
Atlanta, GA 30333
(404) 639-3311
http://www.cdc.gov/

Health Care Financing Administration
7500 Security Boulevard
Baltimore, MD 21244
(410) 786-3000
http://www.hcfa.gov/

Internal Revenue Service
1111 Constitution Ave., NW
Washington, DC 20224
(202) 622-5000
http://www.irs.ustreas.gov/

National Center for Health Statistics
6525 Belcrest Road
Room 1064
Hyattsville, MD 20782
(301) 458-4636
http://www.cdc.gov/nchs/

National Health Information Center
P.O. Box 1133
Washington, DC 20013-1133
(800) 336-4797 or
(301) 565-4167
http://www.nhic-nt.health.org/

Appendix A

National Institutes of Health
9000 Rockville Pike
Bethesda, MD 20892
(301) 496-4000
http://www.nih.gov/

National Technical Information Service
U.S. Department of Commerce
5285 Port Royal Road
Springfield, VA 22161
(703) 605-6000
http://www.ntis.gov/

Social Security Administration
110 West Road
Suite 500
Towson, MD 21204
(800) 772-1213
http://www.ssa.gov/

U.S. Department of Commerce
1401 Constitution Avenue, NW
Washington, DC 20230
(202) 482-2000
http://www.doc.gov

U.S. Department of Health and Human Services
200 Independence Avenue, SW
Washington, DC 20201
(202) 619-0257
http://www.os.dhhs.gov/

U.S. Department of Labor
Pension and Welfare Benefits Administration
200 Constitution Avenue, NW
Washington, DC 20210
(202) 219-8921
http://www.dol.gov/dol/pwba/

U.S. General Accounting Office
Document Handling and Information Facility
441 G Street, NW
Room 6252 Washington, DC 20548
(202) 512-6000
http://www.gao.gov/

U.S. Government Bookstore
Federal Building
1000 Liberty Avenue
Room 118
Pittsburgh, PA 15222
(412) 395-5021

Associations/Organizations

AFL-CIO Insurance Benefits
Department 815
16th Street, NW
3rd Floor
Washington, DC 20006
(202) 637-5256
http://www.aflcio.org/home.htm

Alcoholics Anonymous
General Services Office
P.O. Box 459
Grand Central Station
New York, NY 10163
(212) 870-3400
http://www.aa.org/

American Association of Health Care Consultants
11208 Waples Mill Road
Suite 109
Fairfax, VA 22030
(703) 691-2242
http://www.aahc.net/

Appendix A

American Association of Health Plans
1129 20th St., NW
Suite 600
Washington, DC 20036
(202) 778-3200
http://www.aahp.org/

American Association of Homes and Services for the Aging
901 E Street, NW
Suite 500
Washington, DC 20004-2011
(202) 783-2242
http://www.aahsa.org/

American Cancer Society
1599 Clifton Road, NE
Atlanta, GA 30329
(404) 320-3333
http://www.cancer.org/

American College of Health Care Administrators
1800 Diagonal Road
Suite 355
Alexandria, VA 22314
(703) 549-5822
http://www.achca.org/

American Health Care Association
1201 L Street, NW
Washington, DC 20005-4014
(202) 842-4444
http://www.ahca.org/

American Health Lawyers Association (AHLA)
1025 Connecticut Avenue, NW
Suite 600
Washington, DC 20036
(202) 833-1100
http://www.healthlawyers.org/

American Heart Association
7272 Greenville Avenue
Dallas, TX 75231-4596
(214) 373-6300
http://www.americanheart.org/

American Hospital Association
One North Franklin
27th Floor
Chicago, IL 60606
(312) 422-3000
http://www.aha.org/

American Insurance Association
1130 Connecticut Ave., NW
Suite 1000
Washington, DC 20036
(202) 828-7100
http://www.aiadc.org/

American Medical Association
515 N. State St.
Chicago, IL 60610
(312) 464-5000
http://www.ama-assn.org/

American Medical Rehabilitation Providers Association
1606 20th Street, NW
3rd Floor
Washington, DC 20009
(202) 265-3916
http://www.amrpa.org/

Blue Cross and Blue Shield Association
225 N. Michigan Avenue
Chicago, IL 60601
(312) 297-6000
http://www.bluecares.com/

Appendix A

Disability Management Employers Coalition
5694 Mission Center Road
#310
San Diego, CA 92108-4328
(800) 789-3632
http://www.dmec.org

Employee Assistance Professionals Association
2101 Wilson Blvd.
Suite 500
Arlington, VA 22201
(703) 522-6272
http://www.eap-association.com/

Employee Benefit Research Institute (EBRI)
2121 K Street, NW
Suite 600
Washington, DC 20037
(202) 659-0670
http://www.ebri.org/

Employers Council on Flexible Compensation (ECFC)
927 15th St., NW
Suite 1000
Washington, DC 20005
(202) 659-4300
http://www.ecfc.org/

ERISA Industry Committee
1400 L Street, NW
Suite 350
Washington, DC 20005
(202) 789-1400
http://www.eric.org

The Financial Accounting Standards Board (FASB)
401 Merritt 7
P.O. Box 5116
Norwalk, CT 06856-5116
(203) 847-0700
http://www.fasb.org/

Healthcare Financial Management Association (HFMA)
Two Westbrook Corporate Center
Suite 700
Westchester, IL 60154
(800) 252-4362
http://www.hfma.org/

Health Insurance Association of America (HIAA)
555 13th St., NW
Suite 600
East Washington, DC 20004
(202) 824-1600
http://www.hiaa.org/

Institute for a Drug-Free Workplace
1225 I Street, NW
Suite 1000
Washington, DC 20005
(202) 842-7400
http://www.drugfreeworkplace.org/

International Foundation of Employee Benefit Plans (IFEBP)
18700 West Bluemound Road
Brookfield, WI 53045
(262) 786-6700
http://www.ifebp.org/

International Society of Certified Employee Benefit Specialists
P.O. Box 209
Brookfield, WI 53008-0209
(262) 786-8771
http://www.iscebs.org

InterStudy Publications
2610 University Avenue
Suite 350
St. Paul, MN 55114
(612) 858-9291
http://www.hmodata.com/

Appendix A

March of Dimes Birth Defects Foundation
1275 Mamaroneck Avenue
White Plains, NY 10605
(888) 663-4637
http://www.modimes.org

Midwest Business Group on Health
8765 West Higgins Road
Suite 280
Chicago, IL 60631
(773) 380-9090
http://www.mbgh.org/

National Association of Health Data Organizations
391 Chipeta Way
Suite G
Salt Lake City, UT 84108
(801) 587-9104
http://www.nahdo.org/nahdo/index.html

National Association of Health Underwriters
2000 North 14th Street
Suite 450
Arlington, VA 22201
(703) 276-0220
http://www.nahu.org

National Association of Insurance Commissioners
2301 McGee
Suite 800
Kansas City, MO 64108-2604
(816) 842-3600
http://www.naic.org

National Association of Psychiatric Health Systems
325 7th Street, NW
Suite 625
Washington, DC 20004-2802
(202) 393-6700
http://www.naphs.org/

National Business Coalition on Health
1015 18th Street, NW
Suite 450
Washington, DC 20036
(202) 775-9300
http://www.nbch.org/

National Coalition on Health Care
1200 G Street, NW
Suite 750
Washington, DC 20005
(202) 638-7151
http://www.nchc.org/

National Council on Alcoholism and Drug Dependence, Inc. (NCADD)
12 West 21st St.
7th Floor
New York, NY 10010
(212) 206-6770
http://www.ncadd.org/

National Council on Compensation Insurance
750 Park of Commerce Drive
Boca Raton, FL 33487
(561) 997-1000
http://www.ncci.com/ncciweb/

National Health Council
1730 M Street, NW
Suite 500
Washington, DC 20036
(202) 785-3910
http://www.nhcouncil.org/

National Heart, Lung, and Blood Institute
Health Information Center
P.O. Box 30105
Bethesda, MD 20824-0105
(301) 592-8573
http://www.nhlbi.nih.gov

Appendix A

National Safety Council
1121 Spring Lake Drive
Itasca, IL 60143-3201
(630) 285-1121
http://www.nsc.org/

The National Wellness Institute
P.O. Box 827
Stevens Point, WI 54481-0827
(715) 342-2969
http://www.nationalwellness.org/

New York Business Group on Health, Inc.
386 Park Avenue South
Suite 508
New York, NY 10016-8804
(212) 252-7440
http://www.nybgh.org/

Self Insurance Institute of America, Inc.
12241 Newport Avenue
Suite 100
Santa Ana, CA 92705
(714) 508-4920
http://www.siia.org/

Society for Human Resource Management
1800 Duke Street
Alexandria, VA 22314
(703) 548-3440
http://www.shrm.org/

Society of Professional Benefit Administrators
2 Wisconsin Circle
Suite 670
Chevy Chase, MD 20815
(301) 718-7722

U.S. Chamber of Commerce
1615 H Street, NW
Washington, DC 20062
(202) 659-6000
http://www.uschamber.org/

Washington Business Group on Health
777 N. Capitol St., NE
Suite 800
Washington, DC 20002
(202) 408-9320
http://www.wbgh.com/

Workgroup for Electronic Data Interchange
12020 Sunrise Valley Drive
Suite 100
Reston, VA 20191
(703) 391-2716
http://www.wedi.org

Accreditation Agencies/HMO Quality Review Organizations

Accreditation Association for Ambulatory Health Care
3201 Old Glenview Road
Suite 300
Wilmette, IL 60091
(847) 853-6060
http://www.aaahc.org

The American Accreditation HealthCare Commission/URAC
1275 K Street, NW
Suite 1100
Washington, DC 20005
(202) 216-9010
http://www.urac.org/

Appendix A

Joint Commission on Accreditation of Healthcare Organizations
1 Renaissance Blvd.
Oak Brook Terr., IL 60181
(630) 792-5000
http://www.jcaho.org/

National Committee for Quality Assurance
2000 L Street, NW
Suite 500
Washington, DC 20036
(202) 955-3500
http://www.ncqa.org/

National League for Nursing
61 Broadway
33rd Floor
New York, NY 10006
(212) 363-5555
http://www.nln.org/

Appendix B

DOL Model COBRA Initial Notice

The following is the Department of Labor Model Statement for providing a COBRA Initial Notice to employees and spouses. The italicized wording is for use where one notice is being provided to both the employee and spouse simultaneously.

VERY IMPORTANT NOTICE

On April 7, 1986, a new Federal law was enacted [Public Law 99-272, Title X] requiring that most employers sponsoring group health plans offer employees and their families the opportunity for a temporary extension of health coverage (called "continuation coverage") at group rates in certain instances where coverage under the plan would otherwise end. This notice is intended to inform you, in a summary fashion, of your rights and obligations under the continuation coverage provisions of the new law. *Both you and your spouse should take time to read this notice carefully.*

If you are an employee of [employer's name] covered by [Group Health Plan Name] you have a right to choose this continuation coverage if you lose your group health coverage because of a reduction in hours of employment or the termination of your employment (for reasons other than gross misconduct on your part).

If you are the spouse of an employee covered by [Group Health Plan Name], you have the right to choose continuation coverage for yourself if you lose group health coverage under [Group Health Plan Name] for any of the following four reasons:

(1) The death of your spouse;

(2) A termination of your spouse's employment (for reasons other than gross misconduct) or reduction in your spouse's hours of employment;

(3) Divorce or legal separation from your spouse; or

(4) Your spouse becomes eligible for Medicare.

In the case of a dependent child of an employee covered by [Name of Group Health Plan], he or she has the right to continuation coverage if group health coverage under [Name of Group Health Plan] is lost for any of the following five reasons:

(1) The death of a parent;

(2) The termination of a parent's employment (for reasons other than gross misconduct) or reduction in a parent's hours of employment with [Name of Employer];

(3) Parents' divorce or separation;

(4) A parent becomes eligible for Medicare; or

(5) The dependent ceases to be a "dependent child" under [Name of Group Health Plan].

Under the new law, the employee or a family member has the responsibility to inform [Name of Plan Administrator] of a divorce, legal separation, or a child losing dependent status under [Name of Group Health Plan]. [Name of Employer] has the responsibility to notify [Name of Plan Administrator] of the employee's death, termination of employment or reduction in hours, or Medicare eligibility.

When [Name of Plan Administrator] is notified that one of these events has happened, [Name of Plan Administrator] will in turn notify you that you have the right to choose continuation coverage. Under the new law, you have at least 60 days from the date you would lose coverage because of one of the events described above to inform [Name of Plan Administrator] that you want continuation coverage.

If you do not choose continuation coverage, your group health insurance coverage will end.

Appendix B

If you choose continuation coverage, [Name of Employer] is required to give you coverage which, as of the time coverage is being provided, is identical to the coverage provided under the plan to similarly situated employees or family members. The new law requires that you be afforded the opportunity to maintain continuation coverage for 3 years unless you lost group health coverage because of a termination of employment or reduction in hours. In that case, the required continuation coverage period is 18 months. However, the law also provides that your continuation coverage may be cut short for any of the following four reasons:

(1) [Name of Employer] no longer provides group health coverage to any of its employees;

(2) The premium for your continuation coverage is not paid;

(3) You become an employee covered under another group health plan; and

(4) You become eligible to Medicare:

(5) You were divorced from a covered employee and subsequently remarry and are covered under your spouse's group health plan.

You do not have to show that you are insurable to choose continuation coverage. However, under the new law, you may have to pay all or part of the premium for your continuation coverage. [The new law also says that, at the end of the 18 month or 3 year continuation coverage period, you must be allowed to enroll in an individual conversion health plan provided under [Name of Group Health Plan].]

This new law applies to [Name of Group Health Plan] beginning on [applicable date under § 10002(d) of COBRA]. If you have any questions about the new law, please contact [Plan Administrator name and business address]. Also, if you have changed marital status, or you or your spouse have changed addresses, please notify [Plan Administrator] at the above address.

Appendix C

DOL Model COBRA Initial Notice Incorporating Revisions

Following is the Department of Labor model COBRA initial notice, revised to incorporate final and new proposed regulations, technical amendments, etc. Revisions are shown in italics.

VERY IMPORTANT NOTICE

On April 7, 1986, a new Federal law was enacted [Public Law 99-272, Title X] requiring that most employers sponsoring group health plans offer employees and their families the opportunity for a temporary extension of health coverage (called "continuation coverage") at group rates in certain instances where coverage under the plan would otherwise end. This notice is intended to inform you, in a summary fashion, of your rights and obligations under the continuation coverage provisions of the new law. Both you and your spouse should take time to read this notice carefully.

If you are an employee of [employer's name] covered by [Group Health Plan Name] you have a right to choose this continuation coverage if you lose your group health coverage because of a reduction in hours of employment or the termination of your employment (for reasons other than gross misconduct on your part).

If you are the spouse of an employee covered by [Group Health Plan Name], you have the right to choose continuation coverage for yourself if you lose group health coverage under [Group Health Plan Name] for any of the following four reasons:

(1) The death of your spouse;
(2) A termination of your spouse's employment (for reasons other than gross misconduct) or reduction in your spouse's hours of employment;
(3) Divorce or legal separation from your spouse; or
(4) Your spouse becomes *entitled to* Medicare.

In the case of a dependent child of an employee covered by [Name of Group Health Plan], he or she has the right to continuation coverage if group health coverage under [Name of Group Health Plan] is lost for any of the following five reasons:

(1) The death of a parent;
(2) The termination of a parent's employment (for reasons other than gross misconduct) or reduction in a parent's hours of employment with [Name of Employer];
(3) Parents' divorce or separation;
(4) A parent becomes *entitled to* Medicare; or
(5) The dependent ceases to be a "dependent child" under [Name of Group Health Plan].

Under the law, the employee or a family member has the responsibility to inform [Name of Plan Administrator] of a divorce, legal separation, or a child losing dependent status under [Name of Group Health Plan]. *You have 60 days from the date of the event, or the date coverage would be lost because of the event in which to notify the Plan Administrator.* [Name of Employer] has the responsibility to notify [Name of Plan Administrator] of the employee's death, termination of employment or reduction in hours, or Medicare *entitlement.*

If the employer commences a bankruptcy proceeding, retirees, spouses, and dependents who lose coverage as a result of the bankruptcy may have rights similar to those described previously.

When [Name of Plan Administrator] is notified that one of these events has happened, [Name of Plan Administrator] will in turn notify you that you have the right to choose continuation coverage. Under the law, you have at least 60 days from the date you would

Appendix C

lose coverage because of one of the events described above to inform [Name of Plan Administrator] that you want continuation coverage.

If you do not choose continuation coverage, your group health insurance coverage will end.

If you choose continuation coverage, [Name of Employer] is required to give you coverage which, as of the time coverage is being provided, is identical to the coverage provided under the plan to similarly situated employees or family members. The law requires that you be afforded the opportunity to maintain continuation coverage for 3 years unless you lost group health coverage because of a termination of employment or reduction in hours. In that case, the required continuation coverage period is 18 months. *These 18 months may be extended if other events occur during this time. If, for example, a divorce or legal separation occurs, coverage could be extended due to that event.*

If the Social Security Administration determines that you or a dependent were disabled at the time of termination or a reduction in hours or during the first 60 days of COBRA coverage, you and your dependents may be eligible for an additional 11 months of coverage if you notify [Name of Plan Administrator] within 60 days of the date of the Social Security determination and before the end of the 18-month period.

In no case will continuation be extended beyond three years from the date of the event which caused the initial period of continuation to begin. However, the law also provides that your continuation coverage may be cut short for any of the following reasons:

(1) [Name of Employer] no longer provides group health coverage to any of its employees;

(2) The premium for your continuation coverage is not paid;

(3) You *first* become *covered* under another group health plan unless that plan excludes a preexisting condition that applies to you or a dependent;

(4) You *first* become *entitled to Medicare;* or

(5) *If Social Security determines that you or a dependent receiving the 11-month extension for disability is no longer disabled.*

You do not have to show that you are insurable to choose continuation coverage. However, under the law, you may have to pay all or part of the premium for your continuation coverage. *There is a grace period of at least 30 days for payment of regularly scheduled premiums.* [The law also says that, at the end of the 18 month, *29 month,* or 3 year continuation coverage period, you must be allowed to enroll in an individual conversion health plan provided under [Name of Group Health Plan].]

If you choose continuation coverage and then acquire a new dependent(s), you must notify [Name of Plan Administrator] within 30 days to obtain coverage for your dependent(s).

This law applies to [Name of Group Health Plan] beginning on [applicable date under § 10002(d) of COBRA]. If you have any questions about the law, please contact [Plan Administrator name and business address]. Also, if you have changed marital status, or you or your spouse have changed addresses, please notify [Plan Administrator] at the above address.

Appendix D

Sample COBRA Notice Upon Occurrence of a Qualifying Event

(TO BE TYPED ON COMPANY LETTERHEAD)

Date

(Qualified Beneficiary's Name)

(Qualified Beneficiary's Address)

(   )

RE: Notice of COBRA rights to continue Health Plan coverage

Your participation in the (name of health plan or HMO), (will terminate) (has terminated) on (enter date). As a result of this termination, your (medical, dental, vision, hearing) coverage is being made available to you for continuation at your expense. If you elect to continue coverage, you may continue paying for the coverage, and continue it for up to (18, 29 or 36) months, until (end date). However, should one of the events listed below occur, the (18, 29 or 36) month period may not apply, and your coverage will end on the earliest of the following dates:

1. The date the Plan Sponsor ceases to provide any group medical coverage;
2. The date you become covered under another group medical plan, or under Medicare; or

3. The last day of the grace period for which a monthly premium remains unpaid.

If social security determines that you were disabled when COBRA began or became disabled at any time during the first 60 days of COBRA continuation coverage, you may continue your coverage for an additional 11 months, if you notify us within 60 days of the determination and before the end of the 18-month period. Higher premiums will apply during the additional 11 months.

You have 60 days from (the date of the notice, or the date coverage will terminate, whichever is later) to elect continuation coverage. To do so, you should complete, sign and return the enclosed copy of this letter (or complete the enclosed election form, etc.) within the 60-day period, and return it to:

(Name)
(Address)

If you elect to continue coverage, (employer, plan administrator, etc.) must receive the first premium payment at the above address within 45 days from the date you complete this election form. The first premium payment must include premium for all months from the date your coverage terminated, through the month you elect continuation coverage. Thereafter, premium payments must be made by you monthly, and are due at the above address on the first of each month for that month's coverage. For example, coverage for the month of April will be due on April 1st. If payment is not received within (30, 31) days after the due date, your coverage will be terminated as of the last day of the last month for which timely premium had been received. If the coverage is cancelled, it cannot be reinstated for any reason.

The monthly premium is:

	Medical	Dental	Vision	Hearing
Employee only:	$	$	$	$
Employee and Spouse:	$	$	$	$
Employee and Child:	$	$	$	$
Spouse and Child:	$	$	$	$
Full Family:	$	$	$	$

[Note: Employers should modify this grid as need be to reflect the appropriate types of coverage and premium categories as is applicable.]

Appendix D

APPLICANT DATA: Please complete the items below. Be sure to retain a copy for your records.

Name: _____.

Social Security No. _____.

Relationship to Employee:

_____ Self _____ Spouse _____ Child

I am electing to continue the following health coverages: (check all that apply)

____ Medical ____ Dental ____ Hearing ____ Vision

I am electing coverage for my eligible dependents listed below, in addition to myself:

Name: _____. Name: _____.

Name: _____. Name: _____.

Signature _____.

Date _____.

Appendix E

Model Certificate of Coverage

On April 1, 1997, the Departments of Labor, Health and Human Services, and Treasury issued interim, final regulations under the Health Insurance Portability and Accountability Act of 1996. The regulations included the following model certificate.

Model Certificate

CERTIFICATE OF GROUP HEALTH PLAN COVERAGE

IMPORTANT—This certificate provides evidence of your prior health coverage. You may need to furnish this certificate if you become eligible under a group health plan that excludes coverage for certain medical conditions that you have before you enroll. This certificate may need to be provided if medical advice, diagnosis, care, or treatment was recommended or received for the condition within the 6-month period prior to your enrollment in the new plan. If you become covered under another group health plan, check with the plan administrator to see if you need to provide this certificate. You may also need this certificate to buy, for yourself or your family, an insurance policy that does not exclude coverage for medical conditions that are present before you enroll.

1. Date of this certificate: _____

2. Name of group health plan: _____

3. Name of participant:_____

Health Insurance Answer Book

4. Identification number of participant: _____

5. Name of any dependents to whom this certificate applies:
_____

6. Name, address, and telephone number of plan administrator or issuer responsible for providing this certificate:

_____

_____

_____

_____

7. For further information, call: _____

8. If the individual(s) identified in line 3 and line 5 has at least 18 months of creditable coverage (disregarding periods of coverage before a 63-day break), check here ____ and skip lines 9 and 10.

9. Date waiting period or affiliation period (if any) began:_____

10. Date coverage began:_____

11. Date coverage ended: _____ (or check if coverage is continuing as of the date of this certificate: ___).

Note. Separate certificates will be furnished if information is not identical for the participant and each beneficiary.

Appendix F
Internet Resources

The following is a list of web sites that can provide information on various aspects of health care and insurance.

Government

Code of Federal Regulations
http://www.access.gpo.gov/nara/cfr/index.html

Congressional Record
http://www.access.gpo.gov/su_docs/aces/aces150.html

Federal Register
http://www.access.gpo.gov/su_docs/aces/aces140.html

Federal Web Locator
http://www.infoctr.edu/fwl/fedweb.new.html

Library of Congress
http://lcweb.loc.gov/homepage/lchp.html

Medicare
http://www.Medicare.gov

National Library of Medicine
http://www.nlm.nih.gov/

U.S. House of Representatives
http://www.house.gov/

U.S. Senate
http://www.senate.gov/

White House
http://www.whitehouse.gov/WH/welcome.html

Other

Insurance News Net
http://www.insurancenewsnet.com

The National Employee Benefits Web Site
http://www.benefitslink.com/

University of Michigan Documents Center Federal Government Resources on the Web
http://www.lib.umich.edu/libhome/Documents.center/federal.html

Yahoo Health/Medicine
http://dir.yahoo.com/health/medicine/

Index

[*References are to question numbers.*]

A

A. Foster Higgins. *See* Survey
A. M. Best. *See* Survey
AAPCC. *See* Adjusted average per capita cost (AAPCC)
Abortion coverage, 4:7
  PDA, 4:60
Absenteeism
  preventive care and, 12:66
  quality assurance and, 19:8
Acceleration. *See* Benefit
Acceptable loss ratio (ALR), defined, 5:36
Accidental death and dismemberment (AD&D), 1:13, 1:14
Accident and health plans
  nondiscrimination rules, 11:1–11:10
    aggregation, 11:9
    benefit test for self-insured plan, 11:6, 11:9
    eligibility tests for self-insured plans, 11:4, 11:5, 11:9
    5 percent owner, 11:3
    highly compensated employee, 11:3
    penalty, 11:7, 11:8
    retiree plans, 11:10
    self-insured plans, 11:1, 11:2
Accommodation, ADA and, 22:63
  reasonable accommodation, 4:83
Accounting
  audit, self-accounting employees, 6:36
  FASB rules, retiree health benefits, 15:11–15:25
  self-accounting, 6:33, 6:36
Accreditation
  American Accreditation HealthCare Commission/URAC, 19:11
  American Medical Accreditation Program, 19:10
  home health care, 20:17
  Joint Commission, 19:23
  National Committee for Quality Assurance (NCQA), 19:6, 19:8
    HEDIS, use of, 19:25
Acquired Immune Deficiency Syndrome. *See* AIDS
Acquisition of company
  consequence to cafeteria plan, 9:96
Actuary
  actuarial formulas, retiree health benefits, 15:16
  group health insurance definition, 5:6

Actuary (cont'd)
  group health insurance (cont'd)
    estimate of which individuals will receive claims, 5:7
    finding actuary, 5:8
Acupuncture, coverage, 3:28
ADA. See Americans with Disabilities Act
ADEA. See Age Discrimination in Employment Act of 1976 (ADEA)
Adjusted average per capita cost (AAPCC), 15:44, 15:45
Administration
  billing, 6:33–6:36
    self-accounting, 6:36
  claims, 6:37–6:51
    self-funding and, 17:46, 17:47
  computerized, 6:64–6:74
  cost reduction approaches, 7:22
  enrollment, 6:23–6:32
  flexible spending accounts, COBRA and, 13:74
  Form 5500, 14:10–14:19
  interactive communication systems, 21:17
  reporting and disclosure, 6:10–6:22
  setting up the plan, 6:1–6:9
    announcement materials, 6:7
    certificate of insurance, defined, 6:8
    effective date of coverage, 6:2
    identification cards, 6:9
    materials issued to employees, 6:9
    not approved by underwriter, 6:3, 6:4
    plan administrator vs TPA, 6:6
    putting coverage into effect, 6:1
    required coverage information before policy issuance, 6:5
    summary of material reduction (SMR), distribution of, 6:9
  third party
    performance standards, 18:8, 18:9
    role of TPA, 18:1–18:7
    TPA market, 18:18–18:28

Administrative services only (ASO) arrangement, 17:29
  classification of plans, 17:32
  services, 17:31
  TPA vs, 17:30
Adolph Coors, 12:72
Adopted children
  COBRA, qualified beneficiary, 13:54, 13:56
  flexible benefits plans, adoption assistance, 9:34
Adult day care, 20:32
Advance dividends. See Retrospective premium arrangement
Adverse selection
  defined, 2:9
  flexible benefits plans, 9:80
  HMOs, 8:39–8:44
    conventional plan cost, effect on, 8:41
    defined, 8:39
    health status of employee and, 8:42
    obviousness to employers, 8:33
    occurrence of, 8:40
Advisor as group insurance intermediary, 2:21
Aetna Life Insurance Company. See Survey
After-acquired, COBRA beneficiary, 13:5, 13:56
Age 65, over
  percentage of population, 15:1
Age Discrimination in Employment Act of 1976 (ADEA)
  group health insurance plans, 4:37, 4:44
  requirements, 4:2
  20-employee cutoff for coverage requirements, 13:6
Agency for Health Care Policy and Research. See Survey
Agent
  broker vs, 2:14
  decision to use, 2:16

I-2

Index

Aggregation
  accident and health plans, eligibility and benefits tests, 11:9
AIDS
  ADA and, 7:124
  corporate policy, 7:125
  coverage, 7:121
    limitations, 3:44
  employer response to, 7:125
  insurance, impact on, 7:117–7:125
    actual costs, 7:118
    ADA and, 7:124
    coverage for patients, 7:121
    employer response, 7:125
    expensive drugs, 7:119
    hospital stays, 7:119
    information restrictions, 7:120
    legal protections for persons with, 7:122
    life expectancy, lengthening, 7:119
    reasons for high costs, 7:119
    testing for AIDS, 7:123
  legal protections for persons with, 7:122
  testing for AIDS, permissibility, 7:123
Alcohol abuse. *See also* Substance abuse
  ADA and, 22:59
  programs, 12:69
Alternative health care systems. *See* Health maintenance organization; Preferred provider organization
Alternative therapy coverage, 3:28
  costs of, 3:31
  popularity of, 3:30
  types of, 3:28
AMA. *See* American Medical Association (AMA)
AMAP. *See* American Medical Accreditation Program
Ambulatory care utilization review. *See* Utilization review
Ambulatory surgery centers, Medicare reimbursement, 10:43

American Accreditation HealthCare Commission/URAC, 19:11
American Association of Health Plans. *See also* Survey
  "Putting Patients First" policies, 8:119
American Association of Retired Persons (AARP). *See* Survey
American Cancer Society, 12:64
American College of Physicians
  medical examinations, guidelines, 12:63
American Council of Life Insurance, 20:36
American Hospital Association, 2:31
American Institute of Certified Public Accountants
  SAS 70, 14:22
American Journal of Public Health. *See* Survey
American Legislative Exchange Council, 17:66
American Managed Care Pharmacy Association (AMCPA). *See* Survey
American Medical Accreditation Program, 19:10
American Medical Association (AMA), 2:31, 3:28
  antitrust laws and, 8:110
  collective bargaining unit, 8:104
  current procedural technology (CPT) coding system, 7:113
  HMOs, 8:12
American Subacute Care Association (ASCA), 20:39
Americans with Disabilities Act (ADA), 4:74–4:91
  accommodation, 4:83, 22:63
  AIDS and, 7:124
  alcohol abuse, 22:59
  businesses affected, 4:76
  compliance, 4:77
  confidentiality, 22:62
  cosmetic disfigurement, 4:79
  current drug abuse, defined, 22:60
  defined, 4:74

I-3

Americans with Disabilities Act (ADA) *(cont'd)*
  disability defined, 4:79
  drug-related questions during hiring process, 22:61
  drug-testing program, 22:57–22:63
  EEOC guidance, 4:90
  effect of
    business, 4:84
    employers and employees, 4:75
    health insurance benefits, 4:87
  essential job function, 4:82
  exemptions, 4:88, 22:58
  generally, 4:37
  health promotion programs, incentives, 12:87
  hiring process, 4:85
  information, obtaining, 4:91
  leave policies, 4:89
  preemployment physicals, 4:86
  qualified individual with disability, 4:81
  substance abuse and, 4:80, 22:57–22:63
  undue business hardship, 4:78
  who is protected by, 22:57
AmeriHealth, 8:104
Announcement materials
  informing employees about the plan, 6:7
Antidiscrimination laws. *See* Nondiscrimination rules; *specific law by name*
Antidisparagement provision. *See* Gag rule; Managed care
Antitrust
  physicians and, 8:110
  PPOs, 8:86
Any willing provider (AWP) laws
  defined, 8:107
  states passing, 8:108
Aon Consulting. *See* Survey
Appeals
  claim determination
    plan administrator obligation, 6:49

  process, 6:48, 6:50, 6:51
  reason for appeal, 6:48
  managed care plans, 8:105, 8:106
Apple Computer Inc., 3:11
Applicable premium, COBRA, 13:5
Application for coverage, approval denied, 6:3, 6:4
Approval, underwriter, 6:3, 6:4
Aragon Consulting Group. *See* Survey
Arizona
  marijuana, legalization of use of, 9:20
Aromatherapy, coverage, 3:28
Art supplies
  dependent care reimbursement accounts, 9:27
Asbestos, removal of, 9:23
ASCA. *See* American Subacute Care Association (ASCA)
Assets, including guaranteed investment contract, 14:18
Assignment of benefits, 6:37
  defined, 6:40
Association
  association plans, 1:17, 1:21
  insurers, HIPAA, 4:131
AT&T, 3:6
Audit
  claim audit, defined, 7:110
  hospital bill audit defined, 7:97
  self-accounting employees, 6:36
Average benefits test, dependent care assistance plans, 11:35
Ayurveda, coverage, 3:28

B

Balance billing
  defined, 10:19
  federal Medicare limits, 10:20
  state requirements, 10:21
Balanced Budget Act of 1997
  Medicare
    beneficiaries, 8:12
    cost containment, 10:35, 10:36

Index

disabled, rules for, 10:27
Medigap insurance policy, 10:44
preventive care, 10:8
Medicare + Choice, 10:51–10:53
quality assurance and, 19:9
Bankruptcy of Medicare, 10:36
Base-plus plans
defined, 3:25
nonsurgical physicians' services, 3:39
Bed wetting alarms
health care reimbursement accounts, 9:23
Behavioral health plans
cost control, 22:16
cost-cutting, 22:51
managed care
benefits of, 22:33
carve-outs, 22:35–22:41
development of, employer considerations, 22:34
pre-paid mental health plan, defined, 22:30
substance abuse benefit programs, effect on, 22:31
trend toward, what is driving, 22:32
outcomes measurement, 22:55, 22:56
physician, role of, 22:15
Beneficiary
COBRA, qualified beneficiary. *See* COBRA (Consolidated Omnibus Budget Reconciliation Act of 1985)
domestic partner benefits, reciprocal beneficiaries, 3:15–3:17
ERISA disclosure, HIPAA, 4:122
Medicare, 8:12
Balanced Budget Act of 1997, 8:12
election of HMO coverage by beneficiaries, 10:34, 10:54, 10:55
typical beneficiary spending, 10:15
Benefit
ADA, effect of, 4:87
assignment, 6:39, 6:40

cash chosen instead, cafeteria plan, 9:65
check, who receives, 6:46
communicating
bad news, 21:29
basic principles, 21:23
electronic media, use to communicate information, 21:25
enrollment campaign, 21:26
legal trends, 21:24
new employees, to, 21:27
retiring employees, 21:28
consultant. *See* Employee benefit consultant
coordination of benefits, 7:83–7:92
death benefits, acceleration, 4:127
dental. *See* Dental benefits
disability. *See* Disability benefits
domestic partner, 9:7. *See* Domestic partner benefit
electronic media, use to communicate information, 21:25
employee-pay-all, and FMLA, 4:71
explanation, 6:47
in SPD, 6:20
group health plan, taxable to employees, 4:140
guaranteed, change of jobs, 4:107
HIPAA requirements, 4:112
life insurance, 12:21–12:25
long-term care
adjustment for inflation, 20:33
duration of, 20:37
levels, 20:37
Medicaid, 20:29
Medicare, 20:28
loss, change in health status, 4:110
mandated. *See also* State law
self-funding, 17:52
Medicaid, long-term care, 20:29
Medicare, long-term care, 20:28
mental health. *See* Mental health benefit
order, Medicare, 10:22–10:33
periodic reports. *See* Periodic benefit reports

I-5

Benefit (*cont'd*)
  pharmacy benefit management, 16:1–16:72
  qualified, 9:4
  reduction
    before COBRA qualifying event, 13:59
    HIPAA rules, 4:119, 6:9
    60-day notice requirements, 4:122, 4:123
    summary of material reduction (SMR), distribution of, 6:9
  reservist. *See* Reservist benefits
  retiree. *See* Retiree health benefits
  survivor, group plan, 12:21–12:25
  vision care coverage. *See* Vision care coverage
Benefit statements
  reasons for, 21:9
  usefulness, 21:10
Benefit test
  cafeteria plans, 11:24
  dependent care assistance plans, 11:33
  group term life insurance, 11:16
  self-insured plans, 11:6, 11:9
Billing, 6:33–6:36
  audit of employees who self-account, 6:36
  balance billing
    defined, 10:19
    federal Medicare limits, 10:20
    state requirements, 10:21
  COBRA notice, 13:40
  current procedural technology (CPT) coding system, 7:113
  flexible benefits plans, 9:94
  hospital bill audit defined, 7:97
  medical billing codes
    code gaming, 7:114–7:116
    defined, 7:113
  premiums
    calculation, getting help, 6:34
    group insurance, 6:33
    late payment and coverage lapse, 6:35
    roster or list billing, 6:33
Biofeedback, coverage, 3:28
Birthday rule, COB, 7:91
Blue Cross/Blue Shield, 2:31–2:34
  defined, 2:31
  establishment of, 2:31
  history, 8:66
  major medical supplements and, 2:33
  medical examinations, guidelines, 12:63
  PPO vs, 8:68
  premium rate, 5:29
  private insurance companies
    differences, 2:34
    similarities, 2:32
  retrospective premium arrangements, 5:54
  self-funding, 17:46
  termination of coverage, 6:57
  Viagra, coverage, 16:30
  wraparound major medical, 2:33, 5:21
Bonus in lieu of TPA performance standards, 18:9
Boston Dispensary, 20:2
Breast pumps
  health care reimbursement accounts, 9:23
The Broadcaster Newsletter, 20:39
Broker
  agent vs, 2:14
  decision to use, 2:16
  insurance, 2:13
Brokerage firms, largest, 2:19
Buck Consultants. *See* Survey
Bundled plans or coverage, COBRA, 13:5, 13:21
Bureau of Labor Statistics. *See* Survey
Business advisor. *See* Advisor
Business Insurance magazine
  costs, forecasts, 5:10

Index

Buyers HealthCare Action Group. *See* Survey

C

Cafeteria plans
  benefit types, 9:53
  cash instead of benefits, 9:65
  Code definition, 9:3
  company acquired, 9:96
  court order to commence medical coverage, 9:44
  default or negative elections, 9:88
  401(k) plans and, 9:34, 9:66, 9:67
  nondiscrimination rules, 11:20–11:28
    benefits test, 11:24
    concentration test, 11:25
    discrimination penalty, 11:27
    eligibility test, 11:22, 11:23
    health benefit test, 11:26
    highly compensated employee, 11:21
    more than one set of discrimination rules, 11:28
  options. *See* Flexible benefits plans
  reimbursement for individual policy purchase, 9:60
  tax advantages, 9:6
    domestic partner benefits, 9:7
    employer contributions, 9:8
  vacation trading, 9:54–9:58
CAHPS. *See* Consumer Assessment of Health Plans (CAHPS)
California
  domestic partners, benefits for, 3:6
  marijuana, legalization of use of, 9:20
California Medical Association, 8:12
CalPERS
  managed competition, 3:103
  report card movement, 19:22
Camps, specialty, 9:27
Capitation
  HMOs, 8:6
    factors affecting, 8:17
    fee-for-service payment structure, differences, 8:16
  pharmacy benefit management role, 16:54
CareData Reports, Inc. *See* Survey
CARF. *See* Commission on Accreditation of Rehabilitation Facilities (CARF)
Carryover deductibles, 3:62
Carve-outs
  EAPs, integrated carve-out, 22:52
  generally, 3:75
  Medicare, 10:22
  mental health
    advantages, 22:30
    appropriateness for behavioral health care, 22:36
    cost control, 22:39
    defined, 22:35
    disadvantages, 22:31
    limits on access, 22:37
    nontraditional services, 22:38
  retiree health benefits and Medicare, 15:43
Case management
  changes in, 7:40
  defined, 7:38
  hospital discharge planning vs, 7:41
  managed care and, 7:40
  mental health benefits, 22:17, 22:21
  process, 7:39
Cash flow
  insurance, conventional, 7:93
  self-funding and, 17:14, 17:48
Cash instead of benefits, 9:65
Cash-or-deferred arrangement (CODA), as qualified benefit, 9:4
Center for Health Dispute Resolution, 3:51
Centers of excellence
  cost savings, 7:101
  defined, 7:99
  procedures, 7:100
Certificate
  HIPAA
    coverage, Appendix E

Certificate (cont'd)
  HIPAA (cont'd)
    group health plans and issuers, 4:100–4:104
    from insurer or HMO, 4:100
    minimum coverage period, 4:104
    nonreceipt, 4:98
    no preexisting condition clause, 4:99
  insurance, of
    defined, 6:8
    medical claim after plan effective date, 6:38
  preadmission, 7:42, 7:43
CHAMPUS. *See also* TRICARE
  defined, 4:147
  group plan under COBRA, 13:78
Charles D. Spencer & Associates. *See* Survey
Checkups. *See* Medical examination
Children. *See also* Dependents; Newborns and Mothers Health Protection Act of 1996
  adopted children
    COBRA, qualified beneficiary, 13:54, 13:56
    flexible benefits plans, adoption assistance, 9:34
  dependent, COB birthday rule, 7:91
  OBRA '93 enrollment requirement, 6:14
  uninsured, extension of coverage to, 1:6
Chinese medicine, coverage, 3:28
Chiropractic, coverage, 3:28
Cholesterol reduction programs, COBRA and, 13:15
Choosing and Using an HMO, 8:62
Church plans, exclusion from COBRA, 13:16
Civil charges, fiduciaries, 18:17
Civilian Health and Medical Program of the Uniformed Services. *See* CHAMPUS
Civil Rights Act of 1964, Title VII, 4:37

Claims
  administration choices, self-funding, 17:46, 17:47
  assignment of benefits, 6:39, 6:40
  audits, defined, 7:110
  benefit check recipient, 6:46
  cost management
    coordination of benefits, 7:84
    retrospective review, 7:46
  cost projections, employer with several locations, 5:12
  credibility, 5:21
  determination, appeal, 6:48–6:51
  expected, types of, 5:3
  explanation of benefits, 6:47
  extended benefits, liability of insurer, 5:4
  help completing claim form, 6:41
  higher than anticipated, margin calculation, 5:13
  incurred
    defined, 5:26
    paid claims, differences, 5:27
    stop-loss coverage, 17:56, 17:57
    when to use, 5:28
  insurer knowledge of expected claims, 5:5
  integrated processing, 16:52
  lag
    defined, 5:38
    report, 5:28
    study, 5:39
  later reimbursement, after paying heath care provider, 6:39
  manual rate, 5:22
  medical care, for, after plan effective date, 6:38
  paid
    defined, 5:25
    incurred claims, differences, 5:27
    when to use, 5:28
  pool, 5:23
  processing, 6:43–6:45
  prospective rating, 5:14
  reimbursement
    stop-loss coverage, 17:60

I-8

Index

timing, 6:42
reserves
  defined, 5:17
  necessary, 5:18
retrospective rating, 5:15
self-administration, 17:40
shock claims, 5:64, 7:94
submitting, 6:37
termination of contract, payment after, 5:4

Client service representative, defined, 2:9

Clinics
"quick clinics," 3:40

Coalition
cost management, 7:135–7:137
defined, 7:105
employer health care coalition defined, 2:41
local governments, joint purchasing, 1:26
participants, 7:106
state-sponsored group insurance coalitions
  defined, 1:24
  success of, 1:25

COBRA (Consolidated Omnibus Budget Reconciliation Act of 1985), 13:1–13:85
administration features, 6:66
adopted children, 13:54, 13:56
after-acquired dependent, defined, 13:5
amendments, 13:1
applicable premium, defined, 13:5
beneficiary. *See* Qualified beneficiary *below, this group*
bundled plans or coverage, 13:21
  defined, 13:5
change of benefits, active employees and, 13:25
changing elected coverage, 13:63
cholesterol reduction programs, 13:15
commencement, 13:58
compliance, 9:35
continuation coverage, defined, 13:5
continuation of one plan dependent on another, 13:21
continuation period, defined, 13:5
continuation requirements, change by HIPAA, 4:114
continuee, defined, 13:5
conversion privilege and, 6:62
core and noncore plans, 13:20
counseling programs, 13:15
covered employees
  changing elected coverage, 13:63
  creditable coverage, under HIPAA, 4:106
  defined, 13:5
  retiring employees, 13:67, 13:68
  sale of company, 13:11
  switching from family to single coverage, 13:82
  terminating employees, employer advisory to take COBRA, 13:75
covered employers, 13:6–13:11
  controlled groups, 13:9
  definition of employer, 13:7
  generally, 13:6
  more than 20 employers, growth to, 13:8
  multiple employer welfare arrangements (MEWAs), 13:10
  small-employer exemption, 13:10
covered plans, 13:12–13:22
  continuation of one plan dependent on another, 13:21
  core and noncore plans, 13:20
  excluded plans, 13:16
  excluded services, 13:15
  flexible spending accounts, 13:13
  group health plan defined, 13:14
  "involvement" in plan, defined, 13:17
  maintenance of plan by employer, 13:17
  more than one, 13:19
  Puerto Rico, plans in, 13:22
  types covered, 13:12
  union plans, 13:18

I-9

COBRA (Consolidated Omnibus Budget Reconciliation Act of 1985) *(cont'd)*
  deductibles
    handling, 13:69
    pay-based, 13:70
  deferred premium arrangement, 5:47
  defined, 13:1
  dependent, employee premium payment for, 13:64
  disability, extension of COBRA due to, 13:57
    family members, 13:57
    state law, 13:84
  disabled qualified beneficiary, defined, 13:5
  disclosures by plan to health care providers about coverage for qualified beneficiary, 13:27
  discount programs, 13:15
  election and grace periods, 13:47–13:53
    coverage during grace period, 13:50
    coverage without payment, 13:51
    date of election or payment, 13:48
    family coverage not specified, 13:53
    first payment, determination, 13:52
    45-day grace period, 13:47
    payment one day after grace period expiration, 13:49
    postmarked one day after grace period expired, 13:49
    60-day election period, 13:47, 13:63
    30-day grace period, 13:47
    time period, 13:47
  elimination of benefits, active employees and, 13:25
  employee assistance plans (EAPs), 13:12
  ERISA, penalties under, 13:61
  excise taxes on employers, 13:61
  exhaustion of COBRA, obtaining individual policies and, 4:117
  exhaustion of coverage, 6:31
  Family and Medical Leave Act of 1993 (FMLA) and, 13:30
  federal coverage continuation rules, 13:4
  flexible benefits plan and, 13:72
  flexible spending accounts and, 13:13, 13:73, 13:74
  generally, 4:2
  general requirements, 13:23–13:30
  grace period. *See* Election and grace periods *above, this group*
  gross misconduct defined, 13:60
  health maintenance organizations (HMOs), 13:12, 13:26
  impact on employers, 13:85
  "involvement" in plan, defined, 13:17
  loss of coverage
    commencement of COBRA, 13:58
    defined, 13:5
  maintenance of plan by employer, 13:17
  Medicaid or CHAMPUS, as group plan, 13:78
  Medicare entitlement, 13:77, 13:80
  minimizing financial exposure by reducing benefits before qualifying event, 13:59
  model initial notice, Appendix B
    revisions, incorporating, Appendix C
  more than one covered plans, 13:19
  movement of beneficiary out of HMO service area, 13:26
  multiemployer plan, withdrawal of employee from, 13:29
  multiple employer welfare arrangements (MEWAs), 13:10, 13:14
  multiple qualifying events, defined, 13:5
  newborns, 13:54

Index

new regulations
  effective dates, 13:3, 13:5
  highlights, 13:2
noncompliance penalty, 13:61
nonqualified beneficiary, 13:55
nonresident aliens, 13:55
notification requirements, 13:31–13:41
  bills or payment reminders to continuees, 13:40
  compliance responsibility, 13:32
  components of notice, 13:36
  employees, spouses, or dependents, 13:38
  initial notice, 13:37
  model initial notice, Appendix B, Appendix C
  model notice, DOL, 13:36
  qualifying event, 13:39
  recipient of notice, 13:35
  rights, notice of, 21:27
  sample notice upon qualifying event, Appendix D
  software package, COBRA administration, 13:41
  spouse, notification of COBRA rights after qualifying event, 13:34
  summary plan description, initial notice placed in, 13:37
  when employees must receive, 13:33
OBRA '93 effect, 13:24
physical or health examination programs, annual, 13:15
plan design for COBRA continuation only, 13:66
plan limits, 13:71
preferred provider organizations (PPOs), 13:12
premiums, 13:42–13:46
  frequency of rate changes, 13:42
  how determined, 13:43
  IRS guidance, 13:45
  less than amount due is paid, 13:46
  rate, determination of, 13:44
  self-funded employers, 13:44
  "similarly situated" individuals, 13:43
  spouse or dependent, for, 13:64
Puerto Rico, plans in, 13:22
qualified beneficiary, 13:54–13:57
  adopted children, 13:54, 13:56
  after-acquired dependents, 13:56
  changing elected coverage, 13:63
  classification, 13:54
  defined, 13:5
  disability, extension of COBRA due to, 13:57
  disabled qualified beneficiary, defined, 13:5
  disallowed individuals, 13:55
  disclosures by plan to health care providers, 13:27
  evidence of insurability, 13:65
  family members, extension of COBRA to due to disability, 13:57
  independent election, 13:62
  moving outside service area, 13:26
qualifying event
  commencement of COBRA, 13:58
  defined, 13:5
  minimizing financial exposure by reducing benefits before, 13:59
  notice of, 13:39
  sample notice, Appendix D
  spouse, notice of rights after, 13:34
requirements, 4:2
reserve benefits and, 4:142
  USERRA and COBRA compared, 4:142
retiring employees, 13:67, 13:68
sample notice upon qualifying event, Appendix D
similarly situated, defined, 13:5

I-11

COBRA (Consolidated Omnibus Budget Reconciliation Act of 1985) *(cont'd)*
   simultaneous coverage by new plan with preexisting condition exclusion and old plan, 13:81, 13:82
   small-employer exemption, 13:10
   smoking cessation programs, 13:15
   software package, COBRA administration notification requirements and, 13:41
   spouse, employee premium payment for, 13:64
   state law and, 13:84
     state-by-state list, 13:83
   TAMRA, penalties under, 13:61
   termination
     early, 13:76
     prematurely, 13:78
   terminology, 13:5
   20-employee cutoff for coverage requirements, 13:6
     controlled groups, treatment of members of, 13:9
     growth of employer, 13:8
     multiple employer welfare arrangements (MEWAs), 13:10
     unbundled plans or coverage, 13:21
     defined, 13:5
   USERRA
     comparison, 4:142
     relationship between COBRA and, 13:28
   weight reduction programs, 13:15
Code creep, 7:115
Code gaming
   detecting, 7:116
   kinds of, 7:115
   providers, by, 7:114
Code Section 79, group term life plans, 11:11
Code Section 416(i), key employee, 11:12

Coinsurance
   costs, Massachusetts surcharge and, 4:34
   defined, 3:65
   forgiveness, 3:89
   indexed requirements, 10:10
   maximum out-of-pocket limit, 3:67–3:69
   typical percentages, 3:66
   utilization, effect on, 3:90
COLI. *See* Corporate-owned life insurance (COLI)
Collective bargaining agreement, FMLA and, 4:70
Colorado
   managed care plans, exceeding scheduled fees, 3:36
Combining plans, Form 5500, 14:13–14:16
Commission
   schedules, 2:23
   vesting, 2:24
Commission on Accreditation of Rehabilitation Facilities (CARF), 20:40
Communication, 21:1–21:29. *See also* Information
   benefit statements
     reasons for, 21:9
     usefulness, 21:10
   computerized, programs available, 6:68
   electronic media, use to communicate benefit information, 21:25
   e-mail, HIPAA disclosure, 4:124
   employee benefits, 21:23–21:29
   event-based communications, 21:8
   flexible benefits plans, implementation, 9:86
   interactive systems
     administrative advantages, 21:17
     benefits of using, 21:15
     customized programs, 21:18
     expense, 21:18
     preference, 21:16

Index

lack of, as medical cost factor, 7:17
new employees, to, 21:27
on-line services
  enrollment, for, 21:20–21:22
  usage, 21:19
periodic benefit reports, 21:11–21:14
strategies, developing, 21:1–21:8
  budget, 21:5
  event-based communications, 21:8
  human resources, 21:7
  media considerations, 21:4
  plan changes, 21:6
  process, 21:3
  reason for focus on communications, 21:1
  successful effort, 21:2
  written communication or human resources, 21:7
Community rating
  defined, 2:33
  HMOs, 8:48
Comparability rule, medical savings accounts, 7:73, 7:74
Compensation. *See also* Commission; Pay
  flexible spending account administration, 13:74
  intermediaries, 2:22–2:24
  pharmacy benefit management, 16:53
  total compensation, 3:2
  TPAs, 2:30
Competition. *See also* Managed competition
  managed competition, 3:2, 3:99–3:107
  plan cuts and, 7:130
Complaints, 8:105, 8:106
Comprehensive plans, defined, 3:26
Computerized administration, 6:64–6:74
  advantages of, 6:73
  buying or leasing a system, 6:69
  COBRA administration system features, 6:66

communication programs available, 6:68
electronic communications, advantages of, 6:73
financial projection systems, 6:68
flexible benefits plans, 6:67
interactive programs, 6:68
Internet, use of, 6:70–6:72
Intranet, use of, 6:70–6:72
outsourcing, 6:74
role of computer systems
  nondiscrimination testing, 6:65
  plan management, 6:64
statement and correspondence systems, 6:68
Computer-scannable forms
  EFAST, Form 5500, 14:27
Concentration test
  cafeteria plans, 11:25
  dependent care assistance plans, 11:34
Concurrent review, process, 7:45
Conditions. *See* Preexisting condition
Confidentiality
  ADA, 22:62
  EAPs, 22:49
  Form 5500, 14:4
  managed care plans, 8:105
Congressional Budget Office. *See* Survey
Congressional Research Service. *See* Survey
Connecticut
  alternative therapies, coverage, 3:28
Consolidated Omnibus Budget Reconciliation Act of 1985. *See* COBRA
Constructive receipt. *See also* Receipt
  flexible benefits plans, 9:11
Consultants. *See* Employee benefit consultant
Consulting firms, largest, 2:20
Consumer Assessment of Health Plans (CAHPS), 19:20
Consumer Bill of Rights, managed care plans, 8:105

I-13

Consumer protection laws, managed care plans, 8:115
Consumers Union. *See* Survey
Containing costs. *See* Cost
Continuation of coverage. *See* COBRA (Consolidated Omnibus Budget Reconciliation Act of 1985)
Contraception, coverage, 16:65
Contracting. *See also* Hospital
  direct contracting arrangements, cost management, 7:104
Contributions
  dependent care reimbursement accounts, average rate, 9:28
  employee
    ERISA requirements, 4:47
    flexible benefits plans, 9:9
    HIPAA requirements, 4:112
    MSAs, 7:68
    premiums, toward, 3:77–3:79
  employer
    cafeteria plans, state tax, 9:8
    MSAs, 7:68
    taxable income, 4:138
  extensive coverage, 4:12
  health care reimbursement accounts, 9:24
  MSAs, 7:68
    deadline for, 7:72
    maximum annual contribution, 7:70
  reimbursements exceeding, 9:33
  VEBAs
    deductions, 17:81
    key employees, 17:83
Controlled group, COBRA coverage, 13:9
Control over insurers, legislating, 2:6
Conventional insurance. *See* Insurance
Conversion privilege
  COBRA effect, 6:62
  defined, 6:61
  other group plans, 6:63

Coordination of benefits (COB), 7:83–7:92
  birthday rule, 7:91
  claim cost management, 7:84
  defined, 7:83
  ERISA control, 7:86
  forms of coordination, 7:89, 7:90
  innovations, 7:92
  maintenance of benefits, 7:88
  multiple plan coverage, payment priority, 7:85
  states adopting rules, 7:87
Copayments, 3:39
  generic drugs, mail service, 16:41
  prescription drug plans
    average prescription drug copays, 16:71
    flat, 16:70
    three-tier copay, 16:72
Core-plus plan, defined, 9:47
Corporate-owned life insurance (COLI)
  retiree health benefits, pre-funding, 15:30
  trust-owned life insurance (TOLI), differences, 15:31
Cosmetic drugs, formularies and, 16:24
Cosmetic surgery, 3:45
  flexible benefits plans, 9:20
  exceptions, 9:21
  procedures considered elective, 9:22
Cost. *See also* Medical savings account
  alternative therapy coverage, 3:31
  annual, payment by employer, 3:19
  behavioral health carve-out, 22:39
  claim projections, employer with several locations, 5:12
  comparison, health plans, 8:55
  containment. *See* Cost containment; Cost management
  contributory plans, 3:20, 3:21
  control. *See also* Cost containment; Cost management
    education, 7:96

Index

flexible benefits plans, 9:13–9:15
hospice care, 20:46
pharmacy benefit management, 16:14–16:39
poor quality of care resulting, 7:102
prescription drug plan, 16:46
risk reduction, 7:103
covered expense
    limiting, 3:43, 3:44
    reimbursement, 3:42
crisis, and HMOs enrollment, 8:31
dental plans
    cost-control considerations, 12:10
    cost-management, 12:7
EAPs, 22:44
effectiveness
    HMOs, 8:29
    substance abuse, 2:39
expense projection, 5:19
factors affecting. *See* Cost management
fully insured plans, 5:2
health care reimbursement accounts expenses, 9:20
HMOs, 8:29
    effect on conventional plan, 8:41
    other health care plans vs, 8:32
home health care, long-term care, 20:27
hospital charges, group plan coverage, 3:32
hospital outpatient expenses, coverage, 3:41
impact of uninsured on insurance costs, 1:8
legal constraints, 3:23
long-term care insurance, 20:36
management. *See* Cost management
MSAs, medical expenses defined, 7:78
noncontributory plans, 3:20, 3:21
pharmacy benefit management, 16:13, 16:14–16:39
    increases, 16:11, 16:12
physician fees, RBRVS effect, 10:42

plan design, effect on, 3:19–3:23
PPOs, vs quality of care, 8:89
prescription drug plans, typical cost, 16:63
projection, insurer, 5:10
reasonable and customary charge, 3:36
    coverage, 3:34, 3:92
    defined, 3:34
    exceeding by physicians, 3:37
    scheduled benefit structure, change to, 3:92
reduction
    centers of excellence, 7:101
    EAPs, 22:51
    fundamental approaches, 7:22
    new and expensive medical technology, 7:131
    outcomes data, 19:29
    quality measures and, 19:4
reimbursement. *See* Reimbursement
retiree health benefits, 15:7–15:10
risk financing, reducing by self-funding, 17:45
savings
    centers of excellence, 7:101
    home health care, 20:12
    medical savings account, 7:62
    physician profiling, 7:54
    self-funding, 17:9
    UR, 7:47
self-funding, 3:24
sharing, hospital stays in connection with childbirth, 4:40
shifting, 7:7
    self-funding to avoid, 17:44
TPAs, 18:18
utilization review, expense vs savings, 7:47

Cost containment
coinsurance
    forgiveness, 3:89
    utilization, effect on, 3:90
coverage options, 4:5
managed competition, 3:107

Cost containment (cont'd)
  plan design and, 3:71–3:98
    carving out coverage, 3:75
    coinsurance, 3:90
    coinsurance forgiveness, 3:89
    cost-sharing increases, 3:76
    deductibles, 3:80–3:88, 3:90
    design philosophy, 3:71
    design theory, 3:72
    employee contributions toward premiums, 3:77–3:79
    encouragement to use most cost-effective care, 3:91
    inappropriately designed plans, combating problem of, 3:98
    outpatient surgery, 3:93
    preexisting conditions, exclusions, 3:74
    preventive care programs, 3:94
    redesign of plan, 3:73, 3:96
    reducing benefits, legal factors, 3:95
    scheduled benefit structure, change to, 3:92
    specific factors, 3:71
Cost effectiveness
  PPOs, 8:78
  TPAs, 2:29
Cost management, 7:1–7:134
  AIDS, impact on insurance, 7:117–7:125
  billing codes, 7:113–7:116
  case management, 7:38–7:41
  centers of excellence, 7:99–7:101
  claim audits defined, 7:110
  coalitions, 7:135–7:137
  conventional insurance, 7:93–7:95
  coordination of benefits, 7:83–7:92.
    See also Coordination of benefits for detailed treatment
  cost shifting defined, 7:7
  defensive medicine, 7:4, 7:14
  direct contracting arrangements, 7:104
  education, 7:96
  employees' expectations and, 7:134

  employer's role, 7:129–7:134
    competition and cost-cutting, 7:130
    employees' expectations and, 7:134
    high costs and, 7:20, 7:21
    inappropriate use of medical services, 7:133
    individual employers, 7:129
    overprovision of services, 7:132
    reduction of costs, steps, 7:131
  escalation of health care costs, 7:1, 7:4
  experience rating, 7:22
  extended care facilities, coverage, 20:11
  factors affecting cost, 7:1–7:22
    communication, lack of, 7:17
    consumer lack of medical understanding, 7:16
    cost shifting defined, 7:7
    defensive medicine, 7:4, 7:14
    employers, role in high costs, 7:20, 7:21
    excessive use of medical services, 7:4
    first dollar coverage medical insurance, 7:4
    fraud, 7:4
    higher claims, 7:8
    inappropriate use of medical services, 7:12
    insulation of consumers from cost exposure, 7:15
    legal liability and, 7:6
    less care, purchase of, 7:11
    mandated coverage, 7:19
    overprovision of services, 7:9
    oversupply of medical professionals and facilities, 7:13
    physicians' decisions, 7:21
    plan design, inappropriate, 7:18
    rate of increase in cost, 7:2
    reduction approaches, 7:22
    rising costs, 7:3

Index

technology, new and expensive, 7:5
unnecessary care, 7:10
health care data, 7:23–7:31
   analysis, effective, 7:26
   design features to implement without data, 7:31
   employer-specific, 7:25
   inpatient and outpatient charges vs comparative norms, 7:30
   inpatient charges by type of service, 7:30
   insurance company, 7:30
   kinds of data useful, 7:27
   plan redesign purposes, 7:28
   programs to implement, 7:24
   self-analysis, 7:29
   TPAs, 7:30
HMO considerations, 7:109
home health care, coverage, 20:11
inappropriate use of medical services, 7:12, 7:133
individual employers, 7:129
legal liability issues, 7:6
less care, purchase of, 7:11
malpractice insurance, 7:6
managed competition. *See* Managed competition
medical billing codes, 7:113–7:116
medical savings accounts, 7:60–7:82. *See also* Medical savings accounts *for detailed treatment*
negotiations with providers, 7:98
options other than plan design features, 7:95
overprovision of services, 7:9, 7:132
performance guarantees, 7:12, 7:111
plan cuts, competition and, 7:130
poor quality of care resulting, 7:102
provisions, 6:56
rationing health care, 7:126–7:128
retrospective review, 7:46
risk reduction, 7:103
scheduled approach, change to, 7:22

technology
   effect on costs, 7:5
   new and expensive, 7:131
   unnecessary care and, 7:10
   utilization review, 7:32–7:37, 7:42–7:59. *See also* Utilization review *for detailed treatment*
   value-based purchasing, 7:108
Cost-of-living adjustments (COLAs)
   long-term disability plan, 12:34
Cost sharing
   increases, 3:76
   mental health plans, 22:22
Counseling
   COBRA and, 13:15
   employee assistance programs (EAPs), 22:49
Coverage
   abortions, 4:7
   acupuncture, 3:28
   AIDS patients, 7:121
   alternative therapies, 3:28
      costs of, 3:31
      popularity of alternative therapy, 3:30
      types of, 3:28
   application, underwriter not approving, 6:3, 6:4
   aromatherapy, 3:28
   ayurveda, 3:28
   base-plus plans, 3:25
   biofeedback, 3:28
   carving out, 3:75
   changing, 6:53
   chiropractic, 3:28
   choosing option not offering best coverage, 9:68
   classes of employees covered, 3:54
   comprehensive plans, 3:26
   cost limitations, 3:43, 3:44
   denial of, 3:60
   dental benefits. *See* Dental benefits
   different service waiting periods, 3:61
   duplicating benefits, drawbacks, 3:56

I-17

Coverage (cont'd)
  effective date, 6:2
  election change, COBRA qualified beneficiary, 13:63
  exclusions
    dental services, 12:13
    legitimate experimental treatments, 3:47
    reasons for, 3:53
  experimental treatment, 3:46
  extended care facilities, 3:52, 20:11
  extensive use, and premium or contribution amount, 4:12
  external review, 3:49–3:51
  flexible benefits plans, proof of coverage, 9:71
  gems and magnets, 3:28
  generally, 3:27
  guided imagery, 3:28
  HMOs, employer payment, 8:50
  home health care, 20:11
    procedure for installing, 20:16
  homeopathy, 3:28
  hospital and surgical care, recent changes, 3:38
  hospital charges
    group plan, 3:32
    outpatient expenses, 3:41
  information, required before issuing policy, 6:5
  initial decline and subsequent enrollment, 6:30
  intensive care charges, 3:32
  key employees, enhanced health care coverage, 3:59
  late premium, 6:35
  long-term care benefits, 20:32
    ages covered, 20:37
  mandated
    cost factor, as, 7:19
    federal requirement, 4:1
    state requirement, 4:3, 4:4
  massage therapy, 3:28
  maternity or family, single employees, 4:8
  Medicare, 10:2–10:8
  Medigap insurance policy, 10:45
  mental illnesses, 22:1, 22:8
    limitations, 22:4
    what constitutes coverage, 22:11
  model certificate, HIPAA, Appendix E
  MSA participants, 7:69
  multiple plan, COB, 7:85
  naturopathy, 3:28
  nonsurgical physician's services, 3:39
  options, for cost containment, 4:5
  orthodontics, 12:9
  part-time employees, 3:57, 3:58
  pediatric vaccines, 3:95, 4:53
  plan design and, 3:24–3:52
    restrictions on coverage, 3:53–3:61
  prescription drug. *See* Prescription drug coverage
  preventive care, 3:45, 12:58
  primary, employer plan, 4:10
  prior, HIPAA, 4:97
  putting into effect, 6:1
  QMCSOs, 6:14
  reasonable and customary charge
    defined, 3:34
    exceeding, by physicians, 3:37
    reasons for, 3:36
  reimbursement of covered expense, 3:42–3:44
  requirement, HIPAA, 4:111
  restrictions on, 3:53–3:61
  retired employees, federal law, 4:45
  secondary, Medicare eligibility, 4:9
  self-funded plans, 17:43
  service or benefit
    generally, 3:27
    services not covered, group plans, 3:45
    60-day notice of material reduction, 4:122, 4:123
  skilled nursing facilities, 3:40, 3:52
  spouse, mandatory, 4:13
  surgery, 3:33
    outpatient surgery, 3:93
  temporary employees, 3:57

Index

termination, 6:57–6:63
  middle of plan year, 6:57
  protection against medical expense, 6:59, 6:60
  year-end only, 6:58
traditional Chinese medicine, 3:28
treatment decision, insurer, 3:48
types of plan available, 3:24
vasectomies, 4:7
vision care. *See* Vision care coverage
waiting periods, 3:61
yoga, 3:28
Credentialing. *See also* Accreditation
Credibility, defined, 5:21
Credit
  COBRA coverage, 4:106
  preexisting conditions, HIPAA, 4:105
Criminal charges, fiduciaries, 18:17
Current procedural technology (CPT) coding system, 7:113
Custodial care
  long-term care, 20:24
  tax status, 20:34
Customer satisfaction measures
  report card movement, 19:18
  surveys, 19:8

D

Damage awards, prevention, 6:51
Dartmouth Atlas of Health Care, 19:9
Day care
  adult day care, 20:32
  flexible benefit plans, mid-year election changes
    change of provider, 9:41
    change of rate, 9:40
Death benefit. *See* Benefit; Group term life insurance; Life insurance
  employee, disposition of MSA, 7:77
Deductibles. *See also* Tax considerations
  carryover deductibles, 3:62
  cost containment and, 3:80–3:88
    front-end deductibles, 3:87, 3:88
    pay-based deductibles, 3:83–3:85
    per-condition deductibles, 3:86
    typical deductibles, 3:81
    utilization, effect on, 3:90
    waivers, 3:82
  defined, 3:62
  front-end deductibles, 3:87, 3:88
  maximum out-of-pocket limit, 3:67–3:69
  pay-based deductibles
    advantages, 3:84
    defined, 3:83
    disadvantages, 3:85
  per-condition deductibles, 3:86
  reimbursement and, 3:64
  typical deductibles, 3:81
  utilization, effect on, 3:90
  waivers of, 3:82
Deep cut retros, defined, 5:54
Default elections, flexible benefits plans, 9:88
Defense of Marriage Act, 3:10
Defensive medicine. *See also* Preventive care
  costs, effect on, 7:4, 7:14
Deferred premium arrangements. *See also* Premiums
  defined, 5:45
  reason for electing, 5:46
  reason for not electing, 5:47
Deficit Reduction Act of 1984, 11:19
Defined contribution plans
  retirement benefit financing, 15:36, 15:42
Defined dollar approach, defined, 15:25
Delinquent Filer Voluntary Compliance program, 14:35, 14:36
Delivery systems. *See also* Hospitals
Demographically adjusted, defined, 2:34
Demographics
  flexible benefits plans and, 9:12
  plan design and, 3:1
Dental benefits, 12:1–12:13
  cost-control considerations, 12:10

Dental benefits (*cont'd*)
   cost-management features, 12:7
   coverage, 12:1
   direct reimbursement, 12:4
   evidence of insurability, 12:8
   excluded services, 12:13
   HIPAA, 4:132
   how provided, 12:3
   incentives, 12:11
   insurance coverage, 12:6, 12:8
   lag time, payment of claims, 5:38
   numbers of employers offering, 12:2
   orthodontics, 9:22, 12:9
   precertification, 12:12
   services typically provided, 12:5
Department of Defense
   reservists benefits, 4:145
Department of Labor (DOL)
   notice
      COBRA initial notice, Appendix B, Appendix C
   401(h) transfers, 15:34
Dependent care assistance plans. *See also* Day care
   eligibility test, 11:30
   highly compensated employee, 11:31
   nondiscrimination rules, 11:29–11:36
      benefit test, 11:33
      concentration test, 11:34
      excluded employees, 11:32
      penalty for discrimination, 11:36
      separate-line-of-business basis, 11:29
   qualified benefit, as, 9:4
Dependent care reimbursement accounts
   art supplies, 9:27
   camps, specialty, 9:27
   contribution rates, average, 9:28
   defined, 9:25
   eligible expenses, 9:27
   field trips, 9:27
   ineligible expenses, 9:27
   participation rates, average, 9:28
   registration fees, 9:27
   services, when incurred, 9:26

   structure of, 9:29
   summer camps, 9:27
   termination of employment, 9:30
   tuition, 9:27
Dependent rates, fully insured plans, 5:34
Dependents
   after-acquired, COBRA beneficiary, 13:5, 13:56
   children, COB birthday rule, 7:91
   claim appeal process, 6:50
   COBRA
      notice rules, 13:38
      premium payment by employee, 13:64
   dependent care assistance plans. *See* Dependent care assistance plans
   dependent care reimbursement accounts. *See* Dependent care reimbursement accounts
   HIPAA certificate, 4:103
   PDA coverage, 4:59
   reservist benefits, 4:146
   TRICARE, employer responsibility to, 4:148
Design. *See* Plan design
Diagnosis-related group (DRGs)
   all claims paid on DRG basis, 10:37
   home health care and, 20:3
   Medicare payment determination, 10:37–10:39
Diet pills, 16:48
Direct contracting. *See also* Hospitals
   cost management, 7:104
Direct reimbursement. *See* Reimbursement
Disability. *See also* Preexisting conditions
   benefits. *See* Disability benefits
   defined, ADA, 4:79
   disabled individual, ADA, 4:81
   management. *See* Disability management
Disability benefits
   amount received, 12:35

Index

causes of claims, 12:28
COBRA
   continuation and state law, 13:84
   disabled qualified beneficiary defined, 13:5
   extension of coverage, qualified beneficiary, 13:57
compensation programs, 12:29
disability, defined, 12:33
dual-purpose deferred compensation/accident and health plans, 12:37
long-term disability plans, 12:32–12:34
   amount received from, 12:35
   components of, 12:34
   contributions, pre- or post-tax, 9:73
   cost-of-living adjustments (COLAs), 12:34
   defined, 12:32
   disability, defined, 12:33
   eligibility period, 12:34
   elimination period, 12:34
   integration with other benefits, 12:34
   payment period, 12:34
   preexisting conditions, 12:34
Medicare rules
   generally, 10:27
   secondary requirements, 10:31
   who is considered disabled, 10:30
payroll of employer, amount used to pay benefits, 12:26
pervasiveness of disabilities, 12:27
short-term disability plans, 12:30, 12:31
   amount received from, 12:35
taxation, 12:36, 12:37
total disability, leaving service of employer due to, 12:36
Disability management, 12:38–12:49
   coordination of approach by employers, 12:49
   effective, achieving, 12:38
   independent living program, 12:48

independent medical examination defined, 12:40
job accommodation program, 12:47
prevention program implementation, 12:39
rehabilitation, 12:41–12:46
   actuality of rehabilitation, 12:43
   benefit, vs pay, 12:42
   candidates, 12:44
   disability management, 12:41–12:46
   ingredients of program, 12:45
   staff, 12:46
return-to-work programs, 12:47
Discharge planning, case management vs, 7:41
Disclosure. *See also* Information; Reporting
   COBRA to health care providers, 13:27
   ERISA, 4:122
   HIPAA, 4:122, 4:133
   HMOs, pharmaceutical plans, 16:48, 16:49
   managed care plans, 8:105
   retiree health benefits, 15:14, 15:15
   small employers, HIPAA, 4:133
Discounts
   COBRA and, 13:15
   PPOs, 8:88, 8:93
Discount vision plans, 12:19
Discrimination. *See* Nondiscrimination rules; *related laws by name*
Disease state management (DSM) programs
   cutting drug costs, 16:38
   defined, 16:35
   evaluation, 16:39
   value to plan sponsors, 16:36
Distributions
   MSAs, who governs, 7:76
DOL. *See* Department of Labor (DOL)
Domestic partner benefits, 3:5–3:17
   cities, requirements, 3:12, 3:13
   civil union laws, 3:14

I-21

Domestic partner benefits (*cont'd*)
  criteria used to determine validity of domestic partnership, 3:8
  Defense of Marriage Act and, 3:10
  diversity, 3:7
  fairness and, 3:7
  generally, 3:5
  IRS position on, 3:9, 3:10
  market competition, 3:7
  private employers, 3:6
  public reaction, 3:11
  reasons for offering, 3:7
  reciprocal beneficiaries (Hawaii)
    defined, 3:15
    reaction to, 3:17
    rights of, 3:16
  spouse, defined, 3:9
  tax advantages, 9:7
Drug abuse. *See also* Substance abuse
  current, ADA definition, 22:60
  questions during hiring process, 22:61
Drug testing, ADA and, 22:57–22:63
Drug utilization review (DUR), 16:4
DSM programs. *See* Disease state management (DSM) programs
Dual choice option
  HMO Act of 1973, 4:2, 4:48, 8:45, 8:49
Dual-purpose deferred compensation/accident and health plans, 12:37
Duplication of benefits. *See* Benefit

E

EAPs. *See* Employee assistance programs (EAPs)
EBRI. *See* Survey
Education. *See also* Information
  educational assistance plan. *See* Educational assistance plan
  health, on, 12:69
  health care cost control and, 7:96
  medical understanding for consumers, 7:16
  pharmacy benefit manager, 16:7
  PPO, incorporating into health plan, 8:94
Educational assistance plans, 9:4
EEOC. *See* Equal Employment Opportunity Commission
EFAST, Form 5500, 14:25–14:36
  computer-scannable forms, 14:27
  definition, 14:25
  Delinquent Filer Voluntary Compliance program, 14:35, 14:36
  edit checks, 14:33, 14:34
  hand print format, difference, 14:31
  how to become electronic filer, 14:32
  machine print forms, 14:30, 14:31
  payments owed, 14:35
  reasons for development, 14:26
  software, 14:28, 14:29
Elections
  COBRA. *See* COBRA (Consolidated Omnibus Budget Reconciliation Act of 1985)
  deferred premium arrangement, 5:46, 5:47
  flexible benefits plan. *See* Flexible benefits plan
  shared funding arrangement, 5:49
Electronic communications, advantages of, 6:73
Electronic data interchange
  HIPAA, 4:125
  pharmacy benefit management, 16:57
Electronic filing (EFAST)
  Form 5500, 14:25–14:36
    computer-scannable forms, 14:27
    definition, 14:25
    Delinquent Filer Voluntary Compliance program, 14:35, 14:36
    edit checks, 14:33, 14:34
    hand print format, difference, 14:31

Index

how to become electronic filer, 14:32
machine print forms, 14:30, 14:31
payments owed, 14:35
reasons for development, 14:26
software, 14:28, 14:29
Electronic media, use to communicate benefit information, 21:25
Eligibility. *See also* Coverage
HIPAA, 4:108, 4:109
Medicaid, considerations when enrolling employees, 6:25
Medicare, 10:2
MSA, 7:64, 7:67
nondiscrimination tests, group term life plans, 11:13
retiree health benefits, 15:1–15:6
how eligibility is determined, 15:4
Eligibility test
cafeteria plans, 11:22
excluded employees, 11:23
dependent care assistance plans, 11:30
group term life insurance, 11:14
self-insured accident and health plans, 11:4, 11:5, 11:9
Eligible dependent, defined, 3:4
Eligible employee, defined, 3:3
E-mail, communicating HIPAA disclosures, 4:124
Emergency services
emergency room deductible, 7:22
managed care plans, 8:105
Employee assistance programs (EAPs), 22:42–22:54
advantages of integrated carve-out, 22:52
behavioral health cost-cutting, 22:51
carve-out, advantages, 22:52
COBRA and, 13:12
confidentiality, 22:49
cost-effectiveness, 22:44, 22:54
counseling, 22:49
defined, 22:42

effective components, 22:48
elements of good design, 22:49
employee attitudes towards, 22:53
ERISA welfare plan, as, 22:46
evaluation, 22:49
expense, 22:44
external resources, 22:47
failure to enter into or cooperate with, 22:49
financing, 22:45
follow-up, 22:49
in-house counselors or external resources, 22:47
management training, 22:49
monitoring, 22:49
prevalence, 22:43
provision of services, 22:50
surveys, 22:49
timeliness, 22:49
Employee benefit consultants
decision to use, 2:16
defined, 2:15
Employee Benefit News. *See* Survey
Employee Benefit Research Institute (EBRI). *See* Survey
Employee contributions. *See* Contributions
Employee-pay-all benefits, FMLA and, 4:71
Employee Retirement Income Security Act. *See* ERISA
Employees. *See specific topic*
Employee savings accounts
retiree benefit financing, 15:41
Employee stock ownership plans (ESOPs)
retiree benefit financing, 15:38
Employer contributions. *See* Contributions
Employer health care coalitions, 1:29
Employer quality partnerships (EQPs), 19:14
Employers. *See specific topic*
Employers Council on Flexible Compensation, 9:83

I-23

End-stage renal disease, Medicare coverage, 10:22
  primary coverage, as, 10:24, 10:30
Enrollment, 6:23–6:32
  benefit programs, on-line technology, 21:20–21:22
  children, 6:14
  communication, campaigns, 21:26
  encouraging, reason for, 6:23
  flexible benefits plans
    communication in advance of, 9:86
    confirmation, 9:89
    how employees enroll, 9:87
  forms
    completion period, 6:28
    late submission, 6:29
  group plans, 6:27
  HIPAA
    date, 4:93, 4:95
    special enrollment periods, 4:113
  HMOs, 8:9, 8:25–8:31
    geographic differentials, 8:11
    hospitalization and, 8:23
    trends, 8:10
    unlimited health care entitlement, 8:20
  information required, 6:24
  late, 4:95, 6:29
  managed care plans, 8:5
  Medicaid eligibility consideration, 6:25
  Medicare, age one may enroll, 10:16
  noncontributory plan, 6:26
  person initially declining coverage, 6:30
  reenrollment in group plans, 6:32
  special enrollment period, defined, 6:31
EPOs. *See* Exclusive provider organizations (EPOs)
Equal Employment Opportunity Commission (EEOC)
  abortion coverage, guidelines, 4:60
  ADA, guidance, 4:90
  AIDS and, 7:124
  testing for, 7:123
ERISA (Employee Retirement Income Security Act)
  claims processing requirements, 6:43
  COBRA, noncompliance, 13:61
  coordination of benefits and, 7:86
  disclosure requirements, HIPAA, 4:122
  EAPs as welfare plans, 22:46
  employee contributions, 4:47
  establishing self-funding, 17:5
  fiduciary responsibility, 18:13–18:17
  flexible benefit plan and, 9:5
  generally, 4:37
  group plan requirements, 4:46
  mandated benefit rules, self-funding, 17:52
  noncompliance penalty, TPA, 18:10
  preemption
    HMOs, 8:53, 8:54
    state law, 4:17, 4:18
  requirements, 4:2
  TPAs, noncompliance penalty, 18:10
  written communication, 21:7
ERISA Industry Committee, 19:8
Essential job function, ADA, 4:82
Ethics in Patient Referrals Act, 20:22
Evaluation, EAPs, 22:49
Evidence of insurability
  dental benefits, 12:8
  qualified beneficiary, COBRA, 13:65
Examination. *See* Medical examination
Excise taxes
  COBRA, noncompliance, 13:61
Exclusive provider organizations (EPOs)
  defined, 8:70
  PPOs, compared, 8:71
Exercise clubs, 9:23
Expense projection, fully insured plans, 5:19
Expenses. *See* Cost
Experience gain, flexible benefits plans, 9:31

Index

Experience rate
  combined with manual rate, 5:29
  cost and, 7:22
  definition, 5:24, 17:36
  fully insured plan, 5:14
  pooling of claims, 5:30
Experimental treatment, 3:46
  legitimate experimental treatments, 3:47
Exploding (code gaming), 7:115
Express Scripts/Value Rx. *See* Survey
Extended care. *See* Home health care; Medical facilities
External review
  defined, 3:49
  managed care plans, 8:117, 8:118
  prevalence of, 3:51
  reason for process, 3:50

F

FACCT. *See* Foundation for Accountability (FACCT)
Facilities. *See* Medical facilities
Fallon Community Plan, 16:30
Families USA. *See* Survey
Family and Medical Leave Act of 1993 (FMLA), 4:62–4:73
  cafeteria plans, 9:95
  COBRA, applicability, 13:30
  collective bargaining agreement, 4:70
  compliance, 9:35
  effect on benefits, 4:64
  employee-pay-all benefits, 4:71
  employer payment of employee premiums, 4:69
  final regulations, 4:63
  generally, 4:2, 4:62
  maternity vs parental or family leave, 4:72
  noncompliance, consequences, 4:66
  notices about benefits, 4:65
  part-time schedule, employee switch to, 4:67
  plan changes during leave, 4:68
  requirements, 4:2
  typical employer family leave policies, 4:73
Family coverage
  mandatory for single employees, 4:8
Family law. *See also* Newborns and Mothers Health Protection Act of 1996
Family leave. *See also* Family and Medical Leave Act; Leave
  maternity leave vs, 4:72
  state law, 4:31
  typical employer leave policies, 4:73
Family status, change in
  flexible benefit plans, 9:34
    mid-year election changes and, 9:35
FASB accounting rules, retiree health benefits
  accumulated postretirement benefit obligation (APBO), 15:14
  actuarial formulas, 15:16
  changes to rules, 15:20
  company response, 15:19
  determining costs to be reported, 15:14
  effective dates, 15:17
  FAS 106, 15:1, 15:3
    changes created by, 15:5
    changes to, 15:20
    explained, 15:11
    government entities, 15:21
    minimizing impact of rules, 15:18
    responses by companies, 15:19
  government entities, 15:21
  minimizing impact of rules, 15:18
  multiemployer welfare plans, applicability of FAS 106, 15:22
  pre-funding rules, 15:26
  SOP 92-6, multiemployer welfare plans, 15:22
  substantive plan defined, 15:13
FDA, generic drugs and, 16:33
Federal Employees Health Benefit Plan, 3:103, 13:16

Federal law
ADEA and group health insurance plans, 4:44
affecting group insurance plans, 4:37
change, employer's plan obligations, 4:15
coverage continuation requirement, 13:4
direct requirements, 4:2
ERISA. *See* ERISA
group health plans, 4:37–4:53
generally, 4:37
taxes, 4:136
HMO Act of 1973. *See* HMO Act of 1973
HMOs, 8:46
prevalence of federally qualified HMOs, 8:47
influence on plan design. *See lines throughout this topic*
mandatory coverage, 4:1
maternity stay, preauthorization of, 4:43
MEWAs, 4:14
Newborns and Mothers Health Protection Act of 1996, 4:38–4:42
PPOs, 8:83
reporting, 6:10
retiree coverage, mandate, 4:45
self-funded plans, 4:15, 4:17
state health insurance, division between, 4:18

Federally qualified HMOs
mirror image HMOs vs, 2:38

FICA contributions
flexible benefits plans, 9:6

Fiduciary responsibility, ERISA
classes of fiduciaries, 18:16
defined, 18:13
named fiduciaries, 18:16
prudence, 18:13, 18:15
quality assurance, 19:4
requirements, strictness, 18:14
risks, 18:17

Field trips, dependent care reimbursement accounts, 9:27
"Field underwritten" policies, 6:5
Financial Accounting Standards Board (FASB). *See* FASB accounting rules, retiree health benefits
Financial Services Online. See Survey
Financing. *See* Plan funding; Self-funding
FIND/SVP. *See* Survey
First dollar coverage medical treatment, 7:4
Fitness programs, 12:69
Flat copayments, 16:70
Flexible benefits plans, 9:1–9:96
acquisition of plan by another company, 9:96
administrator selection, 9:93
adoption assistance, 9:34
adverse election, 9:80
automatic cost changes, mid-year election changes and, 9:35
billing arrangement, 9:94
cafeteria plans
defined, 9:3
types of benefits, 9:53
cash in lieu of benefits, 9:43
changes to plan, developments regarding, 9:34
COBRA and, 13:72
computerized administration, 6:67
contributions
how made, 9:77
level of, determination, 9:75, 9:76
pre- or post-tax, 9:73
reimbursements exceeding, 9:33
contributory requirement, 9:74
core-plus plans, defined, 9:47
cosmetic surgery, 9:20
exceptions, 9:21
procedures considered elective, 9:22
cost and pricing, compared with traditional plan, 9:90
cost control, 9:13–9:15

Index

cost increases, mid-year election changes and, 9:35
court order to commence medical coverage, 9:44
coverage
  curtailment of, mid-year election changes and, 9:35
  dependent or spouse, change in, 9:35
  proof of, 9:71
day care providers
  change of provider, 9:41
  change of rate, mid-year election changes and, 9:40
decision pools, 9:77
default elections, 9:88
defined, 9:1
demographic changes and, 9:12
dependent care reimbursement accounts, 9:25–9:29
domestic partner benefits, 9:7
employee communications, types advisable, 9:86
employment status, change in, 9:35
enrollment
  communication in advance of, 9:86
  confirmation, 9:89
  how employees enroll, 9:87
ERISA and, 9:5
experience gain, 9:31
family status, change in, 9:34
  mid-year election changes and, 9:35
FICA contributions, 9:6
first introduction, 9:10
flexible spending or reimbursement accounts, 9:18
FMLA rules, 9:35, 9:95
full-menu or total flexible benefits plans, 9:49, 9:50
funding, 9:72
  self-funding, 9:78
FUTA contributions, 9:6

health care reimbursement accounts
  changes in what is considered, 9:20
  defined, 9:19
HMOs, inclusion in plan, 9:61
home office billing, 9:94
implementation, 9:72–9:96
  acquisition of plan by another company, 9:96
  administrator selection, 9:93
  adverse election, 9:80
  billing arrangement, 9:94
  communications, types advisable, 9:86
  contributory requirement, 9:74
  cost management, 9:90
  decision pools, 9:77
  default or negative elections, 9:88
  enrollment, 9:87, 9:89
  FMLA rules, 9:95
  funding, 9:72
  how are implemented, 9:84
  issues to address, 9:81
  level of contributions, determination, 9:75, 9:76
  needs of employees, determining, 9:82
  post-tax contributions, 9:73
  pre-tax contributions, 9:73
  purchase of plan, compared to purchase of traditional plan, 9:79
  renewal of, 9:91
  reports, 9:92
  resources for researching, 9:83
  self-funding, 9:78
  specific issues, 9:81
  time frame, 9:85
issues to address in purchase of, 9:81
laetrile, 9:20
life cycle flex plan, 9:51
  life cycle allowance, 9:52
lockouts, mid-year election changes and, 9:35
marital status, change in, 9:35

I-27

Flexible benefits plans (cont'd)
  Medicaid entitlement, mid-year election changes and, 9:35
  medical care, changes in costs of, 9:37
  Medicare entitlement, mid-year election changes and, 9:35
  mid-year election changes, 9:35–9:45
    automatic cost changes, 9:35
    cash in lieu of benefits, 9:43
    cost increases, 9:35
    court order to commence medical coverage, 9:44
    coverage, curtailment of, 9:35
    coverage of dependent or spouse, change in, 9:35
    day care providers and, 9:40, 9:41
    effective before election, 9:45
    employment status, change in, 9:35
    lockouts, 9:35
    Medicaid entitlement, 9:35
    medical care, changes in costs of, 9:37
    Medicare entitlement, 9:35
    mistaken first election, 9:39
    nanny, increase in salary, 9:42
    new benefit introduced mid-year, 9:38
    number of dependents, change in, 9:35
    option, addition or elimination of, 9:35
    residence, change of, 9:35
    status changes permitting, 9:36
    strikes, 9:35
  mistaken first election, mid-year election changes and, 9:39
  modular plan, defined, 9:46
  nanny, increase in salary, 9:42
  needs of employees, determining, 9:82
  negative elections, 9:88
  new benefit introduced mid-year, 9:38
  number of dependents, change in, 9:35
  options, 9:59–9:71
    cash instead of benefits, 9:65
    HMOs, inclusion in plan, 9:61
    insurance carrier, 9:63, 9:64
    integration of 401(k) into cafeteria plan, 9:66, 9:67
    medical insurance, 9:59
    not choosing best coverage option, 9:68
    PPOs, inclusion in plan, 9:62
    reimbursement for individual health insurance policy, 9:60
    waiver, 9:69–9:71
  post-tax contributions, 9:73
  PPOs, inclusion in plan, 9:62
  pre-tax contributions, 9:73
  prevalence, 9:2
  proof of coverage, 9:71
  purchase of plan, compared to purchase of traditional plan, 9:79
  qualified benefits defined, 9:4
  reasons first developed, 9:12
  renewal of, compared with traditional plan, 9:91
  residence, change of, 9:35
  resources for researching, 9:83
  salary reduction premium conversion plan, 9:17
  self-accounting, 9:94
  self-funding, 9:78
  strikes, mid-year election changes and, 9:35
  tax advantages, 9:6–9:12
    cafeteria plan, 9:6
    constructive receipt, 9:11
    domestic partner benefits, 9:7
    employee contributions, 9:9
    first introduction of flexible benefits plans, 9:10
    reason for development of plan, 9:12
    state income tax, 9:8
  types of plans, 9:16–9:53

Index

uniform reimbursement approach, 9:32
vacation trading, 9:54–9:58
waiver, 9:69–9:71
working spouse plan, 9:48
Flexible/market-driven plan design, 3:2
Flexible spending accounts (FSAs)
  COBRA and, 13:13, 13:73, 13:74
  health care reimbursement accounts. *See* Health care reimbursement accounts
  HIPAA, 4:94
  MSAs vs, 7:61
  "use it or lose it" rule, 7:61
FMLA. *See* Family and Medical Leave Act of 1993 (FMLA)
Form M-1, 1:23
Form 5500, 6:10, 14:1–14:36
  administration, 14:10–14:19
    assigning plan numbers, 14:12
    attachments included, 14:17
    combining plans, 14:13–14:16
    errors, common, 14:19
    guaranteed investment contracts, 14:18
    1999 or later, plan years beginning, 14:17
    plan administrator defined, 14:11
    plan sponsor defined, 14:10
    Schedules, described, 14:17
  combining plans, 14:13–14:16
  completing, 14:20–14:24
    extension of time to file, 14:24
    private delivery service, use to file, 14:21
    schedules not to be completed, 14:20
    stop-loss policy, instructions for Schedule A, 14:23
    third party administrators, 14:22
  confidentiality, 14:4
  defined, 14:1
  electronic filing (EFAST), 14:25–14:36
    computer-scannable forms, 14:27
    definition, 14:25
    Delinquent Filer Voluntary Compliance program, 14:35, 14:36
    edit checks, 14:33, 14:34
    hand print format, difference, 14:31
    how to become electronic filer, 14:32
    machine print forms, 14:30, 14:31
    payments owed, 14:35
    reasons for development, 14:26
    software, 14:28, 14:29
  errors, common, 14:19
  extension of time to file, 14:24
  filing date, 14:5
  goal of filing forms, 14:3
  long plan year, 14:9
  multiemployer welfare plans, 15:22
  1999 or later, plan years beginning, 14:17
  plan years, 14:6–14:9
    defined, 14:7
    short plan year, 14:8
  private delivery service, use to file, 14:21
  Schedule A
    combining plans, 14:13
    completing, 14:20
    described, 14:17
    guaranteed investment contract included in assets, 14:18
    more than one required, 14:14
    short plan years, 14:8
    stop-loss policy, 14:23
  Schedule C, 14:17
    completing, 14:20
  Schedule D, 14:17
  Schedule F, 14:17
    completing, 14:20
  Schedule G, 14:17
  Schedule H, 14:17
    completing, 14:20
  Schedule I, 14:17
    completing, 14:20

I-29

Form 5500 (cont'd)
  stop-loss policy, instructions for Schedule A, 14:23
  time for filing, 14:5
  welfare plans excluded, 14:2
Former employees
  nondiscrimination rules, group term life plans, 11:19
Formularies
  advantages to closed formularies, 16:20
  controversy, 16:28
  cosmetic drugs, 16:24
  defined, 16:17
  disadvantages to closed formularies, 16:21
  excluded drugs, 16:24
  hair-loss, drugs used for, 16:24
  most commonly found, 16:19
  new drugs, effect of, 16:29
  open vs closed, 16:18
  over-the-counter drugs, 16:24
  PBM influence over, 16:23
  physicians
    and role of, 16:26
    support, 16:25
Foster Higgins. *See* Survey
Foundation for Accountability (FACCT), 19:8, 19:9
401(h) accounts
  defined, 15:32
  transfers, 15:33, 15:34
401(k) plans, cafeteria plans and, 9:34, 9:66, 9:67
Fraud
  costs, effect on, 7:4
  home health care, 20:20–20:22
Front-end deductibles, 3:87, 3:88
FSAs. *See* Flexible spending accounts (FSAs)
Full-menu plans
  defined, 9:49
  restricted to large employers, 9:50
Full outsourcing, 6:74

Fully insured plans. *See also* Plan funding
  alternatives to, 5:40–5:44
  claims
    expected, 5:3
    extended benefits, liability of insurer, 5:4
    incurred, 5:26–5:28
    insurer knowledge of expected claims, 5:5
    lag report, 5:28
    paid, 5:25, 5:27, 5:28
    paid after contract termination, 5:4
    and plan design, 5:9
    termination of contract, payment after, 5:4
  cost components, 5:2
  credibility, defined, 5:21
  deficit reimbursement, 5:16
  dependent rates, 5:34
  distinguishing characteristics, 17:34
  expected cost of claims, employer with several locations, 5:12
  expense projection, 5:19
  experience rating, 5:14
    combined with manual rate, 5:29
    defined, 5:24
    pooling of claims, 5:30
  geography, impact on cost, 5:10
  group health insurance actuary, 5:6
    estimate of which individuals will receive claims, 5:7
    finding actuary, 5:8
  insurance company profit, 5:20
  insurer cost projections, 5:10
  lag
    defined, 5:38
    studies, 5:18, 5:39
  "life years" formula, 5:29
  loss ratio
    defined, 5:35
    tolerable. *See* Tolerable loss ratio (TLR)
  manual rate, 5:22, 5:29

Index

margin for higher-than-anticipated claims, 5:13
pool, 5:23, 5:30
   charge, 5:31
premium rate, 5:29–5:34
prospective rating, 5:14
rate-guarantee period, 5:10
reserves
   defined, 5:17
   necessary, 5:18
retention, 5:32
retrospective rating, 5:15
"spreadsheet" quotes, 5:33
TPAs, 2:27
utilization review, 5:9
Funding. *See* Plan funding; Self-funding
FUTA contributions
flexible benefits plans, 9:6

G

Gag rule, 8:112
defined, 8:111
Gallup Organization, Inc. *See* Survey
Gaming. *See* Code gaming
Gatekeeper, HMOs, 8:21
Gems and magnets, coverage, 3:28
General Accounting Office (GAO), 1:10
General Motors. *See* Survey
Generic drugs, 16:22
copayments, mail service, 16:41
FDA's position on, 16:33
Geography, impact on cost, 5:10
Georgia
domestic partners, benefits for, 3:11
Global fees, centers of excellence, 7:101
Government agencies, home health care, 20:4
Governmental plans, exclusion from COBRA, 13:16

Grace period, COBRA. *See* COBRA (Consolidated Omnibus Budget Reconciliation Act of 1985)
Grand Coulee Dam, 8:7, 8:11
Gross misconduct, defined, 13:60
Group health insurance plans, 1:1–1:29
actuary, 5:6
   estimate of which individuals will receive claims, 5:7
   finding, 5:8
ADEA and, 4:44
advantages over individual insurance, 1:3
association plans, 1:17, 1:21
availability to single employers, 1:18
benefits, taxable to employees, 4:140
certificate, HIPAA, 4:100–4:104
change in state and federal laws, employer obligations, 4:15
characteristics, 1:15
COBRA
   definition, 13:14
   Medicaid or CHAMPUS, 13:78
   new regulations, 13:2, 13:3, 13:5
   plans excluded, 13:16
   services excluded, 13:15
coverage
   denial of, 3:60
   different service waiting periods, 3:61
   part-time employees, 3:57, 3:58
   restrictions on, 3:53–3:61
   for retired employees, federal law, 4:45
   temporary employees, 3:57
   waiting periods, 3:61
employer health care coalitions, 1:29
enrollment, 6:27
ERISA requirements, 4:46
excluding workers over age 65, 10:23
federal law, 4:37–4:53
fringe benefit, as, 1:17
generally, 1:1

I-31

Group health plans (*cont'd*)
  growth of, 1:16
  HIPAA disclosures, information to participant and beneficiary, 4:122
  history of, 1:16
  HMO Act of 1973, 4:48
  hospital charges covered, 3:32
  importance to employees, 1:17
  imposing deductible or cost-sharing for childbirth hospital stays, 4:40
  individual insurance vs, 1:2
  joint purchasing, 1:27, 1:28
    local governments, 1:26
  law of large numbers, 1:2
  maximum participants, 4:30
  minimum participants, 4:29
  multiple employer trust, 1:19
  multiple employer welfare arrangements (MEWAs)
    defined, 1:22
    generally, 1:21
    requirements, 1:23
  multiple individual policies, 1:4
  participation, state requirements, 4:28
  physical examination requirement, 4:109
  premium billing, 6:33
  prevalence in United States, 1:5
  protection, 1:12
  reason for providing, 1:12
  reenrollment, 6:32
  sale, intermediary services, 2:12
  self-employed individuals, deductions, 4:137
  self-funded, HIPAA, 4:121
  services not covered, 3:45
  similarities among state laws, 4:20
  small groups, HIPAA insurer requirements, 4:130
  state law, 4:16–4:36
  state mandates, 4:28–4:30
  state-sponsored coalitions
    defined, 1:24
    success of, 1:25
  survivor benefits, 12:21–12:25
  tax considerations
    federal tax status, 4:136
    state tax laws, 4:135
  types provided, 1:13, 1:14
  underwriter, 2:6
  union, 1:20
  wage controls of, 1:16
Group sales representatives
  defined, 2:8
  interaction with intermediary in sale of group plan, 2:11
Group term life insurance
  coverage, self-funding, 17:28
  nondiscrimination rules, 11:11–11:19
    Code Section 79, 11:11
    Code Section 416(i) key employee, 11:12
    former employees, 11:19
    nondiscrimination tests, 11:13
    penalty for discrimination, 11:18
    retired employees, nondiscrimination rules, 11:19
Group-to-individual portability, HIPAA, 4:116
Guaranteed investment contract (GIC), 14:18
Guarantees. *See* Guaranteed investment contract; Performance; State insurance guaranty funds
Guided imagery, coverage, 3:28

H

Habit-breaking programs, 12:69
Hardship
  undue business hardship, ADA, 4:78
Harvard Pilgrim Health Care, 16:30
Hawaii
  managed care plans, exceeding scheduled fees, 3:37
  reciprocal beneficiaries, 3:15–3:17

Index

HCFA. *See* Health Care Financing Administration (HCFA)
Health and Human Services Department
    Advisory Committee on Immigration Practices, 4:53
Health audits, 12:69
Health benefit test, cafeteria plans, 11:26
Health care. *See also specific health care topics*
    claims, after plan effective date, 6:38
    coalition, employer health care coalition defined, 2:41
    data. *See* Cost management
    rationing, 7:126–7:128
    self-referral, vs SSO panel referral, 7:57
Healthcare Financial Management Association. *See* Survey
Health Care Financing Administration (HCFA)
    appeals process, 6:50
    HMOs, nondiscrimination requirements, 8:51
    Medicare + Choice HMOs, 15:44
    Operation Data Match. *See* Operation Data Match
    rationing health care, 7:128
    transplants
        Medicare coverage, 10:7
Health Care Plan Employer Data and Information Set (HEDIS), 19:8
    accreditation process, 19:25
    defined, 19:13, 19:24
    financial measures, 19:26
    generally, 19:20
Health care reimbursement accounts
    asbestos, removal of, 9:23
    average participation rate, 9:24
    bed wetting alarms, 9:23
    breast pumps, 9:23
    changes, 9:20
    cosmetic surgery, 9:20
        exceptions, 9:21
    procedures considered elective, 9:22
    defined, 9:19
    exercise clubs, 9:23
    hospital charges, 9:23
    laetrile, 9:20
    Lamaze classes, 9:20
    lead paint, removal of, 9:23
    marijuana, legalization of use of, 9:20
    orthodontia, 9:22
    smoking cessation programs, 9:20, 9:23
    special education, 9:23
    structure of, 9:29
    surrogate mother, in-vitro expenses, 9:23
    termination of employment, 9:30
    tooth capping, 9:22
    vitamins, 9:23
    weight loss drugs and treatment, 9:23
Health Insurance Association of America (HIAA)
    AIDS, impact on insurance, 7:117
    long-term care, 20:30
Health insurance marketplace
    agents, 2:14, 2:16
    Blue Cross/Blue Shield plans, 2:31–2:34
    brokers, 2:13, 2:16
    choosing and compensating intermediaries, 2:17–2:30
    client service representative, defined, 2:9
    employee benefit consultants, 2:15, 2:16
    group sales representatives
        defined, 2:8
        interaction with intermediary in sale of group plan, 2:11
    HMOs, PPOs, and health care coalitions, 2:30–2:41
    information, obtaining from principal rating companies, 2:4

I-33

Health insurance marketplace *(cont'd)*
  intermediaries
    defined, 2:10
    group sales representative, interaction with, 2:12
    professional designations, 2:17
    types of insurance professionals, 2:1–2:16
Health Insurance Plan of California (HIPC)
  model, cited as, 1:25
Health insurance plans. *See specific plan type by name*
Health Insurance Portability and Accountability Act of 1996. *See* HIPAA
Health Maintenance Organization Act of 1973. *See* HMO Act of 1973
Health maintenance organizations (HMOs), 8:6–8:38
  advantages, 8:95
  adverse selection, 8:39–8:44
    conventional plan cost, effect of HMOs, 8:41
    defined, 8:39
    health status of employee and, 8:42
    obviousness to employers, 8:33
    occurrence of, 8:40
  capitated payment structure, 8:6
    factors affecting, 8:17
    fee-for-service payment structure, differences, 8:16
  care received outside HMOs, reimbursement for, 8:24
  certificate, HIPAA, 4:100
  Choosing and Using an HMO, 8:62
  COBRA and, 13:12
    qualified beneficiary moving outside service area, 13:26
  community rating system, 2:33, 8:48
  cost effectiveness, 8:29
  costs
    management of, considerations, 7:109

  other health care plans vs, 8:32
  deductible, 8:22
  defined, 2:30, 8:6
  demographically adjusted, defined, 2:34
  developers of, 8:8
  disadvantages, 8:95
  enrollment
    choice, 8:26
    conventional plan participation requirement, effect on, 8:30
    cost effectiveness, 8:29
    geographic differentials, 8:11
    hospitalization, subsequent, 8:23
    increase during health care cost crisis, 8:31
    number of people enrolled, 8:9
    timing, 8:25
    traditional plan and HMOs, in both, 8:28
    trends, 8:10
    unlimited health care entitlement, 8:20
    yearly change of plans, 8:27
  evaluating, 8:55–8:64
    checklist, 8:61
    costs of health plans compared, 8:55
    excellence, indicators of, 8:62
    financial difficulty, reason for, 8:60
    managed care plans, 8:57, 8:58
    multiple option plans, 8:64
    quality of care compared with conventional plan, 8:56
    rating by HMOs participant, 8:59
    triple option plans, 8:63, 8:64
  excellence, indicators of, 8:62
  financial difficulty, reason for, 8:60
  financial nondiscrimination rules, 2:39
  flexible/market-driven plan design, 3:2
  flexible plan, inclusion in, 9:61
  gatekeeper, defined, 8:21
  group model, 8:13

I-34

Index

HMO Act of 1973. *See* HMO Act of 1973
hybrid arrangements, 8:97
importance of participation by certain employees, 2:35
imposing deductible or cost-sharing for childbirth hospital stays, 4:40
independent practice association (IPA) model, 8:13, 8:15
"leaky HMOs," 8:97
legal standards, 8:45–8:54
   community rating system, 8:48
   coverage payment, 8:50
   dual choice mandate, 4:2, 4:48, 8:45, 8:49
   ERISA preemption, 8:53, 8:54
   federally qualified HMOs, 8:46, 8:47
   Health Maintenance Organization Act of 1973. *See* HMO Act of 1973
   nondiscrimination requirements, 8:51
   state regulations, 8:52–8:54
   supplemental health services, 8:46
managed competition, 3:104, 3:105
Medicare, election of HMO coverage by beneficiaries
   generally, 10:34
   number of beneficiaries, 10:55
Medicare + Choice. *See* Medicare + Choice HMOs
mental health benefits, 22:6, 22:7
mirror image
   federally qualified vs., 2:38
   self-funded HMOs, 8:38
mixed model, 8:13
models, differences, 8:13
most popular type, 8:14
multiple option plans, 8:64
negligent care, employer liability for, 8:100
network model, 8:13
nondiscrimination requirements, 8:51
only plan offered by employer, 8:33
organization, 8:13
pharmaceutical plans, disclosure, 16:48, 16:49
physicians
   different treatment of patients by, 8:34
   ownership and, 8:12
POS plans, advantages and disadvantages, 8:98
PPOs, differences, 8:67, 8:95
prepayment
   health services, for, 8:18
   payroll deductions, through, 8:19
self-funded, 2:31, 8:35–8:38, 17:3
   advantageous conversion to self-funded HMO, 2:32
   federally qualified HMO, 2:37
self-insured, 2:36
self-referral option, 8:20
sponsors of, 8:8
staff model, 8:13, 8:14
state regulations, 8:52
   ERISA preemption, 8:53, 8:54
summary plan description (SPD), 6:17–6:19, 6:19
supplemental health services, 8:46
top ten by size, 8:9
triple option plans, 8:63, 8:64
when developed, 8:7

Health Net, 16:30

Health promotion programs, 12:50–12:88. *See also* Preventive care; Wellness programs
achievement, as incentive, 12:84
common types of activities, 12:51
defined, 12:50
dissatisfaction with information, 12:57
growing interest in, 12:56
health risk appraisal, 12:80–12:84
incentives, 12:84
   financial incentives, 12:88
   government issues with, 12:87
   positive vs negative, 12:85, 12:86

Health promotion programs (cont'd)
  information, employee satisfaction with, 12:57
  insured, 12:79
  life-style cost index, 12:55
  participation, as incentive, 12:84
  policies by companies, 12:76
  preventive care coverage, 12:58. *See also* Preventive care
  reasons for programs, 12:52
  selection of, 12:54
  worksite, advantages of offering, 12:53
Health risk appraisals, 3:94, 12:51, 12:69, 12:80–12:84
Health screening. *See* Screening
Health status, change in, 4:110
Hearing, evaluations and hearing aids, 12:20
HEDIS. *See* Health Care Plan Employer Data and Information Set (HEDIS)
Hewitt Associates. *See* Survey
Higgins. *See* Survey
Highly compensated employees. *See also* Key employees
  cafeteria plan nondiscrimination rules, 11:21
  defined, 11:3
  dependent care assistance plans, 11:31
HIPAA (Health Insurance Portability and Accountability Act of 1996), 4:92–4:134
  accelerated death benefits, 4:127
  associations, insurers of, 4:131
  availability, renewability, and portability provisions, 4:132
  benefits, requirements, 4:112
  certificate
    insurer or HMO, from, 4:100
    minimum coverage period, 4:104
    model certificate, 4:102
    nonreceipt, 4:98
    no preexisting condition clause, 4:99

change in health status, loss of benefits, 4:110
change of jobs, guaranteed benefits, 4:107
COBRA
  amendments, 13:1
  changes in requirements, 4:114
  as creditable coverage, 4:106
compliance, 9:35
dental benefits, 4:132, 12:8
effective date, 4:92
electronic data interchange, 4:125
eligibility, 4:108
  physical exam requirement, 4:109
e-mail, disclosures by, 4:124
employee contributions, requirements, 4:112
employees, acceptance for medical coverage, 6:2
enforcement, 4:134
enrollment
  date, 4:93
  late, 4:95, 6:29
  person initially declining coverage, 6:30
  special enrollment periods, 4:113, 6:31
ERISA disclosure requirements and, 4:122
exhaustion of COBRA, obtaining individual policies and, 4:117
flexible spending account, 4:94
generally, 4:2
group and individual insurance compared, 1:2
group-to-individual portability, 4:116
health coverage requirement, 4:111
health promotion programs, incentives, 12:87
home health care fraud, 20:22
individual policies, changes, 4:115
IRA medical withdrawals, 4:128
late enrollee, 4:95
limited scope dental or vision benefits, 4:132

I-36

Index

long-term care insurance, 4:126, 9:4, 20:34
look-back period, 4:93
material reduction, notice of, 4:122, 4:123
MEWAs, 4:129
model certificate of coverage, Appendix E
MSAs, 9:4
multiemployer plans, 4:129
notice requirements, 21:27
policy renewal, 4:118
preexisting conditions, 3:74, 4:93
prior coverage, proving, 4:97
reduction in benefits, 4:119
renewal of policy, 6:54
reporting rules, 6:11
requirements, overview, 4:2
retiree health benefits, applicability, 15:6
self-funded group health plans, 4:121
significant break in coverage, 4:93
small employers
  application to, 4:120
  change in health plans, 4:115
  market disclosures, 4:133
small group insurers, 4:130
special enrollment periods, 4:113
summary of material reduction (SMR), 6:9
summary plan description (SPD), 6:16
third-party administrator (TPA), 18:20
vision benefits, 4:132
waiting periods, 4:93, 4:96
HIPC. *See* Health Insurance Plan of California (HIPC)
Hiring process, ADA, 4:85
HIV (human immunodeficiency virus). *See* AIDS
HMO Act of 1973
care received outside HMOs, reimbursement for, 8:24
described, 8:45

dual choice option, 4:2, 4:48, 8:45, 8:49
effect on group health insurance plans, 4:48
employer payment of coverage, amount, 8:50
generally, 4:37
HMO Amendments Act of 1988, 8:45, 8:50
  nondiscrimination requirements, 8:51
passing of, 8:7
HMOs. *See* Health maintenance organizations (HMOs)
Hold-harmless agreements, 5:60
Home Care Accreditation Program, 20:10
Home health care, 20:1–20:19. *See also* Long-term care
accreditation
  information, 20:17
  information not learned, 20:18
advantages, 20:6
availability in plans, 20:14
coverage
  cost management and, 20:11
  procedure for installing, 20:16
dealing directly with agency, 20:19
defined, 20:1
diagnostic-related groups (DRGs) and, 20:3
exclusion, reasons for, 20:13
fostering use, 20:9
fraud, 20:20–20:22
  prevention, 20:22
  who pays, 20:21
government agencies, 20:4
history, 20:2
hospice care
  cost-effectiveness, 20:46
  defined, 20:44
  payor, 20:45
institution-based agencies, 20:4
long-term care. *See* Long-term care
market for, 20:3
medical equipment, 20:7

Home health care *(cont'd)*
  monitoring agencies, 20:10
  private nonprofit agencies, 20:4
  procedure for installing coverage, 20:16
  professional services, 20:7
  proprietary agencies, 20:4
  providers, 20:4
  savings, 20:12
  services
    frequency and duration, 20:8
    most provided, 20:15
    provided, 20:7
  skilled nursing services, 20:7
  social or custodial services, 20:7
  subacute care
    chronic subacute, 20:41
    defined, 20:39
    general subacute, 20:41
    levels of, 20:41
    payment for, 20:43
    skilled nursing facilities, objections to using, 20:42
    standards for assessing, 20:40
    transitional hospital, 20:41
    transitional subacute, 20:41
  users, 20:5
  visiting nurse associations (VNAs), 20:4
Home office
  accounting, 6:33
  billing, flexible benefits plans, 9:94
Homeopathy, coverage, 3:28
Hospice care
  cost-effectiveness, 20:46
  defined, 20:44
  payor, 20:45
Hospital Insurance (HI) trust fund
  Medicare, 10:35
Hospitals. *See also* Medical facilities
  bill audit, defined, 7:97
  care
    alternatives, 3:40
    outpatient expenses, coverage, 3:41
    recent changes, 3:38

  charges, health care reimbursement accounts, 9:23
  discharge planning, vs case management, 7:41
  expenses
    lag time, payment of claims, 5:38
  intensive care charges, 3:32
  Joint Commission. *See* Joint Commission on Accreditation of Healthcare Organizations
  managed care plans exclusion, 8:107
  Part A deductible, Medicare, 10:9
  Part B deductible, Medicare, 10:12
  room and board, 3:32
  stays
    AIDS, persons with, 7:119
    criteria for length of care, 7:44
    HMOs, individual enrolled in, 8:23
  surgery, charges, 3:33
HRAs. *See* Health risk appraisals
HSOPs
  defined, 15:39
  IRS position, 15:40
Humana, 16:30
Human resources, communications strategies, 21:7
Hybrid HMOs arrangements, 8:97

I

Identification cards, 6:9
Implementation. *See* Administration
Incentives
  dental plan, 12:11
  health promotion programs, 12:84
    financial incentives, 12:88
    government issues with, 12:87
    positive vs negative, 12:85, 12:86
  in lieu of TPA performance standards, 18:9
  PPOs
    employers, 8:87
    providers, 8:79

Index

Incurred claim date, 17:56, 17:57
Indemnity plan
  self-funding, 17:3
  vision plans, 12:17
Independent living program, 12:48
Independent medical examination.
  See Medical examination
Individual insurance
  group insurance vs, 1:2, 1:3
  HIPAA changes, 4:115
Individual (or independent) practice associations, 8:13, 8:15
Inflation
  long-term care, 20:33
  premium increase and, 5:10
Influenza vaccinations, 12:51
Information. *See also* Communication
  ADA, 4:91
  administrative material provided by insurer to employer, 6:22
  announcement materials, 6:7
  data collection, quality measures, 19:6
  electronic data interchange
    HIPAA, 4:125
    pharmacy benefit management, 16:57
    quality assurance, 16:57
  electronic media, use to communicate benefit information, 21:25
  enrollment, 6:24
  health care data, 7:23–7:31
  home health care accreditation, through, 20:17
  long-term care, 20:38
  Medicare and Medicaid Coverage Data Bank, 10:50
  mental health benefits, 22:14
  outcomes data, and cost reduction, 19:29
  principal rating companies, 2:4
  required before policy issuance, 6:5
  resources, Appendix A
  systems, mental health benefit data, 22:14

Inpatients
  benefits, substance abuse, 22:28
  UR, vs ambulatory care UR, 7:49
Institution-based agencies, home health care, 20:4
Insurance. *See also* Coinsurance; *specific type of insurance*
  agent. *See* Agent
  AIDS, impact on, 7:117–7:125
  broker. *See* Broker
  company. *See* Insurance company
  contract
    termination, paying claims after, 5:4
    termination, reserve decrease, 5:58
  conventional
    cash flow, predictable, 7:93
    shock claim protection, 7:94
  guaranty funds. *See* State insurance guaranty funds
  long-term care, HIPAA, 4:126
  marketplace. *See* Health insurance marketplace
  medical, cafeteria plan, 9:59
  plan design. *See* Plan design
  policy, individual, HIPAA changes, 4:115
  professionals. *See also specific types of professionals*; State law
  types of, 2:1–2:16
  uncertainty in industry, 2:2
Insurance company
  administrative material provided to employer, 6:22
  association insurers, HIPAA, 4:131
  certificate, HIPAA, 4:100–4:104
  coverage, treatment decision, 3:48
  direct work with employer, 2:1
  disability prevention program, 12:39
  eliminating liability after contract termination, reserve decrease, 5:58
  failure, employer protection against, 2:3
  flexible benefits plans, 9:63
    one carrier, advantages of, 9:64

I-39

Insurance company (*cont'd*)
  imposing deductible or cost-sharing for childbirth hospital stays, 4:40
  insurability, requiring evidence, 13:65
  legislating tighter control, 2:6
  long-term care, 20:35
  merging health care service, 8:4
  plan funding, medical cost projection, 5:10
  profit, 5:20
  requiring detailed coverage information, 6:5
  reserves
    defined, 5:17
    necessary, 5:18
  small employer disclosures, HIPAA, 4:133
  small group insurers, HIPAA rules, 4:130
Integrated claims processing
  pharmacy benefit management, 16:52
Intensive care charges, 3:32
Interactive systems. *See* Communication
Intermediaries
  advisor as, 2:21
  brokerage firms, largest, 2:19
  choosing and compensating, 2:17–2:30
  commissions
    schedules, 2:23
    vesting, 2:24
  compensation, 2:22–2:24
  consulting firms, largest, 2:20
  defined, 2:10
  laws regulating business practices of, 2:25
  plan administration, 2:28
  selection of particular intermediary, 2:19, 2:21
  self-funding, 2:26
  services
    interaction with group sales representative, 2:11

    prior to purchase of group health insurance plan, 2:12
  size of, 2:18–2:30
  TPAs, 2:27–2:30
Internal Revenue Code (IRC)
  cafeteria plan definition, 9:3
  Section 79 group term life plans, 11:11
  Section 416(i) key employee, 11:12
Internal Revenue Service (IRS)
  COBRA premium guidance, 13:45
  Delinquent Filer Voluntary Compliance program, 14:35, 14:36
  domestic partners, benefits for, 3:9, 3:10
  HSOP, position on, 15:40
International Foundation of Employee Benefit Plans, 7:107
International Society of Certified Employee Benefit Specialists. *See* Survey
International Subacute Healthcare Association, 20:41
Internet, 21:20
  administration and, 6:70–6:72
  resources, Appendix F
InterStudy. *See* Survey
Intracorp. *See* Survey
Intranet, 21:20
  administration and, 6:70–6:72
IPA. *See* Individual (or independent) practice association
IRA medical withdrawals, HIPAA, 4:128
IRC. *See* Internal Revenue Code (IRC)
IRS. *See* Internal Revenue Service (IRS)

J

Job accommodation program, 12:47
Johnson & Johnson, 12:72
Joint Commission on Accreditation of Healthcare Organizations
  defined, 19:23

Index

home health care, 20:10, 20:17
   subacute care, 20:39, 20:40
Joint purchasing
   defined, 1:27
   focus of, 1:28
Journal of Family Practice. See Survey
Journal of the American Medical Association. See Survey

K

Kaiser Family Foundation. *See* Survey
Kaiser Health Plan, 8:11
Kaiser Permanente, 16:30
Key employees. *See also* Highly compensated employees
   enhanced health care coverage, 3:59
   nondiscrimination rules
      Code Section 416(i), under, 11:12
   retiree health benefits, VEBA rules, 15:28
   survivor benefits in group plan, 12:23
   VEBA contributions, 17:83
KPMG Peat Marwick. *See* Survey

L

Labor union. *See* Union
Laetrile, 9:20
Lag
   defined, 5:38
   report, 5:28
   studies, 5:18, 5:39
Laid-off employees, age 55 through 64, 10:17
Lamaze classes, 9:20
Large employers, full-menu plan, 9:50
Large group health plan, defined, 10:33
Late enrollment. *See* Enrollment
Law of large numbers
   group health insurance plans, 1:2

Lead paint, removal of, 9:23
"Leaky HMOs," 8:97
Lease
   computerized administration system, 6:69
Leave. *See also specific type of leave*
   ADA, policies, 4:89
   FMLA, 4:62–4:73, 9:95
   maternity. *See also* Newborns and Mothers Health Protection Act of 1996; Pregnancy Discrimination Act
      parental or family leave vs, 4:72
   returning veterans, training leave, 4:154
   return-to-work program, 12:47
   state law, 4:31
Legal Action Center, 22:58, 22:60, 22:62, 22:63
Legal issues. *See also* Federal law; State law
   liability, health care costs, 7:6
   plan design and, 3:23, 4:1–4:15
Legal standards, HMOs, 8:45–8:54
Legislation, tighter control over insurance companies, 2:6
Life cycle flex plans
   allowance, 9:52
   defined, 9:51
Life expectancy, AIDS and, 7:119
Life insurance. *See also* Group term life insurance
   contributions, pre- or post-tax, 9:73
   survivor benefits in group plan, 12:21–12:25
      state taxes, 12:25
      taxation, 12:23–12:25
   VEBAs, 17:82
Life-style cost index, 12:55
Lifestyle drugs, coverage for, 16:31
Lifetime maximums, mental health benefits, 22:9
Living wage ordinance, state law, 4:35

Local governments
  coalitions, group health insurance plan, 1:26
Long-term care, 20:23–20:38. *See also* Home health care
  adult day care, 20:32
  advantages, 20:26
  benefit levels, 20:37
  care levels, 20:37
  contributions to, 20:31
  coverage
    ages, 20:37
    typical, 20:32
  custodial care, 20:24
  defined, 20:23
  duration of benefits, 20:37
  elimination periods, 20:37
  exclusions, 20:37
  expense, 20:27
  facilities, 20:37
  inflation, adjusted for, 20:33
  information, 20:38
  insurance
    cost, 20:36
    HIPAA, 4:126, 9:4
    provider, 20:35
  intermediate care, 20:24
  levels, 20:24, 20:37
  Medicaid and, 20:29
  Medicare and, 20:28
  policy considerations, 20:37
  premiums, 20:37
  prevalence, 20:30
  renewability, 20:37
  skilled nursing care, 20:24
  special issues, 20:25
  tax status of custodial care, 20:34
Long-term disability. *See* Disability benefits
Look-back period, HIPAA, 4:93
Los Angeles
  City Department of Water and Power, HMOs, 8:7
  City Task Force on Family Diversification, 3:5
  domestic partners, benefits for, 3:13

Los Angeles Times. *See* Survey
Loss ratio
  defined, 5:35
  tolerable. *See* Tolerable loss ratio (TLR)
Louis Harris. *See* Survey

M

Machine print forms
  EFAST, Form 5500, 14:30, 14:31
Mail service, prescription drugs, 16:40–16:45
  appropriateness, 16:43
  effectiveness of, 16:42
  generic drugs, copayments, 16:41
  incentives to use, 16:45
  safety, 16:44
  underutilization of, 16:41
Maintenance of benefits. *See* Coordination of benefits
Major medical, 2:33
  lag time, payment of claims, 5:38
Malpractice insurance
  cost management and, 7:6
Mammograms
  frequency, recommended, 12:64
Managed care plans, 8:1–8:119
  anti-managed care legislation, 8:113
    state law, 8:114
  any willing provider (AWP) laws
    defined, 8:107
    states passing, 8:108
  appeals, 8:105
  backlash, 8:102–8:119
    anti-managed care legislation, 8:113, 8:114
    consumer protection laws, 8:115
    employers, feelings of, 8:103
    expanded liability legislation, 8:116
    external reviews, 8:117, 8:118
    forms of, 8:105
    gag rule, 8:111, 8:112

Index

health care providers, feelings of, 8:104
network exclusion, 8:109
physicians, 8:104, 8:110
public, feelings of, 8:102
response from industry, 8:119
cause of shift toward, 8:2
choice of providers or plans, 8:105
complaints, 8:105
confidentiality, 8:105
Consumer Bill of Rights, 8:105
consumer protection laws, 8:115
consumer responsibilities, 8:105
defined, 8:2
emergency services, 8:105
employers, feelings on, 8:103
enrollment in, numbers, 8:5
excluding physicians, hospitals, or other providers, 8:107
expanded liability legislation, 8:116
external reviews, 8:117, 8:118
gag rule, 8:112
    defined, 8:111
growth, change in case management, 7:40
health care providers, feelings on, 8:104
HMOs, 8:6–8:38. *See also* Health maintenance organizations (HMOs) *for detailed treatment*
hospital charges, 3:32
information disclosure, 8:105
mental health plans
    benefits of managed care, 22:33
    carve-outs, 22:35–22:41
    development of, employer considerations, 22:34
    pre-paid mental health plan, defined, 22:30
    substance abuse benefit programs, effect on, 22:31
    trend toward, what is driving, 22:32
network exclusion, 8:109
nondiscrimination, 8:105
nonsurgical physician, coverage, 3:39
number of people enrolled, 8:5
PPOs. *See* Preferred provider organizations (PPOs)
prudent layperson standard, 8:115
public opinion, 8:102
"Putting Patients First" policies, 8:119
quality measurement, 8:57, 8:58
report card movement
    criticisms, 19:17
    effect of, 19:16
    satisfaction of enrollees, 19:21
respect and, 8:105
scheduled approach to fees, 3:36
    exceeding scheduled fees, 3:37
shift toward, cause of, 8:3
surgery, charges, 3:33
treatment decisions, participation in, 8:105
utilization review and, 7:35
Managed care TPAs
    defined, 18:26
    value of using, 18:27
Managed competition, 3:2, 3:99–3:107
    advantages, 3:106
    common elements, 2:3, 2:5
    companies using, 3:103
    considerations of employers before incorporating, 3:101
    cost containment and, 3:107
    defined, 3:99
    disadvantages, 3:105
    elements of, 3:100
    groups of employees, 3:106
    health maintenance organizations (HMOs), 3:104, 3:105
    key features, 3:100
    quality improvement measures and, 3:104
    reasons for not adopting, 3:102
Managed Healthcare. See Survey
Managed vision plans, 12:18
Management training, EAPs, 22:49

Managing costs. *See* Cost management

Managing health insurance costs. *See* Cost

Mandated benefit rules. *See also* State law
   self-funding, 17:52

Mandated coverage. *See* Coverage; Federal law; State law

Mandated offering, defined, 4:27

Manual rate, defined, 5:22

Margin, higher-than-anticipated claims, 5:13

Marijuana, legalization of use of, 9:20

Marital status, change in
   flexible benefit plans, 9:35

Marketplace. *See* Health insurance marketplace

Maryland
   managed care plans, 8:114

Massachusetts
   mandated coverage, 4:3
   self-funded plans, 4:18
   surcharge
     coinsurance costs and, 4:34
     defined, 4:33

Massage therapy, coverage, 3:28

Material reduction
   60-day notice requirements, 4:122, 4:123

Maternity
   coverage, mandatory for single employees, 4:8
   leave. *See also* Newborns and Mothers Health Protection Act of 1996; Pregnancy Discrimination Act
     parental or family leave vs maternity leave, 4:72
   stay, preauthorization of, 4:43

Maximum allowable cost (MAC), prescription drugs, 16:34

Maximum out-of-pocket limit, 3:67–3:69
   Medicare coinsurance payable for Part B, 10:11

McDonnell Douglas Corporation. *See* Survey

Meals and lodging, 9:4

Medicaid
   eligibility, 4:9, 6:25
   flexible benefit plans, mid-year election changes and, 9:35
   group plan under COBRA, as, 13:78
   long-term care benefits, 20:29
   Medicare and Medicaid Coverage Data Bank, 10:50
   rationing health care and, 7:128

Medi-Cal, 8:66

Medical benefits. *See* Benefit

Medical billing. *See* Billing

Medical care. *See* Health care

Medical equipment, home health care, 20:7

Medical examinations, 4:109
   annual programs, COBRA and, 13:15
   drug testing, 22:58
   guidelines, 12:63–12:65
   independent medical examination defined, 12:40
   preemployment, ADA, 4:86
   routine checkups, coverage, 12:60–12:62

Medical expense plans
   financing, 17:33
   stop-loss coverage, effect on, 17:54

Medical expenses, defined, 7:78

Medical facilities. *See also* Hospitals
   extended care, 3:52, 20:11
   oversupply, cost factors, 7:13

Medical Practice Management. *See* Survey

Medical professionals. *See also* Nursing; Physicians
   oversupply, effect on cost, 7:13

Index

Medical review organization. *See* Review
Medical savings accounts, 7:60–7:82
Medical savings accounts (MSAs)
  comparability rule, 7:73, 7:74
    noncompliance, 7:74
  contributions
    deadline, 7:72
    employee and employer, 7:68
    maximum annual contribution, 7:70
  cost savings, 7:62
  coverage, 7:69
  death of employee, 7:77
  defined, 7:60
  distributions, who governs, 7:76
  eligibility, 7:64, 7:67
  employee and employer contributions, 7:68
  flexible spending account vs, 7:61
  high-deductible plan, 7:71, 7:73–7:76
  HIPAA, 9:4
  medical expenses, defined, 7:78
  nondiscrimination, 7:73
  opposition to, 7:63
  participant limit, 7:79
  pilot project termination, 7:82
  small employers, 7:65
    growth of, 7:66
  unpopularity of, 7:80, 7:81
Medical withdrawals
  IRA, HIPAA, 4:128
MEDICA performance report, 19:5
Medicare, 10:1–10:55. *See also* Resource-based relative value scale (RBRVS) *for detailed treatment*
  adjusted average per capita cost, 15:44
  age one may enroll, 10:16
  balance billing
    defined, 10:19
    limits, 10:20
    state requirements, 10:21
  bankruptcy, impending, 10:36
  basic information, 10:1–10:21

  care not covered, 10:22
  carve-out, 10:22
  coinsurance requirements, 10:10, 10:12
  cost containment, 10:34–10:43
    bankruptcy of Medicare, impending, 10:36
    diagnosis-related groups (DRGs), 10:37–10:39
    generally, 10:34
    importance of, 10:35
    RBRVS, 10:34, 10:40–10:42
    reimbursing ambulatory surgery centers, 10:43
    steps to limit costs, 10:34
  coverage, 10:2–10:8
    Medigap insurance policy, 10:45
  current employment status, 10:31
  defined, 10:1
  diagnosis-related groups (DRGs), 10:37–10:39
  disability, rules
    generally, 10:27
    secondary requirements, 10:31
    who is considered disabled, 10:30
  eligibility
    individuals, 10:2
    secondary coverage election, 4:9
  end-stage renal disease
    order of benefit determination, 10:22
    primary coverage, Medicare as, 10:24, 10:30
  enrollment, age one may enroll, 10:16
  entitlement
    flexible benefit plans, mid-year election changes and, 9:35
  entitlement, and COBRA, 13:77, 13:80
  extension of, 10:17
  HMO coverage, election of, 10:34
  home health care, 20:2
    fraud, 20:21

Medicare (cont'd)
  hospital deductible
    Part A, 10:9
    Part B, 10:12
  Hospital Insurance (HI) trust fund, 10:35
  indexed coinsurance requirements, 10:10
  laid-off employees, age 55 through 64, 10:17
  large group health plans
    coverage of disabled persons, 10:22
    defined, 10:33
  long-term care benefits, 20:28
  low-income elderly, typical spending, 10:15
  Medigap insurance policy, 10:44, 10:45. See Medigap insurance policy
  National Bipartisan Committee on the Future of Medicare, 10:18
  "near elderly," 10:17, 10:18
  new premiums, 10:13
  noncompliance, 10:28
  number of people covered by, 10:3
  Operation Data Match, 10:46–10:50
    causes of, 10:47
    defined, 10:46
    employer's responsibility, 10:48
    Medicare and Medicaid Coverage Data Bank, 10:50
    process involved, 10:49
  order of benefits
    determination, 10:22–10:33
    disabled individuals, 10:27, 10:30, 10:31
    excluding workers over age 65, 10:23
    integration with employer-provided benefits, 10:22
    large group health plan, defined, 10:33
    noncompliance, 10:28
  secondary payor rules, 10:25–10:27, 10:31, 10:32
  Part A
    cost containment, 10:35
    defined, 10:1
    hospital deductible, 10:9
    premiums, 10:13
    services covered under, 10:4
  Part B
    coinsurance requirements, 10:12
    defined, 10:1
    hospital deductible, 10:12
    maximum out-of-pocket limit, 10:11
    premiums, 10:13
    services covered under, 10:5
  payroll tax, 10:14
  preventive services covered, 10:8
  primary coverage, employee election, 4:9–4:11
  provider contracts, vs PPO, 8:68
  reimbursing ambulatory surgery centers, 10:43
  retiree health benefits and, 15:43–15:53
    carve-out, 15:43
    coordination of benefits, 15:43
    Medicare + Choice HMO, 15:44–15:53. See also Medicare + Choice HMO for detailed treatment
  retirees age 62 through 64, 10:18
  secondary payor rules, 10:25–10:27, 10:31, 10:32
    disabled, rules for, 10:27
    enforcement, 10:26
  services
    Part A, 10:4
    Part B, 10:5
  supplement policies, 10:44
  transplants, coverage, 10:7
  typical beneficiary spending, 10:15
Medicare + Choice, 10:44, 10:51–10:55
  defined, 10:51
  success of, 10:52

Index

Medicare + Choice HMOs, 10:53–10:55, 15:44–15:53
  adjusted average per capita cost, 15:44, 15:45
  changing back to traditional Medicare and supplemental plan, 15:53
  communication on, 15:51
  costs, 15:9
    reduction, 15:47
  defined, 15:44
  disadvantages of, 15:48
  educating employees, 15:51
  enrollment procedures, 15:52
  explained, 15:18
  number of employers using, 15:46
  Part C, 15:45
  prescription drug coverage, 15:49
  primary care physicians, use of, 15:47
  selection of, criteria, 15:50
Medicare + Choice Plans. *See also* Medicare + Choice HMOs
  generally, 15:7
Medigap insurance policy
  coverage, 10:45
  rules, 10:44
MEDSTATE Group. *See* Survey
Mental health benefits, 22:1–22:74
  Americans with Disabilities Act, 22:57–22:63
  benefit coverage, 22:8
  case management, 22:17, 22:21
  changes in clinical practice, impact of, 22:5
  cost control, 22:16–22:22
    behavioral health, 22:16
    case management, 22:17, 22:21
    coinsurance level, increasing, 22:19
    cost sharing, 22:22
    length of stay, limiting, 22:19
    methods considered by employers, 22:19
    outpatient care, substituting, 22:19
    partial hospitalization, substituting, 22:19
    premiums, increasing, 22:19
    reducing benefits, 22:19, 22:20
    size of payment, limiting, 22:19
    strategies, 22:18
    utilization review, 22:18
  cost sharing, 22:22
  coverage
    assumptions, 22:11
    limitations, 22:4
  EAPs, 22:42–22:54
  HMOs, 22:6, 22:7
  information systems, data from, 22:14
  in-network coverage, 22:8
  lifetime maximums, 22:9
  managed care
    benefits of managed care, 22:33
    carve-outs, 22:35–22:41
    development of, employer considerations, 22:34
    pre-paid mental health plan, defined, 22:30
    substance abuse benefit programs, effect on, 22:31
    trend toward, what is driving, 22:32
  Mental Health Parity Act. *See* Mental Health Parity Act of 1996
  outcome measurements, 22:55, 22:56
  out-of-network coverage, 22:8
  plan design, employer concerns, 22:2
  primary physician's role, 22:15
  reason for focus, 22:12
  structures of plan, reason for differences, 22:3
  substance abuse, 22:2, 22:23–22:29
  30-day limit on treatment length, 22:4
  trends affecting, 22:10
  usual coverage, 22:1
  utilization, increase in, 22:13
  utilization review, 22:18

I-47

Mental Health Parity Act of 1996
  claims, 22:69
  cost to employers, 22:73, 22:74
  exempt employers, 22:68
  generally, 4:37
  inpatient treatment, limiting, 22:71
  limiting inpatient or outpatient treatment, 22:71
  medical benefits, similarity to mental health benefits, 22:67
  mental health coverage, 22:66
  1 percent exemption, 22:69, 22:70
  outpatient treatment, limiting, 22:71
  regulations published regarding, 22:65
  requirements, 4:2, 22:64–22:74
  substance abuse, 22:23, 22:24, 22:72
Mercer/Foster Higgins. See Survey
MEWAs. See Multiple employer welfare arrangements (MEWAs)
Military benefits. See Reservist benefits
Milliman & Robertson. See Survey
Minimum premium plans (MPPs), 5:48
  defined, 5:62
  employer benefit, 5:66
  employers typically electing, 5:68
  level of responsibility, 5:63
  payment, 5:65
  reason for not electing, 5:67
  shock claims, 5:64
  third-party administrative services, 5:68
Minimum-premium product, self-funding, 17:38
Mirror image HMOs
  federally qualified HMO vs, 2:38
  self-funded, 8:38
Miscellaneous Revenue Act of 1980, 9:66
Misconduct. See Gross misconduct
Missouri
  managed care plans, 8:115

Modular plan, defined, 9:46
Monitoring, EAPs, 22:49
Montefiore Medical Center, 3:8
Mortality data. See Information
MPPs. See Minimum premium plans (MPPs)
MSAs. See Medical savings accounts
Multiemployer plans
  multiple-employer plans, differences, 18:6
  welfare plans
    FASB accounting rules, retiree health benefits, 15:22
    withdrawal from, COBRA and, 13:29
Multiple employer plans
  multiemployer plans, differences, 18:6
Multiple employer trust, defined, 1:19
Multiple employer welfare arrangements (MEWAs)
  COBRA, small-employer exemption, 13:10
  defined, 1:22, 18:5
  federal law, governed by, 4:14
  generally, 1:21
  HIPAA, 4:129
  requirements, 1:23
  state law, governed by, 4:14
Multiple option plans, 8:64
Multiple plan coverage, payment priority, 7:85
Multiple qualifying events, COBRA, 13:5

N

NAIC. See National Association of Insurance Commissioners (NAIC)
NAIC Stop-Loss Model Act, 17:66
National Association of Dental Plans. See Survey
National Association of Insurance Commissioners (NAIC)
  health insurance marketplace, 2:3

Index

health maintenance organizations (HMOs), 8:52
Medigap insurance policy, 10:44
self-funding, position on, 17:66
third-party administrators (TPA), 18:1
National Association of Life Underwriters, 20:30
National Bipartisan Committee on the Future of Medicare, 10:18
National Business Coalition on Health, 7:107
National Cancer Institute, 12:64
National Center for Health Promotion, 12:55
National Center for Policy Analysis, 7:15
National Committee for Quality Assurance (NCQA), 19:2, 19:3, 19:8. *See also* Survey
  accreditation process, 19:6, 19:8
    HEDIS, use of, 19:25. *See also* Health Care Plan Employer Data and Information Set (HEDIS)
  Quality Compass, 19:7
National Council on Aging, 20:25
National League for Nursing, 20:10, 20:17
National Underwriter. *See* Survey
Naturopathy, coverage, 3:28
NCQA. *See* National Committee for Quality Assurance (NCQA)
Negative elections, flexible benefits plans, 9:88
Negligent care
  employer liability, HMOs or PPOs, 8:100
Network, exclusions, 8:109
Newborns
  COBRA, qualified beneficiary, 13:54
Newborns and Mothers Health Protection Act of 1996
  compliance guidelines, 4:41
  cost containment and, 4:6
  deductibles or cost-sharing provisions, 4:40
  generally, 4:2
  minimum hospital stays, 4:39
  notice requirements, 4:42, 21:27
  requirements, 4:2, 4:38
New employees, communication, 21:27
New Jersey
  alternative therapies, coverage, 3:28
  flexible benefits plans, 9:8
  managed care plans, 8:114
New Mexico
  managed care plans, 8:115
New York
  alternative therapies, coverage, 3:28
New York City
  domestic partners, benefits for, 3:8, 3:11
  Small Business Health Insurance Program, 1:26
New York surcharge, 4:18, 4:32
New York Times. See Survey
Nicotine patches, 16:48
NMHPA. *See* Newborns and Mothers Health Protection Act of 1996
Noncontributory plan, enrollment, 6:26
Nondiscrimination rules, 11:1–11:41. *See also* Nondiscrimination testing; *specific law by name*
  accident and health plans, 11:1–11:10
    aggregation, 11:9
    benefit test for self-insured plan, 11:6, 11:9
    discrimination in health plans, 11:1
    discrimination penalty, 11:7, 11:8
    eligibility tests for self-insured plans, 11:4, 11:5, 11:9
    5 percent owner, 11:3
    highly compensated employee, 11:3
    retiree plans, 11:10
    self-insured plans, 11:1, 11:2
    attribution rules for ownership, 11:3

Nondiscrimination rules (cont'd)
  cafeteria plans, 11:20–11:28. See also Cafeteria plans for detailed treatment
  dependent care assistance plans, 11:29–11:36
    excluded employees, 11:32
    penalty for discrimination, 11:36
    separate-line-of-business basis, 11:29
  group term life insurance, 11:11–11:19
    former employees, 11:19
    penalty for discrimination, 11:18
    retired employees, 11:19
  HMOs, 2:39, 8:51
  managed care plans, 8:105
  MSA-holding employers, 7:73
  testing. See Nondiscrimination testing
  20 percent, top paid, 11:3
  VEBAs, 17:85
    compensation limits, 11:38
    defined, 11:37
    penalty for discrimination, 11:39
Nondiscrimination testing
  average benefits test, dependent care assistance plans, 11:35
  benefits test
    cafeteria plans, 11:24
    dependent care assistance plans, 11:33
    group term life insurance, 11:16
    self-insured accident and health plans, 11:6, 11:9
  computer systems, role of, 6:65
  concentration test
    cafeteria plans, 11:25
    dependent care assistance plans, 11:34
  eligibility test
    dependent care assistance plans, 11:30
    group term life insurance, 11:14
    self-insured accident and health plans, 11:4, 11:5, 11:9

  group term life insurance, 11:13–11:17
    benefit test, 11:16
    combining of plans for testing purposes, 11:17
    eligibility test, 11:14
    excluded employees, 11:15
  health benefit test, cafeteria plans, 11:26
  nondiscriminatory classification test, 11:40, 11:41
  self-insured accident and health plans, 11:2
Nondiscriminatory classification test, 11:40, 11:41
Nonresident aliens
  COBRA, 13:55
  VEBAs, 11:37
Notice
  COBRA. See also COBRA (Consolidated Omnibus Budget Reconciliation Act of 1985) for detailed treatment
    model initial notice, Appendix B, Appendix C
    requirements, 13:31–13:41
    sample notice upon qualifying event, Appendix D
  DOL, 401(h) transfers, 15:34
  FMLA, 4:65
  NMHPA, 4:42
  QMCSOs, 6:15
  60-day, material reduction in covered services or benefits, 4:122, 4:123
  Women's Health and Cancer Rights Act, 4:50
    guidance, 4:51
Nursing
  skilled nursing facilities, 3:40, 3:52, 20:24
  skilled nursing services
    home health care, 20:7
    long-term care, 20:24
  visiting nurse associations (VNAs), 20:4

Index

O

OASDI. *See* Old Age, Survivors' and Disability Insurance Act (OASDI)
OBRA '86
  COBRA, amendments, 13:1
OBRA '89
  COBRA, amendments, 13:1
OBRA '90
  COBRA, amendments, 13:1
  flexible benefits plans, 9:20
  home health care, 20:4
  Medicare
    benefit incentives, 10:22
OBRA '93
  child enrollment requirement, 6:14
  COBRA, 13:24
    amendments, 13:1
  eligible dependent, defined, 3:4
  Medicaid eligibility, taking into account, 4:9
  Medicare
    current employment status, 10:31
    disabled individuals, 10:31
    Medicare and Medicaid Coverage Data Bank, 10:50
    Medigap insurance policy, 10:44
    payroll tax, 10:14
  Medicare and Medicaid Coverage Data Bank, 10:50
  notice requirements, 6:15
  pediatric vaccines coverage, 4:53
  QMCSOs, 6:12
    certain children, plans covering, 6:14
    notice requirements, 6:15
  reducing benefits, 3:95
  requirements, 4:2
Ohio
  domestic partners, benefits for, 3:6
Old Age, Survivors' and Disability Insurance Act (OASDI), 4:37
Omnibus Budget Reconciliation Acts. *See* OBRA '86; OBRA '89; OBRA '90; OBRA '93
One Health Plan, 16:30

On-line services
  advantages, 21:21
  disadvantages, 21:22
  enrollment, for, 21:20–21:22
  usage, 21:19
Operation Data Match, 10:46–10:50
  causes of, 10:47
  defined, 10:46
  employer's responsibility, 10:48
  Medicare and Medicaid Coverage Data Bank, 10:50
  process involved, 10:49
Order of benefits. *See* Medicare
Oregon
  domestic partners, benefits for, 3:5
  Patient Protection Act, 8:114
Orthodontics
  health care reimbursement accounts, 9:22
  as special coverage category, 12:9
Outcomes measurement
  behavioral health plans
    performance indicators, 22:55
    types of measures, 22:56
  defined, 19:27
  measurement systems needed, 19:28
  quality improvement organization (QIO), defined, 19:30
  reducing cost of obtaining, 19:29
Out-of-pocket limit. *See* Maximum out-of-pocket limit
  maximum out-of-pocket limit, 3:67–3:69
Outpatients
  expenses, coverage, 3:41
  Mental Health Parity Act, 22:71
  surgery, 3:93
Outsourcing, types of, 6:74
Over-the-counter drugs, formularies and, 16:24
Oxford Health Plans, coverage for alternative therapies, 3:28, 3:31

P

PacAdvantage, 1:25

I-51

PacifiCare. *See* Survey
Pacific Business Group on Health (PBGC), 19:5
Pacific Health Advantage, 1:25
Parental leave
  maternity leave vs, 4:72
  state law, 4:31
Part A or B. *See* Medicare
Partial outsourcing, 6:74
Participant
  coalitions, 7:106
  ERISA disclosure, HIPAA, 4:122
  existing, locating, 7:107
  HMOs
    importance of participation by certain employees, 2:35
    rating HMOs, 8:59
  MSAs
    limit, 7:79
    other coverage and, 7:69
  nonemployee, VEBAs, 17:77
Participation. *See also* Coverage; Participant
  average rate, health care reimbursement accounts, 9:24
  conventional plan, HMOs enrollment effect on, 8:30
  group insurance plan, state rules, 4:28–4:30
  late enrollment, 6:29
  limits, group health insurance plan, 4:28–4:30
  POS plans, 8:99
  PPO plans, 8:99
Partnerships, self-funding, 17:23
Part-time employees
  coverage, 3:57, 3:58
  FMLA and switch from full-time status, 4:67
Paternalistic plan design, 3:2
Pay-as-you-go method, retiree health benefits, 15:3
Pay-based deductibles
  advantages, 3:84
  defined, 3:83
  disadvantages, 3:85

Payment. *See also* Billing
  claim, submitting, 6:37
  COBRA notice, 13:40
  HMO coverage, 8:50
  minimum premium plan, 5:65
  priority, COB, 7:85
  rehabilitation benefit, 12:42
  subacute care, 20:43
Payroll
  deductions, self-funding, 17:27
  tax, Medicare and, 10:14
PBM. *See* Pharmacy benefit management
PCS Health Systems. *See* Survey
PDA. *See* Pregnancy Discrimination Act
Pediatric vaccines coverage, 3:95, 4:53
Penalties
  COBRA noncompliance, 13:61
  damage awards, preventing by improving appeal process, 6:51
  discrimination
    cafeteria plans, 11:27
    dependent care assistance plan, 11:36
    group term life plans, 11:18
    VEBA, 11:39
  ERISA noncompliance, TPA, 18:10
Pennsylvania
  flexible benefits plans, 9:8
  managed care plans, 8:115
Pennsylvania Motor Vehicle Financial Responsibility Law, 4:18
Per-condition deductibles, 3:86
Performance guarantees, 7:12, 7:111
Periodic benefit reports
  defined, 21:11
  excluded information, 21:13
  risks, 21:14
  value of benefits, communicating, 21:12
Pharmacoeconomic research, 16:46
Pharmacy benefit management, 16:1–16:72
  capitation, role of, 16:54

Index

charge, 16:13
compensation, 16:53
considering, most important element, 16:50
cost control, 16:14–16:39
  disease state management programs, 16:35
  formularies, 16:17–16:29, 16:29
  generic drugs, 16:22, 16:33
  influence over formularies, 16:23
  lifestyle drugs, 16:31
  maximum allowable cost (MAC), defined, 16:34
  open vs closed formularies, 16:18
  proper drug usage, 16:37
  recommendations, 16:14
  therapeutic interchange protocols, 16:25, 16:32
  UR role, 16:16
  Viagra, coverage for, 16:30
  without closed formularies, 16:27
cost increases, 16:11, 16:12
direct-to-consumer advertising, 16:11
drug utilization review, 16:4
educational programs, 16:4, 16:7
enrollees, 16:8
growth, 16:8–16:13
largest PBMs, 16:69
nationwide service, 16:9
ownership concern, 16:6
pharmacy benefit manager defined, 16:2
point of dispensing, 16:58
prescription benefit concerns, 16:10
prescription drug management, 16:40–16:54
prescription drug plans, 16:63–16:72
  largest PBMs, 16:69
proper drug usage, cost control and, 16:37
quality assurance, 16:55–16:62
  duplicates, 16:55
  electronic data interchange, 16:57
  error detection and reporting, 16:47, 16:56

  measuring quality, 16:61
  point of dispensing, 16:58
  receiving coverage, 16:59
  satisfaction rates, 16:61
  size of company participating, 16:60
questions to ask, 16:4, 16:5
reporting, 16:51
satisfaction with, 16:61
Pharmacy Benefit Management Institute. *See* Survey
Philadelphia
  domestic partners, benefits for, 3:11
PHSA. *See* Public Health Service Act
Physical examinations. *See* Medical examinations
Physicians
  behavioral health care, primary role, 22:15
  costs of health care and, 7:21
  fees, RBRVS effect, 10:42
  formularies
    and role of physicians, 16:26
    support of, 16:25
  HMO ownership, 8:12
  managed care plans, exclusion, 8:107, 8:109, 8:110
  negotiations, and cost management, 7:98
  nonsurgical, coverage, 3:39
  primary care physicians, Medicare + Choice HMOs, 15:47
  profiling
    cost savings, 7:54
    defined, 7:53
  scheduled approach to fees, exceeding, 3:37
  unionizing, attempts, 8:104, 8:110
Plan administrators. *See also* Third-party administrators
  claim appeal obligation, 6:49
  defined, 14:11
  flexible benefits plans, 9:93
  notice of COBRA qualifying event, 13:39

Plan administrators (cont'd)
services provided where TPA used, 6:6
Plan design, 3:1–3:107
ADA, 4:74–4:91
claim calculation, fully insured plan, 5:9
company structure and, 3:3
contributory plans, 3:20, 3:21
costs
  containment, 3:71–3:98. *See also* Cost containment *for detailed treatment*
  effect of, 3:19–3:23
  reduction approaches, 7:22
coverage and, 3:24–3:52
  restrictions on, 3:53–3:61
deductibles, 3:62–3:64
demographics and, 3:1
diversity of workforce and, 3:18
domestic partners, benefits for, 3:5–3:17
EAPs, 22:49
eligible dependent, defined, 3:4
eligible employee, defined, 3:3
factors affecting, 3:1–3:107
  coinsurance, 3:65–3:69
  cost containment, 3:71–3:98
  costs, 3:19–3:23
  coverage, 3:24–3:61
  deductibles, 3:62–3:64
  non-legal factors affecting, 3:1–3:18
flexible/market-driven, 3:2
health care data, features to implement without, 7:31
HIPAA, 4:92–4:134
inappropriate, 7:18
legal factors affecting, 4:1–4:15
  cost, 3:23
managed competition, 3:2, 3:99–3:107
mental health benefit plans
  employer concerns, 22:2
  lifetime maximums, 22:9
noncontributory plans, 3:20, 3:21

nonlegal factors affecting, 3:1–3:18
domestic partners. *See* Domestic partner benefit
paternalistic, 3:2
paying for insurance. *See* Payment
PDA, 4:54–4:61
purchasing process, 3:1
redesign, health care data, 7:28
state law, 4:16–4:36
substance abuse benefits, 22:26
total compensation, 3:2
typical employer strategies, 3:2
Plan funding
alternatives to fully insured plans
  appropriateness of, 5:42
  conventional funding vs, 5:41
  employer size, 5:43
  self-funded/stop-loss combination and small employers, 5:44
cost reduction approaches, 7:22
deferred premium arrangements, 5:45–5:47
defined, 5:1
employee assistance program, 22:45
flexible benefits plans, 9:72
fully insured plans, 5:2–5:39
  alternatives to fully insured plan, 5:40–5:44
minimum premium plans, 5:62–5:69
reserve reduction agreements, 5:57–5:61
retrospective premium arrangements, 5:52–5:56
shared funding arrangements, 5:48–5:51
Plan rating. *See* Premiums
Plan sponsors
defined, 14:10
HMOs, 8:8
PPOs, 8:73
value of DSM program, 16:36
Plan years, Form 5500, 14:6–14:9
PM Group, 16:30
Point of dispensing, pharmacy benefit management, 16:58

Index

Point-of-service HMOs (POS plans)
advantages and disadvantages, 8:98
hybrid arrangements, 8:97
negligent care, employer liability for, 8:100
participation decision, 8:99
prevalence, 8:101

Policy
"field underwritten" policies, 6:5
individual insurance, HIPAA changes, 4:115
individual purchase, cafeteria plan reimbursement for, 9:60
long-term care, considerations, 20:37
renewal
   automatic coverage of employees, 6:54
   HIPAA, 4:118
   options available, 6:55
   process, 6:52
requiring detailed coverage information before issuing, 6:5
stop-loss, mid-year termination, 17:64

Policyholder, deficit reimbursement, 5:16

Poll. *See* Survey

Pooling, 5:30
defined, 5:23
pool charge, defined, 5:31
stop-loss insurance vs, 17:69

Post-retirement benefits, VEBA funding restrictions, 17:82

PPOs. *See* Preferred provider organizations (PPOs)

Preadmission certification
process, 7:42
UR, necessity for, 7:43

Precertification, dental plans, 12:12

Preemployment physical. *See* Medical examination

Preemption of state law
by ERISA, 4:17, 4:18, 8:53, 8:54
by PDA, 4:61

Preexisting conditions
COBRA, exclusions, simultaneous coverage by two types of plans, 13:81, 13:82
HIPAA
   certificate requirement and, 4:99
   credit, 4:105
   exclusions, 3:74, 4:93
   long-term disability plan, 12:34

Preferred provider arrangements, PPOs vs, 8:69

Preferred provider organizations (PPOs), 8:65–8:101
advantages, 8:95
antitrust issues, 8:86
Blues and Medicare contracts with providers vs, 8:68
case mix discounts, 8:93
COBRA and, 13:12
concept development, 8:66
cost-effective treatment, ensuring, 8:78
cost vs quality considerations, 8:89
defined, 2:40, 8:65
disadvantages, 8:95
discounts
   employers with largest, 8:88
   types available, 8:93
establishing, 8:76
evaluating, prospective employer or trust, 8:91
exclusive provider organizations (EPOs)
   comparison between EPOs and PPOs, 8:71
   defined, 8:70
federally qualified, 8:83
first dollar discounts, 8:93
flexible/market-driven plan design, 3:2
flexible plan, inclusion in, 9:62
freezing of fee levels, 8:93
HMOs vs, 8:67, 8:95
hybrid HMO arrangements, 8:97
incentives
   inclusion of PPOs in plans, 8:87

I-55

Preferred provider organizations (PPOs) *(cont'd)*
  incentives *(cont'd)*
    providers, 8:79
  included by any employer, 8:90
  incorporation into existing program, 8:92, 8:94
  inflation trend, 5:10
  large network, advantages and disadvantages, 8:96
  materials issued to employees, 6:9
  nationwide PPOs, 8:75
  negligent care, employer liability for, 8:100
  other health care delivery arrangements, 8:95
  percentage of UCR discounts, 8:93
  POS plans, 8:97–8:101
  preferred provider arrangements vs, 8:69
  prevalence, 8:74
  quality vs cost considerations, 8:89
  rate regulations, 8:85
  relative value study (RVS), 8:93
  scheduled discounts, 8:93
  selecting providers, 8:77
  self-funding, 17:3
  services offered, 8:72
  sponsor, 8:73
  state standards or laws, 8:84
  utilization review
    controls, 8:80
    importance of controls, 8:81
    reviewer, 8:82
  vertical integration, 8:95
  volume discounts, 8:93
Pregnancy Discrimination Act (PDA), 4:54–4:61
  abortion coverage, 4:60
  applicability of, 4:57
  covered employers, 4:56
  defined, 4:54
  dependent coverage, 4:59
  generally, 4:37
  requirements, 4:2
  same treatment defined, 4:55
  single persons, 4:57
  spouses of employees, benefits for, 4:58
  state law preemption, 4:61
Premiums
  calculation, getting help, 6:34
  COBRA
    determination, 13:43, 13:44
    frequency of rate change, 13:42
    IRS guidance, 13:45
    payment by employee for spouse or dependent, 13:64
    self-funded employer, 13:44
  deferred premium arrangement, 5:45–5:47
  experience rating, 5:24
  extensive coverage, for, 4:12
  group insurance, billing, 6:33
  insurance company profit component, 5:20
  late payment, coverage considerations, 6:35
  long-term care, 20:37
  minimum premium plans
    defined, 5:62
    employer benefit, 5:66
    employers typically electing, 5:68
    level of responsibility, 5:63
    payment, 5:65
    reason for not electing, 5:67
    shock claims, 5:64
    third-party administrative services, 5:68
  minimum-premium product, defined, 17:38
  payment by employer while employee on FMLA leave, 4:69
  rates, 5:29–5:34
    frequency of COBRA rate change, 13:42
    guarantee period, 5:10
  reasonableness of rate, determination, 5:33
  reserves, reserve reduction agreement, 5:57–5:61
  retention, 5:32

Index

retrospective premium arrangements
    availability, 5:56
    deep cut retro defined, 5:54
    defined, 5:52
    negotiating, 5:53
    not negotiating, 5:55
retrospective rating, 5:15
self-employed individuals,
    deductions, 4:137
taxes, self-funding, 17:51
Prenatal care programs, 12:70, 12:71
Prescription drug card plan, defined, 16:47
Prescription drug coverage. *See also* Prescription drug plans
    costs, increasing, 16:11
    DSM program cost cutting, 16:38
    generic drugs, FDA's position, 16:33
    lifestyle drugs, 16:31
    managed prescription programs, 16:16
    maximum allowable cost (MAC), defined, 16:34
    Medicare + Choice HMO, 15:49
    prescription benefit concerns, 16:10
    prescription drug card plans, 6:9, 16:47
    therapeutic interchange protocols, 16:25, 16:32
    Viagra, 16:30
Prescription drug plans, 16:63–16:72. *See also* Prescription drug coverage
    benefit concerns, 16:10
    cash-carry and reimburse, 16:1
    contraceptives, 16:65
    copayments
        flat, 16:70
        three-tier copays, 16:72
    cost of coverage, typical, 16:63
    defined, 16:1
    disclosure in HMO pharmaceutical plans, 16:48, 16:49
    drugs covered, 16:64
    duplicate prescriptions, 16:55
    excluded drugs, 16:64
    filling prescriptions, locations, 16:59
    free-standing plan vs major medical or comprehensive plan, 16:67
    generic drugs, 16:22
    important consideration, 16:50
    integrated claims information processing, defined, 16:52
    largest PBMs, 16:69
    mail service
        appropriateness, 16:43
        effectiveness studies, 16:42
        incentives to use, 16:45
        prescriptions, 16:40–16:54
        program underuse, 16:41
        safety, 16:43
    options, 16:3
    pharmacoeconomic research to cut costs, 16:46
    pharmacy benefit manager defined, 16:2
    prescription drug card plans, 16:9, 16:47
    reason for separate plan, 16:66
    reporting, 16:51
    separate plans, 16:66
    who offers, 16:68
Preventive care, 12:58–12:79. *See also* Health promotion programs; Wellness programs
    absenteeism and, 12:66
    benefits provided by, 12:59
    cost containment and, 3:94
    cost savings and, 12:66
    coverage, 3:45, 12:58
    disability prevention programs, 12:39
    group insurance plans, reasons for providing in, 12:77
    mammograms, 12:64
    medical examinations
        guidelines, 12:63–12:65
        routine checkups, coverage, 12:60–12:62
    Medicare, coverage, 10:8
    recommended tests, 12:65

Preventive care (cont'd)
routine checkups, coverage, 12:60–12:62
self-funding and, 4:6
Primary care physicians, Medicare + Choice HMOs, 15:47
Primary coverage. *See* Coverage; Medicare
Private delivery service, use to file, 14:21
Processing of claims, 6:43–6:45
Producer-owner reinsurance company, 17:50
Professional designations, list of, 2:17
Professionals. *See* Insurance; Medical professional; Nursing; Physicians
Professional services, home health care, 20:7
Profiling. *See* Physicians
Profits, insurance companies, 5:20
Profit sharing plan account, 15:37
Proprietary agencies, home health care, 20:4
Prospective rating, defined, 5:14
Provider-sponsored organizations (PSOs), 8:12
Prudence, ERISA fiduciary, 18:13, 18:15
Prudential HealthCare, 16:30
Prudent layperson standard, managed care plans, 8:115
PSOs. *See* Provider-sponsored organizations (PSOs)
Public Health Service Act, 13:14
Public opinion, managed care plans, 8:102
Puerto Rico
COBRA coverage, 13:22
flexible benefits plans, 9:8
Purchasing, joint. *See* Joint purchasing
"Putting Patients First" policies, 8:119

Q

Qualified beneficiary, COBRA. *See* COBRA (Consolidated Omnibus Budget Reconciliation Act of 1985)
Qualified benefit, defined, 9:4
Qualified medical child support orders (QMCSOs)
compliance, 9:35
coverage, 6:14
defined, 6:12
new benefit requirement, 6:13
notice, 6:15
Qualifying event. *See* COBRA (Consolidated Omnibus Budget Reconciliation Act of 1985)
Quality
assurance. *See* Quality assurance
care, of
poor quality as result of cost control, 7:102
PPO, vs cost, 8:89
HMOs vs conventional plan, 8:56
managed care plans, 8:57, 8:58
Quality assurance, 19:1–19:30
absenteeism and, 19:8
accreditation, 19:6, 19:8, 19:10
American Accreditation HealthCare Commission/URAC, 19:11
American Medical Accreditation Program, 19:10
choice of health plan and, 19:12
cost pressures and, 19:15
customer satisfaction surveys, 19:8
data, collection of, 19:6
definition of quality, 19:1
employees
measures by to ensure, 19:8
relations, 19:4
understanding of issues, 19:14
employer-driven data collection efforts, 19:6
employer quality partnership (EQPs), 19:14
fiduciary responsibility, 19:4
Foundation for Accountability (FACCT), 19:8, 19:9

I-58

Index

health-plan driven data collection efforts, 19:6
HEDIS, use of. *See* Health Care Plan Employer Data and Information Set (HEDIS)
importance of quality measures, 19:4
Joint Commission, 19:23
market-driven data collection efforts, 19:6
measures, defined, 19:2
MEDICA performance report, 19:5
National Committee for Quality Assurance (NCQA), 19:2, 19:3, 19:8
outcomes measurement, 19:27–19:30
pharmacy benefit management, 16:55–16:62
Quality Compass, 19:7, 19:21
quality improvement organization (QIO), defined, 19:30
quality measures, 19:1–19:15
  concerns by employers, 19:13
  cost pressures and, 19:15
  employees, measures by to ensure, 19:8
  employee understanding, 19:14
  importance of, 19:4
  prevalence of, 19:5
  Quality Compass, 19:7
  reduced costs, 19:4
report card movement, 19:8, 19:16–19:22
  Consumer Assessment of Health Plans (CAHPS), 19:20
  criticisms, 19:17
  effect of, 19:16
  examples, 19:22
  HEDIS, 19:13
  managed care, satisfaction of enrollees, 19:21
  national report card projects, 19:20
  patient satisfaction studies, 19:19
  Quality Compass, 19:21
  Report on Report Cards, 19:22

Quality Compass, 19:7, 19:21
Quality improvement measures
  managed competition and, 3:104
"Quick clinics," 3:40

R

Racketeer Influenced and Corrupt Organizations Act, 4:37
Rand Corporation. *See* Survey
Rating. *See also* Accreditation; Premium
  company, information from, 2:4
Rationing health care, 7:126–7:128
RBRVS. *See* Resource-based relative value scale (RBRVS)
Reasonable accommodation. *See* Accommodation
Reasonable and customary charge
  coverage, 3:34, 3:92
  defined, 3:34
  exceeding by physicians, 3:37
  reasons for, 3:36
  scheduled benefit structure, change to, 3:92
Receipt
  certificate, HIPAA, 4:98
  constructive. *See* Constructive receipt
Reciprocal beneficiaries (Hawaii)
  defined, 3:15
  reaction to, 3:17
  rights of, 3:16
Reduction
  cost. *See* Cost
  covered services and benefits before COBRA qualifying event, 13:59
  HIPAA rules, 4:119, 6:9
  60-day notice requirements, 4:122, 4:123
  summary of material reduction (SMR), distribution of, 6:9

I-59

Registration fees, dependent care reimbursement accounts, 9:27
Regulation. *See* Federal law; *individual laws by name*; State law
Rehabilitation
  actuality of rehabilitation, 12:43
  benefit, vs pay, 12:42
  candidates, 12:44
  disability management, 12:41–12:46
  ingredients of program, 12:45
  staff, 12:46
Reimbursement. *See also* Dependent care reimbursement account; Health care reimbursement account
  after paying heath care provider, 6:39
  ambulatory surgery centers, by Medicare, 10:43
  claims
    expenses, timing, 6:42
    stop-loss coverage, 17:60
  contributions, exceeding, 9:33
  covered expense, 3:42
  deductibles and, 3:64
  deficit, 5:16
  direct, dental care, 12:4
  escalating health care cost and, 8:1
  HMOs, care received outside of, 8:24
  individual limit, 3:43, 3:44
  individual policy purchase, for, 9:60
  uniform reimbursement approach, 9:32
Reimbursement accounts. *See* Dependent care reimbursement accounts
Reinsurance, 17:50
Relative value study (RVS), 8:93
Renal disease. *See* End-stage renal disease
Renewal, policy
  automatic coverage of employees, 6:54
  HIPAA, 4:118
  options available, 6:55
  process, 6:52

Report card movement, 19:16–19:22
  Consumer Assessment of Health Plans (CAHPS), 19:20
  criticisms, 19:17
  customer satisfaction measures, 19:18
  effect on quality, 19:16
  examples, 19:22
  managed care, satisfaction of enrollees, 19:21
  national report card projects, 19:20
  patient satisfaction studies, 19:19
  quality assurance and, 19:8
  Quality Compass, 19:21
  Report on Report Cards, 19:22
  satisfaction with, 19:18
Reporting
  benefits, periodic benefits reports, 21:11–21:14
  flexible benefit plan implementation and administration, 9:92
  HIPAA rules, 6:11
  periodic benefits reports, 21:11–21:14
  pharmacy benefit management errors, 16:56
  QMCSOs, 6:12–6:15
  report card movement. *See* Report card movement
  retiree benefit costs, 15:14
  state or federal government, 6:10
  summary plan description (SPD), 6:16
    changes pending, 6:17, 6:18
Representative. *See* Client service representative; Group sales representative
Reserves
  defined, 5:17
  necessary, 5:18
  reserve reduction agreement
    defined, 5:57
    reason for negotiating, 5:59
    reason for not negotiating, 5:60
    small employer, 5:61
    termination of contract, 5:58

Index

Reservist benefits, 4:141–4:155
  CHAMPUS, 4:147
  Department of Defense, provided by, 4:145
  dependents, 4:146
  employer discontinuing benefits for active duty employees, 4:144
  generally, 4:141
  health benefits, 4:152
  military benefit eligibility, 4:143
  reinstatement rules, 4:150
  rights at return to civilian life, 4:149
  sick leave, 4:153
  specific benefits reemployed veterans are entitled to, 4:151–4:154
  state laws, effect of, 4:155
  training leave, 4:154
  TRICARE, 4:147, 4:148
  Veterans Administration, provided by, 4:145

Resource-based relative value scale (RBRVS)
  Medicare cost limitation, 10:34, 10:40–10:42
  physician fees, effect on, 10:42

Retention, defined, 5:32

Retiree health benefits, 15:1–15:55
  accumulated postretirement benefit obligation (APBO), 15:14
  age requirements, changing to reduce liability of company, 15:24
  COBRA coverage, 13:67, 13:68
  communication, 21:28
  defined contribution benefits, 15:25
  defined dollar benefits, 15:25
  determining and allocating costs
    annual cost, 15:8
    cost differences between younger than 65 and older than 65, 15:9
    cost reduction efforts, 15:10
    cost sharing, 15:7–15:10
  eligibility, determining, 15:1–15:6
  factors employer should consider, 15:3
  HIPAA, applicability of, 15:6
  level of benefits, changing to reduce liability of company, 15:24
  liability of company, reduction of, 15:24
  mandatory federal coverage, 4:45
  medical liabilities, FASB accounting rules, 15:11–15:25
  Medicare and
    carve-out, 15:43
    coordination of benefits, 15:43
    Medicare + Choice HMO, 15:44–15:53. *See also* Medicare + Choice HMO *for detailed treatment*
    plan integration with Medicare, 15:43
  nondiscrimination rules
    accident and health plans, 11:10
    group term life plans, 11:19
  number of employers providing, 15:2
  pay-as-you-go method, 15:3
  pre-funding, 15:26–15:42
    company stock plan, 15:38
    contribution orientation, 15:35
    corporate-owned life insurance (COLI), 15:30, 15:31
    defined contribution approaches, 15:35, 15:36, 15:42
    employee savings accounts, 15:41
    FASB rules, 15:26
    401(h) account, 15:32
    HSOPs, 15:39, 15:40
    options, 15:27
    permissibility, 15:1
    profit sharing plan accounts, 15:37
    trust-owned life insurance (TOLI), differences, 15:31
    VEBA rules, 15:28, 15:29
  regulatory issues, 15:54, 15:55
  service requirements, changing to reduce liability of company, 15:24
  structure of, 15:5

Retirement Protection Act of 1994, 15:33

Retrospective premium arrangements
 availability, 5:56
 deep cut retro defined, 5:54
 defined, 5:52
 negotiating, 5:53
 not negotiating, 5:55
Retrospective rating
 agreements, 17:37
 defined, 5:15
Retrospective review, claim cost management, 7:46
Return to work, defined, 12:47
Revenue Act of 1978, 9:10, 9:11
Review. See also Utilization review
 retrospective review, claim cost management, 7:46
Risk
 COBRA, minimizing by reducing benefits before qualifying event, 13:59
 cost control, 7:103
 defined, 2:7
 excess-risk coverage, 17:25
 fiduciary, 18:17
 financing costs, reducing by self-funding, 17:45
 periodic benefits reports, 21:14
Robert Wood Johnson Foundation Employer Health Insurance Survey. See Survey
Rogaine, formularies and, 16:24
Ross-Loos Medical Group, 8:7, 8:11
Roster or list billing, 6:33
Routine checkups, 12:60–12:62. See also Medical examination

S

Safe harbors, nondiscriminatory classification test, 11:40

Salary reduction premium conversion plan defined, 9:17
Sale of company, COBRA coverage, 13:11
Sales representative. See Group sales representative
San Francisco
 domestic partners, benefits for, 3:12
Satisfaction
 PBM services, 16:61
 report card movement
  customer satisfaction, 19:18
  managed care, enrollees, 19:21
  patient satisfaction, 19:19
Savings. See Cost
Savings accounts. See Employee savings account
SBJPA. See Small Business Job Protection Act of 1996 (SBJPA)
Schedule
 benefit
  change to structure, 3:92
  exceeding by physicians, 3:37
 commissions, 2:23
 insurance, of, defined, 3:35
Scholarships and fellowships, 9:4
Screening
 AIDS, testing for, 7:123
 preventive care, health screening, 12:63–12:65
Seattle
 domestic partners, benefits for, 3:13
Secondary coverage. See Coverage; Medicare
Secondary payor. See Medicare; OBRA '89
Second surgical opinion programs. See Surgery
The Segal Company. See Survey
Selection. See also Adverse selection
 intermediaries, 2:17–2:30
Self-accounting, 6:33, 6:36
 flexible benefits plans, 9:94
Self-employed individuals
 as employers, premium deduction, 4:137

I-62

Index

Self-funding, 17:1–17:85. *See also* Plan funding
  administration, 17:29–17:34
    ASOs, 17:29–17:31
    classifying self-funded plans, 17:32
    fully insured plan, distinguishing characteristics, 17:34
    medical expense plans, financing, 17:33
    TPAs, 17:29–17:31
  advantages, 17:14, 17:16
  asset exposure, 17:18
  benefits to employees, 17:17
  cash flow, 17:14, 17:48
  challenges to benefits, 17:15
  claim processing, 17:14
  COBRA premium rate determination, 13:44
  cost containment and, 4:6
  cost savings, 17:9
  cost shifting, avoidance of, 17:44
  decision to self-fund, 17:10
    application to all companies, 17:19
    criteria, 17:21
    excess-risk coverage, 17:25
    first year of self-funding, 17:24
    group term life insurance coverage, 17:28
    large companies, 17:20
    partnerships, 17:23
    and payroll deductions, 17:27
    redesign of existing plan, 17:26
    smaller companies, 17:19–17:21
    stop-loss coverage, 17:75
  defined, 17:1
  disadvantages, 17:18
  employer types, 17:3
  federal and state laws, application of, 4:15, 4:17
  federally qualified HMOs, 2:37
  first year expectations, 17:24
  flexibility, enhancing, 4:6
  flexible benefits plans, 9:78
  fully insured health plan, defined, 17:4
  generally, 3:24
  group health plans, 4:121
  history, 17:2
  HMOs, 17:3
    advantages of conversion to, 2:32
    defined, 2:31
  indemnity plans, 17:3
  insurance professionals, 2:26
  laws governing, 17:6
  legal basis, 17:5
  marketplace
    approaches used, 17:39
    cash flow, 17:48
    claim administration, 17:46, 17:47
    cost shifting, avoidance of, 17:44
    covered employees, 17:43
    experience-rated plans, 17:36
    minimum-premium product, 17:38
    primary characteristic of self-funded plan, 17:42
    producer-owner reinsurance company, 17:50
    product modification to meet demand, 17:35–17:50
    retrospective-rating agreements, 17:37
    risk financing costs, reduction, 17:45
    self-administration of claims, 17:40
    separate trust, 17:41
    stop-loss intermediary, 17:49
  partnerships, 17:23
  PPOs, 17:3
  primary characteristic, 17:42
  process, 17:13
  producer-owner reinsurance company, 17:50
  provision of services, 17:18
  reasons for, 17:8–17:18
    generally, 17:7
  regulations, effect on health plan revisions, 17:53

I-63

Self-funding (cont'd)
  regulations, effect on (cont'd)
    mandated benefit rules, 17:52
    premium taxes, 17:51
    stop-loss insurance, 17:65
  restrictions, VEBA, 17:82
  risk assumption, 17:18
  risk financing costs, reduction, 17:45
  self-funded health plan defined, 17:11
  self-insurance vs self-funding, 17:12
  state mandate exemption, 4:22
  stop-loss insurance, 17:54–17:69. *See also* Stop-loss insurance *for detailed treatment*
    generally, 17:13
  stop-loss intermediary, 17:49
  third-party administrators (TPAs), laws governing, 18:12
  utilization controls, 17:14
  VEBAs, 17:70–17:85. *See also* Voluntary employees' beneficiary associations (VEBAs)
Self-Insurance Institute of America. *See* Survey
Self-insured plans. *See also* Plan funding
  aggregation, 11:9
  benefit test, 11:6, 11:9
  discrimination penalty, 11:7, 11:8
  HMO, vs other HMOs, 2:36
  nondiscrimination eligibility tests, 11:4, 11:5, 11:9
  nondiscrimination rules, 11:1, 11:2
Self-referral
  SSO panel referral vs, 7:57
Separate-line-of-business
  dependent care assistance plans, nondiscrimination rules, 11:29
Separate trust, self-funding, 17:41
Services
  claim for payment for, 6:39
  covered, HIPAA notice requirements, 4:123
  dental
    coverage exclusions, 12:13

  types covered, 12:6
  typically provided, 12:5
  dependent care reimbursement accounts, 9:26
  EAPs, 22:50
  fee-for-service, vs capitated payment structure, 8:16
  group health plans, COBRA exclusions, 13:15
  health care
    merging insurers and providers, 8:4
    prepayment, 8:18, 8:19
  home health care, 20:7, 20:8, 20:15
  inappropriate use
    affecting costs, 7:12
    combating, 7:133
  incentives, in lieu of TPA performance standards, 18:9
  insurer cost projections, 5:10
  Medicaid, long-term care benefits, 20:29
  Medicare, 10:4, 10:5
  nonsurgical physician, coverage, 3:39
  nontraditional, carve-outs, 22:38
  not covered by group plan, 3:45
  overprovision of, and cost management, 7:9, 7:132
  pharmacy benefit management, 16:9
  plan administrator, where TPA used, 6:6
  PPOs, 8:72
  TPAs, 17:31, 18:25
Setting up the plan. *See* Administration
Shared funding arrangement
  conventionally funded plan vs, 5:48
  reason for electing, 5:49
  reason for not electing, 5:50, 5:51
Shock claims, 5:64, 7:94
Short-term disability. *See* Disability benefits
Sick leave, reservist benefits, 4:153

Index

Single employee
mandatory maternity or family coverage, 4:8
Skilled nursing facilities, 3:40, 3:52
subacute care, objectives to using for, 20:42
Skilled nursing services
home health care, 20:7
long-term care, 20:24
Small Business Job Protection Act of 1996 (SBJPA)
COBRA, amendments, 13:1
nondiscrimination rules
accident and health plans, 11:3
highly compensated employee defined, 11:3, 11:31
Small employers
COBRA coverage
more than 20 employers, growth to, 13:8
disclosures, HIPAA, 4:133
funding alternative to fully insured plan, 5:43, 5:44
HIPAA applicability, 4:120
medical savings account, 7:65
growth of, 7:66
more than 50 employees, MSA and, 7:66
plans, HIPAA changes, 4:115
reserve reduction agreement, 5:61
underwriter not approving application for insurance, 6:3
uninsured persons, 1:9
Small group insurers, HIPAA rules, 4:130
Smoking cessation programs, 12:69, 12:70
COBRA and, 13:15
health care reimbursement accounts, 9:20, 9:23
Social or custodial services, home health care, 20:7
Society for Human Resource Management. *See* Survey

Software
COBRA administration, notification requirements and, 13:41
EFAST, Form 5500, 14:28, 14:29
Special education
health care reimbursement accounts, 9:23
Sponsor. *See* Plan sponsor
Spouse. *See also* Dependent
COBRA
notice rules, 13:38
premium payment by employee, 13:64
defined, domestic partner benefits, 3:9
mandatory coverage, 4:13
PDA coverage, 4:58
working spouse plan defined, 9:48
"Spreadsheet" quotes, 5:33
SSOs (second surgical opinion programs). *See* Surgery
Staff outsourcing, 6:74
Standard & Poor. *See* Survey
Standards. *See also* Accreditation
HMOs, 8:45–8:54
Joint Commission. *See* Joint Commission on Accreditation of Healthcare Organizations
PPOs, 8:84
TPA performance, 18:8, 18:9
Stark Bill. *See* Ethics in Patient Referrals Act
State insurance guaranty funds, 2:5
State Joint Task Force on the Changing Family. *See* Survey
State law, 4:16–4:36
ADA exemptions, 4:88
anti-managed care legislation, 8:114
any willing provider law, 8:108
change, employer's plan obligations, 4:15
COBRA and, 13:84
state-by-state list, 13:83
coordination of benefits, 7:87
division between federal law and, 4:18

State law (cont'd)
 ERISA fiduciary requirements vs, 18:14
 group health plans, taxation, 4:135
 HMOs, 8:52
  ERISA preemption, 8:53, 8:54
 influence on plan design, 4:16–4:36
 living wage ordinance, 4:35
 mandated benefit rules
  common mandates, 4:24
  cost increases and, 4:26
  defined, 4:21
  extensiveness, 4:25
  rationale, 4:23
  self-funded plans, 4:22, 17:52
 mandated coverage, 4:3, 4:4
  coping with, 4:36
 mandated offering, defined, 4:27
 Massachusetts surcharge
  coinsurance costs and, 4:34
  defined, 4:33
 MEWAs, 4:14
 New York surcharge, 4:18, 4:32
 parental or family leave, 4:31
 participation in group insurance plan, 4:28–4:30
 PPOs, 8:84
 preemption
  ERISA, 4:17, 4:18, 8:53, 8:54
  PDA, 4:61
 reporting, 6:10
 reservist benefits, 4:155
 self-funded plans, 4:15, 4:17
 similarities among group health insurance laws, 4:20
 state insurance department, responsibilities, 4:19
 state-sponsored coalitions, group health insurance plan, 1:24, 1:25
 stop-loss insurance, 17:67
 Supreme Court and, 4:18
 utilization review, 7:34

State-sponsored coalitions or plans. See State law

State tax. See Tax considerations

Stop-loss insurance, 17:54–17:69
 aggregate, 17:58, 17:75
 alternative, 17:68
 American Legislative Exchange Council, 17:66
 benefit period, 17:61, 17:62
 claim reimbursement, 17:60
 defined, 17:25
 employer responsibility to workers, 17:59
 Form 5500, 14:23
 generally, 17:13
 incurred claim date, 17:56, 17:57
 intermediary, 17:49
 medical expense plans, effect on, 17:54
 mid-year termination, 17:64
 NAIC position, 17:66
 plan types available, 17:56
 pooling vs, 17:69
 problematical nature of, 17:63
 regulatory environment, 17:65
 specific coverage, 17:55, 17:75
 state regulation, 17:67
 stop-loss intermediary, 17:49
 termination, mid-year, 17:64
 VEBAs, 15:29
 volatility of claims and, 17:19

Stress prevention programs, 12:69

Subacute care. See Home health care

Substance abuse. See also Drug testing
 ADA, 4:80, 22:57–22:63
 cost to companies, 22:25
 mental health benefit, 22:2
 treatment
  benefits typically offered, 22:24
  inpatient benefits, 22:28
  Mental Health Parity Act, 22:72
  plan design, 22:26
  reasons for restricting, 22:27
  treatable illness, as, 22:29
  typical coverage, 22:23

Successor employers, COBRA coverage, 13:11

Index

Summary of material reduction (SMR), 6:9

Summary plan description (SPD)
changes pending, 6:17, 6:18
COBRA initial notice, 13:37
defined, 6:16
explaining plan benefits, 6:20
health maintenance organization (HMOs), 6:17–6:19
multiple purpose, 6:21
requirement to file, 6:10

Summer camps
dependent care reimbursement accounts, 9:27

Surcharge. *See* New York surcharge

Surgery
ambulatory surgery centers, Medicare reimbursement, 10:43
coverage, 3:33
elective cosmetic, 9:20
 exceptions, 9:21
 procedures considered elective, 9:22
outpatient surgery, 3:93
second surgical opinion program
 current thinking, 7:59
 defined, 7:55
 mandatory programs, 7:58
 procedures requiring, 7:56
 self-referral vs referral by SSO panel, 7:57
surgical care, recent changes, 3:38

Surgicenters, 3:40

Surrogate mother, in-vitro expenses, 9:23

Survey
AIDS, impact on insurance
 Employee Benefit Research Institute (EBRI), 7:118
 Pharmaceutical Research and Manufacturers of America, 7:118
alternative therapy coverage
 Employee Benefit News, 3:28
 Los Angeles Times, 3:30

COBRA, impact on employers
 Charles D. Spencer & Associates, 13:85
computerized administration
 International Foundation of Employee Benefit Plans, 6:71, 6:72
 International Society of Certified Employee Benefit Specialists, 6:71
 Society for Human Resource Management, 6:70
contributory or noncontributory plans
 Bureau of Labor Statistics, 3:21
cost containment
 Charles D. Spencer & Associates, 3:74
cost management
 Deloitte & Touche, 7:112
 Journal of the American Medical Association, 7:133
 Midwest Business Group on Health, 7:108
costs
 Mercer/Foster Higgins, 3:19, 3:79, 7:1
coverage
 Business Insurance, 3:57
 Government Accounting Office (GAO), 3:48
 Hewitt Associates, 3:57
deductibles
 Mercer/Foster Higgins, 3:81
dental benefits
 Mercer/Foster Higgins, 12:2, 12:3
 National Association of Dental Plans, 12:3
 Tillinghast-Towers Perrin, 12:2
dependent care reimbursement accounts
 Mercer/Foster Higgins, 9:28
disability
 Aetna, 12:28
 Social Security Administration, 12:27

I-67

Survey (cont'd)
  disability benefits
    Washington Business Group on Health, 12:26
  disability management
    Washington Business Group on Health, 12:49
  disease state management (DSM) programs
    MEDSTATE Group, 16:36
    PCS Health Systems, 16:36
    William M. Mercer, 16:35
  domestic partners, benefits for
    Census Bureau, 3:5
    Employee Benefit Research Institute (EBRI), 3:7
    Hewitt Associates, 3:6
    New York Times, 3:8
    Society for Human Resource Management, 3:6, 3:8
    State Joint Task Force on the Changing Family, 3:5
  electronic communications, advantages of
    William M. Mercer, Inc., 6:73
  employee assistance programs (EAPs), 22:49
    Aon Consulting, 22:53
    Bureau of Labor Statistics, 22:43
    McDonnell Douglas Corporation, 22:54
    Mercer/Foster Higgins, 22:43
  employee contributions
    Mercer/Foster Higgins, 3:79
  external review
    Bureau of National Affairs, 3:51
    Kaiser Family Foundation, 8:118
  factors affecting costs
    Bureau of Labor Statistics, 7:2
  flexible benefits plans
    Mercer/Foster Higgins, 9:2, 9:14, 9:15, 9:24, 9:28, 9:71
    Towers Perrin, 9:71
  geography, impact on costs
    Mercer/Foster Higgins, 5:10
  group insurance
    Employee Benefits Research Institute (EBRI), 1:5, 1:17
    Fidelity Benefits Center, 1:17
    Gallup Organization, Inc., 1:17
  health care reimbursement accounts
    Mercer/Foster Higgins, 9:24
  health insurance marketplace
    A. M. Best, 2:3
    Standard & Poor, 2:3
  health maintenance organizations (HMOs)
    American Association of Health Plans, 8:33
    Aragon Consulting Group, 8:59
    Congressional Research Service, 8:34
    Hewitt Associates, 8:59
    InterStudy, 8:9, 8:47
    Journal of Family Practice, 8:58
    Journal of the American Medical Association, 8:34
    PacifiCare, 8:59
  health promotion programs
    Care Data, 12:57
    Hewitt Associates, 12:50, 12:51
    Intracorp, 12:57
  hearing, evaluations and hearing aids
    Hewitt Associates, 12:20
  inflation
    The Segal Company, 5:10
  long-term care
    Bureau of Labor Statistics, 20:30
    Financial Services Online, 20:27
    Gallup Organization, Inc., 20:30
    Health Insurance Association of America, 20:36
    Hewitt Associates, 20:30
    MetLife, 20:27
    The Wall Street Journal, 20:27
    William A. Mercer Inc., 20:31, 20:32
  mail service pharmacy
    William M. Mercer, Inc., 16:42

I-68

Index

managed care plans
  Employee Benefit News, 8:5
  Families USA, 8:115
  Kaiser Family Foundation, 8:118
  National Committee for Quality Assurance (NCQA), 8:57
managed care plans, feelings of employers
  Washington Business Group on Health, 8:103
managed care plans, feelings of health care providers
  Healthcare Financial Management Association, 8:104
managed care plans, public opinion
  American Association of Health Plans, 8:102
  Employee Benefits Research Institute (EBRI), 8:102
  Hewitt Associates, 8:102
  Kaiser Family Foundation, 8:102
managed competition
  General Motors, 3:104
  Medical Practice Management, 3:107
  Robert Wood Johnson Foundation Employer Health Insurance Survey, 3:103
mandated benefits
  Blue Cross and Blue Shield Association, 4:24
  Milliman & Robertson, 4:26
  National Underwriter, 4:24
Medicare, coverage
  Employee Benefit Research Institute, 10:3
Medicare, election of HMO coverage by beneficiaries
  American Association of Health Plans, 10:55
  CareData Reports, Inc., 10:54
  Towers-Perrin, 10:54
Medicare, typical beneficiary spending
  American Association of Retired Persons (AARP), 10:15

Medicare + Choice
  General Accounting Office, 11:53
Medicare + Choice HMOs
  A. Foster Higgins, 15:46
  Towers Perrin, 15:46
  William Mercer, 15:46
Medigap insurance policy
  Families USA, 10:45
  Weiss Ratings Inc., 10:45
mental health benefits
  Bureau of Labor Statistics, 22:43
  Congressional Budget Office, 22:73
  Hay Group, 22:16
  Mathematica Policy Research, 22:74
  Mercer/Foster Higgins, 22:4, 22:6, 22:13, 22:18, 22:23, 22:43
  Rand Corporation, 22:73
on-line communication technology
  International Society of Certified Employee Benefit Specialists, 21:19
outsourcing
  Buck Consultants, 6:74
participant
  Agency for Health Care Policy and Research (AHCPR), 7:107
PBM
  CareData Reports, Inc., 16:62
pharmacy benefit management
  Express Scripts, 16:12
  Mercer/Foster Higgins, 16:12
  Merck-Medco Managed Care, 16:15
  William M. Mercer, Inc., 16:8
point-of-service plans
  Mercer/Foster Higgins, 8:101
preferred provider organizations (PPOs)
  Managed Healthcare, 8:75
  Mercer/Foster Higgins, 8:74
premium increase
  Towers Perrin, 5:10

Survey (cont'd)
  prescription drug coverage
    Employee Benefit Research Institute, 16:10
  prescription drug plans
    American Managed Care Pharmacy Association (AMCPA), 16:41
    Boston Consulting Group, 16:42
    Express Scripts/Value Rx, 16:63
    FIND/SVP, 16:42
    Mercer/Foster Higgins, 16:41, 16:63, 16:70, 16:71
    Pharmacy Benefit Management Institute, 16:70, 16:71
    The Segal Company, 16:63
    Wyatt Company, 16:42
  quality assurance
    Brandeis University, 19:12
    MEDSTAT Group, 19:12
    Mercer/Foster Higgins, 19:5
    United HealthCare, 19:1
    Washington Business Group on Health, 19:13
  rationing health care
    Louis Harris, 7:128
    Rand Corporation, 7:126
  report card movement
    Buyers HealthCare Action Group, 19:18
    KPMG Peat Marwick, 19:19
    Quality Compass, 19:21
  reservist benefits
    Hewitt Associates, 4:144
  retiree health benefits
    Charles D. Spencer and Associates, 15:5, 15:19
    Employee Benefits Research Institute (EBRI), 15:19
    Mercer/Foster Higgins, 15:2, 15:7–15:10, 15:46
    Towers Perrin, 15:46
    William Mercer, 15:46
  second surgical opinion program
    Aetna Life Insurance Company, 7:59
  self-funded plans
    A. Foster Higgins, 17:47
    Employee Benefit Research Institute, 17:3
    Mercer/Foster Higgins, 17:3
  stop-loss insurance
    Mercer/Foster Higgins, 17:55
  substance abuse
    Mercer/Foster Higgins, 22:23
  third-party administrator (TPA)
    Charles D. Spencer & Associates, Inc., 18:25
    Self-Insurance Institute of America, 18:28
  uniform reimbursement approach
    Mercer/Foster Higgins, 9:32
  uninsured
    Agency for Health Care Policy and Research, 1:10
    Census Bureau, 1:7
    Consumers Union, 1:11
    Current Population Survey (CPS), 1:7
    Employee Benefits Research Institute (EBRI), 1:6, 1:7
    Kaiser Family Foundation, 1:9
    Lewin-VHI, Inc., 1:8
    UCLA School of Public Health, 1:10
  utilization review
    United HealthCare, 7:43
  vacation trading
    Mercer/Foster Higgins, 9:54
  vision care coverage
    Mercer/Foster Higgins, 12:15
  wellness programs
    American Journal of Public Health, 12:74
    Journal of the American Medical Association, 12:74
Survivor benefits. *See* Benefit; Dependents; Spouse
System outsourcing, 6:74

Index

T

Taft-Hartley Act of 1946, 18:4, 18:6
TAMRA. *See* Technical and Miscellaneous Revenue Act of 1988; Technical and Miscellaneous Revenue Act of 1988 (TAMRA)
Tax considerations
  custodial care, 20:34
  death benefits, 12:23, 12:24
    state taxes, 12:25
  deduction
    COBRA, 13:69, 13:70
    high-deductible plan defined, 7:71
    self-employed individual, 4:137
    VEBA, 17:81
  disability benefits, 12:36, 12:37
  flexible benefits plans, 9:6–9:12
    cafeteria plan, 9:6
    constructive receipt, 9:11
    domestic partner benefits, 9:7
    employee contributions, 9:9
    first introduction of, 9:10
    reason for development of plan, 9:12
    state income tax, 9:8
  group health plan
    benefits, 4:140
    federal tax status, 4:136
    state tax laws, 4:135
  income tax, employer contributions, 4:138
  long-term care, 20:34
  payroll tax, Medicare, 10:14
  reimbursement of employee for costs of individual health insurance, 4:139
  self-funding and premium taxes, 17:51
  state tax, flexible benefits plans, 9:8
  vacation trading, 9:55
  VEBAs
    benefits, 17:71
    tax-exempt, 17:74, 17:75

Tax Equity and Fiscal Responsibility Act of 1984, 4:37
Taxpayer Relief Act of 1997, 6:10, 6:16
Tax Reform Act of 1986, 13:1
Technical and Miscellaneous Revenue Act of 1988 (TAMRA)
  COBRA
    amendments, 13:1
    penalties, noncompliance, 13:61
  generally, 4:37
Technology
  benefit program enrollment on-line, 21:20–21:22
  new and expensive, cost reduction, 7:131
  rising costs and, 7:5
TEFRA. *See* Tax Equity and Fiscal Responsibility Act of 1984
Temporary employees, coverage, 3:57
Termination
  coverage, 6:57–6:63
    COBRA, 13:76, 13:78
    middle of plan year, 6:57
    protection against medical expense, 6:59, 6:60
    year-end only, options, 6:58
  employment
    COBRA coverage advisory, 13:75
    conversion privilege, 6:61–6:63
    reimbursement accounts and, 9:30
  insurance, reserve decrease, 5:58
  insurance contract, paying claims after, 5:4
  MSA pilot project, 7:82
  stop-loss policy, mid-year, 17:64
Testing, nondiscrimination. *See* Nondiscrimination testing
Tests, medical. *See* Medical examination
Texas
  managed care plans, 8:114, 8:115
Therapeutic interchange protocols, 16:25, 16:32

I-71

Third-party administration. See also Administration
  defined, 18:1
  minimum premium plan, 5:68
Third-party administrators (TPAs), 18:1–18:28. See also Administration
  bonuses and incentives for good service, 18:9
  common guarantees, 18:8
  compensation, 2:30
  cost, effect on, 7:22
  cost-effectiveness, 2:29
  defined, 18:2
  ERISA noncompliance penalty, 18:10
  Form 5500, completing, 14:22
  fully insured plan, use by, 2:27
  future of TPA business, 18:24
  government compliance, 18:20
  health care data, 7:30
  history of use, 18:4
  laws governing, 18:12
  legal issues, 18:10–18:17
  legal opinions, 18:11
  managed care TPA, 18:26, 18:27
  market, 18:18–18:28
    changes underway, 18:23
    future of TPA business, 18:24
    growth, 18:20, 18:21
    individuals served, 18:19
    major markets, 18:22
    managed care TPA, 18:26, 18:27
    prevalence of TPA use, 18:28
    services provided, 18:25
    TPA charge, 18:18
  MEWAs, defined, 18:5
  minimum premium plan, 5:68
  multiemployer plans and multiple-employer plans, regulatory differences, 18:6
  performance guarantees, 18:7
  performance standards
    ERISA fiduciary responsibility, 18:13–18:17
    examples, 18:8
  plan administrator, as, 2:28
  plan administrator vs, 6:6
  prevalence of TPA use, 18:28
  role of, 18:3
  selection considerations, 18:7
  self-funded plans, 17:29
    ASO arrangement vs, 17:30
    classification of plans, 17:32
    laws governing, 18:12
    marketplace, 17:39
  services, 17:31
  services provided, 18:25
  Taft-Hartley Act of 1946, 18:4, 18:6
Three-tier copayments, 16:72
Tillinghast-Towers Perrin. See Survey
Tolerable loss ratio (TLR)
  defined, 5:36
  variation from year to year and employer to employer, 5:37
TOLI. See Trust-owned life insurance (TOLI)
Tooth capping
  health care reimbursement accounts, 9:22
Total compensation, 3:2
Total flexible benefits plans. See Full menu plans
Towers Perrin. See Survey
TPAs. See Third-party administrators
Traditional Chinese medicine (TCM), coverage, 3:28
Training leave, returning veterans, 4:154
Transfers, 401(h) account, 15:33, 15:34
Transplants, Medicare coverage, 10:7
Transportation Equity Act of 1998, 9:4
Treatment
  experimental treatment, 3:46
    legitimate experimental treatments, 3:47
  external review, 3:49–3:51
  inpatient
    Mental Health Parity Act, 22:71
    substance abuse, 22:28
  insurer decision, 3:48

Index

outpatient
  coverage, 3:41
  Mental Health Parity Act, 22:71
  substance abuse, 22:23–22:29
  Mental Health Parity Act, 22:72
Treatment protocols, utilization review, 7:36
TRICARE
  employer responsibility to dependents covered by TRICARE, 4:148
  reservists benefits, 4:147
Triple option plan, defined, 8:63
Trust-owned life insurance (TOLI), 15:31
Trusts
  multiple employer, defined, 1:19
  PPO, evaluating, 8:91
  separate, self-funding, 17:41
Tufts Health Plan, 16:30
Tuition
  dependent care reimbursement accounts, 9:27
20 percent, top paid
  nondiscrimination rules, 11:3

U

UCLA School of Public Health. *See* Survey
Unbundled plans or coverage, COBRA, 7:115, 13:5, 13:21
Underinsurance, defined, 1:11
Underwriters
  "field underwritten" policies, 6:5
  group health insurance, 2:6
  not approving application for coverage, 6:3, 6:4
Undue business hardship. *See* Hardship
Uniformed Services Employment and Reemployment Rights Act of 1994 (USERRA)
  COBRA
    comparison, 4:142

    relationship with, 13:28
  generally, 4:141
  rights of returning military personnel, 4:149
Uniform reimbursement approach, 9:32. *See* Reimbursement
Uninsured, 1:6–1:11
  characteristics, 1:7
  children, extension of coverage to, 1:6
  impact on health insurance costs, 1:8
  portion of U.S. population, 1:6
  reasons for lack of coverage, 1:9, 1:10
  small companies, members of, 1:9
  underinsurance, defined, 1:11
Unions
  claim processing, 6:43
  COBRA rules or exceptions, 13:18
  coverage, exclusions, 3:53
  disability prevention program, 12:39
  group health insurance, 1:20
  physicians, 8:104, 8:110
United HealthCare. *See* Survey
Unrelated business income, VEBAs, 17:84
Upcoding, 7:115
URAC. *See* American Accreditation HealthCare Commission/URAC
Urgent care claims, processing, 6:44
USERRA. *See* Uniformed Services Employment and Reemployment Rights Act of 1994 (USERRA)
Usual, customary, and reasonable charge, coverage, 3:34
Usual and prevailing charge, coverage, 3:34
Utilization review, 7:32–7:37
  ambulatory care
    cost savings, 7:52
    defined, 7:48
    inpatient UR vs, 7:49
    prevalence, 7:51
    review techniques, 7:50
  concurrent review, 7:45

Utilization review (*cont'd*)
  cost savings vs additional expense, 7:47
  defined, 7:32
  fully insured plan, 5:9
  indicators, 7:27
  inpatient, vs ambulatory care, 7:49
  length of hospitalization, 7:44
  managed care, growth of, 7:35
  managed prescription program, 16:16
  mental health plans, 22:18
  necessity for, 7:43
  physician profiling, 7:53, 7:54
  PPOs
    controls, 8:80
    importance of controls, 8:81
    reviewers, 8:82
  preadmission certification process, 7:42
  process, 7:33
  retrospective review, 7:46
  second surgical opinion program, 7:55–7:59
  state regulation, 7:34
  treatment protocols, 7:36
  types of, 7:37

V

Vacation trading, 9:54–9:58
  advantages to employer, 9:56
  costs of, 9:57
  disadvantages to employer, 9:57
  prevalence, 9:54
  restrictions, suggested, 9:58
  tax consequences, 9:55
Vaccinations
  influenza, 12:51
  pediatric vaccines, 3:95, 4:53
Value-based purchasing, cost management, 7:108
Van pooling, 9:4
Vasectomies, coverage, 4:7

VEBAs. *See* Voluntary employees' beneficiary associations (VEBAs)
Vermont
  managed care plans, 8:115
Vermont Civil Union Law, 3:14
Vertical integration, PPOs, 8:95
Vesting, commissions, 2:24
Veterans. *See* Reservist benefits
Veterans Administration
  reservists benefits, 4:145
Viagra, coverage for, 16:30
Virginia
  domestic partners, benefits for, 3:11
Vision care coverage, 12:14–12:19
  discount vision plans, 12:19
  generally, 12:14
  HIPAA, 4:132
  indemnity vision plans, 12:17
  managed vision plans, 12:18
  prevalence of, 12:15
  types of delivery systems, 12:16
Visit churning (code gaming), 7:115
Visiting nurse associations (VNAs), 20:4
Vitamins
  health care reimbursement accounts, 9:23
VNAs. *See* Visiting nurse associations (VNAs)
Voluntary employees' beneficiary associations (VEBAs), 4:136, 15:24, 17:70–17:85
  benefits, 17:72
    not provided, 17:73
  compensation limits, 11:38
  controller of, 17:80
  deductible limit, 17:81
  defined, 17:70
  employee, defined, 17:78
  key employee rules, 17:83
  life insurance benefits, restrictions, 17:82
  medical benefits, restrictions, 17:82
  membership restrictions, 17:79
  nondiscrimination rules, 17:85
    compensation limits, 11:38

definition of VEBA, 11:37
nonemployees benefiting, 17:77
one person benefiting, 17:76
penalties for discrimination, 11:39
post-retirement benefits, funding restrictions, 17:82
pre-funding retiree health benefits, 15:28
  stop-loss insurance and VEBA combined, 15:29
tax benefits, 17:71
tax-exempt
  establishing, 17:74
  obtaining status, 17:75
unrelated business income, 17:84

W

Waiting periods, 3:61
  HIPAA, 4:93, 4:96
Waivers
  deductibles, 3:82
  flexible benefits plans
    controls, 9:70
    employer policies, 9:71
    purpose of waiver, 9:69
The Wall Street Journal. See Survey
Washington
  alternative therapies, coverage, 3:28
Washington, D.C.
  workers' compensation law, 4:18
Washington Business Group on Health. *See* Survey
Waste. *See also* Cost
Weight loss drugs, treatment and programs
  COBRA and, 13:15
  health care reimbursement accounts, 9:23
Weiss Ratings Inc. *See* Survey
Welfare plans
  ERISA, EAPs as, 22:46
  Form 5500, exclusion, 14:2

Wellness programs. *See also* Health promotion programs; Preventive care
  advantages, 12:68
  alcohol abuse programs, 12:69
  components of, 12:70
  defined, 12:67
  disadvantages, 12:68
  education, health, 12:69
  effectiveness of, 12:74, 12:75
  fitness programs, 12:69
  habit-breaking programs, 12:69
  health audits, 12:69
  health risk appraisals, 12:69
  information on, obtaining, 12:78
  insured, 12:79
  prenatal care, 12:70, 12:71
  prevalence of, 12:73
  smoking cessation programs, 12:69, 12:70
  stress prevention programs, 12:69
  types of, 12:69
  typical components of, 12:70
WHCRA. *See* Women's Health and Cancer Rights Act (WHCRA)
William M. Mercer. *See* Survey
Withdrawal
  medical, from IRA, HIPAA, 4:128
Women's Health and Cancer Rights Act (WHCRA)
  applicability of, 4:52
  described, 4:49
  notice requirements, 4:50, 21:27
    guidance, 4:51
  requirements, 4:2
Working spouse. *See* Spouse
Workplace accommodation. *See* Accommodation
Wraparound major medical, 2:33, 5:21
Written communication, ERISA, 21:7
Wyatt Company. *See* Survey

Y

Yoga, coverage, 3:28